Microeconomic Analysis

Third Edition

Microeconomic Analysis

Third Edition

Hal R. Varian

University of Michigan

W. W. Norton & Company • New York • London

To my parents

Copyright © 1992, 1984, 1978 by W. W. Norton & Company, Inc.

THIRD EDITION

Library of Congress Cataloging-in-Publication Data

Varian, Hal R.
   Microeconomic analysis / Hal R. Varian. -- 3rd ed.
      p.   cm.
   Includes bibliographical references and index.
   1. Microeconomics.   I. Title.
   HB172.V35 1992   91-42241
   338.5--dc20

ISBN 0-393-95735-7

W. W. Norton & Company, Inc., 500 Fifth Avenue, New York, N.Y. 10110
W. W. Norton & Company, Ltd., 10 Coptic Street, London WC1A 1PU

2 3 4 5 6 7 8 9 0

CONTENTS

3 Profit Function

4 Cost Minimization

5 Cost Function

6 Duality

7 Utility Maximization

8 Choice

9 Demand

10 Consumers' Surplus

11 Uncertainty

12 Econometrics

13 Competitive Markets

14 Monopoly

15 Game Theory

16 Oligopoly

17 Exchange

18 Production

19 Time

20 Asset Markets

21 Equilibrium Analysis

22 Welfare

23 Public goods

24 Externalities

25 Information

26 Mathematics

27 Optimization

PREFACE

The first edition of *Microeconomic Analysis* was published in 1977. After 15 years, I thought it was time for a major revision. There are two types of changes I have made for this third edition, structural changes and substantive changes.

The structural changes involve a significant rearrangement of the material into "modular" chapters. These chapters have, for the most part, the same titles as the corresponding chapters in my undergraduate text, *Intermediate Microeconomics*. This makes it easy for the student to go back to the undergraduate book to review material when appropriate. It also works the other way around: if an intermediate student wants to pursue more advanced work on a topic, it is easy to turn to the appropriate chapter in *Microeconomic Analysis*. I have found that this modular structure also has two further advantages: it is easy to traverse the book in various orders, and it makes it more convenient to use the book for reference.

In addition to this reorganization, there are several substantive changes. First, I have rewritten substantial sections of the book. The material is now less terse, and, I hope, more accessible. Second, I have brought a lot of material up to date. In particular, the material on monopoly and oligopoly has been completely updated, following the major advances in the theory of industrial organization during the eighties.

Third, I have added lots of new material. There are now chapters on game theory, asset markets, and information. These chapters can serve as an appropriate introduction to this material for first-year economics students. I haven't tried to provide in-depth treatments of these topics since I've found that is better pursued in the second or third year of graduate studies, after facility with the standard tools of economic analysis have been mastered.

Fourth, I've added a number of new exercises, along with complete answers to all odd-numbered problems. I must say that I am ambivalent about putting the answers in the book—but I hope that most graduate students will have sufficient willpower to avoid looking at the answer until they have put some effort into solving the problems for themselves.

Organization of the book

As I mentioned above, the book is organized into a number of short chapters. I suspect that nearly everyone will want to study the material in the first half of the book systematically since it describes the fundamental tools of microeconomics that will be useful to all economists. The material in the second half of the book consists of introductions to a number of topics in microeconomics. Most people will want to pick and choose among these topics. Some professors will want to emphasize game theory; others will want to emphasize general equilibrium. Some courses will devote a lot of time to dynamic models; others will spend several weeks on welfare economics.

It would be impossible to provide in-depth treatment of all of these topics, so I have decided to provide introductions to the subjects. I've tried to use the notation and methods described in the first part of the book so that these chapters can pave the way to a more thorough treatment in books or journal articles. Luckily, there are now several book-length treatments of asset markets, game theory, information economics, and general equilibrium theory. The serious student will have no shortage of materials in which he or she can pursue the study of these topics.

Production of the book

In the process of rewriting the book, I have moved everything over to Donald Knuth's TEX system. I think that the book now looks a lot better; furthermore, cross-referencing, equation numbering, indexing, and so on are now a lot easier for both the author and the readers. Since the cost to the author of revising the book is now much less, the reader can expect to see more frequent revisions. (Perhaps that last sentence can be turned into an exercise for the next edition...)

Part of the book was composed on MS-DOS equipment, but the majority of it was composed and typeset on a NeXT computer. I used Emacs as the primary editor, operating in Kresten Thorup's auc-tex mode. I use ispell for spell-checking, and the standard makeindex and bibtex tools for indexing and bibliographic management. Tom Rokicki's TEXview was the tool of choice for previewing and printing. Preliminary versions of the diagrams were produced using Designer and Top Draw. An artist rendered final versions using FreeHand and sent me the Encapsulated Postscript files which were then incorporated into the TeX code using Trevor Darrell's `psfig` macros. I owe a special debt of gratitude to the authors of these software tools, many of which have been provided to users free of charge.

Acknowledgments

Many people have written to me with typos, comments, and suggestions over the years. Here is a partial list of names: Tevfik Aksoy, Jim Andreoni, Gustavo Angeles, Ken Binmore, Soren Blomqvist, Kim Border, Gordon Brown, Steven Buccola, Mark Burkey, Lea Verdin Carty, Zhiqi Chen, John Chilton, Francisco Armando da Costa, Giacomo Costa, David W. Crawford, Peter Diamond, Karen Eggleston, Maxim Engers, Sjur Flam, Mario Forni, Marcos Gallacher, Jon Hamilton, Barbara Harrow, Kevin Jackson, Yi Jiang, John Kennan, David Kiefer, Rachel Kranton, Bo Li, George Mailath, David Malueg, Duhamel Marc, John Miller, V. A. Noronha, Martin Osborne, Marco Ottaviani, Attila Ratfai, Archie Rosen, Jan Rutkowski, Michael Sandfort, Marco Sandri, Roy H. M. Sembel, Mariusz Shatba, Bert Schoonbeek, Carl Simon, Bill Sjostrom, Gerhard Sorger, Jim Swanson, Knut Sydsater, A. J. Talman, Coenraad Vrolijk, Richard Woodward, Frances Wooley, Ed Zajac, and Yong Zhu. If my filing system were better, there would probably be several more names. I appreciate being notified of errata and will usually be able to correct such bugs in the next printing. You can send me e-mail about bugs at `Hal.Varian@umich.edu`.

Several people have contributed suggestions on the new third edition, including Eduardo Ley, Pat Reagan, John Weymark, and Jay Wilson. Eduardo Ley also provided some of the exercises and several of the answers.

Finally, I want to end with a comment to the student. As you read this work, it is important to keep in mind the immortal words of Sir Richard Steele (1672–1729): "It is to be noted that when any part of this paper appears dull there is a design in it."

Ann Arbor
November 1991

Microeconomic Analysis

Third Edition

CHAPTER **1**

TECHNOLOGY

The simplest and most common way to describe the technology of a firm is the **production function**, which is generally studied in intermediate courses. However, there are other ways to describe firm technologies that are both more general and more useful in certain settings. We will discuss several of these ways to represent firm production possibilities in this chapter, along with ways to describe economically relevant aspects of a firm's technology.

1.1 Measurement of inputs and outputs

A firm produces outputs from various combinations of inputs. In order to study firm choices we need a convenient way to summarize the production possibilities of the firm, i.e., which combinations of inputs and outputs are **technologically feasible**.

It is usually most satisfactory to think of the inputs and outputs as being measured in terms of *flows:* a certain amount of inputs per time period are used to produce a certain amount of outputs per unit time period. It is a good idea to explicitly include a time dimension in a specification of inputs and outputs. If you do this you will be less likely to use incommensurate units, confuse stocks and flows, or make other elementary errors. For example, if we measure labor time in hours per week, we would want to be sure to measure capital services in hours per week, and the production of output in units per week. However, when discussing technological choices in the abstract, as we do in this chapter, it is common to omit the time dimension.

We may also want to distinguish inputs and outputs by the calendar time in which they are available, the location in which they are available, and even the circumstances under which they become available. By defining the inputs and outputs with regard to when and where they are available, we can capture some aspects of the temporal or spatial nature of production. For example, concrete available in a given year can be used to construct a building that will be completed the following year. Similarly, concrete purchased in one location can be used in production in some other location.

An input of "concrete" should be thought of as a concrete of a particular grade, available in a particular place at a particular time. In some cases we might even add to this list qualifications such as "if the weather is dry"; that is, we might consider the circumstances, or state of nature, in which the concrete is available. The level of detail that we will use in specifying inputs and outputs will depend on the problem at hand, but we should remain aware of the fact that a particular input or output good can be specified in arbitrarily fine detail.

1.2 Specification of technology

Suppose the firm has n possible goods to serve as inputs and/or outputs. If a firm uses y_j^i units of a good j as an input and produces y_j^o of the good as an output, then the **net output** of good j is given by $y_j = y_j^o - y_j^i$. If the net output of a good j is positive, then the firm is producing more of good j than it uses as an input; if the net output is negative, then the firm is using more of good j than it produces.

A **production plan** is simply a list of net outputs of various goods. We can represent a production plan by a vector $\mathbf{y}$ in R^n where y_j is negative if the jth good serves as a net input and positive if the jth good serves as a net output. The set of all technologically feasible production plans is called the firm's **production possibilities set** and will be denoted by Y, a subset of R^n. The set Y is supposed to describe all patterns of inputs and outputs that are technologically feasible. It gives us a complete description of the technological possibilities facing the firm.

When we study the behavior of a firm in certain economic environments, we may want to distinguish between production plans that are "immediately feasible" and those that are "eventually" feasible. For example, in the short run, some inputs of the firm are fixed so that only production plans compatible with these fixed factors are possible. In the long run, such factors may be variable, so that the firm's technological possibilities may well change.

We will generally assume that such restrictions can be described by some vector $\mathbf{z}$ in R^n. For example, $\mathbf{z}$ could be a list of the maximum amount of the various inputs and outputs that can be produced in the time period under consideration. The **restricted** or **short-run production possibilities set** will be denoted by $Y(\mathbf{z})$; this consists of all feasible net output bundles consistent with the constraint level $\mathbf{z}$. Suppose, for example, that factor n is fixed at $\bar{y}_n$ in the short run. Then $Y(\bar{y}_n) = \{\mathbf{y} \text{ in } Y : y_n = \bar{y}_n\}$. Note that $Y(\mathbf{z})$ is a subset of Y, since it consists of all production plans that are feasible—which means that they are in Y—and that also satisfy some additional conditions.

EXAMPLE: Input requirement set

Suppose we are considering a firm that produces only one output. In this case we write the net output bundle as $(y, -\mathbf{x})$ where $\mathbf{x}$ is a vector of inputs that can produce y units of output. We can then define a special case of a restricted production possibilities set, the **input requirement set**:

$$V(y) = \{\mathbf{x} \text{ in } R^n_+ : (y, -\mathbf{x}) \text{ is in } Y\}$$

The input requirement set is the set of all input bundles that produce *at least* y units of output.

Note that the input requirement set, as defined here, measures inputs as positive numbers rather than negative numbers as used in the production possibilities set.

EXAMPLE: Isoquant

In the case above we can also define an **isoquant**:

$$Q(y) = \{\mathbf{x} \text{ in } R^n_+ : \mathbf{x} \text{ is in } V(y) \text{ and } \mathbf{x} \text{ is not in } V(y') \text{ for } y' > y\}.$$

The isoquant gives all input bundles that produce exactly y units of output.

EXAMPLE: Short-run production possibilities set

Suppose a firm produces some output from labor and some kind of machine which we will refer to as "capital." Production plans then look like $(y, -l, -k)$ where y is the level of output, l the amount of labor input, and k the amount of capital input. We imagine that labor can be varied immediately but that capital is fixed at the level $\bar{k}$ in the short run. Then

$$Y(\bar{k}) = \{(y, -l, -k) \text{ in } Y : k = \bar{k}\}$$

is an example of a **short-run production possibilities set**.

EXAMPLE: Production function

If the firm has only one output, we can define the **production function**:

$$f(\mathbf{x}) = \{y \text{ in } R : y \text{ is the maximum output associated with } -\mathbf{x} \text{ in } Y\}.$$

EXAMPLE: Transformation function

There is an n-dimensional analog of a production function that will be useful in our study of general equilibrium theory. A production plan $\mathbf{y}$ in Y is **(technologically) efficient** if there is no $\mathbf{y}'$ in Y such that $\mathbf{y}' \geq \mathbf{y}$ and $\mathbf{y}' \neq \mathbf{y}$; that is, a production plan is efficient if there is no way to produce more output with the same inputs or to produce the same output with less inputs. (Note carefully how the sign convention on inputs works here.) We often assume that we can describe the set of technologically efficient production plans by a **transformation function** $T : R^n \rightarrow R$ where $T(\mathbf{y}) = 0$ if and only if $\mathbf{y}$ is efficient. Just as a production function picks out the maximum *scalar* output as a function of the inputs, the transformation function picks out the maximal *vectors* of net outputs.

EXAMPLE: Cobb-Douglas technology

Let a be a parameter such that $0 < a < 1$. Then the **Cobb-Douglas technology** is defined in the following manner. See Figure 1.1A.

$$Y = \{(y, -x_1, -x_2) \text{ in } R^3 : y \leq x_1^a x_2^{1-a}\}$$
$$V(y) = \{(x_1, x_2) \text{ in } R_+^2 : y \leq x_1^a x_2^{1-a}\}$$
$$Q(y) = \{(x_1, x_2) \text{ in } R_+^2 : y = x_1^a x_2^{1-a}\}$$
$$Y(z) = \{(y, -x_1, -x_2) \text{ in } R^3 : y \leq x_1^a x_2^{1-a}, x_2 = z\}$$
$$T(y, x_1, x_2) = y - x_1^a x_2^{1-a}$$
$$f(x_1, x_2) = x_1^a x_2^{1-a}.$$

EXAMPLE: Leontief technology

Let $a > 0$ and $b > 0$ be parameters. Then the **Leontief technology** is defined in the following manner. See Figure 1.1B.

$$Y = \{(y, -x_1, -x_2) \text{ in } R^3 : y \leq \min(ax_1, bx_2)\}$$
$$V(y) = \{(x_1, x_2) \text{ in } R_+^2 : y \leq \min(ax_1, bx_2)\}$$
$$Q(y) = \{(x_1, x_2) \text{ in } R_+^2 : y = \min(ax_1, bx_2)\}$$
$$T(y, x_1, x_2) = y - \min(ax_1, bx_2)$$
$$f(x_1, x_2) = \min(ax_1, bx_2).$$

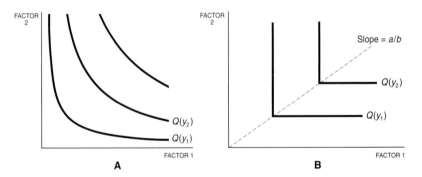

Cobb-Douglas and Leontief technologies. Panel A depicts the general shape of a Cobb-Douglas technology, and panel B depicts the general shape of a Leontief technology.

Figure 1.1

In this chapter we will deal primarily with firms that produce only one output; therefore, we will generally describe their technology by input requirement sets or production functions. Later on we will use the production set and the transformation function.

1.3 Activity analysis

The most straightforward way of describing production sets or input requirement sets is simply to list the feasible production plans. For example, suppose that we can produce an output good using factor inputs 1 and 2. There are two different **activities** or **techniques** by which this production can take place:

Technique A: one unit of factor 1 and two units of factor 2 produces one unit of output.

Technique B: two units of factor 1 and one unit of factor 2 produces one unit of output.

Let the output be good 1, and the factors be goods 2 and 3. Then we can represent the production possibilities implied by these two activities by the production set

$$Y = \{(1, -1, -2), (1, -2, -1)\}$$

or the input requirement set

$$V(1) = \{(1, 2), (2, 1)\}.$$

This input requirement set is depicted in Figure 1.2A.

It may be the case that to produce y units of output we could just use y times as much of each input for $y = 1, 2, \ldots$. In this case you might think that the set of feasible ways to produce y units of output would be given by

$$V(y) = \{(y, 2y), (2y, y)\}.$$

However, this set does not include all the relevant possibilities. It is true that $(y, 2y)$ will produce y units of output if we use technique A and that $(2y, y)$ will produce y units of output if we use technique B—but what if we use a mixture of techniques A and B?

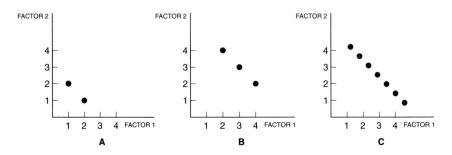

Figure 1.2

Input requirement sets. Panel A depicts $V(1)$, panel B depicts $V(2)$, and panel C depicts $V(y)$ for a larger value of y.

In this case we have to let y_A be the amount of output produced using technique A and y_B the amount of output produced using technique B. Then $V(y)$ will be given by the set

$$V(y) = \{(y_A + 2y_B, y_B + 2y_A) : y = y_A + y_B\}.$$

So, for example, $V(2) = \{(2, 4), (4, 2), (3, 3)\}$, as depicted in Figure 1.2B. Note that the input combination $(3, 3)$ can produce two units of output by producing one unit using technique A and one unit using technique B.

1.4 Monotonic technologies

Let us continue to examine the two-activity example introduced in the last section. Suppose that we had an input vector $(3,2)$. Is this sufficient to produce one unit of output? We may argue that since we could dispose of 2 units of factor 1 and be left with $(1,2)$, it would indeed be possible to produce 1 unit of output from the inputs $(3,2)$. Thus, if such **free disposal** is allowed, it is reasonable to argue that if $\mathbf{x}$ is a feasible way to produce y units of output and $\mathbf{x}'$ is an input vector with at least as much of each input, then $\mathbf{x}'$ should be a feasible way to produce y. Thus, the input requirement sets should be **monotonic** in the following sense:

MONOTONICITY.   *If* **x** *is in* $V(y)$ *and* $\mathbf{x}' \geq \mathbf{x}$, *then* $\mathbf{x}'$ *is in* $V(y)$.

If we assume monotonicity, then the input requirement sets depicted in Figure 1.2 become the sets depicted in Figure 1.3.

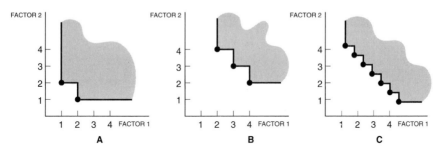

Monotonicity.   Here are the same three input requirement sets if we also assume monotonicity.

Figure 1.3

Monotonicity is often an appropriate assumption for production sets as well. In this context, we generally want to assume that if **y** is in Y and $\mathbf{y}' \leq \mathbf{y}$, then $\mathbf{y}'$ must also be in Y. Note carefully how the sign convention works here. If $\mathbf{y}' \leq \mathbf{y}$, it means that every component of vector $\mathbf{y}'$ is less than or equal to the corresponding component of **y**. This means that the production plan represented by $\mathbf{y}'$ produces an equal or smaller amount of all outputs by using at least as much of all inputs, as compared to **y**. Hence, it is natural to suppose that if **y** is feasible, $\mathbf{y}'$ is also feasible.

1.5 Convex technologies

Let us now consider what the input requirement set looks like if we want to produce 100 units of output. As a first step, we might argue that if we multiply the vectors (1,2) and (2,1) by 100, we should be able just to *replicate* what we were doing before and thereby produce 100 times as much. It is clear that not all production processes will necessarily allow for this kind of replication, but it seems to be plausible in many circumstances.

If such replication is possible, then we can conclude that (100,200) and (200,100) are in V(100). Are there any other possible ways to produce 100 units of output? Well, we could operate 50 processes of activity A and 50 processes of activity B. This would use 150 units of good 1 and 150 units of good 2 to produce 100 units of output; hence, (150,150) should be in the input requirement set. Similarly, we could operate 25 processes of activity A and 75 processes of type B. This implies that

$$.25(100, 200) + .75(200, 100) = (175, 125)$$

should be in $V(100)$. More generally,

$$t(100, 200) + (1 - t)(200, 100) = (100t + 200(1 - t), 200t + (1 - t)100)$$

should be in $V(100)$ for $t = 0, .01, .02, \ldots, 1$.

We might as well make the obvious approximation here and let t take on any fractional value between 0 and 1. This leads to a production set of the form depicted in Figure 1.4A. The precise statement of this property is given in the next definition.

CONVEXITY. *If* $\mathbf{x}$ *and* $\mathbf{x}'$ *are in* $V(y)$, *then* $t\mathbf{x} + (1 - t)\mathbf{x}'$ *is in* $V(y)$ *for all* $0 \leq t \leq 1$. *That is,* $V(y)$ *is a* **convex set**.

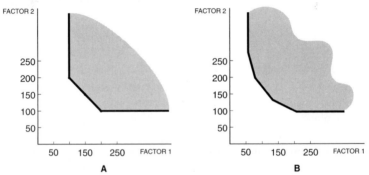

Figure 1.4

Convex input requirement sets. If $\mathbf{x}$ and $\mathbf{x}'$ can produce y units of output, then any weighted average $t\mathbf{x} + (1 - t)\mathbf{x}'$ can also produce y units of output. Panel A depicts a convex input requirement set with two underlying activities; panel B depicts a convex input requirement set with many activities.

We have motivated the convexity assumption by a replication argument. If we want to produce a "large" amount of output and we can replicate "small" production processes, then it appears that the technology should be modeled as being convex. However, if the scale of the underlying activities is large relative to the desired amount of output, convexity may not be a reasonable hypothesis.

However, there are also other arguments about why convexity is a reasonable assumption in some circumstances. For example, suppose that we are considering output per month. If one vector of inputs $\mathbf{x}$ produces y

units of output per month, and another vector $\mathbf{x}'$ also produces y units of output per month, then we might use $\mathbf{x}$ for half a month and $\mathbf{x}'$ for half a month. If there are no problems introduced by switching production plans in the middle of the month, we might reasonably expect to get y units of output.

We applied the arguments given above to the input requirement sets, but similar arguments apply to the production set. It is common to assume that if $\mathbf{y}$ and $\mathbf{y}'$ are both in Y, then $t\mathbf{y} + (1-t)\mathbf{y}'$ is also in Y for $0 \le t \le 1$; in other words, Y is a convex set. However, it should be noted that the convexity of the production set is a much more problematic hypothesis than the convexity of the input requirement set. For example, convexity of the production set rules out "start up costs" and other sorts of returns to scale. This will be discussed in greater detail shortly. For now we will describe a few of the relationships between the convexity of $V(y)$, the curvature of the production function, and the convexity of Y.

Convex production set implies convex input requirement set.   *If the production set Y is a convex set, then the associated input requirement set, $V(y)$, is a convex set.*

Proof. If Y is a convex set then it follows that for any $\mathbf{x}$ and $\mathbf{x}'$ such that $(y, -\mathbf{x})$ and $(y, -\mathbf{x}')$ are in Y, we must have $(ty + (1-t)y, -t\mathbf{x} - (1-t)\mathbf{x}')$ in Y. This is simply requiring that $(y, -(t\mathbf{x} + (1-t)\mathbf{x}'))$ is in Y. It follows that if $\mathbf{x}$ and $\mathbf{x}'$ are in $V(y)$, $t\mathbf{x} + (1-t)\mathbf{x}'$ is in $V(y)$ which shows that $V(y)$ is convex. ∎

Convex input requirement set is equivalent to quasiconcave production function. $V(y)$ *is a convex set if and only if the production function $f(\mathbf{x})$ is a quasiconcave function.*

Proof. $V(y) = \{\mathbf{x} : f(\mathbf{x}) \ge y\}$, which is just the upper contour set of $f(\mathbf{x})$. But a function is quasiconcave if and only if it has a convex upper contour set; see Chapter 27, page 496. ∎

1.6 Regular technologies

Finally, we consider a weak regularity condition concerning $V(y)$.

REGULAR. $V(y)$ *is a closed, nonempty set for all $y \ge 0$.*

The assumption that $V(y)$ is nonempty requires that there is some conceivable way to produce any given level of output. This is simply to avoid qualifying statements by phrases like "assuming that y can be produced."

The assumption that $V(y)$ is closed is made for technical reasons and is innocuous in most contexts. One implication of the assumption that $V(y)$ is a closed set is as follows: suppose that we have a sequence $(\mathbf{x}^i)$ of input bundles that can each produce y and this sequence converges to an input bundle $\mathbf{x}^0$. That is to say, the input bundles in the sequence get arbitrarily close to $\mathbf{x}^0$. If $V(y)$ is a closed set then this limit bundle $\mathbf{x}^0$ must be capable of producing y. Roughly speaking, the input requirement set must "include its own boundary."

1.7 Parametric representations of technology

Suppose that we have many possible ways to produce some given level of output. Then it might be reasonable to summarize this input set by a "smoothed" input set as in Figure 1.5. That is, we may want to fit a nice curve through the possible production points. Such a smoothing process should not involve any great problems, if there are indeed many slightly different ways to produce a given level of output.

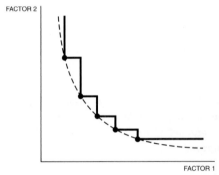

FACTOR 2

FACTOR 1

Figure 1.5   **Smoothing an isoquant**. An input requirement set and a "smooth" approximation to it.

If we do make such an approximation to "smooth" the input requirement set, it is natural to look further for a convenient way to represent the technology by a parametric function involving a few unknown parameters. For example, the Cobb-Douglas technology mentioned earlier implies that any input bundle (x_1, x_2) that satisfies $x^a x^{1-a} \geq y$ can produce at least y units of output.

These parametric technological representations should not necessarily be thought of as a literal depiction of production possibilities. The production possibilities are the engineering data describing the physically possible production plans. It may well happen that this engineering data can be reasonably well described by a convenient functional form such as the Cobb-Douglas function. If so, such a parametric description can be very useful.

In most applications we only care about having a parametric approximation to a technology over some particular range of input and output levels, and it is common to use relatively simple functional forms to make such a parametric approximation. These parametric representations are very convenient as pedagogic tools, and we will often take our technologies to have such a representation. We can then bring the tools of calculus and algebra to investigate the production choices of the firm.

1.8 The technical rate of substitution

Assume that we have some technology summarized by a smooth production function and that we are producing at a particular point $y^* = f(x_1^*, x_2^*)$. Suppose that we want to increase the amount of input 1 and decrease the amount of input 2 so as to maintain a constant level of output. How can we determine this **technical rate of substitution** between these two factors?

In the two-dimensional case, the technical rate of substitution is just the slope of the isoquant: how one has to adjust x_2 to keep output constant when x_1 changes by a small amount, as depicted in Figure 1.6. In the n-dimensional case, the technical rate of substitution is the slope of an isoquant surface, measured in a particular direction.

Let $x_2(x_1)$ be the (implicit) function that tells us how much of x_2 it takes to produce y if we are using x_1 units of the other input. Then by definition, the function $x_2(x_1)$ has to satisfy the identity

$$f(x_1, x_2(x_1)) \equiv y$$

We are after an expression for $\partial x_2(x_1^*)/\partial x_1$. Differentiating the above identity, we find:

$$\frac{\partial f(\mathbf{x}^*)}{\partial x_1} + \frac{\partial f(\mathbf{x}^*)}{\partial x_2}\frac{\partial x_2(x_1^*)}{\partial x_1} = 0$$

or

$$\frac{\partial x_2(x_1^*)}{\partial x_1} = -\frac{\partial f(\mathbf{x}^*)/\partial x_1}{\partial f(\mathbf{x}^*)/\partial x_2}.$$

This gives us an explicit expression for the technical rate of substitution.

Here is another way to derive the technical rate of substitution. Think of a vector of (small) changes in the input levels which we write as $\mathbf{dx} = (dx_1, dx_2)$. The associated change in the output is approximated by

$$dy = \frac{\partial f}{\partial x_1}\,dx_1 + \frac{\partial f}{\partial x_2}\,dx_2.$$

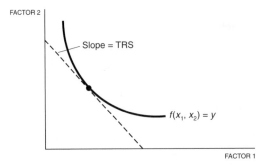

FACTOR 2

Slope = TRS

$f(x_1, x_2) = y$

FACTOR 1

Figure 1.6   **The technical rate of substitution.**   The technical rate of substitution measures how one of the inputs must adjust in order to keep output constant when another input changes.

This expression is known as the **total differential** of the function $f(\mathbf{x})$. Consider a particular change in which only factor 1 and factor 2 change, and the change is such that output remains constant. That is, dx_1 and dx_2 adjust "along an isoquant."

Since output remains constant, we have

$$0 = \frac{\partial f}{\partial x_1}\, dx_1 + \frac{\partial f}{\partial x_2}\, dx_2,$$

which can be solved for

$$\frac{dx_2}{dx_1} = -\frac{\partial f/\partial x_1}{\partial f/\partial x_2}.$$

Either the implicit function method or the total differential method may be used to calculate the technical rate of substitution. The implicit function method is a bit more rigorous, but the total differential method is perhaps more intuitive.

EXAMPLE: TRS for a Cobb-Douglas technology

Given that $f(x_1, x_2) = x_1^a x_2^{1-a}$, we can take the derivatives to find

$$\frac{\partial f(\mathbf{x})}{\partial x_1} = a x_1^{a-1} x_2^{1-a} = a \left[\frac{x_2}{x_1}\right]^{1-a}$$

$$\frac{\partial f(\mathbf{x})}{\partial x_2} = (1-a) x_1^a x_2^{-a} = (1-a) \left[\frac{x_1}{x_2}\right]^{a}.$$

It follows that

$$\frac{\partial x_2(x_1)}{\partial x_1} = -\frac{\partial f/\partial x_1}{\partial f/\partial x_2} = -\frac{a}{1-a}\frac{x_2}{x_1}.$$

1.9 The elasticity of substitution

The technical rate of substitution measures the slope of an isoquant. The **elasticity of substitution** measures the *curvature* of an isoquant. More specifically, the elasticity of substitution measures the percentage change in the factor ratio divided by the percentage change in the TRS, with output being held fixed. If we let $\Delta(x_2/x_1)$ be the change in the factor ratio and ΔTRS be the change in the technical rate of substitution, we can express this as

$$\sigma = \frac{\frac{\Delta(x_2/x_1)}{x_2/x_1}}{\frac{\Delta TRS}{TRS}}.$$

This is a relatively natural measure of curvature: it asks how the ratio of factor inputs changes as the slope of the isoquant changes. If a small change in slope gives us a large change in the factor input ratio, the isoquant is relatively flat which means that the elasticity of substitution is large.

In practice we think of the percent change as being very small and take the limit of this expression as Δ goes to zero. Hence, the expression for σ becomes

$$\sigma = \frac{TRS}{(x_2/x_1)} \frac{d(x_2/x_1)}{dTRS}.$$

It is often convenient to calculate σ using the **logarithmic derivative**. In general, if $y = g(x)$, the elasticity of y with respect to x refers to the percentage change in y induced by a (small) percentage change in x. That is,

$$\epsilon = \frac{\frac{dy}{y}}{\frac{dx}{x}} = \frac{dy}{dx}\frac{x}{y}.$$

Provided that x and y are positive, this derivative can be written as

$$\epsilon = \frac{d\ln y}{d\ln x}.$$

To prove this, note that by the chain rule

$$\frac{d\ln y}{d\ln x}\frac{d\ln x}{dx} = \frac{d\ln y}{dx}.$$

Carrying out the calculation on the left-hand and the right-hand side of the equals sign, we have

$$\frac{d\ln y}{d\ln x}\frac{1}{x} = \frac{1}{y}\frac{dy}{dx},$$

or

$$\frac{d\ln y}{d\ln x} = \frac{x}{y}\frac{dy}{dx}.$$

Alternatively, we can use total differentials to write

$$d \ln y = \frac{1}{y} dy$$
$$d \ln x = \frac{1}{x} dx,$$

so that

$$\epsilon = \frac{d \ln y}{d \ln x} = \frac{dy}{dx} \frac{x}{y}.$$

Again, the calculation given first is more rigorous, but the second calculation is more intuitive.

Applying this to the elasticity of substitution, we can write

$$\sigma = \frac{d \ln(x_2/x_1)}{d \ln |TRS|}.$$

(The absolute value sign in the denominator is to convert the TRS to a positive number so that the logarithm makes sense.)

EXAMPLE: The elasticity of substitution for the Cobb-Douglas production function

We have seen above that

$$TRS = -\frac{a}{1-a} \frac{x_2}{x_1},$$

or

$$\frac{x_2}{x_1} = -\frac{1-a}{a} TRS.$$

It follows that

$$\ln \frac{x_2}{x_1} = \ln \frac{1-a}{a} + \ln |TRS|.$$

This in turn implies

$$\sigma = \frac{d \ln(x_2/x_1)}{d \ln |TRS|} = 1.$$

1.10 Returns to scale

Suppose that we are using some vector of inputs $\mathbf{x}$ to produce some output y and we decide to scale all inputs up or down by some amount $t \geq 0$. What will happen to the level of output?

In the cases we described earlier, where we wanted only to scale output *up* by some amount, we typically assumed that we could simply replicate what we were doing before and thereby produce t times as much output as before. If this sort of scaling is always possible, we will say that the technology exhibits **constant returns to scale**. More formally,

CONSTANT RETURNS TO SCALE. *A technology exhibits* **constant returns to scale** *if any of the following are satisfied:*

(1) $\mathbf{y}$ *in Y implies* $t\mathbf{y}$ *is in Y, for all $t \geq 0$;*

(2) $\mathbf{x}$ *in $V(y)$ implies* $t\mathbf{x}$ *is in $V(ty)$ for all $t \geq 0$;*

(3) $f(t\mathbf{x}) = tf(\mathbf{x})$ *for all $t \geq 0$; i.e., the production function $f(\mathbf{x})$ is homogeneous of degree 1.*

The replication argument given above indicates that constant returns to scale is often a reasonable assumption to make about technologies. However, there are situations where it is not a plausible assumption.

One circumstance where constant returns to scale may be violated is when we try to "subdivide" a production process. Even if it is always possible to scale operations up by integer amounts, it may not be possible to scale operations *down* in the same way. For example, there may be some minimal scale of operation so that producing output below this scale involves different techniques. Once the minimal scale of operation is reached, larger levels of output can be produced by replication.

Another circumstance where constant returns to scale may be violated is when we want to scale operations up by noninteger amounts. Certainly, replicating what we did before is simple enough, but how do we do one and one half times what we were doing before?

These two situations in which constant returns to scale is not satisfied are only important when the scale of production is small relative to the minimum scale of output.

A third circumstance where constant returns to scale is inappropriate is when doubling all inputs allows for a *more* efficient means of production to be used. Replication says that doubling our output by doubling our inputs is feasible, but there may be a better way to produce output. Consider, for example, a firm that builds an oil pipeline between two points and uses as inputs labor, machines, and steel to construct the pipeline. We may take the relevant measure of output for this firm to be the capacity of the resulting line. Then it is clear that if we double all inputs to the production process, the output may more than double since increasing the surface area of a pipe by 2 will increase the volume by a factor of 4.[1] In

---

[1] Of course, a larger pipe may be more difficult to build, so we may not think of output

this case, when output increases by more than the scale of the inputs, we say the technology exhibits **increasing returns to scale**.

INCREASING RETURNS TO SCALE. *A technology exhibits increasing returns to scale if $f(t\mathbf{x}) > tf(\mathbf{x})$ for all $t > 1$.*

A fourth way that constant returns to scale may be violated is by being *unable* to replicate some input. Consider, for example, a 100-acre farm. If we wanted to produce twice as much output, we could use twice as much of each input. But this would imply using twice as much land as well. It may be that this is impossible to do since more land may not be available. Even though the technology exhibits constant returns to scale if we increase *all* inputs, it may be convenient to think of it as exhibiting **decreasing returns to scale** with respect to the inputs under our control. More precisely, we have:

DECREASING RETURNS TO SCALE. *A technology exhibits decreasing returns to scale if $f(t\mathbf{x}) < tf(\mathbf{x})$ for all $t > 1$.*

The most natural case of decreasing returns to scale is the case where we are unable to replicate some inputs. Thus, we should expect that *restricted* production possibility sets would typically exhibit decreasing returns to scale. It turns out that it can always be assumed that decreasing returns to scale is due to the presence of some fixed input.

To show this, suppose that $f(\mathbf{x})$ is a production function for some k inputs that exhibits decreasing returns to scale. Then we can introduce a new "mythical" input and measure its level by z. Define a new production function $F(z, \mathbf{x})$ by

$$F(z, \mathbf{x}) = zf(\mathbf{x}/z).$$

Note that F exhibits constant returns to scale. If we multiply all inputs—the $\mathbf{x}$ inputs and the z input—by some $t \geq 0$, we have output going up by t. And if z is fixed at 1, we have exactly the same technology that we had before. Hence, the original decreasing returns technology $f(\mathbf{x})$ can be thought of as a restriction of the constant returns technology $F(z, \mathbf{x})$ that results from setting $z = 1$.

Finally, let us note that the various kinds of returns to scale defined above are global in nature. It may well happen that a technology exhibits increasing returns to scale for some values of $\mathbf{x}$ and decreasing returns to scale for other values. Thus in many circumstances a local measure of returns to scale is useful. The **elasticity of scale** measures the percent increase in output due to a one percent increase in all inputs—that is, due to an increase in the *scale* of operations.

necessarily increasing exactly by a factor of 4. But it may very well increase by more than a factor of 2.

Let $y = f(\mathbf{x})$ be the production function. Let t be a positive scalar, and consider the function $y(t) = f(t\mathbf{x})$. If $t = 1$, we have the current scale of operation; if $t > 1$, we are scaling all inputs up by t; and if $t < 1$, we are scaling all inputs down by t.

The elasticity of scale is given by

$$e(\mathbf{x}) = \frac{\frac{dy(t)}{y(t)}}{\frac{dt}{t}},$$

evaluated at $t = 1$. Rearranging this expression, we have

$$e(\mathbf{x}) = \frac{dy(t)}{dt}\frac{t}{y}\bigg|_{t=1} = \frac{df(t\mathbf{x})}{dt}\frac{t}{f(t\mathbf{x})}\bigg|_{t=1}.$$

Note that we must evaluate the expression at $t = 1$ to calculate the elasticity of scale at the point $\mathbf{x}$. We say that the technology exhibits locally increasing, constant, or decreasing returns to scale as $e(\mathbf{x})$ is greater, equal, or less than 1.

EXAMPLE: Returns to scale and the Cobb-Douglas technology

Suppose that $y = x_1^a x_2^b$. Then $f(tx_1, tx_2) = (tx_1)^a(tx_2)^b = t^{a+b}x_1^a x_2^b = t^{a+b}f(x_1, x_2)$. Hence, $f(tx_1, tx_2) = tf(x_1, x_2)$ if and only if $a + b = 1$. Similarly, $a + b > 1$ implies increasing returns to scale, and $a + b < 1$ implies decreasing returns to scale.

In fact, the elasticity of scale for the Cobb-Douglas technology turns out to be precisely $a + b$. To see this, we apply the definition:

$$\frac{d(tx_1)^a(tx_2)^b}{dt} = \frac{dt^{a+b}x_1^a x_2^b}{dt} = (a + b)t^{a+b-1}x_1^a x_2^b.$$

Evaluating this derivative at $t = 1$ and dividing by $f(x_1, x_2) = x_1^a x_2^b$ gives us the result.

1.11 Homogeneous and homothetic technologies

A function $f(\mathbf{x})$ is **homogeneous of degree** k if $f(t\mathbf{x}) = t^k f(\mathbf{x})$ for all $t > 0$. The two most important "degrees" in economics are the zeroth and first degree.[2] A zero-degree homogeneous function is one for which

---

[2] However, it is sometimes thought that the Masters and the Ph.D. are even more important.

$f(t\mathbf{x}) = f(\mathbf{x})$, and a first-degree homogeneous function is one for which $f(t\mathbf{x}) = tf(\mathbf{x})$.

Comparing this definition to the definition of constant returns to scale, we see that a technology has constant returns to scale if and only if its production function is homogeneous of degree 1.

A function $g : R \to R$ is said to be a **positive monotonic transformation** if g is a strictly increasing function; that is, a function for which $x > y$ implies that $g(x) > g(y)$. (The "positive" is usually implied by the context.) A **homothetic function** is a monotonic transformation of a function that is homogeneous of degree 1. In other words, $f(\mathbf{x})$ is homothetic if and only if it can be written as $f(\mathbf{x}) = g(h(\mathbf{x}))$ where $h(\cdot)$ is homogeneous of degree 1 and $g(\cdot)$ is a monotonic function. See Figure 1.7 for a geometric interpretation.

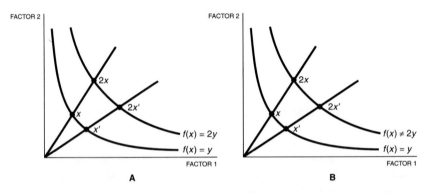

Figure 1.7   **Homogeneous and homothetic functions.** Panel A depicts a function that is homogeneous of degree 1. If $\mathbf{x}$ and $\mathbf{x}'$ can both produce y units of output, then $2\mathbf{x}$ and $2\mathbf{x}'$ can both produce $2y$ units of output. Panel B depicts a homothetic function. If $\mathbf{x}$ and $\mathbf{x}'$ produce the *same* level of output, y, then $2\mathbf{x}$ and $2\mathbf{x}'$ can produce the *same* level of output, but not necessarily $2y$.

Think of a monotonic transformation as a way to measure output in different units. For example, we could measure the output of a chemical process in pints or quarts. Changing from one unit to another in this case is pretty simple—we just multiply or divide by two. A more exotic monotonic transformation would be one in which we measure the output in the *square* of the number of quarts. Given this interpretation, a homothetic technology is one for which there is some way to measure output so that the technology "looks like" constant returns to scale.

Homogeneous and homothetic functions are of interest due to the simple ways that their isoquants vary as the level of output varies. In the case of a homogeneous function, the isoquants are all just "blown up" versions of a single isoquant. If $f(\mathbf{x})$ is homogeneous of degree 1, then if $\mathbf{x}$ and $\mathbf{x}'$ can produce y units of output it follows that $t\mathbf{x}$ and $t\mathbf{x}'$ can produce ty units of output, as depicted in Figure 1.7A. A homothetic function has almost the same property: if $\mathbf{x}$ and $\mathbf{x}'$ produce the same level of output, then $t\mathbf{x}$ and $t\mathbf{x}'$ can produce the same level of output—but it won't necessarily be t times as much as the original output. The isoquants for a homothetic technology look just like the isoquants for a homogeneous technology, only the output levels associated with the isoquants are different.

Homogeneous and homothetic technologies are of interest since they put specific restrictions on how the technical rate of substitution changes as the scale of production changes. In particular, for either of these functions the technical rate of substitution is independent of the scale of production.

This follows immediately from the remarks in Chapter 26, page 482, where we show that if $f(\mathbf{x})$ is homogeneous of degree 1, then $\partial f(\mathbf{x})/\partial x_i$ is homogeneous of degree 0. It follows that the ratio of any two derivatives is homogeneous of degree zero, which is the result we seek.

EXAMPLE: The CES production function

The **constant elasticity of substitution** or **CES production function** has the form

$$y = [a_1 x_1^\rho + a_2 x_2^\rho]^{\frac{1}{\rho}}.$$

It is easy to verify that the CES function exhibits constant returns to scale. The CES function contains several other well-known production functions as special cases, depending on the value of the parameter ρ. These are described below and illustrated in Figure 1.8. In our discussion, it is convenient to set the parameters $a_1 = a_2 = 1$.

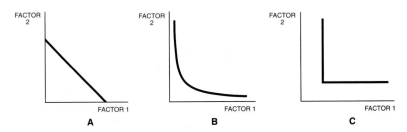

The CES production function. The CES production function takes on a variety of shapes depending on the value of the parameter ρ. Panel A depicts the case where $\rho = 1$, panel B the case where $\rho = 0$, and panel C the case where $\rho = -\infty$.

Figure 1.8

(1) The linear production function ($\rho = 1$). Simple substitution yields

$$y = x_1 + x_2.$$

(2) The Cobb-Douglas production function ($\rho = 0$). When $\rho = 0$ the CES production function is not defined, due to division by zero. However, we will show that as ρ approaches zero, the isoquants of the CES production function look very much like the isoquants of the Cobb-Douglas production function.

This is easiest to see using the technical rate of substitution. By direct calculation,

$$TRS = - \left(\frac{x_1}{x_2} \right)^{\rho - 1}. \tag{1.1}$$

As ρ approaches zero, this tends to a limit of

$$TRS = - \frac{x_2}{x_1},$$

which is simply the TRS for the Cobb-Douglas production function.

(3) The Leontief production function ($\rho = -\infty$). We have just seen that the TRS of the CES production function is given by equation (1.1). As ρ approaches $-\infty$, this expression approaches

$$TRS = - \left(\frac{x_1}{x_2} \right)^{-\infty} = - \left(\frac{x_2}{x_1} \right)^{\infty}.$$

If $x_2 > x_1$ the TRS is (negative) infinity; if $x_2 < x_1$ the TRS is zero. This means that as ρ approaches $-\infty$, a CES isoquant looks like an isoquant associated with the Leontief technology. ∎

It will probably not surprise you to discover that the CES production function has a constant elasticity of substitution. To verify this, note that the technical rate of substitution is given by

$$TRS = - \left(\frac{x_1}{x_2} \right)^{\rho - 1},$$

so that

$$\frac{x_2}{x_1} = |TRS|^{\frac{1}{1-\rho}}.$$

Taking logs, we see that

$$\ln \frac{x_2}{x_1} = \frac{1}{1 - \rho} \ln |TRS|.$$

Applying the definition of σ using the logarithmic derivative,

$$\sigma = \frac{d \ln x_2 / x_1}{d \ln |TRS|} = \frac{1}{1 - \rho}.$$

Notes

The elasticity of substitution is due to Hicks (1932). For a discussion of generalizations of the elasticity of substitution to the n-input case, see Blackorby & Russell (1989) and the references cited therein. The elasticity of scale is due to Frisch (1965).

Exercises

1.1. True or false? If $V(y)$ is a convex set, then the associated production set Y must be convex.

1.2. What is the elasticity of substitution for the general CES technology $y = (a_1 x_1^\rho + a_2 x_2^\rho)^{1/\rho}$ when $a_1 \neq a_2$?

1.3. Define the **output elasticity of a factor** i to be

$$\epsilon_i(\mathbf{x}) = \frac{\partial f(\mathbf{x})}{\partial x_i} \frac{x_i}{f(\mathbf{x})}.$$

If $f(\mathbf{x}) = x_1^a x_2^b$, what is the output elasticity of each factor?

1.4. If $\epsilon(\mathbf{x})$ is the elasticity of scale and $\epsilon_i(\mathbf{x})$ is the output elasticity of factor i, show that $\epsilon(\mathbf{x}) = \sum_{i=1}^{n} \epsilon_i(\mathbf{x})$.

1.5. What is the elasticity of scale of the CES technology, $f(x_1, x_2) = (x_1^\rho + x_2^\rho)^{\frac{1}{\rho}}$?

1.6. True or false? A differentiable function $g(x)$ is a strictly increasing function if and only if $g'(x) > 0$.

1.7. In the text it was claimed that if $f(\mathbf{x})$ is a homothetic technology and $\mathbf{x}$ and $\mathbf{x}'$ produce the same level of output, then $t\mathbf{x}$ and $t\mathbf{x}'$ must also produce the same level of output. Can you prove this rigorously?

1.8. Let $f(x_1, x_2)$ be a homothetic function. Show that its technical rate of substitution at (x_1, x_2) equals its technical rate of substitution at (tx_1, tx_2).

1.9. Consider the CES technology $f(x_1, x_2) = [a_1 x_1^\rho + a_2 x_2^\rho]^{\frac{1}{\rho}}$. Show that we can always write this in the form $f(x_1, x_2) = A(\rho)[bx_1^\rho + (1-b)x_2^\rho]^{\frac{1}{\rho}}$.

1.10. Let Y be a production set. We say that the technology is **additive** if $\mathbf{y}$ in Y and $\mathbf{y}'$ in Y implies that $\mathbf{y} + \mathbf{y}'$ is in Y. We say that the technology is **divisible** if $\mathbf{y}$ in Y and $0 \leq t \leq 1$ implies that $t\mathbf{y}$ is in Y. Show that if a technology is both additive and divisible, then Y must be convex and exhibit constant returns to scale.

1.11. For each input requirement set determine if it is regular, monotonic, and/or convex. Assume that the parameters a and b and the output levels are strictly positive.

(a) $V(y) = \{x_1, x_2 : ax_1 \geq \log y, bx_2 \geq \log y\}$

(b) $V(y) = \{x_1, x_2 : ax_1 + bx_2 \geq y, x_1 > 0\}$

(c) $V(y) = \{x_1, x_2 : ax_1 + \sqrt{x_1 x_2} + bx_2 \geq y\}$

(d) $V(y) = \{x_1, x_2 : ax_1 + bx_2 \geq y\}$

(e) $V(y) = \{x_1, x_2 : x_1(1 - y) \geq a, x_2(1 - y) \geq b\}$

(f) $V(y) = \{x_1, x_2 : ax_1 - \sqrt{x_1 x_2} + bx_2 \geq y\}$

(g) $V(y) = \{x_1, x_2 : x_1 + \min(x_1, x_2) \geq 3y\}$

CHAPTER **2**

PROFIT MAXIMIZATION

Economic **profit** is defined to be the difference between the revenue a firm
receives and the costs that it incurs. It is important to understand that *all*
costs must be included in the calculation of profit. If a small businessman
owns a grocery store and he also works in the grocery, his salary as an
employee should be counted as a cost. If a group of individuals loans a
firm money in return for a monthly payment, these interest payments must
be counted as a cost of production.

Both revenues and costs of a firm depend on the actions taken by the
firm. These actions may take many forms: actual production activities,
purchases of factors, and purchases of advertising are all examples of actions
undertaken by a firm. At a rather abstract level, we can imagine that a firm
can engage in a large variety of actions such as these. We can write revenue
as a function of the level of operations of some n actions, $R(a_1, \ldots, a_n)$,
and costs as a function of these same n activity levels, $C(a_1, \ldots, a_n)$.

A basic assumption of most economic analysis of firm behavior is that
a firm acts so as to maximize its profits; that is, a firm chooses actions
$(a_1, \ldots, a_n)$ so as to maximize $R(a_1, \ldots, a_n) - C(a_1, \ldots, a_n)$. This is the
behavioral assumption that will be used throughout this book.

Even at this broad level of generality, two basic principles of profit maximization emerge. The first follows from a simple application of calculus. The profit maximization problem facing the firm can be written as

$$\max_{a_1,\ldots,a_n} R(a_1,\ldots,a_n) - C(a_1,\ldots,a_n).$$

A simple application of calculus shows that an optimal set of actions, $\mathbf{a}^* = (a_1^*,\ldots,a_n^*)$, is characterized by the conditions

$$\frac{\partial R(\mathbf{a}^*)}{\partial a_i} = \frac{\partial C(\mathbf{a}^*)}{\partial a_i} \qquad i = 1,\ldots,n.$$

The intuition behind these conditions should be clear: if marginal revenue were greater than marginal cost, it would pay to increase the level of the activity; if marginal revenue were less than marginal cost, it would pay to decrease the level of the activity.

This fundamental condition characterizing profit maximization has several concrete interpretations. For example, one decision the firm makes is to choose its level of output. The fundamental condition for profit maximization tells us that the level of output should be chosen so that the production of one more unit of output should produce a marginal revenue equal to its marginal cost of production. Another decision of the firm is to determine how much of a specific factor—say labor—to hire. The fundamental condition for profit maximization tells us that the firm should hire an amount of labor such that the marginal revenue from employing one more unit of labor should be equal to the marginal cost of hiring that additional unit of labor.

The second fundamental condition of profit maximization is the condition of equal long-run profits. Suppose that two firms have identical revenue functions and cost functions. Then it is clear that in the long run the two firms cannot have unequal profits—since each firm could imitate the actions of the other. This condition is very simple, but its implications are often surprisingly powerful.

In order to apply these conditions in a more concrete way, we need to break up the revenue and cost functions into more basic parts. Revenue is composed of two parts: how much a firm sells of various outputs times the price of each output. Costs are also composed of two parts: how much a firm uses of each input times the price of each input.

The firm's profit maximization problem therefore reduces to the problem of determining what prices it wishes to charge for its outputs or pay for its inputs, and what levels of outputs and inputs it wishes to use. Of course, it cannot set prices and activity levels unilaterally. In determining its optimal policy, the firm faces two kinds of constraints: technological constraints and market constraints.

Technological constraints are simply those constraints that concern the feasibility of the production plan. We have examined ways to describe technological constraints in the previous chapter.

Market constraints are those constraints that concern the effect of actions of other agents on the firm. For example, the consumers who buy output from the firm may only be willing to pay a certain price for a certain amount of output; similarly, the suppliers of a firm may accept only certain prices for their supplies of inputs.

When the firm determines its optimal actions, it must take into account both sorts of constraints. However, it is convenient to begin by examining the constraints one at a time. For this reason the firms described in the following sections will exhibit the simplest kind of market behavior, namely that of **price-taking behavior**. Each firm will be assumed to take prices as given, exogenous variables to the profit-maximizing problem. Thus, the firm will be concerned only with determining the profit-maximizing levels of outputs and inputs. Such a price-taking firm is often referred to as a **competitive firm**.

The reason for this terminology will be discussed later on; however, we can briefly indicate here the kind of situation where price-taking behavior might be an appropriate model. Suppose we have a collection of well-informed consumers who are buying a homogeneous product that is produced by a large number of firms. Then it is reasonably clear that all firms must charge the same price for their product—any firm that charged more than the going market price for its product would immediately lose all of its customers. Hence, each firm must take the market price as given when it determines its optimal policy. In this chapter we will study the optimal choice of production plans, given a configuration of market prices.

2.1 Profit maximization

Let us consider the problem of a firm that takes prices as given in both its output and its factor markets. Let $\mathbf{p}$ be a vector of prices for inputs and outputs of the firm.[1] The profit maximization problem of the firm can be stated as

$$\pi(\mathbf{p}) = \max \mathbf{p}\mathbf{y}$$

$$\text{such that } \mathbf{y} \text{ is in } Y.$$

Since outputs are measured as positive numbers and inputs are measured as negative numbers, the objective function for this problem is profits: revenues minus costs. The function $\pi(\mathbf{p})$, which gives us the maximum profits as a function of the prices, is called the **profit function** of the firm.

---

[1] In general we will take prices to be row vectors and quantities to be column vectors.

There are several useful variants of the profit function. For example, if we are considering a short-run maximization problem, we might define the **short-run profit function**, also known as the **restricted profit function**:

$$\pi(\mathbf{p}, \mathbf{z}) = \max \ \mathbf{p}\mathbf{y}$$

such that $\mathbf{y}$ is in $Y(\mathbf{z})$.

If the firm produces only one output, the profit function can be written as

$$\pi(p, \mathbf{w}) = \max \ pf(\mathbf{x}) - \mathbf{w}\mathbf{x}$$

where p is now the (scalar) price of output, $\mathbf{w}$ is the vector of factor prices, and the inputs are measured by the (nonnegative) vector $\mathbf{x} = (x_1, \ldots, x_n)$. In this case we can also define a variant of the restricted profit function, the **cost function**

$$c(\mathbf{w}, y) = \min \ \mathbf{w}\mathbf{x}$$

such that $\mathbf{x}$ is in $V(y)$.

In the short run, we may want to consider the **restricted** or **short-run cost function**:

$$c(\mathbf{w}, y, \mathbf{z}) = \min \ \mathbf{w}\mathbf{x}$$

such that $(y, -\mathbf{x})$ is in $Y(\mathbf{z})$.

The cost function gives the minimum cost of producing a level of output y when factor prices are $\mathbf{w}$. Since only the factor prices are taken as exogenous in this problem, the cost function can be used to describe firms that are price takers in factor markets but do not take prices as given in the output markets. This observation will prove useful in our study of monopoly.

Profit-maximizing behavior can be characterized by calculus. For example, the first-order conditions for the single output profit maximization problem are

$$p\frac{\partial f(\mathbf{x}^*)}{\partial x_i} = w_i \qquad i = 1, \cdots, n.$$

This condition simply says that the value of the marginal product of each factor must be equal to its price. Using vector notation, we can also write these conditions as

$$p\mathbf{D}f(\mathbf{x}^*) = \mathbf{w}.$$

Here

$$\mathbf{D}f(\mathbf{x}^*) = \left(\frac{\partial f(\mathbf{x}^*)}{\partial x_1}, \ldots, \frac{\partial f(\mathbf{x}^*)}{\partial x_n} \right)$$

is the **gradient** of f: the vector of partial derivatives of f with respect to each of its arguments.

The first-order conditions state that the "value marginal product of each factor must be equal to its price." This is just a special case of the optimization rule we stated earlier: that the marginal revenue of each action be equal to its marginal cost.

This first-order condition can also be exhibited graphically. Consider the production possibilities set depicted in Figure 2.1. In this two-dimensional case, profits are given by $\Pi = py - wx$. The level sets of this function for fixed p and w are straight lines which can be represented as functions of the form: $y = \Pi/p + (w/p)x$. Here the slope of the isoprofit line gives the wage measured in units of output, and the vertical intercept gives us profits measured in units of output.

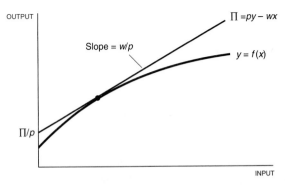

Profit maximization. The profit-maximizing amount of input occurs where the slope of the isoprofit line equals the slope of the production function.

Figure 2.1

A profit-maximizing firm wants to find a point on the production set with the maximal level of profits—this is a point where the vertical axis intercept of the associated isoprofit line is maximal. By inspection it can be seen that such an optimal point can be characterized by the tangency condition

$$\frac{df(x^*)}{dx} = \frac{w}{p}.$$

In this two-dimensional case it is easy to see the appropriate second-order condition for profit maximization, namely that the second derivative of the production function with respect to the input must be nonpositive:

$$\frac{d^2 f(x^*)}{dx^2} \le 0.$$

Geometrically, this means that at a point of maximal profits the production function must lie below its tangent line at x^*; i.e., it must be "locally concave." It is often useful to assume that the second derivative will be strictly negative.

A similar second-order condition holds in the multiple-input case. In this case the second-order condition for profit maximization is that the matrix of second derivatives of the production function must be **negative semidefinite** at the optimal point; that is, the second-order condition requires that the Hessian matrix

$$\mathbf{D}^2 f(\mathbf{x}^*) = \left(\frac{\partial^2 f(\mathbf{x}^*)}{\partial x_i \partial x_j} \right)$$

must satisfy the condition that $\mathbf{h}\mathbf{D}^2 f(\mathbf{x}^*)\mathbf{h}^t \leq 0$ for all vectors $\mathbf{h}$. (The superscript t indicates the transpose operation.) Note that if there is only a single input, the Hessian matrix is a scalar and this condition reduces to the second-order condition we examined earlier for the single-input case.

Geometrically, the requirement that the Hessian matrix is negative semidefinite means that the production function must be locally concave in the neighborhood of an optimal choice—that is, the production function must lie below its tangent hyperplane.

In many applications we will be concerned with the case of a regular maximum, so that the relevant condition to check is whether the Hessian matrix is negative definite. In Chapter 26, page 476, we show that a necessary and sufficient test for this is that the leading principal minors of the Hessian must alternate in sign. This algebraic condition is sometimes useful for checking second-order conditions, as we will see below.

2.2 Difficulties

For each vector of prices $(p, \mathbf{w})$ there will in general be some optimal choice of factors $\mathbf{x}^*$. The function that gives us the optimal choice of inputs as a function of the prices is called the **factor demand function** of the firm. This function is denoted by $\mathbf{x}(p, \mathbf{w})$. Similarly, the function $y(p, \mathbf{w}) = f(\mathbf{x}(p, \mathbf{w}))$ is called the **supply function** of the firm. We will often assume that these functions are well-defined and nicely behaved, but it is worthwhile considering problems that may arise if they aren't.

First, it may happen that the technology cannot be described by a differentiable production function, so that the derivatives described above are inappropriate. The Leontief technology is a good example of this problem.

Second, the calculus conditions derived above make sense only when the choice variables can be varied in an open neighborhood of the optimal choice. In many economic problems the variables are naturally nonnegative; and if some variables have a value of zero at the optimal choice, the calculus conditions described above may be inappropriate. The above conditions are valid only for **interior solutions**—where each of the factors is used in a positive amount.

The necessary modifications of the conditions to handle **boundary solutions** are not difficult to state. For example, if we constrain $\mathbf{x}$ to be nonnegative in the profit maximization problem, the relevant first-order conditions turn out to be

$$p\frac{\partial f(\mathbf{x})}{\partial x_i} - w_i \leq 0 \quad \text{if } x_i = 0$$

$$p\frac{\partial f(\mathbf{x})}{\partial x_i} - w_i = 0 \quad \text{if } x_i > 0.$$

Thus the marginal profit from increasing x_i must be nonpositive, otherwise the firm would increase x_i. If $x_i = 0$, the marginal profit from increasing x_i may be negative—which is to say, the firm would like to decrease x_i. But since x_i is already zero, this is impossible. Finally, if $x_i > 0$ so that the nonnegativity constraint is not binding, we will have the usual conditions for an interior solution.

Cases involving nonnegativity constraints or other sorts of inequality constraints can be handled formally by means of the Kuhn-Tucker Theorem described in Chapter 27, page 503. We will present some examples of the application of this theorem in the chapter on cost minimization.

The third problem that can arise is that there may exist no profit-maximizing production plan. For example, consider the case where the production function is $f(x) = x$ so that one unit of x produces one unit of output. It is not hard to see that for $p > w$ no profit-maximizing plan will exist. If you want to maximize $px - wx$ when $p > w$, you would want to choose an indefinitely large value of x. A maximal profit production plan will exist for this technology only when $p \leq w$, in which case the maximal level of profits will be zero.

In fact, this same phenomenon will occur for any constant-returns-to-scale technology. To demonstrate this, suppose that we can find some $(p, \mathbf{w})$ where optimal profits are strictly positive so that

$$pf(\mathbf{x}^*) - \mathbf{w}\mathbf{x}^* = \pi^* > 0.$$

Suppose that we scale up production by a factor $t > 1$; our profits will now be

$$pf(t\mathbf{x}^*) - \mathbf{w}t\mathbf{x}^* = t[pf(\mathbf{x}^*) - \mathbf{w}\mathbf{x}^*] = t\pi^* > \pi^*.$$

This means that, if profits are *ever* positive, they can be made larger—hence, profits are unbounded and no maximal profit production plan will exist in this case.

It is clear from this example that the only nontrivial profit-maximizing position for a constant-returns-to-scale firm is one involving zero profits. If the firm is producing some positive level of output and it makes zero profits, then it is indifferent about the level of output at which it produces.

This brings up the fourth difficulty: even when a profit-maximizing production plan exists, it may not be unique. If $(y, \mathbf{x})$ yields maximal profits of zero for some constant returns technology, then $(ty, t\mathbf{x})$ will also yield zero profits and will therefore also be profit-maximizing. In the case of constant returns to scale, if there exists a profit-maximizing choice at some $(p, \mathbf{w})$ at all, there will typically be a whole range of production plans that are profit-maximizing.

EXAMPLE: The profit function for Cobb-Douglas technology

Consider the problem of maximizing profits for the production function of the form $f(x) = x^a$ where $a > 0$. The first-order condition is

$$pax^{a-1} = w,$$

and the second-order condition reduces to

$$pa(a - 1)x^{a-2} \leq 0.$$

The second-order condition can only be satisfied when $a \leq 1$, which means that the production function must have constant or decreasing returns to scale for competitive profit maximization to be meaningful.

If $a = 1$, the first-order condition reduces to $p = w$. Hence, when $w = p$ any value of x is a profit-maximizing choice. When $a < 1$, we use the first-order condition to solve for the factor demand function

$$x(p, w) = \left(\frac{w}{ap}\right)^{\frac{1}{a-1}}.$$

The supply function is given by

$$y(p, w) = f(x(p, w)) = \left(\frac{w}{ap}\right)^{\frac{a}{a-1}},$$

and the profit function is given by

$$\pi(p, w) = py(p, w) - wx(p, w) = w\left(\frac{1-a}{a}\right)\left(\frac{w}{ap}\right)^{\frac{1}{a-1}}.$$

2.3 Properties of demand and supply functions

The functions that give the optimal choices of inputs and outputs as a function of the prices are known as the **factor demand** and **output supply** functions. The fact that these functions are the solutions to a maximization problem of a specific form, the profit maximization problem, will imply certain restrictions on the behavior of the demand and supply functions.

For example, it is easy to see that if we multiply all of the prices by some positive number t, the vector of factor inputs that maximizes profits will not change. (Can you prove this rigorously?) Hence, the factor demand functions $x_i(p, \mathbf{w})$ for $i = 1, \cdots, n$ must satisfy the restriction that

$$x_i(tp, t\mathbf{w}) = x_i(p, \mathbf{w}).$$

In other words the factor demand functions must be homogeneous of degree zero. This property is an important implication of profit-maximizing behavior: an immediate way to check whether some observed behavior could come from the profit-maximizing model is to see if the demand functions are homogeneous of degree zero. If they aren't, the firm in question couldn't possibly be maximizing profits.

We would like to find other such restrictions on demand functions. In fact, we would like to find a *complete* list of such restrictions. We could use such a list in two ways. First, we could use it to examine theoretical statements about how a profit-maximizing firm would respond to changes in its economic environment. An example of such a statement would be: "If all prices are doubled, the levels of goods demanded and supplied by a profit-maximizing firm will not change." Second, we could use such restrictions empirically to decide whether a particular firm's observed behavior is consistent with the profit maximization model. If we observed that some firm's demands and supplies changed when all prices doubled and nothing else changed, we would have to conclude (perhaps reluctantly) that this firm was not a profit maximizer.

Thus both theoretical and empirical considerations suggest the importance of determining the properties that demand and supply functions possess. We will attack this problem in three ways. The first way is by examining the first-order conditions that characterize the optimal choices. The second approach is to examine the maximizing properties of the demand and supply functions directly. The third way is to examine the properties of the profit and cost functions and relate these properties to the demand functions. This approach is sometimes referred to as the "dual approach." Each of these methods of examining optimizing behavior is useful for other sorts of problems in economics, and the manipulations involved should be carefully studied.

Economists refer to the study of how an economic variable responds to changes in its environment as **comparative statics**. For example, we could ask how the supply of output of a profit-maximizing firm responds to a change in the output price. This would be part of a study of the comparative statics of the supply function.

The term *comparative* refers to comparing a "before" and an "after" situation. The term *statics* refers to the idea that the comparison is made after all adjustments have been "worked out;" that is, we must compare one *equilibrium* situation to another.

The term "comparative statics" is not especially descriptive, and it seems to be used only by economists. A better term for this sort of analysis would be **sensitivity analysis**. This has the additional advantage that this term is used in other fields of study. However, the comparative statics terminology is the traditional one in economics and seems so embedded in economic analysis that it would be futile to attempt to change it.

2.4 Comparative statics using the first-order conditions

Let us first consider the simple example of a firm maximizing profits with one output and one input. The problem facing the firm is

$$\max_x \ pf(x) - wx.$$

If $f(x)$ is differentiable, the demand function $x(p, w)$ must satisfy the necessary first-order and second-order conditions

$$pf'(x(p, w)) - w \equiv 0$$
$$pf''(x(p, w)) \leq 0.$$

Notice that these conditions are an *identity* in p and w. Since $x(p, w)$ is by definition the choice that maximizes profits at (p, w), $x(p, w)$ must satisfy the necessary conditions for profit maximization for *all* values of p and w. Since the first-order condition is an identity, we can differentiate it with respect to w, say, to get

$$pf''(x(p, w)) \frac{dx(p, w)}{dw} - 1 \equiv 0.$$

Assuming that we have a **regular** maximum so that $f''(x)$ is not zero, we can divide through to get

$$\frac{dx(p, w)}{dw} \equiv \frac{1}{pf''(x(p, w))}. \tag{2.1}$$

This identity tells us some interesting facts about how the factor demand $x(p, w)$ responds to changes in w. First, it gives us an explicit expression for dx/dw in terms of the production function. If the production function is very curved in a neighborhood of the optimum—so that the second derivative is large in magnitude—then the change in factor demand as the factor price changes will be small. (You might draw a diagram similar to Figure 2.1 and experiment a bit to verify this fact.)

Second, it gives us important information about the *sign* of the derivative: since the second-order condition for maximization implies that the second derivative of the production function, $f''(x(p, w))$, is negative, equation (2.1) implies that $dx(p, w)/dw$ is negative. In other words: *the factor demand curve slopes downward.*

This procedure of differentiating the first-order conditions can be used to examine profit-maximizing behavior when there are many inputs. Let us consider for simplicity the case of two inputs. For notational convenience we will normalize $p = 1$ and just look at how the factor demands behave with respect to the factor prices. The factor demand functions must satisfy the first-order conditions

$$\frac{\partial f(x_1(w_1, w_2), x_2(w_1, w_2))}{\partial x_1} \equiv w_1$$

$$\frac{\partial f(x_1(w_1, w_2), x_2(w_1, w_2))}{\partial x_2} \equiv w_2.$$

Differentiating with respect to w_1, we have

$$f_{11}\frac{\partial x_1}{\partial w_1} + f_{12}\frac{\partial x_2}{\partial w_1} = 1$$

$$f_{21}\frac{\partial x_1}{\partial w_1} + f_{22}\frac{\partial x_2}{\partial w_1} = 0.$$

Differentiating with respect to w_2, we have

$$f_{11}\frac{\partial x_1}{\partial w_2} + f_{12}\frac{\partial x_2}{\partial w_2} = 0$$

$$f_{21}\frac{\partial x_1}{\partial w_2} + f_{22}\frac{\partial x_2}{\partial w_2} = 1.$$

Writing these equations in matrix form yields

$$\begin{pmatrix} f_{11} & f_{12} \\ f_{21} & f_{22} \end{pmatrix} \begin{pmatrix} \frac{\partial x_1}{\partial w_1} & \frac{\partial x_1}{\partial w_2} \\ \frac{\partial x_2}{\partial w_1} & \frac{\partial x_2}{\partial w_2} \end{pmatrix} = \begin{pmatrix} 1 & 0 \\ 0 & 1 \end{pmatrix}.$$

Let us assume that we have a regular maximum. This means that the Hessian matrix is strictly negative definite, and therefore nonsingular. (This assumption is analogous to the assumption that $f''(x) < 0$ in the one-dimensional case.) Solving for the matrix of first derivatives, we have

$$\begin{pmatrix} \frac{\partial x_1}{\partial w_1} & \frac{\partial x_1}{\partial w_2} \\ \frac{\partial x_2}{\partial w_1} & \frac{\partial x_2}{\partial w_2} \end{pmatrix} = \begin{pmatrix} f_{11} & f_{12} \\ f_{21} & f_{22} \end{pmatrix}^{-1}.$$

The matrix on the left of this last equation is known as a **substitution matrix** since it describes how the firm substitutes one input for another as the factor prices change. According to our calculation, the substitution matrix is simply the inverse of the Hessian matrix. This has several important implications.

Recall that the second-order condition for (strict) profit maximization is that the Hessian matrix is a symmetric negative definite matrix. It is a standard result of linear algebra that the inverse of a symmetric negative definite matrix is a symmetric negative definite matrix. This means that the substitution matrix itself must be a symmetric, negative definite matrix. In particular:

1) $\partial x_i/\partial w_i < 0$, for $i = 1, 2$, since the diagonal entries of a negative definite matrix must be negative.

2) $\partial x_i/\partial w_j = \partial x_j/\partial w_i$ by the symmetry of the matrix.

Although it is quite intuitive that the factor demand curves should have a negative slope, the fact that the substitution matrix is symmetric is not very intuitive. Why should the change in a firm's demands for good i when price j changes necessarily be equal to the change in the firm's demand for good j when price i changes? There is no obvious reason ... but it is implied by the model of profit-maximizing behavior.

The same sorts of calculations can be made for an arbitrary number of inputs. Normalizing $p = 1$, the first-order conditions for profit maximization are

$$\mathbf{D}f(\mathbf{x}(\mathbf{w})) - \mathbf{w} \equiv \mathbf{0}.$$

If we differentiate with respect to $\mathbf{w}$, we get

$$\mathbf{D}^2 f(\mathbf{x}(\mathbf{w}))\mathbf{D}\mathbf{x}(\mathbf{w}) - \mathbf{I} \equiv \mathbf{0}.$$

Solving this equation for the substitution matrix, we find

$$\mathbf{D}\mathbf{x}(\mathbf{w}) \equiv [\mathbf{D}^2 f(\mathbf{x}(\mathbf{w}))]^{-1}.$$

Since $\mathbf{D}^2 f(\mathbf{x}(\mathbf{w}))$ is a symmetric negative definite matrix, the substitution matrix $\mathbf{D}\mathbf{x}(\mathbf{w})$ is a symmetric negative definite matrix. This formula is, of course, a natural analog of the one-good and two-good cases described above.

What is the empirical content of the statement that the substitution matrix is negative semidefinite? We can provide the following interpretation. Suppose that the vector of factor prices change from $\mathbf{w}$ to $\mathbf{w} + \mathbf{dw}$. Then the associated change in the factor demands is

$$\mathbf{dx} = \mathbf{D}\mathbf{x}(\mathbf{w})\mathbf{dw}^t.$$

Multiplying both sides of this equation by $\mathbf{dw}$ yields

$$\mathbf{dw}\,\mathbf{dx} = \mathbf{dw}\mathbf{Dx}(\mathbf{w})\mathbf{dw}^t \leq 0.$$

The inequality follows from the definition of a negative semidefinite matrix. We see that negative semidefiniteness of the substitution matrix means that the inner product of the change in factor prices and the change in factor demands must always be nonpositive, at least for infinitesimal changes in factor prices. If, for example, the price of the ith factor increases, and no other prices change, it follows that the demand for the ith factor must decrease. In general, the change in quantities, $\mathbf{dx}$, must make an obtuse angle with the change in prices, $\mathbf{dw}$. Roughly speaking, the direction of the quantity change must be more-or-less "opposite" the direction of the price change.

2.5 Comparative statics using algebra

In this section we will examine the consequences of profit-maximizing behavior that follow *directly* from the definition of maximization itself. We will do this in a slightly different setting than before. Instead of taking the behavior of the firm as being described by its demand and supply functions, we will think of just having a finite number of observations on a firm's behavior. This allows us to avoid some tedious details involved in taking limits and gives us a more realistic setting for empirical analysis. (Who has ever had an infinite amount of data anyway?)

Thus, suppose that we are given a list of observed price vectors $\mathbf{p}^t$, and the associated net output vectors $\mathbf{y}^t$, for $t = 1, \ldots, T$. We refer to this collection as the *data*. In terms of the net supply functions we described before, the data are just $(\mathbf{p}^t, \mathbf{y}(\mathbf{p}^t))$ for some observations $t = 1, \ldots, T$.

The first question we will ask is what the model of profit maximization implies about the set of data. If the firm is maximizing profits, then the observed net output choice at price $\mathbf{p}^t$ must have a level of profit at least as great as the profit at any other net output the firm could have chosen. We don't know *all* the other choices that are feasible in this situation, but we do know some of them—namely, the other choices $\mathbf{y}^s$ for $s = 1, \ldots, T$ that we have observed. Hence, a *necessary* condition for profit maximization is that

$$\mathbf{p}^t \mathbf{y}^t \geq \mathbf{p}^t \mathbf{y}^s \text{ for all } t \quad \text{and } s = 1, \ldots, T.$$

We will refer to this condition as the **Weak Axiom of Profit Maximization (WAPM)**.

In Figure 2.2A we have drawn two observations that *violate* WAPM, while Figure 2.2B depicts two observations that *satisfy* WAPM.

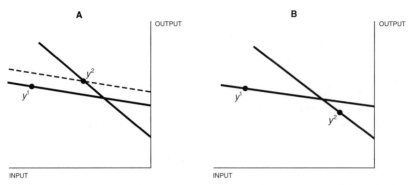

**Figure
2.2**

WAPM. Panel A shows two observations that violate WAPM, since $\mathbf{p}^1\mathbf{y}^2 > \mathbf{p}^1\mathbf{y}^1$. Panel B shows two observations that satisfy WAPM.

WAPM is a simple, but very useful, condition; let us derive some of its consequences. Fix two observations t and s, and write WAPM for each one. We have

$$\mathbf{p}^t(\mathbf{y}^t - \mathbf{y}^s) \geq 0$$
$$-\mathbf{p}^s(\mathbf{y}^t - \mathbf{y}^s) \geq 0.$$

Adding these two inequalities gives us

$$(\mathbf{p}^t - \mathbf{p}^s)(\mathbf{y}^t - \mathbf{y}^s) \geq 0.$$

Letting $\Delta\mathbf{p} = (\mathbf{p}^t - \mathbf{p}^s)$ and $\Delta\mathbf{y} = (\mathbf{y}^t - \mathbf{y}^s)$, we can rewrite this expression as

$$\Delta\mathbf{p}\Delta\mathbf{y} \geq 0. \tag{2.2}$$

In other words, *the inner product of a vector of price changes with the associated vector of changes in net outputs must be nonnegative.*

For example, if $\Delta\mathbf{p}$ is the vector $(1, 0, \ldots, 0)$, then this inequality implies that Δy_1 must be nonnegative. If the first good is an output good for the firm, and thus a positive number, then the supply of that good cannot decrease when its price rises. On the other hand, if the first good is an input for the firm, and thus measured as a negative number, then the demand for that good must not increase when its price goes up.

Of course, equation (2.2) is simply a "delta" version of the infinitesimal inequality derived in the previous section. But it is stronger in that it applies for *all* changes in prices, not just infinitesimal changes. Note that (2.2) follows directly from the *definition* of profit maximization and that no regularity assumptions about the technology are necessary.

2.6 Recoverability

Does WAPM exhaust all of the implications of profit-maximizing behavior, or are there other useful conditions implied by profit maximization? One way to answer this question is to try to construct a technology that generates the observed behavior $(\mathbf{p}^t, \mathbf{y}^t)$ as profit-maximizing behavior. If we can find such a technology for *any* set of data that satisfy WAPM, then WAPM must indeed exhaust the implications of profit-maximizing behavior. We refer to the operation of constructing a technology consistent with the observed choices as the operation of **recoverability**.

We will show that if a set of data satisfies WAPM it is always possible to find a technology for which the observed choices are profit-maximizing choices. In fact, it is always possible to find a production set Y that is closed and convex. The remainder of this section will sketch the proof of this assertion.

Our task is to construct a production set that will generate the observed choices $(\mathbf{p}^t, \mathbf{y}^t)$ as profit-maximizing choices. We will actually construct two such production sets, one that serves as an "inner bound" to the true technology and one that serves as an "outer bound." We start with the inner bound.

Suppose that the true production set Y is convex and monotonic. Since Y must contain $\mathbf{y}^t$ for $t = 1, \ldots, T$, it is natural to take the inner bound to be the *smallest* convex, monotonic set that contains $\mathbf{y}^1, \ldots, \mathbf{y}^t$. This set is called the convex, monotonic **hull** of the points $\mathbf{y}^1, \ldots, \mathbf{y}^T$ and is denoted by

$$YI = \text{ convex, monotonic hull of } \{\mathbf{y}^t : t = 1, \cdots, T\}$$

The set YI is depicted in Figure 2.3A.

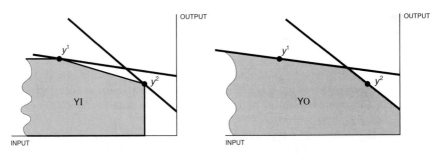

The sets YI and YO. The set YI is the smallest convex, monotonic set that could be a production set consistent with the data. The set YO is the largest convex, monotonic set that could be a production set consistent with the data.

Figure 2.3

It is easy to show that for the technology YI, $\mathbf{y}^t$ is a profit-maximizing choice at prices $\mathbf{p}^t$. All we have to do is to check that for all t,

$$\mathbf{p}^t \mathbf{y}^t \geq \mathbf{p}^t \mathbf{y} \text{ for all } \mathbf{y} \text{ in } YI.$$

Suppose that this is not the case. Then for some observation t, $\mathbf{p}^t\mathbf{y}^t < \mathbf{p}^t\mathbf{y}$ for some $\mathbf{y}$ in YI. But inspecting the diagram shows that there must then exist some observation s such that $\mathbf{p}^t\mathbf{y}^t < \mathbf{p}^t\mathbf{y}^s$. But this inequality violates WAPM.

Thus the set YI **rationalizes** the observed behavior in the sense that it is one possible technology that could have generated that behavior. It is not hard to see that YI must be contained in any convex technology that generated the observed behavior: if Y generated the observed behavior and it is convex, then it must contain the observed choices $\mathbf{y}^t$ and the convex hull of these points is the smallest such set. In this sense, YI gives us an "inner bound" to the true technology that generated the observed choices.

It is natural to ask if we can find an outer bound to this "true" technology. That is, can we find a set YO that is guaranteed to *contain* any technology that is consistent with the observed behavior?

The trick to answering this question is to rule out all of the points that couldn't possibly be in the true technology and then take everything that is left over. More precisely, let us define $NOTY$ by

$$NOTY = \{\mathbf{y} : \mathbf{p}^t\mathbf{y} > \mathbf{p}^t\mathbf{y}^t \text{ for some } t\}.$$

$NOTY$ consists of all those net output bundles that yield higher profits than some observed choice. If the firm is a profit maximizer, such bundles couldn't be technologically feasible; otherwise they would have been chosen. Now as our outer bound to Y we just take the complement of this set:

$$YO = \{\mathbf{y} : \mathbf{p}^t\mathbf{y} \leq \mathbf{p}^t\mathbf{y}^t \text{ for all } t = 1, \cdots, T\}.$$

The set YO is depicted in Figure 2.3B.

In order to show that YO rationalizes the observed behavior we must show that the profits at the observed choices are at least as great as the profits at any other $\mathbf{y}$ in YO. Suppose not. Then there is some $\mathbf{y}^t$ such that $\mathbf{p}^t\mathbf{y}^t < \mathbf{p}^t\mathbf{y}$ for some $\mathbf{y}$ in YO. But this contradicts the definition of YO given above.

It is clear from the construction of YO that it must contain any production set consistent with the data $(\mathbf{y}^t)$. Hence, YO and YI form the tightest inner and outer bounds to the true production set that generated the data.

Notes

For more on comparative statics methodology, see Silberberg (1974) and Silberberg (1990). The algebraic approach described here was inspired by Afriat (1967) and Samuelson (1947); for further development see Varian (1982b).

Exercises

2.1. Use the Kuhn-Tucker theorem to derive conditions for profit maximization and cost minimization that are valid even for boundary solutions, i.e., when some factor is not used.

2.2. Show that a profit-maximizing bundle will typically not exist for a technology that exhibits increasing returns to scale as long as there is some point that yields a positive profit.

2.3. Calculate explicitly the profit function for the technology $y = x^a$, for $0 < a < 1$ and verify that it is homogeneous and convex in (p, w).

2.4. Let $f(x_1, x_2)$ be a production function with two factors and let w_1 and w_2 be their respective prices. Show that the elasticity of the factor share $(w_2 x_2 / w_1 x_1)$ with respect to (x_1 / x_2) is given by $1/\sigma - 1$.

2.5. Show that the elasticity of the factor share with respect to (w_2/w_1) is $1 - \sigma$.

2.6. Let $(\mathbf{p}^t, \mathbf{y}^t)$ for $t = 1, \ldots, T$ be a set of observed choices that satisfy WAPM, and let YI and YO be the inner and outer bounds to the true production set Y. Let $\pi^+(\mathbf{p})$ be the profit function associated with YO and $\pi^-(\mathbf{p})$ be the profit function associated with YI, and $\pi(\mathbf{p})$ be the profit function associated with Y. Show that for all $\mathbf{p}$, $\pi^+(\mathbf{p}) \geq \pi(\mathbf{p}) \geq \pi^-(\mathbf{p})$.

2.7. The production function is $f(x) = 20x - x^2$ and the price of output is normalized to 1. Let w be the price of the x-input. We must have $x \geq 0$.

(a) What is the first-order condition for profit maximization if $x > 0$?

(b) For what values of w will the optimal x be zero?

(c) For what values of w will the optimal x be 10?

(d) What is the factor demand function?

(e) What is the profit function?

(f) What is the derivative of the profit function with respect to w?

CHAPTER 3

PROFIT FUNCTION

Given any production set Y, we have seen how to calculate the profit function, $\pi(\mathbf{p})$, which gives us the maximum profit attainable at prices $\mathbf{p}$. The profit function possesses several important properties that follow directly from its definition. These properties are very useful for analyzing profit-maximizing behavior.

Recall that the profit function is, by definition, the maximum profits the firm can make as a function of the vector of prices of the net outputs:

$$\pi(\mathbf{p}) = \max_{\mathbf{y}} \mathbf{p}\mathbf{y}$$

such that $\mathbf{y}$ is in Y.

From the viewpoint of the mathematical results that follow, what is important is that the objective function in this problem is a *linear* function of prices.

3.1 Properties of the profit function

We begin by outlining the properties of the profit function. It is important to recognize that these properties follow solely from the assumption of profit maximization. No assumptions about convexity, monotonicity, or other sorts of regularity are necessary.

Properties of the profit function.

1) Nondecreasing in output prices, nonincreasing in input prices. If $p'_i \geq p_i$ for all outputs and $p'_j \leq p_j$ for all inputs, then $\pi(\mathbf{p}') \geq \pi(\mathbf{p})$.

2) Homogeneous of degree 1 in $\mathbf{p}$. $\pi(t\mathbf{p}) = t\pi(\mathbf{p})$ for all $t \geq 0$.

3) Convex in $\mathbf{p}$. Let $\mathbf{p}'' = t\mathbf{p} + (1-t)\mathbf{p}'$ for $0 \leq t \leq 1$. Then $\pi(\mathbf{p}'') \leq t\pi(\mathbf{p}) + (1-t)\pi(\mathbf{p}')$.

4) Continuous in $\mathbf{p}$. *The function* $\pi(\mathbf{p})$ *is continuous, at least when* $\pi(\mathbf{p})$ *is well-defined and* $p_i > 0$ *for* $i = 1, \ldots, n$.

Proof. We emphasize once more that the proofs of these properties follow from the definition of the profit function alone and do not rely on any properties of the technology.

1) Let $\mathbf{y}$ be a profit-maximizing net output vector at $\mathbf{p}$, so that $\pi(\mathbf{p}) = \mathbf{py}$ and let $\mathbf{y}'$ be a profit-maximizing net output vector at $\mathbf{p}'$ so that $\pi(\mathbf{p}') = \mathbf{p}'\mathbf{y}'$. Then by definition of profit maximization we have $\mathbf{p}'\mathbf{y}' \geq \mathbf{p}'\mathbf{y}$. Since $p'_i \geq p_i$ for all i for which $y_i \geq 0$ and $p'_i \leq p_i$ for all i for which $y_i \leq 0$, we also have $\mathbf{p}'\mathbf{y} \geq \mathbf{py}$. Putting these two inequalities together, we have $\pi(\mathbf{p}') = \mathbf{p}'\mathbf{y}' \geq \mathbf{py} = \pi(\mathbf{p})$, as required.

2) Let $\mathbf{y}$ be a profit-maximizing net output vector at $\mathbf{p}$, so that $\mathbf{py} \geq \mathbf{py}'$ for all $\mathbf{y}'$ in Y. It follows that for $t \geq 0$, $t\mathbf{py} \geq t\mathbf{py}'$ for all $\mathbf{y}'$ in Y. Hence $\mathbf{y}$ also maximizes profits at prices $t\mathbf{p}$. Thus $\pi(t\mathbf{p}) = t\mathbf{py} = t\pi(\mathbf{p})$.

3) Let $\mathbf{y}$ maximize profits at $\mathbf{p}$, $\mathbf{y}'$ maximize profits at $\mathbf{p}'$, and $\mathbf{y}''$ maximize profits at $\mathbf{p}''$. Then we have

$$\pi(\mathbf{p}'') = \mathbf{p}''\mathbf{y}'' = (t\mathbf{p} + (1-t)\mathbf{p}')\mathbf{y}'' = t\mathbf{py}'' + (1-t)\mathbf{p}'\mathbf{y}''. \qquad (3.1)$$

By the definition of profit maximization, we know that

$$t\mathbf{py}'' \leq t\mathbf{py} = t\pi(\mathbf{p})$$
$$(1-t)\mathbf{p}'\mathbf{y}'' \leq (1-t)\mathbf{p}'\mathbf{y}' = (1-t)\pi(\mathbf{p}').$$

Adding these two inequalities and using (3.1), we have

$$\pi(\mathbf{p}'') \leq t\pi(\mathbf{p}) + (1-t)\pi(\mathbf{p}'),$$

as required.

4) The continuity of $\pi(\mathbf{p})$ follows from the Theorem of the Maximum described in Chapter 27, page 506. ∎

The facts that the profit function is homogeneous of degree 1 and increasing in output prices are not terribly surprising. The convexity property, on the other hand, does not appear to be especially intuitive. Despite this appearance there is a sound economic rationale for the convexity result, which turns out to have very important consequences.

Consider the graph of profits versus the price of a single output good, with the factor prices held constant, as depicted in Figure 3.1. At the price vector $(p^*, \mathbf{w}^*)$ the profit-maximizing production plan $(y^*, \mathbf{x}^*)$ yields profits $p^* y^* - \mathbf{w}^* \mathbf{x}^*$. Suppose that p increases, but the firm continues to use the *same* production plan $(y^*, \mathbf{x}^*)$. Call the profits yielded by this passive behavior the "passive profit function" and denote it by $\Pi(p) = py^* - \mathbf{w}^* \mathbf{x}^*$. This is easily seen to be a straight line. The profits from pursuing an *optimal* policy must be at least as large as the profits from pursuing the passive policy, so the graph of $\pi(p)$ must lie above the graph of $\Pi(p)$. The same argument can be repeated for any price p, so the profit function must lie above its tangent lines at every point. It follows that $\pi(p)$ must be a convex function.

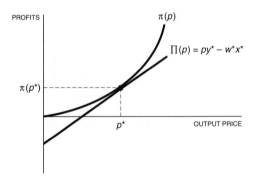

Figure 3.1   **The profit function**. As the output price increases, the profit function increases at an increasing rate.

The properties of the profit function have several uses. At this point we will satisfy ourselves with the observation that these properties offer several *observable* implications of profit-maximizing behavior. For example, suppose that we have access to accounting data for some firm and observe that when all prices are scaled up by some factor $t > 0$ profits do not scale up proportionally. If there were no other apparent changes in the environment, we might suspect that the firm in question is not maximizing profits.

EXAMPLE: The effects of price stabilization

Suppose that a competitive industry faces a randomly fluctuating price for its output. For simplicity we imagine that the price of output will be p_1 with probability q and p_2 with probability $(1-q)$. It has been suggested that it may be desirable to stabilize the price of output at the average price $\bar{p} = qp_1 + (1-q)p_2$. How would this affect profits of a typical firm in the industry?

We have to compare average profits when p fluctuates to the profits at the average price. Since the profit function is convex,

$$q\pi(p_1) + (1-q)\pi(p_2) \geq \pi(qp_1 + (1-q)p_2) = \pi(\bar{p}).$$

Thus average profits with a fluctuating price are at least as large as with a stabilized price.

At first this result seems counterintuitive, but when we remember the economic reason for the convexity of the profit function it becomes clear. Each firm will produce more output when the price is high and less when the price is low. The profit from doing this will exceed the profits from producing a fixed amount of output at the average price.

3.2 Supply and demand functions from the profit function

If we are given the net supply function $\mathbf{y}(\mathbf{p})$, it is easy to calculate the profit function. We just substitute into the definition of profits to find

$$\pi(\mathbf{p}) = \mathbf{p}\mathbf{y}(\mathbf{p}).$$

Suppose that instead we are given the profit function and are asked to find the net supply functions. How can that be done? It turns out that there is a very simple way to solve this problem: just differentiate the profit function. The proof that this works is the content of the next proposition.

Hotelling's lemma.   *(The derivative property) Let $y_i(\mathbf{p})$ be the firm's net supply function for good i. Then*

$$y_i(\mathbf{p}) = \frac{\partial \pi(\mathbf{p})}{\partial p_i} \qquad \text{for } i = 1, \ldots, n,$$

assuming that the derivative exists and that $p_i > 0$.

Proof. Suppose $(\mathbf{y}^*)$ is a profit-maximizing net output vector at prices $(\mathbf{p}^*)$. Then define the function

$$g(\mathbf{p}) = \pi(\mathbf{p}) - \mathbf{p}\mathbf{y}^*.$$

Clearly, the profit-maximizing production plan at prices **p** will always be at least as profitable as the production plan **y***. However, the plan **y*** will be a profit-maximizing plan at prices **p***, so the function g reaches a minimum value of 0 at **p***. The assumptions on prices imply this is an interior minimum.

The first-order conditions for a minimum then imply that

$$\frac{\partial g(\mathbf{p}^*)}{\partial p_i} = \frac{\partial \pi(\mathbf{p}^*)}{\partial p_i} - y_i^* = 0 \text{ for } i = 1, \dots, n.$$

Since this is true for all choices of **p***, the proof is done. ∎

The above proof is just an algebraic version of the relationships depicted in Figure 3.1. Since the graph of the "passive" profit line lies below the graph of the profit function and coincides at one point, the two lines must be tangent at that point. But this implies that the derivative of the profit function at p^* must equal the profit-maximizing factor supply at that price: $y(p^*) = \partial \pi(p^*)/\partial p$.

The argument given for the derivative property is convincing (I hope!) but it may not be enlightening. The following argument may help to see what is going on.

Let us consider the case of a single output and a single input. In this case the first-order condition for a maximum profit takes the simple form

$$p\frac{df(x)}{dx} - w = 0. \tag{3.2}$$

The factor demand function $x(p, w)$ must satisfy this first-order condition.

The profit function is given by

$$\pi(p, w) \equiv pf(x(p, w)) - wx(p, w).$$

Differentiating the profit function with respect to w, say, we have

$$\frac{\partial \pi}{\partial w} = p\frac{\partial f(x(p, w))}{\partial x}\frac{\partial x}{\partial w} - w\frac{\partial x}{\partial w} - x(p, w)$$
$$= \left[p\frac{\partial f(x(p, w))}{\partial x} - w\right]\frac{\partial x}{\partial w} - x(p, w).$$

Substituting from (3.2), we see that

$$\frac{\partial \pi}{\partial w} = -x(p, w).$$

The minus sign comes from the fact that we are increasing the price of an input—so profits must decrease.

This argument exhibits the economic rationale behind Hotelling's lemma. When the price of an output increases by a small amount there will be two effects. First, there is a direct effect: because of the price increase the firm will make more profits, even if it continues to produce the same level of output.

But secondly, there will be an indirect effect: the increase in the output price will induce the firm to change its level of output by a small amount. However, the change in profits resulting from any infinitesimal change in output must be zero since we are already at the profit-maximizing production plan. Hence, the impact of the indirect effect is zero, and we are left only with the direct effect.

3.3 The envelope theorem

The derivative property of the profit function is a special case of a more general result known as the **envelope theorem**, described in Chapter 27, page 491. Consider an arbitrary maximization problem where the objective function depends on some parameter a:

$$M(a) = \max_x \ f(x, a).$$

The function $M(a)$ gives the maximized value of the objective function as a function of the parameter a. In the case of the profit function a would be some price, x would be some factor demand, and $M(a)$ would be the maximized value of profits as a function of the price.

Let $x(a)$ be the value of x that solves the maximization problem. Then we can also write $M(a) = f(x(a), a)$. This simply says that the optimized value of the function is equal to the function evaluated at the optimizing choice.

It is often of interest to know how $M(a)$ changes as a changes. The envelope theorem tells us the answer:

$$\frac{dM(a)}{da} = \frac{\partial f(x, a)}{\partial a}\bigg|_{x=x(a)}.$$

This expression says that the derivative of M with respect to a is given by the partial derivative of f with respect to a, *holding x fixed at the optimal choice*. This is the meaning of the vertical bar to the right of the derivative. The proof of the envelope theorem is a relatively straightforward calculation given in Chapter 27, page 491. (You should try to prove the result yourself before you look at the answer.)

Let's see how the envelope theorem works in the case of a simple one-input, one-output profit maximization problem. The profit maximization problem is

$$\pi(p, w) = \max_x \ pf(x) - wx.$$

The a in the envelope theorem is p or w, and $M(a)$ is $\pi(p,w)$. According to the envelope theorem, the derivative of $\pi(p,w)$ with respect to p is simply the *partial* derivative of the objective function, evaluated at the optimal choice:

$$\frac{\partial \pi(p,w)}{\partial p} = f(x)\Big|_{x=x(p,w)} = f(x(p,w)).$$

This is simply the profit-maximizing supply of the firm at prices (p,w). Similarly,

$$\frac{\partial \pi(p,w)}{\partial w} = -x\Big|_{x=x(p,w)} = -x(p,w),$$

which is the profit-maximizing net supply of the factor.

3.4 Comparative statics using the profit function

At the beginning of this chapter we proved that the profit function must satisfy certain properties. We have just seen that the net supply functions are the derivatives of the profit function. It is of interest to see what the properties of the profit function imply about the properties of the net supply functions. Let us examine the properties one by one.

First, the profit function is a monotonic function of the prices. Hence, the partial derivative of $\pi(\mathbf{p})$ with respect to price i will be negative if good i is an input and positive if good i is an output. This is simply the sign convention for net supplies that we have adopted.

Second, the profit function is homogeneous of degree 1 in the prices. We have seen that this implies that the partial derivatives of the profit function must be homogeneous of degree 0. Scaling all prices by a positive factor t won't change the optimal choice of the firm, and therefore profits will scale by the same factor t.

Third, the profit function is a convex function of $\mathbf{p}$. Hence, the matrix of second derivatives of π with respect to $\mathbf{p}$—the Hessian matrix—must be a positive semidefinite matrix. But the matrix of second derivatives of the profit function is just the matrix of *first* derivatives of the net supply functions. In the two-good case, for example, we have

$$\begin{pmatrix} \frac{\partial^2 \pi}{\partial p_1^2} & \frac{\partial^2 \pi}{\partial p_1 \partial p_2} \\ \frac{\partial^2 \pi}{\partial p_1 \partial p_2} & \frac{\partial^2 \pi}{\partial p_2^2} \end{pmatrix} = \begin{pmatrix} \frac{\partial y_1}{\partial p_1} & \frac{\partial y_1}{\partial p_2} \\ \frac{\partial y_2}{\partial p_1} & \frac{\partial y_2}{\partial p_2} \end{pmatrix}.$$

The matrix on the right is just the substitution matrix—how the net supply of good i changes as the price of good j changes. It follows from the properties of the profit function that this must be a symmetric, positive semidefinite matrix.

The fact that the net supply functions are the derivatives of the profit function gives us a handy way to move between properties of the profit function and properties of the net supply functions. Many propositions about profit-maximizing behavior become much easier to derive by using this relationship.

EXAMPLE: The LeChatelier principle

Let us consider the short-run response of a firm's supply behavior as compared to the long-run response. It seems plausible that the firm will respond more to a price change in the long run since, by definition, it has more factors to adjust in the long run than in the short run. This intuitive proposition can be proved rigorously.

For simplicity, we suppose that there is only one output and that the input prices are all fixed. Hence the profit function only depends on the (scalar) price of output. Denote the short-run profit function by $\pi_S(p, z)$ where z is some factor that is fixed in the short run. Let the long-run profit-maximizing demand for this factor be given by $z(p)$ so that the long-run profit function is given by $\pi_L(p) = \pi_S(p, z(p))$. Finally, let p^* be some given output price, and let $z^* = z(p^*)$ be the optimal long-run demand for the z-factor at p^*.

The long-run profits are always at least as large as the short-run profits since the set of factors that can be adjusted in the long run includes the subset of factors that can be adjusted in the short run. It follows that

$$h(p) = \pi_L(p) - \pi_S(p, z^*) = \pi_S(p, z(p)) - \pi_S(p, z^*) \geq 0$$

for all prices p. At the price p^* the difference between the short-run and long-run profits is zero, so that $h(p)$ reaches a minimum at $p = p^*$. Hence, the first derivative must vanish at p^*. By Hotelling's lemma, we see that the short-run and the long-run net supplies for each good must be equal at p^*.

But we can say more. Since p^* is in fact a *minimum* of $h(p)$, the second derivative of $h(p)$ is nonnegative. This means that

$$\frac{\partial^2 \pi_L(p^*)}{\partial p^2} - \frac{\partial^2 \pi_S(p^*, z^*)}{\partial p^2} \geq 0.$$

Using Hotelling's lemma once more, it follows that

$$\frac{dy_L(p^*)}{dp} - \frac{\partial y_S(p^*, z^*)}{\partial p} = \frac{\partial^2 \pi_L(p^*)}{\partial p^2} - \frac{\partial^2 \pi_S(p^*, z^*)}{\partial p^2} \geq 0.$$

This expression implies that the long-run supply response to a change in price is at least as large as the short-run supply response at $z^* = z(p^*)$.

Notes

The properties of the profit function were developed by Hotelling (1932), Hicks (1946), and Samuelson (1947).

Exercises

3.1. A competitive profit-maximizing firm has a profit function $\pi(w_1, w_2) = \phi_1(w_1) + \phi_2(w_2)$. The price of output is normalized to be 1.

(a) What do we know about the first and second derivatives of the functions $\phi_i(w_i)$?

(b) If $x_i(w_1, w_2)$ is the factor demand function for factor i, what is the sign of $\partial x_i / \partial w_j$?

(c) Let $f(x_1, x_2)$ be the production function that generated the profit function of this form. What can we say about the form of this production function? (Hint: look at the first-order conditions.)

3.2. Consider the technology described by $y = 0$ for $x \leq 1$ and $y = \ln x$ for $x > 1$. Calculate the profit function for this technology.

3.3. Given the production function $f(x_1, x_2) = a_1 \ln x_1 + a_2 \ln x_2$, calculate the profit-maximizing demand and supply functions, and the profit function. For simplicity assume an interior solution. Assume that $a_i > 0$.

3.4. Given the production function $f(x_1, x_2) = x_1^{a_1} x_2^{a_2}$, calculate the profit-maximizing demand and supply functions, and the profit function. Assume $a_i > 0$. What restrictions must a_1 and a_2 satisfy?

3.5. Given the production function $f(x_1, x_2) = \min\{x_1, x_2\}^a$, calculate the profit-maximizing demand and supply functions, and the profit function. What restriction must a satisfy?

CHAPTER 4

COST MINIMIZATION

In this chapter we will study the behavior of a cost-minimizing firm. This is of interest for two reasons: first it gives us another way to look at the supply behavior of a firm facing competitive output markets, and second, the cost function allows us to model the production behavior of firms that don't face competitive output markets. In addition, the analysis of cost minimization gives us a taste of the analytic methods used in examining constrained optimization problems.

4.1 Calculus analysis of cost minimization

Let us consider the problem of finding a cost-minimizing way to produce a given level of output:

$$\min_{\mathbf{x}} \mathbf{w}\mathbf{x}$$

such that $f(\mathbf{x}) = y$.

We analyze this constrained minimization problem using the method of Lagrange multipliers. Begin by writing the Lagrangian

$$\mathcal{L}(\lambda, \mathbf{x}) = \mathbf{w}\mathbf{x} - \lambda(f(\mathbf{x}) - y),$$

and differentiate it with respect to each of the choice variables, x_i, and the Lagrange multiplier, λ. The first-order conditions characterizing an interior solution $\mathbf{x}^*$ are

$$w_i - \lambda \frac{\partial f(\mathbf{x}^*)}{\partial x_i} = 0 \quad \text{for } i = 1, \ldots, n$$

$$f(\mathbf{x}^*) = y.$$

These conditions can also be written in vector notation. Letting $\mathbf{D}f(\mathbf{x})$ be the gradient vector, the vector of partial derivatives of $f(\mathbf{x})$, we can write the derivative conditions as

$$\mathbf{w} = \lambda \mathbf{D}f(\mathbf{x}^*).$$

We can interpret these first-order conditions by dividing the ith condition by the jth condition to get

$$\frac{w_i}{w_j} = \frac{\dfrac{\partial f(\mathbf{x}^*)}{\partial x_i}}{\dfrac{\partial f(\mathbf{x}^*)}{\partial x_j}} \qquad i, j = 1, \cdots, n. \tag{4.1}$$

The right-hand side of this expression is the technical rate of substitution, the rate at which factor j can be substituted for factor i while maintaining a constant level of output. The left-hand side of this expression is the economic rate of substitution—at what rate factor j can be substituted for factor i while maintaining a constant cost. The conditions given above require that the technical rate of substitution be equal to the economic rate of substitution. If this were not so, there would be some kind of adjustment that would result in a lower cost way of producing the same output.

For example, suppose

$$\frac{w_i}{w_j} = \frac{2}{1} \neq \frac{1}{1} = \frac{\dfrac{\partial f(\mathbf{x}^*)}{\partial x_i}}{\dfrac{\partial f(\mathbf{x}^*)}{\partial x_j}}.$$

Then if we use one unit less of factor i and one unit more of factor j, output remains essentially unchanged but costs have gone down. For we have saved two dollars by hiring one unit less of factor i and incurred an additional cost of only one dollar by hiring more of factor j.

This first-order condition can also be represented graphically. In Figure 4.1, the curved lines represent isoquants and the straight lines represent constant cost curves. When y is fixed, the problem of the firm is to find a cost-minimizing point on a given isoquant. The equation of a constant cost curve, $C = w_1 x_1 + w_2 x_2$, can be written as $x_2 = C/w_2 - (w_1/w_2)x_1$. For fixed w_1 and w_2 the firm wants to find a point on a given isoquant

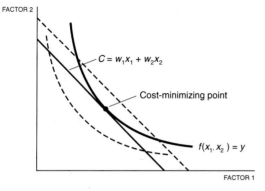

FACTOR 2

$C = w_1 x_1 + w_2 x_2$

Cost-minimizing point

$f(x_1, x_2) = y$

FACTOR 1

Cost minimization.   At a point that minimizes costs, the   **Figure**
isoquant must be tangent to the constant cost line.   **4.1**

where the associated constant cost curve has minimal vertical intercept. It
is clear that such a point will be characterized by the tangency condition
that the slope of the constant cost curve must be equal to the slope of the
isoquant. Substituting the algebraic expressions for these two slopes gives
us equation (4.1).

Examination of Figure 4.1 indicates that there is also a second-order
condition that must be satisfied at a cost-minimizing choice, namely, that
the isoquant must lie above the isocost line. Another way to say this
is that any change in factor inputs that keeps costs constant—that is,
a movement along the isocost line—must result in output decreasing or
remaining constant.

What are the local implications of this condition? Let (h_1, h_2) be a small
change in factors 1 and 2 and consider the associated change in output.
Assuming the necessary differentiability, we can write the second-order
Taylor series expansion

$$f(x_1 + h_1, x_2 + h_2) \approx f(x_1, x_2) + \frac{\partial f}{\partial x_1} h_1 + \frac{\partial f}{\partial x_2} h_2$$

$$+ \frac{1}{2} \left[\frac{\partial^2 f}{\partial x_1^2} h_1^2 + 2 \frac{\partial^2 f}{\partial x_1 \partial x_2} h_1 h_2 + \frac{\partial^2 f}{\partial x_2^2} h_2^2 \right].$$

This is more conveniently written in matrix form as

$$f(x_1 + h_1, x_2 + h_2) \approx f(x_1, x_2) + (f_1 \quad f_2) \begin{pmatrix} h_1 \\ h_2 \end{pmatrix}$$

$$+ \frac{1}{2} (h_1 \quad h_2) \begin{pmatrix} f_{11} & f_{12} \\ f_{21} & f_{22} \end{pmatrix} \begin{pmatrix} h_1 \\ h_2 \end{pmatrix}.$$

A change (h_1, h_2) that keeps costs constant must satisfy $w_1 h_1 + w_2 h_2 = 0$.
Substituting for w_i from the first-order condition for cost minimization, we
can write this as

$$w_1 h_1 + w_2 h_2 = \lambda f_1 h_1 + \lambda f_2 h_2 = \lambda [f_1 h_1 + f_2 h_2] = 0.$$

Hence, the first-order terms in this Taylor expansion must vanish for movements along the isocost line. Thus, the requirement that output decreases for any movement along the isocost line can be stated as

$$(h_1 \quad h_2) \begin{pmatrix} f_{11} & f_{12} \\ f_{21} & f_{22} \end{pmatrix} \begin{pmatrix} h_1 \\ h_2 \end{pmatrix} \leq 0$$

$$\text{for all } (h_1, h_2) \text{ such that } (f_1 \quad f_2) \begin{pmatrix} h_1 \\ h_2 \end{pmatrix} = 0.$$

(4.2)

Intuitively, at the cost-minimizing point, a first-order movement tangent to the isocost curve implies output remains constant, and a second-order movement implies output decreases.

This way of expressing the second-order condition generalizes to the n-factor case; the appropriate second-order condition is that the Hessian matrix of the production function is negative semidefinite subject to a linear constraint

$$\mathbf{h}^t \mathbf{D}^2 f(\mathbf{x}^*) \mathbf{h} \leq 0 \text{ for all } \mathbf{h} \text{ satisfying } \mathbf{wh} = 0.$$

4.2 More on second-order conditions

In Chapter 27, page 498, we show that we can state the second-order conditions in a way involving the Hessian matrix of the Lagrangian. Let us apply that method to the case at hand.

In this case, the Lagrangian is

$$\mathcal{L}(\lambda, x_1, x_2) = w_1 x_1 + w_2 x_2 - \lambda[f(x_1, x_2) - y].$$

The first-order conditions for cost minimization are that the first derivative of the Lagrangian with respect to λ, x_1, and x_2 equals zero. The second-order conditions involve the Hessian matrix of the Lagrangian,

$$\mathbf{D}^2 \mathcal{L}(\lambda^*, x_1^*, x_2^*) = \begin{pmatrix} \dfrac{\partial^2 \mathcal{L}}{\partial \lambda^2} & \dfrac{\partial^2 \mathcal{L}}{\partial \lambda \partial x_1} & \dfrac{\partial^2 \mathcal{L}}{\partial \lambda \partial x_2} \\ \dfrac{\partial^2 \mathcal{L}}{\partial x_1 \partial \lambda} & \dfrac{\partial^2 \mathcal{L}}{\partial x_1^2} & \dfrac{\partial^2 \mathcal{L}}{\partial x_1 \partial x_2} \\ \dfrac{\partial^2 \mathcal{L}}{\partial x_2 \partial \lambda} & \dfrac{\partial^2 \mathcal{L}}{\partial x_2 \partial x_1} & \dfrac{\partial^2 \mathcal{L}}{\partial x_2^2} \end{pmatrix}.$$

It is convenient to use f_{ij} to denote $\partial^2 f / \partial x_i \partial x_j$. Calculating the various second derivatives and using this notation gives us

$$\mathbf{D}^2 \mathcal{L}(\lambda^*, x_1^*, x_2^*) = \begin{pmatrix} 0 & -f_1 & -f_2 \\ -f_1 & -\lambda f_{11} & -\lambda f_{12} \\ -f_2 & -\lambda f_{21} & -\lambda f_{22} \end{pmatrix}.$$

(4.3)

This is the so-called **bordered Hessian** matrix. It follows from Chapter 27, page 498, that the second-order conditions stated in (4.2) can be satisfied as a strict inequality if and only if the determinant of the bordered Hessian is negative. This gives us a relatively simple condition to determine whether or not the second-order conditions are satisfied in a particular case.

In the general case, with n-factor demands, the second-order conditions become a bit more complicated. In this case, we have to check the sign of the determinants of certain submatrices of the bordered Hessian. See the discussion in Chapter 27, page 498.

Suppose, for example, that there are three factors of production. The bordered Hessian will take the form

$$\mathbf{D}^2 \mathcal{L}(\lambda^*, x_1^*, x_2^*, x_3^*) = \begin{pmatrix} 0 & -f_1 & -f_2 & -f_3 \\ -f_1 & -\lambda f_{11} & -\lambda f_{12} & -\lambda f_{13} \\ -f_2 & -\lambda f_{21} & -\lambda f_{22} & -\lambda f_{23} \\ -f_3 & -\lambda f_{31} & -\lambda f_{32} & -\lambda f_{33} \end{pmatrix}. \tag{4.4}$$

The second-order conditions for the three-factor case then require that the determinant of both (4.3) and (4.4) be negative when evaluated at the optimal choice. If there are n factors, *all* of the bordered Hessians of this form must be negative in order to have the second-order conditions satisfied as strict inequalities.

4.3 Difficulties

For each choice of $\mathbf{w}$ and y there will be some choice of $\mathbf{x}^*$ that minimizes the cost of producing y units of output. We will call the function that gives us this optimal choice the **conditional factor demand function** and write it as $\mathbf{x}(\mathbf{w}, y)$. Note that conditional factor demands depend on the level of output produced as well as on the factor prices. The **cost function** is the minimal cost at the factor prices $\mathbf{w}$ and output level y; that is, $c(\mathbf{w}, y) = \mathbf{w}\mathbf{x}(\mathbf{w}, y)$.

The first-order conditions are reasonably intuitive, but simply applying the first-order conditions mechanically may lead to difficulties, as in the case of profit maximization. Let us examine the four possible difficulties that can arise with the profit maximization problem and see how they relate to the cost minimization problem.

First, the technology in question may not be representable by a differentiable production function, so the calculus techniques cannot be applied. The Leontief technology is a good example of this problem. We will calculate its cost function below.

The second problem is that the conditions are valid only for interior operating positions; they must be modified if a cost minimization point occurs on the boundary. The appropriate conditions turn out to be

$$\lambda \frac{\partial f(\mathbf{x}^*)}{\partial x_i} - w_i \leq 0 \text{ if } x_i^* = 0$$

$$\lambda \frac{\partial f(\mathbf{x}^*)}{\partial x_i} - w_i = 0 \text{ if } x_i^* > 0.$$

We will examine this problem further in the context of a specific example below.

The third problem in our discussion of profit maximization had to do with the existence of a profit-maximizing bundle. However, this sort of problem will not generally arise in the case of cost minimization. It is known that a continuous function achieves a minimum and a maximum value on a closed and bounded set. The objective function $\mathbf{w}\mathbf{x}$ is certainly a continuous function and the set $V(y)$ is a closed set by hypothesis. All that we need to establish is that we can restrict our attention to a bounded subset of $V(y)$. But this is easy. Just pick an arbitrary value of $\mathbf{x}$, say $\mathbf{x}'$. Clearly the minimal cost factor bundle must have a cost less than $\mathbf{w}\mathbf{x}'$. Hence, we can restrict our attention to the subset $\{\mathbf{x} \text{ in } V(y): \mathbf{w}\mathbf{x} \leq \mathbf{w}\mathbf{x}'\}$, which will certainly be a bounded subset, as long as $\mathbf{w} \gg 0$.

The fourth problem is that the first-order conditions may not determine a unique operating position for the firm. The calculus conditions are, after all, only necessary conditions. Although they are usually sufficient for the existence of *local* optimum, they will uniquely describe a global optimum only under certain convexity conditions—i.e., requiring $V(y)$ to be convex for cost minimization problems.

EXAMPLE: Cost function for the Cobb-Douglas technology

Consider the cost minimization problem

$$c(\mathbf{w}, y) = \min_{x_1, x_2} w_1 x_1 + w_2 x_2$$

$$\text{such that } A x_1^a x_2^b = y.$$

Solving the constraint for x_2, we see that this problem is equivalent to

$$\min_{x_1} w_1 x_1 + w_2 A^{-\frac{1}{b}} y^{\frac{1}{b}} x_1^{-\frac{a}{b}}.$$

The first-order condition is

$$w_1 - \frac{a}{b} w_2 A^{-\frac{1}{b}} y^{\frac{1}{b}} x_1^{-\frac{a+b}{b}} = 0,$$

which gives us the conditional demand function for factor 1:

$$x_1(w_1, w_2, y) = A^{-\frac{1}{a+b}} \left[\frac{a w_2}{b w_1}\right]^{\frac{b}{a+b}} y^{\frac{1}{a+b}}.$$

The other conditional demand function is

$$x_2(w_1, w_2, y) = A^{-\frac{1}{a+b}} \left[\frac{aw_2}{bw_1}\right]^{-\frac{a}{a+b}} y^{\frac{1}{a+b}}.$$

The cost function is

$$c(w_1, w_2, y) = w_1 x_1(w_1, w_2, y) + w_2 x_2(w_1, w_2, y)$$

$$= A^{-\frac{1}{a+b}} \left[\left(\frac{a}{b}\right)^{\frac{b}{a+b}} + \left(\frac{a}{b}\right)^{\frac{-a}{a+b}}\right] w_1^{\frac{a}{a+b}} w_2^{\frac{b}{a+b}} y^{\frac{1}{a+b}}.$$

When we use the Cobb-Douglas technology for examples, we will usually measure units so that $A = 1$ and use the constant-returns-to-scale assumption that $a + b = 1$. In this case the cost function reduces to

$$c(w_1, w_2, y) = K w_1^a w_2^{1-a} y,$$

where $K = a^{-a}(1-a)^{a-1}$.

EXAMPLE: The cost function for the CES technology

Suppose that $f(x_1, x_2) = (x_1^\rho + x_2^\rho)^{\frac{1}{\rho}}$. What is the associated cost function? The cost minimization problem is

$$\min w_1 x_1 + w_2 x_2$$
$$\text{such that } x_1^\rho + x_2^\rho = y^\rho$$

The first-order conditions are

$$w_1 - \lambda \rho x_1^{\rho-1} = 0$$
$$w_2 - \lambda \rho x_2^{\rho-1} = 0$$
$$x_1^\rho + x_2^\rho = y^\rho.$$

Solving the first two equations for x_1^ρ and x_2^ρ, we have

$$x_1^\rho = w_1^{\frac{\rho}{\rho-1}} (\lambda\rho)^{\frac{-\rho}{\rho-1}}$$
$$x_2^\rho = w_2^{\frac{\rho}{\rho-1}} (\lambda\rho)^{\frac{-\rho}{\rho-1}}. \tag{4.5}$$

Substitute this into the production function to find

$$(\lambda\rho)^{\frac{-\rho}{\rho-1}} \left[w_1^{\frac{\rho}{\rho-1}} + w_2^{\frac{\rho}{\rho-1}}\right] = y^\rho.$$

Solve this for $(\lambda\rho)^{\frac{-\rho}{\rho-1}}$ and substitute into the system (4.5). This gives us the conditional factor demand functions

$$x_1(w_1, w_2, y) = w_1^{\frac{1}{\rho-1}} \left[w_1^{\frac{\rho}{\rho-1}} + w_2^{\frac{\rho}{\rho-1}} \right]^{-\frac{1}{\rho}} y$$

$$x_2(w_1, w_2, y) = w_2^{\frac{1}{\rho-1}} \left[w_1^{\frac{\rho}{\rho-1}} + w_2^{\frac{\rho}{\rho-1}} \right]^{-\frac{1}{\rho}} y.$$

Substituting these functions into the definition of the cost function yields

$$c(w_1, w_2, y) = w_1 x_1(w_1, w_2, y) + w_2 x_2(w_1, w_2, y)$$

$$= y \left[w_1^{\frac{\rho}{\rho-1}} + w_2^{\frac{\rho}{\rho-1}} \right] \left[w_1^{\frac{\rho}{\rho-1}} + w_2^{\frac{\rho}{\rho-1}} \right]^{-\frac{1}{\rho}}$$

$$= y \left[w_1^{\frac{\rho}{\rho-1}} + w_2^{\frac{\rho}{\rho-1}} \right]^{\frac{\rho-1}{\rho}}.$$

This expression looks a bit nicer if we set $r = \rho/(\rho - 1)$ and write

$$c(w_1, w_2, y) = y \left[w_1^r + w_2^r \right]^{\frac{1}{r}}.$$

Note that this cost function has the same form as the original CES production function with r replacing ρ. In the general case where

$$f(x_1, x_2) = \left[(a_1 x_1)^\rho + (a_2 x_2)^\rho \right]^{\frac{1}{\rho}},$$

similar computations can be done to show that

$$c(w_1, w_2, y) = \left[(w_1/a_1)^r + (w_2/a_2)^r \right]^{\frac{1}{r}} y.$$

EXAMPLE: The cost function for the Leontief technology

Suppose $f(x_1, x_2) = \min\{ax_1, bx_2\}$. What is the associated cost function? Since we know that the firm will not waste any input with a positive price, the firm must operate at a point where $y = ax_1 = bx_2$. Hence, if the firm wants to produce y units of output, it must use y/a units of good 1 and y/b units of good 2 no matter what the input prices are. Hence, the cost function is given by

$$c(w_1, w_2, y) = \frac{w_1 y}{a} + \frac{w_2 y}{b} = y \left(\frac{w_1}{a} + \frac{w_2}{b} \right).$$

EXAMPLE: The cost function for the linear technology

Suppose that $f(x_1, x_2) = ax_1 + bx_2$, so that factors 1 and 2 are perfect substitutes. What will the cost function look like? Since the two goods are perfect substitutes, the firm will use whichever is cheaper. Hence, the cost function will have the form $c(w_1, w_2, y) = \min\{w_1/a, w_2/b\}y$.

In this case the answer to the cost-minimization problem typically involves a boundary solution: one of the two factors will be used in a zero amount. Although it is easy to see the answer to this particular problem, it is worthwhile presenting a more formal solution since it serves as a nice example of the Kuhn-Tucker theorem in action. The Kuhn-Tucker theorem is the appropriate tool to use here, since we will almost never have an interior solution. See Chapter 27, page 503, for a statement of this theorem.

For notational convenience we consider the special case where $a = b = 1$. We pose the minimization problem as

$$\min \ w_1 x_1 + w_2 x_2$$

$$\text{s.t. } x_1 + x_2 = y$$

$$x_1 \geq 0$$

$$x_2 \geq 0.$$

The Lagrangian for this problem can be written as

$$\mathcal{L}(\lambda, \mu_1, \mu_2, x_1, x_2) = w_1 x_1 + w_2 x_2 - \lambda(x_1 + x_2 - y) - \mu_1 x_1 - \mu_2 x_2.$$

The Kuhn-Tucker first-order conditions are

$$w_1 - \lambda - \mu_1 = 0$$
$$w_2 - \lambda - \mu_2 = 0$$
$$x_1 + x_2 = y$$
$$x_1 \geq 0$$
$$x_2 \geq 0.$$

and the complementary slackness conditions are

$$\mu_1 \geq 0, \ \mu_1 = 0 \text{ if } x_1 > 0$$
$$\mu_2 \geq 0, \ \mu_2 = 0 \text{ if } x_2 > 0.$$

In order to determine the solution to this minimization problem, we have to examine each of the possible cases where the inequality constraints are binding or not binding. Since there are two constraints and each can be binding or not binding, we have four cases to consider.

1) $x_1 = 0$, $x_2 = 0$. In this case, we cannot satisfy the condition that $x_1 + x_2 = y$ unless $y = 0$.

2) $x_1 = 0$, $x_2 > 0$. In this case, we know that $\mu_2 = 0$. Hence, the first two first-order conditions give us

$$w_1 = \lambda + \mu_1$$
$$w_2 = \lambda$$

Since $\mu_1 \geq 0$, this case can only arise when $w_1 \geq w_2$. Since $x_1 = 0$, it follows that $x_2 = y$.

3) $x_2 = 0$, $x_1 > 0$. Reasoning similar to that in the above case shows that $x_1 = y$ and that this case can only occur when $w_2 \geq w_1$.

4) $x_1 > 0$, $x_2 > 0$. In this case, complementary slackness implies that $\mu_1 = 0$, and $\mu_2 = 0$. Thus, the first-order conditions imply that $w_1 = w_2$.

The above problem, though somewhat trivial, is typical of the methods used in applying the Kuhn-Tucker theorem. If there are k constraints that can be binding or not binding, there will be 2^k configurations possible at the optimum. Each of these must be examined to see if it is actually compatible with all of the required conditions in which case it represents a potentially optimal solution.

4.4 Conditional factor demand functions

Let us now turn to the cost minimization problem and the conditional factor demands. Applying the usual arguments, the conditional factor demand functions $\mathbf{x}(\mathbf{w}, y)$ must satisfy the first-order conditions

$$f(\mathbf{x}(\mathbf{w}, y)) \equiv y$$
$$\mathbf{w} - \lambda \mathbf{Df}(\mathbf{x}(\mathbf{w}, y)) \equiv \mathbf{0}.$$

It is easy to get lost in matrix algebra in the following calculations, so we will consider a simple two-good example. In this case the first-order conditions look like

$$f(x_1(w_1, w_2, y), x_2(w_1, w_2, y)) \equiv y$$
$$w_1 - \lambda \frac{\partial f(x_1(w_1, w_2, y), x_2(w_1, w_2, y))}{\partial x_1} \equiv 0$$
$$w_2 - \lambda \frac{\partial f(x_1(w_1, w_2, y), x_2(w_1, w_2, y))}{\partial x_2} \equiv 0$$

Just as in the last chapter, these first-order conditions are *identities*—by definition of the conditional factor demand functions they are true for all values of w_1, w_2, and y. Therefore, we can differentiate these identities with respect to w_1, say.

We find

$$\frac{\partial f}{\partial x_1}\frac{\partial x_1}{\partial w_1} + \frac{\partial f}{\partial x_2}\frac{\partial x_2}{\partial w_1} \equiv 0$$

$$1 - \lambda\left[\frac{\partial^2 f}{\partial x_1^2}\frac{\partial x_1}{\partial w_1} + \frac{\partial^2 f}{\partial x_1 \partial x_2}\frac{\partial x_2}{\partial w_1}\right] - \frac{\partial f}{\partial x_1}\frac{\partial \lambda}{\partial w_1} \equiv 0$$

$$0 - \lambda\left[\frac{\partial^2 f}{\partial x_2 \partial x_1}\frac{\partial x_1}{\partial w_1} + \frac{\partial^2 f}{\partial x_2^2}\frac{\partial x_2}{\partial w_1}\right] - \frac{\partial f}{\partial x_2}\frac{\partial \lambda}{\partial w_1} \equiv 0.$$

These equations can be written in matrix form as

$$\begin{pmatrix} 0 & -f_1 & -f_2 \\ -f_1 & -\lambda f_{11} & -\lambda f_{21} \\ -f_2 & -\lambda f_{12} & -\lambda f_{22} \end{pmatrix} \begin{pmatrix} \frac{\partial \lambda}{\partial w_1} \\ \frac{\partial x_1}{\partial w_1} \\ \frac{\partial x_2}{\partial w_1} \end{pmatrix} \equiv \begin{pmatrix} 0 \\ -1 \\ 0 \end{pmatrix}.$$

Note the important fact that the matrix on the left-hand side is precisely the bordered Hessian involved in the second-order conditions for maximization. (See Chapter 27, page 498.) We can use a standard technique from matrix algebra, Cramer's rule, which is discussed in Chapter 26, page 477, to solve for $\partial x_1 / \partial w_1$:

$$\frac{\partial x_1}{\partial w_1} = \frac{\begin{vmatrix} 0 & 0 & -f_2 \\ -f_1 & -1 & -\lambda f_{21} \\ -f_2 & 0 & -\lambda f_{22} \end{vmatrix}}{\begin{vmatrix} 0 & -f_1 & -f_2 \\ -f_1 & -\lambda f_{11} & -\lambda f_{21} \\ -f_2 & -\lambda f_{12} & -\lambda f_{22} \end{vmatrix}}.$$

Let H be the determinant of the matrix in the denominator of this fraction. We know that this is a negative number by the second-order conditions for minimization. Carrying out the calculation in the numerator, we have

$$\frac{\partial x_1}{\partial w_1} = \frac{f_2^2}{H} < 0.$$

Hence, the conditional factor demand curve slopes downward.

Similarly, we can derive the expression for $\partial x_2 / \partial w_1$. Applying Cramer's rule again, we have

$$\frac{\partial x_2}{\partial w_1} = \frac{\begin{vmatrix} 0 & -f_1 & 0 \\ -f_1 & -\lambda f_{11} & -1 \\ -f_2 & -\lambda f_{12} & 0 \end{vmatrix}}{\begin{vmatrix} 0 & -f_1 & -f_2 \\ -f_1 & -\lambda f_{11} & -\lambda f_{21} \\ -f_2 & -\lambda f_{12} & -\lambda f_{22} \end{vmatrix}}.$$

Carrying out the indicated calculations,

$$\frac{\partial x_2}{\partial w_1} = -\frac{f_2 f_1}{H} > 0. \tag{4.6}$$

Repeating the same sorts of calculations for $\partial x_1/\partial w_2$, we find

$$\frac{\partial x_1}{\partial w_2} = \frac{\begin{vmatrix} 0 & 0 & -f_2 \\ -f_1 & 0 & -\lambda f_{12} \\ -f_2 & -1 & -\lambda f_{22} \end{vmatrix}}{\begin{vmatrix} 0 & -f_1 & -f_2 \\ -f_1 & -\lambda f_{11} & -\lambda f_{21} \\ -f_2 & -\lambda f_{12} & -\lambda f_{22} \end{vmatrix}}.$$

which implies

$$\frac{\partial x_1}{\partial w_2} = -\frac{f_1 f_2}{H} > 0. \tag{4.7}$$

Comparing expressions (4.6) and (4.7), we see that they are identical. Thus $\partial x_1/\partial w_2$ equals $\partial x_2/\partial w_1$. Just as in the case of profit maximization, we find a symmetry condition: as a consequence of the model of cost minimization the "cross-price effects must be equal."

In the two-input case under examination here, the sign of the cross-price effect must be positive. That is, the two factors must be **substitutes**. This is special to the two-input case; if there are more factors of production, the cross-price effect between any two of them can go either direction.

We now proceed to rephrase the above calculations in terms of matrix algebra. Since y will be held fixed in all the calculations, we will drop it as an argument of the conditional factor demands for notational convenience. The first-order conditions for cost minimization are

$$f(\mathbf{x}(\mathbf{w})) \equiv y$$
$$\mathbf{w} - \lambda \mathbf{D}f(\mathbf{x}(\mathbf{w})) \equiv \mathbf{0}.$$

Differentiating these identities with respect to $\mathbf{w}$ we find:

$$\mathbf{D}f(\mathbf{x}(\mathbf{w}))\mathbf{D}\mathbf{x}(\mathbf{w}) = \mathbf{0}$$
$$\mathbf{I} - \lambda \mathbf{D}^2 f(\mathbf{x}(\mathbf{w}))\mathbf{D}\mathbf{x}(\mathbf{w}) - \mathbf{D}f(\mathbf{x}(\mathbf{w}))\mathbf{D}\lambda(\mathbf{w}) = \mathbf{0}.$$

Rearranging slightly gives us

$$\begin{pmatrix} 0 & -\mathbf{D}f(\mathbf{x}) \\ -\mathbf{D}f(\mathbf{x})^t & -\lambda \mathbf{D}^2 f(\mathbf{x}) \end{pmatrix} \begin{pmatrix} \mathbf{D}\lambda(\mathbf{w}) \\ \mathbf{D}\mathbf{x}(\mathbf{w}) \end{pmatrix} = -\begin{pmatrix} 0 \\ \mathbf{I} \end{pmatrix}.$$

Note that the matrix is simply the bordered Hessian matrix—i.e., the second derivative matrix of the Lagrangian. Assuming that we have a regular optimum so that the Hessian matrix is nondegenerate, we can solve for the substitution matrix $\mathbf{Dx(w)}$ by taking the inverse of the Hessian matrix:

$$\begin{pmatrix} \mathbf{D\lambda(w)} \\ \mathbf{Dx(w)} \end{pmatrix} = \begin{pmatrix} 0 & \mathbf{D}f(\mathbf{x}) \\ \mathbf{D}f(\mathbf{x})^t & \lambda\mathbf{D}^2 f(\mathbf{x}) \end{pmatrix}^{-1} \begin{pmatrix} 0 \\ \mathbf{I} \end{pmatrix}.$$

(We have multiplied through by -1 to eliminate the minus signs from both sides of the expression.) Since the bordered Hessian is symmetric, its inverse is symmetric, which shows that the cross-price effects are symmetric. It can also be shown that the substitution matrix is negative semidefinite. Since we will present a simple proof of this below using other methods, we will omit this demonstration here.

4.5 Algebraic approach to cost minimization

As in the case of profit maximization, we can also apply the algebraic techniques to the problem of cost minimization. We take as our data some observed choices by a firm of output levels y^t, factor prices $\mathbf{w}^t$, and factor levels $\mathbf{x}^t$, for $t = 1, \cdots, T$. When will these data be consistent with the model of cost minimization?

An obvious necessary condition is that the cost of the observed choice of inputs is no greater than the cost of any other level of inputs that would produce at least as much output. Translated into symbols, this says

$$\mathbf{w}^t\mathbf{x}^t \leq \mathbf{w}^t\mathbf{x}^s \text{ for all } s \text{ and } t \text{ such that } y^s \geq y^t.$$

We will refer to this condition as the **Weak Axiom of Cost Minimization (WACM)**.

As in the case of profit maximization, WACM can be used to derive the delta version of downward-sloping demands. Take two different observations with the same output level and note that cost minimization implies that

$$\mathbf{w}^t\mathbf{x}^t \leq \mathbf{w}^t\mathbf{x}^s$$
$$\mathbf{w}^s\mathbf{x}^s \leq \mathbf{w}^s\mathbf{x}^t.$$

The first expression says that the tth observation must have the lower production costs at the tth prices; the second expression says that the sth observation must have the lower production costs at the sth prices.

Write the second inequality as

$$-\mathbf{w}^s\mathbf{x}^t \leq -\mathbf{w}^s\mathbf{x}^s,$$

add it to the first, and rearrange the result to get

$$(\mathbf{w}^t - \mathbf{w}^s)(\mathbf{x}^t - \mathbf{x}^s) \leq 0,$$

or

$$\Delta\mathbf{w}\Delta\mathbf{x} \leq 0.$$

Roughly speaking, the vector of factor demands must move "opposite" the vector of factor prices.

One can also construct inner and outer bounds to the true input requirement set that generated the data. We will state the bounds here and leave it to the reader to check the details. The arguments are similar to those presented for the case of profit maximization.

The inner bound is given by:

$$VI(y) = \text{convex monotonic hull of } \{\mathbf{x}^t : y^t \geq y\}.$$

That is, the inner bound is simply the convex monotonic hull of all observations that can produce at least y amount of output. The outer bound is given by:

$$VO(y) = \{\mathbf{x} : \mathbf{w}^t\mathbf{x} \geq \mathbf{w}^t\mathbf{x}^t \text{ for all } t \text{ such that } y^t \leq y\}.$$

These constructions are analogous to the earlier constructions of YO and YI. A picture of VO and VI is given in Figure 4.2.

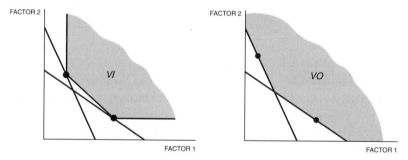

Figure 4.2   **Inner and outer bounds.**   The sets VI and VO give inner and outer bounds to the true input requirement set.

It is pretty obvious that $VI(y)$ is contained in $V(y)$, at least as long as $V(y)$ is convex and monotonic. It is perhaps not quite so obvious that $VO(y)$ contains $V(y)$, so we provide the following proof.

Suppose, contrary to the assertion, that we have some $\mathbf{x}$ that is in $V(y)$ but not in $VO(y)$. Since $\mathbf{x}$ is not in $VO(y)$, there must be some observation t such that $y^t \leq y$ and

$$\mathbf{w}^t\mathbf{x} < \mathbf{w}^t\mathbf{x}^t. \tag{4.8}$$

But since $\mathbf{x}$ is in $V(y)$ it can produce at least y^t units of output and (4.8) shows that it costs less than $\mathbf{x}^t$. This contradicts the assumption that $\mathbf{x}^t$ is a cost-minimizing bundle.

Notes

The algebraic approach to cost minimization is further developed in Varian (1982b).

Exercises

4.1. Prove rigorously that profit maximization implies cost minimization.

4.2. Use the Kuhn-Tucker theorem to derive conditions for cost minimization that are valid even if the optimal solution involves a boundary solution.

4.3. A firm has two plants with cost functions $c_1(y_1) = y_1^2/2$ and $c_2(y_2) = y_2$. What is the cost function for the firm?

4.4. A firm has two plants. One plant produces output according to the production function $x_1^a x_2^{1-a}$. The other plant has a production function $x_1^b x_2^{1-b}$. What is the cost function for this technology?

4.5. Suppose that the firm has two possible activities to produce output. Activity a uses a_1 units of good 1 and a_2 units of good 2 to produce 1 unit of output. Activity b uses b_1 units of good 1 and b_2 units of good 2 to produce 1 unit of output. Factors can only be used in these fixed proportions. If the factor prices are (w_1, w_2), what are the demands for the two factors? What is the cost function for this technology? For what factor prices is the cost function not differentiable?

4.6. A firm has two plants with cost functions $c_1(y_1) = 4\sqrt{y_1}$ and $c_2(y_2) = 2\sqrt{y_2}$. What is its cost of producing an output y?

4.7. The following table shows two observations on factor demand x_1, x_2, factor prices, w_1, w_2, and output, y for a firm. Is the behavior depicted in this table consistent with cost-minimizing behavior?

Obs	y	w_1	w_2	x_1	x_2
A	100	2	1	10	20
B	110	1	2	14	10

4.8. A firm has a production function $y = x_1 x_2$. If the minimum cost of production at $w_1 = w_2 = 1$ is equal to 4, what is y equal to?

CHAPTER 5

COST
FUNCTION

The cost function measures the minimum cost of producing a given level of output for some fixed factor prices. As such it summarizes information about the technological choices available to the firms. It turns out that the behavior of the cost function can tell us a lot about the nature of the firm's technology.

Just as the production function is our primary means of describing the technological possibilities of production, the cost function will be our primary means of describing the economic possibilities of a firm. In the next two sections we will investigate the behavior of the cost function $c(\mathbf{w}, y)$ with respect to its price and quantity arguments. Before undertaking that study we need to define a few related functions, namely the average and the marginal cost functions.

5.1 Average and marginal costs

Let us consider the structure of the cost function. In general, the cost function can always be expressed simply as the value of the conditional factor demands.

$$c(\mathbf{w}, y) \equiv \mathbf{w}\mathbf{x}(\mathbf{w}, y)$$

This just says that the minimum cost of producing y units of output is the cost of the cheapest way to produce y.

In the short run, some of the factors of production are fixed at predetermined levels. Let $\mathbf{x}_f$ be the vector of fixed factors, $\mathbf{x}_v$ the vector of variable factors, and break up $\mathbf{w}$ into $\mathbf{w} = (\mathbf{w}_v, \mathbf{w}_f)$, the vectors of prices of the variable and the fixed factors. The short-run conditional factor demand functions will generally depend on $\mathbf{x}_f$, so we write them as $\mathbf{x}_v(\mathbf{w}, y, \mathbf{x}_f)$. Then the short-run cost function can be written as

$$c(\mathbf{w}, y, \mathbf{x}_f) = \mathbf{w}_v \mathbf{x}_v(\mathbf{w}, y, \mathbf{x}_f) + \mathbf{w}_f \mathbf{x}_f.$$

The term $\mathbf{w}_v \mathbf{x}_v(\mathbf{w}, y, \mathbf{x}_f)$ is called **short-run variable cost** (SVC), and the term $\mathbf{w}_f \mathbf{x}_f$ is the **fixed cost** (FC). We can define various derived cost concepts from these basic units:

$$\text{short-run total cost} = \text{STC} = \mathbf{w}_v \mathbf{x}_v(\mathbf{w}, y, \mathbf{x}_f) + \mathbf{w}_f \mathbf{x}_f$$

$$\text{short-run average cost} = \text{SAC} = \frac{c(\mathbf{w}, y, \mathbf{x}_f)}{y}$$

$$\text{short-run average variable cost} = \text{SAVC} = \frac{\mathbf{w}_v \mathbf{x}_v(\mathbf{w}, y, \mathbf{x}_f)}{y}$$

$$\text{short-run average fixed cost} = \text{SAFC} = \frac{\mathbf{w}_f \mathbf{x}_f}{y}$$

$$\text{short-run marginal cost} = \text{SMC} = \frac{\partial c(\mathbf{w}, y, \mathbf{x}_f)}{\partial y}$$

When all factors are variable, the firm will optimize in the choice of $\mathbf{x}_f$. Hence, the long-run cost function only depends on the factor prices and the level of output as indicated earlier.

We can express this long-run function in terms of the short-run cost function in the following way. Let $\mathbf{x}_f(\mathbf{w}, y)$ be the optimal choice of the fixed factors, and let $\mathbf{x}_v(\mathbf{w}, y) = \mathbf{x}_v(\mathbf{w}, y, \mathbf{x}_f(\mathbf{w}, y))$ be the long-run optimal choice of the variable factors. Then the long-run cost function can be written as

$$c(\mathbf{w}, y) = \mathbf{w}_v \mathbf{x}_v(\mathbf{w}, y) + \mathbf{w}_f \mathbf{x}_f(\mathbf{w}, y) = c(\mathbf{w}, y, \mathbf{x}_f(\mathbf{w}, y)).$$

The long-run cost function can be used to define cost concepts similar to those defined above:

$$\text{long-run average cost} = \text{LAC} = \frac{c(\mathbf{w}, y)}{y}$$

$$\text{long-run marginal cost} = \text{LMC} = \frac{\partial c(\mathbf{w}, y)}{\partial y}.$$

Notice that "long-run average cost" equals "long-run average variable cost" since all costs are variable in the long-run; "long-run fixed costs" are zero for the same reason.

Long run and short run are of course relative concepts. Which factors are considered variable and which are considered fixed depends on the particular problem being analyzed. You must first consider over what time period you wish to analyze the firm's behavior and then ask what factors can the firm adjust during that time period.

EXAMPLE: The short-run Cobb-Douglas cost functions

Suppose the second factor in a Cobb-Douglas technology is restricted to operate at a level k. Then the cost-minimizing problem is

$$\min w_1 x_1 + w_2 k$$
$$\text{such that } y = x_1^a k^{1-a}.$$

Solving the constraint for x_1 as a function of y and k gives

$$x_1 = (yk^{a-1})^{\frac{1}{a}}.$$

Thus

$$c(w_1, w_2, y, k) = w_1 (yk^{a-1})^{\frac{1}{a}} + w_2 k.$$

The following variations can also be calculated:

$$\text{short-run average cost } = w_1 \left(\frac{y}{k}\right)^{\frac{1-a}{a}} + \frac{w_2 k}{y}$$

$$\text{short-run average variable cost } = w_1 \left(\frac{y}{k}\right)^{\frac{1-a}{a}}$$

$$\text{short-run average fixed cost } = \frac{w_2 k}{y}$$

$$\text{short-run marginal cost } = \frac{w_1}{a} \left(\frac{y}{k}\right)^{\frac{1-a}{a}}$$

EXAMPLE: Constant returns to scale and the cost function

If the production function exhibits constant returns to scale, then it is intuitively clear that the cost function should exhibit costs that are linear in the level of output: if you want to produce twice as much output it will cost you twice as much. This intuition is verified in the following proposition:

Constant returns to scale. *If the production function exhibits constant returns to scale, the cost function may be written as $c(\mathbf{w}, y) = yc(\mathbf{w}, 1)$.*

Proof. Let $\mathbf{x}^*$ be a cheapest way to produce one unit of output at prices $\mathbf{w}$ so that $c(\mathbf{w}, 1) = \mathbf{w}\mathbf{x}^*$. Then I claim that $c(\mathbf{w}, y) = \mathbf{w}y\mathbf{x}^* = yc(\mathbf{w}, 1)$. Notice first that $y\mathbf{x}^*$ is feasible to produce y since the technology is constant returns to scale. Suppose that it does not minimize cost; instead let $\mathbf{x}'$ be the cost-minimizing bundle to produce y at prices $\mathbf{w}$ so that $\mathbf{w}\mathbf{x}' < \mathbf{w}y\mathbf{x}^*$. Then $\mathbf{w}\mathbf{x}'/y < \mathbf{w}\mathbf{x}^*$ and $\mathbf{x}'/y$ can produce 1 since the technology is constant returns to scale. This contradicts the definition of $\mathbf{x}^*$. ∎

If the technology exhibits constant returns to scale, then the average cost, the average variable cost, and the marginal cost functions are all the same.

5.2 The geometry of costs

The cost function is the single most useful tool for studying the economic behavior of a firm. In a sense to be made clear later, the cost function summarizes all economically relevant information about the technology of the firm. In the following sections we will examine some of the properties of the cost function. This is most conveniently done in two stages: first, we examine the properties of the cost function under the assumption of fixed factor prices. In this case, we will write the cost function simply as $c(y)$. Second, we will examine the properties of the cost function when factor prices are free to vary.

Since we have taken factor prices to be fixed, costs depend only on the level of output of a firm, and useful graphs can be drawn that relate output and costs. The total cost curve is always assumed to be monotonic in output: the more you produce, the more it costs. The average cost curve, however, can increase or decrease with output, depending on whether total costs rise more than or less than linearly. It is often thought that the most realistic case, at least in the short run, is the case where the average cost curve first decreases and then increases. The reason for this is as follows.

In the short run the cost function has two components: fixed costs and variable costs. We can therefore write short-run average cost as

$$SAC = \frac{c(\mathbf{w}, y, \mathbf{x}_f)}{y} = \frac{\mathbf{w}_f\mathbf{x}_f}{y} + \frac{\mathbf{w}_v\mathbf{x}_v(\mathbf{w}, y, \mathbf{x}_f)}{y} = SAFC + SAVC.$$

In most applications, the short-run fixed factors will be such things as machines, buildings, and other types of capital equipment while the variable factors will be labor and raw materials. Let us consider how the costs attributable to these factors will change as output changes.

As we increase output, average variable costs may initially decrease if there is some initial region of economies of scale. However, it seems reasonable to suppose that the variable factors required will increase more or less linearly until we approach some capacity level of output determined by the amounts of the fixed factors. When we are near to capacity, we need to use more than a proportional amount of the variable inputs to increase output. Thus, the average variable cost function should eventually increase as output increases, as depicted in Figure 5.1A. Average fixed costs must of course decrease with output, as indicated in Figure 5.1B. Adding together the average variable cost curve and the average fixed costs gives us the U-shaped average cost curve in Figure 5.1C. The initial decrease in average costs is due to the decrease in average fixed costs; the eventual increase in average costs is due to the increase in average variable costs. The level of output at which the average cost of production is minimized is sometimes known as the **minimal efficient scale.**

In the long run all costs are variable costs; in such circumstances increasing average costs seems unreasonable since a firm could always replicate its production process. Hence, the reasonable long-run possibilities should be either constant or decreasing average costs. On the other hand, as we mentioned earlier, certain kinds of firms may not exhibit a long-run constant-returns-to-scale technology because of long-run fixed factors. If some factors do remain fixed even in the long run, the appropriate long-run average cost curve should presumably be U-shaped, for essentially the same reasons given in the short-run case.

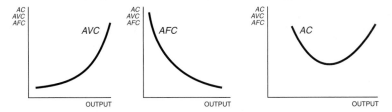

Figure 5.1 **Average cost curves.** The average variable cost curve will eventually rise with output, while the average fixed cost curve always falls with output. The interaction of these two effects produces a U-shaped average cost curve.

Let us now consider the marginal cost curve. What is its relationship to the average cost curve? Let y^* denote the point of minimum average cost; then to the left of y^* average costs are declining so that for $y \leq y^*$

$$\frac{d}{dy}\left(\frac{c(y)}{y}\right) \leq 0.$$

Taking the derivative gives

$$\frac{yc'(y) - c(y)}{y^2} \le 0 \text{ for } y \le y^*,$$

which implies

$$c'(y) \le \frac{c(y)}{y} \text{ for } y \le y^*.$$

This inequality says that marginal cost is less than average cost to the left of the minimum average cost point. A similar analysis shows that

$$c'(y) \ge \frac{c(y)}{y} \text{ for } y \ge y^*.$$

Since both inequalities must hold at y^*, we have

$$c'(y^*) = \frac{c(y^*)}{y^*};$$

that is, marginal costs equal average costs at the point of minimum average costs.

What is the relationship of the marginal cost curve to the average variable cost curve? Simply by changing the notation in the above argument, we can show that the marginal cost curve lies below the average variable cost curve when the average variable cost curve is decreasing, and lies above it when it is increasing. It follows that the marginal cost curve must pass through the minimum point of the average variable cost curve.

It is also not hard to show that marginal cost must equal average variable cost for the first unit of output. After all, the marginal cost of the *first* unit of output is the same as the average variable cost of the first unit of output, since both numbers are equal to $c_v(1) - c_v(0)$. A more formal demonstration is also possible. Average variable cost is defined by

$$AVC(y) = \frac{c_v(y)}{y}.$$

If $y = 0$, this expression becomes $0/0$, which is indeterminate. However, the limit of $c_v(y)/y$ can be calculated using L'Hôpital's rule:

$$\lim_{y \to 0} \frac{c_v(y)}{y} = \frac{c_v'(0)}{1}.$$

(See Chapter 26, page 481, for a statement of this rule.) It follows that average variable cost at zero output is just marginal cost.

All of the analysis just discussed holds in both the long and the short run. However, if production exhibits constant returns to scale in the long run, so that the cost function is linear in the level of output, then average cost, average variable cost, and marginal cost are all equal to each other, which makes most of the relationships just described rather trivial.

EXAMPLE: The Cobb-Douglas cost curves

As calculated in an earlier example, the generalized Cobb-Douglas technology has a cost function of the form

$$c(y) = Ky^{\frac{1}{a+b}} \qquad a+b \le 1$$

where K is a function of factor prices and parameters. Thus,

$$AC(y) = \frac{c(y)}{y} = Ky^{\frac{1-a-b}{a+b}}$$

$$MC(y) = c'(y) = \frac{K}{a+b}y^{\frac{1-a-b}{a+b}}.$$

If $a+b < 1$, the cost curves exhibit increasing average costs; if $a+b = 1$, the cost curves exhibit constant average cost.

We have also seen earlier that the short-run cost function for the Cobb-Douglas technology has the form

$$c(y) = Ky^{\frac{1}{a}} + F.$$

Thus

$$AC(y) = \frac{c(y)}{y} = Ky^{\frac{1-a}{a}} + \frac{F}{y}.$$

5.3 Long-run and short-run cost curves

Let us now consider the relationship between the long-run cost curves and the short-run cost curves. It is clear that the long-run cost curve must never lie above any short-run cost curve, since the short-run cost minimization problem is just a constrained version of the long-run cost minimization problem.

Let us write the long-run cost function as $c(y) = c(y, z(y))$. Here we have omitted the factor prices since they are assumed fixed, and we let $z(y)$ be the cost-minimizing demand for a single fixed factor. Let y^* be some given level of output, and let $z^* = z(y^*)$ be the associated long-run demand for the fixed factor. The short-run cost, $c(y, z^*)$, must be at least as great as the long-run cost, $c(y, z(y))$, for all levels of output, and the short-run cost will equal the long-run cost at output y^*, so $c(y^*, z^*) = c(y^*, z(y^*))$. Hence, the long- and the short-run cost curves must be tangent at y^*.

This is just a geometric restatement of the envelope theorem. The slope of the long-run cost curve at y^* is

$$\frac{dc(y^*, z(y^*))}{dy} = \frac{\partial c(y^*, z^*)}{\partial y} + \frac{\partial c(y^*, z^*)}{\partial z}\frac{\partial z(y^*)}{\partial y}.$$

But since z^* is the *optimal* choice of the fixed factors at the output level y^*, we must have

$$\frac{\partial c(y^*, z^*)}{\partial z} = 0.$$

LMC = SMC
at y^*.

Thus, long-run marginal costs at y^* equal short-run marginal costs at (y^*, z^*).

Finally, we note that if the long- and short-run cost curves are tangent, the long- and short-run *average* cost curves must also be tangent. A typical configuration is illustrated in Figure 5.2.

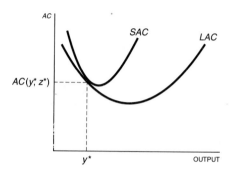

Long-run and short-run average cost curves. Note that the long-run and the short-run average cost curves must be tangent which implies that the long-run and short-run marginal costs must be equal.

**Figure
5.2**

Another way to see the relationship between the long-run and the short-run average cost curves is to start with the family of short-run average cost curves. Suppose, for example, that we have a fixed factor that can be used only at three discrete levels: z_1, z_2, z_3. We depict this family of curves in Figure 5.3. What would be the long-run cost curve? It is simply the lower envelope of these short-run curves since the optimal choice of z to produce output y will simply be the choice that has the minimum cost of producing y. This envelope operation generates a scalloped-shaped long-run average cost curve. If there are many possible values of the fixed factor, these scallops become a smooth curve.

5.4 Factor prices and cost functions

We turn now to the study of the price behavior of cost functions. Several interesting properties follow directly from the definition of the functions. These are summarized in the following remarks. Note the close analogy with the properties of the profit function.

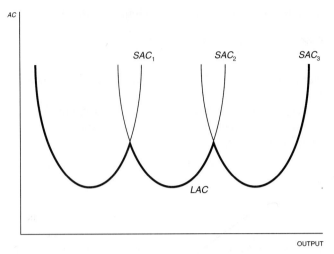

**Figure
5.3**

Long-run average cost curve. The long-run average cost
curve, LAC, is the lower envelope of the short-run average cost
curves, SAC_1, SAC_2, and SAC_3.

Properties of the cost function.

1) Nondecreasing in **w.** *If* $\mathbf{w}' \geq \mathbf{w}$, *then* $c(\mathbf{w}', y) \geq c(\mathbf{w}, y)$.

2) Homogeneous of degree 1 in **w.** $c(t\mathbf{w}, y) = tc(\mathbf{w}, y)$ *for* $t > 0$.

3) Concave in **w.** $c(t\mathbf{w} + (1 - t)\mathbf{w}', y) \geq tc(\mathbf{w}, y) + (1 - t)c(\mathbf{w}', y)$ *for*
$0 \leq t \leq 1$.

4) Continuous in **w.** $c(\mathbf{w}, y)$ *is continuous as a function of* **w**, *for* $\mathbf{w} \gg \mathbf{0}$.

Proof.
1) This is obvious, but a formal proof may be instructive. Let **x** and **x'**
be cost-minimizing bundles associated with **w** and **w'**. Then $\mathbf{wx} \leq \mathbf{wx}'$
by minimization and $\mathbf{wx}' \leq \mathbf{w}'\mathbf{x}'$ since $\mathbf{w} \leq \mathbf{w}'$. Putting these inequalities
together gives $\mathbf{wx} \leq \mathbf{w}'\mathbf{x}'$ as required.

2) We show that if **x** is the cost-minimizing bundle at prices **w**, then **x**
also minimizes costs at prices $t\mathbf{w}$. Suppose not, and let **x'** be a cost-
minimizing bundle at $t\mathbf{w}$ so that $t\mathbf{wx}' < t\mathbf{wx}$. But this inequality implies
$\mathbf{wx}' < \mathbf{wx}$, which contradicts the definition of **x**. Hence, multiplying factor
prices by a positive scalar t does not change the composition of a cost-
minimizing bundle, and, thus, costs must rise by exactly a factor of t:
$c(t\mathbf{w}, y) = t\mathbf{wx} = tc(\mathbf{w}, y)$.

3) Let $(\mathbf{w}, \mathbf{x})$ and $(\mathbf{w}', \mathbf{x}')$ be two cost-minimizing price-factor combinations

and let $\mathbf{w}'' = t\mathbf{w} + (1-t)\mathbf{w}'$ for any $0 \le t \le 1$. Now,

$$c(\mathbf{w}'', y) = \mathbf{w}'' \mathbf{x}'' = t\mathbf{w}\,\mathbf{x}'' + (1-t)\mathbf{w}'\,\mathbf{x}''.$$

Since $\mathbf{x}''$ is not necessarily the cheapest way to produce y at prices $\mathbf{w}'$ or $\mathbf{w}$, we have $\mathbf{w}\mathbf{x}'' \ge c(\mathbf{w}, y)$ and $\mathbf{w}' \cdot \mathbf{x}'' \ge c(\mathbf{w}', y)$. Thus,

$$c(\mathbf{w}'', y) \ge tc(\mathbf{w}, y) + (1-t)c(\mathbf{w}', y).$$

4) The continuity of c follows from the Theorem of the Maximum, in Chapter 27, page 506. ∎

The only property that is surprising here is the concavity. However, we can provide intuition for this property similar to the one presented for the profit function. Suppose we graph cost as a function of the price of a single input, with all other prices held constant. If the price of a factor rises, costs will never go down (property 1), but they will go up at a decreasing rate (property 3). Why? Because as this one factor becomes more expensive and other prices stay the same, the cost-minimizing firm will shift away from it to use other inputs.

This is made more clear by considering Figure 5.4. Let $\mathbf{x}^*$ be a cost-minimizing bundle at prices $\mathbf{w}^*$. Suppose the price of factor 1 changes from w_1^* to w_1. If we just behave passively and continue to use $\mathbf{x}^*$, our costs will be $C = w_1 x_1^* + \sum_{i=2}^{n} w_i^* x_i^*$. The minimal cost of production $c(\mathbf{w}, y)$ must be less than this "passive" cost function; thus, the graph of $c(\mathbf{w}, y)$ must lie below the graph of the passive cost function, with both curves coinciding at w_1^*. It is not hard to see that this implies $c(\mathbf{w}, y)$ is concave with respect to w_1.

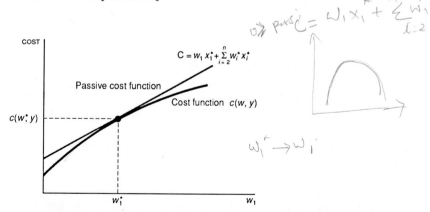

Concavity of the cost function. The cost function will be a concave function of the factor price since it must always lie below the "passive" cost function.

Figure 5.4

The same graph can be used to discover a very useful way to find an expression for the conditional factor demand. We first state the result formally:

Shephard's lemma. *(The derivative property.) Let $x_i(\mathbf{w}, y)$ be the firm's conditional factor demand for input i. Then if the cost function is differentiable at $(\mathbf{w}, y)$, and $w_i > 0$ for $i = 1, \ldots, n$ then*

$$x_i(\mathbf{w}, y) = \frac{\partial c(\mathbf{w}, y)}{\partial w_i} \qquad i = 1, \cdots, n.$$

Proof. The proof is very similar to the proof of Hotelling's lemma. Let $\mathbf{x}^*$ be a cost-minimizing bundle that produces y at prices $\mathbf{w}^*$. Then define the function

$$g(\mathbf{w}) = c(\mathbf{w}, y) - \mathbf{w}\mathbf{x}^*.$$

Since $c(\mathbf{w}, y)$ is the cheapest way to produce y, this function is always nonpositive. At $\mathbf{w} = \mathbf{w}^*$, $g(\mathbf{w}^*) = 0$. Since this is a maximum value of $g(\mathbf{w})$, its derivative must vanish:

$$\frac{\partial g(\mathbf{w}^*)}{\partial w_i} = \frac{\partial c(\mathbf{w}^*, y)}{\partial w_i} - x_i^* = 0 \qquad i = 1, \cdots, n$$

Hence, the cost-minimizing input vector is just given by the vector of derivatives of the cost function with respect to the prices. ∎

Since this proposition is important, we will suggest *four* different ways of proving it. First, the cost function is by definition equal to $c(\mathbf{w}, y) \equiv \mathbf{w}\mathbf{x}(\mathbf{w}, y)$. Differentiating this expression with respect to w_i and using the first-order conditions give us the result. (Hint: $\mathbf{x}(\mathbf{w}, y)$ also satisfies the identity $f(\mathbf{x}(\mathbf{w}, y)) \equiv y$. You will need to differentiate this with respect to w_i.)

Second, the above calculations are really just repeating the derivation of the envelope theorem described in the next section. This theorem can be applied directly to give the desired result.

Third, there is a nice geometrical argument that uses the same Figure 5.4 we used in arguing for concavity of the cost function. Recall in Figure 5.4 that the line $c = w_1 x_1^* + \sum_{i=2}^{n} w_i^* x_i^*$ lay above $c = c(\mathbf{w}, y)$ and both curves coincided at $w_1 = w_1^*$. Thus, the curves must be tangent, so that $x_1^* = \partial c(\mathbf{w}^*, y)/\partial w_1$.

Finally, we consider the basic economic intuition behind the proposition. If we are operating at a cost-minimizing point and the price w_1 increases, there will be a direct effect, in that the expenditure on the first factor will increase. There will also be an indirect effect, in that we will want to change the factor mix. But since we are operating at a cost-minimizing point, any such infinitesimal change must yield zero additional profits.

5.5 The envelope theorem for constrained optimization

Shephard's lemma is another example of the envelope theorem. However, in this case we must apply a version of the envelope theorem that is appropriate for constrained maximization problems. The proof for this case is given in Chapter 27, page 501.

Consider a general parameterized constrained maximization problem of the form

$$M(a) = \max_{x_1, x_2} g(x_1, x_2, a)$$

such that $h(x_1, x_2, a) = 0$.

In the case of the cost function $g(x_1, x_2, a) = w_1 x_1 + w_2 x_2$, $h(x_1, x_2, a) = f(x_1, x_2) - y$, and a could be one of the prices.

The Lagrangian for this problem is

$$\mathcal{L} = g(x_1, x_2, a) - \lambda h(x_1, x_2, a),$$

and the first-order conditions are

$$\frac{\partial g}{\partial x_1} - \lambda \frac{\partial h}{\partial x_1} = 0$$

$$\frac{\partial g}{\partial x_2} - \lambda \frac{\partial h}{\partial x_2} = 0 \tag{5.1}$$

$$h(x_1, x_2, a) = 0.$$

These conditions determine the optimal choice functions $(x_1(a), x_2(a))$, which in turn determine the maximum value function

$$M(a) \equiv g(x_1(a), x_2(a), a). \tag{5.2}$$

The envelope theorem gives us a formula for the derivative of the value function with respect to a parameter in the maximization problem. Specifically, the formula is

$$\frac{dM(a)}{da} = \left. \frac{\partial \mathcal{L}(\mathbf{x}, a)}{\partial a} \right|_{\mathbf{x} = \mathbf{x}(a)}$$

$$= \left. \frac{\partial g(x_1, x_2, a)}{\partial a} \right|_{x_i = x_i(a)} - \lambda \left. \frac{\partial h(x_1, x_2, a)}{\partial a} \right|_{x_i = x_i(a)}$$

As before, the interpretation of the partial derivatives needs special care: they are the derivatives of g and h with respect to a *holding x_1 and x_2 fixed at their optimal values*. The proof of the envelope theorem is given in Chapter 27, page 501. Here we simply apply it to the cost minimization problem.

In this problem the parameter a can be chosen to be one of the factor prices, w_i. The optimal value function $M(a)$ is the cost function $c(\mathbf{w}, y)$. The envelope theorem asserts that

$$\frac{\partial c(\mathbf{w}, y)}{\partial w_i} = \frac{\partial \mathcal{L}}{\partial w_i} = \left. x_i \right|_{x_i = x_i(\mathbf{w}, y)} = x_i(\mathbf{w}, y),$$

which is simply Shephard's lemma.

EXAMPLE: Marginal cost revisited

As another application of the envelope theorem, consider the derivative of the cost function with respect to y. According to the envelope theorem, this is given by the derivative of the Lagrangian with respect to y. The Lagrangian for the cost minimization problem is

$$\mathcal{L} = w_1 x_1 + w_2 x_2 - \lambda[f(x_1, x_2) - y].$$

Hence

$$\frac{\partial c(w_1, w_2, y)}{\partial y} = \lambda.$$

In other words, the Lagrange multiplier in the cost minimization problem is simply marginal cost.

5.6 Comparative statics using the cost function

We have shown earlier that cost functions have certain properties that follow from the structure of the cost minimization problem; we have shown above that the conditional factor demand functions are simply the derivatives of the cost functions. Hence, the properties we have found concerning the cost function will translate into certain restrictions on its derivatives, the factor demand functions. These restrictions will be the same sort of restrictions we found earlier using other methods, but their development using the cost function is quite nice.

Let us go through these restrictions one by one.

1) *The cost function is nondecreasing in factor prices.* It follows from this that $\partial c(\mathbf{w}, y)/\partial w_i = x_i(\mathbf{w}, y) \geq 0$.

2) *The cost function is homogeneous of degree 1 in* $\mathbf{w}$. Therefore, the derivatives of the cost function, the factor demands, are homogeneous of degree 0 in $\mathbf{w}$. (See Chapter 26, page 482).

3) *The cost function is concave in* w. Therefore, the matrix of second derivatives of the cost function—the matrix of first derivatives of the factor demand functions—is a symmetric negative semidefinite matrix. This is not an obvious outcome of cost-minimizing behavior. It has several implications.

a) The cross-price effects are symmetric. That is,

$$\frac{\partial x_i(\mathbf{w}, y)}{\partial w_j} = \frac{\partial^2 c(\mathbf{w}, y)}{\partial w_j \partial w_i} = \frac{\partial^2 c(\mathbf{w}, y)}{\partial w_i \partial w_j} = \frac{\partial x_j(\mathbf{w}, y)}{\partial w_i}.$$

b) The own-price effects are nonpositive. Roughly speaking, the conditional factor demand curves are downward sloping. This follows since $\partial x_i(\mathbf{w}, y)/\partial w_i = \partial^2 c(\mathbf{w}, y)/\partial w_i^2 \leq 0$ where the last inequality comes from the fact that the diagonal terms of a negative semidefinite matrix must be nonpositive.

c) The vector of changes in factor demands moves "opposite" the vector of changes in factor prices. That is, $\mathbf{dw}\,\mathbf{dx} \leq 0$.

Note that since the concavity of the cost function followed solely from the hypothesis of cost minimization, the symmetry and negative semidefiniteness of the first derivative matrix of the factor demand functions follow solely from the hypothesis of cost minimization and do not involve any restrictions on the structure of the technology.

Notes

The properties of the cost function were developed by several authors, but the most systematic treatment is in Shephard (1953) and Shephard (1970). A comprehensive survey is available in Diewert (1974). The treatment here owes much to McFadden (1978).

Exercises

5.1. A firm has two plants. One plant produces according to a cost function $c_1(y_1) = y_1^2$. The other plant produces according to a cost function $c_2(y_2) = y_2^2$. The factor prices are fixed and so are omitted from the discussion. What is the cost function for the firm?

5.2. A firm has two plants with cost functions $c_1(y_1) = 3y_1^2$ and $c_2(y_2) = y_2^2$. What is the cost function for the firm?

5.3. A firm has a production function given by $f(x_1, x_2, x_3, x_4) = \min\{2x_1 + x_2, x_3 + 2x_4\}$. What is the cost function for this technology? What is the conditional demand function for factors 1 and 2 as a function of factor prices (w_1, w_2, w_3, w_4) and output y?

5.4. A firm has a production function given by $f(x_1, x_2) = \min\{2x_1 + x_2, x_1 + 2x_2\}$. What is the cost function for this technology? What is the conditional demand function for factors 1 and 2 as a function of factor prices (w_1, w_2) and output y?

5.5. A firm has a production function of the form $f(x_1, x_2) = \max\{x_1, x_2\}$. Does this firm have a convex or a nonconvex input requirement set? What is the conditional factor demand function for factor 1? What is its cost function?

5.6. Consider a firm with conditional factor demand functions of the form

$$x_1 = 1 + 3w_1^{-\frac{1}{2}}w_2^a$$
$$x_2 = 1 + bw_1^{\frac{1}{2}}w_2^c.$$

Output has been set equal to 1 for convenience. What are the values of the parameters a, b, and c and why?

5.7. A firm has a production function $y = x_1 x_2$. If the minimum cost of production at $w_1 = w_2 = 1$ is equal to 4, what is y equal to?

5.8. A firm has a cost function

$$c(y) = \begin{cases} y^2 + 1 & \text{if } y > 0 \\ 0 & \text{if } y = 0. \end{cases}$$

Let p be the price of output, and let the factor prices be fixed. If $p = 2$ how much will the firm produce? If $p = 1$ how much will the firm produce? What is the profit function of this firm? (Hint: be careful!)

5.9. A typical Silicon Valley firm produces output of chips y using a cost function $c(y)$, which exhibits increasing marginal costs. Of the chips it produces, a fraction $1 - \alpha$ are defective and cannot be sold. Working chips can be sold at a price p and the chip market is highly competitive.

(a) Calculate the derivative of profits with respect to α and its sign.

(b) Calculate the derivative of output with respect to α and its sign.

(c) Suppose that there are n identical chip producers, let $D(p)$ be the demand function, and let $p(\alpha)$ be the competitive equilibrium price. Calculate $(dp/d\alpha)$ and its sign.

5.10. Suppose that a firm behaves competitively in its output market and its factor market. Suppose the price of each input increases, and let dw_i be the increase in factor price i. Under what conditions will the profit maximizing output decrease?

5.11. A firm uses 4 inputs to produce 1 output. The production function is $f(x_1, x_2, x_3, x_4) = \min\{x_1, x_2\} + \min\{x_3, x_4\}$.

(a) What is the vector of conditional factor demands to produce 1 unit of output when the factor price vector is $\mathbf{w} = (1, 2, 3, 4)$?

(b) What is the cost function?

(c) What kind of returns to scale does this technology exhibit?

(d) Another firm has a production function $f(x_1, x_2, x_3, x_4) = \min\{x_1 + x_2, x_3 + x_4\}$. What is the vector of conditional factor demands to produce 1 unit of output when prices are $\mathbf{w} = (1, 2, 3, 4)$?

(e) What is the cost function for this firm?

(f) What kind of returns to scale does this technology represent?

5.12. A factor of production i is called *inferior* if the conditional demand for that factor decreases as output increases; that is, $\partial x_i(\mathbf{w}, y)/\partial y < 0$.

(a) Draw a diagram indicating that inferior factors are possible.

(b) Show that if the technology is constant returns to scale, then no factors can be inferior.

(c) Show that if marginal cost decreases as the price of some factor increases, then that factor must be inferior.

5.13. Consider a profit-maximizing firm that produces a good which is sold in a competitive market. It is observed that when the price of the output good rises, the firm hires more skilled workers but fewer unskilled workers. Now the unskilled workers unionize and succeed in getting their wage increased. Assume that all other prices remain constant.

(a) What will happen to the firm's demand for unskilled workers?

(b) What will happen to the firm's supply of output?

5.14. You have a time series of observations on changes in output, Δy, changes in cost, Δc, changes in factor prices, Δw_i, and the levels of factor demands, x_i for $i = 1 \ldots n$. How would you construct an estimate of marginal cost, $\partial c(\mathbf{w}, y)/\partial y$, in each period?

5.15. Compute the cost function for the technology

$$V(y) = \{(x_1, x_2, x_3) : x_1 + \min(x_2, x_3) \geq 3y\}.$$

5.16. For each cost function determine if it is homogeneous of degree one, monotonic, concave, and/or continuous. If it is, derive the associated production function.

(a) $c(\mathbf{w}, y) = y^{1/2}(w_1 w_2)^{3/4}$

(b) $c(\mathbf{w}, y) = y(w_1 + \sqrt{w_1 w_2} + w_2)$

(c) $c(\mathbf{w}, y) = y(w_1 e^{-w_1} + w_2)$

(d) $c(\mathbf{w}, y) = y(w_1 - \sqrt{w_1 w_2} + w_2)$

(e) $c(\mathbf{w}, y) = (y + \frac{1}{y})\sqrt{w_1 w_2}$

5.17. A firm has an input requirement set given by $V(y) = \{\mathbf{x} \geq \mathbf{0} : ax_1 + bx_2 \geq y^2\}$.

(a) What is the production function?

(b) What are the conditional factor demands?

(c) What is the cost function?

CHAPTER **6**

DUALITY

In the last chapter we investigated the properties of the cost function, the function that measures the minimum cost of achieving a desired level of production. Given any technology, it is straightforward, at least in principle, to derive its cost function: we simply solve the cost minimization problem.

In this chapter we show that this process can be reversed. Given a cost function we can "solve for" a technology that could have generated that cost function. This means that the cost function contains essentially the same information that the production function contains. Any concept defined in terms of the properties of the production function has a "dual" definition in terms of the properties of the cost function and vice versa. This general observation is known as the principle of **duality**. It has several important consequences that we will investigate in this chapter.

The duality between seemingly different ways of representing economic behavior is useful in the study of consumer theory, welfare economics, and many other areas in economics. Many relationships that are difficult to understand when looked at directly become simple, or even trivial, when looked at using the tools of duality.

6.1 Duality

In Chapter 4 we described a set $VO(y)$ which we argued was an "outer bound" to the true input requirement set $V(y)$. Given data $(\mathbf{w}^t, \mathbf{x}^t, y^t)$, $VO(y)$ is defined to be,

$$VO(y) = \{\mathbf{x} : \mathbf{w}^t\mathbf{x} \geq \mathbf{w}^t\mathbf{x}^t \text{ for all } t \text{ such that } y^t \leq y\}.$$

It is straightforward to verify that $VO(y)$ is a closed, monotonic, and convex technology. Furthermore, as we observed in Chapter 4, it contains any technology that could have generated the data $(\mathbf{w}^t, \mathbf{x}^t, y^t)$ for $t = 1, \cdots, T$.

If we observe choices for many different factor prices, it seems that $VO(y)$ should "approach" the true input requirement set in some sense. To make this precise, let the factor prices vary over *all* possible price vectors $\mathbf{w} \geq \mathbf{0}$. Then the natural generalization of VO becomes

$$V^*(y) = \{\mathbf{x} : \mathbf{wx} \geq \mathbf{wx}(\mathbf{w}, y) = c(\mathbf{w}, y) \text{ for all } \mathbf{w} \geq \mathbf{0}\}.$$

What is the relationship between $V^*(y)$ and the true input requirement set $V(y)$? Of course, $V^*(y)$ will contain $V(y)$, as we showed in Chapter 4, page 62. In general, $V^*(y)$ will strictly contain $V(y)$. For example, in Figure 6.1A we see that the shaded area cannot be ruled out of $V^*(y)$ since the points in this area satisfy the condition that $\mathbf{wx} \geq c(\mathbf{w}, y)$.

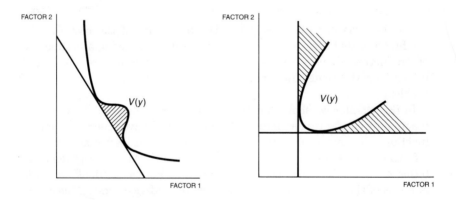

Figure 6.1   **Relationship between $V(y)$ and $V^*(y)$.** In general $V^*(y)$ will strictly contain $V(y)$.

The same is true for Figure 6.1B. The cost function can only contain information about the *economically relevant* sections of $V(y)$, namely, those factor bundles that could actually be the solution to a cost minimization problem, i.e., that could actually be conditional factor demands.

However, suppose that our original technology is convex and monotonic. In this case $V^*(y)$ will equal $V(y)$. This is because, in the convex, monotonic case, each point on the boundary of $V(y)$ is a cost-minimizing factor demand for *some* price vector $\mathbf{w} \geq \mathbf{0}$. Thus, the set of points where $\mathbf{w}\mathbf{x} \geq c(\mathbf{w}, y)$ for all $\mathbf{w} \geq \mathbf{0}$ will precisely describe the input requirement set. More formally:

When $V(y)$ equals $V^*(y)$.   *Suppose $V(y)$ is a regular, convex, monotonic technology. Then $V^*(y) = V(y)$.*

Proof. (Sketch) We already know that $V^*(y)$ contains $V(y)$, so we only have to show that if $\mathbf{x}$ is in $V^*(y)$ then $\mathbf{x}$ must be in $V(y)$. Suppose that $\mathbf{x}$ is not an element of $V(y)$. Then since $V(y)$ is a closed convex set satisfying the monotonicity hypothesis, we can apply a version of the separating hyperplane theorem (see Chapter 26, page 483) to find a vector $\mathbf{w}^* \geq \mathbf{0}$ such that $\mathbf{w}^*\mathbf{x} < \mathbf{w}^*\mathbf{z}$ for all $\mathbf{z}$ in $V(y)$. Let $\mathbf{z}^*$ be a point in $V(y)$ that minimizes cost at the prices $\mathbf{w}^*$. Then in particular we have $\mathbf{w}^*\mathbf{x} < \mathbf{w}^*\mathbf{z}^* = c(\mathbf{w}^*, y)$. But then $\mathbf{x}$ cannot be in $V^*(y)$, according to the definition of $V^*(y)$. ∎

This proposition shows that if the original technology is convex and monotonic, then the cost function associated with the technology can be used to completely reconstruct the original technology. If we know the minimal cost of operation for every possible price vector $\mathbf{w}$, then we know the entire set of technological choices open to the firm.

This is a reasonably satisfactory result in the case of convex and monotonic technologies, but what about less well-behaved cases? Suppose we start with some technology $V(y)$, possibly nonconvex. We find its cost function $c(\mathbf{w}, y)$ and then generate $V^*(y)$. We know from the above results that $V^*(y)$ will not necessarily be equal to $V(y)$, unless $V(y)$ happens to have the convexity and monotonicity properties. However, suppose we define

$$c^*(\mathbf{w}, y) = \min \mathbf{w}\mathbf{x}$$

such that $\mathbf{x}$ is in $V^*(y)$.

What is the relationship between $c^*(\mathbf{w}, y)$ and $c(\mathbf{w}, y)$?

When $c(\mathbf{w}, y)$ equals $c^*(\mathbf{w}, y)$.   *It follows from the definition of the functions that $c^*(\mathbf{w}, y) = c(\mathbf{w}, y)$.*

Proof. It is easy to see that $c^*(\mathbf{w}, y) \leq c(\mathbf{w}, y)$; since $V^*(y)$ always contains $V(y)$, the minimal cost bundle in $V^*(y)$ must be at least as small as the minimal cost bundle in $V(y)$. Suppose that for some prices $\mathbf{w}'$, the cost-minimizing bundle $\mathbf{x}'$ in $V^*(y)$ has the property that $\mathbf{w}'\mathbf{x}' = c^*(\mathbf{w}',y) < c(\mathbf{w}',y)$. But this can't happen, since by definition of $V^*(y)$, $\mathbf{w}'\mathbf{x}' \geq c(\mathbf{w}',y)$. $\blacksquare$

This proposition shows that the cost function for the technology $V(y)$ is the same as the cost function for its convexification $V^*(y)$. In this sense, the assumption of convex input requirement sets is not very restrictive from an economic point of view.

Let us summarize the discussion to date:

(1) Given a cost function we can define an input requirement set $V^*(y)$.

(2) If the original technology is convex and monotonic, the constructed technology will be identical with the original technology.

(3) If the original technology is nonconvex or nonmonotonic, the constructed input requirement will be a convexified, monotonized version of the original set, and, most importantly, the constructed technology will have the same cost function as the original technology.

We can summarize the above three points succinctly with the fundamental principle of duality in production: *the cost function of a firm summarizes all of the economically relevant aspects of its technology.*

6.2 Sufficient conditions for cost functions

We have seen in the last section that the cost function summarizes all of the economically relevant information about a technology. We have seen in the previous chapter that all cost functions are nondecreasing, homogeneous, concave, continuous functions of prices. The question arises: suppose that you are given a nondecreasing, homogeneous, concave, continuous function of prices—is it necessarily the cost function of some technology?

Another way to phrase this question is: are the properties described in the last chapter a *complete* list of the implications of cost-minimizing behavior? Given a function that has those properties, must it necessarily arise from some technology? The answer is yes, and the following proposition shows how to construct such a technology.

When $\phi(\mathbf{w}, y)$ is a cost function. *Let $\phi(\mathbf{w}, y)$ be a differentiable function satisfying*

1) $\phi(t\mathbf{w}, y) = t\phi(\mathbf{w}, y)$ for all $t \geq 0$;

2) $\phi(\mathbf{w}, y) \geq 0$ for $\mathbf{w} \geq 0$ and $y \geq 0$;

3) $\phi(\mathbf{w}', y) \geq \phi(\mathbf{w}, y)$ for $\mathbf{w}' \geq \mathbf{w}$;

4) $\phi(\mathbf{w}, y)$ is concave in $\mathbf{w}$.

Then $\phi(\mathbf{w}, y)$ is the cost function for the technology defined by $V^*(y) = \{\mathbf{x} \geq \mathbf{0} : \mathbf{wx} \geq \phi(\mathbf{w}, y), \text{ for all } \mathbf{w} \geq \mathbf{0}\}$.

Proof. Given a $\mathbf{w} \geq 0$ we define

$$\mathbf{x}(\mathbf{w}, y) = \left(\frac{\partial \phi(\mathbf{w}, y)}{\partial w_1}, \ldots, \frac{\partial \phi(\mathbf{w}, y)}{\partial w_n} \right)$$

and note that since $\phi(\mathbf{w}, y)$ is homogeneous of degree 1 in w, Euler's law implies that $\phi(\mathbf{w}, y)$ can be written as

$$\phi(\mathbf{w}, y) = \sum_{i=1}^{n} w_i \frac{\partial \phi(\mathbf{w}, y)}{\partial w_i} = \mathbf{wx}(\mathbf{w}, y).$$

(For Euler's law, see Chapter 26, page 481.) Note that the monotonicity of $\phi(\mathbf{w}, y)$ implies $\mathbf{x}(\mathbf{w}, y) \geq 0$.

What we need to show is that for any given $\mathbf{w}' \geq 0$, $\mathbf{x}(\mathbf{w}', y)$ actually minimizes $\mathbf{w}'\mathbf{x}$ over all $\mathbf{x}$ in $V^*(y)$:

$$\phi(\mathbf{w}', y) = \mathbf{w}'\mathbf{x}(\mathbf{w}', y) \leq \mathbf{w}'\mathbf{x} \text{ for all } \mathbf{x} \text{ in } V^*(y).$$

First, we show that $\mathbf{x}(\mathbf{w}', y)$ is feasible; that is, $\mathbf{x}(\mathbf{w}', y)$ is in $V^*(y)$. By the concavity of $\phi(\mathbf{w}, y)$ in $\mathbf{w}$ we have

$$\phi(\mathbf{w}', y) \leq \phi(\mathbf{w}, y) + \mathbf{D}\phi(\mathbf{w}, y)(\mathbf{w}' - \mathbf{w})$$

for all $\mathbf{w} \geq 0$. (See Chapter 27, page 496.)
Using Euler's law as above, this reduces to

$$\phi(\mathbf{w}', y) \leq \mathbf{w}'\mathbf{x}(\mathbf{w}, y) \text{ for all } \mathbf{w} \geq 0.$$

It follows from the definition of $V^*(y)$, that $\mathbf{x}(\mathbf{w}', y)$ is in $V^*(y)$.
Next we show that $\mathbf{x}(\mathbf{w}, y)$ actually minimizes $\mathbf{wx}$ over all $\mathbf{x}$ in $V^*(y)$. If $\mathbf{x}$ is in $V^*(y)$, then by definition it must satisfy

$$\mathbf{wx} \geq \phi(\mathbf{w}, y).$$

But by Euler's law,

$$\phi(\mathbf{w}, y) = \mathbf{wx}(\mathbf{w}, y).$$

The above two expressions imply

$$\mathbf{wx} \geq \mathbf{wx}(\mathbf{w}, y)$$

for all $\mathbf{x}$ in $V^*(y)$ as required. ∎

6.3 Demand functions

The proposition proved in the last section raises an interesting question. Suppose you are given a set of functions $(g_i(\mathbf{w}, y))$ that satisfy the properties of conditional factor demand functions described in the last chapter, namely, that they are homogeneous of degree 0 in prices and that

$$\left(\frac{\partial g_i(\mathbf{w}, y)}{\partial w_j}\right)$$

is a symmetric negative semidefinite matrix. Are these functions necessarily factor demand functions for some technology?

Let us try to apply the above proposition. First, we construct a candidate for a cost function:

$$\phi(\mathbf{w}, y) = \sum_{i=1}^{n} w_i g_i(\mathbf{w}, y).$$

Next, we check whether it satisfies the properties required for the proposition just proved.

1) Is $\phi(\mathbf{w}, y)$ homogeneous of degree 1 in $\mathbf{w}$? To check this we look at $\phi(t\mathbf{w}, y) = \sum_i tw_i g_i(t\mathbf{w}, y)$. Since the functions $g_i(\mathbf{w}, y)$ are by assumption homogeneous of degree 0, $g_i(t\mathbf{w}, y) = g_i(\mathbf{w}, y)$ so that

$$\phi(t\mathbf{w}, y) = t \sum_{i=1}^{n} w g_i(\mathbf{w}, y) = t\phi(\mathbf{w}, y).$$

2) Is $\phi(\mathbf{w}, y) \geq 0$ for $\mathbf{w} \geq 0$? Since $g_i(\mathbf{w}, y) \geq 0$, the answer is clearly yes.

3) Is $\phi(\mathbf{w}, y)$ nondecreasing in w_i? Using the product rule, we compute

$$\frac{\partial \phi(\mathbf{w}, y)}{\partial w_i} = g_i(\mathbf{w}, y) + \sum_{j=1}^{n} w_j \frac{\partial g_j(\mathbf{w}, y)}{\partial w_i} = g_i(\mathbf{w}, y) + \sum_{j=1}^{n} w_j \frac{\partial g_i(\mathbf{w}, y)}{\partial w_j}.$$

Since $g_i(\mathbf{w}, y)$ is homogeneous of degree 0, the last term vanishes and $g_i(\mathbf{w}, y)$ is clearly greater than or equal to 0.

4) Finally is $\phi(\mathbf{w}, y)$ concave in $\mathbf{w}$? To check this we differentiate $\phi(\mathbf{w}, y)$ twice to get

$$\left(\frac{\partial^2 \phi}{\partial w_i \partial w_j}\right) = \left(\frac{\partial g_i(\mathbf{w}, y)}{\partial w_j}\right).$$

For concavity we want these matrices to be symmetric and negative semidefinite, which they are by hypothesis.

Hence, the proposition proved in this section applies and there is a technology $V^*(y)$ that yields $(g_i(\mathbf{w}, y))$ as its conditional factor demands. This means that the properties of homogeneity and negative semidefiniteness form a complete list of the restrictions on demand functions imposed by the model of cost-minimizing behavior.

Of course, essentially the same results hold for profit functions and (unconditional) demand and supply functions. If the profit function obeys the restrictions described in Chapter 3, page 40, or, equivalently, if the demand and supply functions obey the restrictions in Chapter 3, page 46, then there must exist a technology that generates this profit function or these demand and supply functions.

EXAMPLE: Applying the duality mapping

Suppose we are given a specific cost function $c(\mathbf{w}, y) = y w_1^a w_2^{1-a}$. How can we solve for its associated technology? According to the derivative property

$$x_1(\mathbf{w}, y) = a y w_1^{a-1} w_2^{1-a} = ay \left(\frac{w_2}{w_1} \right)^{1-a}$$

$$x_2(\mathbf{w}, y) = (1-a) y w_1^a w_2^{-a} = (1-a) y \left(\frac{w_2}{w_1} \right)^{-a}.$$

We want to eliminate w_2/w_1 from these two equations and get an equation for y in terms of x_1 and x_2. Rearranging each equation gives

$$\frac{w_2}{w_1} = \left(\frac{x_1}{ay} \right)^{\frac{1}{1-a}}$$

$$\frac{w_2}{w_1} = \left(\frac{x_2}{(1-a)y} \right)^{-\frac{1}{a}}.$$

Setting these equal to each other and raising both sides to the $-a(1-a)$ power,

$$\frac{x_1^{-a}}{a^{-a} y^{-a}} = \frac{x_2^{1-a}}{(1-a)^{(1-a)} y^{1-a}},$$

or,

$$[a^a (1-a)^{1-a}] y = x_1^a x_2^{1-a}.$$

This is just the Cobb-Douglas technology.

EXAMPLE: Constant returns to scale and the cost function

Since the cost function tells us all of the economically relevant information about the technology, we can try to interpret various restrictions on costs in terms of restrictions on technology. In Chapter 5, page 66, we showed that *if* the technology exhibited constant returns to scale, then the cost function would have the form $c(\mathbf{w})y$. Here we show that the reverse implication is also true.

Constant returns to scale. *Let $V(y)$ be convex and monotonic; then if $c(\mathbf{w}, y)$ can be written as $yc(\mathbf{w}), V(y)$ must exhibit constant returns to scale.*

Proof. Using convexity, monotonicity, and the assumed form of the cost function assumptions, we know that

$$V(y) = V^*(y) = \{\mathbf{x} : \mathbf{w} \cdot \mathbf{x} \ge yc(\mathbf{w}) \text{ for all } \mathbf{w} \ge \mathbf{0}\}.$$

We want to show that, if $\mathbf{x}$ is in $V^*(y)$, then $t\mathbf{x}$ is in $V^*(ty)$. If $\mathbf{x}$ is in $V^*(y)$, we know that $\mathbf{wx} \ge yc(\mathbf{w})$ for all $\mathbf{w} \ge \mathbf{0}$. Multiplying both sides of this equation by t we get: $\mathbf{wtx} \ge tyc(\mathbf{w})$ for all $\mathbf{w} \ge \mathbf{0}$. But this says $t\mathbf{x}$ is in $V^*(ty)$. ∎

EXAMPLE: Elasticity of scale and the cost function

Given a production function $f(\mathbf{x})$ we can consider the local measure of returns to scale known as the **elasticity of scale**:

$$e(\mathbf{x}) = \frac{df(t\mathbf{x})}{dt} \frac{t}{f(\mathbf{x})}\bigg|_{t=1}$$

which was defined in Chapter 1, page 16. The technology exhibits locally decreasing, constant, or increasing returns to scale as $e(\mathbf{x})$ is less than, equal to, or greater than one.

Given some vector of factor prices we can compute the cost function of the firm $c(\mathbf{w}, y)$. Let $\mathbf{x}^*$ be the cost-minimizing bundle at $(\mathbf{w}, y)$. Then we can calculate $e(\mathbf{x}^*)$ by the following formula:

$$e(\mathbf{x}^*) = \frac{c(\mathbf{w}, y)/y}{\partial c(\mathbf{w}, y)/\partial y} = \frac{AC(y)}{MC(y)}.$$

To see this, we perform the differentiation indicated in the definition of $e(\mathbf{x})$:

$$e(\mathbf{x}^*) = \frac{\sum_{i=1}^n \frac{\partial f(\mathbf{x}^*)}{\partial x_i} x_i^*}{f(\mathbf{x}^*)}.$$

Since $\mathbf{x}^*$ minimizes costs it satisfies the first-order conditions that $w_i = \lambda \frac{\partial f(x^*)}{\partial x_i}$. Furthermore, by the envelope theorem, $\lambda = \partial c(\mathbf{w}, y)/\partial y$. (See Chapter 5, page 76.) Thus,

$$e(\mathbf{x}^*) = \frac{\sum_{i=1}^n w_i x_i^*}{\lambda f(\mathbf{x}^*)} = \frac{c(\mathbf{w}, y)/f(\mathbf{x}^*)}{\partial c(\mathbf{w}, y)/\partial y} = \frac{AC(y)}{MC(y)}.$$

6.4 Geometry of duality

In this section we will examine geometrically the relationship between a firm's technology as summarized by its production function and its economic behavior as summarized by its cost function.

In Figure 6.2 we have illustrated the isoquant of a firm and an isocost curve for the same level of output y. The slope at a point (w_1^*, w_2^*) on this isocost curve is given by

$$\frac{dw_2(w_1^*)}{dw_1} = -\frac{\dfrac{\partial c(\mathbf{w}^*, y)}{\partial w_1}}{\dfrac{\partial c(\mathbf{w}^*, y)}{\partial w_2}} = -\frac{x_1(\mathbf{w}^*, y)}{x_2(\mathbf{w}^*, y)}.$$

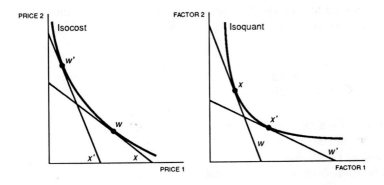

Curvature of isoquant and isocost curves.   The more curved the isoquant, the less curved the isocost curve.

Figure 6.2

On the other hand, an isoquant is defined by:

$$f(\mathbf{x}) \equiv y.$$

The slope of an isoquant at a point $\mathbf{x}^*$ is given by

$$\frac{dx_2(x_1^*)}{dx_1} = -\frac{\dfrac{\partial f(\mathbf{x}^*)}{\partial x_1}}{\dfrac{\partial f(\mathbf{x}^*)}{\partial x_2}}.$$

Now if (x_1^*, x_2^*) is a cost-minimizing point at prices (w_1^*, w_2^*), we know it satisfies the first-order condition

$$\frac{w_1^*}{w_2^*} = \frac{\dfrac{\partial f(\mathbf{x}^*)}{\partial x_1}}{\dfrac{\partial f(\mathbf{x}^*)}{\partial x_2}}.$$

Notice the nice **duality**: the slope of the isoquant curve gives the ratio of the factor prices while the slope of the isocost curve gives the ratio of the factor levels.

What about the *curvature* of the isoquant and the isocost curves? It turns out that their curvatures are inversely related: if the isocost curve is very curved, the isoquant will be rather flat and vice versa. We can see this by considering some specific (w_1, w_2) on the isocost curve and then moving to some (w_1', w_2') on the isocost curve that is fairly far away. Suppose we find that the slope of the isocost curve doesn't change very much—i.e., the isocost curve has little curvature. Since the slope of the isocost curve gives us the ratio of factor demands, this means that the cost-minimizing bundles must be rather similar. Referring to Figure 6.2 we see that this means that the isoquant must be rather sharply curved. In the extreme case we find that the cost function of the Leontief technology is a linear function and that an L-shaped cost function corresponds to a linear technology.

EXAMPLE: Production functions, cost functions, and conditional factor demands

Suppose we have a nice smooth convex isoquant. Then the isocost curve is also convex and smooth and the conditional factor demand curves are well behaved as in Figure 6.3.

Suppose that the isoquant has a flat spot, so that at some combination of factor prices there is no unique bundle of factor demands. Then the isocost curve must be nondifferentiable at this level of factor prices, and the conditional factor demand functions are multivalued as in Figure 6.4.

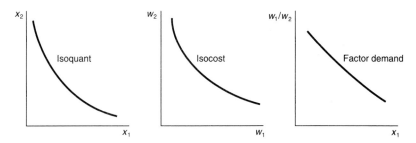

Technology, costs, and demand. Case of smooth, convex isoquant.

Figure 6.3

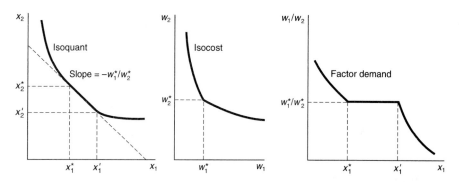

Technology, costs, and demand. Case of isoquant with flat spot. There is a kink at the isocost curve at the prices equal to the *slope* of the flat spot. At these factor prices, there are several cost-minimizing bundles.

Figure 6.4

Suppose that the isoquant has a kink at some point. Then for some *range* of prices, a fixed bundle of inputs will be demanded. This means that the isocost curve must have a flat spot as depicted in Figure 6.5.

Suppose the isoquant is nonconvex over some range. Then the isocost curve has a kink at some point and the conditional factor demands are discontinuous and multivalued as depicted in Figure 6.6. Notice how the cost function for this technology is indistinguishable from the cost function for the convexification of this technology by comparing Figures 6.4 and 6.6.

6.5 The uses of duality

The fact that there is a dual relationship between the description of a technology and its associated cost function has several important consequences for production economics. We have touched on some of these briefly in passing, but it is worthwhile to summarize them here.

First, having two different ways to describe technological properties is very convenient theoretically since some sorts of arguments are much easier

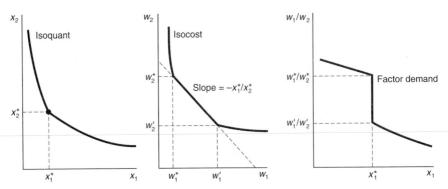

Figure 6.5

Technology, costs, and demand. Case of kinked isoquant. There is a flat spot in the isocost curve and several prices at which the same bundle will minimize costs.

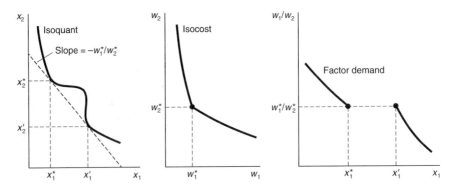

Figure 6.6

Technology, costs, and demand. Case of nonconvex isoquant. The isocost curve looks just the same as if there were a flat spot, but the factor demand function is now discontinuous.

to demonstrate by using a cost function or profit function than by using a direct representation of technology. For example, consider the example given earlier that expected profits would be higher with a fluctuating price than with a price stabilized at the expected value. This is a trivial consequence of the convexity of the profit function; the argument is substantially less trivial if we approach this situation using a direct representation of the technology.

Second, dual representations of behavior such as the cost function and the profit function are very useful in equilibrium analysis since they subsume the behavioral assumptions in the functional specification. If we want to examine the way in which a particular tax policy affects firm profits, for example, we can investigate how the taxes affect the prices the firm faces and then see how those particular changes in prices affect the profit function. We don't have to solve any maximization problems—they are already "solved" in the specification of the profit function.

Third, the fact that the homogeneity, monotonicity and curvature properties exhaust the properties of the cost and profit functions makes it much simpler to verify certain sorts of propositions about firm behavior. We can simply ask whether the particular property in question is a consequence of the homogeneity, monotonicity, or curvature of the cost or profit function. If it is not, then the property does not follow simply from maximizing behavior.

Fourth, the fact that the profit and cost functions can be characterized by three relatively simple mathematical conditions is of great help in generating parametric forms for representing technologies. In order to completely specify a technology, for example, all that is necessary to do is to specify a continuous homogeneous, monotonic, concave function of factor prices. This may be much more convenient than specifying a production function representation of a technology. Such parametric representations may be of considerable help in calculating examples or in econometric work.

Fifth, dual representations usually turn out to be more satisfactory for econometric work. The reason is that the variables that enter into the dual specification—the price variables—are generally thought to be exogenous variables with respect to the choice problem of the firm. If factor markets are competitive, then the firm is supposed to take factor prices as given and choose levels of inputs, so that the factor prices may not be correlated with the error terms in the statistical production relationship. This property is very desirable from a statistical point of view. We will investigate further in Chapter 12.

Notes

The basic duality between cost and production functions was first shown rigorously by Shephard (1953). See Diewert (1974) for the historical development of this topic and a general modern treatment.

Exercises

6.1. The cost function is $c(w_1, w_2, y) = \min\{w_1, w_2\}y$. What is the production function? What are the conditional factor demands?

6.2. The cost function is $c(w_1, w_2, y) = y[w_1 + w_2]$. What are the conditional factor demands? What is the production function?

6.3. The cost function is $c(w_1, w_2, y) = w_1^a w_2^b y$. What do we know about a and b?

CHAPTER 7

UTILITY MAXIMIZATION

In this chapter we begin our examination of consumer behavior. In the theory of a competitive firm, the supply and demand functions were derived from a model of profit-maximizing behavior and a specification of the underlying technological constraints. In the theory of the consumer we will derive demand functions by considering a model of utility-maximizing behavior coupled with a description of underlying economic constraints.

7.1 Consumer preferences

We consider a consumer faced with possible consumption bundles in some set X, his **consumption set**. In this book we usually assume that X is the nonnegative orthant in R^k, but more specific consumption sets may be used. For example, we might only include bundles that would give the consumer at least a subsistence existence. We will always assume that X is a closed and convex set.

The consumer is assumed to have preferences on the consumption bundles in X. When we write $\mathbf{x} \succeq \mathbf{y}$, we mean "the consumer thinks that the bundle $\mathbf{x}$ is at least as good as the bundle $\mathbf{y}$." We want the preferences to *order* the set of bundles. Therefore, we need to assume that they satisfy certain standard properties.

COMPLETE.   *For all* **x** *and* **y** *in* X, *either* $\mathbf{x} \succeq \mathbf{y}$ *or* $\mathbf{y} \succeq \mathbf{x}$ *or both.*

REFLEXIVE.   *For all* **x** *in* X, $\mathbf{x} \succeq \mathbf{x}$.

TRANSITIVE.   *For all* **x**, **y**, *and* **z** *in* X, *if* $\mathbf{x} \succeq \mathbf{y}$ *and* $\mathbf{y} \succeq \mathbf{z}$, *then* $\mathbf{x} \succeq \mathbf{z}$.

The first assumption just says that any two bundles can be compared, the second is trivial, and the third is necessary for any discussion of preference *maximization*; if preferences were not transitive, there might be sets of bundles which had no best elements.

Given an ordering $\succeq$ describing "weak preference," we can define an ordering $\succ$ of **strict preference** simply by defining $\mathbf{x} \succ \mathbf{y}$ to mean not $\mathbf{y} \succeq \mathbf{x}$. We read $\mathbf{x} \succ \mathbf{y}$ as "**x** is strictly preferred to **y**." Similarly, we define a notion of **indifference** by $\mathbf{x} \sim \mathbf{y}$ if and only if $\mathbf{x} \succeq \mathbf{y}$ and $\mathbf{y} \succeq \mathbf{x}$.

We often wish to make other assumptions on consumers' preferences; for example.

CONTINUITY.   *For all* **y** *in* X, *the sets* $\{\mathbf{x} : \mathbf{x} \succeq \mathbf{y}\}$ *and* $\{\mathbf{x} : \mathbf{x} \preceq \mathbf{y}\}$ *are closed sets. It follows that* $\{\mathbf{x} : \mathbf{x} \succ \mathbf{y}\}$ *and* $\{\mathbf{x} : \mathbf{x} \prec \mathbf{y}\}$ *are open sets.*

This assumption is necessary to rule out certain discontinuous behavior; it says that if $(\mathbf{x}^i)$ is a sequence of consumption bundles that are all at least as good as a bundle **y**, and if this sequence converges to some bundle $\mathbf{x}^*$, then $\mathbf{x}^*$ is at least as good as **y**.

The most important consequence of continuity is this: if **y** is strictly preferred to **z** and if **x** is a bundle that is close enough to **y**, then **x** must be strictly preferred to **z**. This is just a restatement of the assumption that the set of strictly preferred bundles is an open set. For a brief discussion of open and closed sets, see Chapter 26, page 478.

In economic analysis it is often convenient to summarize a consumer's behavior by means of a **utility function**; that is, a function $u : X \to R$ such that $\mathbf{x} \succ \mathbf{y}$ if and only if $u(\mathbf{x}) > u(\mathbf{y})$. It can be shown that if the preference ordering is complete, reflexive, transitive, and continuous, then it can be represented by a continuous utility function. We will prove a weaker version of this assertion below. A utility function is often a very convenient way to describe preferences, but it should not be given any psychological interpretation. The only relevant feature of a utility function is its ordinal character. If $u(\mathbf{x})$ represents some preferences $\succeq$ and $f : R \to R$ is a monotonic function, then $f(u(\mathbf{x}))$ will represent exactly the same preferences since $f(u(\mathbf{x})) \geq f(u(\mathbf{y}))$ if and only if $u(\mathbf{x}) \geq u(\mathbf{y})$.

There are other assumptions on preferences that are often useful; for example:

WEAK MONOTONICITY. *If* $\mathbf{x} \geq \mathbf{y}$ *then* $\mathbf{x} \succeq \mathbf{y}$.

STRONG MONOTONICITY. *If* $\mathbf{x} \geq \mathbf{y}$ *and* $\mathbf{x} \neq \mathbf{y}$, *then* $\mathbf{x} \succ \mathbf{y}$.

Weak monotonicity says that "at least as much of everything is at least as good." If the consumer can costlessly dispose of unwanted goods, this assumption is trivial. Strong monotonicity says that at least as much of every good, and strictly more of some good, is strictly better. This is simply assuming that goods are good.

If one of the goods is a "bad," like garbage, or pollution, then strong monotonicity will not be satisfied. But in these cases, redefining the good to be the *absence* of garbage, or the *absence* of pollution, will often result in preferences over the re-defined good that satisfies the strong monotonicity postulate.

Another assumption that is weaker than either kind of monotonicity is the following:

LOCAL NONSATIATION. *Given any* $\mathbf{x}$ *in* X *and any* $\epsilon > 0$, *then there is some bundle* $\mathbf{y}$ *in* X *with* $|\mathbf{x} - \mathbf{y}| < \epsilon$ *such that* $\mathbf{y} \succ \mathbf{x}$.[1]

Local nonsatiation says that one can always do a little bit better, even if one is restricted to only small changes in the consumption bundle. You should verify that strong monotonicity implies local nonsatiation but not vice versa. Local nonsatiation rules out "thick" indifference curves.

Here are two more assumptions that are often used to guarantee nice behavior of consumer demand functions:

CONVEXITY. *Given* $\mathbf{x}$, $\mathbf{y}$, *and* $\mathbf{z}$ *in* X *such that* $\mathbf{x} \succeq \mathbf{z}$ *and* $\mathbf{y} \succeq \mathbf{z}$, *then it follows that* $t\mathbf{x} + (1-t)\mathbf{y} \succeq \mathbf{z}$ *for all* $0 \leq t \leq 1$.

STRICT CONVEXITY. *Given* $\mathbf{x} \neq \mathbf{y}$ *and* $\mathbf{z}$ *in* X, *if* $\mathbf{x} \succeq \mathbf{z}$ *and* $\mathbf{y} \succeq \mathbf{z}$, *then* $t\mathbf{x} + (1-t)\mathbf{y} \succ \mathbf{z}$ *for all* $0 < t < 1$.

Given a preference ordering, we often display it graphically. The set of all consumption bundles that are indifferent to each other is called an **indifference curve**. One can think of indifference curves as being **level sets** of the utility function; they are analogous to the isoquants used in production theory. The set of all bundles on or above an indifference curve, $\{\mathbf{x} \text{ in } X : \mathbf{x} \succeq \mathbf{y}\}$, is called an **upper contour set**. This is analogous to the input requirement set used in production theory.

Convexity implies that an agent prefers averages to extremes, but, other than that, it has little economic content. Convex preferences may have indifference curves that exhibit "flat spots," while strictly convex preferences

---

[1] The notation $|\mathbf{x} - \mathbf{y}|$ means the Euclidean distance between $\mathbf{x}$ and $\mathbf{y}$.

have indifference curves that are strictly rotund. Convexity is a general-ization of the neoclassical assumption of "diminishing marginal rates of substitution."

EXAMPLE: The existence of a utility function

Existence of a utility function.   *Suppose preferences are complete, re-flexive, transitive, continuous, and strongly monotonic. Then there exists a continuous utility function $u : R_+^k \rightarrow R$ which represents those preferences.*

Proof. Let $\mathbf{e}$ be the vector in R_+^k consisting of all ones. Then given any vector $\mathbf{x}$ let $u(\mathbf{x})$ be that number such that $\mathbf{x} \sim u(\mathbf{x})\mathbf{e}$. We have to show that such a number exists and is unique.

Let $B = \{t \text{ in } R : t\mathbf{e} \succeq \mathbf{x}\}$ and $W = \{t \text{ in } R : \mathbf{x} \succeq t\mathbf{e}\}$. Then strong monotonicity implies B is nonempty; W is certainly nonempty since it contains 0. Continuity implies both sets are closed. Since the real line is connected, there is some t_x such that $t_x\mathbf{e} \sim \mathbf{x}$. We have to show that this utility function actually represents the underlying preferences. Let

$$u(\mathbf{x}) = t_x \quad \text{where } t_x\mathbf{e} \sim \mathbf{x}$$
$$u(\mathbf{y}) = t_y \quad \text{where } t_y\mathbf{e} \sim \mathbf{y}.$$

Then if $t_x < t_y$, strong monotonicity shows that $t_x\mathbf{e} \prec t_y\mathbf{e}$, and transitivity shows that

$$\mathbf{x} \sim t_x\mathbf{e} \prec t_y\mathbf{e} \sim \mathbf{y}.$$

Similarly, if $\mathbf{x} \succ \mathbf{y}$, then $t_x\mathbf{e} \succ t_y\mathbf{e}$ so that t_x must be greater than t_y.

The proof that $u(\mathbf{x})$ is a continuous function is somewhat technical and is omitted. ∎

EXAMPLE: The marginal rate of substitution

Let $u(x_1, \ldots, x_k)$ be a utility function. Suppose that we increase the amount of good i; how does the consumer have to change his consump-tion of good j in order to keep utility constant?

Following the construction in Chapter 1, page 11, we let dx_i and dx_j be the changes in x_i and x_j. By assumption, the change in utility must be zero, so

$$\frac{\partial u(\mathbf{x})}{\partial x_i} dx_i + \frac{\partial u(\mathbf{x})}{\partial x_j} dx_j = 0.$$

Hence

$$\frac{dx_j}{dx_i} = -\frac{\frac{\partial u(\mathbf{x})}{\partial x_i}}{\frac{\partial u(\mathbf{x})}{\partial x_j}}.$$

This expression is known as the **marginal rate of substitution** between goods i and j.

The marginal rate of substitution does not depend on the utility function chosen to represent the underlying preferences. To prove this, let $v(u)$ be a monotonic transformation of utility. The marginal rate of substitution for this utility function is

$$\frac{dx_j}{dx_i} = -\frac{v'(u)\frac{\partial u(\mathbf{x})}{\partial x_i}}{v'(u)\frac{\partial u(\mathbf{x})}{\partial x_j}} = -\frac{\frac{\partial u(\mathbf{x})}{\partial x_i}}{\frac{\partial u(\mathbf{x})}{\partial x_j}}.$$

7.2 Consumer behavior

Now that we have a convenient way to represent preferences we can begin to investigate consumer behavior. Our basic hypothesis is that a rational consumer will always choose a most preferred bundle from the set of affordable alternatives.

In the basic problem of preference maximization, the set of affordable alternatives is just the set of all bundles that satisfy the consumer's budget constraint. Let m be the fixed amount of money available to a consumer, and let $\mathbf{p} = (p_1, \cdots, p_k)$ be the vector of prices of goods, $1, \cdots, k$. The set of affordable bundles, the budget set of the consumer, is given by

$$B = \{\mathbf{x} \text{ in } X : \mathbf{px} \le m.\}$$

The problem of preference maximization can then be written as:

$$\max u(\mathbf{x})$$
$$\text{such that } \mathbf{px} \le m$$
$$\mathbf{x} \text{ is in } X.$$

Let us note a few basic features of this problem. The first issue is whether there will exist a solution to this problem. According to Chapter 27, page 506, we need to verify that the objective function is continuous and that the constraint set is closed and bounded. The utility function is continuous by assumption, and the constraint set is certainly closed. If $p_i > 0$ for $i = 1, \ldots, k$ and $m \ge 0$, it is not difficult to show that the constraint set will be bounded. If some price is zero, the consumer might want an infinite amount of the corresponding good. We will generally ignore such boundary problems.

The second issue we examine concerns the representation of preferences. Here we can observe that the maximizing choice $\mathbf{x}^*$ will be independent of the choice of utility function used to represent the preferences. This is because the optimal $\mathbf{x}^*$ must have the property that $\mathbf{x}^* \succeq \mathbf{x}$ for any $\mathbf{x}$ in B, so any utility function that represents the preferences $\succeq$ must pick out $\mathbf{x}^*$ as a constrained maximum.

Third, if we multiply all prices and income by some positive constant, we will not change the budget set, and thus we cannot change the set of optimal choices. That is, if $\mathbf{x}^*$ has the property that $\mathbf{x}^* \succeq \mathbf{x}$ for all $\mathbf{x}$ such that $\mathbf{px} \leq m$, then $\mathbf{x}^* \succeq \mathbf{y}$ for all $\mathbf{y}$ such that $t\mathbf{py} \leq tm$. Roughly speaking, the optimal choice set is "homogeneous of degree zero" in prices and income.

By making a few regularity assumptions on preferences, we can say more about the consumer's maximizing behavior. For example, suppose that preferences satisfy local nonsatiation; can we ever get an $\mathbf{x}^*$ where $\mathbf{px}^* < m$? Suppose that we could; then, since $\mathbf{x}^*$ costs strictly less than m, every bundle in X close enough to $\mathbf{x}^*$ also costs less than m and is therefore feasible. But, according to the local nonsatiation hypothesis, there must be some bundle $\mathbf{x}$ which is close to $\mathbf{x}^*$ and which is preferred to $\mathbf{x}^*$. But this means that $\mathbf{x}^*$ could not maximize preferences on the budget set B.

Therefore, under the local nonsatiation assumption, a utility-maximizing bundle $\mathbf{x}^*$ must meet the budget constraint with equality. This allows us to restate the consumer's problem as

$$v(\mathbf{p}, m) = \max u(\mathbf{x})$$
$$\text{such that } \mathbf{px} = m.$$

The function $v(\mathbf{p}, m)$ that gives us the maximum utility achievable at given prices and income is called the **indirect utility function**. The value of $\mathbf{x}$ that solves this problem is the consumer's **demanded bundle**: it expresses how much of each good the consumer desires at a given level of prices and income. We assume that there is a unique demanded bundle at each budget; this is for purposes of convenience and is not essential to the analysis.

The function that relates $\mathbf{p}$ and m to the demanded bundle is called the consumer's **demand function**. We denote the demand function by $\mathbf{x}(\mathbf{p}, m)$. As in the case of the firm, we need to make a few assumptions to make sure that this demand function is well-defined. In particular, we will want to assume that there is a *unique* bundle that maximizes utility. We will see later on that strict convexity of preferences will ensure this behavior.

Just as in the case of the firm, the consumer's demand function is homogeneous of degree 0 in $(\mathbf{p}, m)$. As we have seen above, multiplying all prices and income by some positive number does not change the budget set at all and thus cannot change the answer to the utility maximization problem.

As in the case of production we can characterize optimizing behavior by calculus, as long as the utility function is differentiable. The Lagrangian for the utility maximization problem can be written as

$$\mathcal{L} = u(\mathbf{x}) - \lambda(\mathbf{px} - m),$$

where λ is the Lagrange multiplier. Differentiating the Lagrangian with respect to x_i gives us the first-order conditions

$$\frac{\partial u(\mathbf{x})}{\partial x_i} - \lambda p_i = 0 \quad \text{for } i = 1, \dots, k.$$

In order to interpret these conditions we can divide the ith first-order condition by the jth first-order condition to eliminate the Lagrange multiplier. This gives us

$$\frac{\frac{\partial u(\mathbf{x}^*)}{\partial x_i}}{\frac{\partial u(\mathbf{x}^*)}{\partial x_j}} = \frac{p_i}{p_j} \quad \text{for } i, j = 1, \dots, k.$$

The fraction on the left is the marginal rate of substitution between good i and j, and the fraction on the right might be called the **economic rate of substitution** between goods i and j. Maximization implies that these two rates of substitution be equal. Suppose they were not; for example, suppose

$$\frac{\frac{\partial u(\mathbf{x}^*)}{\partial x_i}}{\frac{\partial u(\mathbf{x}^*)}{\partial x_j}} = \frac{1}{1} \neq \frac{2}{1} = \frac{p_i}{p_j}.$$

Then, if the consumer gives up one unit of good i and purchases one unit of good j, he or she will remain on the same indifference curve and have an extra dollar to spend. Hence, total utility can be increased, contradicting maximization.

Figure 7.1 illustrates the argument geometrically. The budget line of the consumer is given by $\{\mathbf{x} : p_1 x_1 + p_2 x_2 = m\}$. This can also be written as the graph of an implicit function: $x_2 = m/p_2 - (p_1/p_2)x_1$. Hence, the budget line has slope $-p_1/p_2$ and vertical intercept m/p_2. The consumer wants to find the point on this budget line that achieves highest utility. This must clearly satisfy the tangency condition that the slope of the indifference curve equals the slope of the budget line. Translating this into algebra gives the above condition.

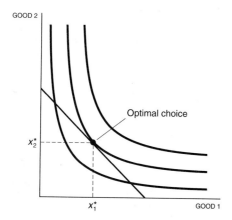

GOOD 2

Optimal choice

x_2^*

x_1^* GOOD 1

Preference maximization. The optimal consumption bundle
will be at a point where an indifference curve is tangent to the
budget constraint.

**Figure
7.1**

Finally, we can state the condition using vector terminology. Let $\mathbf{x}^*$ be
an optimal choice, and let $\mathbf{dx}$ be a perturbation of $\mathbf{x}^*$ that satisfies the
budget constraint. Hence, we must have

$$\mathbf{p}(\mathbf{x}^* \pm \mathbf{dx}) = m.$$

Since $\mathbf{px} = m$, this equation implies that $\mathbf{p}\,\mathbf{dx} = 0$, which in turn implies
that $\mathbf{dx}$ must be orthogonal to $\mathbf{p}$.

For any such perturbation $\mathbf{dx}$, utility cannot change, or else $\mathbf{x}^*$ would
not be optimal. Hence, we also have

$$\mathbf{D}u(\mathbf{x}^*)\mathbf{dx} = 0$$

which says that $\mathbf{D}u(\mathbf{x}^*)$ is also orthogonal to $\mathbf{dx}$. Since this is true for all
perturbations for which $\mathbf{p}\,\mathbf{dx} = 0$, we must have $\mathbf{D}u(\mathbf{x}^*)$ proportional to
$\mathbf{p}$, just as we found in the first-order conditions.

The second-order conditions for utility maximization can be found by
applying the results of Chapter 27, page 494. The second derivative of the
Lagrangian with respect to goods i and j is $\partial^2 u(\mathbf{x})/\partial x_i \partial x_j$. Hence, the
second-order condition can be written as

$$\mathbf{h}^t \mathbf{D}^2 u(\mathbf{x}^*)\mathbf{h} \leq 0 \quad \text{for all } \mathbf{h} \text{ such that } \mathbf{ph} = 0. \tag{7.1}$$

This condition requires that the Hessian matrix of the utility function is
negative semidefinite for all vectors $\mathbf{h}$ orthogonal to the price vector. This is

essentially equivalent to the requirement that $u(\mathbf{x})$ be locally quasiconcave. Geometrically, the condition means that the upper contour set must lie above the budget hyperplane at the optimal $\mathbf{x}^*$.

As usual the second-order condition can also be expressed as a condition involving the bordered Hessian. Examining Chapter 27, page 500, we see that this formulation says that (7.1) can be satisfied as a strict inequality if and only if the naturally ordered principal minors of the bordered Hessian alternate in sign. Hence,

$$\begin{vmatrix} 0 & -p_1 & -p_2 \\ -p_1 & u_{11} & u_{12} \\ -p_2 & u_{21} & u_{22} \end{vmatrix} > 0,$$

$$\begin{vmatrix} 0 & -p_1 & -p_2 & -p_3 \\ -p_1 & u_{11} & u_{12} & u_{13} \\ -p_2 & u_{21} & u_{22} & u_{23} \\ -p_3 & u_{31} & u_{32} & u_{33} \end{vmatrix} < 0,$$

and so on.

7.3 Indirect utility

Recall the indirect utility function defined earlier. This function, $v(\mathbf{p}, m)$, gives maximum utility as a function of $\mathbf{p}$ and m.

Properties of the indirect utility function.

(1) $v(\mathbf{p}, m)$ is nonincreasing in $\mathbf{p}$; that is, if $\mathbf{p}' \geq \mathbf{p}, v(\mathbf{p}', m) \leq v(\mathbf{p}, m)$. Similarly, $v(\mathbf{p}, m)$ is nondecreasing in m.

(2) $v(\mathbf{p}, m)$ is homogeneous of degree 0 in $(\mathbf{p}, m)$.

(3) $v(\mathbf{p}, m)$ is quasiconvex in $\mathbf{p}$; that is, $\{\mathbf{p} : v(\mathbf{p}, m) \leq k\}$ is a convex set for all k.

(4) $v(\mathbf{p}, m)$ is continuous at all $\mathbf{p} \gg 0, m > 0$.

Proof.

(1) Let $B = \{\mathbf{x} : \mathbf{px} \leq m\}$ and $B' = \{\mathbf{x} : \mathbf{p'x} \leq m\}$ for $\mathbf{p}' \geq \mathbf{p}$. Then B' is contained in B. Hence, the maximum of $u(\mathbf{x})$ over B is at least as big as the maximum of $u(\mathbf{x})$ over B'. The argument for m is similar.

(2) If prices and income are both multiplied by a positive number, the budget set doesn't change at all. Thus, $v(t\mathbf{p}, tm) = v(\mathbf{p}, m)$ for $t > 0$.

(3) Suppose $\mathbf{p}$ and $\mathbf{p}'$ are such that $v(\mathbf{p}, m) \leq k$, $v(\mathbf{p}', m) \leq k$. Let $\mathbf{p}'' = t\mathbf{p} + (1-t)\mathbf{p}'$. We want to show that $v(\mathbf{p}'', m) \leq k$. Define the budget sets:

$$B = \{\mathbf{x} : \mathbf{px} \leq m\}$$
$$B' = \{\mathbf{x} : \mathbf{p}'\mathbf{x} \leq m\}$$
$$B'' = \{\mathbf{x} : \mathbf{p}''\mathbf{x} \leq m\}$$

We will show that any $\mathbf{x}$ in B'' must be in either B or B'; that is, that $B \cup B' \supset B''$. Assume not; then $\mathbf{x}$ is such that $t\mathbf{px} + (1-t)\mathbf{p}'\mathbf{x} \leq m$ but $\mathbf{px} > m$ and $\mathbf{p}'\mathbf{x} > m$. These two inequalities can be written as

$$t\mathbf{px} > tm$$
$$(1-t)\mathbf{p}'\mathbf{x} > (1-t)m.$$

Summing, we find that

$$t\mathbf{px} + (1-t)\mathbf{p}'\mathbf{x} > m$$

which contradicts our original assumption.

Now note that

$$v(\mathbf{p}'', m) = \max\ u(\mathbf{x}) \text{ such that } \mathbf{x} \text{ is in } B''$$
$$\leq \max\ u(\mathbf{x}) \text{ such that } \mathbf{x} \text{ is in } B \cup B'$$
$$\text{since } B \cup B' \supset B''$$
$$\leq k \text{ since } v(\mathbf{p}, m) \leq k \text{ and } v(\mathbf{p}', m) \leq k.$$

(4) This follows from the theorem of the maximum in Chapter 27, page 506.
∎

In Figure 7.2 we have depicted a typical set of "price indifference curves." These are just the level sets of the indirect utility function. By property (1) of the above theorem utility is nondecreasing as we move towards the origin, and by property (3) the lower contour sets are convex. Note that the lower contour sets lie to the northeast of the price indifference curves since indirect utility declines with higher prices.

We note that if preferences satisfy the local nonsatiation assumption, then $v(\mathbf{p}, m)$ will be *strictly* increasing in m. In Figure 7.3 we have drawn the relationship between $v(\mathbf{p}, m)$ and m for constant prices. Since $v(\mathbf{p}, m)$ is strictly increasing in m, we can invert the function and solve for m as a function of the level of utility; that is, given any level of utility, u, we can read off of Figure 7.3 the minimal amount of income necessary to achieve utility u at prices $\mathbf{p}$. The function that relates income and utility in this way—the inverse of the indirect utility function—is known as the **expenditure function** and is denoted by $e(\mathbf{p}, u)$.

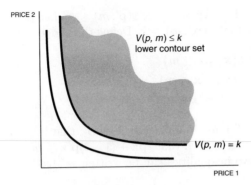

**Figure
7.2**

Price indifference curves. The indifference curve is all those prices such that $v(\mathbf{p}, m) = k$, for some constant k. The lower contour set consists of all prices such that $v(\mathbf{p}, m) \leq k$.

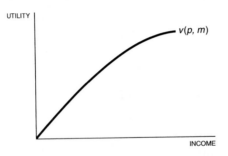

**Figure
7.3**

Utility as a function of income. As income increases indirect utility must increase.

An equivalent definition of the expenditure function is given by the following problem:

$$e(\mathbf{p}, u) = \min \ \mathbf{px}$$
$$\text{such that } u(\mathbf{x}) \geq u.$$

The expenditure function gives the minimum cost of achieving a fixed level of utility.

The expenditure function is completely analogous to the cost function we considered in studying firm behavior. It therefore has all the properties we derived in Chapter 5, page 71. These properties are repeated here for convenience.

Properties of the expenditure function.

(1) $e(\mathbf{p}, u)$ is nondecreasing in $\mathbf{p}$.

(2) $e(\mathbf{p}, u)$ is homogeneous of degree 1 in $\mathbf{p}$.

(3) $e(\mathbf{p}, u)$ is concave in $\mathbf{p}$.

(4) $e(\mathbf{p}, u)$ is continuous in $\mathbf{p}$, for $\mathbf{p} \gg 0$.

(5) If $\mathbf{h}(\mathbf{p}, u)$ is the expenditure-minimizing bundle necessary to achieve utility level u at prices $\mathbf{p}$, then $h_i(\mathbf{p}, u) = \dfrac{\partial e(\mathbf{p}, u)}{\partial p_i}$ for $i = 1, \ldots, k$ assuming the derivative exists and that $p_i > 0$.

Proof. These are exactly the same properties that the cost function exhibits. See in Chapter 5, page 71 for the arguments. ∎

The function $\mathbf{h}(\mathbf{p}, u)$ is called the **Hicksian demand function**. The Hicksian demand function is analogous to the conditional factor demand functions examined earlier. The Hicksian demand function tells us what consumption bundle achieves a target level of utility and minimizes total expenditure.

A Hicksian demand function is sometimes called a **compensated demand function**. This terminology comes from viewing the demand function as being constructed by varying prices *and income* so as to keep the consumer at a fixed level of utility. Thus, the income changes are arranged to "compensate" for the price changes.

Hicksian demand functions are not directly observable since they depend on utility, which is not directly observable. Demand functions expressed as a function of prices and income are observable; when we want to emphasize the difference between the Hicksian demand function and the usual demand function, we will refer to the latter as the **Marshallian demand function**, $\mathbf{x}(\mathbf{p}, m)$. The Marshallian demand function is just the ordinary market demand function we have been discussing all along.

7.4 Some important identities

There are some important identities that tie together the expenditure function, the indirect utility function, the Marshallian demand function, and the Hicksian demand function.

Let us consider the utility maximization problem

$$v(\mathbf{p}, m^*) = \max u(\mathbf{x})$$
$$\text{such that } \mathbf{px} \leq m^*.$$

Let $\mathbf{x}^*$ be the solution to this problem and let $u^* = u(\mathbf{x}^*)$. Consider the expenditure minimization problem

$$e(\mathbf{p}, u^*) = \min \mathbf{px}$$
$$\text{such that } u(\mathbf{x}) \geq u^*.$$

An inspection of Figure 7.4 should convince you that in nonperverse cases the answers to these two problems should be the same $\mathbf{x}^*$. (A more rigorous argument is given in the appendix to this chapter.) This simple observation leads to four important identities:

(1) $e(\mathbf{p}, v(\mathbf{p}, m)) \equiv m$. The minimum expenditure necessary to reach utility $v(\mathbf{p}, m)$ is m.

(2) $v(\mathbf{p}, e(\mathbf{p}, u)) \equiv u$. The maximum utility from income $e(\mathbf{p}, u)$ is u.

(3) $x_i(\mathbf{p}, m) \equiv h_i(\mathbf{p}, v(\mathbf{p}, m))$. The Marshallian demand at income m is the same as the Hicksian demand at utility $v(\mathbf{p}, m)$.

(4) $h_i(\mathbf{p}, u) \equiv x_i(\mathbf{p}, e(\mathbf{p}, u))$. The Hicksian demand at utility u is the same as the Marshallian demand at income $e(\mathbf{p}, u)$.

This last identity is perhaps the most important since it ties together the "observable" Marshallian demand function with the "unobservable" Hicksian demand function. Identity (4) shows that the Hicksian demand function—the solution to the expenditure minimization problem—is equal to the Marshallian demand function at an appropriate level of income— namely, the minimum income necessary at the given prices to achieve the desired level of utility. Thus, any demanded bundle can be expressed *either* as the solution to the utility maximization problem or the expenditure minimization problem. In the appendix to this chapter we give the exact conditions under which this equivalence holds. For now, we simply explore the consequences of this duality.

It is this link that gives rise to the term "compensated demand function." The Hicksian demand function is simply the Marshallian demand functions for the various goods if the consumer's income is "compensated" so as to achieve some target level of utility.

A nice application of one of these identities is given in the next proposition:

Roy's identity. *If $\mathbf{x}(\mathbf{p}, m)$ is the Marshallian demand function, then*

$$x_i(\mathbf{p}, m) = -\frac{\dfrac{\partial v(\mathbf{p}, m)}{\partial p_i}}{\dfrac{\partial v(\mathbf{p}, m)}{\partial m}} \quad for \quad i = 1, \cdots, k$$

provided, of course, that the right-hand side is well defined and that $p_i > 0$ and $m > 0$.

Proof. Suppose that $\mathbf{x}^*$ yields a maximal utility of u^* at $(\mathbf{p}^*, m^*)$. We know from our identities that

$$\mathbf{x}(\mathbf{p}^*, m^*) \equiv \mathbf{h}(\mathbf{p}^*, u^*). \tag{7.2}$$

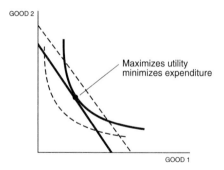

GOOD 2

Maximizes utility
minimizes expenditure

GOOD 1

Maximize utility and minimize expenditure. Normally, a consumption bundle that maximizes utility will also minimize expenditure and vice versa.

**Figure
7.4**

From another one of the fundamental identities, we also know that

$$u^* \equiv v(\mathbf{p}, e(\mathbf{p}, u^*)).$$

This identity says that no matter what prices are, if you give the consumer the minimal income to get utility u^* at those prices, then the maximal utility he can get is u^*.

Since this is an identity we can differentiate it with respect to p_i to get

$$0 = \frac{\partial v(\mathbf{p}^*, m^*)}{\partial p_i} + \frac{\partial v(\mathbf{p}^*, m^*)}{\partial m} \frac{\partial e(\mathbf{p}^*, u^*)}{\partial p_i}.$$

Rearranging, and combining this with identity (7.2), we have

$$x_i(\mathbf{p}^*, m^*) \equiv h_i(\mathbf{p}^*, u^*) \equiv \frac{\partial e(\mathbf{p}^*, u^*)}{\partial p_i} \equiv -\frac{\partial v(\mathbf{p}^*, m^*)/\partial p_i}{\partial v(\mathbf{p}^*, m^*)/\partial m}.$$

Since this identity is satisfied for all $(\mathbf{p}^*, m^*)$ and since $\mathbf{x}^* = \mathbf{x}(\mathbf{p}^*, m^*)$, the result is proved. ∎

The above proof, though elegant, is not particularly instructive. Here is an alternative direct proof of Roy's identity. The indirect utility function is given by

$$v(\mathbf{p}, m) \equiv u(\mathbf{x}(\mathbf{p}, m)). \tag{7.3}$$

If we differentiate this with respect to p_j, we find

$$\frac{\partial v(\mathbf{p}, m)}{\partial p_j} = \sum_{i=1}^{k} \frac{\partial u(\mathbf{x})}{\partial x_i} \frac{\partial x_i}{\partial p_j}. \tag{7.4}$$

Since $\mathbf{x}(\mathbf{p}, m)$ is the demand function, it satisfies the first-order conditions for utility maximization. Substituting the first-order conditions into expression (7.4) gives

$$\frac{\partial v(\mathbf{p}, m)}{\partial p_j} = \lambda \sum_{i=1}^{k} p_i \frac{\partial x_i}{\partial p_j}. \tag{7.5}$$

The demand functions also satisfy the budget constraint $\mathbf{px}(\mathbf{p}, m) \equiv m$. Differentiating this identity with respect to p_j, we have

$$x_j(\mathbf{p}, m) + \sum_{i=1}^{k} p_i \frac{\partial x_i}{\partial p_j} = 0. \tag{7.6}$$

Substitute (7.6) into (7.5) to find

$$\frac{\partial v(\mathbf{p}, m)}{\partial p_j} = -\lambda x_j(\mathbf{p}, m). \tag{7.7}$$

Now we differentiate (7.3) with respect to m to find

$$\frac{\partial v(\mathbf{p}, m)}{\partial m} = \lambda \sum_{i=1}^{k} p_i \frac{\partial x_i}{\partial m}. \tag{7.8}$$

Differentiating the budget constraint with respect to m, we have

$$\sum_{i=1}^{k} p_i \frac{\partial x_i}{\partial m} = 1. \tag{7.9}$$

Substituting (7.9) into (7.8) gives us

$$\frac{\partial v(\mathbf{p}, m)}{\partial m} = \lambda. \tag{7.10}$$

This equation simply says that the Lagrange multiplier in the first-order condition is the marginal utility of income. Combining (7.7) and (7.10) gives us Roy's identity.

Finally, for one last proof of Roy's identity, we note that it is an immediate consequence of the envelope theorem described in Chapter 27, page 501. The argument given above is just going through the steps of the proof of this theorem.

7.5 The money metric utility functions

There is a nice construction involving the expenditure function that comes up in a variety of places in welfare economics. Consider some prices $\mathbf{p}$ and some given bundle of goods **x**. We can ask the following question: how much money would a given consumer need at the prices **p** to be as well off as he could be by consuming the bundle of goods **x**?

Figure 7.5 tells us how to construct the answer to this question graphically if we know the consumer's preferences. We just see how much money the consumer would need to reach the indifference curve passing through **x**. Mathematically, we simply solve the following problem:

$$\min_{\mathbf{z}} \mathbf{p}\mathbf{z}$$

$$\text{such that } u(\mathbf{z}) \geq u(\mathbf{x})$$

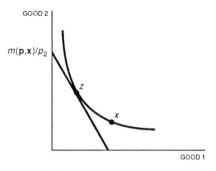

Direct money metric utility function.   The money metric utility function gives the minimum expenditure at prices **p** necessary to purchase a bundle at least as good as **x**.

Figure 7.5

This type of function occurs so often that it is worthwhile giving it a special name; following Samuelson (1974) we call it the **money metric utility function**. It is also known as the "minimum income function," the "direct compensation function," and by a variety of other names. An alternative definition is

$$m(\mathbf{p}, \mathbf{x}) \equiv e(\mathbf{p}, u(\mathbf{x})).$$

It is easy to see that for fixed **x**, $u(\mathbf{x})$ is fixed, so $m(\mathbf{p}, \mathbf{x})$ behaves exactly like an expenditure function: it is monotonic, homogeneous, concave in **p**, and so on. What is not as obvious is that when **p** is fixed, $m(\mathbf{p}, \mathbf{x})$ is in fact a utility function. The proof is simple: for fixed prices the expenditure function is increasing in the level of utility: if you want to get a higher utility level, you have to spend more money. In fact, the expenditure function is strictly increasing in u for continuous, locally nonsatiated preferences.

Hence, for fixed $\mathbf{p}$, $m(\mathbf{p}, \mathbf{x})$ is simply a monotonic transform of the utility function and is therefore itself a utility function.

This is easily seen in Figure 7.5. All points on the indifference curve passing through $\mathbf{x}$ will be assigned the same level of $m(\mathbf{p}, \mathbf{x})$, and all points on higher indifference curves will be assigned a higher level. This is all it takes to be a utility function.

There is a similar construct for indirect utility known as the **money metric indirect utility function**. It is given by

$$\mu(\mathbf{p}; \mathbf{q}, m) \equiv e(\mathbf{p}, v(\mathbf{q}, m)).$$

That is, $\mu(\mathbf{p}; \mathbf{q}, m)$ measures how much money one would need at prices $\mathbf{p}$ to be as well off as one would be facing prices $\mathbf{q}$ and having income m. Just as in the direct case, $\mu(\mathbf{p}; \mathbf{q}, m)$ behaves like an expenditure function with respect to $\mathbf{p}$, but now it behaves like an indirect utility function with respect to $\mathbf{q}$ and m, since it is, after all, simply a monotonic transformation of an indirect utility function. See Figure 7.6 for a graphical example.

A nice feature of the direct and indirect compensation functions is that they contain only *observable* arguments. They are *specific* direct and indirect utility functions that measure something of interest, and there is no ambiguity regarding monotonic transformations. We will find this feature to be useful in our discussion of integrability theory and welfare economics.

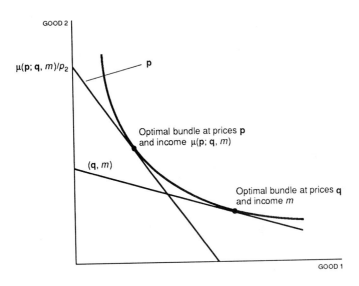

Figure 7.6   **Indirect money metric utility function.**   This function gives the minimum expenditure at prices $\mathbf{p}$ for the consumer to be as well off as he would be facing prices $\mathbf{q}$ and having income m.

EXAMPLE: The Cobb-Douglas utility function

The Cobb-Douglas utility function is given by: $u(x_1, x_2) = x_1^a x_2^{1-a}$. Since any monotonic transform of this function represents the same preferences, we can also write $u(x_1, x_2) = a \ln x_1 + (1-a) \ln x_2$.

The expenditure function and Hicksian demand functions are the same, up to a change in notation, as the cost function and conditional factor demands derived in Chapter 4, page 54. The Marshallian demand functions and the indirect utility function can be derived by solving the following problem:

$$\max a \ln x_1 + (1-a) \ln x_2$$
$$\text{such that } p_1 x_1 + p_2 x_2 = m.$$

The first–order conditions are

$$\frac{a}{x_1} - \lambda p_1 = 0$$
$$\frac{1-a}{x_2} - \lambda p_2 = 0,$$

or

$$\frac{a}{p_1 x_1} = \frac{1-a}{p_2 x_2}.$$

Cross multiply and use the budget constraint to get

$$a p_2 x_2 = p_1 x_1 - a p_1 x_1$$
$$am = p_1 x_1$$
$$x_1(p_1, p_2, m) = \frac{am}{p_1}.$$

Substitute into the budget constraint to get the second Marshallian demand:

$$x_2(p_1, p_2, m) = \frac{(1-a)m}{p_2}.$$

Substitute into the objective function and eliminate constants to get the indirect utility function:

$$v(p_1, p_2, m) = \ln m - a \ln p_1 - (1-a) \ln p_2. \qquad (7.11)$$

A quicker way to derive the indirect utility function is to invert the Cobb-Douglas cost/expenditure function we derived in Chapter 4, page 54. This gives us

$$e(p_1, p_2, u) = K p_1^a p_2^{1-a} u,$$

where K is some constant depending on a. Inverting the expression by replacing $e(p_1, p_2, u)$ by m, and u by $v(p_1, p_2, m)$, we get

$$v(p_1, p_2, m) = \frac{m}{K p_1^a p_2^{1-a}}.$$

This is just a monotonic transform of (7.11) as can be seen by taking the logarithm of both sides.

The money metric utility functions can be derived by substitution. We have

$$m(\mathbf{p}, \mathbf{x}) = K p_1^a p_2^{1-a} u(x_1, x_2)$$
$$= K p_1^a p_2^{1-a} x_1^a x_2^{1-a}$$

and

$$\mu(\mathbf{p}; \mathbf{q}, m) = K p_1^a p_2^{1-a} v(q_1, q_2, m)$$
$$= p_1^a p_2^{1-a} q_1^{-a} q_2^{a-1} m.$$

EXAMPLE: The CES utility function

The CES utility function is given by $u(x_1, x_2) = (x_1^\rho + x_2^\rho)^{1/\rho}$. Since preferences are invariant with respect to monotonic transforms of utility, we could just as well choose $u(x_1, x_2) = \frac{1}{\rho} \ln(x_1^\rho + x_2^\rho)$.

We have seen earlier that the cost function for the CES technology has the form $c(w, y) = (w_1^r + w_2^r)^{1/r} y$ where $r = \rho/(\rho-1)$. Thus the expenditure function for the CES utility function must have the form

$$e(\mathbf{p}, u) = (p_1^r + p_2^r)^{1/r} u.$$

We can find the indirect utility function by inverting the above equation:

$$v(\mathbf{p}, m) = (p_1^r + p_2^r)^{-1/r} m.$$

The demand functions can be found by Roy's law:

$$x_1(\mathbf{p}, m) = \frac{-\partial v(\mathbf{p}, m)/\partial p_1}{\partial v(\mathbf{p}, m)/\partial m} = \frac{\frac{1}{r}(p_1^r + p_2^r)^{-\left(1 + \frac{1}{r}\right)} m r p_1^{r-1}}{(p_1^r + p_2^r)^{-1/r}}$$
$$= \frac{p_1^{r-1} m}{(p_1^r + p_2^r)}.$$

The money metric utility functions for the CES utility function can also be found by substitution:

$$m(\mathbf{p}, \mathbf{x}) = (p_1^r + p_2^r)^{\frac{1}{r}} (x_1^\rho + x_2^\rho)^{\frac{1}{\rho}}$$
$$\mu(\mathbf{p}; \mathbf{q}, m) = (p_1^r + p_2^r)^{\frac{1}{r}} (q_1^r + q_2^r)^{-1/r} m.$$

APPENDIX

Consider the following two problems:

$$\max u(\mathbf{x})$$
$$\text{such that } \mathbf{px} \leq m. \tag{7.12}$$

$$\min \mathbf{px}$$
$$\text{such that } u(\mathbf{x}) \geq u. \tag{7.13}$$

Assume that

(1) the utility function is continuous;

(2) preferences satisfy local nonsatiation;

(3) answers to both problems exist.

Utility maximization implies expenditure minimization.   *Suppose that the above assumptions are satisfied. Let* $\mathbf{x}^*$ *be a solution to (7.12), and let* $u = u(\mathbf{x}^*)$. *Then* $\mathbf{x}^*$ *solves (7.13).*

Proof.   Suppose not, and let $\mathbf{x}'$ solve (7.13). Hence, $\mathbf{px}' < \mathbf{px}^*$ and $u(\mathbf{x}') \geq u(\mathbf{x}^*)$. By local nonsatiation there is a bundle $\mathbf{x}''$ close enough to $\mathbf{x}'$ so that $\mathbf{px}'' < \mathbf{px}^* = m$ and $u(\mathbf{x}'') > u(\mathbf{x}^*)$. But then $\mathbf{x}^*$ cannot be a solution to (7.12). ∎

Expenditure minimization implies utility maximization.   *Suppose that the above assumptions are satisfied and that* $\mathbf{x}^*$ *solves (7.13). Let* $m = \mathbf{px}^*$ *and suppose that* $m > 0$. *Then* $\mathbf{x}^*$ *solves (7.12).*

Proof.   Suppose not, and let $\mathbf{x}'$ solve (7.12) so that $u(\mathbf{x}') > u(\mathbf{x}^*)$ and $\mathbf{px}' = \mathbf{px}^* = m$. Since $\mathbf{px}^* > 0$ and utility is continuous, we can find $0 < t < 1$ such that $\mathbf{pt}\mathbf{x}' < \mathbf{px}^* = m$ and $u(t\mathbf{x}') > u(\mathbf{x}^*)$. Hence, $\mathbf{x}^*$ cannot solve (7.13). ∎

Notes

The argument for the existence of a utility function is based on Wold (1943). A general theorem on the existence of a utility function can be found in Debreu (1964).

The importance of the indirect utility function was first recognized by Roy (1942), Roy (1947). The expenditure function seems to be due to Hicks (1946). The dual approach to consumer theory described follows that of McFadden & Winter (1968). The money metric utility function was used by McKenzie (1957) and Samuelson (1974).

Exercises

7.1. Consider preferences defined over the nonnegative orthant by $(x_1, x_2) \succ (y_1, y_2)$ if $x_1 + x_2 < y_1 + y_2$. Do these preferences exhibit local nonsatiation? If these are the only two consumption goods and the consumer faces positive prices, will the consumer spend all of his income? Explain.

7.2. A consumer has a utility function $u(x_1, x_2) = \max\{x_1, x_2\}$. What is the consumer's demand function for good 1? What is his indirect utility function? What is his expenditure function?

7.3. A consumer has an indirect utility function of the form

$$v(p_1, p_2, m) = \frac{m}{\min\{p_1, p_2\}}.$$

What is the form of the expenditure function for this consumer? What is the form of a (quasiconcave) utility function for this consumer? What is the form of the demand function for good 1?

7.4. Consider the indirect utility function given by

$$v(p_1, p_2, m) = \frac{m}{p_1 + p_2}.$$

(a) What are the demand functions?

(b) What is the expenditure function?

(c) What is the direct utility function?

7.5. A consumer has a direct utility function of the form

$$U(x_1, x_2) = u(x_1) + x_2.$$

Good 1 is a discrete good; the only possible levels of consumption of good 1 are $x_1 = 0$ and $x_1 = 1$. For convenience, assume that $u(0) = 0$ and $p_2 = 1$.

(a) What kind of preferences does this consumer have?

(b) The consumer will definitely choose $x_1 = 1$ if p_1 is strictly less than what?

(c) What is the algebraic form of the indirect utility function associated with this direct utility function?

7.6. A consumer has an indirect utility function of the form $v(\mathbf{p}, m) = A(\mathbf{p})m$.

(a) What kind of preferences does this consumer have?

(b) What is the form of this consumer's expenditure function, $e(\mathbf{p}, u)$?

(c) What is the form of this consumer's indirect money metric utility function, $\mu(\mathbf{p}; \mathbf{q}, m)$?

(d) Suppose instead that the consumer had an indirect utility function of the form $v(\mathbf{p}, m) = A(\mathbf{p})m^b$ for $b > 1$. What will be the form of the consumer's indirect money metric utility function now?

CHAPTER **8**

CHOICE

In this chapter we will examine the comparative statics of consumer demand behavior: how the consumer's demand changes as prices and income change. As in the case of the firm, we will approach this problem in three different ways: by differentiating the first-order conditions, by using the properties of the expenditure and indirect utility functions, and by using the algebraic inequalities implied by the optimizing model.

8.1 Comparative statics

Let us examine the two-good consumer maximization problem in a bit more detail. It is of interest to look at how the consumer's demand changes as we change the parameters of the problem. Let's hold prices fixed and allow income to vary; the resulting locus of utility-maximizing bundles is known as the **income expansion path**. From the income expansion path, we can derive a function that relates income to the demand for each commodity (at constant prices). These functions are called **Engel curves**. Several possibilities arise:

(1) The income expansion path (and thus each Engel curve) is a straight line through the origin. In this case the consumer is said to have demand

curves with unit income elasticity. Such a consumer will consume the same proportion of each commodity at each level of income.

(2) The income expansion path bends towards one good or the other—i.e., as the consumer gets more income, he consumes more of both goods but proportionally more of one good (the **luxury good**) than of the other (the **necessary good**).

(3) The income expansion path could bend backwards—in this case an increase in income means the consumer actually wants to consume less of one of the goods. For example, one might argue that as income increases I would want to consume fewer potatoes. Such goods are called **inferior goods**; goods for which more income means more demand are called **normal goods**. (See Figure 8.1.)

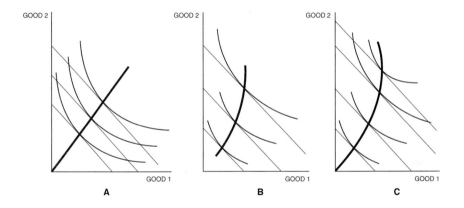

Income expansion paths. Panel A depicts unit elastic demands, in panel B good 2 is a luxury good, and in panel C, good 1 is an inferior good.

Figure 8.1

We can also hold income fixed and allow prices to vary. If we let p_1 vary and hold p_2 and m fixed, our budget line will tilt, and the locus of tangencies will sweep out a curve known as the **price offer curve**. In the first case in Figure 8.2 we have the ordinary case where a lower price for good 1 leads to greater demand for the good; in the second case we have a situation where a decrease in the price of good 1 brings about a *decreased* demand for good 1. Such a good is called a **Giffen good**. An example might again be potatoes; if the price of potatoes goes down I can buy just as many of them as I could before and still have some money left over. I could use this leftover money to buy more pasta. But now that I am consuming more pasta I don't even want to consume as many potatoes as I did before.

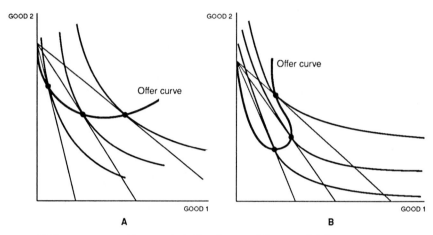

GOOD 2   GOOD 2

Offer curve

Offer curve

GOOD 1   GOOD 1

A   B

Figure 8.2   **Offer curves.** In panel A the demand for good 1 increases as the price decreases so it is an ordinary good. In panel B the demand for good 1 decreases as its price decreases, so it is a Giffen good.

In the above example we see that a fall in the price of a good may have two sorts of effects—one commodity will become less expensive than another, and total "purchasing power" may change. A fundamental result of the theory of the consumer, the Slutsky equation, relates these two effects. We will derive the Slutsky equation later in several ways.

EXAMPLE: Excise and income taxes

Suppose we wish to tax a utility-maximizing consumer to obtain a certain amount of revenue. Initially, the consumer's budget constraint is $p_1x_1 + p_2x_2 = m$, but after we impose a tax on sales of good 1, the consumer's budget constraint becomes $(p_1 + t)x_1 + p_2x_2 = m$. The effect of this excise tax is illustrated in Figure 8.3. If we denote the after-tax level of consumption by (x_1^*, x_2^*), then the revenue collected by the tax is tx_1^*.

Suppose now that we decide to collect this same amount of revenue by a tax on income. The budget constraint of the consumer would then be $p_1x_1 + p_2x_2 = m - tx_1^*$. This is a line with slope $-p_1/p_2$ that passes through

(x_1^*, x_2^*), as shown in Figure 8.3. Notice that since this budget line cuts the indifference curve through (x_1^*, x_2^*), the consumer can achieve a higher level of utility from an income tax than from a commodity tax, even though they both generate the same revenue.

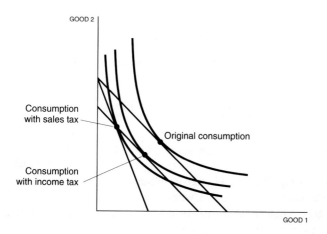

Excise tax and income tax. A consumer is always worse off facing an excise tax than an income tax that generates the same revenue.

Figure 8.3

8.2 The Slutsky equation

We have seen that the Hicksian, or compensated demand curve, is formally the same as the conditional factor demand discussed in the theory of the firm. Hence it has all the same properties; in particular, it has a symmetric, negative semidefinite substitution matrix.

In the case of the firm, this sort of restriction was an observable restriction on firm behavior, since the output of the firm is an observable variable. In the case of the consumer, this sort of restriction does not appear to be of much use since utility is not directly observable.

However, it turns out that this appearance is misleading. Even though the compensated demand function is not *directly* observable, we shall see that its derivative can be easily calculated from observable things, namely, the derivative of the Marshallian demand with respect to price and income. This relationship is known as the **Slutsky equation**.

Slutsky equation.

$$\frac{\partial x_j(\mathbf{p}, m)}{\partial p_i} = \frac{\partial h_j(\mathbf{p}, v(\mathbf{p}, m))}{\partial p_i} - \frac{\partial x_j(\mathbf{p}, m)}{\partial m} x_i(\mathbf{p}, m)$$

Proof. Let $\mathbf{x}^*$ maximize utility at $(\mathbf{p}^*, m^*)$ and let $u^* = u(\mathbf{x}^*)$. It is identically true that

$$h_j(\mathbf{p}, u^*) \equiv x_j(\mathbf{p}, e(\mathbf{p}, u^*)).$$

We can differentiate this with respect to p_i and evaluate the derivative at $\mathbf{p}^*$ to get

$$\frac{\partial h_j(\mathbf{p}^*, u^*)}{\partial p_i} = \frac{\partial x_j(\mathbf{p}^*, m^*)}{\partial p_i} + \frac{\partial x_j(\mathbf{p}^*, m^*)}{\partial m} \frac{\partial e(\mathbf{p}^*, u^*)}{\partial p_i}.$$

Note carefully the meaning of this expression. The left-hand side is how the compensated demand changes when p_i changes. The right-hand side says that this change is equal to the change in demand holding expenditure fixed at m^* *plus* the change in demand when income changes *times* how much income has to change to keep utility constant. But this last term, $\partial e(\mathbf{p}^*, u^*)/\partial p_i$, is just x_i^*; rearranging gives us

$$\frac{\partial x_j(\mathbf{p}^*, m^*)}{\partial p_i} = \frac{\partial h_j(\mathbf{p}^*, u^*)}{\partial p_i} - \frac{\partial x_j(\mathbf{p}^*, m^*)}{\partial m} x_i^*$$

which is the Slutsky equation. ∎

The Slutsky equation decomposes the demand change induced by a price change Δp_i into two separate effects: the **substitution effect** and the **income effect**:

$$\Delta x_j \approx \frac{\partial x_j(\mathbf{p}, m)}{\partial p_i} \Delta p_i = \frac{\partial h_j(\mathbf{p}, u)}{\partial p_i} \Delta p_i - \frac{\partial x_j(\mathbf{p}, m)}{\partial m} x_i \Delta p_i$$

We can also consider the effects from all prices changing at once; in this case we just interpret the derivatives as generalized n–dimensional derivatives rather than partial derivatives. In the two-good case the Slutsky equation looks like this:

$$\mathbf{D_p x}(\mathbf{p}, m) = \mathbf{D_p h}(\mathbf{p}, u) - \mathbf{D_m x}(\mathbf{p}, m)\mathbf{x}$$

$$\begin{bmatrix} \dfrac{\partial x_1(\mathbf{p}, m)}{\partial p_1} & \dfrac{\partial x_1(\mathbf{p}, m)}{\partial p_2} \\ \dfrac{\partial x_2(\mathbf{p}, m)}{\partial p_1} & \dfrac{\partial x_2(\mathbf{p}, m)}{\partial p_2} \end{bmatrix} = \begin{bmatrix} \dfrac{\partial h_1(\mathbf{p}, u)}{\partial p_1} & \dfrac{\partial h_1(\mathbf{p}, u)}{\partial p_2} \\ \dfrac{\partial h_2(\mathbf{p}, u)}{\partial p_1} & \dfrac{\partial h_2(\mathbf{p}, u)}{\partial p_2} \end{bmatrix}$$

$$\begin{bmatrix} \dfrac{\partial x_1(\mathbf{p}, m)}{\partial m} \\ \dfrac{\partial x_2(\mathbf{p}, m)}{\partial m} \end{bmatrix} [x_1, x_2]$$

where $u = v(\mathbf{p}, m)$.

Expanding the last term gives

$$\begin{bmatrix} \dfrac{\partial x_1(\mathbf{p}, m)}{\partial m} \\ \dfrac{\partial x_2(\mathbf{p}, m)}{\partial m} \end{bmatrix} [x_1, x_2] = \begin{bmatrix} \dfrac{\partial x_1(\mathbf{p}, m)}{\partial m} x_1 & \dfrac{\partial x_1(\mathbf{p}, m)}{\partial m} x_2 \\ \dfrac{\partial x_2(\mathbf{p}, m)}{\partial m} x_1 & \dfrac{\partial x_2(\mathbf{p}, m)}{\partial m} x_2 \end{bmatrix}.$$

Suppose we consider a price change $\Delta\mathbf{p} = (\Delta p_1, \Delta p_2)$ and we are interested in the approximate change in demand $\Delta\mathbf{x} = (\Delta x_1, \Delta x_2)$. According to the Slutsky equation, we can calculate this change using the expression

$$\begin{bmatrix} \Delta x_1 \\ \Delta x_2 \end{bmatrix} \approx \begin{bmatrix} \dfrac{\partial h_1}{\partial p_1} & \dfrac{\partial h_1}{\partial p_2} \\ \dfrac{\partial h_2}{\partial p_1} & \dfrac{\partial h_2}{\partial p_2} \end{bmatrix} \begin{bmatrix} \Delta p_1 \\ \Delta p_2 \end{bmatrix} - \begin{bmatrix} \dfrac{\partial x_1}{\partial m} x_1 & \dfrac{\partial x_1}{\partial m} x_2 \\ \dfrac{\partial x_2}{\partial m} x_1 & \dfrac{\partial x_2}{\partial m} x_2 \end{bmatrix} \begin{bmatrix} \Delta p_1 \\ \Delta p_2 \end{bmatrix}.$$

$$= \begin{bmatrix} \Delta x_1^s \\ \Delta x_2^s \end{bmatrix} - \begin{bmatrix} \Delta x_1^m \\ \Delta x_2^m \end{bmatrix}.$$

The first vector is the substitution effect. It indicates how the Hicksian demands change. Since changes in Hicksian demands keep utility constant, $(\Delta x_1^s, \Delta x_2^s)$ will be tangent to the indifference curve. The second vector is the income effect. The price change has caused "purchasing power" to change by $x_1 \Delta p_1 + x_2 \Delta p_2$ and the vector $(\Delta x_1^m, \Delta x_2^m)$ measures the impact of this change on demand, with prices held constant at the initial level. This vector therefore lies along the income expansion path.

We can do a similar decomposition for finite changes in demand as illustrated in Figure 8.4. Here prices change from $\mathbf{p}^0$ to $\mathbf{p}'$, and demand changes from $\mathbf{x}$ to $\mathbf{x}'$. To construct the Hicks decomposition, we first pivot the budget line around the indifference curve to find the optimal bundle at prices $\mathbf{p}'$ with utility fixed at the original level. Then we shift the budget line out to the $\mathbf{x}'$ to find the income effect. The total effect is the sum of these two movements.

EXAMPLE: The Cobb-Douglas Slutsky equation

Let us check the Slutsky equation in the Cobb-Douglas case. As we've seen, in this case we have

$$v(p_1, p_2, m) = m p_1^{-a} p_2^{a-1}$$
$$e(p_1, p_2, u) = u p_1^a p_2^{1-a}$$
$$x_1(p_1, p_2, m) = \frac{am}{p_1}$$
$$h_1(p_1, p_2, u) = a p_1^{a-1} p_2^{1-a} u.$$

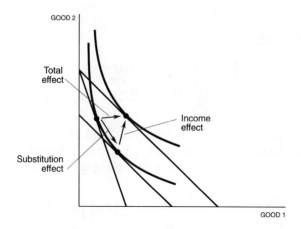

GOOD 2

Total
effect

Income
effect

Substitution
effect

GOOD 1

**Figure
8.4**

The Hicks decomposition of a demand change. We can
decompose the change in demand into two movements: the substitution effect and the income effect.

Thus

$$\frac{\partial x_1(\mathbf{p}, m)}{\partial p_1} = -\frac{am}{p_1^2}$$

$$\frac{\partial x_1(\mathbf{p}, m)}{\partial m} = \frac{a}{p_1}$$

$$\frac{\partial h_1(\mathbf{p}, u)}{\partial p_1} = a(a-1)p_1^{a-2}p_2^{1-a}u$$

$$\frac{\partial h_1(\mathbf{p}, v(\mathbf{p}, m))}{\partial p_1} = a(a-1)p_1^{a-2}p_2^{1-a}mp_1^{-a}p_2^{a-1}$$

$$= a(a-1)p_1^{-2}m.$$

Now plug into the Slutsky equation to find

$$\frac{\partial h_1}{\partial p_1} - \frac{\partial x_1}{\partial m}x_1 = \frac{a(a-1)m}{p_1^2} - \frac{a}{p_1}\frac{am}{p_1}$$

$$= \frac{[a(a-1)-a^2]m}{p_1^2}$$

$$= \frac{-am}{p_1^2} = \frac{\partial x_1}{\partial p_1}.$$

8.3 Properties of demand functions

The properties of the expenditure function give us an easy way to develop
the main propositions of the neoclassical theory of consumer behavior:

(1) *The matrix of substitution terms* $(\partial h_j(\mathbf{p}, u)/\partial p_i)$ *is negative semidefinite.* This follows because

$$(\partial h_j(\mathbf{p}, u)/\partial p_i) = (\partial^2 e(\mathbf{p}, u)/\partial p_i \partial p_j),$$

which is negative semidefinite because the expenditure function is concave. (See Chapter 27, page 496.)

(2) *The matrix of substitution terms is symmetric*—since

$$\frac{\partial h_j(\mathbf{p}, u)}{\partial p_i} = \frac{\partial^2 e(\mathbf{p}, u)}{\partial p_j \partial p_i} = \frac{\partial^2 e(\mathbf{p}, u)}{\partial p_i \partial p_j} = \frac{\partial h_i(\mathbf{p}, u)}{\partial p_j}.$$

(3) *In particular, "the compensated own-price effect is nonpositive";* that is, the Hicksian demand curves slope downward:

$$\frac{\partial h_i(\mathbf{p}, u)}{\partial p_i} = \frac{\partial^2 e(\mathbf{p}, u)}{\partial p_i^2} \leq 0,$$

since the substitution matrix is negative semidefinite and thus has nonpositive diagonal terms.

These restrictions all concern the Hicksian demand functions, which are not directly observable. However, as we indicated earlier the Slutsky equation allows us to express the derivatives of $\mathbf{h}$ with respect to $\mathbf{p}$ as derivatives of $\mathbf{x}$ with respect to $\mathbf{p}$ and m, and these are observable. For example, Slutsky's equation and the above remarks yield

(4) *The substitution matrix* $\left(\dfrac{\partial x_j(\mathbf{p}, m)}{\partial p_i} + \dfrac{\partial x_j(\mathbf{p}, m)}{\partial m} x_i\right)$ *is a symmetric, negative semidefinite matrix.*

This is a rather nonintuitive result: a particular combination of price and income derivatives has to result in a negative semidefinite matrix. However, it follows inexorably from the logic of maximizing behavior.

8.4 Comparative statics using the first-order conditions

The Slutsky equation can also be derived by differentiating the first-order conditions. Since the calculations are a bit tedious, we will limit ourselves to the case of two goods and just sketch the broad outlines of the argument.
    In this case the first-order conditions take the form

$$p_1 x_1(p_1, p_2, m) + p_2 x_2(p_1, p_2, m) - m \equiv 0$$

$$\frac{\partial u(x_1(p_1, p_2, m), x_2(p_1, p_2, m))}{\partial x_1} - \lambda p_1 \equiv 0$$

$$\frac{\partial u(x_1(p_1, p_2, m), x_2(p_1, p_2, m))}{\partial x_2} - \lambda p_2 \equiv 0.$$

Differentiating with respect to p_1, and arranging in matrix form, we have

$$
\begin{bmatrix}
0 & -p_1 & -p_2 \\
-p_1 & u_{11} & u_{12} \\
-p_2 & u_{21} & u_{22}
\end{bmatrix}
\begin{bmatrix}
\dfrac{\partial \lambda}{\partial p_1} \\[2mm]
\dfrac{\partial x_1}{\partial p_1} \\[2mm]
\dfrac{\partial x_2}{\partial p_1}
\end{bmatrix}
\equiv
\begin{bmatrix}
x_1 \\
\lambda \\
0
\end{bmatrix}.
$$

Solving for $\partial x_1/\partial p_1$ via Cramer's rule gives us

$$
\frac{\partial x_1}{\partial p_1} =
\frac{
\begin{vmatrix}
0 & x_1 & -p_2 \\
-p_1 & \lambda & u_{12} \\
-p_2 & 0 & u_{22}
\end{vmatrix}
}{H},
$$

where $H > 0$ is the determinant of the bordered Hessian.

Expanding this determinant by cofactors on the second column, we have

$$
\frac{\partial x_1}{\partial p_1} = \lambda
\frac{
\begin{vmatrix}
0 & -p_2 \\
-p_2 & u_{22}
\end{vmatrix}
}{H}
- x_1
\frac{
\begin{vmatrix}
-p_1 & u_{12} \\
-p_2 & u_{22}
\end{vmatrix}
}{H}.
$$

This is beginning to look a bit like Slutsky's equation already. Note that the first term—which turns out to be the substitution effect—is negative as required. Now go back to the first-order conditions and differentiate them with respect to m. We have

$$
\begin{bmatrix}
0 & -p_1 & -p_2 \\
-p_1 & u_{11} & u_{12} \\
-p_2 & u_{21} & u_{22}
\end{bmatrix}
\begin{bmatrix}
\dfrac{\partial \lambda}{\partial m} \\[2mm]
\dfrac{\partial x_1}{\partial m} \\[2mm]
\dfrac{\partial x_2}{\partial m}
\end{bmatrix}
=
\begin{bmatrix}
-1 \\
0 \\
0
\end{bmatrix}.
$$

So, by Cramer's rule,

$$
\frac{\partial x_1}{\partial m} =
\frac{
\begin{vmatrix}
-p_1 & u_{12} \\
-p_2 & u_{22}
\end{vmatrix}
}{H}.
$$

Substituting into the equation for $\partial x_1/\partial p_1$ derived above, we have the income-effect part of Slutsky's equation. In order to derive the substitution effect, we need to set up the expenditure minimization problem and calculate $\partial h_1/\partial p_1$. This calculation is analogous to the calculation of the conditional factor demand functions in Chapter 4, page 59. The resulting expression can be shown to be equal to the substitution term in the above equation, which establishes Slutsky's equation.

8.5 The integrability problem

We have seen that the utility maximization hypothesis imposes certain observable restrictions on consumer behavior. In particular, we know that the matrix of substitution terms,

$$\left(\frac{\partial h_i(\mathbf{p}, u)}{\partial p_j}\right) = \left(\frac{\partial x_i(\mathbf{p}, m)}{\partial p_j} + \frac{\partial x_i(\mathbf{p}, m)}{\partial m} x_j(\mathbf{p}, m)\right),$$

must be a symmetric, negative semidefinite matrix.

Suppose that we were given a system of demand functions which had a symmetric, negative semidefinite substitution matrix. Is there necessarily a utility function from which these demand functions can be derived? This question is known as the **integrability problem**.

As we have seen, there are several equivalent ways to describe consumer preferences. We can use a utility function, an indirect utility function, an expenditure function, and so on. The indirect utility function and the expenditure function are quite convenient ways to solve the integrability problem.

For example, Roy's law tells us that

$$x_i(\mathbf{p}, m) = -\frac{\partial v(\mathbf{p}, m)/\partial p_i}{\partial v(\mathbf{p}, m)/\partial m}. \tag{8.1}$$

Generally, we have been given an indirect utility function and then used this identity to calculate the demand functions. However, the integrability problem asks the reverse question: given the demand functions, and the $i = 1, \ldots, k$ relationships in (8.1), how can we solve these equations to find $v(\mathbf{p}, m)$? Or, more fundamentally, how do we even know if a solution exists?

The system of equations given in (8.1) is a system of **partial differential equations**. The integrability problem asks us to determine a solution of this set of equations.

As it turns out, it is somewhat easier to pose this question in terms of the expenditure function rather than the indirect utility function. Suppose that we are given some set of demand functions $(x_i(\mathbf{p}, m))$ for $i = 1, \ldots, k$. Let us pick some point $\mathbf{x}^0 = \mathbf{x}(\mathbf{p}^0, m)$ and arbitrarily assign it utility u^0. How can we construct the expenditure function $e(\mathbf{p}, u^0)$? Once we have found an expenditure function consistent with the demand functions, we can use it to solve for the implied direct or indirect utility function.

If such an expenditure function does exist, it certainly must satisfy the system of partial differential equations given by

$$\frac{\partial e(\mathbf{p}, u^0)}{\partial p_i} = h_i(\mathbf{p}, u^0) = x_i(\mathbf{p}, e(\mathbf{p}, u^0)) \quad i = 1, \cdots, k, \tag{8.2}$$

and initial condition

$$e(\mathbf{p}^0, u^0) = \mathbf{p}^0 \mathbf{x}(\mathbf{p}^0, m^0).$$

These equations simply state that the Hicksian demand for each good at utility u is the Marshallian demand at income $e(\mathbf{p}, u)$. Now the **integrability condition** described in Chapter 26, page 484, says that a system of partial differential equations of the form

$$\frac{\partial f(\mathbf{p})}{\partial p_i} = g_i(\mathbf{p}) \qquad i = 1, \cdots, k$$

has a (local) solution if and only if

$$\frac{\partial g_i(\mathbf{p})}{\partial p_j} = \frac{\partial g_j(\mathbf{p})}{\partial p_i} \qquad \text{all } i \text{ and } j.$$

Applying this condition to the above problem, we see that it reduces to requiring that the matrix

$$\left(\frac{\partial x_i(\mathbf{p}, m)}{\partial p_j} + \frac{\partial x_i(\mathbf{p}, m)}{\partial m} \frac{\partial e(\mathbf{p}, u)}{\partial p_j} \right)$$

is symmetric. But this is just the Slutsky restriction! Thus the Slutsky restrictions imply that the demand functions can be "integrated" to find an expenditure function consistent with the observed choice behavior.

This symmetry condition is enough to ensure that there will exist a function $e(\mathbf{p}, u^0)$ that will satisfy the equations (8.2) at least over some range. (Conditions that ensure a solution exists *globally* are somewhat more involved.) However, in order for this to be a bona fide expenditure function it must also be concave in prices. That is, the second derivative matrix of $e(\mathbf{p}, u)$ must be negative semidefinite. But, we have already seen that the second derivative matrix of $e(\mathbf{p}, u)$ is simply the Slutsky substitution matrix. If this is negative semidefinite, then the solution to the above partial differential equations must be concave.

These observations give us a solution to the integrability problem. Given a set of demand functions $(x_i(\mathbf{p}, m))$, we simply have to verify that they have a symmetric, negative semidefinite substitution matrix. If they do, we can, in principle, solve the system of equations given in (8.2) to find an expenditure function consistent with those demand functions.

There is a nice trick that will allow us to recover the indirect utility function from demand functions, at the same time that we recover the expenditure function. Equation (8.2) is valid for all utility levels u^0, so let us choose some base prices $\mathbf{q}$ and income level m, and let $u^0 = v(\mathbf{q}, m)$. With this substitution, we can write (8.2) as

$$\frac{\partial e(\mathbf{p}, v(\mathbf{q}, m))}{\partial p_i} = x_i(\mathbf{p}, e(\mathbf{p}, v(\mathbf{q}, m))),$$

where the boundary condition now becomes

$$e(\mathbf{q}, v(\mathbf{q}, m)) = m.$$

Recall the definition of the (indirect) money metric utility function in Chapter 7, page 109: $\mu(\mathbf{p}; \mathbf{q}, m) \equiv e(\mathbf{p}, v(\mathbf{q}, m))$. Using this definition, we can also write this system of equations as follows:

$$\frac{\partial \mu(\mathbf{p}; \mathbf{q}, m)}{\partial p_i} = x_i(\mathbf{p}, \mu(\mathbf{p}; \mathbf{q}, m)) \quad i = 1, \cdots, k$$

$$\mu(\mathbf{q}; \mathbf{q}, m) = m.$$

We refer to this system as the **integrability equations**. A function $\mu(\mathbf{p}; \mathbf{q}, m)$ that solves this problem gives us an indirect utility function—a particular indirect utility function—that describes the observed demand behavior $\mathbf{x}(\mathbf{p}, m)$. This money metric utility function is often very convenient for applied welfare analysis.

EXAMPLE: Integrability with two goods

If there are only two goods being consumed, the integrability equations take a very simple form since there is only *one* independent variable, the relative price of the two goods. Similarly, there is only one independent equation since if we know the demand for one good, we can find the demand for the other through the budget constraint.

Let us normalize the price of good 2 to be 1, and write p for the price of the first good and $x(p, m)$ for its demand function. Then the integrability equations become a single equation plus a boundary condition:

$$\frac{d\mu(p; q, m)}{dp} = x(p, \mu(p; q, m))$$

$$\mu(q; q, m) = m$$

This is just an ordinary differential equation with boundary condition which can be solved using standard techniques.

For example, suppose that we have a log-linear demand function:

$$\ln x = a \ln p + b \ln m + c$$

$$x = p^a m^b e^c$$

The integrability equation is

$$\frac{d\mu(p; q, m)}{dp} = p^a e^c \mu^b.$$

Rearranging, we have

$$\mu^{-b} \frac{d\mu(p; q, m)}{dp} = p^a e^c.$$

Integrating this expression,

$$\int_p^q \mu^{-b} \frac{\partial \mu}{\partial t} dt = e^c \int_p^q t^a dt$$

$$\frac{\mu^{1-b}}{1-b} \Big]_p^q = \frac{q^{a+1} - p^{a+1}}{a+1} e^c$$

for $b \neq 1$. Solving this equation yields

$$\frac{m^{1-b} - \mu(p; q, m)^{1-b}}{1-b} = \frac{q^{a+1} - p^{a+1}}{a+1} e^c,$$

or,

$$\mu(p; q, m) = \left[m^{1-b} + \frac{(b-1)}{(1+a)} e^c [q^{a+1} - p^{a+1}] \right]^{\frac{1}{1-b}}.$$

EXAMPLE: Integrability with several goods

We now consider a case where there are three goods and thus two independent demand equations. For definiteness consider the Cobb-Douglas system:

$$x_1 = \frac{a_1 m}{p_1}$$

$$x_2 = \frac{a_2 m}{p_2}$$

We verified earlier that this system satisfies Slutsky symmetry so that we know that the integrability equations will have a solution. We simply have to solve the following system of partial differential equations:

$$\frac{\partial \mu}{\partial p_1} = \frac{a_1 \mu}{p_1}$$

$$\frac{\partial \mu}{\partial p_2} = \frac{a_2 \mu}{p_2}$$

$$\mu(q_1, q_2; q_1, q_2, m) = m$$

The first equation implies that

$$\ln \mu = a_1 \ln p_1 + C_1$$

for some constant of integration C_1, and the second equation implies that

$$\ln \mu = a_2 \ln p_2 + C_2.$$

So it is natural to look for a solution of the form

$$\ln \mu = a_1 \ln p_1 + a_2 \ln p_2 + C_3,$$

where C_3 is independent of p_1 and p_2.

Substituting into the boundary condition, we have

$$\ln \mu(\mathbf{q}; \mathbf{q}, m) = \ln m = a_1 \ln q_1 + a_2 \ln q_2 + C_3.$$

Solving this equation for C_3 and substituting into the proposed solution, we have

$$\ln \mu(\mathbf{p}; \mathbf{q}, m) = a_1 \ln p_1 + a_2 \ln p_2 - a_1 \ln q_1 - a_2 \ln q_2 + \ln m.$$

which is indeed the money metric indirect utility function for the Cobb-Douglas utility function. See Chapter 7, page 111, for another derivation of this function.

8.6 Duality in consumption

We have seen how one can recover an indirect utility function from observed demand functions by solving the integrability equations. Here we see how to solve for the direct utility function.

The answer exhibits quite nicely the duality between direct and indirect utility functions. It is most convenient to describe the calculations in terms of the normalized indirect utility function, where we have prices divided by income so that expenditure is identically one. Thus the normalized indirect utility function is given by

$$v(\mathbf{p}) = \max_{\mathbf{x}} u(\mathbf{x})$$

such that $\mathbf{px} = 1$.

It turns out that if we are given the indirect utility function $v(\mathbf{p})$, we can find the direct utility function by solving the following problem:

$$u(\mathbf{x}) = \min_{\mathbf{p}} v(\mathbf{p})$$

such that $\mathbf{px} = 1$

The proof is not difficult, once you see what is going on. Let $\mathbf{x}$ be the demanded bundle at the prices $\mathbf{p}$. Then by definition $v(\mathbf{p}) = u(\mathbf{x})$. Let

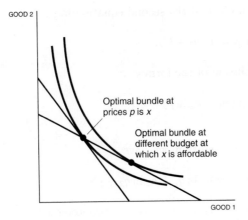

GOOD 2

Optimal bundle at
prices *p* is *x*

Optimal bundle at
different budget at
which *x* is affordable

GOOD 1

**Figure
8.5**

Solving for the direct utility function. The utility associated with the bundle **x** must be no larger than the utility that
can be achieved at any prices **p** at which **x** is affordable.

$\mathbf{p}'$ be any other price vector that satisfies the budget constraint so that
$\mathbf{p}'\mathbf{x} = 1$. Then since **x** is always a *feasible* choice at the prices $\mathbf{p}'$, due to
the form of the budget set, the utility-maximizing choice must yield utility
at least as great as the utility yielded by **x**; that is, $v(\mathbf{p}') \geq u(\mathbf{x}) = v(\mathbf{p})$.
Hence, the minimum of the indirect utility function over all **p**'s that satisfy
the budget constraint gives us the utility of **x**.

The argument is depicted in Figure 8.5. Any price vector **p** that satisfies
the budget constraint $\mathbf{px} = 1$ must yield a higher utility than $u(\mathbf{x})$, which
is simply to say that $u(\mathbf{x})$ solves the minimization problem posed above.

EXAMPLE: Solving for the direct utility function

Suppose that we have an indirect utility function given by $v(p_1, p_2) =
-a \ln p_1 - b \ln p_2$. What is its associated direct utility function? We set up
the minimization problem:

$$\min_{p_1, p_2} \quad -a \ln p_1 - b \ln p_2$$

$$\text{such that } p_1 x_1 + p_2 x_2 = 1.$$

The first-order conditions are

$$-a/p_1 = \lambda x_1$$
$$-b/p_2 = \lambda x_2,$$

or,

$$-a = \lambda p_1 x_1$$
$$-b = \lambda p_2 x_2.$$

Adding together and using the budget constraint yields

$$\lambda = -a - b.$$

Substitute back into the first-order conditions to find

$$p_1 = \frac{a}{(a+b)x_1}$$

$$p_2 = \frac{b}{(a+b)x_2}.$$

These are the choices of (p_1, p_2) that minimize indirect utility. Now substitute these choices into the indirect utility function:

$$u(x_1, x_2) = -a \ln \frac{a}{(a+b)x_1} - b \ln \frac{b}{(a+b)x_2}$$

$$= a \ln x_1 + b \ln x_2 + \text{constant}.$$

This is the familiar Cobb-Douglas utility function.

8.7 Revealed preference

In our study of consumer behavior we have taken preferences as the primitive concept and derived the restrictions that the utility maximization model imposes on the observed demand functions. These restrictions are basically the Slutsky restrictions that the matrix of substitution terms be symmetric and negative semidefinite.

These restrictions are in principle observable, but in practice they leave something to be desired. After all, who has really seen a demand function? The best that we may hope for in practice is a list of the choices made under different circumstances. For example, we may have some observations on consumer behavior that take the form of a list of prices, $\mathbf{p}^t$, and the associated chosen consumption bundles, $\mathbf{x}^t$ for $t = 1, \ldots, T$. How can we tell whether these data could have been generated by a utility-maximizing consumer?

We will say that a utility function **rationalizes** the observed behavior $(\mathbf{p}^t, \mathbf{x}^t)$ for $t = 1, \cdots, T$ if $u(\mathbf{x}^t) \geq u(\mathbf{x})$ for all $\mathbf{x}$ such that $\mathbf{p}^t \mathbf{x}^t \geq \mathbf{p}^t \mathbf{x}$. That is, $u(\mathbf{x})$ rationalizes the observed behavior if it achieves its maximum value on the budget set at the chosen bundles. Suppose that the data were generated by such a maximization process. What observable restrictions must the observed choices satisfy?

Without any assumptions about $u(\mathbf{x})$ there is a trivial answer to this question, namely, no restrictions. For suppose that $u(\mathbf{x})$ were a constant function, so that the consumer was indifferent to all observed consumption bundles. Then there would be no restrictions imposed on the patterns of observed choices: anything is possible.

To make the problem interesting, we have to rule out this trivial case. The easiest way to do this is to require the underlying utility function to be locally nonsatiated. Our question now becomes: what are the observable restrictions imposed by the maximization of a locally nonsatiated utility function?

First, we note that if $\mathbf{p}^t\mathbf{x}^t \geq \mathbf{p}^t\mathbf{x}$, then it must be the case that $u(\mathbf{x}^t) \geq u(\mathbf{x})$. Since $\mathbf{x}^t$ was chosen when $\mathbf{x}$ could have been chosen, the utility of $\mathbf{x}^t$ must be at least as large as the utility of $\mathbf{x}$. In this case we will say that $\mathbf{x}^t$ is **directly revealed preferred** to $\mathbf{x}$, and write $\mathbf{x}^t R^D \mathbf{x}$. As a consequence of this definition and the assumption that the data were generated by utility maximization, we can conclude that "$\mathbf{x}^t R^D \mathbf{x}$ implies $u(\mathbf{x}^t) \geq u(\mathbf{x})$."

Suppose that $\mathbf{p}^t\mathbf{x}^t > \mathbf{p}^t\mathbf{x}$. Does it follow that $u(\mathbf{x}^t) > u(\mathbf{x})$? It is not hard to show that local nonsatiation implies this conclusion. For we know from the previous paragraph that $u(\mathbf{x}^t) \geq u(\mathbf{x})$; if $u(\mathbf{x}^t) = u(\mathbf{x})$, then by local nonsatiation there would exist some other $\mathbf{x}'$ close enough to $\mathbf{x}$ so that $\mathbf{p}^t\mathbf{x}^t > \mathbf{p}^t\mathbf{x}'$ and $u(\mathbf{x}') > u(\mathbf{x}) = u(\mathbf{x}^t)$. This contradicts the hypothesis of utility maximization.

If $\mathbf{p}^t\mathbf{x}^t > \mathbf{p}^t\mathbf{x}$, we will say that $\mathbf{x}^t$ is **strictly directly revealed preferred** to $\mathbf{x}$ and write $\mathbf{x}^t P^D \mathbf{x}$.

Now suppose that we have a sequence of such revealed preference comparisons such that $\mathbf{x}^t R^D \mathbf{x}^j, \mathbf{x}^j R^D \mathbf{x}^k, \ldots, \mathbf{x}^n R^D \mathbf{x}$. In this case we will say that $\mathbf{x}^t$ is **revealed preferred** to $\mathbf{x}$ and write $\mathbf{x}^t R \mathbf{x}$. The relation R is sometimes called the **transitive closure** of the relation R^D. If we assume that the data were generated by utility maximization, it follows that "$\mathbf{x}^t R \mathbf{x}$ implies $u(\mathbf{x}^t) \geq u(\mathbf{x})$."

Consider two observations $\mathbf{x}^t$ and $\mathbf{x}^s$. We now have a way to determine whether $u(\mathbf{x}^t) \geq u(\mathbf{x}^s)$ and an observable condition to determine whether $u(\mathbf{x}^s) > u(\mathbf{x}^t)$. Obviously, these two conditions should not both be satisfied. This condition can be stated as the

GENERALIZED AXIOM OF REVEALED PREFERENCE. *If* $\mathbf{x}^t$ *is revealed preferred to* $\mathbf{x}^s$, *then* $\mathbf{x}^s$ *cannot be strictly directly revealed preferred to* $\mathbf{x}^t$.

Using the symbols defined above, we can also write this axiom as

GARP. $\mathbf{x}^t R \mathbf{x}^s$ *implies not* $\mathbf{x}^s P^D \mathbf{x}^t$. *In other words,* $\mathbf{x}^t R \mathbf{x}^s$ *implies* $\mathbf{p}^s\mathbf{x}^s \leq \mathbf{p}^s\mathbf{x}^t$.

As the name implies, GARP is a generalization of various other revealed preference tests. Here are two standard conditions.

WEAK AXIOM OF REVEALED PREFERENCE (WARP).   *If* $\mathbf{x}^t \; R^D \; \mathbf{x}^s$ *and* $\mathbf{x}^t$ *is not equal to* $\mathbf{x}^s$, *then it is not the case that* $\mathbf{x}^s \; R^D \; \mathbf{x}^t$.

STRONG AXIOM OF REVEALED PREFERENCE (SARP).   *If* $\mathbf{x}^t \; R \; \mathbf{x}^s$ *and* $\mathbf{x}^t$ *is not equal to* $\mathbf{x}^s$, *then it is not the case that* $\mathbf{x}^s \; R \; \mathbf{x}^t$.

Each of these axioms requires that there be a *unique* demand bundle at each budget, while GARP allows for multiple demanded bundles. Thus, GARP allows for flat spots in the indifference curves that generated the observed choices.

8.8 Sufficient conditions for maximization

If the data $(\mathbf{p}^t, \mathbf{x}^t)$ were generated by a utility-maximizing consumer with nonsatiated preferences, the data must satisfy GARP. Hence, GARP is an observable consequence of utility maximization. But does it express all the implications of that model? If some data satisfy this axiom, is it necessarily true that it must come from utility maximization, or at least be thought of in that way? Is GARP a *sufficient* condition for utility maximization?

It turns out that it is. If a finite set of data is consistent with GARP, then there exists a utility function that rationalizes the observed behavior—i.e., there exists a utility function that could have generated that behavior. Hence, GARP exhausts the list of restrictions imposed by the maximization model.

The following theorem is the nicest way to state this result.

Afriat's theorem.   *Let* $(\mathbf{p}^t, \mathbf{x}^t)$ *for* $t = 1, \ldots, T$ *be a finite number of observations of price vectors and consumption bundles. Then the following conditions are equivalent.*

(1) There exists a locally nonsatiated utility function that rationalizes the data;

(2) The data satisfy GARP;

(3) There exist positive numbers (u^t, λ^t) *for* $t = 1, \ldots, T$ *that satisfy the Afriat inequalities:*

$$u^s \leq u^t + \lambda^t \mathbf{p}^t (\mathbf{x}^s - \mathbf{x}^t) \quad \text{for all } t, s;$$

(4) There exists a locally nonsatiated, continuous, concave, monotonic utility function that rationalizes the data.

Proof. We have already seen that (1) implies (2). The proof that (2) implies (3) is omitted; see Varian (1982a) for the argument. The proof that (4) implies (1) is trivial. All that is left is the proof that (3) implies (4).

We establish this implication constructively by exhibiting a utility function that does the trick. Define

$$u(\mathbf{x}) = \min_t \{u^t + \lambda^t \mathbf{p}^t(\mathbf{x} - \mathbf{x}^t)\}.$$

Note that this function is continuous. As long as $\mathbf{p}^t \geq \mathbf{0}$ and no $\mathbf{p}^t = \mathbf{0}$, the function will be locally nonsatiated and monotonic. It is also not difficult to show that it is concave. Geometrically, this function is just the lower envelope of a finite number of hyperplanes.

We need to show that this function rationalizes the data; that is, when prices are $\mathbf{p}^t$, this utility function achieves its constrained maximum at $\mathbf{x}^t$. First we show that $u(\mathbf{x}^t) = u^t$. If this were not the case, we would have

$$u(\mathbf{x}^t) = u^m + \lambda^m \mathbf{p}^m (\mathbf{x}^t - \mathbf{x}^m) < u^t.$$

But this violates one of the Afriat inequalities. Hence, $u(\mathbf{x}^t) = u^t$.

Now suppose that $\mathbf{p}^s \mathbf{x}^s \geq \mathbf{p}^s \mathbf{x}$. It follows that

$$u(\mathbf{x}) = \min_t \{u^t + \lambda^t \mathbf{p}^t(\mathbf{x} - \mathbf{x}^t)\} \leq u^s + \lambda^s \mathbf{p}^s(\mathbf{x} - \mathbf{x}^s) \leq u^s = u(\mathbf{x}^s).$$

This shows that $u(\mathbf{x}^s) \geq u(\mathbf{x})$ for all $\mathbf{x}$ such that $\mathbf{p}^s \mathbf{x} \leq \mathbf{p}^s \mathbf{x}^s$. In other words, $u(\mathbf{x})$ rationalizes the observed choices. ∎

The utility function defined in the proof of Afriat's theorem has a natural interpretation. Suppose that $u(\mathbf{x})$ is a concave, differentiable utility function that rationalizes the observed choices. The fact that $u(\mathbf{x})$ is differentiable implies it must satisfy the T first-order conditions

$$\mathbf{D}u(\mathbf{x}^t) = \lambda^t \mathbf{p}^t. \tag{8.3}$$

The fact that $u(\mathbf{x})$ is concave implies that it must satisfy the concavity conditions

$$u(\mathbf{x}^t) \leq u(\mathbf{x}^s) + \mathbf{D}u(\mathbf{x}^s)(\mathbf{x}^t - \mathbf{x}^s). \tag{8.4}$$

Substituting from (8.3) into (8.4), we have

$$u(\mathbf{x}^t) \leq u(\mathbf{x}^s) + \lambda^s \mathbf{p}^s(\mathbf{x}^t - \mathbf{x}^s).$$

Hence, the Afriat numbers u^t and λ^t can be interpreted as utility levels and marginal utilities that are consistent with the observed choices.

The most remarkable implication of Afriat's theorem is that (1) implies (4): if there is any locally nonsatiated utility function at all that rationalizes the data, there must exist a continuous, monotonic, and concave utility function that rationalizes the data. This is similar to the observation made in Chapter 6, page 83, where we showed that if there were nonconvex parts of the input requirement set, no cost minimizer would ever choose to operate there.

The same is true for utility maximization. If the underlying utility function had the "wrong" curvature at some points, we would never observe choices being made at such points because they wouldn't satisfy the right second-order conditions. Hence market data do not allow us to reject the hypotheses of convexity and monotonicity of preferences.

8.9 Comparative statics using revealed preference

Since GARP is a necessary and sufficient condition for utility maximization, it must imply conditions analogous to comparative statics results derived earlier. These include the Slutsky decomposition of a price change into the income and the substitution effects and the fact that the own substitution effect is negative.

Let us begin with the latter result. When we consider finite changes in a price rather than just infinitesimal changes, there are two possible definitions of the compensated demand. The first definition is the natural extension of our earlier definition—namely, the demand for the good in question if we change the level of income so as to restore the original level of utility. That is, the value of the compensated demand for good i when prices change from $\mathbf{p}$ to $\mathbf{p} + \mathbf{\Delta p}$ is just $x_i(\mathbf{p} + \mathbf{\Delta p}, m + \Delta m) \equiv x_i(\mathbf{p} + \mathbf{\Delta p}, e(\mathbf{p} + \mathbf{\Delta p}, u))$, where u is the original level of utility achieved at $(\mathbf{p}, m)$. This notion of compensation is known as the **Hicksian compensation**.

The second notion of compensated demand when prices change from $\mathbf{p}$ to $\mathbf{p} + \mathbf{\Delta p}$ is known as the **Slutsky compensation**. It is the level of demand that arises when income is changed so as to make the original level of *consumption* possible. This is easily described by the following equations. We want the change in income, Δm, necessary to allow for the old level of consumption, $\mathbf{x}(\mathbf{p}, m)$, to be feasible at the new prices, $\mathbf{p} + \mathbf{\Delta p}$. That is

$$(\mathbf{p} + \mathbf{\Delta p})\mathbf{x}(\mathbf{p}, m) = m + \Delta m.$$

Since $\mathbf{p}\,\mathbf{x}(\mathbf{p}, m) = m$, this reduces to $\mathbf{\Delta p}\,\mathbf{x}(\mathbf{p}, m) = \Delta m$.

The difference between the two notions of compensation is illustrated in Figure 8.6. The Slutsky notion is directly measurable without knowledge of the preferences, but Hicksian notion is more convenient for analytic work.

For infinitesimal changes in price there is no need to distinguish between the two concepts since they coincide. We can prove this simply by examining the expenditure function. If the price of good j changes by dp_j, we need to change expenditure by $(\partial e(\mathbf{p}, u)/\partial p_j)dp_j$ to keep utility constant.

If we want to keep the old level of consumption feasible, we need to change income by $x_j dp_j$. By the derivative property of the expenditure function, these two magnitudes are the same.

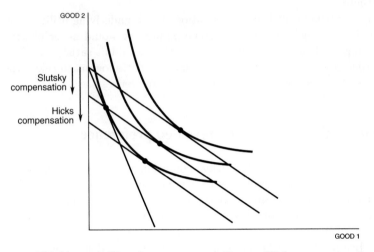

Figure 8.6   **Hicks and Slutsky compensation.** Hicks compensation is an amount of money that makes the original level of utility affordable. Slutsky compensation is an amount of money that makes the original consumption bundle achievable.

Whichever definition you prefer, we can still use revealed preference to prove that "the compensated own-price effect is negative." Suppose we consider the Hicksian definition. We start with a price vector $\mathbf{p}$ and let $\mathbf{x} = \mathbf{x}(\mathbf{p}, m)$ be the demanded bundle. The price vector changes to $\mathbf{p} + \boldsymbol{\Delta}\mathbf{p}$, and the compensated demand, therefore, changes to $\mathbf{x}(\mathbf{p} + \boldsymbol{\Delta}\mathbf{p}, m + \Delta m)$, where Δm is the amount necessary to make $\mathbf{x}(\mathbf{p} + \boldsymbol{\Delta}\mathbf{p}, m + \Delta m)$ indifferent to $\mathbf{x}(\mathbf{p}, m)$.

Since $\mathbf{x}(\mathbf{p}, m)$ and $\mathbf{x}(\mathbf{p} + \boldsymbol{\Delta}\mathbf{p}, m + \Delta m)$ are indifferent to each other, neither can be strictly directly revealed preferred to the other. That is, we must have

$$\mathbf{p}\,\mathbf{x}(\mathbf{p}, m) \le \mathbf{p}\,\mathbf{x}\,(\mathbf{p} + \boldsymbol{\Delta}\mathbf{p}, m + \Delta m)$$
$$(\mathbf{p} + \boldsymbol{\Delta}\mathbf{p})\mathbf{x}(\mathbf{p} + \boldsymbol{\Delta}\mathbf{p}, m + \Delta m) \le (\mathbf{p} + \boldsymbol{\Delta}\mathbf{p})\mathbf{x}(\mathbf{p}, m).$$

Adding these inequalities together, we have

$$\boldsymbol{\Delta}\mathbf{p}[\mathbf{x}(\mathbf{p} + \boldsymbol{\Delta}\mathbf{p}, m + \Delta m) - \mathbf{x}(\mathbf{p}, m)] \le 0.$$

Letting $\boldsymbol{\Delta}\mathbf{x} = \mathbf{x}(\mathbf{p} + \boldsymbol{\Delta}\mathbf{p}, m + \Delta m) - \mathbf{x}(\mathbf{p}, m)$, this becomes

$$\boldsymbol{\Delta}\mathbf{p}\,\boldsymbol{\Delta}\mathbf{x} \le 0.$$

Suppose that only one price has changed so that $\mathbf{\Delta p} = (0, \cdots, \Delta p_i, \cdots, 0)$. Then this inequality implies that x_i must change in the opposite direction.

We now turn to the Slutsky definition. We keep the same notation as before, but now interpret Δm as the change in income necessary to make the old consumption bundle affordable. Since $\mathbf{x}(\mathbf{p}, m)$ is thus by hypothesis a feasible level of consumption at $\mathbf{p} + \mathbf{\Delta p}$, the bundle actually chosen at $\mathbf{p} + \mathbf{\Delta p}$ cannot be revealed worse than $\mathbf{x}(\mathbf{p}, m)$. That is,

$$\mathbf{p} \, \mathbf{x}(\mathbf{p}, m) \le \mathbf{p} \, \mathbf{x}(\mathbf{p} + \mathbf{\Delta p}, m + \Delta m).$$

Since $(\mathbf{p} + \mathbf{\Delta p})\mathbf{x}(\mathbf{p} + \mathbf{\Delta p}, m + \Delta m) = (\mathbf{p} + \mathbf{\Delta p})\mathbf{x}(\mathbf{p}, m)$ by construction of Δm, we can subtract this equality from the above inequality to find

$$\mathbf{\Delta p} \, \mathbf{\Delta x} \le 0,$$

just as before.

8.10 The discrete version of the Slutsky equation

We turn now to the task of deriving the Slutsky equation. We derived this equation earlier by differentiating an identity involving Hicksian and Marshallian demands. We start by writing the following arithmetic identity:

$$x_i(\mathbf{p} + \mathbf{\Delta p}, m) - x_i(\mathbf{p}, m) = x_i(\mathbf{p} + \mathbf{\Delta p}, m + \Delta m) - x_i(\mathbf{p}, m)$$
$$- [x_i(\mathbf{p} + \mathbf{\Delta p}, m + \Delta m) - x_i(\mathbf{p} + \mathbf{\Delta p}, m)].$$

Note that this is true by the ordinary rule of algebra.

Suppose that $\mathbf{\Delta p} = (0, \cdots, \Delta p_j, \cdots, 0)$. Then the compensating change in income—in the Slutsky sense—is $\Delta m = x_j(\mathbf{p}, m)\Delta p_j$. If we divide each side of the above identity by Δp_j and use the fact that $\Delta p_j = \Delta m / x_j(\mathbf{p}, m)$, we have

$$\frac{x_i(\mathbf{p} + \mathbf{\Delta p}, m) - x_i(\mathbf{p}, m)}{\Delta p_j} = \frac{x_i(\mathbf{p} + \mathbf{\Delta p}, m + \Delta m) - x_i(\mathbf{p}, m)}{\Delta p_j}$$
$$- x_j(\mathbf{p}, m)\frac{[x_i(\mathbf{p} + \mathbf{\Delta p}, m + \Delta m) - x_i(\mathbf{p} + \mathbf{\Delta p}, m)]}{\Delta m}.$$

Interpreting each of the terms in this expression, we can write

$$\frac{\Delta x_i}{\Delta p_j} = \frac{\Delta x_i}{\Delta p_j}\bigg|_{\text{comp}} - x_j\frac{\Delta x_i}{\Delta m}.$$

Note that this last equation is simply a discrete analog of the Slutsky equation. The term on the left-hand side is how the demand for good i changes as price j changes. This is decomposed into the substitution effect—how the demand for good i changes when price j changes and income is also changed so as to keep the original level of consumption possible—and the income effect—how the demand for good i changes when prices are held constant but income changes times the demand for good j. The Slutsky decomposition of a price change is illustrated in Figure 8.7.

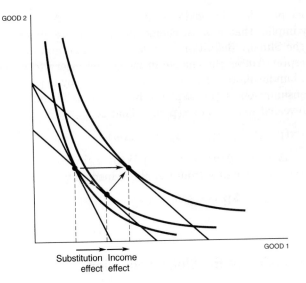

GOOD 2

Substitution Income
effect effect

GOOD 1

**Figure
8.7**

Slutsky decomposition of a price change. First pivot the
budget line around the original consumption bundle and then
shift it out to the final choice.

8.11 Recoverability

Since the revealed preference conditions are a complete set of the restrictions imposed by utility-maximizing behavior, they must contain all of the
information available about the underlying preferences. It is more-or-less
obvious how to use the revealed preference relations to determine the preferences among the *observed* choices, $\mathbf{x}^t$, for $t = 1, \ldots, T$. However, it is less
obvious to use the revealed preference relations to tell you about preference
relations between choices that have never been observed.

This is easiest to see using an example. Figure 8.8 depicts a a single
observation of choice behavior, $(\mathbf{p}^1, \mathbf{x}^1)$. What does this choice imply about
the indifference curve through a bundle $\mathbf{x}^0$? Note that $\mathbf{x}^0$ has not been
previously observed; in particular, we have no data about the prices at
which $\mathbf{x}^0$ would be an optimal choice.

Let's try to use revealed preference to "bound" the indifference curve
through $\mathbf{x}^0$. First, we observe that $\mathbf{x}^1$ is revealed preferred to $\mathbf{x}^0$. Assume
that preferences are convex and monotonic. Then all the bundles on the
line segment connecting $\mathbf{x}^0$ and $\mathbf{x}^1$ must be at least as good as x^0, and all
the bundles that lie to the northeast of this bundle are at least as good
as $\mathbf{x}^0$. Call this set of bundles $RP(x^0)$, for "revealed preferred" to $\mathbf{x}^0$. It
is not difficult to show that this is the best "inner bound" to the upper
contour set through the point $\mathbf{x}^0$.

To derive the best outer bound, we must consider all possible budget lines

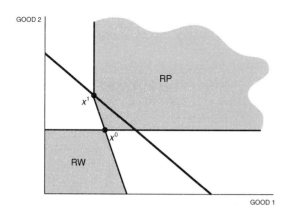

GOOD 2

RP

x^1

x^0

RW

GOOD 1

Figure 8.8

Inner and outer bounds. RP is the inner bound to the indifference curve through $\mathbf{x}^0$; the complement of RW is the outer bound.

passing through $\mathbf{x}^0$. Let RW be the set of all bundles that are revealed worse than $\mathbf{x}^0$ for *all* these budget lines. The bundles in RW are certain to be worse than $\mathbf{x}^0$ no matter what budget line is used.

The outer bound to the upper contour set at $\mathbf{x}^0$ is then defined to be the complement of this set: $NRW = $ all bundles not in RW. This is the best outer bound in the sense that any bundle not in this set cannot ever be revealed preferred to $\mathbf{x}^0$ by a consistent utility-maximizing consumer. Why? Because by construction, a bundle that is not in $NRW(\mathbf{x}^0)$ must be in $RW(\mathbf{x}^0)$ in which case it would be revealed *worse* than $\mathbf{x}^0$.

In the case of a single observed choice, the bounds are not very tight. But with many choices, the bounds can become quite close together, effectively trapping the true indifference curve between them. See Figure 8.9 for an illustrative example. It is worth tracing through the construction of these bounds to make sure that you understand where they come from. Once we have constructed the inner and outer bounds for the upper contour sets, we have recovered essentially all the information about preferences that is contained in the observed demand behavior. Hence, the construction of RP and RW is analogous to solving the integrability equations.

Our construction of RP and RW up until this point has been graphical. However, it is possible to generalize this analysis to multiple goods. It turns out that determining whether one bundle is revealed preferred or revealed worse than another involves checking to see whether a solution exists to a particular set of linear inequalities.

Notes

The dual proof of the Slutsky equation given here follows McKenzie (1957) and Cook (1972).   A detailed treatment of integrability may be found

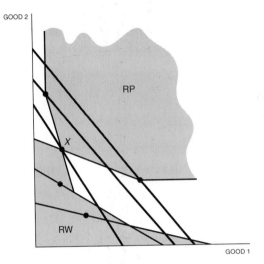

GOOD 2

RP

X

RW

GOOD 1

Figure
8.9 **Inner and outer bounds.** When there are several observations, the inner and outer bounds can be quite tight.

in Hurwicz & Uzawa (1971). The idea of revealed preferences is due to
Samuelson (1948). The approach taken here follows that of Afriat (1967)
and Varian (1982a). The derivation of the Slutsky equation using revealed
preference follows Yokoyama (1968).

Exercises

8.1. Frank Fisher's expenditure function is $e(\mathbf{p}, u)$. His demand function
for jokes is $x_j(\mathbf{p}, m)$, where $\mathbf{p}$ is vector of prices and $m \gg 0$ is his income.
Show that jokes are a normal good for Frank if and only if $\partial^2 e / \partial p_j \partial u > 0$.

8.2. Calculate the substitution matrix for the Cobb-Douglas demand system
with two goods. Verify that the diagonal terms are negative and the cross-
price effects are symmetric.

8.3. Suppose that a consumer has a linear demand function $x = ap + bm + c$.
Write down the differential equation you would need to solve to find the
money metric utility function. If you can, solve this differential equation.

8.4. Suppose that a consumer has a semi-log demand function $\ln x = ap +
bm + c$. Write down the differential equation you would need to solve to
find the money metric utility function. If you can, solve this differential
equation.

8.5. Find the demanded bundle for a consumer whose utility function is $u(x_1, x_2) = x_1^{\frac{3}{2}} x_2$ and her budget constraint is $3x_1 + 4x_2 = 100$.

8.6. Use the utility function $u(x_1, x_2) = x_1^{\frac{1}{2}} x_2^{\frac{1}{3}}$ and the budget constraint $m = p_1 x_1 + p_2 x_2$ to calculate $\mathbf{x}(\mathbf{p}, m)$, $v(\mathbf{p}, m)$, $\mathbf{h}(\mathbf{p}, u)$ and $e(\mathbf{p}, u)$.

8.7. Extend the previous exercise to the case where $u(x_1, x_2) = (x_1 - \alpha_1)^{\beta_1} (x_2 - \alpha_2)^{\beta_2}$ and check the symmetry of the matrix of substitution terms $\left(\dfrac{\partial h_j(\mathbf{p}, u)}{\partial p_i} \right)$.

8.8. Repeat the previous exercise using $u^*(x_1, x_2) = \frac{1}{2} \ln x_1 + \frac{1}{3} \ln x_2$ and show that all the previous formulae hold provided u is replaced by e^{u^*}.

8.9. Preferences are represented by $u = \phi(\mathbf{x})$ and a expenditure function, indirect utility function and demands are calculated. If the same preferences are now represented by $u^* = \psi(\phi(\mathbf{x}))$ for a monotone increasing function $\psi(\cdot)$, show that $e(\mathbf{p}, u)$ is replaced by $e(\mathbf{p}, \psi^{-1}(u^*))$, $v(\mathbf{p}, m)$ by $\psi(v(\mathbf{p}, m))$, and $\mathbf{h}(\mathbf{p}, u)$ by $\mathbf{h}(\mathbf{p}, \psi^{-1}(u^*))$. Also, check that the Marshallian demands $\mathbf{x}(\mathbf{p}, m)$ are unaffected.

8.10. Consider a two-period model with Dave's utility given by $u(x_1, x_2)$ where x_1 represents his consumption during the first period and x_2 is his second period's consumption. Dave is endowed with $(\bar{x}_1, \bar{x}_2)$ which he could consume in each period, but he could also trade present consumption for future consumption and vice versa. Thus, his budget constraint is

$$p_1 x_1 + p_2 x_2 = p_1 \bar{x}_1 + p_2 \bar{x}_2,$$

where p_1 and p_2 are the first and second period prices respectively.

(a) Derive the Slutsky equation in this model. (Note that now Dave's income depends on the value of his endowment which, in turn, depends on prices: $m = p_1 \bar{x}_1 + p_2 \bar{x}_2$.)

(b) Assume that Dave's optimal choice is such that $x_1 < \bar{x}_1$. If p_1 goes down, will Dave be better off or worse off? What if p_2 goes down?

(c) What is the rate of return on the consumption good?

8.11. Consider a consumer who is demanding goods 1 and 2. When the price of the goods are $(2, 4)$, he demands $(1, 2)$. When the prices are $(6, 3)$, he demands $(2, 1)$. Nothing else of significance changed. Is this consumer maximizing utility?

8.12. Suppose that the indirect utility function takes the form $v(p, y) = f(p)y$. What is the form of the expenditure function? What is the form of the indirect compensation function, $\mu(p; q, y)$ in terms of the function $f(\cdot)$ and y?

8.13. The utility function is $u(x_1, x_2) = \min\{x_2 + 2x_1, x_1 + 2x_2\}$.

(a) Draw the indifference curve for $u(x_1, x_2) = 20$. Shade the area where $u(x_1, x_2) \geq 20$.

(b) For what values of p_1/p_2 will the unique optimum be $x_1 = 0$?

(c) For what values of p_1/p_2 will the unique optimum $x_2 = 0$?

(d) If neither x_1 nor x_2 is equal to zero, and the optimum is unique, what must be the value of x_1/x_2?

8.14. Under current tax law some individuals can save up to $2,000 a year in an Individual Retirement Account (I.R.A.), a savings vehicle that has an especially favorable tax treatment. Consider an individual at a specific point in time who has income Y, which he or she wants to spend on consumption, C, I.R.A. savings, S_1, or ordinary savings S_2. Suppose that the "reduced form" utility function is taken to be:

$$U(C, S_1, S_2) = S_1^\alpha S_2^\beta C^\gamma.$$

(This is a reduced form since the parameters are not truly exogenous taste parameters, but also include the tax treatment of the assets, etc.) The budget constraint of the consumer is given by:

$$C + S_1 + S_2 = Y,$$

and the limit that he or she can contribute to the I.R.A. is denoted by L.

(a) Derive the demand functions for S_1 and S_2 for a consumer for whom the limit L is *not* binding.

(b) Derive the demand function for S_1 and S_2 for a consumer for whom the limit L *is* binding.

8.15. If leisure is an inferior good, what is the slope of the supply function of labor?

8.16. A utility-maximizing consumer has strictly convex, strictly monotonic preferences and consumes two goods, x_1 and x_2, each of which has a price of 1. He cannot consume negative amounts of either good. The consumer has an income of m every year. His current level of consumption is (x_1^*, x_2^*), where $x_1^* > 0$ and $x_2^* > 0$. Suppose that next year he will be given a grant of $g_1 \leq x_1^*$ which must be spent entirely on good 1. (If he wishes, he can refuse to accept the grant.)

(a) True or False? If good 1 is a normal good, then the effect of the grant on his consumption must be the same as the effect of an unconstrained lump sum grant of an equal amount. If this is true, prove it. If this is false, prove that it is false.

(b) True or False? If good 1 is an inferior good for the above consumer at all incomes $m > x_1^* + x_2^*$, then if he is given a grant of g_1 which must be spent on good 1, the effect must be the same as an unconstrained grant of an equal amount. If this is true, prove it. If this is false, show what he will do if he is given the grant.

(c) Suppose that the consumer discussed above has homothetic preferences and is currently consuming $x_1^* = 12$ and $x_2^* = 36$. Draw a graph with g_1 on the horizontal axis and the amount of good 1 on the vertical axis. Use this graph to show the amount of good 1 that the consumer will demand if his ordinary income is $m = 48$ and if he is given a grant of g_1 which must be spent on good 1. At what level of g_1 will this graph have a kink? (Think for a minute before you answer this. Give a numerical answer.)

CHAPTER **9**

DEMAND

In this chapter we investigate several topics in demand behavior. Most of these have to do with special forms of the budget constraint or preferences that lead to special forms of demand behavior. There are many circumstances where such special cases are very convenient for analysis, and it is useful to understand how they work.

9.1 Endowments in the budget constraint

In our study of consumer behavior we have taken income to be exogenous. But in more elaborate models of consumer behavior it is necessary to consider how income is generated. The standard way to do this is to think of the consumer as having some **endowment** $\boldsymbol{\omega} = (\omega_1, \ldots, \omega_k)$ of various goods which can be sold at the current market prices $\mathbf{p}$. This gives the consumer income $m = \mathbf{p}\boldsymbol{\omega}$ which can be used to purchase other goods.

The utility maximization problem becomes

$$\max_{\mathbf{x}} u(\mathbf{x})$$

such that $\mathbf{px} = \mathbf{p}\boldsymbol{\omega}$.

This can be solved by the standard techniques to find a demand function $\mathbf{x}(\mathbf{p}, \mathbf{p\omega})$. The **net demand** for good i is $x_i - \omega_i$. The consumer may have positive or negative net demands depending on whether he wants more or less of something than is available in his endowment.

In this model prices influence the value of what the consumer has to sell as well as the value of what the consumer wants to sell. This shows up most clearly in Slutsky's equation, which we now derive. First, differentiate demand with respect to price:

$$\frac{dx_i(\mathbf{p}, \mathbf{p\omega})}{dp_j} = \left.\frac{\partial x_i(\mathbf{p}, \mathbf{p\omega})}{\partial p_j}\right|_{\mathbf{p\omega}=\text{constant}} + \frac{\partial x_i(\mathbf{p}, \mathbf{p\omega})}{\partial m}\omega_j.$$

The first term in the right-hand side of this expression is the derivative of demand with respect to price, holding income fixed. The second term is the derivative of demand with respect to income, times the change in income. The first term can be expanded using Slutsky's equation. Collecting terms we have

$$\frac{dx_i(\mathbf{p}, \mathbf{p\omega})}{dp_j} = \frac{\partial h_i(\mathbf{p}, u)}{\partial p_j} + \frac{\partial x_i(\mathbf{p}, \mathbf{p\omega})}{\partial m}(\omega_j - x_j).$$

Now the income effect depends on the net demand for good j rather than the gross demand.

Think about the case of a normal good. When the price of the good goes up, the substitution effect and the income effect both push towards reduced consumption. But suppose that this consumer is a net seller of this good. Then his actual income increases and this additional **endowment income effect** may actually lead to an increase in consumption of the good.

Labor supply

Suppose that a consumer chooses two goods, consumption and labor. She also has some nonlabor income m. Let $v(c, \ell)$ be the utility of consumption and labor and write the utility maximization problem as

$$\max_{c,\ell} v(c, \ell)$$

such that $pc = w\ell + m$.

This problem looks a bit different than the problems we have been studying: labor is probably a "bad" rather than a good, and labor appears on the right-hand side of the budget constraint.

However, it is not too hard to change it into a problem that has the standard form that we have been working with. Let $\overline{L}$ be the maximum number of hours that the consumer can work and think of $L = \overline{L} - \ell$ as being "leisure." The utility function for consumption and leisure is

$u(c, \overline{L} - \ell) = v(c, \ell)$. Using this we can rewrite the utility maximization problem as

$$\max_{c,\ell} u(c, \overline{L} - \ell)$$

such that $pc + w(\overline{L} - \ell) = w\overline{L} + m.$

Or, using the definition $L = \overline{L} - \ell$, we write

$$\max_{c,L} u(c, L)$$

such that $pc + wL = w\overline{L} + m.$

This is essentially the same form that we have seen before. Here the consumer "sells" her endowment of labor at the price w and then buys some back as leisure.

Slutsky's equation allows us to calculate how the demand for leisure changes as the wage rate changes. We have

$$\frac{dL(p, w, m)}{dw} = \frac{\partial L(p, w, u)}{\partial w} + \frac{\partial L(p, w, m)}{\partial m}[\overline{L} - L].$$

Note that the term in brackets is nonnegative by definition, and almost surely positive in practice.[1] This means that the derivative of leisure demand is the sum of a negative number and a positive number and is inherently ambiguous in sign. In other words, an increase in the wage rate can lead to either an increase or a decrease in labor supply.

Essentially an increase in the wage rate tends to increase the supply of labor since it makes leisure more expensive—you can get more consumption by working more. But, at the same time, the increase in the wage rate makes you potentially richer, and this presumably increases your demand for leisure.

9.2 Homothetic utility functions

A function $f: R^n \to R$ is **homogeneous of degree 1** if $f(t\mathbf{x}) = tf(\mathbf{x})$ for all $t > 0$. A function $f(\mathbf{x})$ is **homothetic** if $f(\mathbf{x}) = g(h(\mathbf{x}))$ where g is a strictly increasing function and h is a function which is homogeneous of degree 1. See Chapter 26, page 482, for further discussion of the mathematical properties of such functions.

Economists often find it useful to assume that utility functions are homogeneous or homothetic. In fact, there is little distinction between the two concepts in utility theory. A homothetic function is simply a monotonic transformation of a homogeneous function, but utility functions are only

---

[1] Except, possibly, at final exam time.

defined up to a monotonic transformation. Thus assuming that preferences can be represented by a homothetic function is equivalent to assuming that they can be represented by a function that is homogeneous of degree 1. If a consumer has preferences that can be represented by a homothetic utility function, economists say that the consumer has **homothetic preferences**.

We saw in our discussion of production theory that if a production function was homogeneous of degree 1, then the cost function could be written as $c(\mathbf{w}, y) = c(\mathbf{w})y$. It follows from this observation that if the utility function is homogeneous of degree 1, then the expenditure function can be written as $e(\mathbf{p}, u) = e(\mathbf{p})u$.

This in turn implies that the indirect utility function can be written as $v(\mathbf{p}, m) = v(\mathbf{p})m$. Roy's identity then implies that the demand functions take the form $x_i(\mathbf{p}, m) = x_i(\mathbf{p})m$—i.e., they are linear functions of income. The fact that the "income effects" take this special form is often useful in demand analysis, as we will see below.

9.3 Aggregating across goods

In many circumstances it is reasonable to model consumer choice by certain "partial" maximization problems. For example, we may want to model the consumer's choice of "meat" without distinguishing how much is beef, pork, lamb, etc. In most empirical work, some kind of aggregation of this sort is necessary.

In order to describe some useful results concerning this kind of separability of consumption decisions, we will have to introduce some new notation. Let us think of partitioning the consumption bundle into two "subbundles" so that the consumption bundle takes the form $(\mathbf{x}, \mathbf{z})$. For example, $\mathbf{x}$ could be the vector of consumptions of different kinds of meat, and $\mathbf{z}$ could be the vector of consumptions of all other goods.

We partition the price vector analogously into $(\mathbf{p}, \mathbf{q})$. Here $\mathbf{p}$ is the price vector for the different kinds of meat, and $\mathbf{q}$ is the price vector for the other goods. With this notation the standard utility maximization problem can be written as

$$\max_{\mathbf{x}, \mathbf{z}} u(\mathbf{x}, \mathbf{z}) \tag{9.1}$$

$$\text{such that } \mathbf{px} + \mathbf{qz} = m.$$

The problem of interest is under what conditions we can study the demand problem for the x-goods, say, as a group, without worrying about how demand is divided among the various components of the x-goods.

One way to formulate this problem mathematically is as follows. We would like to be able to construct some scalar **quantity index**, X, and some scalar **price index**, P, that are functions of the vector of quantities and the vector of prices:

$$P = f(\mathbf{p})$$
$$X = g(\mathbf{x}). \tag{9.2}$$

In this expression P is supposed to be some kind of "price index" which gives the "average price" of the goods, while X is supposed to be a quantity index that gives the average "amount" of meat consumed. Our hope is that we can find a way to construct these price and quantity indices so that they behave like ordinary prices and quantities.

That is, we hope to find a new utility function $U(X, \mathbf{z})$, which depends only on the quantity index of x-consumption, that will give us the same answer as if we solved the entire maximization problem in (9.1). More formally, consider the problem

$$\max_{X, \mathbf{z}} U(X, \mathbf{z})$$

$$\text{such that } PX + \mathbf{qz} = m.$$

The demand function for the quantity index X will be some function $X(P, \mathbf{q}, m)$. We want to know when it will be the case that

$$X(P, \mathbf{q}, m) \equiv X(f(\mathbf{p}), \mathbf{q}, m) = g(\mathbf{x}(\mathbf{p}, \mathbf{q}, m)).$$

This requires that we get to the same value of X via two different routes:

1) first aggregate prices using $P = f(\mathbf{p})$ and then maximize $U(X, \mathbf{z})$ subject to the budget constraint $PX + \mathbf{qz} = m$.

2) first maximize $u(\mathbf{x}, \mathbf{z})$ subject to $\mathbf{px} + \mathbf{qz} = m$ and then aggregate quantities to get $X = g(\mathbf{x})$.

As it happens there are two situations under which this kind of aggregation is possible. The first situation, which imposes constraints on the price movements, is known as **Hicksian separability**. The second, which imposes constraints on the structure of preferences, is known as **functional separability**.

Hicksian separability

Suppose that the price vector $\mathbf{p}$ is always proportional to some fixed base price vector $\mathbf{p}^0$ so that $\mathbf{p} = t\mathbf{p}^0$ for some scalar t. If the x-goods are various kinds of meat, this condition requires that the relative prices of the various kinds of meat remain constant—they all increase and decrease in the same proportion.

Following the general framework described above, let us define the price and quantity indices for the x-goods by

$$P = t$$

$$X = \mathbf{p}^0 \mathbf{x}.$$

We define the *indirect* utility function associated with these indices as

$$V(P, \mathbf{q}, m) = \max_{\mathbf{x}, \mathbf{z}} u(\mathbf{x}, \mathbf{z})$$

$$\text{such that } P\mathbf{p}^0\mathbf{x} + \mathbf{q}\mathbf{z} = m.$$

It is straightforward to check that this indirect utility function has all the usual properties: it is quasiconvex, homogeneous in price and income, etc. In particular, a straightforward application of the envelope theorem shows that we can recover the demand function for the x-good by Roy's identity:

$$X(P, \mathbf{q}, m) = -\frac{\partial V(P, \mathbf{q}, m)/\partial P}{\partial V(P, \mathbf{q}, m)/\partial m} = \mathbf{p}^0\mathbf{x}(\mathbf{p}, \mathbf{q}, m).$$

This calculation shows that $X(P, \mathbf{q}, m)$ is an appropriate quantity index for the x-goods consumption: we get the same result if we first aggregate prices and then maximize $U(X, \mathbf{z})$ as we get if we maximize $u(\mathbf{x}, \mathbf{z})$ and then aggregate quantities.

We can solve for the direct utility function that is dual to $V(P, \mathbf{q}, m)$ by the usual calculation:

$$U(X, \mathbf{z}) = \min_{P, \mathbf{q}} V(P, \mathbf{q}, m)$$

$$\text{such that } PX + \mathbf{q}\mathbf{z} = m.$$

By construction this direct utility function has the property that

$$V(P, \mathbf{q}, m) = \max_{X, \mathbf{z}} U(X, \mathbf{z})$$

$$\text{such that } PX + \mathbf{q}\mathbf{z} = m.$$

Hence, the price and quantity indices constructed this way behave just like ordinary prices and quantities.

The two-good model

One common application of Hicksian aggregation is when we are studying the demand for a single good. In this case, think of the z-goods as being a single good, z, and the x-goods as "all other goods." The actual maximization problem is then

$$\max_{\mathbf{x}, z} u(\mathbf{x}, z)$$

$$\text{such that } \mathbf{p}\mathbf{x} + qz = m.$$

Suppose that the relative prices of the x-goods remains constant, so that $\mathbf{p} = P\mathbf{p}^0$. That is the vector of prices $\mathbf{p}$ is some base price vector $\mathbf{p}^0$ times some price index P. Then Hicksian aggregation says that we can write the demand function for the z-good as

$$z = z(P, q, m).$$

Since this demand function is homogeneous of degree zero, with some abuse of notation, we can also write

$$z = z(q/P, m/P).$$

This says that the demand for the z-good depends on the relative price of the z-good to "all other goods" and income, divided by the price of "all other goods." In practice, the price index for all other goods is usually taken to be some standard consumer price index. The demand for the z-good becomes a function of only two variables: the price of the z-good relative to the CPI and income relative to the CPI.

Functional separability

The second case in which we can decompose the consumer's consumption decision is known as the case of **functional separability**. Let us suppose that the underlying preference ordering has the property that

$$(\mathbf{x}, \mathbf{z}) \succ (\mathbf{x}', \mathbf{z}) \text{ if and only if } (\mathbf{x}, \mathbf{z}') \succ (\mathbf{x}', \mathbf{z}')$$

for all consumption bundles $\mathbf{x}$, $\mathbf{x}'$, $\mathbf{z}$ and $\mathbf{z}'$. This condition says that if $\mathbf{x}$ is preferred to $\mathbf{x}'$ for some choices of the other goods, then $\mathbf{x}$ is preferred to $\mathbf{x}'$ for all choices of the other goods. Or, even more succinctly, the preferences over the x-goods are independent of the z-goods.

If this "independence" property is satisfied and the preferences are locally nonsatiated, then it can be shown that the utility function for $\mathbf{x}$ and $\mathbf{z}$ can be written in the form $u(\mathbf{x}, \mathbf{z}) = U(v(\mathbf{x}), \mathbf{z})$, where $U(v, \mathbf{z})$ is an increasing function of v. That is, the overall utility from $\mathbf{x}$ and $\mathbf{z}$ can be written as a function of the **subutility** of $\mathbf{x}$, $v(\mathbf{x})$, and the level of consumption of the z-goods.

If the utility function can be written in this form, we will say that the utility function is **weakly separable**. What does separability imply about the structure of the utility maximization problem? As usual, we will write the demand function for the goods as $\mathbf{x}(\mathbf{p}, \mathbf{q}, m)$ and $\mathbf{z}(\mathbf{p}, \mathbf{q}, m)$. Let $m_x = \mathbf{px}(\mathbf{p}, \mathbf{q}, m)$ be the optimal expenditure on the x-goods.

It turns out that if the overall utility function is weakly separable, the optimal choice of the x-goods can be found by solving the following subutility maximization problem:

$$\max v(\mathbf{x})$$
$$\text{such that } \mathbf{px} = m_x \tag{9.3}$$

This means that if we know the *expenditure* on the x-goods, $m_x = \mathbf{px}(\mathbf{p}, \mathbf{q}, m)$, we can solve the subutility maximization problem to determine the optimal choice of the x-goods. In other words, the demand for the x-goods is only a function of the prices of the x-goods and the expenditure on the x-goods m_x. The prices of the *other* goods are only relevant insofar as they determine the expenditure on the x-goods.

The proof of this is straightforward. Assume that $\mathbf{x}(\mathbf{p}, \mathbf{q}, m)$ does not solve the above problem. Instead, let $\mathbf{x}'$ be another value of $\mathbf{x}$ that satisfies the budget constraint and yields strictly greater subutility. Then the bundle $(\mathbf{x}', \mathbf{z})$ would give higher overall utility than $(\mathbf{x}(\mathbf{p}, \mathbf{q}, m), \mathbf{z}(\mathbf{p}, \mathbf{q}, m))$, which contradicts the definition of the demand function.

The demand functions $\mathbf{x}(\mathbf{p}, m_x)$ are sometimes known as **conditional demand functions** since they give demand for the x-goods conditional on the level of expenditure on these goods. Thus, for example, we may consider the demand for beef as a function of the prices of beef, pork, and lamb and the total expenditure on meat.

Let $e(\mathbf{p}, v)$ be the expenditure function for the subutility maximization problem given in (9.3). This tells us how much expenditure on the x-goods is necessary at prices $\mathbf{p}$ to achieve the subutility v.

It is not hard to see that we can write the overall maximization problem of the consumer as

$$\max_{v, \mathbf{z}} U(v, \mathbf{z})$$

such that $e(\mathbf{p}, v) + \mathbf{qz} = m$.

This is almost in the form we want: v is a suitable quantity index for the x-goods, but the price index for the x-goods isn't quite right. We want P times X, but we have some nonlinear function of $\mathbf{p}$ and $X = v$.

In order to have a budget constraint that is linear in quantity index, we need to assume that subutility function has a special structure. For example, suppose that the subutility function is homothetic. Then we know from Chapter 5, page 66, that we can write $e(\mathbf{p}, v)$ as $e(\mathbf{p})v$. Hence, we can choose our quantity index to be $X = v(\mathbf{x})$, our price index to be $P = e(\mathbf{p})$, and our utility function to be $U(X, \mathbf{z})$. We get the same X if we solve

$$\max_{X, \mathbf{z}} U(X, \mathbf{z})$$

such that $PX + \mathbf{qz} = m$

as if we solve

$$\max_{\mathbf{x}, \mathbf{z}} u(v(\mathbf{x}), \mathbf{z})$$

such that $\mathbf{px} + \mathbf{qz} = m$,

and then aggregate using $X = v(\mathbf{x})$.

In this formulation we can think of the consumption decision as taking place in two stages: first the consumer considers how much of the composite commodity (e.g., meat) to consume as a function of a price index of meat by solving the overall maximization problem; then the consumer considers how much beef to consume given the prices of the various sorts of meat and the total expenditure on meat, which is the solution to the subutility maximization problem. Such a two-stage budgeting process is very convenient in applied demand analysis.

9.4 Aggregating across consumers

We have studied the properties of a consumer's demand function, $\mathbf{x}(\mathbf{p}, m)$. Now let us consider some collection of $i = 1, \ldots, n$ consumers, each of whom has a demand function for some k commodities, so that consumer i's demand function is a vector $\mathbf{x}_i(\mathbf{p}, m_i) = (x_i^1(\mathbf{p}, m_i), \cdots, x_i^k(\mathbf{p}, m_i))$ for $i = 1, \cdots, n$. Note that we have changed our notation slightly: goods are now indicated by superscripts while consumers are indicated by subscripts. The aggregate demand function is defined by $\mathbf{X}(\mathbf{p}, m_1, \cdots, m_n) = \sum_{i=1}^n \mathbf{x}_i(\mathbf{p}, m_i)$. The aggregate demand for good j is denoted by $X^j(\mathbf{p}, \mathbf{m})$ where $\mathbf{m}$ denotes the vector of incomes $(m_1, \cdots, m_n)$.

The aggregate demand function inherits certain properties of the individual demand functions. For example, if the individual demand functions are continuous, the aggregate demand function will certainly be continuous.

Continuity of the individual demand functions is a sufficient but not necessary condition for continuity of the aggregate demand functions. For example, consider the demand for washing machines. It seems reasonable to suppose that most consumers want one and only one washing machine. Hence, the demand function for an individual consumer i would look like the function depicted in Figure 9.1.

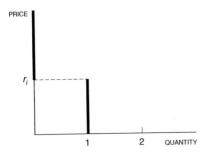

Figure 9.1   **Demand for a discrete commodity.** At any price greater than r_i, consumer i demands zero of the good. If the price is less than or equal to r_i, consumer i will demand one unit of the good.

The price r_i is called the ith consumer's **reservation price**. If consumers' incomes and tastes vary, we would expect to see several different reservation prices. The aggregate demand for washing machines is given by $X(p) =$ number of consumers whose reservation price is at least p. If there are a lot of consumers with dispersed reservation prices, it would make sense to think of this as a continuous function: if the price goes up by a small amount, only a few of the consumers—the "marginal" consumers—will decide to stop buying the good. Even though their demand changes discontinuously, the *aggregate* demand will change only by a small amount.

What other properties does the aggregate demand function inherit from the individual demands? Is there an aggregate version of Slutsky's equation or of the Strong Axiom of Revealed Preference? Unfortunately, the answer to these questions is no. In fact the aggregate demand function will in general possess no interesting properties other than homogeneity and continuity. Hence, the theory of the consumer places no restrictions on aggregate behavior in general.

However, in certain cases it may happen that the aggregate behavior may look as though it were generated by a single "representative" consumer. Below, we consider a circumstance where this may happen.

Suppose that all individual consumers' indirect utility functions take the **Gorman form**:

$$v_i(\mathbf{p}, m_i) = a_i(\mathbf{p}) + b(\mathbf{p})m_i.$$

Note that the $a_i(\mathbf{p})$ term can differ from consumer to consumer, but the $b(\mathbf{p})$ term is assumed to be identical for all consumers. By Roy's identity the demand function for good j of consumer i will then take the form

$$x_i^j(\mathbf{p}, m_i) = \alpha_i^j(\mathbf{p}) + \beta^j(\mathbf{p})m_i. \tag{9.4}$$

where,

$$\alpha_i^j(\mathbf{p}) = -\frac{\dfrac{\partial a_i(\mathbf{p})}{\partial p_j}}{b(\mathbf{p})}$$

$$\beta^j(\mathbf{p}) = -\frac{\dfrac{\partial b(\mathbf{p})}{\partial p_j}}{b(\mathbf{p})}.$$

Note that the marginal propensity to consume good j, $\partial x_i^j(\mathbf{p}, m_i)/\partial m_i$, is independent of the level of income of any consumer and also constant across consumers since $b(\mathbf{p})$ is constant across consumers. The aggregate demand for good j will then take the form

$$X^j(\mathbf{p}, m^1, \cdots, m^n) = -\left[\sum_{i=1}^{n} \frac{\dfrac{\partial a_i}{\partial p_j}}{b(\mathbf{p})} + \frac{\dfrac{\partial b(\mathbf{p})}{\partial p_j}}{b(\mathbf{p})} \sum_{i=1}^{n} m_i \right].$$

This demand function can in fact be generated by a representative consumer. His representative indirect utility function is given by

$$V(\mathbf{p}, M) = \sum_{i=1}^{n} a_i(\mathbf{p}) + b(\mathbf{p})M = A(\mathbf{p}) + B(\mathbf{p})M,$$

where $M = \sum_{i=1}^{n} m_i$.

The proof is simply to apply Roy's identity to this indirect utility function and to note that it yields the demand function given in equation (9.4). In fact it can be shown that the Gorman form is the most general form of the indirect utility function that will allow for aggregation in the sense of the representative consumer model. Hence, the Gorman form is not only *sufficient* for the representative consumer model to hold, but it is also *necessary*.

Although a complete proof of this fact is rather detailed, the following argument is reasonably convincing. Suppose, for the sake of simplicity, that there are only two consumers. Then by hypothesis the aggregate demand for good j can be written as

$$X^j(\mathbf{p}, m_1 + m_2) \equiv x_1^j(\mathbf{p}, m_1) + x_2^j(\mathbf{p}, m_2).$$

If we first differentiate with respect to m_1 and then with respect to m_2, we find the following identities

$$\frac{\partial X^j(\mathbf{p}, M)}{\partial M} \equiv \frac{\partial x_1^j(\mathbf{p}, m_1)}{\partial m_1} \equiv \frac{\partial x_2^j(\mathbf{p}, m_2)}{\partial m_2}.$$

Hence, the marginal propensity to consume good j must be the same for all consumers. If we differentiate this expression once more with respect to m_1, we find that

$$\frac{\partial^2 X^j(\mathbf{p}, M)}{\partial M^2} \equiv \frac{\partial^2 x_1^j(\mathbf{p}, m_1)}{\partial m_1^2} \equiv 0.$$

Thus, consumer 1's demand for good j—and, therefore, consumer 2's demand—is affine in income. Hence, the demand functions for good j take the form $x_i^j(\mathbf{p}, m_i) = \alpha_i^j(\mathbf{p}) + \beta^j(\mathbf{p})m_i$. If this is true for all goods, the indirect utility function for each consumer must have the Gorman form.

One special case of a utility function having the Gorman form is a utility function that is homothetic. In this case the indirect utility function has the form $v(\mathbf{p}, m) = v(\mathbf{p})m$, which is clearly of the Gorman form. Another special case is that of a quasilinear utility function. In this case $v(\mathbf{p}, m) = v(\mathbf{p}) + m$, which obviously has the Gorman form. Many of the properties possessed by homothetic and/or quasilinear utility functions are also possessed by the Gorman form.

9.5 Inverse demand functions

In many applications it is of interest to express demand behavior by describing prices as a function of quantities. That is, given some vector of goods $\mathbf{x}$, we would like to find a vector of prices $\mathbf{p}$ and an income m at which $\mathbf{x}$ would be the demanded bundle.

Since demand functions are homogeneous of degree zero, we can fix income at some given level, and simply determine prices relative to this income level. The most convenient choice is to fix $m = 1$.

In this case the first-order conditions for the utility maximization problem are simply

$$\frac{\partial u(\mathbf{x})}{\partial x_i} - \lambda p_i = 0 \quad \text{for } i = 1, \ldots, k$$

$$\sum_{i=1}^{k} p_i x_i = 1.$$

We want to eliminate λ from this set of equations.

To do so, multiply each of the first set of equalities by x_i and sum them over the number of goods to get

$$\sum_{i=1}^{k} \frac{\partial u(\mathbf{x})}{\partial x_i} x_i = \lambda \sum_{i=1}^{k} p_i x_i = \lambda.$$

Substitute the value of λ back into the first expression to find $\mathbf{p}$ as function of $\mathbf{x}$:

$$p_i(\mathbf{x}) = \frac{\dfrac{\partial u(\mathbf{x})}{\partial x_i}}{\sum_{j=1}^{k} \dfrac{\partial u(\mathbf{x})}{\partial x_j} x_j}. \tag{9.5}$$

Given any vector of demands $\mathbf{x}$, we can use this expression to find the price vector $\mathbf{p}(\mathbf{x})$ which will satisfy the necessary conditions for maximization. If the utility function is quasiconcave so that these necessary conditions are indeed sufficient for maximization, then this will give us the inverse demand relationship.

What happens if the utility function is not everywhere quasiconcave? Then there may be some bundles of goods that will not be demanded at any price; any bundle on a nonconvex part of an indifference curve will be such a bundle.

There is a dual version of the above formula for inverse demands that can be obtained from the expression given in Chapter 8, page 129. The argument given there shows that the demanded bundle $\mathbf{x}$ must *minimize* indirect utility over all prices that satisfy the budget constraint. Thus $\mathbf{x}$

must satisfy the first-order conditions

$$\frac{\partial v(\mathbf{p})}{\partial p_i} - \mu x_i = 0 \quad \text{for } i = 1, \cdots, k$$

$$\sum_{i=1}^{k} p_i x_i = 1.$$

Now multiply each of the first equations by p_i and sum them to find that $\mu = \sum_{i=1}^{k} \frac{\partial v(\mathbf{p})}{\partial p_i} p_i$. Substituting this back into the first-order conditions, we have an expression for the demanded bundle as a function of the normalized indirect utility function:

$$x_i(\mathbf{p}) = \frac{\dfrac{\partial v(\mathbf{p})}{\partial p_i}}{\sum_{j=1}^{k} \dfrac{\partial v(\mathbf{p})}{\partial p_j} p_j}. \tag{9.6}$$

Note the nice duality: the expression for the direct demand function, (9.6), and the expression for the indirect demand function (9.5) have the same form. This expression can also be derived from the definition of the normalized indirect utility function and Roy's identity.

9.6 Continuity of demand functions

Up until now we have blithely been assuming that the demand functions we have been analyzing are nicely behaved; that is, that they are continuous and even differentiable functions. Are these assumptions justifiable?

Referring to the Theorem of the Maximum in Chapter 27, page 506, we see that, as long as the demand functions are well defined, they will be continuous, at least when $\mathbf{p} \gg 0$ and $m > 0$; that is, as long as $\mathbf{x}(\mathbf{p}, m)$ is the *unique* maximizing bundle at prices $\mathbf{p}$ and income m, then demand will vary continuously with $\mathbf{p}$ and m.

If we want to ensure that demand is continuous for all $\mathbf{p} \gg 0$ and $m > 0$, then we need to ensure that demand is always unique. The condition we need is that of strict convexity.

Unique demanded bundle. *If preferences are strictly convex, then for each $\mathbf{p} \gg 0$ there is a unique bundle $\mathbf{x}$ that maximizes u on the consumer's budget set, $B(\mathbf{p}, m)$.*

Proof. Suppose $\mathbf{x}'$ and $\mathbf{x}''$ both maximize u on $B(\mathbf{p}, m)$. Then $\frac{1}{2}\mathbf{x}' + \frac{1}{2}\mathbf{x}''$ is also in $B(\mathbf{p}, m)$ and is strictly preferred to $\mathbf{x}'$ and $\mathbf{x}''$, which is a contradiction. ∎

Loosely speaking, if demand functions are well defined and everywhere continuous and are derived from preference maximization, then the underlying preferences must be strictly convex. If not, there would be some point where there was more than one optimal bundle at some set of prices, as illustrated in Figure 9.2. Note that, in the case depicted in Figure 9.2, a small change in the price brings about a large change in the demanded bundles: the demand "function" is discontinuous.

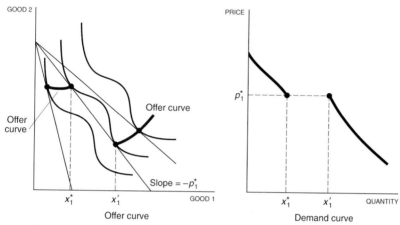

Discontinuous demand. Demand is discontinuous due to nonconvex preferences.

Figure 9.2

Notes

See Pollak (1969) for conditional demands. Separability is treated in Blackorby, Primont & Russell (1979). See Deaton & Muellbauer (1980) for further development and applications to consumer demand estimation. The aggregation section is based on Gorman (1953). See Shafer & Sonnenschein (1982) for a survey of positive and negative results in aggregation.

Exercises

9.1. Suppose preferences are homothetic. Show that

$$\frac{\partial x_i(\mathbf{p}, m)}{\partial p_j} = \frac{\partial x_j(\mathbf{p}, m)}{\partial p_i}.$$

9.2. The demand function for a particular good is $x = a + bp$. What are the associated direct and indirect utility functions?

9.3. The demand function for a particular good is $x = a + bp + cm$. What are the associated direct and indirect utility functions? (Hint: You have to know how to solve a linear, nonhomogeneous differential equation to solve this problem completely. If you can't remember how to do this, just write down the equation.)

9.4. The demand functions for two goods are

$$x_1 = a_1 + b_1 p_1 + b_{12} p_2$$
$$x_2 = a_2 + b_{21} p_1 + b_2 p_2.$$

What restrictions on the parameters does the theory imply? What is the associated money metric utility function?

9.5. What is the direct utility function for the previous problem?

9.6. Let $(\mathbf{q}, m)$ be prices and income, and let $\mathbf{p} = \mathbf{q}/m$. Use Roy's identity to derive the formula

$$x_i(\mathbf{p}) = \frac{\frac{\partial v(\mathbf{p})}{\partial p_i}}{\sum_{j=1}^{k} \frac{\partial v(\mathbf{p})}{\partial p_j} p_j}.$$

9.7. Consider the utility function $u(x_1, z_2, z_3) = x_1^a z_2^b z_3^c$. Is this utility function (weakly) separable in (z_2, z_3)? What is the subutility function for the z-good consumption? What are the conditional demands for the z-goods, given the expenditure on the z-goods, m_z?

9.8. Two goods are available, x and y. The consumer's demand function for the x-good is given by $\ln x = a - bp + cm$, where p is the price of the x-good relative to the y-good, and m is money income divided by the price of the y-good.

(a) What equation would you solve to determine the indirect utility function that would generate this demand behavior?

(b) What is the boundary condition for this differential equation?

9.9. A consumer has a utility function $u(x, y, z) = \min\{x, y\} + z$. The prices of the three goods are given by (p_x, p_y, p_z) and the money the consumer has to spend is given by m.

(a) It turns out that this utility function can be written in the form $U(V(x, y), z)$. What is the function $V(x, y)$? What is the function $U(V, z)$?

(b) What are the demand functions for the three goods?

(c) What is the indirect utility function?

9.10. Suppose that there are two goods, x_1 and x_2. Let the price of good 1 be denoted by p_1 and set the price of good 2 equal to 1. Let income be denoted by y. A consumer's demand for good 1 is given by

$$x_1 = 10 - p_1.$$

(a) What is the demand function for good 2?

(b) What equation would you solve to calculate the income compensation function that would generate these demand functions?

(c) What is the income compensation function associated with these demand functions?

9.11. Consumer 1 has expenditure function $e_1(p_1, p_2, u_1) = u_1 \sqrt{p_1 p_2}$ and consumer 2 has utility function $u_2(x_1, x_2) = 43x_1^3 x_2^a$.

(a) What are the Marshallian (market) demand functions for each of the goods by each of the consumers? Denote the income of consumer 1 by m_1 and the income of consumer 2 by m_2.

(b) For what value(s) of the parameter a will there exist an aggregate demand function that is independent of the distribution of income?

CHAPTER 10

CONSUMERS' SURPLUS

When the economic environment changes a consumer may be made better off or worse off. Economists often want to measure how consumers are affected by changes in the economic environment, and have developed several tools to enable them to do this.

The classical measure of welfare change examined in elementary courses is consumer's surplus. However, consumer's surplus is an exact measure of welfare change only in special circumstances. In this chapter we describe some more general methods for measuring welfare change. These more general methods will include consumer's surplus as a special case.

10.1 Compensating and equivalent variations

Let us first consider what an "ideal" measure of welfare change may be. At the most fundamental level, we would like to have a measure of the change in utility resulting from some policy. Suppose that we have two budgets, $(\mathbf{p}^0, m^0)$ and $(\mathbf{p}', m')$, that measure the prices and incomes that a given consumer would face under two different policy regimes. It is convenient to think of $(\mathbf{p}^0, m^0)$ as being the status quo and $(\mathbf{p}', m')$ as being a proposed change, although this is not the only interpretation.

Then the obvious measure of the welfare change involved in moving from $(\mathbf{p}^0, m^0)$ to $(\mathbf{p}', m')$ is just the difference in indirect utility:

$$v(\mathbf{p}', m') - v(\mathbf{p}^0, m^0).$$

If this utility difference is positive, then the policy change is worth doing, at least as far as this consumer is concerned; and if it is negative, the policy change is not worth doing.

This is about the best we can do in general; utility theory is purely ordinal in nature and there is no unambiguously right way to quantify utility changes. However, for some purposes it is convenient to have monetary measure of changes in consumer welfare. Perhaps the policy analyst wants to have some rough idea of the magnitude of the welfare change for purposes of establishing priorities. Or perhaps the policy analyst wants to compare the benefits and costs accruing to different consumers. In circumstances such as these, it is convenient to choose a "standard" measure of utility differences. A reasonable measure to adopt is the (indirect) money metric utility function described in Chapter 7, page 109.

Recall that $\mu(\mathbf{q}; \mathbf{p}, m)$ measures how much income the consumer would need at prices $\mathbf{q}$ to be as well off as he or she would be facing prices $\mathbf{p}$ and having income m. That is, $\mu(\mathbf{q}; \mathbf{p}, m)$ is defined to be $e(\mathbf{q}, v(\mathbf{p}, m))$. If we adopt this measure of utility, we find that the above utility difference becomes

$$\mu(\mathbf{q}; \mathbf{p}', m') - \mu(\mathbf{q}; \mathbf{p}^0, m^0).$$

It remains to choose the base prices $\mathbf{q}$. There are two obvious choices: we may set $\mathbf{q}$ equal to $\mathbf{p}^0$ or to $\mathbf{p}'$. This leads to the following two measures for the utility difference:

$$EV = \mu(\mathbf{p}^0; \mathbf{p}', m') - \mu(\mathbf{p}^0; \mathbf{p}^0, m^0) = \mu(\mathbf{p}^0; \mathbf{p}', m') - m^0$$
$$CV = \mu(\mathbf{p}'; \mathbf{p}', m') - \mu(\mathbf{p}'; \mathbf{p}^0, m^0) = m' - \mu(\mathbf{p}'; \mathbf{p}^0, m^0). \quad (10.1)$$

The first measure is known as the **equivalent variation**. It uses the current prices as the base and asks what income change at the current prices would be equivalent to the proposed change in terms of its impact on utility. The second measure is known as the **compensating variation**. It uses the new prices as the base and asks what income change would be necessary to compensate the consumer for the price change. (Compensation takes place after some change, so the compensating variation uses the after-change prices.)

Both of these numbers are reasonable measures of the welfare effect of a price change. Their magnitudes will generally differ because the value of a dollar will depend on what the relevant prices are. However, their sign will always be the same since they both measure the same utility differences, just using a different utility function. Figure 10.1 depicts an example of the equivalent and compensating variations in the two-good case.

Which measure is the most appropriate depends on the circumstances involved and what question you are trying to answer. If you are trying to arrange for some compensation scheme at the new prices, then the compensating variation seems reasonable. However, if you are simply trying to get a reasonable measure of "willingness to pay," the equivalent variation is probably better. This is so for two reasons. First, the equivalent variation measures the income change at current prices, and it is much easier for decision makers to judge the value of a dollar at current prices than at some hypothetical prices. Second, if we are comparing more than one proposed policy change, the compensating variation uses different base prices for each new policy while the equivalent variation keeps the base prices fixed at the status quo. Thus, the equivalent variation is more suitable for comparisons among a variety of projects.

Given, then, that we accept the compensating and equivalent variations as reasonable indicators of utility change, how can we measure them in practice? This is equivalent to the question: how can we measure $\mu(\mathbf{q}; \mathbf{p}, m)$ in practice?

We have already answered this question in our study of integrability theory in Chapter 8. There we investigated how to recover the preferences represented by $\mu(\mathbf{q}; \mathbf{p}, m)$ by observing the demand behavior $\mathbf{x}(\mathbf{p}, m)$. Given any observed demand behavior one can solve the integrability equations, at least in principle, and derive the associated money metric utility function.

We have seen in Chapter 8 how to derive the money metric utility functions for several common functional forms for demand functions including linear, log-linear, semilog, and so on. In principle, we can do similar calculations for any demand function that satisfies the integrability conditions.

However, in practice it is usually simpler to make the parametric specification in the *other* direction: first specify a functional form for the indirect utility function and then derive the form of the demand functions by Roy's identity. After all, it is usually a lot easier to differentiate a function than to solve a system of partial differential equations!

If we specify a parametric form for the indirect utility function, then estimating the parameters of the associated system of demand equations immediately gives us the parameters of the underlying utility function. We can derive the money metric utility function—and the compensating and equivalent variations—either algebraically or numerically without much difficulty once we have the relevant parameters. See Chapter 12 for a more detailed description of this approach.

Of course this approach only makes sense if the estimated parameters satisfy the various restrictions implied by the optimization model. We may want to test these restrictions, to see if they are plausible in our particular empirical example, and, if so, estimate the parameters subject to these

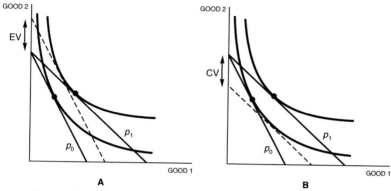

**Figure
10.1**

Equivalent variation and compensating variation. In this
diagram $p_2 = 1$ and the price of good 1 decreases from p_0 to p_1.
Panel A depicts the equivalent variation in income—how much
additional money is needed at the original price p_0 to make the
consumer as well off as she would be facing p_1. Panel B depicts
the compensating variation in income—how much money should
be taken away from the consumer to leave him as well off as he
was facing price p_0.

restrictions.

In summary: the compensating and equivalent variations are in fact observable if the demand functions are observable and if the demand functions
satisfy the conditions implied by utility maximization. The observed demand behavior can be used to construct a measure of welfare change, which
can then be used to analyze policy alternatives.

10.2 Consumer's surplus

The classic tool for measuring welfare changes is **consumer's surplus**.
If $x(p)$ is the demand for some good as a function of its price, then the
consumer's surplus associated with a price movement from p^0 to p' is

$$CS = \int_{p^0}^{p'} x(t)\, dt.$$

This is simply the area to the left of the demand curve between p^0 and
p'. It turns out that when the consumer's preferences can be represented
by a quasilinear utility function, consumer's surplus is an exact measure
of welfare change. More precisely, when utility is quasilinear, the compensating variation equals the equivalent variation, and both are equal to the
consumer's surplus integral. For more general forms of the utility function,

the compensating variation will be different from the equivalent variation and consumer's surplus will not be an exact measure of welfare change. However, even when utility is not quasilinear, consumer's surplus may be a reasonable approximation to more exact measures. We investigate these ideas further below.

10.3 Quasilinear utility

Suppose that there exists a monotonic transformation of utility that has the form

$$U(x_0, x_1, \ldots, x_k) = x_0 + u(x_1, \ldots, x_k).$$

Note that the utility function is linear in one of the goods, but (possibly) nonlinear in the other goods. For this reason we call this a **quasilinear utility function**.

In this section we will focus on the special case where $k = 1$, so that the utility function takes the form $x_0 + u(x_1)$, although everything that we say will work if there are an arbitrary number of goods. We will assume that $u(x_1)$ is a strictly concave function.

Let us consider the utility maximization problem for this form of utility:

$$\max_{x_0, x_1} x_0 + u(x_1)$$

$$\text{such that } x_0 + p_1 x_1 = m.$$

It is tempting to substitute into the objective function and reduce this problem to the unconstrained maximization problem

$$\max_{x_1} u(x_1) + m - p_1 x_1.$$

This has the obvious first-order condition

$$u'(x_1) = p_1,$$

which simply requires that the marginal utility of consumption of good 1 be equal to its price.

By inspection of the first-order condition, the demand for good 1 is only a function of the price of good 1, so we can write the demand function as $x_1(p_1)$. The demand for good 0 is then determined from the budget constraint, $x_0 = m - p_1 x_1(p_1)$. Substituting these demand functions into the utility function gives us the indirect utility function

$$V(p_1, m) = u(x_1(p_1)) + m - p_1 x_1(p_1) = v(p_1) + m,$$

where $v(p_1) = u(x_1(p_1)) - p_1 x_1(p_1)$.

This approach is perfectly fine, but it hides a potential problem. Upon reflection, it is clear that demand for good 1 can't be independent of income for *all* prices and income levels. If income is small enough, the demand for good 1 must be constrained by income.

Suppose that we write the utility maximization problem in a way that explicitly recognizes the nonnegativity constraint on x_0:

$$\max_{x_0, x_1} u(x_1) + x_0$$

$$\text{such that } p_1 x_1 + x_0 = m$$

$$x_0 \geq 0.$$

Now we see that we will get two classes of solutions, depending on whether $x_0 > 0$ or $x_0 = 0$. If $x_0 > 0$, we have the solution that we described above—the demand for good 1 depends only on the price of good 1 and is independent of income. If $x_0 = 0$, then indirect utility will just be given by $u(m/p_1)$.

Think of starting the consumer at $m = 0$ and increasing income by a small amount. The increment in utility is then $u'(m/p_1)/p_1$. If this is larger than 1, then the consumer is better off spending the first dollar of income on good 1 rather than good 0. We continue to spend on good 1 until the marginal utility of an extra dollar spent on that good just equals 1; that is, until the marginal utility of consumption equals price. All additional income will then be spent on the x_0 good.

The quasilinear utility function is often used in applied welfare economics since it has such a simple demand structure. Demand only depends on price—at least for large enough levels of income—and there are no income effects to worry about. This turns out to simplify the analysis of market equilibrium. You should think of this as modeling a situation where the demand for a good isn't very sensitive to income. Think of your demand for paper or pencils: how much would your demand change as your income changes? Most likely, any increases in income would go into consumption of other goods.

Furthermore, with quasilinear utility the integrability problem is very simple. Since the inverse demand function is given by $p_1(x_1) = u'(x_1)$, it follows that the utility associated with a particular level of consumption of good 1 can be recovered from the inverse demand curve by a simple integration:

$$u(x_1) - u(0) = \int_0^{x_1} u'(t)\, dt = \int_0^{x_1} p_1(t)\, dt.$$

The total utility from choosing to consume x_1 will consist of the utility from the consumption good 1, plus the utility from the consumption of good 0:

$$u(x_1(p_1)) + m - p_1 x_1(p_1) = \int_0^{x_1} p_1(t)\, dt + m - p_1 x_1(p_1).$$

If we disregard the constant m, the expression on the right-hand side of this equation is simply the area *under* the demand curve for good 1 minus the expenditure on good 1. Alternatively, this is the area to the left of the demand curve.

Another way to see this is to start with the indirect utility function, $v(p_1) + m$. By Roy's law, $x_1(p_1) = -v'(p_1)$. Integrating this equation, we have

$$v(p_1) + m = \int_{p_1}^{\infty} x_1(t)\, dt + m.$$

This is the area to the left of the demand curve down to the price p_1, which is just another way of describing the same area as described in the last paragraph.

10.4 Quasilinear utility and money metric utility

Suppose that utility takes the quasilinear form $u(x_1) + x_0$. We have seen that for such a utility function the demand function $x_1(p_1)$ will be independent of income. We saw above that we could recover an indirect utility function consistent with this demand function simply by integrating with respect to p_1.

Of course, any monotonic transformation of this indirect utility function is also an indirect utility function that describes the consumer's behavior. If the consumer makes choices that maximize consumer's surplus, then he also maximizes the square of consumer's surplus.

We saw above that the money metric utility function was a particularly convenient utility function for many purposes. It turns out that for quasilinear utility function, the integral of demand is essentially the money metric utility function.

This follows simply by writing down the integrability equations and verifying that consumer's surplus is the solution to these equations. If $x_1(p_1)$ is the demand function, the integrability equation is

$$\frac{d\mu(t; q, m)}{dt} = x_1(t)$$

$$\mu(q; q, m) = m.$$

It can be verified by direct calculation that the solution to these equations is given by

$$\mu(p; q, m) = \int_{q}^{p} x_1(t)\, dt + m.$$

The expression on the right is simply the consumer's surplus associated with a price change from p to q plus income.

For this form of the money metric utility function the compensating and equivalent variations take the form

$$EV = \mu(p^0; p', m') - \mu(p^0; p^0, m^0) = A(p^0, p') + m' - m^0$$
$$CV = \mu(p'; p', m') - \mu(p'; p^0, m^0) = A(p^0, p') + m' - m^0.$$

In this special case the compensating and equivalent variations coincide. It is not hard to see the intuition behind this result. Since the compensation function is linear in income the value of an extra dollar—the marginal utility of income—is independent of price. Hence the value of a compensating or equivalent change in income is independent of the prices at which the value is measured.

10.5 Consumer's surplus as an approximation

We have seen that consumer's surplus is an exact measure of the compensating and equivalent variation only when the utility function is quasilinear. However, it may be a reasonable approximation in more general circumstances.

For example, consider a situation where only the price of good 1 changes from p^0 to p' and income is fixed at $m = m^0 = m'$. In this case, we can use the equation (10.1) and the fact that $\mu(\mathbf{p}; \mathbf{p}, m) \equiv m$ to write

$$EV = \mu(p^0; p', m) - \mu(p^0; p^0, m) = \mu(p^0; p', m) - \mu(p'; p', m)$$
$$CV = \mu(p'; p', m) - \mu(p'; p^0, m) = \mu(p^0; p^0, m) - \mu(p'; p^0, m).$$

We have written these expressions as a function of p alone, since all other prices are assumed to be fixed. Letting $u^0 = v(p^0, m)$ and $u' = v(p', m)$ and using the definition of the money metric utility function given in Chapter 7, page 109, we have

$$EV = e(p^0, u') - e(p', u')$$
$$CV = e(p^0, u^0) - e(p', u^0).$$

Finally, using the fact that the Hicksian demand function is the derivative of the expenditure function, so that $h(p, u) \equiv \partial e / \partial p$, we can write these expressions as

$$EV = e(p^0, u') - e(p', u') = \int_{p'}^{p^0} h(p, u') \, dp$$

$$CV = e(p^0, u^0) - e(p', u^0) = \int_{p'}^{p^0} h(p, u^0) \, dp.$$

(10.2)

It follows from these expressions that the compensating variation is the integral of the *Hicksian* demand curve associated with the initial level of utility, and the equivalent variation is the integral of the Hicksian demand curve associated with the final level of utility. The correct measure of welfare *is* an integral of a demand curve—but you have to use the Hicksian demand curve rather than the Marshallian demand curve.

However, we can use (10.2) to derive a useful bound. The Slutsky equation tells us that

$$\frac{\partial h(p, u)}{\partial p} = \frac{\partial x(p, m)}{\partial p} + \frac{\partial x(p, m)}{\partial m} x(p, m).$$

If the good in question is a normal good, the derivative of the Hicksian demand curve will be larger than the derivative of the Marshallian demand curve, as depicted in Figure 10.2.

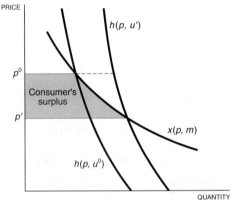

Figure
10.2

Bounds on consumer's surplus. For a normal good, the Hicksian demand curves are steeper than the Marshallian demand curve. Hence, the area to the left of the Marshallian demand curve is bounded by the areas under the Hicksian demand curves.

It follows that the area to the left of the Hicksian demand curves will bound the area to the left of the Marshallian demand curve. In the case depicted, $p^0 > p'$ so all of the areas are positive. It follows that $EV >$ consumer's surplus $> CV$.

10.6 Aggregation

The above relationships among compensating variation, equivalent variation, and consumer's surplus all hold for a single consumer. Here we investigate some issues involving many consumers.

We have seen in Chapter 9, page 153, that aggregate demand for a good will be a function of price and aggregate income only when the indirect utility function for agent i has the Gorman form

$$v_i(\mathbf{p}, m_i) = a_i(\mathbf{p}) + b(\mathbf{p})m_i.$$

In this case the aggregate demand function for each good will be derived from an aggregate indirect utility function that has the form

$$V(\mathbf{p}, M) = \sum_{i=1}^{n} a_i(\mathbf{p}) + b(\mathbf{p})M,$$

where $M = \sum_{i=1}^{n} m_i$.

We saw above that the indirect utility function associated with quasilinear preferences has a form

$$v_i(\mathbf{p}) + m_i.$$

This is clearly a special case of the Gorman form with $b(\mathbf{p}) \equiv 1$. Hence, the aggregate indirect utility function that will generate aggregate demand is simply $V(\mathbf{p}) + M = \sum_{i=1}^{n} v_i(\mathbf{p}) + \sum_{i=1}^{n} m_i$.

How does this relate to aggregate consumers' surplus? Reverting to the case of a single price for simplicity, Roy's law shows that the function $v_i(p)$ is given by

$$v_i(p) = \int_{p}^{\infty} x_i(t) \, dt.$$

It follows that

$$V(p) = \sum_{i=1}^{n} v_i(p) = \sum_{i=1}^{n} \int_{p}^{\infty} x_i(t) \, dt = \int_{p}^{\infty} \sum_{i=1}^{n} x_i(t) \, dt.$$

That is, the indirect utility function that generates the aggregate demand function is simply the integral of the aggregate demand function.

If all consumers have quasilinear utility functions, then the aggregate demand function will appear to maximize aggregate consumer's surplus. However, it is not entirely obvious that aggregate consumer's surplus is appropriate for welfare comparisons. Why should the unweighted sum of a particular representation of utility be a useful welfare measure? We examine this issue in Chapter 13, page 225. As it turns out, aggregate consumers' surplus is the appropriate welfare measure for quasilinear utility, but this case is rather special. In general, aggregate consumers' surplus will not be an exact welfare measure. However, it is often used as an approximate measure of consumer welfare in applied work.

10.7 Nonparametric bounds

We've seen how Roy's identity can be used to calculate the demand function given a parametric form for indirect utility. Integrability theory can be used to calculate a parametric form for the money metric utility function if we are given a parametric form for the demand function. However, each of these operations requires that we specify a parametric form for either the demand function or the indirect utility function.

It is of interest to ask how far we can go without having to specify a parametric form. As it turns out it is possible to derive tight nonparametric bounds on the money metric utility function in an entirely nonparametric way.

We've seen in the discussion of recoverability in Chapter 8 that it is possible to construct sets of consumption bundles that are "revealed preferred" or "revealed worse" than a given consumption bundle. These sets can be thought of as inner and outer bounds to the consumer's preferred set.

Let $NRW(\mathbf{x}_0)$ be the set of points "not revealed worse" than $\mathbf{x}_0$. This is just the complement of the set $RW(\mathbf{x}_0)$. We know from Chapter 8 that the true preferred set associated with $\mathbf{x}_0$, $P(\mathbf{x}_0)$, must contain $RP(\mathbf{x}_0)$ and be contained in the set of points $NRW(\mathbf{x}_0)$.

We illustrate this situation in Figure 10.3. In order not to clutter the diagram, we've left out many of the budget lines and observed choices and have only depicted $RP(\mathbf{x}_0)$ and $RW(\mathbf{x}_0)$. We've also shown the "true" indifference curve through $\mathbf{x}_0$. By definition, the money metric utility of $\mathbf{x}_0$ is defined by

$$m(\mathbf{p}, \mathbf{x}_0) = \min_{\mathbf{x}} \mathbf{p}\mathbf{x}$$

such that $u(\mathbf{x}) \geq u(\mathbf{x}_0)$.

This is the same problem as

$$m(\mathbf{p}, \mathbf{x}_0) = \min_{\mathbf{x}} \mathbf{p}\mathbf{x}$$

such that $\mathbf{x}$ in $P(\mathbf{x}_0)$.

Define $m^+(\mathbf{p}, \mathbf{x}_0)$ and $m^-(\mathbf{p}, \mathbf{x}_0)$ by

$$m^-(\mathbf{p}, \mathbf{x}_0) = \min_{\mathbf{x}} \mathbf{p}\mathbf{x}$$

such that $\mathbf{x}$ in $NRW(\mathbf{x}_0)$,

and

$$m^+(\mathbf{p}, \mathbf{x}_0) = \min_{\mathbf{x}} \mathbf{p}\mathbf{x}$$

such that $\mathbf{x}$ in $RP(\mathbf{x}_0)$.

Since $NRW(\mathbf{x}_0) \supset P(\mathbf{x}_0) \supset RP(\mathbf{x}_0)$, it follows from the standard sort of argument that $m^+(\mathbf{p}, \mathbf{x}_0) \geq m(\mathbf{p}, \mathbf{x}_0) \geq m^-(\mathbf{p}, \mathbf{x}_0)$. Hence, the **overcompensation function**, $m^+(\mathbf{p}, \mathbf{x}_0)$, and the **undercompensation function**, $m^-(\mathbf{p}, \mathbf{x}_0)$, bound the true compensation function, $m(\mathbf{p}, \mathbf{x}_0)$.

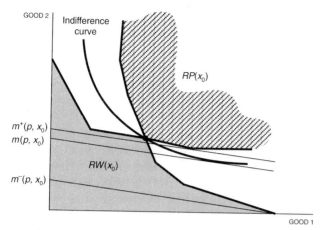

GOOD 2

Indifference curve

$RP(x_0)$

$m^+(p, x_0)$
$m(p, x_0)$

$RW(x_0)$

$m^-(p, x_0)$

GOOD 1

Bounds on the money metric utility. The true preferred set, $P(\mathbf{x}_0)$, contains $RP(\mathbf{x}_0)$ and is contained in $NRW(\mathbf{x}_0)$. Hence the minimum expenditure over $P(\mathbf{x}_0)$ lies between the two bounds, as illustrated.

Figure 10.3

Notes

The concepts of compensating and equivalent variation and their relationship to consumer's surplus is due to Hicks (1956). See Willig (1976) for tighter bounds on consumer's surplus. The nonparametric bounds on the money metric utility function are due to Varian (1982a).

Exercises

10.1. Suppose that utility is quasilinear. Show that the indirect utility function is a convex function of prices.

10.2. Ellsworth's utility function is $U(x, y) = \min\{x, y\}$. Ellsworth has $150 and the price of x and the price of y are both 1. Ellsworth's boss is thinking of sending him to another town where the price of x is 1 and the price of y is 2. The boss offers no raise in pay. Ellsworth, who understands compensating and equivalent variation perfectly, complains bitterly. He says that although he doesn't mind moving for its own sake and the new town is just as pleasant as the old, having to move is as bad as a cut in pay of A. He also says he wouldn't mind moving if when he moved he got a raise of B. What are A and B equal to?

CHAPTER 11

UNCERTAINTY

Until now, we have been concerned with the behavior of a consumer under conditions of certainty. However, many choices made by consumers take place under conditions of uncertainty. In this section we explore how the theory of consumer choice can be used to describe such behavior.

11.1 Lotteries

The first task is to describe the set of choices facing the consumer. We shall imagine that the choices facing the consumer take the form of **lotteries**. A lottery is denoted by $p \circ x \oplus (1 - p) \circ y$. This notation means: "the consumer receives prize x with probability p and prize y with probability $(1 - p)$." The prizes may be money, bundles of goods, or even further lotteries. Most situations involving behavior under risk can be put into this lottery framework.

We will make several assumptions about the consumer's perception of the lotteries open to him.

L1. $1 \circ x \oplus (1 - 1) \circ y \sim x$. Getting a prize with probability one is the same as getting the prize for certain.

L2. $p \circ x \oplus (1 - p) \circ y \sim (1 - p) \circ y \oplus p \circ x$. The consumer doesn't care about the order in which the lottery is described.

L3. $q \circ (p \circ x \oplus (1 - p) \circ y) \oplus (1 - q) \circ y \sim (qp) \circ x \oplus (1 - qp) \circ y$. A consumer's perception of a lottery depends only on the net probabilities of receiving the various prizes.

Assumptions (L1) and (L2) appear to be innocuous. Assumption (L3), sometimes called "reduction of compound lotteries," is somewhat suspect since there is some evidence to suggest that consumers treat compound lotteries different than one-shot lotteries. However, we do not pursue this point here.

Under these assumptions we can define $\mathcal{L}$, the space of lotteries available to the consumer. The consumer is assumed to have preferences on this lottery space: given any two lotteries, he can choose between them. As usual we will assume the preferences are complete, reflexive, and transitive.

The fact that lotteries have only two outcomes is not restrictive since we have allowed the outcomes to be further lotteries. This allows us to construct lotteries with arbitrary numbers of prizes by compounding two-prize lotteries. For example, suppose we want to represent a situation with three prizes x, y, and z where the probability of getting each prize is one third. By the reduction of compound lotteries, this lottery is equivalent to the lottery

$$\frac{2}{3} \circ \left[\frac{1}{2} \circ x \oplus \frac{1}{2} \circ y \right] \oplus \frac{1}{3} \circ z.$$

According to assumption $L3$ above, the consumer only cares about the net probabilities involved, so this is indeed equivalent to the original lottery.

11.2 Expected utility

Under minor additional assumptions, the theorem concerning the existence of a utility function described in Chapter 7, page 95, may be applied to show that there exists a continuous utility function u which describes the consumer's preferences; that is, $p \circ x \oplus (1 - p) \circ y \succ q \circ w \oplus (1 - q) \circ z$ if and only if

$$u(p \circ x \oplus (1 - p) \circ y) > u(q \circ w \oplus (1 - q) \circ z).$$

Of course, this utility function is not unique; any monotonic transform would do as well. Under some additional hypotheses, we can find a particular monotonic transformation of the utility function that has a very convenient property, the **expected utility property**:

$$u(p \circ x \oplus (1 - p) \circ y) = pu(x) + (1 - p)u(y).$$

The expected utility property says that the utility of a lottery is the expectation of the utility from its prizes. We can compute the utility of any lottery by taking the utility that would result from each outcome, multiplying that utility times the probability of occurrence of that outcome, and then summing over the outcomes. Utility is additively separable over the outcomes and linear in the probabilities.

It should be emphasized that the *existence* of a utility function is not at issue; any well-behaved preference ordering can be represented by a utility function. What is of interest here is the existence of a utility function with the above convenient property. For that we need these additional axioms:

U1. $\{p \text{ in } [0,1]: p \circ x \oplus (1-p) \circ y \succeq z\}$ and $\{p \text{ in } [0,1]: z \succeq p \circ x \oplus (1-p) \circ y\}$ are closed sets for all x, y, and z in $\mathcal{L}$.

U2. If $x \sim y$, then $p \circ x \oplus (1-p) \circ z \sim p \circ y \oplus (1-p) \circ z$.

Assumption (U1) is an assumption of continuity; it is relatively innocuous. Assumption (U2) says that lotteries with indifferent prizes are indifferent. That is, if we are given a lottery $p \circ x \oplus (1-p) \circ z$ and we know that $x \sim y$, then we can substitute y for x to construct a lottery $p \circ y \oplus (1-p) \circ z$ that the consumer regards as being equivalent to the original lottery. This assumption appears quite plausible.

In order to avoid some technical details we will make two further assumptions.

U3. There is some best lottery b and some worst lottery w. For any x in $\mathcal{L}$, $b \succeq x \succeq w$.

U4. A lottery $p \circ b \oplus (1-p) \circ w$ is preferred to $q \circ b \oplus (1-q) \circ w$ if and only if $p > q$.

Assumption (U3) is purely for convenience. Assumption (U4) can be derived from the other axioms. It just says that if one lottery between the best prize and the worse prize is preferred to another it must be because it gives higher probability of getting the best prize.

Under these assumptions we can state the main theorem.

Expected utility theorem. *If $(\mathcal{L}, \succeq)$ satisfy the above axioms, there is a utility function u defined on $\mathcal{L}$ that satisfies the expected utility property:*

$$u(p \circ x \oplus (1-p) \circ y) = pu(x) + (1-p)u(y)$$

Proof. Define $u(b) = 1$ and $u(w) = 0$. To find the utility of an arbitrary lottery z, set $u(z) = p_z$ where p_z is defined by

$$p_z \circ b \oplus (1-p_z) \circ w \sim z. \tag{11.1}$$

In this construction the consumer is indifferent between z and a gamble between the best and the worst outcomes that gives probability p_z of the best outcome.

To ensure that this is well defined, we have to check two things.

(1) Does p_z exist? The two sets $\{p \text{ in } [0,1] : p \circ b \oplus (1-p) \circ w \succeq z\}$ and $\{p \text{ in } [0,1] : z \succeq p \circ b \oplus (1-p) \circ w\}$ are closed and nonempty, and every point in $[0,1]$ is in one or the other of the two sets. Since the unit interval is connected, there must be some p in both—but this will just be the desired p_z.

(2) Is p_z unique? Suppose p_z and p_z' are two distinct numbers and that each satisfies (11.1). Then one must be larger than the other. By assumption (U4), the lottery that gives a bigger probability of getting the best prize cannot be indifferent to one that gives a smaller probability. Hence, p_z is unique and u is well defined.

We next check that u has the expected utility property. This follows from some simple substitutions:

$$p \circ x \oplus (1-p) \circ y$$
$$\sim_1 p \circ [p_x \circ b \oplus (1-p_x) \circ w] \oplus (1-p) \circ [p_y \circ b \oplus (1-p_y) \circ w]$$
$$\sim_2 [pp_x + (1-p)p_y] \circ b \oplus [1 - pp_x - (1-p)p_y] \circ w$$
$$\sim_3 [pu(x) + (1-p)u(y)] \circ b \oplus [1 - pu(x) - (1-p)u(y)] \circ w.$$

Substitution 1 uses (U2) and the definition of p_x and p_y. Substitution 2 uses (L3), which says only the net probabilities of obtaining b or w matter. Substitution 3 uses the construction of the utility function.

It follows from the construction of the utility function that

$$u(p \circ x \oplus (1-p) \circ y) = pu(x) + (1-p)u(y).$$

Finally, we verify that u is a utility function. Suppose that $x \succ y$. Then

$$u(x) = p_x \text{ such that } x \sim p_x \circ b \oplus (1-p_x) \circ w$$
$$u(y) = p_y \text{ such that } y \sim p_y \circ b \oplus (1-p_y) \circ w.$$

By axiom (U4), we must have $u(x) > u(y)$. ∎

11.3 Uniqueness of the expected utility function

We have now shown that there exists an expected utility function $u: \mathcal{L} \to R$. Of course, any monotonic transformation of u will also be a utility function that describes the consumer's choice behavior. But will such a monotonic transform preserve the expected utility property? Does the construction described above *characterize* expected utility functions in any way?

It is not hard to see that, if $u(\cdot)$ is an expected utility function describing some consumer, then so is $v(\cdot) = au(\cdot) + c$ where $a > 0$; that is, any affine transformation of an expected utility function is also an expected utility function. This is clear since

$$\begin{aligned}
v(p \circ x \oplus (1-p) \circ y) &= au(p \circ x \oplus (1-p) \circ y) + c \\
&= a[pu(x) + (1-p)u(y)] + c \\
&= p[au(x) + c] + (1-p)[au(y) + c] \\
&= pv(x) + (1-p)v(y).
\end{aligned}$$

It is not much harder to see the converse: that any monotonic transform of u that has the expected utility property must be an affine transform. Stated another way:

Uniqueness of expected utility function. *An expected utility function is unique up to an affine transformation.*

Proof. According to the above remarks we only have to show that, if a monotonic transformation preserves the expected utility property, it must be an affine transformation. Let $f : R \to R$ be a monotonic transform of u that has the expected utility property. Then

$$f(u(p \circ x \oplus (1-p) \circ y)) = pf(u(x)) + (1-p)f(u(y)),$$

or

$$f(pu(x) + (1-p)u(y)) = pf(u(x)) + (1-p)f(u(y)).$$

But this is equivalent to the definition of an affine transformation. (See Chapter 26, page 482.) ∎

11.4 Other notations for expected utility

We have proved the expected utility theorem for the case where there are two outcomes to the lotteries. As indicated earlier, it is straightforward to extend this proof to the case of a finite number of outcomes by using compound lotteries. If outcome x_i is received with probability p_i for $i = 1, \ldots, n$, then the expected utility of this lottery is simply

$$\sum_{i=1}^{n} p_i u(x_i). \tag{11.2}$$

Subject to some minor technical details, the expected utility theorem also holds for *continuous* probability distributions. If $p(x)$ is a probability density function defined on outcomes x, then the expected utility of this gamble can be written as

$$\int u(x)p(x)\, dx. \qquad (11.3)$$

We can subsume both of these cases by using the expectation operator. Let X be a **random variable** that takes on values denoted by x. Then the utility of X is also a random variable, $u(X)$. The **expectation** of this random variable, $Eu(X)$ is simply the expected utility associated with the lottery X. In the case of a discrete random variable, $Eu(X)$ is given by (11.2), and in the case of a continuous random variable $Eu(X)$ is given by (11.3).

11.5 Risk aversion

Let us consider the case where the lottery space consists solely of gambles with money prizes. We know that if the consumer's choice behavior satisfies the various required axioms, we can find a representation of utility that has the expected utility property. This means that we can describe the consumer's behavior over all money gambles if we only know this particular representation of his utility function for money. For example, to compute the consumer's expected utility of a gamble $p \circ x \oplus (1-p) \circ y$, we just look at $pu(x) + (1-p)u(y)$.

This construction is illustrated in Figure 11.1 for $p = \frac{1}{2}$. Notice that in this example the consumer prefers to get the expected value of the lottery. That is, the utility of the lottery $u(p \circ x \oplus (1-p) \circ y)$ is less than the utility of the expected value of the lottery, $px + (1-p)y$. Such behavior is called **risk aversion**. A consumer may also be **risk loving**; in such a case, the consumer prefers a lottery to its expected value.

If a consumer is risk averse over some region, the chord drawn between any two points of the graph of his utility function in this region must lie below the function. This is equivalent to the mathematical definition of a concave function. Hence, concavity of the expected utility function is equivalent to risk aversion.

It is often convenient to have a measure of risk aversion. Intuitively, the more concave the expected utility function, the more risk averse the consumer. Thus, we might think we could measure risk aversion by the second derivative of the expected utility function. However, this definition is not invariant to changes in the expected utility function: if we multiply the expected utility function by 2, the consumer's behavior doesn't change, but our proposed measure of risk aversion does. However, if we normalize

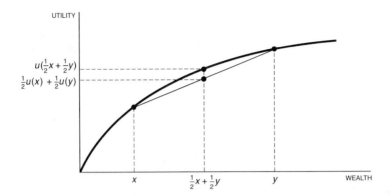

Figure 11.1

Expected utility of a gamble. The expected utility of the gamble is $\frac{1}{2}u(x) + \frac{1}{2}u(y)$. The utility of the expected value of the gamble is $u(\frac{1}{2}x + \frac{1}{2}y)$. In the case depicted the utility of the expected value is higher than the expected utility of the gamble, so the consumer is risk averse.

the second derivative by dividing by the first, we get a reasonable measure, known as the **Arrow-Pratt measure of (absolute) risk aversion**:

$$r(w) = -\frac{u''(w)}{u'(w)}.$$

The following analysis gives further rationale for this measure. Let us represent a gamble now by a pair of numbers (x_1, x_2) where the consumer gets x_1 if some event E occurs and x_2 if not-E occurs. Then we define the consumer's **acceptance set** to be the set of all gambles the consumer would accept at an initial wealth level w. If the consumer is risk averse, the acceptance set will be a convex set. The boundary of this set—the set of indifferent gambles—can be given by an implicit function $x_2(x_1)$, as depicted in Figure 11.2.

Suppose that the consumer's behavior can be described by the maximization of expected utility. Then $x_2(x_1)$ must satisfy the identity:

$$pu(w + x_1) + (1 - p)u(w + x_2(x_1)) \equiv u(w).$$

The slope of the acceptance set boundary at $(0, 0)$ can be found by differentiating this identity with respect to x_1 and evaluating this derivative at $x_1 = 0$:

$$pu'(w) + (1 - p)u'(w)x_2'(0) = 0. \tag{11.4}$$

Solving for the slope of the acceptance set, we find

$$x_2'(0) = -\frac{p}{1 - p}.$$

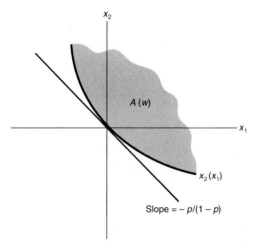

x_2

$A(w)$

x_1

$x_2(x_1)$

Slope $= -p/(1-p)$

The acceptance set. This set describes all gambles that would be accepted by the consumer at his initial level of wealth. If the consumer is risk averse, the acceptance set will be convex.

Figure 11.2

That is, the slope of the acceptance set at $(0,0)$ gives us the odds. This gives us a nice way of eliciting probabilities—find the odds at which a consumer is just willing to accept a small bet on the event in question.

Now suppose that we have two consumers who have identical probabilities on the event E. It is natural to say that consumer i is more risk averse than consumer j if consumer i's acceptance set is contained in consumer j's acceptance set. This is a *global* statement about risk aversion for it says that j will accept *any* gamble that i will accept. If we limit ourselves to small gambles, we get a more useful measure.

It is natural to say that consumer i is **locally more risk averse** than consumer j if i's acceptance set is contained in j's acceptance set in a neighborhood of the point $(0,0)$. This means that j will accept any small gamble that i will accept. If the containment is strict, then i will accept strictly fewer small gambles than j will accept.

It is not hard to see that consumer i is locally more risk averse than consumer j if consumer i's acceptance set is "more curved" than consumer j's acceptance set near the point $(0,0)$. This is useful since we can check the curvature of the acceptance set by calculating the second derivative of $x_2(x_1)$. Differentiating the identity (11.4) once more with respect to x_1, and evaluating the resulting derivative at zero, we find

$$pu''(w) + (1-p)u''(w)x_2'(0)x_2'(0) + (1-p)u'(w)x_2''(0) = 0.$$

Using the fact that $x_2'(0) = -p/(1-p)$, we have

$$x_2''(0) = \frac{p}{(1-p)^2}\left[-\frac{u''(w)}{u'(w)}\right].$$

This expression is proportional to the Arrow-Pratt measure of local risk aversion defined above. We can conclude that an agent j will take more small gambles than agent i if and only if agent i has a larger Arrow-Pratt measure of local risk aversion.

EXAMPLE: The demand for insurance

Suppose a consumer initially has monetary wealth W. There is some probability p that he will lose an amount L—for example, there is some probability his house will burn down. The consumer can purchase insurance that will pay him q dollars in the event that he incurs this loss. The amount of money that he has to pay for q dollars of insurance coverage is πq; here π is the premium per dollar of coverage.

How much coverage will the consumer purchase? We look at the utility maximization problem

$$\max \ pu(W - L - \pi q + q) + (1 - p)u(W - \pi q).$$

Taking the derivative with respect to q and setting it equal to zero, we find

$$pu'(W - L + q^*(1 - \pi))(1 - \pi) - (1 - p)u'(W - \pi q^*)\pi = 0$$

$$\frac{u'(W - L + (1 - \pi)q^*)}{u'(W - \pi q^*)} = \frac{(1 - p)}{p} \ \frac{\pi}{1 - \pi}.$$

If the event occurs, the insurance company receives $\pi q - q$ dollars. If the event doesn't occur, the insurance company receives πq dollars. Hence, the expected profit of the company is

$$(1 - p)\pi q - p(1 - \pi)q.$$

Let us suppose that competition in the insurance industry forces these profits to zero. This means that

$$-p(1 - \pi)q + (1 - p)\pi q = 0,$$

from which it follows that $\pi = p$.

Under the zero-profit assumption the insurance firm charges an *actuarially fair premium:* the cost of a policy is precisely its expected value, so that $p = \pi$. Inserting this into the first-order conditions for utility maximization, we find

$$u'(W - L + (1 - \pi)q^*) = u'(W - \pi q^*).$$

If the consumer is strictly risk averse so that $u''(W) < 0$, then the above equation implies

$$W - L + (1 - \pi)q^* = W - \pi q^*.$$

from which it follows that $L = q^*$. Thus, the consumer will completely insure himself against the loss L.

This result depends crucially on the assumption that the consumer cannot influence the probability of loss. If the consumer's actions do affect the probability of loss, the insurance firms may only want to offer partial insurance, so that the consumer will still have an incentive to be careful. We investigate a model of this sort in Chapter 25, page 455.

11.6 Global risk aversion

The Arrow-Pratt measure seems to be a sensible interpretation of *local* risk aversion: one agent is more risk averse than another if he is willing to accept fewer small gambles. However, in many circumstances we want a *global* measure of risk aversion—that is, we want to say that one agent is more risk averse than another for all levels of wealth. What are natural ways to express this condition?

The first plausible way is to formalize the notion that an agent with utility function $A(w)$ is more risk averse than an agent with utility function $B(w)$ is to require that

$$-\frac{A''(w)}{A'(w)} > -\frac{B''(w)}{B'(w)}$$

for all levels of wealth w. This simply means that agent A has a higher degree of risk aversion than agent B everywhere.

Another sensible way to formalize the notion that agent A is more risk averse than agent B is to say that agent A's utility function is "more concave" than agent B's. More precisely, we say that agent A's utility function is a concave transformation of agent B's; that is, there exists some increasing, strictly concave function $G(\cdot)$ such that

$$A(w) = G(B(w)).$$

A third way to capture the idea that A is more risk averse than B is to say that A would be willing to pay more to avoid a given risk than B would. In order to formalize this idea, let $\tilde{\epsilon}$ be a random variable with expectation of zero: $E\tilde{\epsilon} = 0$. Then define $\pi_A(\tilde{\epsilon})$ to be the maximum amount of wealth that person A would give up in order to avoid facing the random variable $\tilde{\epsilon}$. In symbols, this **risk premium** is

$$A(w - \pi_A(\tilde{\epsilon})) = EA(w + \tilde{\epsilon}).$$

The left-hand side of this expression is the utility from having wealth reduced by $\pi_A(\tilde{\epsilon})$ and the right-hand side is the expected utility from facing the gamble $\tilde{\epsilon}$. It is natural to say that person A is (globally) more risk averse than person B if $\pi_A(\tilde{\epsilon}) > \pi_B(\tilde{\epsilon})$ for all ϵ and w.

It may seem difficult to choose among these three plausible sounding interpretations of what it might mean for one agent to be "globally more risk averse" than another. Luckily, it is not necessary to do so: all three definitions turn out to be equivalent! As one step in the demonstration of this fact we need the following result, which is of great use in dealing with expected utility functions.

Jensen's inequality. *Let X be a nondegenerate random variable and $f(X)$ be a strictly concave function of this random variable. Then $Ef(X) < f(EX)$.*

Proof. This is true in general, but is easiest to prove in the case of a differentiable concave function. Such a function has the property that at any point $\bar{x}$, $f(x) < f(\bar{x}) + f'(\bar{x})(x - \bar{x})$. Let $\overline{X}$ be the expected value of X and take expectations of each side of this expression, we have

$$Ef(X) < f(\overline{X}) + f'(\overline{X})E(X - \overline{X}) = f(\overline{X}),$$

from which it follows that

$$Ef(X) < f(\overline{X}) = f(EX).$$

∎

Pratt's theorem. *Let $A(w)$ and $B(w)$ be two differentiable, increasing and concave expected utility functions of wealth. Then the following properties are equivalent.*

1) $-A''(w)/A'(w) > -B''(w)/B'(w)$ for all w.

2) $A(w) = G(B(w))$ for some increasing strictly concave function G.

3) $\pi_A(\tilde{\epsilon}) > \pi_B(\tilde{\epsilon})$ for all random variables $\tilde{\epsilon}$ with $E\tilde{\epsilon} = 0$.

Proof.

(1) implies (2). Define $G(B)$ implicitly by $A(w) = G(B(w))$. Note that monotonicity of the utility functions implies that G is well defined—i.e., that there is a unique value of $G(B)$ for each value of B. Now differentiate this definition twice to find

$$A'(w) = G'(B)B'(w)$$
$$A''(w) = G''(B)B'(w)^2 + G'(B)B''(w).$$

Since $A'(w) > 0$ and $B'(w) > 0$, the first equation establishes $G'(B) > 0$. Dividing the second equation by the first gives us

$$\frac{A''(w)}{A'(w)} = \frac{G'''(B)}{G'(B)}B'(w) + \frac{B''(w)}{B'(w)}.$$

Rearranging gives us

$$\frac{G''(B)}{G'(B)}B'(w) = \frac{A''(w)}{A'(w)} - \frac{B''(w)}{B'(w)} < 0,$$

where the inequality follows from (1). This shows that $G''(B) < 0$, as required.

(2) implies (3). This follows from the following chain of inequalities:

$$A(w - \pi_A) = EA(w + \tilde{\epsilon}) = EG(B(w + \tilde{\epsilon}))$$
$$< G(EB(w + \tilde{\epsilon})) = G(B(w - \pi_B))$$
$$= A(w - \pi_B).$$

All of these relationships follow from the definition of the risk premium except for the inequality, which follows from Jensen's inequality. Comparing the first and the last terms, we see that $\pi_A > \pi_B$.

(3) implies (1). Since (3) holds for all zero-mean random variables $\tilde{\epsilon}$, it must hold for arbitrarily small random variables. Fix an $\tilde{\epsilon}$, and consider the family of random variables defined by $t\tilde{\epsilon}$ for t in $[0, 1]$. Let $\pi(t)$ be the risk premium as a function of t. The second-order Taylor series expansion of $\pi(t)$ around $t = 0$ is given by

$$\pi(t) \approx \pi(0) + \pi'(0)t + \frac{1}{2}\pi''(0)t^2. \tag{11.5}$$

We will calculate the terms in this Taylor series in order to see how $\pi(t)$ behaves for small t. The definition of $\pi(t)$ is

$$A(w - \pi(t)) \equiv EA(w + t\tilde{\epsilon}).$$

It follows from this definition that $\pi(0) = 0$. Differentiating the definition twice with respect to t gives us

$$-A'(w - \pi(t))\pi'(t) = E[A'(w + t\tilde{\epsilon})\tilde{\epsilon}]$$
$$A''(w - \pi(t))\pi'(t)^2 - A'(w - \pi(t))\pi''(t) = E[A''(w + t\tilde{\epsilon})\tilde{\epsilon}^2].$$

(Some readers may not be familiar with the operation of differentiating an expectation. But taking an expectation is just another notation for a sum or an integral, so the same rules apply: the derivative of an expectation is the expectation of the derivative.)

Evaluating the first expression when $t = 0$, we see that $\pi'(0) = 0$. Evaluating the second expression when $t = 0$, we see that

$$\pi''(0) = -\frac{EA''(w)\tilde{\epsilon}^2}{A'(w)} = -\frac{A''(w)}{A'(w)}\sigma^2,$$

where σ^2 is the variance of $\tilde{\epsilon}$. Plugging the derivatives into equation (11.5) for $\pi(t)$, we have

$$\pi(t) \approx 0 + 0 - \frac{A''(w)}{A'(w)} \frac{\sigma^2}{2} t^2.$$

This implies that for arbitrarily small values of t, the risk premium depends monotonically on the degree of risk aversion, which is what we wanted to show. ∎

EXAMPLE: Comparative statics of a simple portfolio problem

Let us use what we have learned to analyze a simple two-period portfolio problem involving two assets, one with a risky return and one with a sure return. Since the rate of return on the risky asset is uncertain, we denote it by a random variable $\tilde{R}$.

Let w be initial wealth, and let $a \geq 0$ be the dollar amount invested in the risky asset. The budget constraint implies that $w - a$ is the amount invested in the sure asset. For convenience we assume that the sure asset has a zero rate of return.

In this case the second-period wealth can be written as

$$\tilde{W} = a(1 + \tilde{R}) + w - a = a\tilde{R} + w.$$

Note that second-period wealth is a random variable since $\tilde{R}$ is a random variable. The expected utility from investing a in the risky asset can be written as

$$v(a) = Eu(w + a\tilde{R}),$$

and the first two derivatives of expected utility with respect to a are

$$v'(a) = Eu'(w + a\tilde{R})\tilde{R}$$
$$v''(a) = Eu''(w + a\tilde{R})\tilde{R}^2.$$

Note that risk aversion implies that $v''(a)$ is everywhere negative, so the second-order condition will automatically be satisfied.

Let us first consider boundary solutions. Evaluating the first derivative at $a = 0$, we have $v'(0) = Eu'(w)\tilde{R} = u'(w)E\tilde{R}$. It follows that if $E\tilde{R} \leq 0$, $v'(0) \leq 0$, and, given strict risk aversion, $v'(a) < 0$ for all $a > 0$. Hence, $a = 0$ is optimal if and only if $E\tilde{R} \leq 0$. That is, a risk averter will choose zero investment in the risky asset if and only if its expected return is nonpositive.

Conversely, if $E\tilde{R} > 0$, it follows that $v'(0) = u'(w)E\tilde{R} > 0$, so the individual will generally want to invest a positive amount in the risky asset. The *optimal* investment will satisfy the first-order condition

$$Eu'(w + a\tilde{R})\tilde{R} = 0, \tag{11.6}$$

which simply requires that the expected marginal utility of wealth equals zero.

Let us examine the comparative statics of this choice problem. First we look at how a changes as w changes. Let $a(w)$ be the optimal choice of a as a function of w; this must identically satisfy the first-order condition

$$Eu'(w + a(w)\tilde{R})\tilde{R} \equiv 0.$$

Differentiating with respect to w gives us

$$Eu''(w + a\tilde{R})\tilde{R}[1 + a'(w)\tilde{R}] \equiv 0,$$

or

$$a'(w) = -\frac{Eu''(w + a\tilde{R})\tilde{R}}{Eu''(w + a\tilde{R})\tilde{R}^2}.$$

As usual, the denominator is negative because of the second-order condition, so we see that

$$\text{sign } a'(w) = \text{sign } Eu''(w + a\tilde{R})\tilde{R}.$$

The sign of the expression on the right-hand side is not entirely obvious. However, it turns out that it is determined by the behavior of absolute risk aversion, $r(w)$.

Risk aversion. $Eu''(w + a\tilde{R})\tilde{R}$ *is positive, negative, or zero as $r(w)$ is decreasing, increasing, or constant.*

Proof. We show that $r'(w) < 0$ implies that $Eu''(w + a\tilde{R})\tilde{R} > 0$, since this is the most reasonable case. The proofs of the other cases are similar.

Consider first the case where $\tilde{R} > 0$. In this case we have

$$r(w + a\tilde{R}) = -\frac{u''(w + a\tilde{R})}{u'(w + a\tilde{R})} < r(w),$$

which can be rewritten as

$$u''(w + a\tilde{R}) > -r(w)u'(w + a\tilde{R}). \tag{11.7}$$

Since $\tilde{R} > 0$,
$$u''(w + a\tilde{R})\tilde{R} > -r(w)u'(w + a\tilde{R})\tilde{R}. \tag{11.8}$$

Now consider the case where $\tilde{R} < 0$. Examining (11.7), we see that decreasing absolute risk aversion implies

$$u''(w + a\tilde{R}) < -r(w)u'(w + a\tilde{R}).$$

Since $\tilde{R} < 0$, we have

$$u''(w + a\tilde{R})\tilde{R} > -r(w)u'(w + a\tilde{R})\tilde{R}.$$

Comparing this to equation (11.8) we see that (11.8) must hold both for $\tilde{R} > 0$ and $\tilde{R} < 0$. Hence, taking expectation over all values of $\tilde{R}$, we have

$$Eu''(w + a\tilde{R})\tilde{R} > -r(w)Eu'(w + a\tilde{R})\tilde{R} = 0,$$

where the last equality follows from the first-order conditions. ∎

The lemma gives our result: the investment in the risky asset will be increasing, constant, or decreasing in wealth as risk aversion is decreasing, constant, or increasing in wealth.

We turn now to investigating how the demand for the risky asset changes as the probability distribution of its return changes. One way to parameterize shifts in the random rate of return is to write $(1 + h)\tilde{R}$ where h is a shift variable. When $h = 0$ we have the original random variable; if h is positive, this means that every realized return is h percent larger.

Replacing $\tilde{R}$ by $(1 + h)\tilde{R}$ in equation (11.6) and dividing both sides of the expression by $(1 + h)$ gives us

$$Eu'(w + a(1 + h)\tilde{R})\tilde{R} = 0. \qquad (11.9)$$

We could proceed to differentiate this expression with respect to h and sign the result, but there is a much easier way to see what happens to a as h changes. Let $a(h)$ be the demand for the risky asset as a function of h. I claim that

$$a(h) = \frac{a(0)}{1 + h}.$$

The proof is simply to substitute this formula into the first-order condition (11.9).

Intuitively, if the random variable scales up by $1 + h$, the consumer just reduces his holdings by $1/(1 + h)$ and restores exactly the same pattern of returns that he had before the random variable shifted. This kind of linear shift in the random variable can be perfectly offset by a change in the consumer's portfolio.

A more interesting shift in the random variable is a **mean-preserving spread** that increases the variance of $\tilde{R}$ but leaves the mean constant. One way to parameterize such a change is to write $\tilde{R} + h(\tilde{R} - \overline{R})$. The expected value of this random variable is $\overline{R}$, but the variance is $(1 + h)^2\sigma_R^2$, so an increase in h leaves the mean fixed but increases the variance.

We can also write this expression as $(1 + h)\tilde{R} - h\overline{R}$. This shows that this sort of mean-preserving spread can be viewed as multiplying the random variable by $1 + h$ and then subtracting off $h\overline{R}$. According to our earlier results, multiplying the random variable by $1 + h$ scales demand back by $1 + h$, and subtracting wealth reduces demand even more, assuming that absolute risk aversion is decreasing. Hence, a mean preserving spread of this sort reduces investment in the risky asset more than proportionally.

EXAMPLE: Asset pricing

Suppose now that there are many risky assets and one certain asset. Each of the risky assets has a random *total* return $\tilde{R}_i$ for $i = 1, \ldots, n$ and the safe asset has a *total* return R_0. (The total return, R, is one plus the rate of return; in the last section we used R for the rate of return.) The consumer initially has wealth w and chooses to invest a fraction of his wealth x_i in asset i for $i = 0, \ldots, n$. Thus, the wealth of the consumer in the second period—when the random returns are realized—will be given by

$$\tilde{W} = w \sum_{i=0}^{n} x_i \tilde{R}_i. \tag{11.10}$$

We assume that the consumer wants to choose (x_i) to maximize the expected utility of random wealth $\tilde{W}$.

The budget constraint for this problem is that $\sum_{i=0}^{n} x_i = 1$. Since x_i is the fraction of the consumer's wealth invested in asset i, then the sum of the fractions over all the available assets must be 1. We can also write this budget constraint as

$$x_0 + \sum_{i=1}^{n} x_i = 1,$$

so that $x_0 = 1 - \sum_{i=1}^{n} x_i$. Substituting this expression into (11.10) and rearranging, we have

$$\tilde{W} = w \left[x_0 R_0 + \sum_{i=1}^{n} x_i \tilde{R}_i \right]$$

$$= w \left[(1 - \sum_{i=1}^{n} x_i) R_0 + \sum_{i=1}^{n} x_i \tilde{R}_i \right]$$

$$= w \left[R_0 + \sum_{i=1}^{n} x_i (\tilde{R}_i - R_0) \right].$$

With this rearrangement of the budget constraint, we now have an unconstrained maximization problem for $x_1, \ldots, x_n$.

$$\max_{x_1, \ldots, x_n} \ Eu(w[R_0 + \sum_{i=1}^{n} x_i (\tilde{R}_i - R_0)]).$$

Differentiating with respect to x_i we have the first-order conditions

$$Eu'(\tilde{W})(\tilde{R}_i - R_0) = 0,$$

for $i = 1, \ldots, n$. Note that this is essentially the same expression as derived in the preceding section.

This can also be written as

$$Eu'(\tilde{W})\tilde{R}_i = R_0 Eu'(\tilde{W}).$$

Using the covariance identity for random variables, $\text{cov}(X, Y) = EXY - EX\,EY$, we can transform this expression to

$$\text{cov}(u'(\tilde{W}), \tilde{R}_i) + E\tilde{R}_i\, Eu'(\tilde{W}) = R_0 Eu'(\tilde{W}),$$

which can be rearranged to yield

$$E\tilde{R}_i = R_0 - \frac{1}{Eu'(\tilde{W})}\text{cov}(u'(\tilde{W}), \tilde{R}_i). \tag{11.11}$$

This equation says that the expected return on any asset can be written as the sum of two components: the risk-free return plus the **risk premium**. The risk premium depends on the covariance between the marginal utility of wealth and the return of the asset. (Note that this is a different concept of risk premium than that discussed in the proof of Pratt's theorem. Unfortunately, the same term is applied to both concepts.)

Consider an asset whose return is positively correlated with wealth. Since risk aversion implies that the marginal utility of wealth decreases with wealth, it follows that such an asset will be negatively correlated with marginal utility. Hence, such an asset must have an expected return that is higher than the risk-free rate, in order to compensate for its risk.

On the other hand, an asset that is negatively correlated with wealth will have an expected return that is less than the risk-free rate. Intuitively, an asset that is negatively correlated with wealth is an asset that is especially valuable for reducing risk, and therefore people are willing to sacrifice expected returns in order to hold such an asset.

11.7 Relative risk aversion

Consider a consumer with wealth w and suppose that she is offered gambles of the form: with probability p she will receive x percent of her current wealth; with probability $(1 - p)$ she will receive y percent of her current wealth. If the consumer evaluates lotteries using expected utility, the utility of this lottery will be

$$pu(xw) + (1 - p)u(yw).$$

Note that this multiplicative gamble has a different structure than the additive gambles analyzed above. Nevertheless, relative gambles of this sort often arise in economic problems. For example, the return on investments is usually stated relative to the level of investment.

Just as before we can ask when one consumer will accept more small relative gambles than another at a given wealth level. Going through the same sort of analysis used above, we find that the appropriate measure turns out to be the **Arrow-Pratt measure of relative risk aversion**:

$$\rho = -\frac{u''(w)w}{u'(w)}.$$

It is reasonable to ask how absolute and relative risk aversions might vary with wealth. It is quite plausible to assume that absolute risk aversion decreases with wealth: as you become more wealthy you would be willing to accept more gambles expressed in absolute dollars. The behavior of relative risk aversion is more problematic; as your wealth increases would you be more or less willing to risk losing a specific fraction of it? Assuming constant relative risk aversion is probably not too bad an assumption, at least for small changes in wealth.

EXAMPLE: Mean-variance utility

In general the expected utility of a gamble depends on the entire probability distribution of the outcomes. However, in some circumstances the expected utility of a gamble will only depend on certain summary statistics of the distribution. The most common example of this is a **mean-variance utility function**.

For example, suppose that the expected utility function is quadratic, so that $u(w) = w - bw^2$. Then expected utility is

$$Eu(w) = Ew - bEw^2 = \overline{w} - b\overline{w}^2 - b\sigma_w^2.$$

Hence, the expected utility of a gamble is only a function of the mean and variance of wealth.

Unfortunately, the quadratic utility function has some undesirable properties: it is a decreasing function of wealth in some ranges, and it exhibits increasing absolute risk aversion.

A more useful case when mean-variance analysis is justified is the case when wealth is Normally distributed. It is well-known that the mean and variance completely characterize a Normal random variable; hence, choice among Normally distributed random variables reduces to a comparison on their means and variances.

One particular case that is of special interest is when the consumer has a utility function of the form $u(w) = -e^{-rw}$. It can be shown that this utility function exhibits constant absolute risk aversion. Furthermore, when wealth is Normally distributed

$$Eu(w) = -\int e^{-rw} f(w)\, dw = -e^{-r[\overline{w} - r\sigma_w^2/2]}.$$

(To do the integration, either complete the square or else note that this is essentially the calculation that one does to find the moment generating function for the Normal distribution.) Note that expected utility is increasing in $\overline{w} - r\sigma_w^2/2$. This means that we can take a monotonic transformation of expected utility and evaluate distributions of wealth using the utility function $u(\overline{w}, \sigma_w^2) = \overline{w} - \frac{r}{2}\sigma_w^2$. This utility function has the convenient property that it is linear in the mean and variance of wealth.

11.8 State dependent utility

In our original analysis of choice under uncertainty, the prizes were simply abstract bundles of goods; later we specialized to lotteries with only monetary outcomes. However, this is not as innocuous as it appears. After all, the value of a dollar depends on the prevailing prices; a complete description of the outcome of a dollar gamble should include not only the amount of money available in each outcome but also the prevailing prices in each outcome.

More generally, the usefulness of a good often depends on the circumstances or **state of nature** in which it becomes available. An umbrella when it is raining may appear very different to a consumer than an umbrella when it is not raining. These examples show that in some choice problems it is important to distinguish goods by the state of nature in which they are available.

For example, suppose that there are two states of nature, hot and cold, which we index by h and c. Let x_h be the amount of ice cream delivered when it is hot and x_c the amount delivered when it is cold. Then if the probability of hot weather is p, we may write a particular lottery as $pu(h, x_h) + (1 - p)u(c, x_c)$. Here the bundle of goods that is delivered in one state is "hot weather and x_h units of ice cream," and "cold weather and x_c units of ice cream" in the other state.

A more serious example involves health insurance. The value of a dollar may well depend on one's health—how much would a million dollars be worth to you if you were in a coma? In this case we might well write the utility function as $u(h, m_h)$ where h is an indicator of health and m is some amount of money. These are all examples of **state-dependent utility functions**. This simply means that the preferences among the goods under consideration depend on the state of nature under which they become available.

11.9 Subjective probability theory

In the discussion of expected utility theory we have been rather vague about the exact nature of the "probabilities" that enter the expected utility function. The most straightforward interpretation is that they are "objective" probabilities—such as probabilities calculated on the basis of some observed frequencies. Unfortunately, most interesting choice problems involve **subjective probabilities**: a given agent's perception of the likelihood of some event occurring.

In the case of expected utility theory, we asked what axioms about a person's choice behavior would imply the existence of an expected utility function that would represent that behavior. Similarly, we can ask what axioms about a person's choice behavior can be used to infer the existence of subjective probabilities; i.e., that the person's choice behavior can be viewed *as if* he were evaluating gambles according to their expected utility with respect to some subjective probability measures.

As it happens, such sets of axioms exist and are reasonably plausible. Subjective probabilities can be constructed in a way similar to the manner with which the expected utility function was constructed. Recall that the utility of some gamble x was chosen to be that number $u(x)$ such that

$$x \sim u(x) \circ b \oplus (1 - u(x)) \circ w.$$

Suppose that we are trying to ascertain an individual's subjective probability that it will rain on a certain date. Then we can ask at what probability p will the individual be indifferent between the gamble $p \circ b \oplus (1-p) \circ w$ and the gamble "Receive b if it rains and w otherwise."

More formally, let E be some event, and let $p(E)$ stand for the (subjective) probability that E will occur. We *define* the subjective probability that E occurs by the number $p(E)$ that satisfies

$$p(E) \circ b \oplus (1 - p(E)) \circ w \sim \text{receive } b \text{ if } E \text{ occurs and } w \text{ otherwise.}$$

It can be shown that under certain regularity assumptions the probabilities defined in this way have all of the properties of ordinary objective probabilities. In particular, they obey the usual rules for manipulation of conditional probabilities. This has a number of useful implications for economic behavior.

We will briefly explore one such implication. Suppose that $p(H)$ is an individual's subjective probability that a particular hypothesis is true, and that E is an event that is offered as evidence that H is true. How should a rational economic agent adjust his probability belief about H in light of the evidence E? That is, what is the probability of H being true, conditional on observing the evidence E?

We can write the joint probability of observing E and H being true as

$$p(H, E) = p(H|E)p(E) = p(E|H)p(H).$$

Rearranging the right-hand sides of this equation,

$$p(H|E) = \frac{p(E|H)p(H)}{p(E)}.$$

This is a form of **Bayes' law** which relates the **prior probability** $p(H)$, the probability that the hypothesis is true before observing the evidence, to the **posterior probability**, the probability that the hypothesis is true *after* observing the evidence.

Bayes' law follows directly from simple manipulations of conditional probabilities. If an individual's behavior satisfies restrictions sufficient to ensure the existence of subjective probabilities, those probabilities must satisfy Bayes' law. Bayes' law is important since it shows how a rational individual should update his probabilities in the light of evidence, and hence serves as the basis for most models of rational learning behavior.

Thus, both the utility function and the subjective probabilities can be constructed from observed choice behavior, as long as the observed choice behavior follows certain intuitively plausible axioms. However, it should be emphasized that although the axioms are intuitively plausible it does not follow that they are accurate descriptions of how individuals actually behave. *That* determination must be based on empirical evidence.

EXAMPLE: The Allais paradox and the Ellsberg paradox

Expected utility theory and subjective probability theory were motivated by considerations of rationality. The axioms underlying expected utility theory seem plausible, as does the construction that we used for subjective probabilities.

Unfortunately, real-life individual behavior appears to systematically violate some of the axioms. Here we present two famous examples.

The Allais paradox

You are asked to choose between the following two gambles:

Gamble A. A 100 percent chance of receiving 1 million.

Gamble B. A 10 percent chance of 5 million, an 89 percent chance of 1 million, and a 1 percent chance of nothing.

Before you read any further pick one of these gambles, and write it down. Now consider the following two gambles.

Gamble C. An 11 percent chance of 1 million, and an 89 percent chance of nothing.

Gamble D. A 10 percent chance of 5 million, and a 90 percent chance of nothing.

Again, please pick one of these two gambles as your preferred choice and write it down.

Many people prefer A to B and D to C. However, these choices violate the expected utility axioms! To see this, simply write the expected utility relationship implied by $A \succeq B$:

$$u(1) > .1u(5) + .89u(1) + .01u(0).$$

Rearranging this expression gives

$$.11u(1) > .1u(5) + .01u(0),$$

and adding $.89u(0)$ to each side yields

$$.11u(1) + .89u(0) > .1u(5) + .90u(0).$$

It follows that gamble C must be preferred to gamble D by an expected utility maximizer.

The Ellsberg paradox

The Ellsberg paradox concerns subjective probability theory. You are told that an urn contains 300 balls. One hundred of the balls are red and 200 are either blue or green.

Gamble A. You receive $1,000 if the ball is red.

Gamble B. You receive $1,000 if the ball is blue.

Write down which of these two gambles you prefer. Now consider the following two gambles:

Gamble C. You receive $1,000 if the ball is not red.

Gamble D. You receive $1,000 if the ball is not blue.

It is common for people to strictly prefer A to B and C to D. But these preferences violate standard subjective probability theory. To see why, let R be the event that the ball is red, and $\neg R$ be the event that the ball is not red, and define B and $\neg B$ accordingly. By ordinary rules of probability,

$$p(R) = 1 - p(\neg R)$$
$$p(B) = 1 - p(\neg B). \tag{11.12}$$

Normalize $u(0) = 0$ for convenience. Then if A is preferred to B, we must have $p(R)u(1000) > p(B)u(1000)$, from which it follows that

$$p(R) > p(B). \tag{11.13}$$

If C is preferred to D, we must have $p(\neg R)u(1000) > p(\neg B)u(1000)$, from which it follows that

$$p(\neg R) > p(\neg B). \tag{11.14}$$

However, it is clear that expressions (11.12), (11.13), and (11.14) are inconsistent.

The Ellsberg paradox seems to be due to the fact that people think that betting for or against R is "safer" than betting for or against "blue."

Opinions differ about the importance of the Allais paradox and the Ellsberg paradox. Some economists think that these anomalies require new models to describe people's behavior. Others think that these paradoxes are akin to "optical illusions." Even though people are poor at judging distances under some circumstances doesn't mean that we need to invent a new concept of distance.

Notes

The expected utility function is due to Neumann & Morgenstern (1944). The treatment here follows Herstein & Milnor (1953). The measures of risk aversion are due to Arrow (1970) and Pratt (1964). The treatment here follows Yaari (1969). A description of recent work on generalizations of expected utility theory may be found in Machina (1982). Our brief treatment of subjective probability is based on Anscombe & Aumann (1963).

Exercises

11.1. Show that the willingness-to-pay to avoid a small gamble with variance v is approximately $r(w)v/2$.

11.2. What will the form of the expected utility function be if risk aversion is constant? What if relative risk aversion is constant?

11.3. For what form of expected utility function will the investment in a risky asset be independent of wealth?

11.4. Consider the case of a quadratic expected utility function. Show that at some level of wealth marginal utility is decreasing. More importantly, show that absolute risk aversion is increasing at any level of wealth.

11.5. A coin has probability p of landing heads. You are offered a bet in which you will be paid $\$2^j$ if the first head occurs on the jth flip.

(a) What is the expected value of this bet when $p = 1/2$?

(b) Suppose that your expected utility function is $u(x) = \ln x$. Express the utility of this game to you as a sum.

(c) Evaluate the sum. (This requires knowledge of a few summation formulas.)

(d) Let w_0 be the amount of money that would give you the same utility you would have if you played this game. Solve for w_0.

11.6. Esperanza has been an expected utility maximizer ever since she was five years old. As a result of the strict education she received at an obscure British boarding school, her utility function u is strictly increasing and strictly concave. Now, at the age of thirty-something, Esperanza is evaluating an asset with stochastic outcome R which is normally distributed with mean μ and variance σ^2. Thus, its density function is given by

$$ f(r) = \frac{1}{\sigma\sqrt{2\pi}} \exp\left\{ -\frac{1}{2}\left(\frac{r-\mu}{\sigma}\right)^2 \right\}. $$

(a) Show that Esperanza's expected utility from R is a function of μ and σ^2 alone. Thus, show that $E[u(R)] = \phi(\mu, \sigma^2)$.

(b) Show that $\phi(\cdot)$ is increasing in μ.

(c) Show that $\phi(\cdot)$ is decreasing in σ^2.

11.7. Let R_1 and R_2 be the random returns on two assets. Assume that R_1 and R_2 are independently and identically distributed. Show that an expected utility maximizer will divide her wealth between both assets provided she is risk averse; and invest all her wealth in one of the assets if she's risk loving.

11.8. Suppose that a consumer faces two risks and only one of them is to be eliminated. Let $\tilde{w} = w_1$ with probability p and $\tilde{w} = w_2$ with probability $1 - p$. Let $\tilde{\epsilon} = 0$ if $\tilde{w} = w_2$. If $\tilde{w} = w_1$, $\tilde{\epsilon} = \epsilon$ with probability $1/2$ and $\tilde{\epsilon} = -\epsilon$ with probability $1/2$. Now, define a risk premium π_u for $\tilde{\epsilon}$ to satisfy:

$$ E[u(\tilde{w} - \pi_u)] = E[u(\tilde{w} + \tilde{\epsilon})]. \qquad (*) $$

(a) Show that if ϵ is sufficiently small,

$$\pi_u \approx \frac{-\frac{1}{2}pu''(w_1)\epsilon^2}{pu'(w_1) + (1-p)u'(w_2)}.$$

[Hint: Take Taylor expansions of appropriate orders on both sides of $(*)$— first-order on the left and second-order on the right.]

(b) Let $u(w) = -e^{-aw}$ and $v(w) = -e^{-bw}$. Compute the Arrow-Pratt measure for u and v.

(c) Suppose that $a > b$. Show that if $p < 1$ then there exists a value $w_1 - w_2$ large enough to make $\pi_v > \pi_u$. What does this suggest about the usefulness of the Arrow-Pratt measure for problems where risk is only partially reduced?

11.9. A person has an expected utility function of the form $u(w) = \sqrt{w}$. He initially has wealth of \$4. He has a lottery ticket that will be worth \$12 with probability 1/2 and will be worth \$0 with probability 1/2. What is his expected utility? What is the lowest price p at which he would part with the ticket?

11.10. A consumer has an expected utility function given by $u(w) = \ln w$. He is offered the opportunity to bet on the flip of a coin that has a probability π of coming up heads. If he bets \x, he will have $w + x$ if head comes up and $w - x$ if tails comes up. Solve for the optimal x as a function of π. What is his optimal choice of x when $\pi = 1/2$?

11.11. A consumer has an expected utility function of the form $u(w) = -1/w$. He is offered a gamble which gives him a wealth of w_1 with probability p and w_2 with probability $1 - p$. What wealth would he need now to be just indifferent between keeping his current wealth or accepting this gamble?

11.12. Consider an individual who is concerned about monetary payoffs in the states of nature $s = 1, \ldots, S$ which may occur next period. Denote the dollar payoff in state s by x_s and the probability that state s will occur by p_s. The individual is assumed to choose $\mathbf{x} = (x_1, \ldots, x_S)$ so as to maximize the *discounted expected value* of the payoff. The discount factor is denoted by α; i.e., $\alpha = 1/(1 + r)$, where r is the discount rate. The set of feasible payoffs is denoted by X, which we assume to be nonempty.

(a) Write down the individual's maximization problem.

(b) Define $v(\mathbf{p}, \alpha)$ to be the maximum discounted expected value that the individual can achieve if the probabilities are $\mathbf{p} = (p_1, \ldots p_S)$ and the discount factor is α. Show that $v(\mathbf{p}, \alpha)$ is homogeneous of degree 1 in α. (Hint: Does $v(\mathbf{p}, \alpha)$ look like something you have seen before?)

(c) Show that $v(\mathbf{p}, \alpha)$ is a *convex* function of $\mathbf{p}$.

(d) Suppose that you can observe an arbitrarily large number of optimal choices of $\mathbf{x}$ for various values of $\mathbf{p}$ and α. What properties must the set X possess in order for it to be recoverable from the observed choice behavior?

CHAPTER **12**

ECONOMETRICS

In the previous chapters we have examined various models of optimizing behavior. Here we examine how one can use the theoretical insights developed in those chapters to help estimate relationships that may have been generated by optimizing behavior.

Theoretical analysis and econometric analysis can interact in several ways. First, theory can be used to derive hypotheses that can be tested econometrically. Second, the theory can suggest ways to construct better estimates of model parameters. Third, the theory helps to specify the structural relationships in the model in a way that can lead to more appropriate estimation. Finally, the theory helps to specify appropriate functional forms to estimate.

12.1 The optimization hypothesis

We have seen that the model of optimizing choice imposes certain restrictions on observable behavior. These restrictions can be expressed in a number of ways: 1) the algebraic relationships such as WAPM, WACM, GARP, etc.; 2) the derivative relationships such as the conditions that certain substitution matrices must be symmetric and positive or negative semidefinite; 3) the dual relationships such as the fact that profits must be a convex function of prices.

The conditions implied by the maximization models are important for at least two reasons. First, they allow us to test the model of maximizing behavior. If the data don't satisfy the restrictions implied by the particular optimization model we are using, then we generally would not want to use that model to describe the observed behavior.

Second, the conditions allow us to estimate the parameters of our model more precisely. If we find that the theoretical restrictions imposed by optimization are not rejected in some particular data set, we may want to re-estimate our model in a way that requires the estimates to satisfy the restrictions implied by optimization.

Suppose, for example, we have an optimizing model that implies that some parameter α equals zero. First, we might want to test this restriction, and see if the estimated value of α is significantly different from zero. If the parameter is not significantly different from zero, we may want to accept the hypothesis that $\alpha = 0$ and re-estimate the model imposing this hypothesis. If the hypothesis is true, the second set of estimates of the other parameters in the system will generally be more efficient estimates.

Of course, if the hypothesis is false, the re-estimation procedure will not be appropriate. Our faith in the resulting estimates depends to some degree on how much faith we place in the results of the initial test of the optimization restrictions.

12.2 Nonparametric testing for maximizing behavior

If we are given a set of observations on firm choices, we can test the WAPM and/or WACM inequalities described earlier directly. If we have data on consumer choices, the conditions like GARP are only slightly more difficult to check. These conditions give us a definitive answer as to whether the data in question could have been generated by maximizing behavior.

These inequality conditions are easy to check; we simply see if the data in question satisfy certain inequality relationships. If we observe a violation of one of the inequalities, then we can reject the maximizing model. Suppose, for example, that we have several observations on a firm's choice of net outputs at various price vectors: $(\mathbf{p}^t, \mathbf{y}^t)$, for $t = 1, \ldots, T$. We may be interested in the hypothesis that this firm is maximizing profits in a competitive environment. We know that profit maximization implies WAPM: $\mathbf{p}^t \mathbf{y}^t \geq \mathbf{p}^t \mathbf{y}^s$ for all s and t. Testing WAPM simply involves checking to see whether these T^2 inequalities are satisfied.

In this framework a *single* observation where $\mathbf{p}^t \mathbf{y}^t < \mathbf{p}^t \mathbf{y}^s$ is enough to reject the profit-maximizing model. But perhaps this is too strong. Presumably what we really care about is not whether a particular firm is *exactly* maximizing profits, but rather whether its behavior is reasonably well-described by the model of profit maximization. Typically, we want to know not only *whether* the firm fails to maximize, but by *how much* the firm fails to maximize. If it only fails to maximize by a small amount, we may still be willing to accept the theory that the firm is "almost" maximizing profits.

There is a very natural measure of the magnitude of the violation of WAPM, namely the "residuals" $R_t = \max_s\{\mathbf{p}^t\mathbf{y}^s - \mathbf{p}^t\mathbf{y}^t\}$. The residual R_t measures how much more profit the firm could have had at observation t if it had made a different choice. It provides a reasonable measurement of the departure from profit-maximizing behavior. If the average value of R_t is small, then "almost" optimizing behavior may not be a bad model for this firm's behavior.

12.3 Parametric tests of maximizing behavior

The nonparametric tests described above are "exact" tests of optimization: they are necessary and sufficient conditions for data to be consistent with the optimization model. However, economists are often interested in the question of whether a particular parametric form is a good approximation to some underlying production function or utility function.

One way to answer this question is to use regression analysis, or more elaborate statistical techniques, to estimate the parameters of a functional form and see if we satisfy the restrictions imposed by the maximizing model. For example, suppose that we observe prices and choices for k goods. The Cobb-Douglas utility function implies that the demand for good i is a linear function of income divided by price: $x_i = a_i m/p_i$ for $i = 1, \ldots, k$.

It is unlikely that observed demand data will be exactly linear in m/p_i, so we may want to allow for an error term to represent measurement error, misspecification, left-out variables, and so on. Using ϵ_i for the error term on the ith equation, we have the **regression model**

$$x_i = a_i\frac{m}{p_i} + \epsilon_i \quad i = 1, \ldots, k. \tag{12.1}$$

It follows from the maximizing model that $\sum_{i=1}^{k} a_i = 1$. We can estimate the parameters of the model described by (12.1) and see if they satisfy this restriction. If they do, this is some evidence in favor of the Cobb-Douglas model; if the estimated parameters don't satisfy this restriction, this is evidence against the Cobb-Douglas parametric form.

If we use more elaborate functional forms, we get a more elaborate set of testable restrictions. We know from our study of consumer behavior that the fundamental observable restriction imposed by maximization is that the matrix of substitution terms must be negative semidefinite. This condition imposes a number of cross-equation restrictions that can be tested by standard hypothesis testing procedures.

12.4 Imposing optimization restrictions

If our statistical tests do not reject some particular parametric restrictions, we may want to re-estimate the model imposing those restrictions on the estimation procedure. To continue with our above example, the Cobb-Douglas demand system described in (12.1) implies that $\sum_{i=1}^{k} a_i = 1$. We may want to estimate the set of parameters (a_i) imposing this restriction as a maintained hypothesis. If the hypothesis is true, the resulting estimates will generally be better that the unconstrained estimates.

The optimization model often imposes restrictions on the error term as well as on the parameters. For example, another restriction imposed by the theoretical model is that $\sum_{i=1}^{k} p_i x_i(\mathbf{p}, m) = m$. Generally, the observed choices will satisfy the restriction $\sum_{i=1}^{k} p_i x_i = m$ by construction. If this is so, equations (12.1) imply that

$$\sum_{i=1}^{k} p_i x_i = m = \sum_{i=1}^{k} a_i m + \sum_{i=1}^{k} p_i \epsilon_i.$$

If we estimate our system subject to the constraint that $\sum_{i=1}^{k} a_i = 1$, we also would want to impose the restriction $\sum_{i=1}^{k} p_i \epsilon_i = 0$. That is, the k error terms must be orthogonal to the price vector.

12.5 Goodness-of-fit for optimizing models

The parametric tests briefly described in the last section describe how one can statistically test the hypothesis that observed choices were generated by maximization of some particular parametric form. These are "sharp" tests in the sense that we either reject the hypothesis of maximization or not. But in many cases it is often more appropriate to have a goodness-of-fit measure: how *close* are the observed choices to maximizing choices?

In order to answer this question, we need a sensible definition of "close." In the nonparametric analysis of profit maximization, we saw that one reasonable measure of this was how much additional profit the firm could have acquired if it had behaved differently. This idea can be applied more generally: one measure of goodness-of-fit is how far the economic agent fails to optimize the postulated objective function.

This measure can be calculated directly in the case of firm behavior. If our hypothesis is profit maximization or cost minimization, we simply calculate the lost profits or excess costs by comparing the best-fitting optimizing model to the actual choices. The application to utility maximization is slightly more subtle.

Suppose that we are examining consumer choice behavior using a Cobb-Douglas functional form. If the best fitting Cobb-Douglas utility function is described by the parameters $(\hat{a}_i)$, say, we can compare the utility of the *optimal* choices using the estimated utility function to the utility of the *actual* choices.

The problem with this measure is that the units of the utility function are arbitrary. What counts as "close" is not at all obvious. The solution to this problem is to use a *particular* utility function for calculating the goodness-of-fit measure. A natural choice here is the money metric utility function described in Chapter 7, page 109. The money metric utility function measures utility in units of money: how much money a consumer would need at fixed prices to be as well off as he would be consuming a bundle $\mathbf{x}$.

Let's see how to use this to construct a goodness-of-fit measure. Suppose we observe some data $(\mathbf{p}^t, \mathbf{x}^t)$ for $t = 1, \ldots, T$. We hypothesize that the consumer is maximizing a utility function $u(\mathbf{x}, \beta)$, where β is an unknown parameter (or list of parameters). Given $u(\mathbf{x}, \beta)$ we know that we can construct the money metric utility function $m(\mathbf{p}, \mathbf{x}, \beta)$ using standard optimization techniques.

We use the choice data to estimate the utility function $u(\mathbf{x}, \hat{\beta})$ that best describes the observed choice behavior. One way to see how well this utility function "fits" is to calculate the t "residuals"

$$G^t = \frac{m(\mathbf{p}^t, \mathbf{x}^t, \hat{\beta})}{\mathbf{p}^t \mathbf{x}^t}.$$

Here G^t measures the minimal amount of money the consumer needs to spend to get utility $u(\mathbf{x}^t, \hat{\beta})$ compared to the amount of money the consumer *actually* spent. This has a natural interpretation in terms of efficiency: if the average value of G^t is $\overline{G}$, then we can say that on the average the consumer is $\overline{G}$-percent efficient in his choice behavior.

If the consumer is perfectly maximizing the utility function $u(\mathbf{x}, \hat{\beta})$ then $\overline{G}$ will equal 1—the consumer will be 100% efficient in his consumption choice. If $\overline{G}$ is .95, then the consumer is 95% efficient, and so on.

12.6 Structural models and reduced form models

Suppose that we have a theory that suggests some relationships among a number of variables. Typically, there will be two types of variables in our model, **endogenous** variables, whose values are determined by our model, and **exogenous** variables, whose values are predetermined. For example, in our model of profit-maximizing behavior, the prices and the technology are exogenous variables, and the factor choices are endogenous variables.

Typically, a model can be expressed as a system of equations, each equation involving some relationships among the exogenous variables, the endogenous variables, and the parameters. This system of equations is known as a **structural model**.

Consider, for example, a simple demand and supply system:

$$D = a_0 - a_1 p + a_2 z_1 + \epsilon_1$$
$$S = b_0 + b_1 p + b_2 z_2 + \epsilon_2 \tag{12.2}$$
$$D = S$$

Here D and S represent the (endogenous) demand and supply for some good, p is its (endogenous) price, (a_i) and (b_i) are parameters, and z_1 and z_2 are other exogenous variables that affect demand and supply. The variables ϵ_1 and ϵ_2 are error terms. The system (12.2) is a structural system.

We could solve the structural system in a way that expressed the endogenous variable p as a function of the exogenous variables:

$$p = \frac{a_0 - b_0}{a_1 + b_1} + \frac{a_2}{a_1 + b_1} z_1 - \frac{b_2}{a_1 + b_1} z_2 + \frac{\epsilon_2 - \epsilon_1}{a_1 + b_1}. \tag{12.3}$$

This is the **reduced form** of the system.

It is usually not too difficult to estimate the reduced form of a model. In the demand-supply example, we would just estimate a regression of the form

$$p = \beta_0 + \beta_1 z_1 + \beta_2 z_2 + \epsilon_3.$$

The parameters (β_i) are a function of the parameters (a_i, b_i), but in general it will not be possible to recover unique estimates of the structural parameters (a_i, b_i) from the reduced-form parameters (β_i). The reduced-form parameters can be used to predict how the equilibrium price will change as the exogenous variables change. This may be useful for some purposes.

But for other purposes it may be necessary to have estimates of the structural parameters. For example, suppose that we wanted to predict how the equilibrium price in this market would respond to the imposition of a tax on the good. The structural model (12.2) suggests that the equilibrium price received by suppliers, p_s, should be a linear function of the tax:

$$p_s = \frac{a_0 - b_0}{a_1 + b_1} + \frac{a_2}{a_1 + b_1} z_1 - \frac{b_2}{a_1 + b_1} z_2 - \frac{b_1}{a_1 + b_1} t. \tag{12.4}$$

If we had data describing many different choices of taxes and the resulting supply prices, we could estimate the reduced form described by (12.4). But if we don't have such data, there is no way to estimate this reduced form. In order to predict how the equilibrium price will respond to the tax, we need to know the structural parameter $b_1/(a_1 + b_1)$. The reduced form parameters in equation (12.3) just don't provide enough information to answer this question.

This suggests that we must consider methods for estimating structural systems of equations such as (12.2). The simplest method would seem to be simply to estimate the demand equation and the supply equation separately using standard ordinary least squares (OLS) regression techniques. Is this likely to provide acceptable estimates of parameters?

We know from statistics that OLS estimates will have desirable properties if certain assumptions are met. One particular assumption is that the right-hand side variables in the regression should not be correlated with the error term.

However, this is not the case in our problem. The variable p depends on the error terms ϵ_1 and ϵ_2, as can easily be seen in equation (12.3). It can be shown that this dependence will generally result in biased estimates of the parameters.

In order to estimate systems of structural equations, we generally need to use more elaborate estimation techniques such as two-stage least squares or various maximum likelihood techniques. Such methods can be shown to have better statistical properties than OLS for estimation problems involving systems of equations.

In the simple demand-supply example described above, the theoretical relationship among the variables implies that certain estimation techniques are more appropriate than others. This will often be the case; part of the art of econometrics involves using the theory to guide the choice of statistical techniques. We will investigate this further in the context of an extended example in the next section.

12.7 Estimating technological relationships

Suppose that we want to estimate the parameters of a simple Cobb-Douglas production function. To be precise, suppose that we have a sample of farms and we hypothesize that the output of corn on farm i, C_i, depends on the corn planted, K_i, and the number of sunny days in the growing season, S_i. For the moment, we assume that these are the only two variables that affect the output of corn.

We suppose that the production relation is given by a Cobb-Douglas function $C_i = K_i^a S_i^{1-a}$. Taking logs, we can write the relationship between output and inputs as

$$\log C_i = a \log K_i + (1 - a) \log S_i. \qquad (12.5)$$

Suppose that the farmers do not observe the number of sunny days when they make their planting decision. Furthermore, the econometrician does not have data on the number of sunny days at each location. Hence, the econometrician regards (12.5) as a regression model of the form

$$\log C_i = a \log K_i + \epsilon_i, \qquad (12.6)$$

where ϵ_i is the "error term" $(1 - a) \log S_i$.

Econometric theory tells us that OLS will give us good estimates of the parameter a if $\log K_i$ and ϵ_i are uncorrelated. If the farmers don't observe $\log S_i = \epsilon_i$ when they choose K_i, then their choices cannot be affected by it. Hence, this is a reasonable assumption in this case, and OLS is an appropriate estimation technique.

Let us now look at a case where OLS is *not* a good estimation technique. Suppose now that the production relationship also depends on the quality of land at each farm so that $C_i = Q_i K_i^a S_i^{1-a}$, or

$$\log C_i = \log Q_i + a \log K_i + (1 - a) \log S_i.$$

As before, we assume that neither the econometrician nor the farmers observe S_i. However, let us now suppose that the farmers observe Q_i, but the econometrician doesn't. Now is it likely that estimating the regression (12.6) will give us good estimates of a?

The answer is *no*. Since each farmer observes Q_i, his choice of K_i will depend on Q_i. Hence, K_i will be correlated with the error term, and biased estimates are likely to result.

If we assume profit-maximizing behavior, we can be quite explicit about how the farmers will use their information about K_i. The (short-run) profit maximization problem for farmer i is

$$\max\ p_i Q_i K_i^a S_i^{1-a} - q_i K_i,$$

where p_i is the price of output and q_i is the price of seed facing the ith farmer. Taking the derivative with respect to K_i and solving for the factor demand function, we have

$$K_i = \left[a Q_i \frac{p_i}{q_i} \right]^{\frac{1}{1-a}} S_i. \tag{12.7}$$

It is clear that the farmer's knowledge of Q_i directly affects his choice of how much to plant, and thus how much output to produce.

Consider the scatter diagram of $\log K_i$ and $\log C_i$ in Figure 12.1. We have also plotted the function $\log C_i = a \log K_i + \overline{Q}$, where $\overline{Q}$ is the average quality.

It is clear from equation (12.7) that farmers with higher quality land will want to plant more corn. This means that if we observe a farm with a large input of K_i it is likely to be a farm with large Q_i. Hence, the output of the farm will be larger than the output of a farm with average quality land, so that the data points for farms with larger K_i's will lie *above* the true relationship for farms with average Qs. Similarly, farms with small inputs of K_i are likely to be farms with smaller than average Qs.

The result is that a regression line fitted to such data will give us an estimate for a that is larger than the true value of a. The underlying

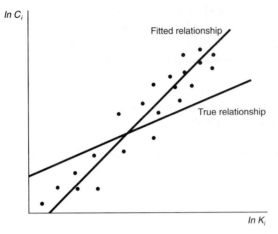

Figure 12.1

Scatter plot. This is a scatter plot of $\log K_i$ and $\log C_i$. Note that a farm with a large K_i will generally be a farm with better than average land, so its output will be larger than that of a farm with average quality land. Hence, such points will lie above the production relationship for a farm with the average quality of land.

problem is that large values of output are not due entirely to large values of inputs. There is a third omitted variable, land quality, that affects both the level of output and the choice of input.

Bias of this sort is very common in econometric work: typically some of the regression variables that influence some choice are themselves chosen by the economic agents. Suppose, for example, that we want to estimate the return to education. Generally people with higher income have higher amounts of education, but education is not a predetermined variable: people *choose* how much education to acquire. If people choose different amounts of education, they are presumably different in other unobserved ways. But these unobserved ways could also easily affect their income.

For example, suppose that people with higher IQ's would earn higher wages, regardless of their education. But people with higher IQ's also find it easier to acquire more education. This implies that people with higher education would have higher wages for two reasons: first, because they have higher IQ's on the average, and, second, because they have more education. A simple regression of wage on education would *overstate* the effect of education on income.

Alternatively, one might postulate that people with wealthy parents tend to have higher incomes. But wealthy parents can afford to purchase more education, and also to contribute more wealth to their children. Again, higher incomes will be associated with higher levels of education, but there may be no direct causal link between the two variables.

Simple regression analysis is appropriate for controlled experiments, but

Simple regression analysis is appropriate for controlled experiments, but often not adequate to deal with situations where the explanatory variables are chosen by the agents. In such cases it is necessary to have a structural model that expresses all relevant choices as a function of truly exogenous variables.

12.8 Estimating factor demands

In the case of production relationships, it may be useful to estimate the parameters of the production relationship indirectly. Consider for example equation (12.7). Taking logs, we can write this as

$$\log K_i = \frac{1}{1-a} \log a + \frac{1}{1-a} \log p_i - \frac{1}{1-a} \log q_i + \frac{1}{1-a} \log Q_i + \log S_i.$$

An appropriate regression for this equation is

$$\log K_i = \beta_0 + \beta_1 \log p_i + \beta_2 \log q_i + \epsilon_i,$$

where the constant term β_0 is some function of a and the mean values of $\log Q_i$ and $\log S_i$. Note that this specification implies that $\beta_2 = -\beta_1$.

Is this equation a likely candidate for OLS estimation? If the farmers are facing competitive markets for the output and inputs, the answer is *yes*, for in competitive markets the prices are outside of the control of the farmers. If the prices are uncorrelated with the error term, then OLS is an appropriate estimation technique.

Furthermore, the fact that $\beta_1 = -\beta_2$ for an optimizing model gives us a way to test optimization of a Cobb-Douglas production function. If we find that β_1 is significantly different from $-\beta_2$, we may be inclined to reject optimization. On the other hand, if we cannot reject the hypothesis that $\beta_1 = -\beta_2$, we may be inclined to impose it as a maintained hypothesis and estimate the model

$$\log K_i = \beta_0 + \beta_1 \log(p_i/q_i) + \epsilon_i.$$

In this case the demand function is a structural equation: it expresses choices as a function of exogenous variables. The estimates of this equation can be used to infer other properties of the technology.

12.9 More complex technologies

Consider the case where we have a production function relating output to several inputs. For simplicity, consider the Cobb-Douglas production function with two inputs: $f(x_1, x_2) = A x_1^a x_2^b$.

We know from Chapter 4, page 54, that the factor demand functions have the form

$$x_1(w_1, w_2, y) = A^{-\frac{1}{a+b}} \left[\frac{aw_2}{bw_1} \right]^{\frac{b}{a+b}} y^{\frac{1}{a+b}}$$

$$x_2(w_1, w_2, y) = A^{-\frac{1}{a+b}} \left[\frac{aw_2}{bw_1} \right]^{-\frac{a}{a+b}} y^{\frac{1}{a+b}}.$$

These demand functions have a linear-in-logarithm form, so we can write the regression model

$$\log x_1 = \beta_{01} + \beta_{11} \log(w_2/w_1) + \beta_{21} \log y + \epsilon_1$$
$$\log x_2 = \beta_{02} + \beta_{12} \log(w_1/w_2) + \beta_{22} \log y + \epsilon_2.$$

Here the parameters of the technology are functions of the regression co-efficients. However, it is important to observe that the *same* parameters a and b enter into the definitions of the coefficients. This means that the parameters of the two equations are not unrestricted, but are related. For example, it is easy to see that $\beta_{01} = \beta_{02}$. The system of equations should be estimated taking account of the **cross-equation restrictions**.

Alternatively, we could combine the two equations to form the cost function, $c(\mathbf{w}, y)$:

$$c(w_1, w_2, y) = A^{\frac{-1}{a+b}} \left[\left(\frac{a}{b} \right)^{\frac{b}{a+b}} + \left(\frac{a}{b} \right)^{\frac{-a}{a+b}} \right] w_1^{\frac{a}{a+b}} w_2^{\frac{b}{a+b}} y^{\frac{1}{a+b}}.$$

This also has a linear-in-logarithms form

$$\log c = \log \gamma_0 + \gamma_1 \log w_1 + \gamma_2 \log w_2 + \gamma_3 \log y.$$

The cross-equation restrictions for the factor demand functions are conveniently incorporated into one equation for the cost function. Furthermore, we know from our theoretical study of the cost function that it should be an increasing, homogeneous, concave function. These restrictions can be tested and imposed, if appropriate.

In fact, the cost function can be regarded as a reduced form of the system of factor demand. Unlike the demand and supply example we studied earlier, the cost function contains all of the relevant information about the structural model. For we know from our study of the cost function that the derivatives of the cost function give us the conditional factor demands. Hence, estimating the parameters of the cost function automatically gives us estimates of the parameters of the conditional factor demand functions.

However, it should be emphasized that this is only true under the maintained hypothesis of cost minimization. If the firms under examination are indeed minimizing costs or maximizing profits, we can use a variety of indirect techniques to estimate the technological parameters. These techniques will generally be preferable to direct techniques, if the optimization hypothesis is true.

12.10 Choice of functional form

All of our examples above have used the Cobb-Douglas functional form. This is for simplicity, not realism. In general, it is desirable to have a more flexible parametric form to represent technological tradeoffs.

One can write down an arbitrary functional form as a production function, but then one has to calculate the implied factor demands and/or cost function. It is much simpler to start with a parametric form for a cost function directly; then it is a simple matter of differentiation to find the appropriate factor demands.

We know from Chapter 6 that any monotonic, homogeneous, concave function of prices is a cost function for *some* well-behaved technology. Hence, all that is necessary is to find a functional form with the required properties.

In general we want to choose a parametric form for which some values of the parameters satisfy the restrictions imposed by optimization and some values don't. Then we can estimate the parameters and test the hypothesis that the estimated parameters satisfy the relevant restrictions imposed by the theory. We describe a few examples below.

EXAMPLE: The Diewert cost function

The **Diewert cost function** takes the form

$$c(\mathbf{w}, y) = y \sum_{i=1}^{k} \sum_{j=1}^{k} b_{ij} \sqrt{w_i w_j}.$$

For this functional form, we require that $b_{ij} = b_{ji}$. Note that we can also write this form as

$$c(\mathbf{w}, y) = y \left[\sum_{i=1}^{k} b_{ii} w_i + \sum_{i \neq j} \sum_{j \neq i} b_{ij} \sqrt{w_i w_j} \right].$$

Since the first part of this expression has the form of a Leontief cost function, this form is also known as a **generalized Leontief cost function**.

The factor demands have the form

$$x_i(\mathbf{w}, y) = y \sum_{j=1}^{k} b_{ij} \sqrt{w_j / w_i}.$$

These demands are linear in the b_{ij} parameters. If $b_{ij} \geq 0$ and some $b_{ij} > 0$, it is easy to verify that this form satisfies the necessary conditions to be a cost function.

The b_{ij} parameters can be related to the elasticities of substitution between the various factors; the larger the b_{ij} term, the greater the elasticity of substitution between factors i and j. The functional form imposes no restrictions on the various elasticities; the Diewert function can serve as a local second-order approximation to an arbitrary cost function.

EXAMPLE: The translog cost function

The **translog cost function** takes the form

$$\log c(\mathbf{w}, y) = a_0 + \sum_{i=1}^{k} a_i \log w_i + \frac{1}{2} \sum_{i=1}^{k} \sum_{j=1}^{k} b_{ij} \log w_i \log w_j + \log y.$$

For this function, we require that

$$\sum_{i=1}^{k} a_i = 1$$

$$b_{ij} = b_{ji}$$

$$\sum_{j=1}^{k} b_{ij} = 0.$$

Under these restrictions, the translog cost function is homogeneous in prices. If $a_i > 0$ and $b_{ij} = 0$ for all i and j, the cost function becomes a Cobb-Douglas function.

The conditional factor demands are not linear in the parameters, but the factor shares $s_i(\mathbf{w}, y) = w_i x_i(\mathbf{w}, y)/c(\mathbf{w}, y)$ are linear in parameters and are given by

$$s_i(\mathbf{w}, y) = a_i + \sum_{j=1}^{k} b_{ij} \ln w_i.$$

12.11 Estimating consumer demands

Our earlier examples have focused on estimating production relationships. These have the convenient feature that the objective function—profit or cost—is observable. In the case of the consumer demand behavior, the objective function is not directly observed. This makes things a bit more complicated conceptually, but doesn't create as many difficulties as one might expect.

Suppose that we are given data $(\mathbf{p}^t, \mathbf{x}^t)$ for $t = 1, \ldots, T$ and want to estimate some parametric demand function. We first investigate the case where we are interested in the demand for a single good, then the many-good case.

Demand functions for a single good

It is important to understand that even when we are only interested in the demand for a single good, there are still two goods involved: the good in which we are interested and "all other goods." We generally model this by thinking of the choice problem as a choice between the good in question and money to be spent on all other goods. See the discussion of Hicksian separability in Chapter 9, page 148.

Suppose that we use x to denote the amount purchased of the good in question and y to denote money to be spent on all other goods. If p is the price of the x-good, and q the price of the y-good, the utility maximization problem becomes

$$\max_{x,y} u(x,y)$$

such that $px + qy = m$.

We denote the demand function by $x(p, q, m)$. Since the demand function is homogeneous of degree zero, we can normalize by q, so that demand becomes a function of the *relative* price of x and real income: $x(p/q, m/q)$. In practice, p is the nominal price of the good in which we are interested and q is usually taken to be some consumer price index. The demand specification then says that the observed quantity demanded is some function of the "real price," p/q, and "real income," m/q.

One convenient feature of the two-good problem is that virtually any functional form is consistent with utility maximization. We know from Chapter 8, page 127, that the integrability equations in the two-good case can be expressed as a single ordinary differential equation. Thus, there will always be an indirect utility function that will generate a single demand equation via Roy's law. Essentially the only requirement imposed by maximization in the two-good case is that the compensated own price effect should be negative.

This means that one has great freedom in choosing functional forms consistent with optimization. Three common forms are

1) linear demand: $x = a + bp + cm$.

2) logarithmic demand: $\ln x = \ln a + b \ln p + c \ln m$.

3) semi-logarithmic demand: $\ln x = a + bp + cm$.

Each of these equations is associated with an indirect utility function. We derived indirect utility functions for logarithmic demand in Chapter 26, page 484, while the linear and semi-log cases were given as exercises. Estimating the parameters of the demand functions automatically gives us estimates of the parameters of the indirect utility function.

Once we have the indirect utility function we can use it to make a variety of predictions. For example, we can use the estimates to calculate the compensating or equivalent variation associated with some price change. For details, see Chapter 10, page 161.

Multiple equations

Suppose that we want to estimate a system of demands for more than two goods. In this case we could start with a functional form for the demand equations and then try to integrate them to find a utility function. However, it is generally much easier to specify a functional form for utility or indirect utility and then differentiate to find the demand functions.

EXAMPLE: Linear expenditure system

Suppose that the utility function takes the form

$$u(\mathbf{x}) = \sum_{i=1}^{k} a_i \ln(x_i - \gamma_i),$$

where $x_i > \gamma_i$. The utility maximization problem is

$$\max_{x_i} \sum_{i=1}^{k} a_i \ln(x_i - \gamma_i)$$

$$\text{such that } \sum_{i=1}^{k} p_i x_i = m.$$

If we let $z_i = x_i - \gamma_i$, we see that we can write the utility maximization problem as

$$\max_{z_i} \sum_{i=1}^{k} a_i \ln z_i$$

$$\text{such that } \sum_{i=1}^{k} p_i z_i = m - \sum_{i=1}^{k} p_i \gamma_i.$$

This is a Cobb-Douglas maximization problem in z_i. The demand functions for x_i can then easily be seen to have the form

$$x_i = \gamma_i + a_i \frac{m - \sum_{i=1}^{k} p_i \gamma_i}{p_i}.$$

EXAMPLE: Almost Ideal Demand System

The **Almost Ideal Demand System** (AIDS) has an expenditure function of the form

$$e(\mathbf{p}, u) = a(p) + b(p)u, \tag{12.8}$$

where

$$a(p) = \alpha_0 + \sum_i a_i \log p_i + \frac{1}{2} \sum_i \sum_j \gamma_{ij}^* \log p_i \log p_m$$

$$b(p) = \beta_0 \prod_i p_i \beta_i.$$

Since $e(\mathbf{p}, u)$ must be homogeneous in $\mathbf{p}$, the parameters must satisfy

$$\sum_{i=1}^{k} a_i = 1$$

$$\sum_{i=1}^{k} \gamma_{ij}^* = \sum_{j=1}^{k} \gamma_{ij}^* = \sum_{i=1}^{k} \beta_i = 0.$$

The demand functions can be derived by differentiating equation (12.8). However, it is usually more convenient to estimate the expenditure shares

$$s_i = \alpha_i + \sum_{j=1}^{k} \gamma_{ij} \log p_j + \beta_i \log \frac{m}{P}, \tag{12.9}$$

where P is a price index given by

$$\log P = \alpha_0 + \sum_{i=1}^{k} \log p_i + \frac{1}{2} \sum_{i=1}^{k} \sum_{j=1}^{k} \gamma_{ij} \log p_i \log p_j,$$

and

$$\gamma_{ij} = \frac{1}{2}(\gamma_{ij}^* + \gamma_{ji}^*).$$

The AIDS system is close to being linear, except for the price index term. In practice, econometricians typically use an arbitrary price index to calculate the m/P terms, and then estimate the rest of the parameters of the system using equation (12.9).

12.12 Summary

We have seen that the theoretical analysis of optimizing models can help to guide econometric investigations in several ways. First, it can provide ways to test the theories, in either a nonparametric or a parametric form. Secondly, the theory can suggest restrictions that can be used to construct more efficient estimates. Third, the theory can specify structural relationships in the models and guide the choice of estimation techniques. Finally, the theory can guide the choice of functional forms.

Notes

See Deaton & Muelbauer (1980) for a textbook discussion of applying consumer theory to estimation of demand systems. Varian (1990) discusses goodness-of-fit in more detail and gives some empirical examples.

CHAPTER 13

COMPETITIVE MARKETS

Up until now we have studied maximizing behavior of individual economic agents: firms and consumers. We have taken the economic environment as given, completely summarized by the vector of market prices. In this chapter we begin our study of how the market prices are determined by the actions of the individual agents. We start with the simplest model: a single competitive market.

13.1 The competitive firm

A **competitive firm** is one that takes the market price of output as being given and outside of its control. In a competitive market each firm takes the price as being independent of its own actions, although it is the actions of all firms taken together that determine the market price.

Let $\bar{p}$ be the market price. Then the demand curve facing an ideal competitive firm takes the form

$$D(p) = \begin{cases} 0 & \text{if } p > \bar{p} \\ \text{any amount} & \text{if } p = \bar{p} \\ \infty & \text{if } p < \bar{p}. \end{cases}$$

A competitive firm is free to set whatever price it wants and produce whatever quantity it is able to produce. However, if a firm is in a competitive market, and it sets a price above the prevailing market price, no one will purchase its product. If it sets its price below the market price, it will have as many customers as it wants; but it will needlessly forego profits, since it can also get as many customers as it wants by pricing at the market price. This is sometimes expressed by saying that a competitive firm faces an infinitely elastic demand curve.

If a competitive firm wants to sell any output at all, it must sell it at the market price. Of course, real world markets seldom achieve this ideal. The question is not whether any particular market is *perfectly* competitive—almost no market is. The appropriate question is to what degree models of perfect competition can generate insights about real-world markets. Just as frictionless models in physics can describe some important phenomena in the physical world, the frictionless model of perfect competition generates useful insights in the economic world.

13.2 The profit maximization problem

Since the competitive firm must take the market price as given, its profit maximization problem is very simple. It must choose output y so as to solve

$$\max_{y} \; py - c(y).$$

The first-order and second-order conditions for an interior solution are

$$p = c'(y^*)$$
$$c''(y^*) \geq 0.$$

We will typically assume that the second-order condition is satisfied as a *strict* inequality. This is not really necessary, but it makes some of the calculations simpler. We refer to this as the **regular** case.

The **inverse supply function**, denoted by $p(y)$, measures the price that must prevail in order for a firm to find it profitable to supply a given amount of output. According to the first-order condition, the inverse supply function is given by

$$p(y) = c'(y),$$

as long as $c''(y) > 0$.

The **supply function** gives the profit-maximizing output at each price. Therefore the supply function, $y(p)$, must identically satisfy the first-order condition

$$p \equiv c'(y(p)), \tag{13.1}$$

and the second-order condition

$$c''(y(p)) \geq 0.$$

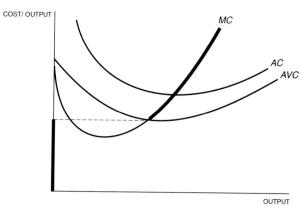

COST/OUTPUT

MC

AC

AVC

OUTPUT

Supply function and cost curves. In well-behaved cases, the supply function of a competitive firm is the upward sloping part of the marginal cost curve that lies above the average variable cost curve.

**Figure
13.1**

The direct supply curve and the inverse supply curve measure the same relationship—the relationship between price and the profit-maximizing supply of output. The two functions simply describe the relationship in different ways.

How does the supply of a competitive firm respond to a change in the price of output? We differentiate expression (13.1) with respect to p to find

$$1 = c''(y(p))y'(p).$$

Since normally $c''(y) > 0$, it follows that $y'(p) > 0$. Hence, the supply curve of a competitive firm has a positive slope, at least in the regular case. We derived this same result earlier in Chapter 2 using different methods.

We have focused on the interior solution to the profit maximization problem, but it is of interest to ask when the interior solution will be chosen. Let us write the cost function as $c(y) = c_v(y) + F$, so that total costs are expressed as the sum of variable costs and fixed costs. We interpret the fixed costs as being truly fixed—they must be paid even if output is zero. In this case, the firm will find it profitable to produce a positive level of output when the profits from doing so exceed the profits (losses) from producing zero:

$$py(p) - c_v(y(p)) - F \geq -F.$$

Rearranging this condition, we find that the firm will produce positive levels of output when

$$p \geq \frac{c_v(y(p))}{y(p)},$$

that is, when price is greater than average variable cost. See Figure 13.1 for a picture.

13.3 The industry supply function

The **industry supply function** is simply the sum of the individual firm supply functions. If $y_i(p)$ is the supply function of the ith firm in an industry with m firms, the industry supply function is given by

$$Y(p) = \sum_{i=1}^{m} y_i(p).$$

The **inverse supply function** for the industry is just the inverse of this function: it gives the minimum price at which the industry is willing to supply a given amount of output. Since each firm chooses a level of output where price equals marginal cost, each firm that produces a positive amount of output must have the same marginal cost. The industry supply function measures the relationship between industry output and the common marginal cost of producing this output.

EXAMPLE: Different cost functions

Consider a competitive industry with two firms, one with cost function $c_1(y) = y^2$, and other with cost function $c_2(y) = 2y^2$. The supply functions are given by

$$y_1 = p/2$$
$$y_2 = p/4.$$

The industry supply curve is therefore $Y(p) = 3p/4$. For any level of industry output Y, the marginal cost of production in each firm is $4Y/3$.

EXAMPLE: Identical cost functions

Suppose that there are m firms that have the common cost function $c(y) = y^2 + 1$. The marginal cost function is simply $MC(y) = 2y$, and the average variable cost function is $AVC(y) = y$. Since in this example the marginal costs are always greater than the average variable costs, the inverse supply function of the firm is given by $p = MC(y) = 2y$.

It follows that the supply function of the firm is $y(p) = p/2$ and the industry supply function is $Y(p, m) = mp/2$. The inverse industry supply function is therefore $p = 2Y/m$. Note that the slope of the inverse supply function is smaller the larger the number of firms.

13.4 Market equilibrium

The industry supply function measures the total output supplied at any price. The **industry demand function** measures the total output demanded at any price. An **equilibrium price** is a price where the amount demanded equals the amount supplied.

Why does such a price deserve to be called an equilibrium? The usual argument is that at any price at which demand does not equal supply, some economic agent would find it in its interest to unilaterally change its behavior. For example, consider a price in which the amount supplied exceeds the amount demanded. In this case some firms will not be able to sell all of the output that they produced. By cutting production these firms can save production costs and not lose any revenue, thereby increasing profits. Hence such a price cannot be an equilibrium.

If we let $x_i(p)$ be the demand function of individual i for $i = 1, \ldots, n$ and $y_j(p)$ be the supply function of firm j for $j = 1, \ldots, m$, then an equilibrium price is simply a solution to the equation

$$\sum_{i=1}^{n} x_i(p) = \sum_{j=1}^{m} y_j(p).$$

EXAMPLE: Identical firms

Suppose that the industry demand curve is linear, $X(p) = a - bp$, and the industry supply curve is that derived in the last example, $Y(p, m) = mp/2$. The equilibrium price is the solution to

$$a - bp = mp/2,$$

which implies

$$p^* = \frac{a}{b + m/2}.$$

Note that in this example the equilibrium price decreases as the number of firms increases.

For an arbitrary industry demand curve, equilibrium is determined by

$$X(p) = my(p).$$

How does the equilibrium price change as m changes? We regard p as an implicit function of m and differentiate to find

$$X'(p)p'(m) = my'(p)p'(m) + y(p),$$

which implies

$$p'(m) = \frac{y(p)}{X'(p) - my'(p)}.$$

Assuming that industry demand has a negative slope, the equilibrium price must decline as the number of firms increases.

13.5 Entry

The previous section described the computation of the industry supply curve when there was an exogenously given number of firms. However, in the long run, the number of firms in an industry is variable. If a firm expects that it can make a profit by producing a particular good, we might expect that it would decide to do so. Similarly, if an existing firm in an industry found itself persistently losing money, we might expect that it would exit the industry.

Several models of **entry** and **exit** are possible, depending on what sort of assumptions one makes about entry and exit costs, the foresight that potential entrants possess and so on. In this section we will describe a particularly simple model involving zero entry and exit costs and perfect foresight.

Suppose that we have an arbitrarily large number of firms with identical cost functions given by $c(y)$. We can calculate the break-even price p^* where profits are zero at the optimal supply of output. This is simply the level of output where average cost equals marginal cost.

Now we can plot the industry supply curves if there are $1, 2, \ldots$ firms in the industry and look for the largest number of firms so that the firms can break even. This is shown in Figure 13.2. If the equilibrium number of firms is large, then the relevant supply function will be very flat, and the equilibrium price will be close to p^*. Hence, it is often assumed that the supply curve of a competitive industry with free entry is essentially a horizontal line at a price equal to the minimum average cost.

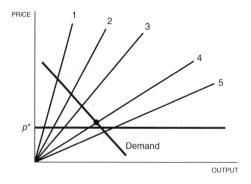

Figure 13.2 **Equilibrium number of firms.** In our model of entry, the equilibrium number of firms is the largest number of firms that can break even. If this number is reasonably large, the equilibrium price must be close to minimum average cost.

In this model of entry, the equilibrium price can be larger than the break-even price. Even though the firms in the industry are making positive profits, entry is inhibited since potential entrants correctly foresee that their entry would result in negative profits.

As usual, positive profits can be regarded as economic rent. In this case, we can view the profits as being the "rent to being first." That is, investors would be willing to pay up to the present value of the stream of profits earned by an incumbent firm in order to acquire that stream of profits. This rent can be counted as an (opportunity) cost of remaining in the industry. If this accounting convention is followed, firms earn zero profits in equilibrium.

EXAMPLE: Entry and long-run equilibrium

If $c(y) = y^2 + 1$, then the breakeven level of output can be found by setting average cost equal to marginal cost:

$$y + 1/y = 2y,$$

which implies that $y = 1$. At this level of output, marginal cost is given by 2, so this is the breakeven price. According to our entry model, firms will enter the industry as long as they determine that they will not drive the equilibrium price below 2.

Suppose that demand is linear, as in the previous example. Then the equilibrium price will be the smallest p^* that satisfies the conditions

$$p^* = \frac{a}{b + m/2}$$
$$p^* \geq 2.$$

As m increases, the equilibrium price must get closer and closer to 2.

13.6 Welfare economics

We have seen how to calculate the competitive equilibrium: the price at which supply equals demand. In this section we investigate the welfare properties of this equilibrium. There are several approaches to this issue, and the one we pursue here, the **representative consumer** approach, is probably the simplest. Later on, in our discussion of general equilibrium theory, we will describe a different and more general approach.

Let us suppose that the market demand curve, $x(p)$, is generated by maximizing the utility of a single representative consumer who has a utility function of the form $u(x) + y$. The x-good is the good under examination in this particular market. The y-good is a proxy for "everything else." The most convenient way to think of the y-good is as money left over for purchasing other goods after the consumer makes the optimal expenditure on the x-good.

We have seen in Chapter 10 that this sort of utility function yields an inverse demand curve of the form

$$p = u'(x).$$

The direct demand function, $x(p)$, is simply the inverse of this function, so it satisfies the first-order condition

$$u'(x(p)) = p.$$

Note the special feature: in the case of quasilinear utility the demand function is independent of income. This feature makes for especially simple equilibrium and welfare analysis.

As long as we've assumed a representative consumer we may as well assume a representative firm, and let it have cost function $c(x)$. We interpret this as saying that the production of x units of output requires $c(x)$ units of the y-good, and make the assumption that $c(0) = 0$. We also assume that $c''(\cdot) > 0$ so that the first-order conditions uniquely determine the profit-maximizing supply of the representative firm.[1]

The profit-maximizing (inverse) supply function of the representative firm is given by $p = c'(x)$. Hence, the **equilibrium** level of output of the x-good is simply the solution to the equation

$$u'(x) = c'(x). \tag{13.2}$$

This is the level of output at which the marginal willingness-to-pay for the x-good just equals its marginal cost of production.

13.7 Welfare analysis

Suppose that instead of using the market mechanism to determine output, we simply determined directly the amount of output that maximized the representative consumer's utility. This problem can be stated as

$$\max_{x,y} u(x) + y$$

$$\text{such that } y = \omega - c(x).$$

---

[1] Of course, competitive behavior is very unreasonable if there is literally a single firm; it is better to think of this as just the "average" or "representative" behavior of the firms in a competitive industry.

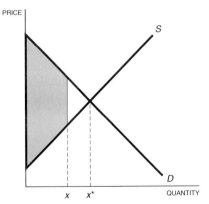

PRICE

S

D

x   x*   QUANTITY

Figure 13.3

Direct utility. The equilibrium quantity maximizes the vertical area between the demand and the supply curve.

Here w is the consumer's initial endowment of the y-good.
Substituting from the constraint, we rewrite this problem as

$$\max_{x} \ u(x) + w - c(x).$$

The first-order condition is

$$u'(x) = c'(x), \tag{13.3}$$

and the second-order condition is automatically satisfied by our earlier curvature assumptions. Note that equations (13.2) and (13.3) determine the same level of output: in this instance the competitive market results in exactly the same level of production and consumption as does maximizing utility directly.

The welfare maximization problem is simply to maximize total utility: the utility of consuming the x-good plus the utility from consuming the y-good. Since x units of the x-good means giving up $c(x)$ units of the y-good, our social objective function is $u(x) + w - c(x)$. The initial endowment w is just a constant, so we may as well take our social objective function to be $u(x) - c(x)$.

We have seen that $u(x)$ is simply the area under the (inverse) demand curve up to x. Similarly, $c(x)$ is simply the area under the marginal cost curve up to x since

$$c(x) - c(0) = \int_{0}^{x} c'(x) \, dx$$

and we are assuming that $c(0) = 0$.

Hence, choosing x to maximize utility minus costs is equivalent to choosing x to maximize the area under the demand curve and above the supply curve, as in Figure 13.3.

Here's another way to look at the same calculation. Let $CS(x) = u(x) - px$ be the **consumer's surplus** associated with a given level of output: this measures the difference between the "total benefits" from the consumption of the x-good and the expenditure on the x-good. Similarly, let $PS(x) = px - c(x)$ be the profits, or the **producer's surplus** earned by the representative firm.

Then the maximization of **total surplus** entails

$$\max_x \ CS(x) + PS(x) = [u(x) - px] + [px - c(x)],$$

or

$$\max_x \ u(x) - c(x).$$

Hence, we can also say that the competitive equilibrium level of output maximizes total surplus.

13.8 Several consumers

The analysis of the last section only dealt with a single consumer and a single firm. However, it is easily extended to multiple consumers and firms. Suppose that there are $i = 1, \dots, n$ consumers and $j = 1, \dots, m$ firms. Each consumer i has a quasilinear utility function $u_i(x_i) + y_i$ and each firm j has a cost function $c_j(x_j)$.

An **allocation** in this context will describe how much each consumer consumes of the x-good and the y-good, (x_i, y_i), for $i = 1, \dots, n$ and how much each firm produces of the x-good, z_j, for $j = 1, \dots, m$. Since we know the cost function of each firm, the amount of the y-good used by each firm j is simply $c_j(z_j)$. The **initial endowment** of each consumer is taken to be some given amount of the y-good, w_i, and 0 of the x-good.

A reasonable candidate for a welfare maximum in this case is an allocation that maximizes the sum of utilities, subject to the constraint that the amount produced be feasible. The sum of utilities is

$$\sum_{i=1}^{n} u_i(x_i) + \sum_{i=1}^{m} y_i.$$

The total amount of the y-good is the sum of the initial endowments, minus the amount used up in production:

$$\sum_{i=1}^{n} y_i = \sum_{i=1}^{n} w_i - \sum_{j=1}^{m} c_j(z_j).$$

Substituting this into the objective function and recognizing the feasibility constraint that the total amount of the x-good produced must equal the total amount consumed, we have the maximization problem

$$\max_{x_i, z_j} \sum_{i=1}^{n} u_i(x_i) + \sum_{i=1}^{n} \omega_i - \sum_{j=1}^{m} c_j(z_j)$$

$$\text{such that } \sum_{i=1}^{n} x_i = \sum_{j=1}^{m} z_j.$$

Letting λ be the Lagrange multiplier on the constraint, the answer to this maximization problem must satisfy

$$u_i'(x_i^*) = \lambda$$
$$c_j'(z_j^*) = \lambda,$$

along with the feasibility constraint.

But note that these are precisely the conditions that must be satisfied by an equilibrium price $p^* = \lambda$. Such an equilibrium price makes marginal utility equal to marginal cost and simultaneously makes demand equal to supply. Hence, the market equilibrium necessarily maximizes welfare, at least as measured by the sum of the utilities.

Of course, this says nothing at all about the distribution of *total* utility, since that will depend on the pattern of initial endowments, (ω_i). In the case of quasilinear utility, the equilibrium price doesn't depend on the distribution of wealth, and any distribution of initial endowments is consistent with the equilibrium conditions given above.

13.9 Pareto efficiency

We have just seen that a competitive equilibrium maximizes the sum of utilities, at least in the case of quasilinear utilities. But it is far from obvious that the sum of utilities is a sensible objective function, even in this restricted case.

A more general objective is the idea of **Pareto efficiency**. A Pareto efficient allocation is one for which there is no way to make all agents better off. Said another way, a Pareto efficient allocation is one for which each agent is as well off as possible, given the utilities of the other agents.

Let us examine the conditions for Pareto efficiency in the case of quasi-linear utility functions. For simplicity, we limit ourselves to the situation where there is some fixed amount of the two goods, $(\bar{x}, \bar{y})$, and there are only two individuals. In this case, a Pareto efficient allocation is one that maximizes the utility of agent 1, say, while holding agent 2 fixed at some given level of utility $\bar{u}$.

$$\max_{x_1, y_1} u_1(x_1) + y_1$$
$$\text{such that } u_2(\bar{x} - x_1) + \bar{y} - y_1 = \bar{u}.$$

Substituting from the constraint into the objective function, we have the unconstrained maximization problem

$$\max_{x_1} u_1(x_1) + u_2(\bar{x} - x_1) + \bar{y} - \bar{u}_2,$$

which has the first-order condition

$$u_1'(x_1) = u_2'(x_2). \tag{13.4}$$

For any given value of x_1, this condition will uniquely determine an efficient level of x_2. However, the distribution of y_1 and y_2 is arbitrary. Transferring the y-good back and forth between the two consumers makes one better off and the other worse off, but doesn't affect the marginal conditions for efficiency at all.

Finally, consider the relationship between (13.4) and the competitive equilibrium. At an equilibrium price p^*, each consumer adjusts his consumption of the x-good so that

$$u_1'(x_1^*) = u_2'(x_2^*) = p^*.$$

Hence, the necessary condition for Pareto efficiency is satisfied. Furthermore, any allocation that is Pareto efficient must satisfy (13.4), which essentially determines a price p^* at which this Pareto efficient allocation would be supported as a competitive equilibrium.

As it happens, essentially the same results hold in general, even if the utility functions are not quasilinear. However, in general the equilibrium prices will depend on the distribution of the y-good. We will investigate this sort of dependency further in the chapter on general equilibrium.

13.10 Efficiency and welfare

On first encounter it seems peculiar that we get the same answer when we maximize a sum of utilities as when we solve the Pareto efficiency problem. Let's explore this a bit more. For simplicity we stick with two consumers and two goods, but everything generalizes to more consumers and goods.

Suppose that there is some initial amount of the x-good, $\bar{x}$, and some initial amount of the y-good, $\bar{y}$. An efficient allocation maximizes one person's utility given a constraint on the other person's utility level:

$$\max_{x_1,y_1} u_1(x_1) + y_1$$
$$\text{such that } u_2(\bar{x} - x_1) + \bar{y} - y_1 = \bar{u}_2. \tag{13.5}$$

An allocation that maximizes the sum of utilities solves

$$\max_{x_1,y_1} u_1(x_1) + u_2(\bar{x} - x_1) + y_1 + \bar{y} - y_1. \tag{13.6}$$

We have already observed that the same x_1^* solves both of these problems. However, the y-good that solves these two problems is different. *Any* pair (y_1, y_2) maximizes the sum of utilities, but there will only be one value of y_1 that satisfies the utility constraint in (13.5). The solution to (13.5) is just *one* of the many solutions to (13.6).

The special structure of quasilinear utility implies that all Pareto efficient allocations can be found by solving (13.6): all Pareto efficient allocations have the same value of (x_1^*, x_2^*) but they differ in (y_1^*, y_2^*). This is why we (apparently) got the same answer by maximizing the sum of utilities as by determining a Pareto efficient allocation directly.[2]

13.11 The discrete good model

The discrete good model is another useful special case for examination of market behavior. In this model, there are again two goods, an x-good and a y-good, but the x-good can only be consumed in discrete amounts. In particular, we suppose that the consumer always purchases either one or zero units of the x-good.

Thus the utility achieved by a consumer with income m facing a price of p if she purchases the good is given by $u(1, m - p)$; if she chooses not to purchase the good she gets utility $u(0, m)$. The reservation price is that price r that just makes the consumer indifferent between purchasing the x-good or not. That is, it is the price r that satisfies the equation

$$u(1, m - r) = u(0, m).$$

The demand curve for a single consumer looks like that depicted in Figure 13.4A; the aggregate demand curve for many consumers with different reservation prices has the staircase shape depicted in Figure 13.4B.

The case with quasilinear preferences and a discrete good is especially simple. In this case the utility if the consumer purchases the good is simply $u(1) + m - p$ and her utility if she doesn't is $u(0) + m$. The reservation price r is the solution to

$$u(1) + m - r = u(0) + m,$$

which is easily seen to be $r = u(1) - u(0)$. Using the convenient normalization that $u(0) = 0$, we see that the reservation price is simply equal to the utility of consumption of the x-good.

If the price of the x-good is p, then a consumer who chooses to consume the good has a utility of $u(1) + m - p = m + r - p$. Hence, the consumer's

---

[2] There is one caveat to these claims: they require that we have an interior solution in (y_1, y_2). If consumer 2's target utility level is so low that it can only be achieved by setting $y_2 = 0$, then the equivalence between the two problems breaks down.

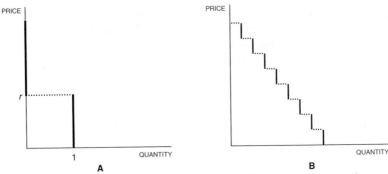

Figure 13.4   **Reservation price.** Panel A depicts the demand curve for a single consumer. Panel B depicts the aggregate demand curve for many consumers with different reservation prices.

surplus $r - p$ is simply a way of measuring the utility achieved by a consumer facing price p.

This special structure makes equilibrium and welfare analysis very simple. The market equilibrium price simply measures the reservation price of the **marginal consumer**—the consumer who is just indifferent between purchasing and not purchasing the good. The marginal consumer gets (approximately) zero consumer's surplus; the **inframarginal consumers** typically get positive consumer's surplus.

13.12 Taxes and subsidies

We have seen that the term comparative statics refers to the analysis of how an economic outcome varies as the economic environment changes. In the context of competitive markets, we generally ask how the equilibrium price and/or quantity changes as some policy variable changes. Taxes and subsidies are a convenient example.

The important thing to remember about a tax is that there are always *two* prices in the system, the **demand price** and the **supply price**. The demand price, p_d, is the price paid by the demanders of a good, and the supply price, p_s, is the price received by the suppliers of the good; they differ by the amount of the tax or subsidy.

For example, a **quantity tax** is a tax levied on the amount of a good consumed. This means that the price paid by the demanders is greater than the price received by the suppliers by the amount of the tax:

$$p_d = p_s + t.$$

A **value tax** is a tax levied on the expenditure of a good. It is usually expressed as a percentage amount, such as a 10 percent sales tax. A value tax at rate τ leads to a specification of the form

$$p_d = (1 + \tau)p_s.$$

Subsidies have a similar structure; a **quantity subsidy** of amount s means that the seller receives s dollars more per unit than the buyer pays, so that $p_d = p_s - s$.

The demander's behavior depends on the price she faces and the supplier's behavior depends on the price that she faces. Hence we write $D(p_d)$ and $S(p_s)$. The typical equilibrium condition is that demand equals supply; this leads to the two equations:

$$D(p_d) = S(p_s)$$
$$p_d = p_s + t.$$

Inserting the second equation into the first, we can solve either

$$D(p_s + t) = S(p_s),$$

or

$$D(p_d) = S(p_d - t).$$

Obviously, the solution for p_d and p_s is independent of which equation we solve.

Another way to solve this kind of tax problem is to use the *inverse* demand and supply functions. In this case the equations become

$$P_d(q) = P_s(q) + t,$$

or

$$P_s(q) = P_d(q) - t.$$

Once we have solved for the equilibrium prices and quantity, it is reasonably straightforward to do the welfare analysis. The utility of consumption accruing to the consumer at the equilibrium x^* is $u(x^*) - p_d x^*$. The profits accruing to the firm are $p_s x^* - c(x^*)$. Finally, the revenues accruing to the government are $tx^* = (p_d - p_s)x^*$. The simplest case is where the profits from the firm and the tax revenues both accrue to the representative consumer, yielding a net welfare of

$$W(x^*) = u(x^*) - c(x^*).$$

This is simply the area below the demand curve minus the area below the marginal cost curve, and is depicted in Figure 13.5. The difference between the surplus achieved with the tax and the welfare achieved in the original equilibrium is known as the **deadweight loss**; it is given by the triangle-shaped region in Figure 13.5. The deadweight loss measures the value to the consumer of the lost output.

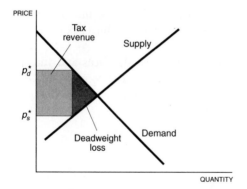

Figure 13.5   **Deadweight loss.**   The lightly shaded region indicates the total revenue from the tax. The darker triangular region is the deadweight loss.

Notes

This is standard neoclassical analysis of a single market. It probably first took the form examined here in Marshall (1920).

Exercises

13.1. Let $v(p) + m$ be the indirect utility function of a representative consumer, and let $\pi(p)$ be the profit function of a representative firm. Let welfare as a function of price be given by $v(p) + \pi(p)$. Show that the competitive price *minimizes* this function. Can you explain why the equilibrium price minimizes this welfare measure rather than maximizes it?

13.2. Show that the integral of the supply function between p_0 and p_1 gives the change in profits when price changes from p_0 to p_1.

13.3. An industry consists of a large number of firms, each of which has a cost function of the form

$$c(w_1, w_2, y) = (y^2 + 1)w_1 + (y^2 + 2)w_2.$$

(a) Find the average cost curve of a firm and describe how it shifts as the factor price w_1/w_2 changes.

(b) Find the short-run supply curve of an individual firm.

(c) Find the long-run industry supply curve.

(d) Describe an input requirement set for an individual firm.

13.4. Farmers produce corn from land and labor. The labor cost in dollars to produce y bushels of corn is $c(y) = y^2$. There are 100 identical farms which all behave competitively.

(a) What is the individual farmer's supply curve of corn?

(b) What is the market supply of corn?

(c) Suppose the demand curve of corn is $D(p) = 200 - 50p$. What is the equilibrium price and quantity sold?

(d) What is the equilibrium rent on the land?

13.5. Consider a model where the U.S. and England engage in trade in umbrellas. The representative firm in England produces the export model umbrella according to a production function $f(K, L)$ where K and L are the amounts of capital and labor used in production. Let r and w be the price of capital and the price of labor respectively in England, and let $c(w, r, y)$ be the cost function associated with the production function $f(K, L)$. Suppose that initially the equilibrium price of umbrellas is p^* and the equilibrium output is y^*. Assume for simplicity that all of the export model umbrellas are exported, that there is no production of umbrellas in the U.S., and that all markets are competitive.

(a) England decides to subsidize the production and export of umbrellas by imposing an export subsidy s on each umbrella, so that each umbrella exported earns the exporter $p + s$. What size import tax $t(s)$ should the U.S. choose so as to offset the imposition of this subsidy; i.e., to keep the production and export of umbrellas constant at y^*? (Hint: This is the easy part; don't get too subtle.)

(b) Since it is so easy for the U.S. to offset the effects of this *export subsidy*, England decides instead to use a *capital subsidy*. In particular, they decide to subsidize capital purchases with a specific subsidy of s so that the price of capital to English umbrella makers is $r - s$. The U.S. decides to retaliate by putting a tax $t(s)$ on imported umbrellas that will be sufficient to keep the number of umbrellas produced constant at y^*. What must be the relationship between the price paid by the consumers, p, the tax, $t(s)$, and the cost function, $c(w, r, y)$?

(c) Calculate an expression for $t'(s)$ involving the conditional factor demand function for capital, $K(w, r, y)$.

(d) Suppose that the production function exhibits constant returns to scale. What simplification does this make to your formula for $t'(s)$?

(e) Suppose that capital is an inferior factor of production in umbrella making. What is unusual about the tariff $t(s)$ that will offset the capital subsidy in England?

13.6. On a tropical island there are 100 boat builders, numbered 1 through 100. Each builder can build up to 12 boats a year and each builder maximizes its profits given the market price. Let y denote the number of boats built per year by a particular builder, and suppose that builder 1 has a cost function $c(y) = 11 + y$, builder 2 has a cost function $c(y) = 11 + 2y$, etc. That is, for each i, from 1 to 100, boat builder i has a cost function $c(y) = 11 + iy$. Assume that the fixed cost of \$11 is a quasifixed cost; i.e., it is only paid if the firm produces a positive level of output. If the price of boats is 25, how many builders will choose to produce a positive amount of output? If the price of boats is 25, how many boats will be built per year in total?

13.7. Consider an industry with the following structure. There are 50 firms that behave in a competitive manner and have identical cost functions given by $c(y) = y^2/2$. There is one monopolist that has 0 marginal costs. The demand curve for the product is given by

$$D(p) = 1000 - 50p.$$

(a) What is the monopolist's profit-maximizing output?

(b) What is the monopolist's profit-maximizing price?

(c) How much does the competitive sector supply at this price?

13.8. U.S. consumers have a demand function for umbrellas which has the form $D(p) = 90 - p$. Umbrellas are supplied by U.S. firms and U.K. firms. For simplicity, assume that there is a single representative firm in each country that behaves competitively. The cost function for producing umbrellas is given by $c(y) = y^2/2$ in each country.

(a) What is the aggregate supply function for umbrellas?

(b) What is the equilibrium price and quantity sold?

(c) Now the domestic industry lobbies for protection and Congress agrees to put a \$3 tariff on foreign umbrellas. What is the new U.S. price for umbrellas paid by the consumers?

(d) How many umbrellas are supplied by foreign firms and how many are supplied by domestic firms?

CHAPTER 14

MONOPOLY

The word **monopoly** originally meant the right of exclusive sale. It has come to be used to describe any situation in which some firm or small group of firms has the exclusive control of a product in a given market. The difficulty with this definition comes in defining what one means by a "given market." There are many firms in the soft-drink market, but only a few firms in the cola market.

The relevant feature of a monopolist from the viewpoint of economic analysis is that a monopolist has market power in the sense that the amount of output that it is able to sell responds continuously as a function of the price it charges. This is to be contrasted to the case of a competitive firm whose sales drop to zero if it charges a price higher than the prevailing market price. A competitive firm is a *price-taker*; a monopoly is a *price-maker*.

The monopolist faces two sorts of constraints when it chooses its price and output levels. First, it faces the standard technological constraints of the sort described earlier—there are only certain patterns of inputs and outputs that are technologically feasible. We will find it convenient to summarize the technological constraints by the use of the cost function,

$c(y)$. (We omit the factor prices as an argument in the cost function since we will assume that they are fixed.)

The second set of constraints that the monopolist faces is that presented by the consumers' behavior. The consumers are willing to purchase different amounts of the good at different prices, and we summarize this relationship using the demand function, $D(p)$.

The monopolist's profit maximization problem can be written as

$$\max_{p,y} py - c(y)$$

$$\text{such that } D(p) \geq y$$

In most cases of interest, the monopolist will want to produce the amount that the consumers demand, so the constraint can be written as the equality $y = D(p)$. Substituting for y in the objective function, we have the problem

$$\max_{p} pD(p) - c(D(p)).$$

Although this is perhaps the most natural way to pose the monopolist's maximization problem, it turns out to be more convenient in most situations to use the *inverse* rather than the direct demand function.

Let $p(y)$ be the inverse demand function—the price that must be charged to sell y units of output. Then the revenue that the monopolist can expect to receive if it produces y units of output is $r(y) = p(y)y$. We can pose the monopolist's maximization problem as

$$\max_{y} p(y)y - c(y).$$

The first- and second-order conditions for this problem are

$$p(y) + p'(y)y = c'(y) \tag{14.1}$$
$$2p'(y) + p''(y)y - c''(y) \leq 0. \tag{14.2}$$

The first-order condition says that at the profit-maximizing choice of output marginal revenue must equal marginal cost. Let us consider this condition more closely. When the monopolist considers selling dy units more output, it has to take into account two effects. First, its revenues increase by $p\,dy$ because it sells more output at the current price. But second, in order to sell this additional output it must reduce its price by $dp = \dfrac{dp}{dy}dy$, and this lower price applies to all the units y it is selling. The additional revenue from selling the additional output is therefore given by

$$p\,dy + dp\,y = \left[p + \frac{dp}{dy}y\right]dy,$$

and it is this quantity that must be balanced against marginal cost.

The second-order condition requires that the derivative of marginal revenue must be less than the derivative of marginal cost; i.e., the marginal revenue curve crosses the marginal cost curve from above.

The first-order condition can be rearranged to take the form

$$r'(y) = p(y)\left[1 + \frac{dp}{dy}\frac{y}{p}\right] = c'(y),$$

or

$$p(y)\left[1 + \frac{1}{\epsilon(y)}\right] = c'(y), \tag{14.3}$$

where

$$\epsilon(y) = \frac{p}{y}\frac{dy}{dp}$$

is the (price) **elasticity of demand** facing the monopolist. Note that the elasticity will be a negative number as long as the consumers' demand curve has a negative slope, which is certainly the standard case.

It follows from the first-order condition that at the optimal level of output the elasticity of demand must be greater than 1 in absolute value. If this were not the case, marginal revenue would be negative and hence could not be equal to the nonnegative marginal cost.

The optimal output of the monopolist is represented graphically in Figure 14.1. The marginal revenue curve is given by $r'(y) = p(y) + p'(y)y$. Since $p'(y) < 0$ by assumption, the marginal revenue curve lies beneath the inverse demand curve.

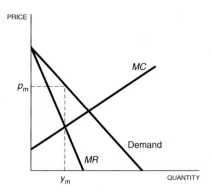

Determination of the monopoly output. The monopolist produces where marginal revenue equals marginal cost.

Figure 14.1

When $y = 0$ the marginal revenue from selling an extra unit of output is just the price $p(0)$. However, when $y > 0$, the marginal revenue from selling an extra unit of output must be less than the price since the only way to sell the additional output is to reduce the price, and this reduction in the price will affect the revenue received from all the inframarginal units sold.

The optimal level of output of the monopolist is where the marginal revenue curve crosses the marginal cost curve. In order to satisfy the second-order condition, the MR curve must cross the MC curve from above. We will typically assume that there is a unique profit-maximizing level of output. Given the level of output, say y^*, the price charged will be given by $p(y^*)$.

14.1 Special cases

There are two special cases for monopoly behavior that are worth mentioning. The first is that of linear demand. If the inverse demand curve is of the form $p(y) = a - by$, then the revenue function will be of the form $r(y) = ay - by^2$ and the marginal revenue takes the form $r'(y) = a - 2by$. Hence, the marginal revenue curve is twice as steep as the demand curve. If firm exhibits constant marginal costs of the form $c(y) = cy$, we can solve the marginal revenue equals marginal cost equations to determine the monopoly price and output directly:

$$y^* = \frac{a - c}{2b}$$
$$p^* = \frac{a + c}{2}.$$

The other case of interest is the constant elasticity demand function, $y = Ap^{-b}$. As we saw earlier, the elasticity of demand is constant and given by $\epsilon(y) = -b$. In this case we can apply (14.3) and write

$$p(y) = \frac{c}{1 - 1/b}.$$

Hence, for the constant elasticity demand function, price is a constant markup over marginal cost, with the amount of the markup depending on the elasticity of demand.

14.2 Comparative statics

It is often of interest to determine how the monopolist's output and price change as its costs change. Suppose for simplicity that the marginal costs are constant. Then the profit maximization problem is

$$\max_{y} \; p(y)y - cy,$$

and the first-order condition is

$$p(y) + p'(y)y - c = 0.$$

We know from the standard comparative statics calculation that the sign of dy/dc is the same as the sign of the derivative of the first-order condition with respect to c. This is easily seen to be negative, so we conclude that a profit-maximizing monopolist will always reduce its output when its marginal costs increase.

It is more interesting to calculate the effect of a cost change on price. We know from the chain rule that

$$\frac{dp}{dc} = \frac{dp}{dy}\frac{dy}{dc}.$$

It is clear from this expression that $dp/dc > 0$, but it is often useful to know the magnitude of dp/dc.

The standard comparative statics calculation tells us that

$$\frac{dy}{dc} = -\frac{\partial^2 \pi / \partial y \partial c}{\partial^2 \pi / \partial y^2}.$$

Taking the appropriate second derivatives of the profit function, we have

$$\frac{dy}{dc} = \frac{1}{2p'(y) + yp''(y)}.$$

It follows that

$$\frac{dp}{dc} = \frac{p'(y)}{2p'(y) + yp''(y)}.$$

This can also be written as

$$\frac{dp}{dc} = \frac{1}{2 + yp''(y)/p'(y)}.$$

From this expression, it is easy to see what happens in the special cases mentioned above. If demand is linear, then $p''(y) = 0$ and $dp/dc = 1/2$. If the demand function exhibits constant elasticity of ϵ, then $dp/dc = \epsilon/(1+\epsilon)$. In the case of a linear demand curve, half of a cost increase is passed along in the form of increased prices. In the case of a constant elasticity demand, prices increase by *more* than the increase in costs—the more inelastic the demand, the more of the cost increase gets passed along.

14.3 Welfare and output

We have seen in Chapter 13 that under certain conditions the level of output at which price equals marginal cost is Pareto efficient. Since the marginal revenue curve always lies under the inverse demand curve, it is clear that a monopoly must produce a level of output which is less than this Pareto efficient amount. In this section we will examine this inefficiency of monopoly in a bit more detail.

For simplicity, let us consider an economy with one consumer, possessing a quasilinear utility function $u(x) + y$. As we've seen in Chapter 13, the inverse demand function for this form of utility function is given by $p(x) = u'(x)$. Let $c(x)$ denote the amount of the y-good necessary to produce x units of the x-good. Then a sensible social objective is to choose x to maximize utility:

$$W(x) = u(x) - c(x).$$

This implies that the socially optimal level of output, x_o, is given by

$$u'(x_o) = p(x_o) = c'(x_o).$$

On the other hand, the level of monopoly output satisfies the condition

$$p(x_m) + p'(x_m)x_m = c'(x_m).$$

Hence, the derivative of the welfare function evaluated at the monopoly level of output is given by

$$W'(x_m) = u'(x_m) - c'(x_m) = -p'(x_m)x_m = -u''(x_m)x_m > 0.$$

It follows from the concavity of $u(x)$ that increasing output will increase utility.

We could make the same argument slightly differently. We can also write the social objective function as consumer's surplus plus profits:

$$W(x) = [u(x) - p(x)x] + [p(x)x - c(x)].$$

The derivative of profits with respect to x is zero at the monopoly output, since the monopolist chooses the level of output that maximizes profits. The derivative of consumer's surplus at x_m is given by

$$u'(x_m) - p(x_m) - p'(x_m)x_m = -p'(x_m)x_m,$$

which is certainly positive.

14.4 Quality choice

Monopolies choose not only output levels, but also other dimensions of the products they produce. Consider, for example, product quality. Let us suppose that we can denote product quality by some numerical level q. We suppose that both utility and costs depend on quality and take the social objective function to be

$$W(x, q) = u(x, q) - c(x, q).$$

(As usual, we assume quasilinear utility for a simple analysis.) We assume that quality is a good, so that $\partial u/\partial q > 0$ and that it is costly to produce, so that $\partial c/\partial q > 0$.

The monopolist maximizes profits:

$$\max_{x,q} \; p(x, q)x - c(x, q).$$

The first-order conditions for this problem are

$$p(x_m, q_m) + \frac{\partial p(x_m, q_m)}{\partial x} x_m = \frac{\partial c(x_m, q_m)}{\partial x}$$

$$\frac{\partial p(x_m, q_m)}{\partial q} x_m = \frac{\partial c(x_m, q_m)}{\partial q}.$$

Let us calculate the derivative of the welfare function at (x_m, q_m). We have

$$\frac{\partial W(x_m, q_m)}{\partial x} = \frac{\partial u(x_m, q_m)}{\partial x} - \frac{\partial c(x_m, q_m)}{\partial x}$$

$$\frac{\partial W(x_m, q_m)}{\partial q} = \frac{\partial u(x_m, q_m)}{\partial q} - \frac{\partial c(x_m, q_m)}{\partial q}.$$

Upon substituting from the first-order conditions, we find

$$\frac{\partial W(x_m, q_m)}{\partial x} = -\frac{\partial p(x_m, q_m)}{\partial x} x_m > 0 \tag{14.4}$$

$$\frac{\partial W(x_m, q_m)}{\partial q} = \frac{\partial u(x_m, q_m)}{\partial q} - \frac{\partial p(x_m, q_m)}{\partial q} x_m. \tag{14.5}$$

The first equation tells us that, holding quality fixed, the monopolist produces too little output, relative to the social optimum. The second equation is not quite so easy to interpret. Since $\partial p/\partial q$ equals the marginal cost of producing more quality, it must be positive, so the derivative of welfare with respect to quality is the difference between two positive numbers and is, on the face of it, ambiguous.

The question is, can we find any plausible conditions on demand behavior that will sign the expression? This is a case where it is much easier to see the answer if we write the social objective function as consumer's surplus plus profits rather than utility minus costs. The social objective function takes the form

$$W(x,q) = [u(x,q) - p(x,q)x] + [p(x,q)x - c(x,q)]$$
$$= \text{consumer's surplus} + \text{profits.}$$

Now differentiate this definition with respect to x and q and evaluate the derivative at the monopolist's profit-maximizing level of output. Since the monopolist is maximizing profits, the derivatives of monopoly profits with respect to output and quality must vanish, indicating that the derivative of welfare with respect to quantity and quality is precisely the derivative of consumer's surplus with respect to quantity and quality.

The derivative of consumer's surplus with respect to quantity is always positive, which is just another way of saying that the monopolist produces too little output. The derivative of consumer's surplus with respect to quality is ambiguous—it may be positive or it may be negative. Its sign depends on the sign of $\partial^2 p(x,q)/\partial x \partial q$.

To see this, consider Figure 14.2. When quality increases, the demand curve shifts up and (possibly) tilts one way or the other. Decompose this movement into a *parallel* shift up and a pivot, as indicated. Consumer's surplus is unaffected by the parallel shift, so the total change simply depends on whether the inverse demand curve becomes flatter or steeper. If the slope of the inverse demand curve gets flatter consumer's surplus goes down and vice-versa.[1]

Another way to interpret equation (14.5) is based on consideration of the reservation price model. Think of $p(x,q)$ as measuring the reservation price of consumer x, so that $u(x,q)$ is just the sum of the reservation prices. In this interpretation, $u(x,q)/x$ is the average willingness to pay and $p(x,q)$ is the marginal willingness to pay. We can rewrite (14.5) as

$$\frac{1}{x_m} \frac{\partial W(x_m, q_m)}{\partial q} = \frac{\partial}{\partial q}\left[\frac{u(x_m, q_m)}{x_m} - p(x_m, q_m)\right].$$

The derivative of welfare with respect to q is now seen to be proportional to the derivative of the *average* willingness to pay for the quality change minus the derivative of the *marginal* willingness to pay for the quality change.

Social welfare depends on the sum of the consumers' utility or willingness to pay; but the monopolist only cares about the willingness to pay of the marginal individual. If these two values are different, the monopolist's quality choice will not be optimal from the social viewpoint.

---

[1] Note that the slope of the demand curve is negative; to say the slope gets flatter means that it gets closer to zero.

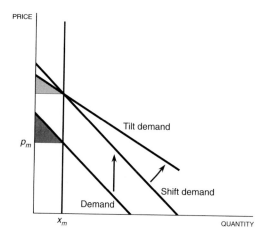

Effect on consumer's surplus of a change in quality.
When the demand curve shifts up and tilts, the effect on consumer's surplus depends only on the direction of the tilt.

**Figure
14.2**

14.5 Price discrimination

Loosely speaking, price discrimination involves selling different units of the
same good at different prices, either to the same or different consumers.
Price discrimination arises naturally in the study of monopoly since we
have seen that a monopolist will typically desire to sell additional output
if it can find a way to do so without lowering the price on the units it is
currently selling.

In order for price discrimination to be a viable strategy for the firm, it
must have the ability to sort consumers and to prevent resale. Preventing
resale is generally not a severe problem, and most of the difficulties associated with price discrimination are concerned with sorting the consumers.
The easiest case is where the firm can explicitly sort consumers with respect to some exogenous category such as age. A more complex analysis is
necessary when the firm must price discriminate on the basis of some *endogenous* category such as the amount of purchase or the time of purchase.
In this case the monopolist faces the problem of structuring its pricing so
that consumers "self select" into appropriate categories.

The traditional classification of the forms of price discrimination is due
to Pigou (1920).

First-degree price discrimination involves the seller charging a different price for each unit of the good in such a way that the price charged
for each unit is equal to the maximum willingness-to-pay for that unit.
This is also known as **perfect price discrimination**

Second-degree price discrimination occurs when prices differ depending on the number of units of the good bought, but not across consumers. This phenomenon is also known as **nonlinear pricing.** Each consumer faces the same price schedule, but the schedule involves different prices for different amounts of the good purchased. Quantity discounts or premia are the obvious examples.

Third-degree price discrimination means that different purchasers are charged different prices, but each purchaser pays a constant amount for each unit of the good bought. This is perhaps the most common form of price discrimination; examples are student discounts, or charging different prices on different days of the week.

We will investigate these three forms of price discrimination in the context of a very simple model. Suppose that there are two potential consumers with utility functions $u_i(x) + y$, for $i = 1, 2$. For simplicity, normalize utility so that $u_i(0) = 0$. Consumer i's maximum willingness-to-pay for some consumption level x will be denoted by $r_i(x)$. It is the solution to the equation

$$u_i(0) + y = u_i(x) - r_i(x) + y.$$

The left-hand side of the equation gives the utility from zero consumption of the good, and the right-hand side gives the utility from consuming x units and paying a price $r_i(x)$. By virtue of our normalization, $r_i(x) \equiv u_i(x)$.

Another useful function associated with the utility function is the marginal willingness-to-pay function, i.e., the (inverse) demand function. This function measures what the per-unit price would have to be to induce the consumer to demand x units of the consumption good. If the consumer faces a per-unit price p and chooses the optimal level of consumption, he or she must solve the utility maximization problem

$$\max_{x,y} u_i(x) + y$$

such that $px + y = m$.

As we have seen several times, the first-order condition for this problem is

$$p = u_i'(x). \tag{14.6}$$

Hence, the inverse demand function is given explicitly by (14.6): the price necessary to induce consumer i to choose consumption level x is $p = p_i(x) = u_i'(x)$.

We will suppose that the maximum willingness-to-pay for the good by consumer 2 always exceeds the maximum willingness-to-pay by consumer 1; i.e., that

$$u_2(x) > u_1(x) \text{ for all } x. \tag{14.7}$$

We will also generally suppose that the *marginal* willingness-to-pay for the good by consumer 2 exceeds the marginal willingness-to-pay by consumer 1; i.e., that

$$u_2'(x) > u_1'(x) \text{ for all } x. \tag{14.8}$$

Thus it is natural to refer to consumer 2 as the **high demand** consumer and consumer 1 as the **low demand** consumer.

We will suppose that there is a single seller of the good in question who can produce it at a constant marginal cost of c per unit. Thus the cost function of the monopolist is $c(x) = cx$.

14.6 First-degree price discrimination

Suppose for the moment that there is only one agent, so that we can drop the subscript distinguishing the agents. A monopolist wants to offer the agent some price and output combination (r^*, x^*) that yields the maximum profits for the monopolist. The price r^* is a take-it-or-leave-it price—the consumer can either pay r^* and consume x^*, or consume zero units of the good.

The profit maximization problem of the monopolist is

$$\max_{r,x} r - cx$$

$$\text{such that } u(x) \geq r.$$

The constraint simply indicates that the consumer must get nonnegative surplus from his consumption of the x-good. Since the monopolist wants r to be as large as possible, this constraint will be satisfied as an equality.

Substituting from the constraint and differentiating, we find the first-order condition determining the optimal level of production to be

$$u'(x^*) = c. \tag{14.9}$$

Given this level of production, the take-it-or-leave-it price is

$$r^* = u(x^*).$$

There are several points worth noting about this solution. First, the monopolist will choose to produce a Pareto efficient level of output—a level of output where the marginal willingness-to-pay equals marginal cost. However, the producer will also manage to capture all the benefits from this efficient level of production—it will achieve the maximum possible profits, while the consumer is indifferent to consuming the product or not.

Second, the monopolist in this market produces the same level of output as would a competitive industry. A competitive industry will produce where price equals marginal cost and supply equals demand. Together, these two conditions imply that $p(x) = c$, which is precisely the equation (14.9) coupled with the definition of the inverse demand function in (14.6). Of course, the gains from trade are divided much differently in the competitive equilibrium. In this case, the consumer gets utility $u(x^*) - cx^*$ and the firm gets zero profits.

Third, the same outcome can be achieved if the monopolist sells each unit of output to the consumer at a different price. Suppose, for example, that the firm breaks up the output into n pieces of size Δx, so that $x = n\Delta x$. Then the willingness-to-pay for the first unit of consumption will be given by

$$u(0) + m = u(\Delta x) + m - p_1,$$

or

$$u(0) = u(\Delta x) - p_1.$$

Similarly, the marginal willingness-to-pay for the second unit of consumption is

$$u(\Delta x) = u(2\Delta x) - p_2.$$

Proceeding this way up to the n units, we have the sequence of equations,

$$u(0) = u(\Delta x) - p_1$$
$$u(\Delta x) = u(2\Delta x) - p_2$$

$$\vdots$$

$$u((n-1)\Delta x) = u(x) - p_n.$$

Adding up these n equations and using the normalization that $u(0) = 0$, we have $\sum_{i=1}^{n} p_n = u(x)$. That is the sum of the marginal willingnesses-to-pay must equal the total willingness-to-pay. So it doesn't matter how the firm price discriminates: making a single take-it-or-leave it offer, or selling each unit of the good at the marginal willingness-to-pay for that unit.

14.7 Second-degree price discrimination

Second-degree price discrimination is also known as **nonlinear pricing**. This involves such practices as quantity discounts, where the revenue a firm collects is a nonlinear function of the amount purchased. In this section we will analyze a simple problem of this type.

Recall the notation introduced earlier. There are two consumers with utility functions $u_1(x_1) + y_1$ and $u_2(x_2) + y_2$, where we assume that $u_2(x) > u_1(x)$ and $u_2'(x) > u_1'(x)$. We refer to consumer 2 as the *high-demand* consumer and consumer 1 as the *low-demand* consumer. The assumption that the consumer with the larger total willingness-to-pay also has the larger marginal willingness-to-pay is sometimes known as the **single crossing property** since it implies that any two indifference curves for the agents can intersect at most once.

Suppose that the monopolist chooses some (nonlinear) function $p(x)$ that indicates how much it will charge if x units are demanded. Suppose that consumer i demands x_i units and spends $r_i = p(x_i)x_i$ dollars. From the viewpoint of both the consumer and the monopolist all that is relevant is that the consumer spends r_i dollars and receives x_i units of output. Hence, the choice of the function $p(x)$ reduces to the choice of (r_i, x_i). Consumer 1 will choose (r_1, x_1) and consumer 2 will choose (r_2, x_2).

The constraints facing the monopolist are as follows. First, each consumer must want to consume the amount x_i and be willing to pay the price r_i:

$$u_1(x_1) - r_1 \geq 0$$
$$u_2(x_2) - r_2 \geq 0.$$

This simply says that each consumer must do at least as well consuming the x-good as not consuming it. Second, each consumer must prefer his consumption to the consumption of the other consumer.

$$u_1(x_1) - r_1 \geq u_1(x_2) - r_2$$
$$u_2(x_2) - r_2 \geq u_2(x_1) - r_1.$$

These are the so-called **self-selection constraints**. If the plan (x_1, x_2) is to be feasible in the sense that it will be voluntarily chosen by the consumers, then each consumer must prefer consuming the bundle intended for him as compared to consuming the other person's bundle.

Rearrange the inequalities in the above paragraph as

$$r_1 \leq u_1(x_1) \tag{14.10}$$
$$r_1 \leq u_1(x_1) - u_1(x_2) + r_2 \tag{14.11}$$

$$r_2 \leq u_2(x_2) \tag{14.12}$$
$$r_2 \leq u_2(x_2) - u_2(x_1) + r_1. \tag{14.13}$$

Of course, the monopolist wants to choose r_1 and r_2 to be as large as possible. It follows that in general one of the first two inequalities will be binding and one of the second two inequalities will be binding. It turns out that the assumptions that $u_2(x) > u_1(x)$ and $u_2'(x) > u_1'(x)$ are sufficient to determine which constraints will bind, as we now demonstrate.

To begin with, suppose that (14.12) is binding. Then (14.13) implies that

$$r_2 \leq r_2 - u_2(x_1) + r_1,$$

or

$$u_2(x_1) \leq r_1.$$

Using (14.7) we can write

$$u_1(x_1) < u_2(x_1) \le r_1,$$

which contradicts (14.10). It follows that (14.12) is not binding and that (14.13) is binding, a fact which we note for future use:

$$r_2 = u_2(x_2) - u_2(x_1) + r_1. \tag{14.14}$$

Now consider (14.10) and (14.11). If (14.11) were binding, we would have

$$r_1 = u_1(x_1) - u_1(x_2) + r_2.$$

Substitute from (14.14) to find

$$r_1 = u_1(x_1) - u_1(x_2) + u_2(x_2) - u_2(x_1) + r_1,$$

which implies

$$u_2(x_2) - u_2(x_1) = u_1(x_2) - u_1(x_1).$$

We can rewrite this expression as

$$\int_{x_1}^{x_2} u_1'(t)\, dt = \int_{x_1}^{x_2} u_2'(t)\, dt.$$

However, this violates the assumption that $u_2'(x) > u_1'(x)$. It follows that (14.11) is not binding and that (14.10) is binding, so

$$r_1 = u_1(x_1). \tag{14.15}$$

Equations (14.14) and (14.15) imply that the low-demand consumer will be charged his maximum willingness-to-pay, and the high-demand consumer will be charged the highest price that will just induce him to consume x_2 rather than x_1.

The profit function of the monopolist is

$$\pi = [r_1 - cx_1] + [r_2 - cx_2],$$

which upon substitution for r_1 and r_2 becomes

$$\pi = [u_1(x_1) - cx_1] + [u_2(x_2) - u_2(x_1) + u_1(x_1) - cx_2].$$

This expression is to be maximized with respect to x_1 and x_2. Differentiating, we have

$$u_1'(x_1) - c + u_1'(x_1) - u_2'(x_1) = 0 \tag{14.16}$$

$$u_2'(x_2) - c = 0. \tag{14.17}$$

Equation (14.16) can be rearranged to give

$$u_1'(x_1) = c + [u_2'(x_1) - u_1'(x_1)] > c, \tag{14.18}$$

which implies that the low-demand consumer has a (marginal) value for the good that exceeds marginal cost. Hence he consumes an inefficiently small amount of the good. Equation (14.17) says that at the optimal nonlinear prices, the high-demand consumer has a marginal willingness-to-pay which is equal to marginal cost. Thus he consumes the socially correct amount.

Note that if the single-crossing property were not satisfied, then the bracketed term in (14.18) would be negative and the low-demand consumer would consume a *larger* amount than he would at the efficient point. This can happen, but it is admittedly rather peculiar.

The result that the consumer with the highest demand pays marginal cost is very general. If the consumer with the highest demand pays a price in excess of marginal cost, the monopolist could lower the price charged to the largest consumer by a small amount, inducing him to buy more. Since price still exceeds marginal cost, the monopolist would make a profit on these sales. Furthermore, such a policy wouldn't affect the monopolist's profits from any other consumers, since they are all optimized at lower values of consumption.

EXAMPLE: A graphical treatment

The price discrimination problem with self-selection can also be treated graphically. Consider Figure 14.3 which depicts the demand curves of the two consumers; for simplicity we assume zero marginal cost. Figure 14.3A depicts the price discrimination if there is no self-selection problem. The firm would simply sell x_h^o to the high-demand consumer and x_l^o to the low-demand consumer at prices that are equal to their respective consumer's surpluses—i.e., the areas under their respective demand curves. Thus the high-demand consumer pays $A+B+C$ to consume x_h^o and the low-demand consumer pays A to consume x_l^o.

However, this policy violates the self-selection constraint. The high-demand consumer prefers the low-demand consumer's bundle, since by choosing it he receives a net surplus equal to the area B. In order to satisfy the self-selection constraint, the monopolist must offer x_h^o at a price equal to $A+C$, which leaves the high-demand consumer a surplus equal to B no matter which bundle he chooses.

This policy is feasible, but is it optimal? The answer is no: by offering the low-demand consumer a slightly smaller bundle, the monopolist loses the profits indicated by the black triangle in Figure 14.3B, and gains the profits indicated by the shaded trapezoid. Reducing the amount offered to the low-demand consumer has no first-order effect on profits since the marginal willingness-to-pay equals zero at x_l^o. However, it increases profits non-marginally since the high-demand consumer's willingness-to-pay is *larger* than zero at this point.

At the profit-maximizing level of consumption for the low-demand consumer, x_l^m in Figure 14.3C, the marginal *decrease* in profits collected from the low-demand consumer from a further reduction, p_1, just equals the marginal *increase* in profits collected from the high-demand consumer, $p_2 - p_1$. (Note that this also follows from equation (14.18).) The final solution has the low-demand consumer consuming at x_l^m and paying A, thereby receiving zero surplus from his purchase. The high-demand consumer consumes at x_h^o, the socially correct amount, and pays $A + C + D$ for this bundle, leaving him with positive surplus in the amount B.

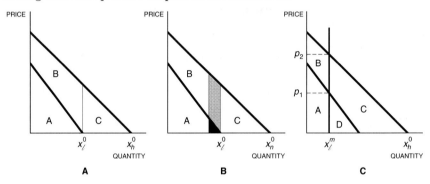

Figure 14.3   **Second-degree price discrimination.** Panel A depicts the solution if self-selection is not a problem. Panel B shows that reducing the bundle of the low-demand consumer will increase profits, and panel C shows the profit-maximizing level of output for the low-demand consumer.

14.8 Third-degree price discrimination

Third-degree price discrimination occurs when consumers are charged different prices, but each consumer faces a constant price for all units of output purchased. This is probably the most common form of price discrimination.

The textbook case is where there are two separate markets, where the firm can easily enforce the division. An example would be discrimination by age, such as youth discounts at the movies. If we let $p_i(x_i)$ be the inverse demand function for group i, and suppose that there are two groups, then the monopolist's profit maximization problem is

$$\max_{x_1, x_2} \; p_1(x_1)x_1 + p_2(x_2)x_2 - cx_1 - cx_2.$$

The first-order conditions for this problem are

$$p_1(x_1) + p_1'(x_1)x_1 = c$$
$$p_2(x_2) + p_2'(x_2)x_2 = c.$$

Let ϵ_i be the elasticity of demand in market i, we can write these expressions as

$$p_1(x_1)\left[1 - \frac{1}{|\epsilon_1|}\right] = c$$

$$p_2(x_2)\left[1 - \frac{1}{|\epsilon_2|}\right] = c.$$

It follows that $p_1(x_1) > p_2(x_2)$ if and only if $|\epsilon_1| < |\epsilon_2|$. Hence, the market with the more elastic demand—the market that is more price sensitive—is charged the lower price.

Suppose now that the monopolist is unable to separate the markets as cleanly as assumed, so that the price charged in one market influences the demand in another market. For example, consider a theater that has a bargain night on Monday; the lower price on Monday would presumably influence demand on Tuesday to some degree.

In this case the profit maximization problem of the firm is

$$\max_{x_1,x_2} \; p_1(x_1,x_2)x_1 + p_2(x_1,x_2)x_2 - cx_1 - cx_2,$$

and the first-order conditions become

$$p_1 + \frac{\partial p_1}{\partial x_1}x_1 + \frac{\partial p_2}{\partial x_1}x_2 = c$$

$$p_2 + \frac{\partial p_2}{\partial x_2}x_2 + \frac{\partial p_1}{\partial x_2}x_1 = c.$$

We can rearrange these conditions to give

$$p_1\left[1 - \frac{1}{|\epsilon_1|}\right] + \frac{\partial p_2}{\partial x_1}x_2 = c$$

$$p_2\left[1 - \frac{1}{|\epsilon_2|}\right] + \frac{\partial p_1}{\partial x_2}x_1 = c.$$

Since we are assuming quasilinear utility, it follows that $\partial p_1/\partial x_2 = \partial p_2/\partial x_1$; i.e., the cross-price effects are symmetric. Subtracting the second equation from the first and rearranging, we have

$$p_1\left[1 - \frac{1}{|\epsilon_1|}\right] - p_2\left[1 - \frac{1}{|\epsilon_2|}\right] = [x_1 - x_2]\frac{\partial p_2}{\partial x_1}.$$

It is natural to suppose that the two goods are substitutes—after all they are the same good being sold to different groups—so that $\partial p_2/\partial x_1 > 0$.

Without loss of generality, assume that $x_1 > x_2$, which, by the equation immediately above, implies that

$$p_1 \left[1 - \frac{1}{|\epsilon_1|}\right] - p_2 \left[1 - \frac{1}{|\epsilon_2|}\right] > 0.$$

Rearranging, we have

$$\frac{p_1}{p_2} > \frac{1 - 1/|\epsilon_2|}{1 - 1/|\epsilon_1|}.$$

It follows from this expression that if $|\epsilon_2| > |\epsilon_1|$ we must have $p_1 > p_2$. That is, if the *smaller* market has the more elastic demand, it must have the lower price. Thus, the intuition of the separate markets carries over to the more general case under these additional assumptions.

Welfare effects

Much of the discussion about third-degree price discrimination has to do with the welfare effects of allowing this form of price discrimination. Would we generally expect consumer's plus producer's surplus to be higher or lower when third-degree price discrimination is present than when it is not?

We begin with formulating a general test for welfare improvement. Suppose for simplicity that there are only two groups and start with an aggregate utility function of the form $u(x_1, x_2) + y$. Here x_1 and x_2 are the consumptions of the two groups and y is money to be spent on other consumption goods. The inverse demand functions for the two goods are given by

$$p_1(x_1, x_2) = \frac{\partial u(x_1, x_2)}{\partial x_1}$$

$$p_2(x_1, x_2) = \frac{\partial u(x_1, x_2)}{\partial x_2}.$$

We assume that $u(x_1, x_2)$ is concave and differentiable, though this is slightly stronger than needed.

Let $c(x_1, x_2)$ be the cost of providing x_1 and x_2, so that social welfare is measured by

$$W(x_1, x_2) = u(x_1, x_2) - c(x_1, x_2).$$

Now consider two configurations of output, (x_1^0, x_2^0) and (x_1', x_2'), with associated prices (p_1^0, p_2^0) and (p_1', p_2'). By the concavity of $u(x_1, x_2)$, we have

$$u(x_1', x_2') \leq u(x_1^0, x_2^0) + \frac{\partial u(x_1^0, x_2^0)}{\partial x_1}(x_1' - x_1^0) + \frac{\partial u(x_1^0, x_2^0)}{\partial x_2}(x_2' - x_2^0).$$

Rearranging and using the definition of the inverse demand functions, we have

$$\Delta u \leq p_1^0 \Delta x_1 + p_2^0 \Delta x_2.$$

By an analogous argument, we have

$$\Delta u \geq p_1' \Delta x_1 + p_2' \Delta x_2.$$

Since $\Delta W = \Delta u - \Delta c$, we have our final result:

$$p_1^0 \Delta x_1 + p_2^0 \Delta x_2 - \Delta c \geq \Delta W \geq p_1' \Delta x_1 + p_2' \Delta x_2 - \Delta c. \qquad (14.19)$$

In the special case of constant marginal cost, $\Delta c = c\Delta x_1 + c\Delta x_2$, so the inequality becomes

$$(p_1^0 - c)\Delta x_1 + (p_2^0 - c)\Delta x_2 \geq \Delta W \geq (p_1' - c)\Delta x_1 + (p_2' - c)\Delta x_2. \quad (14.20)$$

Note that these welfare bounds are perfectly general, based only on the concavity of the utility function, which is, in turn, basically the requirement that demand curves slope down. Varian (1985) derived the inequalities using the indirect utility function, which is slightly more general.

In order to apply these inequalities to the question of price discrimination, let the initial set of prices be the constant monopoly prices so that $p_1^0 = p_2^0 = p^0$, and let (p_1', p_2') be the discriminatory prices. Then the bounds in (14.20) become

$$(p^0 - c)(\Delta x_1 + \Delta x_2) \geq \Delta W \geq (p_1' - c)\Delta x_1 + (p_2' - c)\Delta x_2. \qquad (14.21)$$

The upper bound implies that *a necessary condition for welfare to increase is that total output increase.* Suppose to the contrary that total output decreased so that $\Delta x_1 + \Delta x_2 < 0$. Since $p^0 - c > 0$, (14.21) implies that $\Delta W < 0$. The lower bound gives a sufficient condition for welfare to increase under price discrimination, namely that the sum of the *weighted output* changes is positive, with the weights being given by price minus marginal cost.

The simple geometry of the bounds is shown in Figure 14.4. The welfare gain ΔW is the indicated trapezoid. The area of this trapezoid is clearly bounded above and below by the area of the two rectangles.

As a simple application of the welfare bounds, let us consider the case of two markets with linear demand curves,

$$x_1 = a_1 - b_1 p_1$$
$$x_2 = a_2 - b_2 p_2.$$

For simplicity set marginal costs equal to zero. Then if the monopolist engages in price discrimination, he will maximize revenue by selling halfway down each demand curve, so that $x_1 = a_1/2$ and $x_2 = a_2/2$.

Now suppose that the monopolist sells at a single price to both markets. The total demand curve will be

$$x_1 + x_2 = a_1 + a_2 - (b_1 + b_2)p.$$

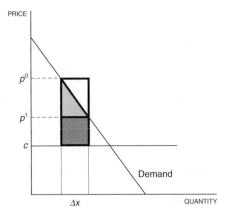

Figure 14.4   **Illustration of the welfare bounds.**   The trapezoid is the true change in consumer's surplus.

To maximize revenue the monopolist will operate halfway down the demand curve which means that

$$x_1 + x_2 = \frac{a_1 + a_2}{2}.$$

Hence, with linear demand curves the total output is the same under price discrimination as under ordinary monopoly. The bound given in (14.21) then implies that welfare must decrease under price discrimination.

However, this result relies on the assumption that both markets are served under the ordinary monopoly. Suppose that market 2 is very small, so that the profit-maximizing firm sells zero to this market if price discrimination is not allowed, as illustrated in Figure 14.5.

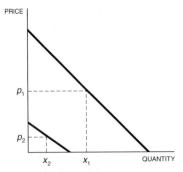

Figure 14.5   **Price discrimination.**   Here the monopolist would optimally choose to serve only the large market if it could not price discriminate.

In this case allowing price discrimination results in $\Delta x_1 = 0$ and $\Delta x_2 > 0$, providing an unambiguous welfare gain by (14.21). Of course, this is not only a welfare gain, but is in fact a Pareto improvement.

This example is quite robust. If a new market is opened up because of price discrimination—a market that was not previously being served under the ordinary monopoly—then we will typically have a Pareto improving welfare enhancement. On the other hand, if linearity of demand is not a bad first approximation, and output does not change too drastically in response to price discrimination, we might well expect that the net impact on welfare is negative.

Notes

The discussion of quality choice is based on Spence (1975). For a survey of price discrimination see Varian (1989a).

Exercises

14.1. The inverse demand curve is given by $p(y) = 10 - y$, and a monopolist has a fixed supply of 4 units of a good available. How much will it sell and what price will it set? What would be the price and output in a competitive market with these demand and supply characteristics? What would happen if the monopolist had 6 units of the good available? (Assume free disposal.)

14.2. Suppose that a monopolist faces a demand curve of $D(p) = 10 - p$ and has a fixed supply of 7 units of output to sell. What is its profit-maximizing price and what are its maximal profits?

14.3. A monopolist faces a demand curve of the form $x = 10/p$, and has a constant marginal cost of 1. What is the profit maximizing level of output?

14.4. For what form of demand curve does $dp/dc = 1$?

14.5. Suppose that the inverse demand curve facing a monopolist is given by $p(y, t)$, where t is a parameter that shifts the demand curve. For simplicity, assume that the monopolist has a technology that exhibits constant marginal costs. Derive an expression showing how output responds to a change in t. How does this expression simplify if the shift parameter takes the special form $p(y, t) = a(y) + b(t)$?

14.6. The demand function facing the monopolist is given by $D(p) = 10/p$, and the monopolist has positive marginal cost of c. What is the profit-maximizing level of output?

14.7. Suppose marginal costs are constant at $c > 0$ and that the demand function is given by

$$D(p) = \begin{cases} 10/p & \text{if } p \leq 20 \\ 0 & \text{if } p > 20. \end{cases}$$

What is the profit-maximizing price?

14.8. For what form of utility function and demand curve does the monopolist produce the optimal level of quality, given its quantity choice?

14.9. In the text we gave a graphical argument that if $\partial^2 p/\partial x \partial q > 0$ then $\partial u/\partial q - x \partial p/\partial q < 0$. Let us prove this algebraically. Here are the steps to follow: 1) Show that the hypothesis implies that if $z < x$ then

$$\frac{\partial p(z, q)}{\partial q} < \frac{\partial p(x, q)}{\partial q}.$$

2) Express the left-hand side of the inequality in terms of the utility function. 3) Integrate both sides of this inequality over z ranging from 0 to x.

14.10. One common way to price discriminate is to charge a lump sum fee to have the *right* to purchase a good, and then charge a per-unit cost for consumption of the good after that. The standard example is an amusement park where the firm charges an entry fee and a charge for the rides inside the park. Such a pricing policy is known as a **two part tariff**. Suppose that all consumers have identical utility functions given by $u(x)$ and that the cost of providing the service is $c(x)$. If the monopolist sets a two part tariff, will it produce more or less than the efficient level of output?

14.11. Consider the graphical treatment of the second-degree price discrimination problem. Look at Figure $14.3C$ carefully and answer the following question: under what conditions would the monopolist sell only to the high-demand consumer?

14.12. If the monopolist chooses to sell to both consumers, show that area B must be less than area A.

14.13. Suppose that there are two consumers who each may purchase one unit of a good. If the good is of quality q, consumer t achieves utility $u(q, t)$. It costs the monopolist zero to provide quality. Let the maximum price that consumer t would be willing to pay for quality q be given by w_t. The monopolist cannot distinguish the two consumers and must therefore offer at most two different qualities between which the consumers can freely choose. Set up the profit maximization problem for the monopolist, and analyze it thoroughly. Hint: does this problem look like anything you've seen before?

14.14. The monopolist can also be thought of as choosing the price and letting the market determine how much is sold. Write down the profit maximization problem and verify that $p[1 + 1/\epsilon] = c'(y)$ at the optimal price.

14.15. There is a single monopolist whose technology exhibits constant marginal costs, i.e., $c(y) = cy$. The market demand curve exhibits constant elasticity, ϵ. There is an *ad valorem* tax on the price of the good sold so that when the consumer pays a price P_D, the monopolist receives a price of $P_S = (1 - \tau)P_D$. (Here P_D is the demand price facing the consumer and P_S is the supply price facing the producer.)

The taxing authority is considering changing the *ad valorem* tax to a tax on output, t, so that we will have $P_D = P_S + t$. You have been hired to calculate the output tax t that is equivalent to the *ad valorem* tax τ in the sense that the final price facing the consumer is the *same* under either scheme.

14.16. Suppose that the inverse demand curve facing a monopolist is given by $p(y, t)$, where t is a parameter that shifts the demand curve. For simplicity, assume that the monopolist has a technology that exhibits constant marginal costs.

(a) Derive an expression showing how output responds to a change in t.

(b) How does this expression simplify if the inverse demand function takes the special form $p(y, t) = a(y) + b(t)$?

14.17. Consider a simple economy which acts as though there is one consumer with utility function $u_1(x_1) + u_2(x_2) + y$, where x_1 and x_2 are the amounts of goods 1 and 2, respectively, and y is money to spend on all other goods. Suppose that good 1 is supplied by a firm that acts competitively and good 2 is supplied by a firm that acts like a monopoly. The cost function for good i is denoted by $c_i(x_i)$, and there is a specific tax of amount t_i on the output of industry i. Assume that $c_i'' > 0$, $p_i'' < 0$, and $p_i' < 0$.

(a) Derive expressions for dx_i/dt_i for $i = 1, 2$ and sign them.

(b) Given a change in outputs (dx_1, dx_2), derive an expression for the change in welfare.

(c) Suppose that we consider taxing one of the two industries and using the proceeds to subsidize the other. Should we tax the competitive industry or the monopoly?

14.18. There are two consumers who have utility functions

$$u_1(x_1, y_1) = a_1 x_1 + y_1$$
$$u_2(x_2, y_2) = a_2 x_2 + y_2.$$

The price of the y-good is 1, and each consumer has a "large" initial wealth. We are given that $a_2 > a_1$. Both goods can only be consumed in nonnegative amounts.

A monopolist supplies the x-good. It has zero marginal costs, but has a capacity constraint: it can supply at most 10 units of the x-good. The monopolist will offer at most two price-quantity packages, (r_1, x_1) and (r_2, x_2). Here r_i is the cost of purchasing x_i units of the good.

(a) Write down the monopolist's profit maximization problem. You should have 4 constraints plus the capacity constraint $x_1 + x_2 \le 10$.

(b) Which constraints will be binding in optimal solution?

(c) Substitute these constraints into the objective function. What is the resulting expression?

(d) What are the optimal values of (r_1, x_1) and (r_2, x_2)?

14.19. A monopolist sells in two markets. The demand curve for the monopolist's product is $x_1 = a_1 - b_1 p_1$ in market 1 and $x_2 = a_2 - b_2 p_2$ in market 2, where x_1 and x_2 are the quantities sold in each market, and p_1 and p_2 are the prices charged in each market. The monopolist has zero marginal costs. Note that although the monopolist can charge different prices in the two markets, it must sell all units within a market at the same price.

(a) Under what conditions on the parameters (a_1, b_1, a_2, b_2) will the monopolist optimally choose not to price discriminate? (Assume interior solutions.)

(b) Now suppose that the demand functions take the form $x_i = A_i p_i^{-b_i}$, for $i = 1, 2$, and the monopolist has some constant marginal cost of $c > 0$. Under what conditions will the monopolist choose not to price discriminate? (Assume interior solutions.)

14.20. A monopolist maximizes $p(x)x - c(x)$. In order to capture some of the monopoly profits, the government imposes a tax on revenue of an amount t so that the monopolist's objective function becomes $p(x)x - c(x) - tp(x)x$. Initially, the government keeps the revenue from this tax.

(a) Does this tax increase or decrease the monopolist's output?

(b) Now government decides to award the revenue from this tax to the consumers of the monopolist's product. Each consumer will receive a "rebate" in the amount of the tax collected from his expenditures. The representative consumer who spends px receives a rebate of tpx from the government. Assuming quasilinear utility, derive an expression for the consumer's inverse demand as a function of x and t.

(c) How does the monopolist's output respond to the tax-rebate program?

14.21. Consider a market with the following characteristics. There is a single monopolist whose technology exhibits constant marginal costs; i.e.,

$$c(y) = cy.$$

The market demand curve exhibits constant elasticity, ϵ. There is an *ad valorem* tax on the price of the good sold so that when the consumer pays a price P_D, the monopolist receives a price of $P_S = (1 - \tau)P_D$. (Here P_D is the demand price facing the consumer and P_S is the supply price facing the producer.)

The taxing authority is considering changing the *ad valorem* tax to a tax on output, t, so that we will have $P_D = P_S + t$. You have been hired to calculate the output tax t that is equivalent to the *ad valorem* tax τ in the sense that the final price facing the consumer is the *same* under either scheme.

14.22. A monopolist has a cost function of $c(y) = y$ so that its marginal costs are constant at \$1 per unit. It faces the following demand curve:

$$D(p) = \begin{cases} 0, & \text{if } p > 20; \\ 100/p & \text{if } p \le 20. \end{cases}$$

(a) What is the profit-maximizing choice of output?

(b) If the government could set a price ceiling on this monopolist in order to force it to act as a competitor, what price should they set?

(c) What output would the monopolist produce if forced to behave as a competitor?

14.23. An economy has two kinds of consumers and two goods. Type A consumers have utility functions $U(x_1, x_2) = 4x_1 - (x_1^2/2) + x_2$ and Type B consumers have utility functions $U(x_1, x_2) = 2x_1 - (x_1^2/2) + x_2$. Consumers can only consume nonnegative quantities. The price of good 2 is 1 and all consumers have incomes of 100. There are N type A consumers and N type B consumers.

(a) Suppose that a monopolist can produce good 1 at a constant unit cost of c per unit and cannot engage in any kind of price discrimination. Find its optimal choice of price and quantity. For what values of c will it be true that it chooses to sell to both types of consumers?

(b) Suppose that the monopolist uses a "two-part tariff" where a consumer must pay a lump sum k in order to be able to buy anything at all. A person who has paid the lump sum k can buy as much as he likes at a price of p per unit purchased. Consumers are not able to resell good 1. For $p < 4$, what is the highest amount k that a type A is willing to pay for the privilege of buying at price p? If a type A does pay the lump sum k to buy at price p, how many units will he demand? Describe the function that determines demand for good 1 by type A consumers as a function of p and k. What is the demand function for good 1 by type B consumers? Now describe the function that determines total demand for good 1 by all consumers as a function of p and k.

(c) If the economy consisted only of N type A consumers and no type B consumers, what would be the profit-maximizing choices of p and k?

(d) If $c < 1$, find the values of p and k that maximize the monopolist's profits subject to the constraint that both types of consumers buy from it.

CHAPTER **15**

GAME THEORY

Game theory is the study of interacting decision makers. In earlier chapters we studied the theory of optimal decision making by a single agent—a firm or a consumer—in very simple environments. The strategic interactions of the agents were not very complicated. In this chapter we will lay the foundations for a deeper analysis of the behavior of economic agents in more complex environments.

There are many directions from which one could study interacting decision makers. One could examine behavior from the viewpoint of sociology, psychology, biology, etc. Each of these approaches is useful in certain contexts. Game theory emphasizes a study of cold-blooded "rational" decision making, since this is felt to be the most appropriate model for most economic behavior.

Game theory has been widely used in economics in the last decade, and much progress has been made in clarifying the nature of strategic interaction in economic models. Indeed, most economic behavior can be viewed as special cases of game theory, and a sound understanding of game theory is a necessary component of any economist's set of analytical tools.

15.1 Description of a game

There are several ways of describing a game. For our purposes, the **strategic form** and the **extensive form** will be sufficient. Roughly speaking the extensive form provides an "extended" description of a game while the strategic form provides a "reduced" summary of a game.[1] We will first describe the strategic form, reserving the discussion of the extensive form for the section on sequential games.

The strategic form of the game is defined by exhibiting a set of **players**, a set of **strategies**, the choices that each player can make, and a set of **payoffs** that indicate the utility that each player receives if a particular combination of strategies is chosen. For purposes of exposition, we will treat two-person games in this chapter. All of the concepts described below can be easily extended to multiperson contexts.

We assume that the description of the game—the payoffs and the strategies available to the players—are **common knowledge**. That is, each player knows his own payoffs and strategies, and the other player's payoffs and strategies. Furthermore, each player knows that the other player knows this, and so on. We also assume that it is common knowledge that each player is "fully rational." That is, each player can choose an action that maximizes his utility given his subjective beliefs, and that those beliefs are modified when new information arrives according to Bayes' law.

Game theory, by this account, is a generalization of standard, one-person decision theory. How should a rational expected utility maximizer behave in a situation in which his payoff depends on the choices of another rational expected utility maximizer? Obviously, each player will have to consider the problem faced by the other player in order to make a sensible choice. We examine the outcome of this sort of consideration below.

EXAMPLE: Matching pennies

In this game, there are two players, Row and Column. Each player has a coin which he can arrange so that either the head side or the tail side is face-up. Thus, each player has two strategies which we abbreviate as Heads or Tails. Once the strategies are chosen there are payoffs to each player which depend on the choices that both players make.

These choices are made independently, and neither player knows the other's choice when he makes his own choice. We suppose that if both players show heads or both show tails, then Row wins a dollar and Column

---

[1] The strategic form was originally known as the **normal form** of a game, but this term is not very descriptive and its use has been discouraged in recent years.

The game matrix of matching pennies.

Table
15.1

		Column	
		Heads	Tails
Row	Heads	$1, -1$	$-1, 1$
	Tails	$-1, 1$	$1, -1$

loses a dollar. If, on the other hand, one player exhibits heads and the other exhibits tails, then Column wins a dollar and Row looses a dollar.

We can depict the strategic interactions in a **game matrix**. The entry in box (Head, Tails) indicates that player Row gets -1 and player Column gets $+1$ if this particular combination of strategies is chosen. Note that in each entry of this box, the payoff to player Row is just the negative of the payoff to player Column. In other words, this is a **zero-sum game**. In zero-sum games the interests of the players are diametrically opposed and are particularly simple to analyze. However, most games of interest to economists are not zero sum games.

EXAMPLE: The Prisoner's Dilemma

Again we have two players, Row and Column, but now their interests are only partially in conflict. There are two strategies: to Cooperate or to Defect. In the original story, Row and Column were two prisoners who jointly participated in a crime. They could cooperate with each other and refuse to give evidence, or one could defect and implicate the other.

In other applications, cooperate and defect could have different meanings. For example, in a duopoly situation, cooperate could mean "keep charging a high price" and defect could mean "cut your price and steal your competitor's market."

An especially simple description used by Aumann (1987) is the game in which each player can simply announce to a referee: "Give me $1,000," or "Give the other player $3,000." Note that the monetary payments come from a third party, not from either of the players; the Prisoner's Dilemma is a **variable-sum game**.

The players can discuss the game in advance but the actual decisions must be independent. The Cooperate strategy is for each person to announce the $3,000 gift, while the Defect strategy is to take the $1,000 (and run!). Table 15.2 depicts the payoff matrix to the Aumann version of the Prisoner's Dilemma, where the units of the payoff are thousands of dollars.

We will discuss this game in more detail below, but we should point out the "dilemma" before proceeding. The problem is that each party has an

The Prisoner's Dilemma

Table
15.2

		Column	
		Cooperate	Defect
Row	Cooperate	3, 3	0, 4
	Defect	4, 0	1, 1

incentive to defect, *regardless* of what he or she believes the other party will do. If I believe that the other person will cooperate and give me a $3,000 gift, then I will get $4,000 in total by defecting. On the other hand, if I believe that the other person will defect and just take the $1,000, then I do better by taking $1,000 for myself.

EXAMPLE: Cournot duopoly

Consider a simple duopoly game, first analyzed by Cournot (1838). We suppose that there are two firms who produce an identical good at zero cost. Each firm must decide how much output to produce without knowing the production decision of the other duopolist. If the firms produce a total of x units of the good, the market price will be $p(x)$; that is, $p(x)$ is the inverse demand curve facing these two producers.

If x_i is the production level of firm i, the market price will then be $p(x_1 + x_2)$, and the profits of firm i are given by $\pi_i = p(x_1 + x_2)x_i$. In this game the strategy of firm i is its choice of production level and the payoff to firm i is its profits.

EXAMPLE: Bertrand duopoly

Consider the same setup as in the Cournot game, but now suppose that the strategy of each player is to announce the price at which he would be willing to supply an arbitrary amount of the good in question. In this case the payoff function takes a radically different form. It is plausible to suppose that the consumers will only purchase from the firm with the lowest price, and that they will split evenly between the two firms if they charge the same price. Letting $x(p)$ represent the market demand function, this leads to a payoff to firm 1 of the form:

$$\pi_1(p_1, p_2) = \begin{cases} p_1 x(p_1) & \text{if } p_1 < p_2 \\ p_1 x(p_1)/2 & \text{if } p_1 = p_2 \\ 0 & \text{if } p_1 > p_2. \end{cases}$$

This game has a similar structure to that of the Prisoner's Dilemma. If both players cooperate, they can charge the monopoly price and each reap half of the monopoly profits. But the temptation is always there for one player to cut its price slightly and thereby capture the entire market for itself. But if both players cut price, then they are both worse off.

15.2 Economic modeling of strategic choices

Note that the Cournot game and the Bertrand game have a radically different structure, even though they purport to model the same economic phenomenon—a duopoly. In the Cournot game, the payoff to each firm is a continuous function of its strategic choice; in the Bertrand game, the payoffs are discontinuous functions of the strategies. As might be expected, this leads to quite different equilibria. Which of these models is "right"?

There is little sense to ask which of these is the "right" model in the abstract. The answer is that it depends on what you are trying to model. It is probably more fruitful to ask what considerations are relevant in modeling the set of strategies used by the agents.

One guide is obviously empirical evidence. If observation of OPEC announcements indicates that they attempt to determine production quotas for each member and allow the price to be set on the world oil markets, then presumably it is more sensible to model the strategies of the game as being production levels rather than prices.

Another consideration is that strategies should be something that can be committed to or that are difficult to change once the opponent's behavior is observed. The games described above are "one-shot" games, but the reality that they are supposed to describe takes place in real time. Suppose that I pick a price for my output and then discover that my opponent has set a slightly smaller price. In this case I can quickly revise my own price. Since the strategic variable can be quickly modified once the opponent's play is known, it doesn't make much sense to try to model this sort of interaction in a one-shot game. It seems that a game with multiple stages must be used to capture the full range of strategic behavior possible in a price-setting game of this sort.

On the other hand, suppose that we interpret output in the Cournot game to be "capacity," in the sense that it is an irreversible capital investment capable of producing the indicated amount of output. In this case, once I discover my opponent's production level, it may be very costly to change my own production level. Here capacity/output seems like a natural choice for the strategic variable, even in a one-shot game.

As in most economic modeling, there is an art to choosing a representation of the strategy choices of the game that captures an element of the real strategic iterations, while at the same time leaving the game simple enough to analyze.

15.3 Solution concepts

In many games the nature of the strategic interaction suggests that a player wants to choose a strategy that is not predictable in advance by the other player. Consider, for example, the Matching Pennies game described above. Here it is clear that neither player wants the other player to be able to predict his choice accurately. Thus, it is natural to consider a random strategy of playing heads with some probability p_h and tails with some probability p_t. Such a strategy is called a **mixed strategy**. Strategies in which some choice is made with probability 1 are called **pure strategies**.

If R is the set of pure strategies available to Row, the set of mixed strategies open to Row will be the set of all probability distributions over R, where the probability of playing strategy r in R is p_r. Similarly, p_c will be the probability that Column plays some strategy c. In order to solve the game, we want to find a set of mixed strategies (p_r, p_c) that are, in some sense, in equilibrium. It may be that some of the equilibrium mixed strategies assign probability 1 to some choices, in which case they are interpreted as pure strategies.

The natural starting point in a search for a solution concept is standard decision theory: we assume that each player has some probability beliefs about the strategies that the other player might choose and that each player chooses the strategy that maximizes his expected payoff.

Suppose for example that the payoff to Row is $u_r(r, c)$ if row plays r and Column plays c. We assume that Row has a **subjective probability distribution** over Column's choices which we denote by (π_c); see Chapter 11, page 191, for the fundamentals of the idea of subjective probability. Here π_c is supposed to indicate the probability, as envisioned by Row, that Column will make the choice c. Similarly, Column has some beliefs about Row's behavior that we can denote by (π_r).

We allow each player to play a mixed strategy and denote Row's *actual* mixed strategy by (p_r) and Column's *actual* mixed strategy by (p_c). Since Row makes his choice without knowing Column's choice, Row's probability that a particular outcome (r, c) will occur is $p_r \pi_c$. This is simply the (objective) probability that Row plays r times Row's (subjective) probability that Column plays c. Hence, Row's objective is to choose a probability distribution (p_r) that maximizes

$$\text{Row's expected payoff} = \sum_r \sum_c p_r \pi_c u_r(r, c).$$

Column, on the other hand, wishes to maximize

$$\text{Column's expected payoff} = \sum_c \sum_r p_c \pi_r u_c(r, c).$$

So far we have simply applied a standard decision-theoretic model to this game—each player wants to maximize his or her expected utility given his or her beliefs. Given my beliefs about what the other player might do, I choose the strategy that maximizes my expected utility.

In this model the beliefs that I hold about the other player's strategic choices are exogenous variables. However, now we add an additional twist to the standard decision model and ask what kinds of beliefs are *reasonable* to hold about the other person's behavior? After all, each player in the game knows that the other player is out to maximize his own payoff, and each should use that information in determining what are reasonable beliefs to have about the other player's behavior.

15.4 Nash equilibrium

In game theory we take as given the proposition that each player is out to maximize his own payoff, and, furthermore, that each player *knows* that this is the goal of each other player. Hence, in determining what might be reasonable beliefs for me to hold about what other players might do, I have to ask what *they* might believe about what *I* will do. In the expected payoff formulas given at the end of the last section, Row's behavior—how likely he is to play each of his strategies—is represented by the probability distribution (p_r) and Column's *beliefs* about Row's behavior are represented by the (subjective) probability distribution (π_r).

A natural consistency requirement is that each player's belief about the other player's choices coincides with the actual choices the other player intends to make. Expectations that are consistent with actual frequencies are sometimes called **rational expectations**. A Nash equilibrium is a certain kind of rational expectations equilibrium. More formally:

Nash equilibrium. *A* **Nash equilibrium** *consists of probability beliefs* (π_r, π_c) *over strategies, and probability of choosing strategies* (p_r, p_c), *such that:*

1) the beliefs are correct: $p_r = \pi_r$ *and* $p_c = \pi_c$ *for all* r *and* c; *and,*

2) each player is choosing (p_r) *and* (p_c) *so as to maximize his expected utility given his beliefs.*

In this definition it is apparent that a Nash equilibrium is an equilibrium in *actions* and *beliefs*. In equilibrium each player correctly foresees how likely the other player is to make various choices, and the beliefs of the two players are mutually consistent.

A more conventional definition of a Nash equilibrium is that it is a pair of mixed strategies (p_r, p_c) such that each agent's choice maximizes his expected utility, given the strategy of the other agent. This is equivalent to the definition we use, but it is misleading since the distinction between the beliefs of the agents and the actions of the agents is blurred. We've tried to be very careful in distinguishing these two concepts.

One particularly interesting special case of a Nash equilibrium is a **Nash equilibrium in pure strategies**, which is simply a Nash equilibrium in which the probability of playing a particular strategy is 1 for each player. That is:

Pure strategies. *A* **Nash equilibrium in pure strategies** *is a pair (r^*, c^*) such that $u_r(r^*, c^*) \geq u_r(r, c^*)$ for all Row strategies r, and $u_c(r^*, c^*) \geq u_c(r^*, c)$ for all Column strategies c.*

A Nash equilibrium is a minimal consistency requirement to put on a pair of strategies: if Row believes that Column will play c^*, then Row's best reply is r^* and similarly for Column. No player would find it in his or her interest to deviate unilaterally from a Nash equilibrium strategy.

If a set of strategies is *not* a Nash equilibrium then at least one player is not consistently thinking through the behavior of the other player. That is, one of the players must expect the other player not to act in his own self-interest—contradicting the original hypothesis of the analysis.

An equilibrium concept is often thought of as a "rest point" of some adjustment process. One interpretation of Nash equilibrium is that it is the adjustment process of "thinking through" the incentives of the other player. Row might think: "If I think that Column is going to play some strategy c_1 then the best response for me is to play r_1. But if Column thinks that I will play r_1, then the best thing for him to do is to play some other strategy c_2. But if Column is going to play c_2, then my best response is to play r_2 ..." and so on. A Nash equilibrium is then a set of beliefs and strategies in which each player's beliefs about what the other player will do are consistent with the other player's actual choice.

Sometimes the "thinking through" adjustment process described in the preceding paragraph is interpreted as an *actual* adjustment process in which each player experiments with different strategies in an attempt to understand the other player's choices. Although it is clear that such experimentation and learning goes on in real-life strategic interaction, this is, strictly speaking, not a valid interpretation of the Nash equilibrium concept. The reason is that if each player knows that the game is going to be repeated some number of times, then each player can plan to base his behavior at time t on observed behavior of the other player up to time t. In this case the correct notion of Nash equilibrium is a sequence of plays that is a best response (in some sense) to a *sequence* of my opponent's plays.

EXAMPLE: Calculating a Nash equilibrium

The following game is known as the "Battle of the Sexes." The story behind the game goes something like this. Rhonda Row and Calvin Column are discussing whether to take microeconomics or macroeconomics this semester. Rhonda gets utility 2 and Calvin gets utility 1 if they both take micro; the payoffs are reversed if they both take macro. If they take different courses, they both get utility 0.

Let us calculate all the Nash equilibria of this game. First, we look for the Nash equilibria in pure strategies. This simply involves a systematic examination of the best responses to various strategy choices. Suppose that Column thinks that Row will play Top. Column gets 1 from playing Left and 0 from playing Right, so Left is Column's best response to Row playing Top. On the other hand, if Column plays Left, then it is easy to see that it is optimal for Row to play Top. This line of reasoning shows that (Top, Left) is a Nash equilibrium. A similar argument shows that (Bottom, Right) is a Nash equilibrium.

The Battle of the Sexes

Table 15.3

		Calvin	
		Left (micro)	Right (macro)
Rhonda	Top (micro)	2, 1	0, 0
	Bottom (macro)	0, 0	1, 2

We can also solve this game systematically by writing the maximization problem that each agent has to solve and examining the first-order conditions. Let (p_t, p_b) be the probabilities with which Row plays Top and Bottom, and define (p_l, p_r) in a similar manner. Then Row's problem is

$$\max_{(p_t, p_b)} \; p_t[p_l 2 + p_r 0] + p_b[p_l 0 + p_r 1]$$

such that $p_t + p_b = 1$

$$p_t \geq 0$$
$$p_b \geq 0.$$

Let λ, μ_t, and μ_b be the Kuhn-Tucker multipliers on the constraints, so that the Lagrangian takes the form:

$$\mathcal{L} = 2p_t p_l + p_b p_r - \lambda(p_t + p_b - 1) - \mu_t p_t - \mu_b p_b.$$

Differentiating with respect to p_t and p_b, we see that the Kuhn-Tucker conditions for Row are

$$2p_l = \lambda + \mu_t$$
$$p_r = \lambda + \mu_b. \qquad (15.1)$$

Since we already know the pure strategy solutions, we only consider the case where $p_t > 0$ and $p_b > 0$. The complementary slackness conditions then imply that $\mu_t = \mu_b = 0$. Using the fact that $p_t + p_b = 1$, we easily see that Row will find it optimal to play a mixed strategy when $p_l = 1/3$ and $p_r = 2/3$.

Following the same procedure for Column, we find that $p_t = 2/3$ and $p_b = 1/3$. The expected payoff to each player from this mixed strategy can be easily computed by plugging these numbers into the objective function. In this case the expected payoff is $2/3$ to each player. Note that each player would prefer either of the pure strategy equilibria to the mixed strategy since the payoffs are higher for each player.

15.5 Interpretation of mixed strategies

It is sometimes difficult to give a behavioral interpretation to the idea of a mixed strategy. For some games, such as Matching Pennies, it is clear that mixed strategies are the only sensible equilibrium. But for other games of economic interest—e.g., a duopoly game—mixed strategies seem unrealistic.

In addition to this unrealistic nature of mixed strategies in some contexts, there is another difficulty on purely logical grounds. Consider again the example of the mixed strategy in the Battle of the Sexes. The mixed strategy equilibrium in this game has the property that if Row is playing his equilibrium mixed strategy, the expected payoff to Column from playing either of his pure strategies must be the same as the expected payoff from playing his equilibrium mixed strategy. The easiest way to see this is to look at the first-order conditions (15.1). Since $2p_l = p_r$, the expected payoff to playing top is the same as the expected payoff to playing bottom.

But this is no accident. It must always be the case that for any mixed strategy equilibrium, if one party believes that the other player will play the equilibrium mixed strategy, then he is indifferent as to whether he plays his equilibrium mixed strategy, or any pure strategy that is part of his mixed strategy. The logic is straightforward: if some pure strategy that is part of the equilibrium mixed strategy had a higher expected payoff than some other component of the equilibrium mixed strategy, then it would pay to increase the frequency with which one played the strategy with the higher expected payoff. But if all of the pure strategies that are played with positive probability in a mixed strategy have the same expected payoff, this must also be the expected payoff of the mixed strategy. And this in turn implies that the agent is indifferent as to which pure strategy he plays or whether he plays the mixed strategy. This "degeneracy" arises since the expected utility function is linear in probabilities. One would like there to be some more compelling reason to "enforce" the mixed strategy outcome.

In some settings this may not pose a serious problem. Suppose that you are part of a large group of people who meet each other randomly and play Matching Pennies once with each opponent. Suppose that initially everyone is playing the unique Nash equilibrium in mixed strategies of $(\frac{1}{2}, \frac{1}{2})$. Eventually some of the players tire of playing the mixed strategy and decide to play heads or tails all of the time. If the number of people who decide to play Heads all the time equals the number who decide to play Tails, then nothing significant has changed in any agent's choice problem: each agent would still rationally believe that his opponent has a 50:50 chance of playing Heads or Tails.

In this way each member of the population is playing a pure strategy, but in a given game the players have no way of knowing which pure strategy their opponent is playing. This interpretation of mixed strategy probabilities as being population frequencies is common in modeling animal behavior.

Another way to interpret mixed strategy equilibria is to consider a given individual's choice of whether to play Heads or play Tails in a one-shot game. This choice may be thought to depend on idiosyncratic factors that cannot be determined by opponents. Suppose for example that one calls Heads if you're in a "heads mood" and one calls tails if you're in a "tails mood." You may be able to observe your own mood, but your opponent cannot. Hence, from the viewpoint of each player, the other person's strategy is random, even though one's own strategy is deterministic. What matters about a player's mixed strategy is the uncertainty it creates in the *other* players of the game.

15.6 Repeated games

We indicated above that it was not appropriate to expect that the outcome of a repeated game with the same players as simply being a repetition of the one-shot game. This is because the strategy space of the repeated game is much larger: each player can determine his or her choice at some point as a function of the entire *history* of the game up until that point. Since my opponent can modify his behavior based on my history of choices, I must take this influence into account when making my own choices.

Let us analyze this in the context of the simple Prisoner's Dilemma game described earlier. Here it is in the "long-run" interest of both players to try to get to the (Cooperate, Cooperate) solution. So it might be sensible for one player to try to "signal" to the other that he is willing to "be nice" and play cooperate on the first move of the game. It is in the short-run interest of the other player to Defect, of course, but is this really in his long-run interest? He might reason that if he defects, the other player may lose patience and simply play Defect himself from then on. Thus, the second player might lose in the long run from playing the short-run optimal strategy. What lies behind this reasoning is the fact that a move that I make now may have repercussions in the future—the other player's future choices may depend on my current choices.

Let us ask whether the strategy of (Cooperate, Cooperate) can be a Nash equilibrium of the repeated Prisoner's Dilemma. First we consider the case of where each player knows that the game will be repeated a fixed number of times. Consider the reasoning of the players just before the last round of play. Each reasons that, at this point, they are playing a one-shot game. Since there is no future left on the last move, the standard logic for Nash equilibrium applies and both parties Defect.

Now consider the move before the last. Here it seems that it might pay each of the players to cooperate in order to signal that they are "nice guys" who will cooperate again in the next and final move. But we've just seen that when the next move comes around, each player will want to play Defect. Hence there is no advantage to cooperating on the next to the last move—as long as both players believe that the other player will Defect on the *final* move, there is no advantage to try to influence future behavior by being nice on the penultimate move. The same logic of **backwards induction** works for two moves before the end, and so on. In a repeated Prisoner's Dilemma with a known number of repetitions, the Nash equilibrium is to Defect in every round.

The situation is quite different in a repeated game with an infinite number of repetitions. In this case, at each stage it is known that the game will be repeated at least one more time and therefore there will be some (potential) benefits to cooperation. Let's see how this works in the case of the Prisoner's Dilemma.

Consider a game that consists of an infinite number of repetitions of the Prisoner's Dilemma described earlier. The strategies in this repeated game are sequences of functions that indicate whether each player will Cooperate or Defect at a particular stage as a function of the history of the game up to that stage. The payoffs in the repeated game are the discounted sums of the payoffs at each stage; that is, if a player gets a payoff at time t of u_t, his payoff in the repeated game is taken to be $\sum_{t=0}^{\infty} u_t/(1+r)^t$, where r is the discount rate.

I claim that as long as the discount rate is not too high there exists a Nash equilibrium pair of strategies such that each player finds it in his interest to cooperate at each stage. In fact, it is easy to exhibit an explicit example of such strategies. Consider the following strategy: "Cooperate on the current move unless the other player defected on the last move. If the other player defected on the last move, then Defect forever." This is sometimes called a **punishment strategy**, for obvious reasons: if a player defects, he will be punished forever with a low payoff.

To show that a pair of punishment strategies constitutes a Nash equilibrium, we simply have to show that if one player plays the punishment strategy the other player can do no better than playing the punishment strategy. Suppose that the players have cooperated up until move T and consider what would happen if a player decided to Defect on this move. Using the numbers from the Prisoner's Dilemma example on page 261, he would get an immediate payoff of 4, but he would also doom himself to an infinite stream of payments of 1. The discounted value of such a stream of payments is $1/r$, so his total expected payoff from Defecting is $4 + 1/r$.

On the other hand, his expected payoff from continuing to cooperate is $3 + 3/r$. Continuing to cooperate is preferred as long as $3 + 3/r > 4 + 1/r$, which reduces to requiring that $r < 2$. As long as this condition is satisfied, the punishment strategy forms a Nash equilibrium: if one party plays the punishment strategy, the other party will also want to play it, and neither party can gain by unilaterally deviating from this choice.

This construction is quite robust. Essentially the same argument works for any payoffs that exceed the payoffs from (Defect, Defect). A famous result known as the Folk Theorem asserts precisely this: in a repeated Prisoner's Dilemma any payoff larger than the payoff received if both parties consistently defect can be supported as a Nash equilibrium. The proof is more-or-less along the lines of the construction given above.

EXAMPLE: Maintaining a cartel

Consider a simple repeated duopoly which yields profits (π_c, π_c) if both firms choose to play a Cournot game and (π_j, π_j) if both firms produce the level of output that maximizes their joint profits—that is, they act as a **cartel**. It is well-known that the levels of output that maximize joint profits are typically not Nash equilibria in a single-period game—each producer has an incentive to dump extra output if he believes that the other producer will keep his output constant. However, as long as the discount rate is not too high, the joint profit-maximizing solution will be a Nash equilibrium of the repeated game. The appropriate punishment strategy is for each firm to produce the cartel output unless the other firm deviates, in which case it will produce the Cournot output forever. An argument similar to the Prisoner's Dilemma argument shows that this is a Nash equilibrium.

15.7 Refinements of Nash equilibrium

The Nash equilibrium concept seems like a reasonable definition of an equilibrium of a game. As with any equilibrium concept, there are two questions of immediate interest: 1) will a Nash equilibrium generally exist; and 2) will the Nash equilibrium be unique?

Existence, luckily, is not a problem. Nash (1950) showed that with a finite number of agents and a finite number of pure strategies, an equilibrium will always exist. It may, of course, be an equilibrium involving mixed strategies.

Uniqueness, however, is very unlikely to occur in general. We have already seen that there may be several Nash equilibria to a game. Game theorists have invested a substantial amount of effort into discovering further criteria that can be used to choose among Nash equilibria. These criteria are known as **refinements** of the concept of Nash equilibrium, and we will investigate a few of them below.

15.8 Dominant strategies

Let r_1 and r_2 be two of Row's strategies. We say that r_1 **strictly dominates** r_2 for Row if the payoff from strategy r_1 is strictly larger than the payoff for r_2 no matter what choice Column makes. The strategy r_1 **weakly dominates** r_2 if the payoff from r_1 is at least as large for all choices Column might make and strictly larger for some choice.

A **dominant strategy equilibrium** is a choice of strategies by each player such that each strategy (weakly) dominates every other strategy available to that player.

One particularly interesting game that has a dominant strategy equilibrium is the Prisoner's Dilemma in which the dominant strategy equilibrium is (Defect, Defect). If I believe that the other agent will Cooperate, then it is to my advantage to Defect; and if I believe that the other agent will Defect, it is still to my advantage to Defect.

Clearly, a dominant strategy equilibrium is a Nash equilibrium, but not all Nash equilibria are dominant strategy equilibria. A dominant strategy equilibrium, should one exist, is an especially compelling solution to the game, since there is a unique optimal choice for each player.

15.9 Elimination of dominated strategies

When there is no dominant strategy equilibrium, we have to resort to the idea of a Nash equilibrium. But typically there will be more than one Nash equilibrium. Our problem then is to try to eliminate some of the Nash equilibria as being "unreasonable."

One sensible belief to have about players' behavior is that it would be unreasonable for them to play strategies that are dominated by other strategies. This suggests that when given a game, we should first eliminate all strategies that are dominated and then calculate the Nash equilibria of the remaining game. This procedure is called **elimination of dominated strategies**; it can sometimes result in a significant reduction in the number of Nash equilibria.

For example consider the game

A game with dominated strategies

Table
15.4

		Column	
		Left	Right
Row	Top	2, 2	0, 2
	Bottom	2, 0	1, 1

Note that there are two pure strategy Nash equilibria, (Top, Left) and (Bottom, Right). However, the strategy Right weakly dominates the strategy Left for the Column player. If the Row agent assumes that Column will never play his dominated strategy, the only equilibrium for the game is (Bottom, Right).

Elimination of *strictly* dominated strategies is generally agreed to be an acceptable procedure to simplify the analysis of a game. Elimination of *weakly* dominated strategies is more problematic; there are examples in which eliminating weakly dominated strategies appears to change the strategic nature of the game in a significant way.

15.10 Sequential games

The games described so far in this chapter have all had a very simple dynamic structure: they were either one-shot games or a repeated sequence of one-shot games. They also had a very simple information structure: each player in the game knew the other player's payoffs and available strategies, but did not know in advance the other player's actual choice of strategies. Another way to say this is that up until now we have restricted our attention to games with **simultaneous moves**.

But many games of interest do not have this structure. In many situations at least *some* of the choices are made sequentially, and one player may know the other player's choice *before* he has to make his own choice. The analysis of such games is of considerable interest to economists since many economic games have this structure: a monopolist gets to observe consumer demand behavior before it produces output, or a duopolist may

The payoff matrix of a simultaneous-move game.

		Column	
		Left	Right
Row	Top	1, 9	1, 9
	Bottom	0, 0	2, 1

observe his opponent's capital investment before making its own output decisions, etc. The analysis of such games requires some new concepts.

Consider for example, the simple game depicted in Table 15.5. It is easy to verify that there are two pure strategy Nash equilibria in this game, (Top, Left) and (Bottom, Right). Implicit in this description of this game is the idea that both players make their choices simultaneously, without knowledge of the choice that the other player has made. But suppose that we consider the game in which Row must choose first, and Column gets to make his choice after observing Row's behavior.

In order to describe such a sequential game it is necessary to introduce a new tool, the **game tree**. This is simply a diagram that indicates the choices that each player can make at each point in time. The payoffs to each player are indicated at the "leaves" of the tree, as in Figure 15.1. This game tree is part of the a description of the game in **extensive form**.

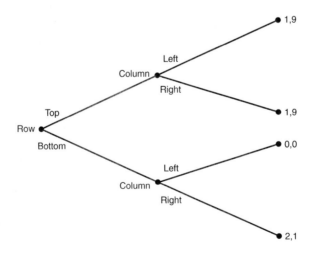

**Figure
15.1**

A game tree. This illustrates the payoffs to the previous game when Row gets to move first.

The nice thing about the tree diagram of the game is that it indicates the dynamic structure of the game—that some choices are made before others. A choice in the game corresponds to the choice of a branch of the tree. Once a choice has been made, the players are in a **subgame** consisting of the strategies and payoffs available to them from then on.

It is straightforward to calculate the Nash equilibria in each of the possible subgames, particularly in this case since the example is so simple. If Row chooses top, he effectively chooses the very simple subgame in which Column has the only remaining move. Column is indifferent between his two moves, so that Row will definitely end up with a payoff of 1 if he chooses Top.

If Row chooses Bottom, it will be optimal for Column to choose Right, which gives a payoff of 2 to Row. Since 2 is larger than 1, Row is clearly better off choosing Bottom than Top. Hence the sensible equilibrium for this game is (Bottom, Right). This is, of course, one of the Nash equilibria in the simultaneous-move game. If Column announces that he will choose Right, then Row's optimal response is Bottom, and if Row announces that he will choose Bottom then Column's optimal response is Right.

But what happened to the *other* equilibrium, (Top, Left)? If Row believes that Column will choose Left, then his optimal choice is certainly to choose Top. But why should Row believe that Column will actually choose Left? Once Row chooses Bottom, the optimal choice in the resulting subgame is for Column to choose Right. A choice of Left at this point is not an equilibrium choice in the relevant subgame.

In this example, only one of the two Nash equilibria satisfies the condition that it is not only an overall equilibrium, *but also an equilibrium in each of the subgames*. A Nash equilibrium with this property is known as a **subgame perfect** equilibrium.

It is quite easy to calculate subgame-perfect equilibria, at least in the kind of games that we have been examining. One simply does a "backwards induction" starting at the last move of the game. The player who has the last move has a simple optimization problem, with no strategic ramifications, so this is an easy problem to solve. The player who makes the second to the last move can look ahead to see how the player with the last move will respond to his choices, and so on. The mode of analysis is similar to that of dynamic programming; see Chapter 19, page 359. Once the game has been understood through this backwards induction, the agents play it going forwards.[2]

The extensive form of the game is also capable of modeling situations where some of the moves are sequential and some are simultaneous. The necessary concept is that of an **information set**. The information set of

---

[2] Compare to Kierkegaard (1938): "It is perfectly true, as philosophers say, that life must be understood backwards. But they forget the other proposition, that it must be lived forwards." [465]

an agent is the set of all nodes of the tree that cannot be differentiated by the agent. For example, the simultaneous-move game depicted at the beginning of this section can be represented by the game tree in Figure 15.2. In this figure, the shaded area indicates that Column cannot differentiate which of these decisions Row made at the time when Column must make his own decision. Hence, it is just as if the choices are made simultaneously.

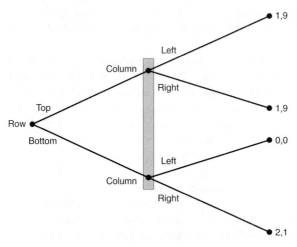

Figure 15.2   **Information set.**   This is the extensive form to the original simultaneous-move game. The shaded information set indicates that Column is not aware of which choice Row made when he makes his own choice.

Thus the extensive form of a game can be used to model everything in the strategic form *plus* information about the sequence of choices and information sets. In this sense the extensive form is a more powerful concept than the strategic form, since it contains more detailed information about the strategic interactions of the agents. It is the presence of this additional information that helps to eliminate some of the Nash equilibria as "unreasonable."

EXAMPLE: A simple bargaining model

Two players, A and B, have $1 to divide between them. They agree to spend at most three days negotiating over the division. The first day, A will make an offer, B either accepts or comes back with a counteroffer the next day, and on the third day A gets to make one final offer. If they cannot reach an agreement in three days, both players get zero.

A and B differ in their degree of impatience: A discounts payoffs in the future at a rate of α per day, and B discounts payoffs at a rate of β per day. Finally, we assume that if a player is indifferent between two offers, he will accept the one that is most preferred by his opponent. This idea is that the opponent could offer some arbitrarily small amount that would make the player strictly prefer one choice, and that this assumption allows us to approximate such an "arbitrarily small amount" by zero. It turns out that there is a unique subgame perfect equilibrium of this bargaining game.[3]

As suggested above, we start our analysis at the end of the game, right before the last day. At this point A can make a take-it-or-leave-it offer to B. Clearly, the optimal thing for A to do at this point is to offer B the smallest possible amount that he would accept, which, by assumption, is zero. So if the game actually lasts three days, A would get 1 and B would get zero (i.e., an arbitrarily small amount).

Now go back to the previous move, when B gets to propose a division. At this point B should realize that A can guarantee himself 1 on the next move by simply rejecting B's offer. A dollar next period is worth α to A this period, so any offer less than α would be sure to be rejected. B certainly prefers $1 - \alpha$ now to zero next period, so he should rationally offer α to A, which A will then accept. So if the game ends on the second move, A gets α and B gets $1 - \alpha$.

Now move to the first day. At this point A gets to make the offer and he realizes that B can get $1 - \alpha$ if he simply waits until the second day. Hence A must offer a payoff that has at least this present value to B in order to avoid delay. Thus he offers $\beta(1 - \alpha)$ to B. B finds this (just) acceptable and the game ends. The final outcome is that the game ends on the first move with A receiving $1 - \beta(1 - \alpha)$ and B receiving $\beta(1 - \alpha)$.

Figure 15.3A illustrates this process for the case where $\alpha = \beta < 1$. The outermost diagonal line shows the possible payoff patterns on the first day, namely all payoffs of the form $x_A + x_B = 1$. The next diagonal line moving towards the origin shows the present value of the payoffs if the game ends in the second period: $x_A + x_B = \alpha$. The diagonal line closest to the origin shows the present value of the payoffs if the game ends in the third period; this equation for this line is $x_A + x_B = \alpha^2$. The right angled path depicts the minimum acceptable divisions each period, leading up to the final subgame perfect equilibrium. Figure 15.3B shows how the same process looks with more stages in the negotiation.

It is natural to let the horizon go to infinity and ask what happens in the infinite game. It turns out that the subgame perfect equilibrium division

---

[3] This is a simplified version of the Rubinstein-Ståhl bargaining model; see the references at the end of the chapter for more detailed information.

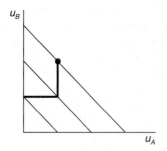 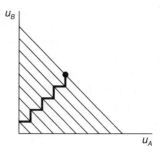

Figure 15.3

A bargaining game. The heavy line connects together the equilibrium outcomes in the subgames. The point on the outermost line is the subgame-perfect equilibrium.

is

$$\text{payoff to } A = \frac{1 - \beta}{1 - \alpha\beta}$$

$$\text{payoff to } B = \frac{\beta(1 - \alpha)}{1 - \alpha\beta}.$$

Note that if $\alpha = 1$ and $\beta < 1$, then player A receives the entire payoff, in accord with the principal expressed in the Gospels: "Let patience have her [subgame] perfect work." (James 1:4).

15.11 Repeated games and subgame perfection

The idea of subgame perfection eliminates Nash equilibria that involve players threatening actions that are not credible—i.e., they are not in the interest of the players to carry out. For example, the Punishment Strategy described earlier is not a subgame perfect equilibrium. If one player actually deviates from the (Cooperate, Cooperate) path, then it is not necessarily in the interest of the other player to actually defect *forever* in response. It may seem reasonable to punish the other player for defection to some degree, but punishing forever seems extreme.

A somewhat less harsh strategy is known as Tit-for-Tat: start out cooperating on the first play and on subsequent plays do whatever your opponent did on the previous play. In this strategy, a player is punished for defection, but he is only punished once. In this sense Tit-for-Tat is a "forgiving" strategy.

Although the punishment strategy is not subgame perfect for the repeated Prisoner's Dilemma, there are strategies that can support the cooperative solution that *are* subgame perfect. These strategies are not easy to describe, but they have the character of the West Point honor code: each player agrees to punish the other for defecting, *and* also punish the other for failing to punish another player for defecting, and so on. The fact that you will be punished if you don't punish a defector is what makes it subgame perfect to carry out the punishments.

Unfortunately, the same sort of strategies can support many other outcomes in the repeated Prisoner's Dilemma. The **Folk Theorem** asserts that essentially all distributions of utility in a repeated one-shot game can be equilibria of the repeated game.

This excess supply of equilibria is troubling. In general, the larger the strategy space, the more equilibria there will be, since there will be more ways for players to "threaten" retaliation for defecting from a given set of strategies. In order to eliminate the "undesirable" equilibria, we need to find some criterion for eliminating strategies. A natural criterion is to eliminate strategies that are "too complex." Although some progress has been made in this direction, the idea of complexity is an elusive one, and it has been hard to come up with an entirely satisfactory definition.

15.12 Games with incomplete information

Up until now we have been investigating games of complete information. In particular, each agent has been assumed to know the payoffs of the other player, and each player knows that the other agent knows this, etc. In many situations, this is not an appropriate assumption. If one agent doesn't know the payoffs of the other agent, then the Nash equilibrium doesn't make much sense. However, there is a way of looking at games of incomplete information due to Harsanyi (1967) that allows for a systematic analysis of their properties.

The key to the Harsanyi approach is to subsume all of the uncertainty that one agent may have about another into a variable known as the agent's **type**. For example, one agent may be uncertain about another agent's valuation of some good, about his or her risk aversion and so on. Each type of player is regarded as a different player and each agent has some prior probability distribution defined over the different types of agents.

A **Bayes-Nash equilibrium** of this game is then a set of strategies for each type of player that maximizes the expected value of each type of player, given the strategies pursued by the other players. This is essentially the same definition as in the definition of Nash equilibrium, except for the additional uncertainty involved about the type of the other player. Each player knows that the other player is chosen from a set of possible types, but doesn't know exactly which one he is playing. Note in order to have a complete description of an equilibrium we must have a list of strategies for *all* types of players, not just the actual types in a particular situation, since each individual player doesn't know the actual types of the other players and has to consider all possibilities.

In a simultaneous-move game, this definition of equilibrium is adequate. In a sequential game it is reasonable to allow the players to update their beliefs about the types of the other players based on the actions they have observed. Normally, we assume that this updating is done in a manner consistent with Bayes' rule.[4] Thus, if one player observes the other choosing some strategy s, the first player should revise his beliefs about what type the other player is by determining how likely it is that s would be chosen by the various types.

EXAMPLE: A sealed-bid auction

Consider a simple sealed-bid auction for an item in which there are two bidders. Each player makes an independent bid without knowing the other player's bid and the item will be awarded to the person with the highest bid. Each bidder knows his own valuation of the item being auctioned, v, but neither knows the other's valuation. However, each player believes that the other person's valuation of the item is uniformly distributed between 0 and 1. (And each person *knows* that each person believes this, etc.)

In this game, the type of the player is simply his valuation. Therefore, a Bayes-Nash equilibrium to this game will be a *function*, $b(v)$, that indicates the optimal bid, b, for a player of type v. Given the symmetric nature of the game, we look for an equilibrium where each player follows an identical strategy.

It is natural to guess that the function $b(v)$ is strictly increasing; i.e., higher valuations lead to higher bids. Therefore, we can let $V(b)$ be its inverse function so that $V(b)$ gives us the valuation of someone who bids b. When one player bids some particular b, his probability of winning is the probability that the other player's bid is less than b. But this is simply the probability that the other player's valuation is less than $V(b)$. Since v is uniformly distributed between 0 and 1, the probability that the other player's valuation is less than $V(b)$ is $V(b)$.

Hence, if a player bids b when his valuation is v, his expected payoff is

$$(v - b)V(b) + 0[1 - V(b)].$$

The first term is the expected consumer's surplus if he has the highest bid; the second term is the zero surplus he receives if he is outbid. The optimal bid must maximize this expression, so

$$(v - b)V'(b) - V(b) = 0.$$

For each value of v, this equation determines the optimal bid for the player as a function of v. Since $V(b)$ is by hypothesis the function that describes the relationship between the optimal bid and the valuation, we must have

$$(V(b) - b)V'(b) \equiv V(b)$$

for all b.

---

[4] See Chapter 11, page 191 for a discussion of Bayes' rule.

The solution to this differential equation is

$$V(b) = b + \sqrt{b^2 + 2C},$$

where C is a constant of integration. (Check this!) In order to determine this constant of integration we note that when $v = 0$ we must have $b = 0$, since the optimal bid when the valuation is zero must be 0. Substituting this into the solution to the differential equation gives us

$$0 = 0 + \sqrt{2C},$$

which implies $C = 0$. It follows that $V(b) = 2b$, or $b = v/2$, is a Bayes-Nash equilibrium for the simple auction. That is, it is a Bayes-Nash equilibrium for each player to bid half of his valuation.

The way that we arrived at the solution to this game is reasonably standard. Essentially, we guessed that the optimal bidding function was invertible and then derived the differential equation that it must satisfy. As it turned out, the resulting bid function had the desired property. One weakness of this approach is that it only exhibits one particular equilibrium to the Bayesian game—there could in principle be many others.

As it happens, in this particular game, the solution that we calculated is unique, but this need not happen in general. In particular, in games of incomplete information it may well pay for some players to try to hide their true type. For example, one type may try to play the same strategy as some other type. In this situation the function relating type to strategy is not invertible and the analysis is much more complex.

15.13 Discussion of Bayes-Nash equilibrium

The idea of Bayes-Nash equilibrium is an ingenious one, but perhaps it is too ingenious. The problem is that the reasoning involved in computing Bayes-Nash equilibria is often very involved. Although it is perhaps not unreasonable that purely *rational* players would play according to the Bayes-Nash theory, there is considerable doubt about whether real players are able to make the necessary calculations.

In addition, there is a problem with the predictions of the model. The choice that each player makes depends crucially on his beliefs about the distribution of various types in the population. Different beliefs about the frequency of different types leads to different optimal behavior. Since we generally don't observe players beliefs about the prevalence of various types of players, we typically won't be able to check the predictions of the model. Ledyard (1986) has shown that essentially *any* pattern of play is a Bayes-Nash equilibrium for some pattern of beliefs.

Nash equilibrium, in its original formulation, puts a consistency requirement on the beliefs of the agents—only those beliefs compatible with maximizing behavior were allowed. But as soon as we allow there to be many types of players with different utility functions, this idea loses much of its force. Nearly any pattern of behavior can be consistent with some pattern of beliefs.

Notes

The concept of Nash equilibrium comes from Nash (1951). The concept of Bayesian equilibrium is due to Harsanyi (1967). More detailed treatments of the simple bargaining model may be found in Binmore & Dasgupta (1987).

This chapter is just a bare-bones introduction to game theory; most students will want to study this subject in more detail. Luckily several fine treatments have recently become available that provide a more rigorous and detailed treatment. For review articles see Aumann (1987), Myerson (1986), and Tirole (1988). For book-length treatments see the works by Kreps (1990), Binmore (1991), Myerson (1991), Rasmusen (1989), and Fudenberg & Tirole (1991).

Exercises

15.1. Calculate all the Nash equilibria in the game of Matching Pennies.

15.2. In a finitely repeated Prisoner's Dilemma game we showed that it was a Nash equilibrium to defect every round. Show that, in fact, this is the dominant strategy equilibrium.

15.3. What are the Nash equilibria of the following game after one eliminates dominated strategies?

		Column		
		Left	Middle	Right
Row	Top	3, 3	0, 3	0, 0
	Middle	3, 0	2, 2	0, 2
	Bottom	0, 0	2, 0	1, 1

15.4. Calculate the expected payoff to each player in the simple auction game described in the text if each player follows the Bayes-Nash equilibrium strategy, conditional on his value v.

15.5. Consider the game matrix given here.

		Column	
		Left	Right
Row	Top	a, b	c, d
	Bottom	e, f	g, h

(a) If (top, left) is a dominant strategy equilibrium, then what inequalities must hold among $a, \ldots, h$?

(b) If (top, left) is a Nash equilibrium, then which of the above inequalities must be satisfied?

(c) If (top, left) is a dominant strategy equilibrium, must it be a Nash equilibrium?

15.6. Two California teenagers Bill and Ted are playing Chicken. Bill drives his hot rod south down a one-lane road, and Ted drives his hot rod north along the same road. Each has two strategies: Stay or Swerve. If one player chooses Swerve he looses face; if both Swerve, they both lose face. However, if both choose Stay, they are both killed. The payoff matrix for Chicken looks like this:

		Column	
		Left	Right
Row	Top	-3,-3	2,0
	Bottom	0,2	1,1

(a) Find all pure strategy equilibria.

(b) Find all mixed strategy equilibria.

(c) What is the probability that both teenagers will survive?

15.7. In a repeated, symmetric duopoly the payoff to both firms is π_j if they produce the level of output that maximizes their joint profits and π_c if they produce the Cournot level of output. The maximum payoff that one player can get if the other chooses the joint profit maximizing output is π_d. The discount rate is r. The players adopt the punishment strategy of reverting to the Cournot game if either player defects from the joint profit-maximizing strategy. How large can r be?

15.8. Consider the game shown below:

		Column		
		Left	Middle	Right
Row	Top	1,0	1,2	2,-1
	Middle	1,1	1,0	0,-1
	Bottom	-3,-3	-3,-3	-3,-3

(a) Which of Row's strategies is strictly dominated no matter what Column does?

(b) Which of Row's strategies is weakly dominated?

(c) Which of Column's strategies is strictly dominated no matter what Row does?

(d) If we eliminate Column's dominated strategies, are any of Row's strategies weakly dominated?

15.9. Consider the following coordination game

		Column	
		Left	Right
Row	Top	2,2	-1,-1
	Bottom	-1,-1	1,1

(a) Calculate all the pure strategy equilibria of this game.

(b) Do any of the pure strategy equilibria dominate any of the others?

(c) Suppose that Row moves first and commits to either Top or Bottom. Are the strategies you described above still Nash equilibria?

(d) What are the subgame perfect equilibria of this game?

CHAPTER 16

OLIGOPOLY

Oligopoly is the study of market interactions with a small number of firms. The modern study of this subject is grounded almost entirely in the theory of games discussed in the last chapter. This is, of course, a very natural development. Many of the earlier *ad hoc* specifications of strategic market interactions have been substantially clarified by using the concepts of game theory. In this chapter we will investigate oligopoly theory primarily, though not exclusively, from this perspective.

16.1 Cournot equilibrium

We begin with the classic model of **Cournot equilibrium**, already mentioned as an example in the last chapter. Consider two firms which produce a homogeneous product with output levels y_1 and y_2, and thus an aggregate output of $Y = y_1 + y_2$. The market price associated with this output (the inverse demand function) is taken to be $p(Y) \equiv p(y_1 + y_2)$. Firm i has a cost function given by $c_i(y_i)$ for $i = 1, 2$.

Firm 1's maximization problem is

$$\max_{y_1} \ \pi_1(y_1, y_2) = p(y_1 + y_2)y_1 - c_1(y_1).$$

Clearly, firm 1's profits depend on the amount of output chosen by firm 2, and in order to make an informed decision firm 1 must forecast firm 2's output decision. This is just the sort of consideration that goes into an abstract game—each player must guess the choices of the other players. For this reason it is natural to think of the Cournot model as being a one-shot game: the profit of firm i is its payoff, and the strategy space of firm i is simply the possible outputs that it can produce. A (pure strategy) Nash equilibrium is then a set of outputs (y_1^*, y_2^*) in which each firm is choosing its profit-maximizing output level given its beliefs about the other firm's choice, and each firm's beliefs about the other firm's choice are actually correct.

Assuming an interior optimum for each firm, this means that a Nash-Cournot equilibrium must satisfy the two first-order conditions:

$$\frac{\partial \pi_1(y_1, y_2)}{\partial y_1} = p(y_1 + y_2) + p'(y_1 + y_2)y_1 - c_1'(y_1) = 0$$

$$\frac{\partial \pi_2(y_1, y_2)}{\partial y_2} = p(y_1 + y_2) + p'(y_1 + y_2)y_2 - c_2'(y_2) = 0.$$

We also have the second-order conditions for each firm which take the form

$$\frac{\partial^2 \pi_i}{\partial y_i^2} = 2p'(Y) + p''(Y)y_i - c_i''(y_i) \leq 0 \quad \text{for } i = 1, 2$$

where $Y = y_1 + y_2$.

The first-order condition for firm 1 determines firm 1's optimal choice of output as a function of its beliefs about firm 2's output choice; this relationship is known as firm 1's **reaction curve**: it depicts how firm 1 will react given various beliefs it might have about firm 2's choice.

Assuming sufficient regularity, the reaction curve of firm 1, $f_1(y_2)$, is defined implicitly by the identity

$$\frac{\partial \pi_1(f_1(y_2), y_2)}{\partial y_1} \equiv 0.$$

In order to determine how firm 1 optimally changes its output as its beliefs about firm 2's output changes, we differentiate this identity and solve for $f_1'(y_2)$:

$$f_1'(y_2) = -\frac{\partial^2 \pi_1 / \partial y_1 \partial y_2}{\partial^2 \pi_1 / \partial y_1^2}.$$

As usual, the denominator is negative due to the second-order conditions so that the slope of the reaction curve is determined by the sign of the mixed partial. This is easily seen to be

$$\partial^2 \pi_1 / \partial y_1 \partial y_2 = p'(Y) + p''(Y)y_1.$$

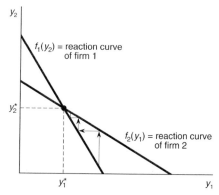

Reaction curves. The intersection of the two reaction curves is a Cournot-Nash equilibrium.

Figure 16.1

If the inverse demand curve is concave, or at least not "too" convex, this expression will be negative, which indicates that a Cournot reaction curve for firm 1 will generally have a negative slope. A typical example is depicted in Figure 16.1.

As we will see below, many important features of duopoly interaction depend on the slope of the reaction curves, which in turn depends on the mixed partial of profit with respect to the two choice variables. If the choice variables are quantities, the "natural" sign of this mixed partial is negative. In this case we say that y_1 and y_2 are **strategic substitutes**. If the mixed partial is positive, then we have a case of **strategic complements**. We'll see an example of these distinctions below.

Stability of the system

Although we have been careful to emphasize the one-shot nature of the Cournot game, Cournot himself thought of it in more dynamic terms. There is, indeed, a natural (if somewhat suspect) dynamic interpretation to the model. Suppose that we think of a learning process in which each firm refines its beliefs about the other firm's behavior by observing its actual choice of output.

Given an arbitrary pattern of outputs at time 0, (y_1^0, y_2^0), firm 1 guesses that firm 2 will continue to produce y_2^0 in period 1, and therefore choose the profit-maximizing output consistent with this guess, namely $y_1^1 = f_1(y_2^0)$. Firm 2 observes this choice y_1^1 and conjectures that firm 1 will maintain the output level y_1^1. Firm 2 therefore chooses $y_2^2 = f_2(y_1^1)$. In general the output choice of firm i in period t is given by $y_i^t = f_i(y_j^{t-1})$.

This gives us a difference equation in outputs that traces out a "cobweb" like that illustrated in Figure 16.1. In the case illustrated, the firm 1's reaction curve is steeper than firm 2's reaction curve and the cobweb converges to the Cournot-Nash equilibrium. We therefore say that the illustrated equilibrium is **stable**. If firm 1's reaction curve were flatter than firm 2's, then the equilibrium would be **unstable**.

A somewhat different dynamic model arises if we imagine that the firms adjust their outputs in the direction of increasing profits, assuming that the other firm keeps its output fixed. This leads to a **dynamical system** of the form

$$\frac{dy_1}{dt} = \alpha_1 \left[\frac{\partial \pi_1(y_1, y_2)}{\partial y_1} \right]$$

$$\frac{dy_2}{dt} = \alpha_2 \left[\frac{\partial \pi_2(y_1, y_2)}{\partial y_2} \right].$$

Here the parameters $\alpha_1 > 0$ and $\alpha_2 > 0$ indicate the speed of adjustment.

A sufficient condition for local stability of this dynamical system is

$$\begin{vmatrix} \dfrac{\partial^2 \pi_1}{\partial y_1^2} & \dfrac{\partial^2 \pi_1}{\partial y_1 \partial y_2} \\ \dfrac{\partial^2 \pi_2}{\partial y_1 \partial y_2} & \dfrac{\partial^2 \pi_2}{\partial y_2^2} \end{vmatrix} > 0. \tag{16.1}$$

This is "almost" a necessary condition for stability; the problem comes in the fact that the determinant may be zero even though the dynamical system is locally stable. We will ignore the complications that arise from consideration of these borderline cases.

This determinant condition turns out to be quite useful in deriving comparative statics results. However, it should be emphasized that the postulated adjustment process is rather *ad hoc*. Each firm expects the other firm to keep its output constant, although it itself expects to change its output. Inconsistent beliefs of this sort are anathema to game theory. The problem is that the one-shot Cournot game cannot be given a dynamic interpretation; in order to analyze the dynamics of a multiple period game, one should really go to the repeated game analysis of the sort considered in the previous chapter. Despite this objection, naive dynamic models of this sort may have some claim to empirical relevance. It is likely that firms will need to experiment in order to learn about how the market responds to their decisions and the particular dynamic adjustment process described above can be thought of as a simple model to decribe this learning process.

16.2 Comparative statics

Suppose that a is some parameter that shifts the profit function of firm 1. The Cournot equilibrium is described by the conditions

$$\frac{\partial \pi_1(y_1(a), y_2(a), a)}{\partial y_1} = 0$$

$$\frac{\partial \pi_2(y_1(a), y_2(a))}{\partial y_2} = 0.$$

Differentiating these equations with respect to a gives us the system

$$\begin{pmatrix} \dfrac{\partial^2 \pi_1}{\partial y_1^2} & \dfrac{\partial^2 \pi_1}{\partial y_1 \partial y_2} \\[2ex] \dfrac{\partial^2 \pi_2}{\partial y_1 \partial y_2} & \dfrac{\partial^2 \pi_2}{\partial y_2^2} \end{pmatrix} \begin{pmatrix} \dfrac{\partial y_1}{\partial a} \\[2ex] \dfrac{\partial y_2}{\partial a} \end{pmatrix} = \begin{pmatrix} -\dfrac{\partial^2 \pi_1}{\partial y_1 \partial a} \\[2ex] 0 \end{pmatrix}.$$

Applying Cramer's rule, in Chapter 26, page 477, we have

$$\frac{\partial y_1}{\partial a} = \frac{\begin{vmatrix} -\dfrac{\partial^2 \pi_1}{\partial y_1 \partial a} & \dfrac{\partial^2 \pi_1}{\partial y_1 \partial y_2} \\[2ex] 0 & \dfrac{\partial^2 \pi_2}{\partial y_2^2} \end{vmatrix}}{\begin{vmatrix} \dfrac{\partial^2 \pi_1}{\partial y_1^2} & \dfrac{\partial^2 \pi_1}{\partial y_1 \partial y_2} \\[2ex] \dfrac{\partial^2 \pi_2}{\partial y_1 \partial y_2} & \dfrac{\partial^2 \pi_2}{\partial y_2^2} \end{vmatrix}}.$$

The sign of the denominator is determined by the stability condition in (16.1); we assume that it is positive. The sign of the numerator is determined by

$$-\frac{\partial^2 \pi_1}{\partial y_1 \partial a} \frac{\partial^2 \pi_2}{\partial y_2^2}.$$

The second term in this expression is negative by the second-order condition for profit maximization. It follows that

$$\text{sign} \; \frac{\partial y_1}{\partial a} = \text{sign} \; \frac{\partial^2 \pi_1}{\partial y_1 \partial a}.$$

This condition says that in order to determine how a shift in profits affects equilibrium output, we simply need to compute the mixed partial $\partial^2 \pi_i / \partial y \partial a$.

Let us apply this result to the duopoly model. Suppose that a is equal to a (constant) marginal cost and profits are given by

$$\pi_1(y_1, y_2, a) = p(y_1 + y_2)y_1 - ay_1.$$

Then $\partial^2 \pi_1 / \partial y_1 \partial a = -1$. This means that increasing the marginal cost for firm 1 will reduce its Cournot equilibrium output.

16.3 Several firms

If there are n firms, the Cournot model has much the same flavor. In this case the first-order condition for firm i becomes

$$p(Y) + p'(Y)y_i = c_i'(y_i), \tag{16.2}$$

where $Y = \sum_i y_i$. It is convenient to rearrange this equation to take the form

$$p(Y)\left[1 + \frac{dp}{dY}\frac{y_i}{p}\right] = c'_i(y_i).$$

Letting $s_i = y_i/Y$ denote firm i's share of industry output, we can write

$$p(Y)\left[1 + \frac{dp}{dY}\frac{Y}{p}s_i\right] = c'_i(y_i),$$

or

$$p(Y)\left[1 + \frac{s_i}{\epsilon}\right] = c'_i(y_i), \tag{16.3}$$

where ϵ is the elasticity of *market* demand.

This last equation illustrates the sense in which the Cournot model is, in some sense, "in between" the case of monopoly and that of pure competition. If $s_i = 1$, we have exactly the monopoly condition, and as s_i approaches zero, so that each firm has an infinitesimal share of the market, the Cournot equilibrium approaches a competitive equilibrium. [1]

There are a couple of special cases of (16.2) and (16.3) that are useful for constructing examples. First, assume that each firm has constant marginal costs of c_i. Then adding up both sides of the equation across all n firms, we have

$$np(Y) + p'(Y)Y = \sum_{i=1}^{n} c_i.$$

Hence, aggregate industry output only depends on the *sum* of the marginal costs, not on their distribution across firms. [2] If all firms have the same constant marginal cost of c, then in a symmetric equilibrium $s_i = 1/n$, and we can write this equation as

$$p(Y)\left[1 + \frac{1}{n\epsilon}\right] = c. \tag{16.4}$$

If, in addition, ϵ is constant, this equation shows that price is a constant markup on marginal cost. For this simple case it is clear that as $n \to \infty$, price must approach marginal cost.

---

[1] Actually, one has to be somewhat careful about such loose statements, as much depends on exactly how the share of each firm goes to zero. For a consistent specification, see Novshek (1980).

[2] Of course, we are *assuming* an interior solution. If the marginal costs are too different, some firms will not want to produce in equilibrium.

Welfare

We have seen earlier that a monopolistic industry produces an inefficiently low level of output since price exceeds marginal cost. The same is true of a Cournot industry. A graphic way to illustrate the nature of the distortion is to ask what it is that a Cournot industry maximizes.

As we have seen earlier, the area under the demand curve, $U(Y) = \int_0^Y p(x)\,dx$, is a reasonable measure of total benefits in certain circumstances. Using this definition, it can be shown that the output level at a symmetric Cournot equilibrium with constant marginal costs maximizes the following expression:

$$W(Y) = [p(Y) - c]Y + (n-1)[U(Y) - cY].$$

The proof is simply to differentiate this expression with respect to Y and note that it satisfies equation (16.4). (We will assume that the relevant second-order conditions are satisfied).

In general we want an industry to maximize utility minus costs. A competitive industry does in fact do this, while a monopoly simply maximizes profits. A Cournot industry maximizes a weighted sum of these two objectives, with the weights depending on the number of firms. As n increases, more and more weight is given to the social objective of utility minus costs as compared to the private objective of profits.

16.4 Bertrand equilibrium

The Cournot model is an attractive one for many of the reasons outlined in the last section, but it is by no means the only possible model of oligopoly behavior. The Cournot model takes the firm's strategy space as being quantities, but it seems equally natural to consider what happens if price is chosen as the relevant strategic variable. This is known as the **Bertrand** model of oligopoly.

Suppose, then, that we have two firms with constant marginal costs of c_1 and c_2 that face a market demand curve of $D(p)$. For definiteness, assume that $c_2 > c_1$. As before, we assume a homogeneous product so that the demand curve facing firm 1, say, is given by

$$d_1(p_1, p_2) = \begin{cases} D(p_1) & \text{if } p_1 < p_2 \\ D(p_1)/2 & \text{if } p_1 = p_2 \\ 0 & \text{if } p_1 > p_2. \end{cases}$$

That is, firm 1 believes that it can capture the entire market by setting a price smaller than the price of firm 2. Of course, firm 2 is assumed to have similar beliefs.

What is the Nash equilibrium of this game? Suppose that firm 1 sets p_1 higher than c_2. This cannot be an equilibrium. Why? If firm 2 expected firm 1 to make such a choice, it would choose p_2 to be between p_1 and c_2. This would yield zero profits to firm 1 and positive profits to firm 2. Similarly, at any price below c_2, firm 1 is "leaving money on the table." At any such price, firm 2 would choose to produce zero but firm 1 could increase its profits by increasing its price slightly.

Thus a Nash equilibrium in this game is for firm 1 to set $p_1 = c_2$ and to produce $D(c_2)$ units of output, while firm 2 sets $p_2 \geq c_2$ and produces zero.

It may seem somewhat nonintuitive that we get price equal to marginal cost in a two-firm industry. Part of the problem is that the Bertrand game is a one-shot game: players choose their prices and then the game ends. This is typically not a standard practice in real-life markets.

One way to think about the Bertrand model is that it is a model of competitive bidding. Each firm submits a sealed bid stating the price at which it will serve all customers; the bids are opened and the lowest bidder gets the customers. Viewed in this way, the Bertrand result is not so paradoxical. It is well-known that sealed bids are a very good way to induce firms to compete vigorously, even if there are only a few firms.

Up until now, we have assumed that fixed costs for each firm are zero. Let us relax this assumption and consider what happens if each firm has fixed costs of $K > 0$. We assume that each firm always has the shut-down option of producing zero output and incurring zero costs. In this case, the logic described above quickly yields the Bertrand equilibrium: the equilibrium price is equal to the marginal cost of firm 2 (the higher cost firm), as long as the profits to firm 1 are nonnegative. If the profits to firm 1 are negative, then no equilibria in pure strategies exist.

However, an equilibrium in mixed strategies will typically exist, and in fact can often be explicitly calculated. In such an equilibrium, each firm has a probability distribution over the prices that the other firm might charge, and chooses its own probability distribution so as to maximize expected profits. This is a case where a mixed strategy may seem implausible; however, as usual, that is in part an artifact of one-shot nature of analysis. Even if we think of a repeated game, one could interpret a mixed strategy as a policy of "sales": each store in a retail market could randomize its price so that in any given week one store would have the lowest price in town, and thereby capture all the customers. However, each week a different store would be the winner.

EXAMPLE: A model of sales

Let us calculate the mixed strategy equilibrium in a duopoly sales model. Suppose for simplicity that each firm has zero marginal costs and fixed costs of k. There are two types of consumers, **informed consumers** know the lowest price being charged and **uninformed consumers** simply choose a store at random. Suppose that there are I informed consumers and $2U$ uninformed consumers. Hence, each store will get U uninformed consumers each period for certain and will get the informed consumers only if they happen to have the lowest price. The reservation price of each consumer is r.

We will consider only the symmetric equilibrium, where each firm uses the same mixed strategy. Let $F(p)$ be the cumulative distribution function of the equilibrium strategy; that is, $F(p)$ is the probability that the chosen price is less than or equal to p. We let $f(p)$ be the associated probability density function which we will assume is a continuous density function, since this allows us to neglect the probability of a tie.[3]

Given this assumption, there are exactly two events that are relevant to a firm when it sets a price p. Either it succeeds in having the lowest price, an event that has probability $1 - F(p)$, or it fails to have the lowest price, an event that has probability $F(p)$. If it succeeds in having the lowest price, it gets a revenue of $p(U + I)$; if it doesn't have the lowest price, it gets revenue pU. In either case it pays a fixed cost of k. Thus, the expected profits of the firm, π, can be written as

$$\pi = \int_0^\infty [p(1 - F(p))(I + U) + pF(p)U - k] f(p)\, dp.$$

Now note the following simple observation: every price that is actually charged in the equilibrium mixed strategy must yield the same expected profit. Otherwise, the firm could increase the frequency with which it charged the more profitable price relative to the less profitable prices and increase its overall expected profit.

This means that we must have

$$p(I + U)(1 - F(p)) + pF(p)U - k = \overline{\pi},$$

or, solving,

$$F(p) = \frac{p(I + U) - k - \overline{\pi}}{pI}. \qquad (16.5)$$

It remains to determine $\overline{\pi}$. The probability that a firm would charge a price less than or equal to r is 1, so we must have $F(r) = 1$. Solving this equation gives us $\overline{\pi} = rU - k$, and substituting back into equation (16.5) yields

$$F(p) = \frac{p(I + U) - rU}{pI}.$$

---

[3] It can be shown by a more elaborate argument that there will be zero probability of a tie in equilibrium.

Letting $u = U/I$, we can write this as

$$F(p) = 1 + u - \frac{ru}{p}.$$

This expression equals zero at $\bar{p} = ru/(1+u)$, so $F(p) = 0$ for $p \leq \bar{p}$, and $F(p) = 1$ for any $p \geq r$.

16.5 Complements and substitutes

In our two models of oligopoly we have assumed that the goods produced by the firms are perfect substitutes. However, it is straightforward to relax that assumption, and by doing so we can point out a nice duality between the Cournot and Bertrand equilibria. The point is most easily exhibited in the case of linear demand functions, although it holds true in general. Let the consumers' inverse demand functions be given by

$$p_1 = \alpha_1 - \beta_1 y_1 - \gamma y_2$$
$$p_2 = \alpha_2 - \gamma y_1 - \beta_2 y_2.$$

Note that the "cross-price effects are symmetric" as is required for well-behaved consumer demand functions.

The corresponding direct demand functions are

$$y_1 = a_1 - b_1 p_1 + c p_2$$
$$y_2 = a_2 + c p_1 - b_2 p_2,$$

where the parameters a_1, a_2, etc., are functions of the parameters α_1, α_2, etc.

When $\alpha_1 = \alpha_2$ and $\beta_1 = \beta_2 = \gamma$, the goods are perfect substitutes. When $\gamma = 0$, the markets are independent. In general, $\gamma^2/\beta_1\beta_2$ can be used as an index of product differentiation. When it is 0, the markets are independent, and when it is 1, the goods are perfect substitutes.

Suppose, for simplicity, that marginal costs are zero. Then if firm 1 is a Cournot competitor, it maximizes

$$(\alpha_1 - \beta_1 y_1 - \gamma y_2) y_1,$$

and if it is a Bertrand competitor, it maximizes

$$(a_1 - b_1 p_1 + c p_2) p_1.$$

Note that the expressions are very similar in structure: we simply interchange α_1 with a_1, β_1 with b_1, and γ with $-c$. Hence, Cournot equilibrium with substitute products (where $\gamma > 0$) has essentially the same mathematical structure as Bertrand equilibrium with complements (where $c < 0$).

This "duality" allows us to prove two theorems for the price of one: when we calculate a result involving Cournot competition, we can simply substitute the Greek for the Roman letters and have a result about Bertrand competition.

For example, we have seen earlier that the slopes of the reaction curves are important in determining comparative statics results in the Cournot model. In the case of heterogeneous goods discussed here, the reaction curve for firm 1 is the solution to the following maximization problem:

$$\max_{y_1} \; [\alpha_1 - \beta_1 y_1 - \gamma y_2] y_1.$$

This is easily seen to be

$$y_1 = \frac{\alpha_1 - \gamma y_2}{2\beta_1}.$$

Translating the Greek to Roman, the reaction curve in the Bertrand model is

$$p_1 = \frac{a_1 + c p_2}{2 b_1}.$$

Note that the reaction curve in the Cournot model has an opposite slope from the reaction curve in the Bertrand model. We have seen that reaction curves are typically downward sloping in the Cournot model, which implies that reaction curves will typically be *upward* sloping in the Bertrand model. This is reasonably intuitive. If firm 2 increases its output, then firm 1 will typically want to reduce output in order to force the price up. However, if firm 2 increases its price, firm 1 will typically find it profitable to increase its price in order to match the price increase.

Another way to make this point is to use the concepts of strategic complements and strategic substitutes introduced earlier. The outputs of the firms are strategic substitutes since increasing y_2 makes it less profitable for firm 1 to increase its output. However, an increase in p_2 makes it more profitable for firm 1 to increase its price. Since the signs of the mixed partials are different, the reaction curves will have slopes of different signs.

16.6 Quantity leadership

Another model of duopoly of some interest is that of **quantity leadership**, also known as the **Stackelberg model**. This is essentially a two-stage model in which one firm gets to move first. The other firm can then observe the first firm's output choice and choose its own optimal level of output. In the terminology of the last chapter, the quantity leadership model is a sequential game.

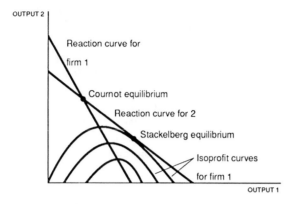

Comparison of Cournot and Stackelberg equilibria. The Nash equilibrium occurs where the two reaction curves intersect. The Stackelberg equilibrium occurs where one reaction curve is tangent to the isoprofit lines of the other firm.

Figure 16.2

As usual, we solve this game "in reverse." Suppose that firm 1 is the leader and firm 2 is the follower. Then firm 2's problem is straightforward: given firm 1's output, firm 2 wants to maximize its profits $p(y_1 + y_2)y_2 - c_2(y_2)$. The first-order condition for this problem is simply

$$p(Y) + p'(Y)y_2 = c_2'(y_2). \qquad (16.6)$$

This is just like the Cournot condition described earlier, and we can use this equation to derive the reaction function of firm 2, $f_2(y_1)$ just as before.

Moving back to the first stage of the game, firm 1 now wants to choose its level of output, looking ahead and recognizing how firm 2 will respond. Thus, firm 1 wants to maximize

$$p(y_1 + f_2(y_1))y_1 - c_1(y_1).$$

This leads to a first-order condition of the form

$$p(Y) + p'(Y)[1 + f_2'(y_1)]y_1 = c_1'(y_1). \qquad (16.7)$$

Equations (16.6) and (16.7) suffice to determine the levels of output of the two firms.

The Stackelberg equilibrium is determined graphically in Figure 16.2. Here the isoprofit lines for firm 1 indicate the combinations of output levels that yield constant profits. Lower isoprofit lines are associated with higher levels of profit. Firm 1 wants to operate at the point on firm 2's reaction curve where firm 1 has the largest possible profits, as depicted.

How does the Stackelberg equilibrium compare to the Cournot equilibrium? One result is immediate from revealed preference: since the Stackelberg leader picks the *optimal* point on his competitor's reaction curve, and the Cournot equilibrium is some "arbitrary" point on his competitor's reaction curve, the profits to the leader in the Stackelberg equilibrium will typically be higher than they would be in the Cournot equilibrium of the same game.

What about the profits of being a leader versus being a follower? Which would a firm prefer to be? There is a nice, general result to be had, but it requires some argument. We will analyze the general case of heterogeneous goods, y_1 and y_2, under the following assumptions. (Of course, these assumptions include the special case of homogeneous goods, where y_1 and y_2 are perfect substitutes.)

A1: Substitute products. $\pi_1(y_1, y_2)$ *is a strictly decreasing function of* y_2 *and* $\pi_2(y_1, y_2)$ *is a strictly decreasing function of* y_1.

A2: Downward sloping reaction curves.   *The reaction curves* $f_i(y_j)$ *are strictly decreasing functions.*

Leadership preferred.   *Under assumptions A1 and A2, a firm always weakly prefers to be a leader rather than a follower.*

Proof. Let $(y_1^*, y_2^*) = (y_1^*, f_2(y_1^*))$ be the Stackelberg equilibrium when firm 1 leads. First, we need to show

$$f_1(y_2^*) \leq y_1^*. \tag{16.8}$$

Suppose not, so that

$$f_1(y_2^*) > y_1^*. \tag{16.9}$$

Applying the function $f_2(\cdot)$ to both sides of this inequality, we find

$$f_2(f_1(y_2^*)) <_1 f_2(y_1^*) =_2 y_2^*. \tag{16.10}$$

Inequality (1) follows from $A2$ and equality (2) follows from the definition of Stackelberg equilibrium.

We now have the following chain of inequalities:

$$\pi_1(y_1^*, y_2^*) \leq_1 \pi_1(f_1(y_2^*), y_2^*) <_2 \pi_1(f_1(y_2^*), f_2(f_1(y_2^*))). \tag{16.11}$$

Inequality (1) follows from the definition of the reaction function and inequality (2) follows from equation (16.10) and assumption $A1$. According to (16.11), the point $(f_1(y_2^*), f_2(f_1(y_2^*)))$ yields higher profits than $(y_1^*, f_2(y_1^*))$, contradicting the claim that $(y_1^*, f_2(y_1^*))$ is the Stackelberg equilibrium. This contradiction establishes (16.8).

The result we are after now follows quickly from the inequalities

$$\max_{y_2} \pi_2(f_1(y_2), y_2) \geq_1 \pi_2(f_1(y_2^*), y_2^*) \geq_2 \pi_2(y_1^*, y_2^*).$$

Inequality (1) follows from maximization, and inequality (2) follows (16.8) and $A1$. The left and right terms in these inequalities show that firm 2's profits are no smaller if it is the leader than if firm 1 is the leader. ∎

Since downward sloping reaction functions and substitutes are usually considered to be the "normal" case, this result indicates that we can typically expect that each Stackelberg firm would prefer to be the leader. Which firm actually is the leader would presumably depend on historical factors, e.g., which firm entered the market first, etc.

16.7 Price leadership

Price leadership occurs when one firm sets the price which the other firm then takes as given. The price leadership model is solved just like the Stackelberg model: first we derive the behavior of the follower, and then derive the behavior of the leader.

In a model with heterogeneous goods, let $x_i(p_1, p_2)$ be the demand for the output of firm i. The follower chooses p_2 taking p_1 as given. That is, the follower maximizes

$$\max_{p_2} \ p_2 x_2(p_1, p_2) - c_2(x_2(p_1, p_2)). \tag{16.12}$$

We let $p_2 = g_2(p_1)$ be the reaction function that gives the optimal choice of p_2 as a function of p_1.

The leader then solves

$$\max_{p_1} \ p_1 x_1(p_1, g_2(p_1)) - c_1(x_1(p_1, g_2(p_1)))$$

to determine his optimal value of p_1.

An interesting special case occurs when the firms are selling identical products. In this case, if firm 2 sells a positive amount of output, it must sell it at $p_2 = p_1$. For each price p_1, the follower will choose to produce the amount of output $S_2(p_1)$ that maximizes its profits, taking p_1 as given. Hence, the reaction function in this case is simply the competitive supply curve.

If firm 1 charges price p_1, firm 1 will sell $r(p_1) = x_1(p_1) - S_2(p_1)$ units of output. The function $r(p_1)$ is known as the **residual demand curve** facing firm 1. Firm 1 wants to choose p_1 so as to maximize

$$\max_{p_1} \ p_1 r(p_1) - c_1(r(p_1)).$$

This is just the problem of a monopolist facing the residual demand curve $r(p_1)$.

The solution is depicted graphically in Figure 16.3. We subtract the supply curve of firm 2 from the market demand curve to get the residual demand curve. Then we use the standard $MR = MC$ condition to solve for the leader's output.

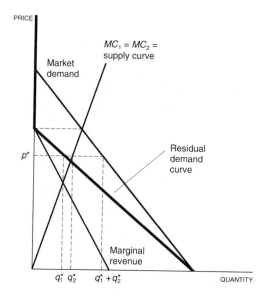

Price leadership. Firm 1 subtracts firm 2's supply curve from the market demand curve to get the residual demand curve. It then chooses the most profitable production level on this curve.

Figure 16.3

Returning to the heterogeneous product case, we can ask whether a firm prefers to be a follower or a leader in this model. First we note that the result proved above can be immediately extended to the price leadership model just by replacing y_i's with p_i's. However, there are two difficulties with this extension. First, it is not necessarily the case that profits will be a decreasing function of the other firm's price. The derivative of profit of firm 1 with respect to price 2 is

$$\frac{\partial \pi_1(p_1, p_2)}{\partial p_2} = [p_1 - c_1'(x_1(p_1, p_2)]\frac{\partial x_1(p_1, p_2)}{\partial p_2}.$$

The sign of this derivative depends on whether price is greater or equal to marginal cost. It turns out that this difficulty can be overcome; leadership is still preferred in a price-leader model, as long as the reaction functions are downward sloping.

However, the assumption of downward sloping price-reaction functions is not at all reasonable. For simplicity, suppose that marginal cost is zero. Then the reaction function for firm 2 must satisfy the first-order condition

$$p_2 \frac{\partial x_2(p_1, g_2(p_1))}{\partial p_2} + x_2(p_1, g_2(p_1)) \equiv 0.$$

By the usual comparative statics calculation,

$$\text{sign } g_2'(p_1) = \text{sign } \left[p_2 \frac{\partial^2 x_2}{\partial p_1 \partial p_2} + \frac{\partial x_2}{\partial p_1} \right].$$

The first term may be positive or negative, but if the two goods are substitutes the sign of the second term will be positive. Hence, as noted earlier, we might well expect *upward* sloping reaction curves in the price-leadership model.

An argument similar to that given above can be used to establish the following proposition.

Consensus. *If both firms have upward sloping reaction functions, then if one prefers to be a leader, the other must prefer to be a follower.*

Proof. See Dowrick (1986). ∎

From this the following observation is immediate.

Following preferred. *If both firms have identical cost and demand functions and reaction curves are upward sloping, then each must prefer to be the follower to being the leader.*

Proof. If one prefers to lead, then by symmetry the other prefers to lead as well. But this contradicts the proposition immediately above. ∎

Here is another argument for this result in the special case where the goods produced by the two firms are identical. The argument uses Figure 16.3. In this figure, firm 1 picks the price p^* and the output level q_1^*. Firm 2 has the *option* of choosing to supply the same output that firm 1 supplies, q_1^*, at the price p^*, but rejects it in favor of producing a different level of output—the output that lies on firm 2's supply curve. Hence firm 2 makes higher profit than firm 1 in equilibrium.

Intuitively, the reason that a firm prefers being a follower in a price setting game is that the leader has to reduce its output to support the price, whereas the follower can take the price as fixed by the leader and produce as much as it wants; i.e., the follower can free-ride on the output restriction of the leader.

16.8 Classification and choice of models

We have discussed four models of duopoly: Cournot, Bertrand, quantity leadership, and price leadership. From a game theoretic viewpoint, these models are distinguished by the definition of the strategy space (prices or quantities) and by the information sets: whether one player knows the other's choice when he makes his move.

Which is the right model? In general, this question has no answer; it can only be addressed in the context of a particular economic situation or industry that one wants to examine. However, we can offer some useful guidelines.

It is important to remember that these models are all "one-shot games." But in applications we are generally trying to model real-time interactions; that is, an industry structure that persists for many periods. Thus it is natural to demand that the strategic variables used to model the industry be variables that cannot immediately be adjusted—once chosen, they will persist for some time period so that the one-shot analysis has some hope of representing economic phenomena that take place in real time.

Consider, for example, the Bertrand equilibrium. Formally speaking this is a one-shot game: the duopolists simultaneously set prices without observing the other's choice. But if it is costless to adjust your price as soon as you see your rival's price (and before the customers see either price!), then the Bertrand model is not very appealing: as soon as the rival firm observes the other firm's price it can respond to it in some way or other, likely leading to a non-Bertrand outcome.

The Cournot model seems appropriate when quantities can only be adjusted slowly. This is especially appealing when "quantity" is interpreted as "capacity." The idea is that each firm chooses, in secret, a production capacity, realizing that once the capacity is chosen they will compete on price—i.e., play a Bertrand game. Kreps & Scheinkman (1983) analyze this two-stage game and show that the outcome is typically a Cournot equilibrium. We will loosely outline a simplified version of their model here.

Assume that each firm simultaneously produces some output level y_i in the first period. In the second period each firm chooses a price at which to sell its output. We are interested in the equilibrium of this two-stage game.

As usual, start with the second period. At this time firm i has a zero marginal cost of selling any output less than y_i and an infinite marginal cost of selling any output more than y_i. In equilibrium, each firm must charge the same price; otherwise the high-price firm would benefit by charging a price slightly lower than that of the low-price firm. Additionally, the price charged can be no greater than $p(y_1 + y_2)$. For if it were, one firm could cut its price slightly and capture the entire market. Finally, the price charged can be no less than $p(y_1 + y_2)$ since raising the price benefits both firms when each is selling at capacity. (The outline of this argument is quite intuitive, but it is surprisingly difficult to establish rigorously.)

The crucial observation is that when each firm is selling at capacity, then neither wants to cut its price. It is true that if it *did* cut its price it would steal all of its rival's customers, but since it is already selling all that it has to sell these extra customers are useless to it.[4]

Once it is known that the equilibrium price in the second period is simply the inverse demand at capacity, it is simple to calculate the first period equilibrium: it is just the standard Cournot equilibrium. Hence, Cournot competition in capacities followed by Bertrand competition in prices lead to the standard Cournot outcome.

16.9 Conjectural variations

The games of price leadership and quantity leadership described above can be generalized in an interesting way. Recall the first-order condition describing the optimal quantity choice of a Stackelberg leader:

$$p(Y) + p'(Y)[1 + f'_2(y_1)]y_1 = c'_1(y_1). \qquad (16.13)$$

The term $f'_2(y_1)$ indicates firm 1's belief about how firm 2's optimal behavior changes as y_1 changes.

In the Stackelberg model, this belief is equal to the slope of the actual reaction function for firm 2. However, we might think of this term as being an arbitrary "conjecture" about how firm 2 responds to firm 1's choice of output. Call this the **conjectural variation** of firm 1 about firm 2, and denote it by ν_{12}. The appropriate first-order condition is now:

$$p(Y) + p'(Y)[1 + \nu_{12}]y_1 = c'_1(y_1). \qquad (16.14)$$

The nice thing about this parameterization is that different choices of the parameters lead directly to the relevant first-order conditions for the various models discussed earlier.

1) $\nu_{12} = 0$ — this is the Cournot model, in which each firm believes that the other firm's choice is independent from its own;

2) $\nu_{12} = -1$ — this is the competitive model, since the first-order condition reduces to price equals marginal cost.

---

[4] However, this does bring up a delicate point: if one firm gets more customers than it can sell to, we must specify a rationing rule to indicate what happens to the extra customers. Davidson & Deneckere (1986) show that specification of the rationing rule can affect the nature of the equilibrium.

3) ν_{12} = slope of firm 2's reaction curve — this is of course the Stackelberg model;

4) $\nu_{12} = y_2/y_1$ — in this case the first-order condition reduces to the condition for maximizing industry profits—the collusive equilibrium.

This table shows that each of the major models discussed earlier is just a special case of the conjectural variations model. In this sense, the idea of a conjectural variation serves as a useful classification scheme for oligopoly models.

However, it is not really satisfactory as a model of behavior. The problem is that it involves a kind of pseudo-dynamics pasted on top of inherently static models. Each of the models examined earlier are specifically one-shot models—in the Cournot model firms choose outputs independently, in the Stackelberg model one firm chooses an output expecting the other to react optimally, and so on. The conjectural variations model indicates that one firm chooses an output because it expects the other firm to respond in some particular way: but how can the other firm respond in a one-shot game? If one wants to model a dynamic situation, where each firm is able to respond to the other firm's output choice, then one should look at the repeated game to begin with.

16.10 Collusion

All of the models described up until now are examples of **non-cooperative** games. Each firm is out to maximize its own profits, and each firm makes its decisions independently of the other firms. What happens if we relax this assumption and consider possibilities of coordinated actions? An industry structure where the firms collude to some degree in setting their prices and outputs is called a **cartel**.

A natural model is to consider what happens if the two firms choose their outputs in order to maximize joint profits. In this case the firms simultaneously choose y_1 and y_2 so as to maximize industry profits:

$$\max_{y_1, y_2} p(y_1 + y_2)[y_1 + y_2] - c_1(y_1) - c_2(y_2).$$

The first-order conditions are

$$p(y_1^* + y_2^*) + p'(y_1^* + y_2^*)[y_1^* + y_2^*] = c_1'(y_1^*)$$
$$p(y_1^* + y_2^*) + p'(y_1^* + y_2^*)[y_1^* + y_2^*] = c_2'(y_2^*).$$

$$(16.15)$$

Since the left-hand sides of these two equations are the same, the right-hand sides must be the same—the firms must equate their marginal costs of production to each other.

The problem with the cartel solution is that it is not "stable." There is always a temptation to cheat: to produce more than the agreed-upon output. To see this, consider what happens if firm 1 contemplates increasing its output by some small amount dy_1, assuming that firm 2 will stick with the cartel agreement level of y_2^*. The change in firm 1's profits as y_1 changes, evaluated at the cartel solution, is

$$\frac{\partial \pi_1(y_1^*, y_2^*)}{\partial y_1} = p(y_1^* + y_2^*) + p'(y_1^* + y_2^*)y_1^* - c_1'(y_1^*) = -p'(y_1^* + y_2^*)y_2^* > 0.$$

The equals sign in this expression comes from the first-order conditions in equations (16.15), and the inequality comes from the fact that demand curves slope downward.

If one firm believes that the other firm will stick to the agreed-upon cartel output, it would benefit it to increase its own output in order to sell more at the high price. But if it doesn't believe that the other firm will stick with the cartel agreement, then it will not in general be optimal for it to maintain the cartel agreement either! It might as well dump its output on the market and take its profits while it can.

The strategic situation is similar to the Prisoner's Dilemma: if you think that other firm will produce its quota, it pays you to defect—to produce more than your quota. And if you think that the other firm will not produce at its quota, then it will in general be profitable for you to produce more than your quota.

In order to make the cartel outcome viable, some way must be found to stabilize the market. This usually takes the form of finding an effective punishment for firms that cheat on the cartel agreement. For example, one firm might announce that if it discovered that the other firm changed its output from the cartel amount it would in turn increase its own output. It is interesting to ask how much would it have to increase its output in response to a deviation by the other firm.

We saw earlier that the conjectural variation that supports the cartel solution is $\nu_{12} = y_1/y_2$. What does this mean? Suppose that firm 1 announces that if firm 2 increases its output by dy_2 then firm 1 will respond by increasing *its* output by $dy_1 = (y_1/y_2)dy_2$. If firm 2 believes this threat, then the change in profits that it expects from an output increase of dy_2 is

$$d\pi_2 = p(y_1^* + y_2^*)dy_2 + p'(y_1^* + y_2^*)\left[dy_2 + \frac{y_1^*}{y_2^*}dy_2\right]y_2^* - c_2'(y_2^*)dy_2$$
$$= [p(y_1^* + y_2^*) + p'(y_1^* + y_2^*)[y_1^* + y_2^*] - c_2'(y_2^*)]dy_2$$
$$= 0.$$

Hence, if firm 2 believes that firm 1 will respond in this way, then firm 2 will not expect to profit from violating its quota.

The nature of firm 1's punishment can be most easily seen by thinking about the case of asymmetric market shares. Suppose that firm 1 produces twice as much output as firm 2 in the cartel equilibrium. Then it has to threaten to punish any deviations from the cartel output by producing twice as much as its rival. On the other hand, firm 2 has to only threaten to produce half as much as any deviations that its rival might consider.

Although suggestive, this sort of analysis suffers from the standard problem with conjectural variations: it is compressing a dynamic interaction into a static model. However, we shall see that a rigorous dynamic analysis involves much the same considerations; the essential problem in supporting a cartel outcome is how to construct the appropriate punishment for deviations.

16.11 Repeated oligopoly games

All of the games up until now have been "one-shot" games. But actual market interactions take place in real time, and a consideration of the repeated nature of the interaction is certainly appropriate. The simplest way to proceed is to imagine the quantity-setting Cournot game as being a repeated game.

The treatment parallels the analysis of the repeated Prisoner's Dilemma given in Chapter 15. The cooperative outcome, in this case, is the cartel solution. The punishment can be chosen to be the Cournot output choice. The strategies that support the cartel solution are then of the following form: choose the cartel output unless your opponent cheats; if he cheats, choose the Cournot output. Just as in the case of the Prisoner's Dilemma, this will be a Nash equilibrium set of strategies, as long as the discount rate is not too high.

Unfortunately, the game has many, many other equilibrium strategies: just as in the case of the repeated Prisoner's Dilemma, almost anything can be a Nash equilibrium. Unlike the repeated Prisoner's Dilemma case, this is also true for the finitely repeated quantity-setting game.

To see this, let us examine a two-period game with identical firms having zero marginal costs. Consider the following strategy for firm 1: produce some output y_1 in the first period. If your opponent produces y_2 first period, produce the Cournot level of output, y_1^c, next period. If your opponent produces an amount other than y_2, then produce an output large enough to drive the market price to zero.

What is firm 2's optimal response to this threat? If it produces y_2 first period and y_2^c second period, it gets a payoff of $\pi_2(y_1, y_2) + \delta\pi_2(y_1^c, y_2^c)$. If it produces an output different from y_2 in the first period—say, an output x—it gets a payoff of $\pi_2(y_1, x)$. Thus, it will be profitable to cooperate with firm 1 when

$$\pi_2(y_1, y_2) + \delta\pi_2(y_1^c, y_2^c) > \max_x \pi_2(y_1, x).$$

This condition will typically hold for a whole range of outputs (y_1, y_2).

The problem is that the threat to actually carry out the punishment strategy is not credible: once the first period is over, it will in general not be in firm 1's interest to flood the market. Said another way, flooding the market is not an equilibrium strategy in the subgame consisting only of the second period. Using the terminology of Chapter 15, this strategy is not **subgame perfect**.

It is not difficult to show that the unique subgame perfect equilibrium in the finitely repeated quantity-setting game is the repeated one-shot Cournot equilibrium, at least as long as the one-shot Cournot equilibrium is unique. The argument is the usual backwards induction: since the Cournot equilibrium is the unique outcome in the last period, the play in the first period cannot credibly influence the last period outcome, and so the "myopic" Cournot equilibrium is the only choice.

One is naturally led to ask whether the cartel output is sustainable as a subgame perfect equilibrium in the infinite repeated game. Friedman (1971) showed that the answer is yes. The strategies that work are similar to the punishment strategies discussed in the last chapter. Let π_i^c be the profits to firm i from the one-period Cournot equilibrium and let π_i^* be the profits from the one-period cartel outcome. Consider the following strategy for firm 1: produce the cartel level of output unless firm 2 produces something other than the cartel output, in which case revert to producing the Cournot output forever.

If firm 2 believes that firm 1 will produce its Cournot level of output in a given period, then its optimal response is to produce the Cournot level of output as well. (This is the definition of the Cournot equilibrium!) Hence, repeating the Cournot output indefinitely is indeed an equilibrium of the repeated game.

To see whether firm 2 finds it profitable to produce the cartel level of output, we must compare the present value of its profits from deviating with its profits from cooperating. Letting π_2^d be the profits from deviating, this condition becomes

$$\pi_2^d + \delta\frac{\pi_2^c}{1-\delta} < \frac{\pi_2^*}{1-\delta}.$$

That is, firm 2 gets the profits from deviating this period plus the present value of the profits from the Cournot equilibrium every period in the future. Rearranging, we have the condition

$$\delta > \frac{\pi_2^d - \pi_2^*}{\pi_2^d - \pi_2^c}. \tag{16.16}$$

As long as δ is sufficiently large—i.e., as long as the discount rate is sufficiently small—this condition will be satisfied. As in the case of the repeated Prisoner's Dilemma, there are a multiplicity of other equilibria in this model.

The basic idea of (subgame perfect) punishment strategies can be extended in a variety of ways by allowing for different kinds of punishment rather than simple Cournot reversion. For example, Abreu (1986) shows that one period of punishment followed by a return to the cartel solution will typically be sufficient to support the cartel output. This is reminiscent of the results about optimal punishment in the conjectural variations model—as long as one firm can punish the other firm quickly enough, it can ensure that the other firm will not profit from its deviation. See Shapiro (1989) for a good survey of results concerning repeated oligopoly games.

16.12 Sequential games

The repeated games described in the last section are simple repetitions of one-shot market games. The choices that a firm makes in one period do not affect its profits in another, except in the indirect way of influencing its rival's behavior. However, in reality, decisions made at one point in time influence output produced at later dates. Investment decisions of this sort play an important strategic role in some games.

In examining models of this sort of behavior the distinction between Nash equilibria and subgame-perfect equilibria is very important. To illustrate this distinction in the simplest possible context, consider a simple model of entry.

Imagine an industry with two firms poised to enter when conditions are ripe. Assume that entry is costless and that there is some sort of exogenous technological progress that reduces the costs of production over time. Let $\pi_1(t)$ be the present value of the profit earned at time t if there is only one firm in the market at that time, and let $\pi_2(t)$ be the profit earned by *each* of the firms if there are two firms in the market at time t. This reduced form profit function glosses over the exact form of competition within the industry; all we need is that $\pi_1(t) > \pi_2(t)$ for all t, which simply means that a monopoly is more profitable than a duopoly.

We illustrate these profit flows in Figure 16.4. We suppose that initially profits rise faster than the rate of interest, leading the discounted profits to increase over time. But eventually technological progress in this industry slows down causing profits to grow less rapidly than the rate of interest, so that the present value of profits falls.

The question of interest to us is the pattern of entry. The obvious candidate is the pair (t_1, t_2); i.e., one of the two firms enters when a monopoly becomes profitable, and the other firm enters when the duopoly becomes profitable. This is the usual sort of positive profit entry condition, and indeed, it is easy to verify that it is a Nash equilibrium. However, somewhat surprisingly, it is not subgame perfect.

For consider what happens if firm 2 (the second entrant) decides to enter slightly before time t_1. It is true that it will lose money for a short time, but now firm 1's threat to enter at time t_1 is no longer credible. Given that

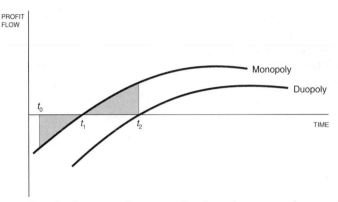

Figure
16.4
Profit flows and entry. In the subgame perfect equilibrium, the first firm enters at t_0, the point where its discounted profits are zero. Entry at t_1 is a Nash equilibrium, but not a subgame perfect equilibrium.

firm 2 is in the market, it is no longer profitable for firm 1 to enter at t_1. Hence, firm 2 will receive positive monopoly profits over the range $[t_1, t_2]$, as well as receiving its duopoly profits after t_2.

Of course if firm 2 contemplates entering slightly before t_1, firm 1 can contemplate this as well. The only subgame perfect equilibria in this model are for one of the firms to enter at time t_0, where the profits from the initial monopoly phase are driven to zero; i.e., the (negative) shaded area above $\pi_1(t)$ between t_0 and t_1 equals the positive area beneath $\pi_1(t)$ between t_1 and t_2. The threat of entry has effectively dissipated the monopoly profits!

In retrospect, this makes a lot of sense. The firms are identically situated and it would be somewhat surprising if they ended up with different profits. In the subgame perfect equilibrium, the profits from early entry are competed away, and all that are left are the profits from the duopoly stage of the game.

16.13 Limit pricing

It is often thought that the threat of entry serves as a disciplining force in oligopolies. Even if there are only a small number of firms currently in an industry, there may be many potential entrants, and hence the "effective" amount of competition could be quite high. Even a monopolist may face a threat of entry that induces it to price competitively. Pricing to prevent entry in this way is known as **limit pricing**.

Although this view has great intuitive appeal, there are some serious problems with it. Let us examine some of these problems by laying out a formal model. Let there be two firms, an **incumbent**, who is currently producing in a market, and a potential **entrant**, who is contemplating entry. The market demand function and the cost functions of both firms are common knowledge. There are two periods: in the first period the monopolist sets a price and quantity, which can be observed by the potential entrant, at which point it decides whether or not to enter the market. If entry occurs, the firms play some duopoly game second period. If entry does not occur, the incumbent charges the monopoly price second period.

What is the nature of limit pricing in this model? Essentially nothing; if entry occurs, the duopoly equilibrium is determined. The only concern of the potential entrant is predicting the profits it can get in that duopoly equilibrium. Since it knows the costs and demand function perfectly, the first-period price conveys no information. Hence the incumbent may as well get its monopoly profits while it can and charge the monopoly price first period.

One is tempted to think that the incumbent might want to charge a low price first period in order to signal that it is "willing to fight" if entry occurs. But this is an empty threat; if the other firm does enter, the incumbent should rationally do the profit-maximizing thing at that point. Since the potential entrant knows all of the relevant information, it can predict *ex ante* what the profit-maximizing action of the incumbent will be, and plan accordingly.

Limit pricing has no role in this framework, since the first-period price conveys no information about the second-period game. However, if we admit some uncertainty into our model, we will find that limit pricing emerges quite readily as an equilibrium strategy.

Consider the following simple model. One unit of some good is demanded if the market price is less than or equal to 3. There is one incumbent who has constant marginal costs of 0 or 2, and there is one potential entrant who has constant marginal costs of 1. In order to enter this market, the entrant must pay an entry fee of $1/4$. If the entrant enters the market, we suppose that the firms engage in Bertrand competition.

Since the firms have different costs, this means that one of the firms is driven out of the market. If the incumbent is a low-cost firm, then it will price (slightly below) the marginal cost of the entrant, 1, and thereby drive the entrant out of the market. In this case, the incumbent makes a profit of 1 and the entrant loses the entry fee, $-1/4$. If the incumbent is a high-cost firm, then the entrant prices the product slightly below 2, making a profit of $2 - 1 - 1/4 = 3/4$, and the incumbent is driven out of the market.

If the incumbent is a high-cost firm and entry does not occur, it will set the monopoly price of 3 and make a profit of 1. The question is, what price should it set in the first period? Essentially, the low-cost incumbent would like to set a price that is not viable for the high-cost incumbent, since this would signal its type to the potential entrant. Suppose that the low-cost incumbent sets a price slightly below 1 in the first period and the monopoly price of 3 the second period. This is still profitable for it since it has zero costs. But this policy is not profitable for the high cost firm—in the first period it would lose a bit more than 1 and in the second period it would only make 1. Overall this policy induces a loss. Since only the low-cost firm can afford to set a price of 1, it is a credible signal. This example shows that limit pricing does play a role in a model with imperfect information: it can serve as a signal to potential entrants about the cost structure of the incumbent, thereby precluding entry, at least in some cases.

Notes

See Shapiro (1989) for a good survey of oligopoly theory. I follow his treatment of repeated games closely. The material on comparative statics in oligopoly was taken from Dixit (1986). The model of sales is from Varian (1980). The discussion of capacity choice in the Cournot model is based on Kreps & Scheinkman (1983). The analysis of profitability in leader-follower games is due to Dowrick (1986). The duality between Cournot and Bertrand equilibria was first noted Sonnenschein (1968) and extended by Singh & Vives (1984). The simple model of limit pricing described here was inspired by Milgrom & Roberts (1982).

Exercises

16.1. Suppose that we have two firms with constant marginal costs of c_1 and two firms with constant marginal costs of c_2, and that $c_2 > c_1$. What is the Bertrand equilibrium in this model? What is the competitive equilibrium in this model?

16.2. Consider the model of sales described on page 294. As U/I increases, what happens to $F(p)$? Interpret this result.

16.3. Given the linear inverse demand functions in the section on page 294 derive formulas for the parameters of the direct demand functions.

16.4. Using the linear demand functions in the previous problem, show that quantities are always lower and prices higher in Cournot competition than in Bertrand competition.

16.5. Show that if both firms have upward sloping reaction functions so that $f_i'(y_j) > 0$, and (y_1^*, y_2^*) is the Stackelberg equilibrium, then $f_2(f_1(y_2^*)) > f_2(y_1^*) = y_2^*$.

16.6. The conjectural variation associated with the competitive model is $\nu = -1$. This means that when one firm increases its output by one unit, the other firm reduces its output by one unit. Intuitively, this hardly seems like competitive behavior. What's wrong?

16.7. Show that if $c_1'(x) < c_2'(x)$ for all $x > 0$, then the cartel solution involves $y_1 > y_2$.

16.8. Suppose that two identical firms are operating at the cartel solution and that each firm believes that if it adjusts its output the other firm will adjust *its* output so as to keep its market share equal to $1/2$. What does this imply about the conjectural variation? What kind of industry structure does this imply?

16.9. Why are there many equilibria in the finitely repeated Cournot game and only one in the finitely repeated Prisoner's Dilemma?

16.10. Consider an industry with 2 firms, each having marginal costs equal to zero. The (inverse) demand curve facing this industry is

$$P(Y) = 100 - Y,$$

where $Y = y_1 + y_2$ is total output.

(a) What is the competitive equilibrium level of industry output?

(b) If each firm behaves as a Cournot competitor, what is firm 1's optimal choice given firm 2's output?

(c) Calculate the Cournot equilibrium amount of output for each firm.

(d) Calculate the cartel amount of output for the industry.

(e) If firm 1 behaves as a follower and firm 2 behaves as a leader, calculate the Stackelberg equilibrium output of each firm.

16.11. Consider a Cournot industry in which the firms' outputs are denoted by $y_1, \ldots, y_n$, aggregate output is denoted by $Y = \sum_{i=1}^{n} y_i$, the industry demand curve is denoted by $P(Y)$, and the cost function of each firm is given by $c_i(y_i) = cy_i$. For simplicity, assume that $P''(Y) < 0$. Suppose that each firm is required to pay a specific tax of t_i.

(a) Write down the first-order conditions for firm i.

(b) Show that the industry output and price only depend on the sum of the tax rates, $\sum_{i=1}^{n} t_i$.

(c) Consider a change in each firm's tax rate that does not change the tax burden on the industry. Letting Δt_i denote the change in firm i's tax rate, we require that $\sum_{i=1}^{n} \Delta t_i = 0$. Assuming that no firm leaves the industry, calculate the change in firm i's equilibrium output, Δy_i. Hint: no derivatives are necessary; this question can be answered by examination of parts (a) and (b).

16.12. Consider an industry with the following structure. There are 50 firms that behave in a competitive manner and have identical cost functions given by $c(y) = y^2/2$. There is one monopolist that has 0 marginal costs. The demand curve for the product is given by

$$D(p) = 1000 - 50p.$$

(a) What is the supply curve of one of the competitive firms?

(b) What is the total supply from the competitive sector?

(c) If the monopolist sets a price p, how much output will it sell?

(d) What is the monopolist's profit-maximizing output?

(e) What is the monopolist's profit-maximizing price?

(f) How much will the competitive sector provide at this price?

(g) What will be the total amount of output sold in this industry?

CHAPTER 17

EXCHANGE

In Chapter 13 we discussed the economic theory of a single market. We saw that when there were many economic agents each might reasonably be assumed to take market prices as outside of their control. Given these exogenous prices, each agent could then determine his or her demands and supplies for the good in question. The price adjusted to clear the market, and at such an equilibrium price, no agent would desire to change his or her actions.

The single-market story described above is a **partial equilibrium** model in that all prices other than the price of the good being studied are assumed to remain fixed. In the **general equilibrium** model *all* prices are variable, and equilibrium requires that *all* markets clear. Thus, general equilibrium theory takes account of all of the interactions between markets, as well as the functioning of the individual markets.

In the interests of exposition, we will examine first the special case of the general equilibrium model where all of the economic agents are consumers. This situation, known as the case of **pure exchange**, contains many of the phenomena present in the more extensive case involving firms and production.

In a pure exchange economy we have several consumers, each described by their preferences and the goods that they possess. The agents trade the goods among themselves according to certain rules and attempt to make themselves better off.

What will be the outcome of such a process? What are desirable outcomes of such a process? What allocative mechanisms are appropriate for achieving desirable outcomes? These questions involve a mixture of both positive and normative issues. It is precisely the interplay between the two types of questions that provides much of the interest in the theory of resource allocation.

17.1 Agents and goods

The concept of good considered here is very broad. Goods can be distinguished by time, location, and state of world. Services, such as labor services, are taken to be just another kind of good. There is assumed to be a market for each good, in which the price of that good is determined.

In the pure exchange model the only kind of economic agent is the consumer. Each consumer i is described completely by his preference, $\succeq_i$ (or his utility function, u_i), and his **initial endowment** of the k commodities, $\boldsymbol{\omega}_i$. Each consumer is assumed to behave competitively—that is, to take prices as given, independent of his or her actions. We assume that each consumer attempts to choose the most preferred bundle that he or she can afford.

The basic concern of the theory of general equilibrium is how goods are allocated among the economic agents. The amount of good j that agent i holds will be denoted by x_i^j. Agent i's **consumption bundle** will be denoted by $\mathbf{x}_i = (x_i^1, \ldots, x_i^k)$; it is a k-vector describing how much of each good agent i consumes. An **allocation** $\mathbf{x} = (\mathbf{x}_1, \cdots, \mathbf{x}_n)$ is a collection of n consumption bundles describing what each of the n agents holds. A **feasible allocation** is one that is physically possible; in the pure exchange case, this is simply an allocation that uses up all the goods, i.e., one in which $\sum_{i=1}^n \mathbf{x}_i = \sum_{i=1}^n \boldsymbol{\omega}_i$. (In some cases it is convenient to consider an allocation feasible if $\sum_{i=1}^n \mathbf{x}_i \leq \sum_{i=1}^n \boldsymbol{\omega}_i$.)

When there are two goods and two agents, we can use a convenient way of representing allocations, preferences, and endowments in a two-dimensional form, known as the **Edgeworth box**. We've depicted an example of an Edgeworth box in Figure 17.1.

Suppose that the total amount of good 1 is $\omega^1 = \omega_1^1 + \omega_2^1$ and that the total amount of good 2 is $\omega^2 = \omega_1^2 + \omega_2^2$. The Edgeworth box has a width of ω^1 and a height of ω^2. A point in the box, (x_1^1, x_1^2), indicates how much agent 1 holds of the two goods. At the same time, it indicates the amount that agent 2 holds of the two goods: $(x_2^1, x_2^2) = (\omega^1 - x_1^1, \omega^2 - x_1^2)$. Geometrically, we measure agent 1's bundle from the lower left-hand corner

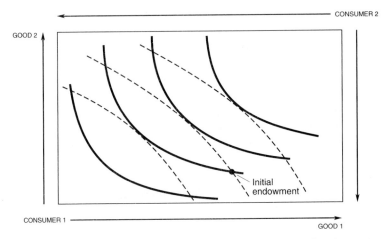

Edgeworth box. The length of the horizontal axis measures the total amount of good 1, and the height of the vertical axis measures the total amount of good 2. Each point in this box is a feasible allocation.

Figure 17.1

of the box. Agent 2's holdings are measured from the upper right-hand corner of the box. In this way, every feasible allocation of the two goods between the two agents can be represented by a point in this box.

We can also illustrate the agents' indifference curves in the box. There will be two sets of indifference curves, one set for each of the agents. All of the information contained in a two-person, two-good pure exchange economy can in this way be represented in a convenient graphical form.

17.2 Walrasian equilibrium

We have argued that, when there are many agents, it is reasonable to suppose that each agent takes the market prices as independent of his or her actions. Consider the particular case of pure exchange being described here. We imagine that there is some vector of market prices $\mathbf{p} = (p_1, \cdots, p_k)$, one price for each good. Each consumer takes these prices as given and chooses the most preferred bundle from his or her consumption set; that is, each consumer i acts as if he or she were solving the following problem:

$$\max_{\mathbf{x}_i} u_i(\mathbf{x}_i)$$

$$\text{such that } \mathbf{p}\mathbf{x}_i = \mathbf{p}\boldsymbol{\omega}_i.$$

The answer to this problem, $\mathbf{x}_i(\mathbf{p}, \mathbf{p}\boldsymbol{\omega}_i)$, is the consumer's **demand function**, which we have studied in Chapter 9. In that chapter the consumer's income or wealth, m_i was exogenous. Here we take the consumer's wealth to be the market value of his or her initial endowment, so that $m_i = \mathbf{p}\boldsymbol{\omega}_i$. We saw in Chapter 9 that under an assumption of strict convexity of preferences, the demand functions will be well-behaved continuous functions.

Of course, for an arbitrary price vector $\mathbf{p}$, it may not be possible actually to make the desired transactions for the simple reason that the aggregate demand, $\sum_i \mathbf{x}_i(\mathbf{p}, \mathbf{p}\boldsymbol{\omega}_i)$, may not be equal to the aggregate supply, $\sum_i \boldsymbol{\omega}_i$.

It is natural to think of an equilibrium price vector as being one that clears all markets; that is, a set of prices for which demand equals supply in every market. However, this is a bit too strong for our purposes. For example, consider the case where some of the goods are undesirable. In this case, they may well be in excess supply in equilibrium.

For this reason, we typically define a **Walrasian equilibrium** to be a pair $(\mathbf{p}^*, \mathbf{x}^*)$, such that

$$\sum_i \mathbf{x}_i(\mathbf{p}^*, \mathbf{p}^*\boldsymbol{\omega}_i) \leq \sum_i \boldsymbol{\omega}_i.$$

That is, $\mathbf{p}^*$ is a Walrasian equilibrium if there is no good for which there is positive excess demand. We show later, in Chapter 17, page 318, that if all goods are desirable—in a sense to be made precise—then in fact demand will equal supply in all markets.

17.3 Graphical analysis

Walrasian equilibria can be examined geometrically by use of the Edgeworth box. Given any price vector, we can determine the budget line of each agent and use the indifference curves to find the demanded bundles of each agent. We then search for a price vector such that the demanded points of the two agents are compatible.

In Figure 17.2 we have drawn such an equilibrium allocation. Each agent is maximizing his utility on his budget line and these demands are compatible with the total supplies available. Note that the Walrasian equilibrium occurs at a point where the two indifference curves are tangent. This is clear, since utility maximization requires that each agent's marginal rate of substitution be equal to the common price ratio.

Another way to describe equilibrium is through the use of **offer curves**. Recall that a consumer's offer curve describes the locus of tangencies between the indifference curves and the budget line as the relative prices vary—i.e., the set of demanded bundles. Thus, at an equilibrium in the Edgeworth box the offer curves of the two agents intersect. At such an intersection the demanded bundles of each agent are compatible with the available supplies.

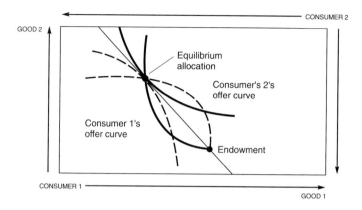

GOOD 2

CONSUMER 2

Equilibrium allocation

Consumer's 2's offer curve

Consumer 1's offer curve

Endowment

CONSUMER 1

GOOD 1

Walrasian equilibrium in the Edgeworth box. Each agent is maximizing utility on his budget line.

Figure 17.2

17.4 Existence of Walrasian equilibria

Will there always exist a price vector where all markets clear? We will analyze this question of the **existence of Walrasian equilibria** in this section.

Let us recall a few facts about this existence problem. First of all, the budget set of a consumer remains unchanged if we multiply all prices by any positive constant; thus, each consumer's demand function has the property that $\mathbf{x}_i(\mathbf{p}, \mathbf{p}\boldsymbol{\omega}_i) = \mathbf{x}_i(k\mathbf{p}, k\mathbf{p}\boldsymbol{\omega}_i)$ for all $k > 0$; i.e., the demand function is homogeneous of degree zero in prices. As the sum of homogeneous functions is homogeneous, the aggregate excess demand function,

$$\mathbf{z}(\mathbf{p}) = \sum_{i=1}^{n} [\mathbf{x}_i(\mathbf{p}, \mathbf{p}\boldsymbol{\omega}_i) - \boldsymbol{\omega}_i],$$

is also homogeneous of degree zero in prices. Note that we ignore the fact that $\mathbf{z}$ depends on the vector of initial endowments, $(\boldsymbol{\omega}_i)$, since the initial endowments remain constant in the course of our analysis.

If all of the individual demand functions are continuous, then $\mathbf{z}$ will be a continuous function, since the sum of continuous functions is a continuous function. Furthermore, the aggregate excess demand function must satisfy a condition known as **Walras' law.**

Walras' law.   *For any price vector* $\mathbf{p}$, *we have* $\mathbf{p}\mathbf{z}(\mathbf{p}) \equiv 0$; *i.e., the value of the excess demand is identically zero.*

Proof. We simply write the definition of aggregate excess demand and multiply by **p**:

$$\mathbf{pz}(\mathbf{p}) = \mathbf{p} \left[\sum_{i=1}^{n} \mathbf{x}_i(\mathbf{p}, \mathbf{p}\omega_i) - \sum_{i=1}^{n} \omega_i \right] = \sum_{i=1}^{n} [\mathbf{p}\mathbf{x}_i(\mathbf{p}, \mathbf{p}\omega_i) - \mathbf{p}\omega_i] = 0,$$

since $\mathbf{x}_i(\mathbf{p}, \mathbf{p}\omega_i)$ must satisfy the budget constraint $\mathbf{p}\mathbf{x}_i = \mathbf{p}\omega_i$ for each agent $i = 1, \ldots, n$. ∎

Walras' law says something quite obvious: if each individual satisfies his budget constraint, so that the value of his excess demand is zero, then the value of the *sum* of the excess demands must be zero. It is important to realize that Walras' law asserts that the value of excess demand is *identically* zero—the value of excess demand is zero for *all* prices.

Combining Walras' law and the definition of equilibrium, we have two useful propositions.

Market clearing. *If demand equals supply in $k-1$ markets, and $p_k > 0$, then demand must equal supply in the kth market.*

Proof. If not, Walras' law would be violated. ∎

Free goods. *If $\mathbf{p}^*$ is a Walrasian equilibrium and $z_j(\mathbf{p}^*) < 0$, then $p_j^* = 0$. That is, if some good is in excess supply at a Walrasian equilibrium it must be a free good.*

Proof. Since $\mathbf{p}^*$ is a Walrasian equilibrium, $\mathbf{z}(\mathbf{p}^*) \leq \mathbf{0}$. Since prices are nonnegative, $\mathbf{p}^*\mathbf{z}(\mathbf{p}^*) = \sum_{i=1}^{k} p_i^* z_i(\mathbf{p}^*) \leq 0$. If $z_j(\mathbf{p}^*) < 0$ and $p_j^* > 0$, we would have $\mathbf{p}^*\mathbf{z}(\mathbf{p}^*) < 0$, contradicting Walras' law. ∎

This proposition shows us what conditions are required for all markets to clear in equilibrium. Suppose that all goods are desirable in the following sense:

Desirability. *If $p_i = 0$, then $z_i(\mathbf{p}) > 0$ for $i = 1, \ldots, k$.*

The desirability assumption says that if some price is zero, the aggregate excess demand for that good is strictly positive. Then we have the following proposition:

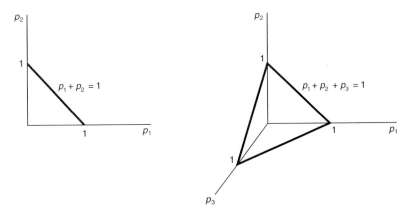

Price simplices. The first panel depicts the one-dimensional price simplex S^1; the second panel depicts S^2.

Figure 17.3

Equality of demand and supply. *If all goods are desirable and* $\mathbf{p}^*$ *is a Walrasian equilibrium, then* $\mathbf{z}(\mathbf{p}^*) = \mathbf{0}$.

Proof. Assume $z_i(\mathbf{p}^*) < 0$. Then by the free goods proposition, $p_i^* = 0$. But then by the desirability assumption, $z_i(\mathbf{p}^*) > 0$, a contradiction. ∎

   To summarize: in general all we require for equilibrium is that there is no excess demand for any good. But the above propositions indicate that if some good is actually in excess supply in equilibrium, then its price must be zero. Thus, if each good is desirable in the sense that a zero price implies it will be in excess demand, then equilibrium will in fact be characterized by the equality of demand and supply in every market.

17.5 Existence of an equilibrium

Since the aggregate excess demand function is homogeneous of degree zero, we can normalize prices and express demands in terms of **relative prices**. There are several ways to do this, but a convenient normalization for our purposes is to replace each absolute price $\hat{p}_i$ by a normalized price

$$p_i = \frac{\hat{p}_i}{\sum_{j=1}^{k} \hat{p}_j}.$$

This has the consequence that the normalized prices p_i must always sum up to 1. Hence, we can restrict our attention to price vectors belonging to the $k - 1$-dimensional unit simplex:

$$S^{k-1} = \left\{ \mathbf{p} \text{ in } R_+^k : \sum_{i=1}^{k} p_i = 1 \right\}.$$

For a picture of S^1 and S^2 see Figure 17.3.

We return now to the question of the existence of Walrasian equilibrium: is there a $\mathbf{p}^*$ that clears all markets? Our proof of existence makes use of the Brouwer fixed-point theorem.

Brouwer fixed-point theorem.   *If* $\mathbf{f} : S^{k-1} \to S^{k-1}$ *is a continuous function from the unit simplex to itself, there is some* $\mathbf{x}$ *in* S^{k-1} *such that* $\mathbf{x} = \mathbf{f}(\mathbf{x})$.

Proof. The proof for the general case is beyond the scope of this book; a good proof is in Scarf (1973). However, we will prove the theorem for $k = 2$.

In this case, we can identify the unit 1-dimensional simplex S^1 with the unit interval. According to the setup of the theorem we have a continuous function $f : [0, 1] \to [0, 1]$ and we want to establish that there is some x in $[0, 1]$ such that $x = f(x)$.

Consider the function g defined by $g(x) = f(x) - x$. Geometrically, g just measures the difference between $f(x)$ and the diagonal in the box depicted in Figure 17.4. A fixed point of the mapping f is an x^* where $g(x^*) = 0$.

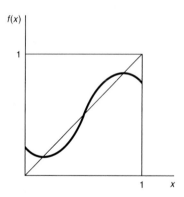

Figure 17.4   **Proof of Brouwer's theorem in two dimensions.**   In the case depicted, there are three points where $x = f(x)$.

Now $g(0) = f(0) - 0 \geq 0$ since $f(0)$ is in $[0, 1]$, and $g(1) = f(1) - 1 \leq 0$ for the same reason. Since f is continuous, we can apply the intermediate value theorem and conclude that there is some x in $[0, 1]$ such that $g(x) = f(x) - x = 0$, which proves the theorem. ∎

We are now in a position to prove the main existence theorem.

Existence of Walrasian equilibria.   *If* $z : S^{k-1} \to R^k$ *is a continuous function that satisfies Walras' law,* $\mathbf{pz(p)} \equiv 0$, *then there exists some* $\mathbf{p}^*$ *in* S^{k-1} *such that* $\mathbf{z(p^*)} \le 0$.

Proof. Define a map $g : S^{k-1} \to S^{k-1}$ by

$$g_i(\mathbf{p}) = \frac{p_i + \max(0, z_i(\mathbf{p}))}{1 + \sum_{j=1}^{k} \max(0, z_j(\mathbf{p}))} \qquad \text{for } i = 1, \dots, k.$$

Notice that this map is continuous since z and the max function are continuous functions. Furthermore, $\mathbf{g(p)}$ is a point in the simplex S^{k-1} since $\sum_i g_i(\mathbf{p}) = 1$. This map also has a reasonable economic interpretation: if there is excess demand in some market, so that $z_i(\mathbf{p}) \ge 0$, then the relative price of that good is increased.

By Brouwer's fixed-point theorem there is a $\mathbf{p}^*$ such that $\mathbf{p}^* = \mathbf{g(p^*)}$; i.e.,

$$p_i^* = \frac{p_i^* + \max(0, z_i(\mathbf{p}^*))}{1 + \sum_j \max(0, z_j(\mathbf{p}^*))} \qquad \text{for } i = 1, \dots, k. \tag{17.1}$$

We will show that $\mathbf{p}^*$ is a Walrasian equilibrium. Cross-multiply equation (17.1) and rearrange to get

$$p_i^* \sum_{j=1}^{k} \max(0, z_j(\mathbf{p}^*)) = \max(0, z_i(\mathbf{p}^*)) \quad i = 1, \dots, k.$$

Now multiply each of these k equations by $z_i(\mathbf{p}^*)$:

$$z_i(\mathbf{p}^*) p_i^* \left[\sum_{j=1}^{k} \max(0, z_j(\mathbf{p}^*)) \right] = z_i(\mathbf{p}^*) \max(0, z_i(\mathbf{p}^*)) \quad i = 1, \dots, k.$$

Sum these k equations to get

$$\left[\sum_{j=1}^{k} \max(0, z_j(\mathbf{p}^*)) \right] \sum_{i=1}^{k} p_i^* z_i(\mathbf{p}^*) = \sum_{i=1}^{k} z_i(\mathbf{p}^*) \max(0, z_i(\mathbf{p}^*)).$$

Now $\sum_{i=1}^{k} p_i^* z_i(\mathbf{p}^*) = 0$ by Walras' law so we have

$$\sum_{i=1}^{k} z_i(\mathbf{p}^*) \max(0, z_i(\mathbf{p}^*)) = 0.$$

Each term of this sum is greater than or equal to zero since each term is either 0 or $(z_i(\mathbf{p}^*))^2$. But if any term were *strictly* greater than zero, the equality wouldn't hold. Hence, every term must be equal to zero, which says

$$z_i(\mathbf{p}^*) \le 0 \quad \text{for } i = 1, \ldots, k.$$

∎

It is worth emphasizing the very general nature of the above theorem. All that is needed is that the excess demand function be continuous and satisfy Walras' law. Walras' law arises directly from the hypothesis that the consumer has to meet some kind of budget constraint; such behavior would seem to be necessary in any type of economic model. The hypothesis of continuity is more restrictive but not unreasonably so. We have seen earlier that if consumers all have strictly convex preferences then their demand functions will be well defined and continuous. The aggregate demand function will therefore be continuous. But even if the individual demand functions display discontinuities it may still turn out the aggregate demand function is continuous if there are a large number of consumers. Thus, continuity of aggregate demand seems like a relatively weak requirement.

However, there is one slight problem with the above argument for existence. It is true that aggregate demand is likely to be continuous for *positive* prices, but it is rather unreasonable to assume it is continuous even when some price goes to zero. If, for example, preferences were monotonic and the price of some good is zero, we would expect that the demand for such a good might be infinite. Thus, the excess demand function might not even be well defined on the boundary of the price simplex—i.e., on that set of price vectors where some prices are zero. However, this sort of discontinuity can be handled by using a slightly more complicated mathematical argument.

EXAMPLE: The Cobb-Douglas Economy

Let agent 1 have utility function $u_1(x_1^1, x_1^2) = (x_1^1)^a (x_1^2)^{1-a}$ and endowment $\boldsymbol{\omega}_1 = (1, 0)$. Let agent 2 have utility function $u_2(x_2^1, x_2^2) = (x_2^1)^b (x_2^2)^{1-b}$ and endowment $\boldsymbol{\omega}_2 = (0, 1)$. Then agent 1's demand function for good 1 is

$$x_1^1(p_1, p_2, m_1) = \frac{a m_1}{p_1}.$$

At prices (p_1, p_2), income is $m_1 = p_1 \times 1 + p_2 \times 0 = p_1$. Substituting, we have

$$x_1^1(p_1, p_2) = \frac{a p_1}{p_1} = a.$$

Similarly, agent 2's demand function for good 1 is

$$x_2^1(p_1, p_2) = \frac{b p_2}{p_1}.$$

The equilibrium price is where total demand for each good equals total supply. By Walras' law, we only need find the price where total demand for good 1 equals total supply of good 1:

$$x_1^1(p_1, p_2) + x_2^1(p_1, p_2) = 1$$

$$a + \frac{bp_2}{p_1} = 1$$

$$\frac{p_2^*}{p_1^*} = \frac{1 - a}{b}.$$

Note that, as usual, only relative prices are determined in equilibrium.

17.6 The first theorem of welfare economics

The existence of Walrasian equilibria is interesting as a positive result insofar as we believe the behavioral assumptions on which the model is based. However, even if this does not seem to be an especially plausible assumption in many circumstances, we may still be interested in Walrasian equilibria for their normative content. Let us consider the following definitions.

Definitions of Pareto efficiency. *A feasible allocation* **x** *is a* **weakly Pareto efficient** *allocation if there is no feasible allocation* **x′** *such that all agents strictly prefer* **x′** *to* **x**. *A feasible allocation* **x** *is a* **strongly Pareto efficient** *allocation if there is no feasible allocation* **x′** *such that all agents weakly prefer* **x′** *to* **x**, *and some agent strictly prefers* **x′** *to* **x**.

It is easy to see that an allocation that is strongly Pareto efficient is also weakly Pareto efficient. In general, the reverse is not true. However, under some additional weak assumptions about preferences the reverse implication *is* true, so the concepts can be used interchangeably.

Equivalence of weak and strong Pareto efficiency. *Suppose that preferences are continuous and monotonic. Then an allocation is weakly Pareto efficient if and only if it is strongly Pareto efficient.*

Proof. If an allocation is strongly Pareto efficient, then it is certainly weakly Pareto efficient: if you can't make one person better off without hurting someone else, you certainly can't make everyone better off.

We need to show that if an allocation is weakly Pareto efficient, then it is strongly Pareto efficient. We prove the logically equivalent claim that if an allocation is *not* strongly efficient, then it is not weakly efficient.

Suppose, then, that it is possible to make some particular agent i better off without hurting any other agents. We must demonstrate a way to make everyone better off. To do this, simply scale back i's consumption bundle by a small amount and redistribute the goods taken from i equally to the other agents. More precisely, replace i's consumption bundle $\mathbf{x}_i$ by $\theta\mathbf{x}_i$ and replace each other agent j's consumption bundle by $\mathbf{x}_j + (1-\theta)\mathbf{x}_i/(n-1)$. By continuity of preferences, it is possible to choose θ close enough to 1 so that agent i is still better off. By monotonicity, all the other agents are made strictly better off by receiving the redistributed bundle. $\blacksquare$

It turns out that the concept of weak Pareto efficiency is slightly more convenient mathematically, so we will generally use this definition: when we say "Pareto efficient" we generally mean "weakly Pareto efficient." However, we will henceforth always assume preferences are continuous and monotonic so that either definition is applicable.

Note that the concept of Pareto efficiency is quite weak as a normative concept; an allocation where one agent gets everything there is in the economy and all other agents get nothing will be Pareto efficient, assuming the agent who has everything is not satiated.

Pareto efficient allocations can easily be depicted in the Edgeworth box diagram introduced earlier. We only need note that, in the two-person case, Pareto efficient allocations can be found by fixing one agent's utility function at a given level and maximizing the other agent's utility function subject to this constraint. Formally, we only need solve the following maximization problem:

$$\max_{\mathbf{x}_1, \mathbf{x}_2} u_1(\mathbf{x}_1)$$

$$\text{such that } u_2(\mathbf{x}_2) \geq \bar{u}_2$$

$$\mathbf{x}_1 + \mathbf{x}_2 = \boldsymbol{\omega}_1 + \boldsymbol{\omega}_2.$$

This problem can be solved by inspection in the Edgeworth box case. Simply find the point on one agent's indifference curve where the other agent reaches the highest utility. By now it should be clear that the resulting Pareto efficient point will be characterized by a tangency condition: the marginal rates of substitution must be the same for each agent.

For each fixed value of agent 2's utility, we can find an allocation where agent 1's utility is maximized and thus the tangency condition will be satisfied. The set of Pareto efficient points—the **Pareto set**—will thus be the locus of tangencies drawn in the Edgeworth box depicted in Figure 17.5. The **Pareto set** is also known as the **contract curve**, since it gives the set of efficient "contracts" or allocations.

The comparison of Figure 17.5 with Figure 17.2 reveals a striking fact: there seems to be a one-to-one correspondence between the set of Walrasian equilibria and the set of Pareto efficient allocations. Each Walrasian equilibrium satisfies the first-order condition for utility maximization that the marginal rate of substitution between the two goods for each agent be equal to the price ratio between the two goods. Since all agents face the

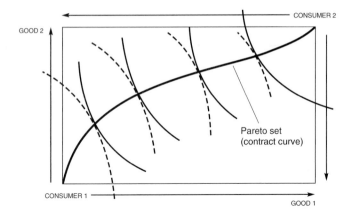

Pareto efficiency in the Edgeworth box. The Pareto set, or the contract curve, is the set of all Pareto efficient allocations.

Figure 17.5

same price ratio at a Walrasian equilibrium, all agents must have the same marginal rates of substitution.

Furthermore, if we pick an arbitrary Pareto efficient allocation, we know that the marginal rates of substitution must be equal across the two agents, and we can thus pick a price ratio equal to this common value. Graphically, given a Pareto efficient point we simply draw the common tangency line separating the two indifference curves. We then pick any point on this tangent line to serve as an initial endowment. If the agents try to maximize preferences on their budget sets, they will end up precisely at the Pareto efficient allocation.

The next two theorems give this correspondence precisely. First, we restate the definition of a Walrasian equilibrium in a more convenient form:

Definition of Walrasian equilibrium.   *An allocation-price pair* $(\mathbf{x}, \mathbf{p})$ *is a* **Walrasian equilibrium** *if (1) the allocation is feasible, and (2) each agent is making an optimal choice from his budget set. In equations:*

(1) $\displaystyle\sum_{i=1}^{n} \mathbf{x}_i = \sum_{i=1}^{n} \boldsymbol{\omega}_i.$

(2) *If* $\mathbf{x}'_i$ *is preferred by agent* i *to* $\mathbf{x}_i$, *then* $\mathbf{p}\mathbf{x}'_i > \mathbf{p}\boldsymbol{\omega}_i.$

This definition is equivalent to the original definition of Walrasian equilibrium, as long as the desirability assumption is satisfied. This definition allows us to neglect the possibility of free goods, which are a bit of a nuisance for the arguments that follow.

First Theorem of Welfare Economics. *If* $(\mathbf{x}, \mathbf{p})$ *is a Walrasian equilibrium, then* $\mathbf{x}$ *is Pareto efficient.*

Proof. Suppose not, and let $\mathbf{x}'$ be a feasible allocation that all agents prefer to $\mathbf{x}$. Then by property 2 of the definition of Walrasian equilibrium, we have

$$\mathbf{p}\mathbf{x}'_i > \mathbf{p}\boldsymbol{\omega}_i \text{ for } i = 1, \ldots, n.$$

Summing over $i = 1, \ldots, n$, and using the fact that $\mathbf{x}'$ is feasible, we have

$$\mathbf{p}\sum_{i=1}^{n}\boldsymbol{\omega}_i = \mathbf{p}\sum_{i=1}^{n}\mathbf{x}'_i > \sum_{i=1}^{n}\mathbf{p}\boldsymbol{\omega}_i,$$

which is a contradiction. ∎

This theorem says that if the behavioral assumptions of our model are satisfied then the market equilibrium is efficient. A market equilibrium is not necessarily "optimal" in any ethical sense, since the market equilibrium may be very "unfair." The outcome depends entirely on the original distribution of endowments. What is needed is some further ethical criterion to choose among the efficient allocations. Such a concept, the concept of a welfare function, will be discussed later in this chapter.

17.7 The second welfare theorem

We have shown that every Walrasian equilibrium is Pareto efficient. Here we show that every Pareto efficient allocation is a Walrasian equilibrium.

Second Theorem of Welfare Economics. *Suppose* $\mathbf{x}^*$ *is a Pareto efficient allocation in which each agent holds a positive amount of each good. Suppose that preferences are convex, continuous, and monotonic. Then* $\mathbf{x}^*$ *is a Walrasian equilibrium for the initial endowments* $\boldsymbol{\omega}_i = \mathbf{x}_i^*$ *for* $i = 1, \ldots, n$.

Proof. Let

$$P_i = \{\mathbf{x}_i \text{ in } R^k : \mathbf{x}_i \succ_i \mathbf{x}_i^*\}.$$

This is the set of all consumption bundles that agent i prefers to $\mathbf{x}_i^*$. Then define

$$P = \sum_{i=1}^{n} P_i = \left\{ \mathbf{z} : \mathbf{z} = \sum_{i=1}^{n} \mathbf{x}_i \text{ with } \mathbf{x}_i \text{ in } P_i \right\}.$$

P is the set of all bundles of the k goods that can be distributed among the n agents so as to make each agent better off. Since each P_i is a convex set by hypothesis and the sum of convex sets is convex, it follows that P is a convex set.

Let $\boldsymbol{\omega} = \sum_{i=1}^{n} \mathbf{x}_i^*$ be the current *aggregate* bundle. Since $\mathbf{x}^*$ is Pareto efficient, there is no redistribution of $\mathbf{x}^*$ that makes everyone better off. This means that $\boldsymbol{\omega}$ is not an element of the set P.

Hence, by the separating hyperplane theorem (Chapter 26, page 483) there exists a $\mathbf{p} \neq \mathbf{0}$ such that

$$\mathbf{pz} \geq \mathbf{p} \sum_{i=1}^{n} \mathbf{x}_i^* \quad \text{for all } \mathbf{z} \text{ in } P.$$

Rearranging this equation gives us

$$\mathbf{p}\left(\mathbf{z} - \sum_{i=1}^{n} \mathbf{x}_i^*\right) \geq \mathbf{0} \quad \text{for all } \mathbf{z} \text{ in } P. \tag{17.2}$$

We want to show that $\mathbf{p}$ is in fact an equilibrium price vector. The proof proceeds in three steps.

(1) $\mathbf{p}$ is nonnegative; that is, $\mathbf{p} \geq \mathbf{0}$.

To see this, let $\mathbf{e}_i = (0, \ldots, 1, \ldots, 0)$ with a 1 in the ith component. Since preferences are monotonic, $\boldsymbol{\omega} + \mathbf{e}_i$ must lie in P; since if we have one more unit of any good, it is possible to redistribute it to make everyone better off. Inequality (17.2) then implies

$$\mathbf{p}(\boldsymbol{\omega} + \mathbf{e}_i - \boldsymbol{\omega}) \geq 0 \quad \text{for } i = 1, \ldots, k.$$

Canceling terms,
$$\mathbf{pe}_i \geq 0 \quad \text{for } i = 1, \ldots, k.$$

This equation implies $p_i \geq 0$ for $i = 1, \ldots, k$.

(2) If $\mathbf{y}_j \succ_j \mathbf{x}_j^*$, then $\mathbf{py}_j \geq \mathbf{px}_j^*$, for each agent $j = 1, \ldots, n$.

We already know that, if *every* agent i prefers $\mathbf{y}_i$ to $\mathbf{x}_i^*$, then

$$\mathbf{p} \sum_{i=1}^{n} \mathbf{y}_i \geq \mathbf{p} \sum_{i=1}^{n} \mathbf{x}_i^*.$$

Now suppose only that some *particular* agent j prefers some bundle $\mathbf{y}_j$ to $\mathbf{x}_j$. Construct an allocation $\mathbf{z}$ by taking some of each good away from agent j and distributing it to the other agents. Formally, let θ be a small number, and define the allocations $\mathbf{z}$ by

$$z_j = (1 - \theta)y_j$$
$$z_i = x_i^* + \frac{\theta y_j}{n - 1} \quad i \neq j.$$

For small enough θ, strong monotonicity implies the allocation $\mathbf{z}$ is Pareto preferred to $\mathbf{x}^*$, and thus $\sum_{i=1}^{n} \mathbf{z}_i$ lies in P. Applying inequality (17.2), we have

$$\mathbf{p} \sum_{i=1}^{n} \mathbf{z}_i \geq \mathbf{p} \sum_{i=1}^{n} \mathbf{x}_i^*$$

$$\mathbf{p} \left[\mathbf{y}_j(1 - \theta) + \sum_{i \neq j} \mathbf{x}_i^* + \mathbf{y}_j \theta \right] \geq \mathbf{p} \left[\mathbf{x}_j^* + \sum_{i \neq j} \mathbf{x}_i^* \right]$$

$$\mathbf{p} \mathbf{y}_j \geq \mathbf{p} \mathbf{x}_j^*.$$

This argument demonstrates that if agent j prefers $\mathbf{y}_j$ to $\mathbf{x}_j^*$, then $\mathbf{y}_j$ can cost no less than $\mathbf{x}_j^*$. It remains to show that we can make this inequality strict.

(3) If $\mathbf{y}_j \succ_j \mathbf{x}_j^*$, we must have $\mathbf{p} \mathbf{y}_j > \mathbf{p} \mathbf{x}_j^*$.

We already know that $\mathbf{p} \mathbf{y}_j \geq \mathbf{p} \mathbf{x}_j^*$; we want to rule out the possibility that the equality case holds. Accordingly, we will assume that $\mathbf{p} \mathbf{y}_j = \mathbf{p} \mathbf{x}_j^*$ and try to derive a contradiction.

From the assumption of continuity of preferences, we can find some θ with $0 < \theta < 1$ such that $\theta \mathbf{y}_j$ is strictly preferred to $\mathbf{x}_j^*$. By the argument of part (2), we know that $\theta \mathbf{y}_j$ must cost at least as much as $\mathbf{x}_j^*$:

$$\theta \mathbf{p} \mathbf{y}_j \geq \mathbf{p} \mathbf{x}_j^*. \tag{17.3}$$

One of the hypotheses of the theorem is that $\mathbf{x}_j^*$ has every component strictly positive; from this it follows that $\mathbf{p} \mathbf{x}_j^* > 0$.

Therefore, if $\mathbf{p} \mathbf{y}_j - \mathbf{p} \mathbf{x}_j^* = 0$, it follows that $\theta \mathbf{p} \mathbf{y}_j < \mathbf{p} \mathbf{x}_j^*$. But this contradicts (17.3), and concludes the proof of the theorem. ∎

It is worth considering the hypotheses of this proposition. Convexity and continuity of preferences are crucial, of course, but strong monotonicity can be relaxed considerably. One can also relax the assumption that $\mathbf{x}_i^* \gg \mathbf{0}$.

A revealed preference argument

There is a very simple but somewhat indirect proof of the Second Welfare Theorem that is based on a revealed preference argument and the existence theorem described earlier in this chapter.

Second Theorem of Welfare Economics.   *Suppose that* $\mathbf{x}^*$ *is a Pareto efficient allocation and that preferences are nonsatiated. Suppose further that a competitive equilibrium exists from the initial endowments* $\boldsymbol{\omega}_i = \mathbf{x}_i^*$ *and let it be given by* $(\mathbf{p}', \mathbf{x}')$. *Then, in fact,* $(\mathbf{p}', \mathbf{x}^*)$ *is a competitive equilibrium.*

Proof. Since $\mathbf{x}_i^*$ is in consumer i's budget set by construction, we must have $\mathbf{x}_i' \succeq_i \mathbf{x}_i^*$. Since $\mathbf{x}^*$ is Pareto efficient, this implies that $\mathbf{x}_i^* \sim_i \mathbf{x}_i'$. Thus if $\mathbf{x}_i'$ is optimal, so is $\mathbf{x}_i^*$. Hence, $(\mathbf{p}', \mathbf{x}^*)$ is a Walrasian equilibrium. ∎

This argument shows that if a competitive equilibrium *exists* from a Pareto efficient allocation, then that Pareto efficient allocation is *itself* a competitive equilibrium. The remarks following the existence theorem in this chapter indicate that the only essential requirement for existence is continuity of the aggregate demand function. Continuity follows from either the convexity of individual preferences or the assumption of a "large" economy. Thus, the Second Welfare Theorem holds under the same circumstances.

17.8 Pareto efficiency and calculus

We have seen in the last section that every competitive equilibrium is Pareto efficient and essentially every Pareto efficient allocation is a competitive equilibrium for some distribution of endowments. In this section we will investigate this relationship more closely through the use of differential calculus. Essentially, we will derive first-order conditions that characterize market equilibria and Pareto efficiency and then compare these two sets of conditions.

The conditions characterizing the market equilibrium are very simple.

Calculus characterization of equilibrium.   *If* $(\mathbf{x}^*, \mathbf{p}^*)$ *is a market equilibrium with each consumer holding a positive amount of every good, then there exists a set of numbers* $(\lambda_1, \dots, \lambda_n)$ *such that:*

$$\mathbf{D}u_i(\mathbf{x}^*) = \lambda_i \mathbf{p}^* \qquad i = 1, \dots, n.$$

Proof. If we have a market equilibrium, then each agent is maximized on his budget set, and these are just the first-order conditions for such utility maximization. The λ_i's are the agents' marginal utilities of income. ∎

The first-order conditions for Pareto efficiency are a bit harder to formulate. However, the following trick is very useful.

Calculus characterization of Pareto efficiency. *A feasible allocation* $\mathbf{x}^*$ *is Pareto efficient if and only if* $\mathbf{x}^*$ *solves the following* n *maximization problems for* $i = 1, \ldots, n$:

$$\max_{(x_i^g, x_j^g)} u_i(\mathbf{x}_i)$$

$$\text{such that } \sum_{h=1}^{n} x_h^g \leq \omega^g \quad g = 1, \ldots, k$$

$$u_j(\mathbf{x}_j^*) \leq u_j(\mathbf{x}_j) \quad j \neq i.$$

Proof. Suppose $\mathbf{x}^*$ solves all maximization problems but $\mathbf{x}^*$ is not Pareto efficient. This means that there is some allocation $\mathbf{x}'$ where everyone is better off. But then $\mathbf{x}^*$ couldn't solve any of the problems, a contradiction.

Conversely, suppose $\mathbf{x}^*$ is Pareto efficient, but it doesn't solve one of the problems. Instead, let $\mathbf{x}'$ solve that particular problem. Then $\mathbf{x}'$ makes one of the agents better off without hurting any of the other agents, which contradicts the assumption that $\mathbf{x}^*$ is Pareto efficient. ∎

Before examining the Lagrange formulation for one of these maximization problems, let's do a little counting. There are $k + n - 1$ constraints for each of the n maximization problems. The first k constraints are resource constraints, and the second $n - 1$ constraints are the utility constraints. In each maximization problem there are kn choice variables: how much each of the n agents has of each of the k goods.

Let q^g, for $g = 1, \ldots, k$, be the Kuhn-Tucker multipliers for the resource constraints, and let a_j, for $j \neq i$, be the multipliers for the utility constraints. Write the Lagrangian for one of the maximization problems.

$$\mathcal{L} = u_i(\mathbf{x}_i) - \sum_{g=1}^{k} q^g \left[\sum_{i=1}^{n} x_i^g - \omega^g \right] - \sum_{j \neq i} a_j [u_j(\mathbf{x}_j^*) - u_j(\mathbf{x}_j)].$$

Now differentiate $\mathcal{L}$ with respect to x_j^g where $g = 1, \ldots, k$ and $j = 1, \ldots, n$. We get first-order conditions of the form

$$\frac{\partial u_i(\mathbf{x}_i^*)}{\partial x_i^g} - q^g = 0 \qquad g = 1, \ldots, k$$

$$a_j \frac{\partial u_j(\mathbf{x}_j^*)}{\partial x_j^g} - q^g = 0 \qquad j \neq i; g = 1, \ldots, k.$$

At first these conditions seem somewhat strange since they seem to be asymmetric. For each choice of i, we get different values for the multipliers (q^g) and (a_j). However, the paradox is resolved when we note that the *relative* values of the qs are independent of the choice of i. This is clear since the above conditions imply

$$\frac{\frac{\partial u_i(\mathbf{x}_i^*)}{\partial x_i^g}}{\frac{\partial u_i(\mathbf{x}_i^*)}{\partial x_i^h}} = \frac{q^g}{q^h} \qquad \text{for } i = 1, \ldots, n \text{ and } g, h = 1, \ldots, k.$$

Since $\mathbf{x}^*$ is given, q^g/q^h must be independent of which maximization problem we solve. The same reasoning shows that a_i/a_j is independent of which maximization problem we solve. The solution to the asymmetry problem now becomes clear: if we maximize agent i's utility and use the other agent's utilities as constraints, then it is just as if we are arbitrarily setting agent i's Kuhn-Tucker multiplier to be $a_i = 1$.

Using the First Welfare Theorem, we can derive nice interpretations of the weights (a_i) and (q^g): if $\mathbf{x}^*$ is a market equilibrium, then

$$\mathbf{D}u_i(\mathbf{x}_i^*) = \lambda_i \mathbf{p}^* \quad i = 1, \ldots, n.$$

However, all market equilibria are Pareto efficient and thus must satisfy

$$a_i \mathbf{D}u_i(\mathbf{x}_i^*) = \mathbf{q} \quad i = 1, \ldots, n.$$

From this it is clear that we can choose $\mathbf{p}^* = \mathbf{q}$ and $a_i = 1/\lambda_i$. In words, the Kuhn-Tucker multipliers on the resource constraints are just the competitive prices, and the Kuhn-Tucker multipliers on the agent's utilities are just the reciprocals of their marginal utilities of income.

If we eliminate the Kuhn-Tucker multipliers in the first-order conditions, we get the following conditions characterizing efficient allocations:

$$\frac{\frac{\partial u_i(\mathbf{x}_i^*)}{\partial x_i^g}}{\frac{\partial u_i(\mathbf{x}_i^*)}{\partial x_i^h}} = \frac{p_g^*}{p_h^*} = \frac{q^g}{q^h} \qquad i = 1, \ldots, n \text{ and } g, h = 1, \ldots, k.$$

This says that each Pareto efficient allocation must satisfy the condition that the marginal rate of substitution between each pair of goods is the same for every agent. This marginal rate of substitution is simply the ratio of the competitive prices.

The intuition behind this condition is fairly clear: if two agents had different marginal rates of substitution between some pair of goods, they could arrange a small trade that would make them both better off, contradicting the assumption of Pareto efficiency.

It is often useful to note that the first-order conditions for a Pareto efficient allocation are the same as the first-order conditions for maximizing a weighted sum of utilities. To see this, consider the problem

$$\max \sum_{i=1}^{n} a_i u_i(\mathbf{x}_i)$$

$$\text{such that } \sum_{i=1}^{n} x_i^g \leq w^g \quad g = 1, \ldots, k.$$

The first-order conditions for a solution to this problem are

$$a_i \mathbf{D} u_i(\mathbf{x}_i^*) = \mathbf{q}, \tag{17.4}$$

which are precisely the same as the necessary conditions for Pareto efficiency.

As the set of "welfare weights" $(a_1, \ldots, a_n)$ varies, we trace out the set of Pareto efficient allocations. If we are interested in conditions that characterize all Pareto efficient allocations, we need to manipulate the equations so that the welfare weights disappear. Generally, this boils down to expressing the conditions in terms of marginal rates of substitution.

Another way to see this is to think of incorporating the welfare weights into the definition of the utility function. If the original utility function for agent i is $u_i(\mathbf{x}_i)$, take a monotonic transformation so that the new utility function is $v_i(\mathbf{x}_i) = a_i u_i(\mathbf{x}_i)$. The resulting first-order conditions characterize a *particular* Pareto efficient allocation—the one that maximizes the sum of utilities for a particular representation of utility. But if we manipulate the first-order conditions so that they are expressed in terms of marginal rates of substitution, we will typically find a condition that characterizes all efficient allocations.

For now we note that this calculus characterization of Pareto efficiency gives us a simple proof of the Second Welfare Theorem. Let us assume that all consumers have concave utility functions, although this is not really required. Then if $\mathbf{x}^*$ is a Pareto efficient allocation, we know from the first-order conditions that

$$\mathbf{D} u_i(\mathbf{x}^*) = \frac{1}{a_i} \mathbf{q} \text{ for } i = 1, \ldots, n.$$

Thus, the gradient of each consumer's utility function is proportional to some fixed vector $\mathbf{q}$. Let us choose $\mathbf{q}$ to be the vector of competitive prices. We need to check that each consumer is maximized on his budget set $\{\mathbf{x}_i : \mathbf{q}\mathbf{x}_i \leq \mathbf{q}\mathbf{x}_i^*\}$. But this follows quickly from concavity; according to the mathematical properties of concave functions:

$$u(\mathbf{x}_i) \leq u(\mathbf{x}_i^*) + \mathbf{D} u(\mathbf{x}_i^*)(\mathbf{x}_i - \mathbf{x}_i^*),$$

so

$$u(\mathbf{x}_i) \leq u(\mathbf{x}_i^*) + \frac{1}{a_i} \mathbf{q}(\mathbf{x}_i - \mathbf{x}_i^*).$$

Thus, if $\mathbf{x}_i$ is in the consumer's budget set, $u(\mathbf{x}) \leq u(\mathbf{x}_i^*)$.

17.9 Welfare maximization

One problem with the concept of Pareto efficiency as a normative criterion is that it is not very specific. Pareto efficiency is only concerned with efficiency and has nothing to say about distribution of welfare. Even if we agree that we should be at a Pareto efficient allocation, we still don't know which one we should be at.

One way to resolve these problems is to hypothesize the existence of some **social welfare function**. This is supposed to be a function that aggregates the individual utility functions to come up with a "social utility." The most reasonable interpretation of such a function is that it represents a social decision maker's preferences about how to trade off the utilities of different individuals. We will refrain from making philosophical comments here and just postulate that some such function exists; that is, we will suppose that we have

$$W : R^n \to R,$$

so that $W(u_1, \ldots, u_n)$ gives us the "social utility" resulting from any distribution $(u_1, \ldots, u_n)$ of private utilities. To make sense of this construction we have to pick a particular representation of each agent's utility which will be held fixed during the course of the discussion.

We will suppose that W is increasing in each of its arguments—if you increase any agent's utility without decreasing anybody else's welfare, social welfare should increase. We suppose that society should operate at a point that maximizes social welfare; that is, we should choose an allocation $\mathbf{x}^*$ such that $\mathbf{x}^*$ solves

$$\max \; W(u_1(\mathbf{x}_1), \ldots, u_n(\mathbf{x}_n))$$

$$\text{such that } \sum_{i=1}^{n} x_i^g \le \omega^g \quad g = 1, \ldots, k.$$

How do the allocations that maximize this welfare function compare to Pareto efficient allocations? The following is a trivial consequence of the monotonicity hypothesis:

Welfare maximization and Pareto efficiency. *If $\mathbf{x}^*$ maximizes a social welfare function, then $\mathbf{x}^*$ is Pareto efficient.*

Proof. If $\mathbf{x}^*$ were not Pareto efficient, then there would be some feasible allocation $\mathbf{x}'$ such that $u_i(\mathbf{x}_i') > u_i(\mathbf{x}_i^*)$ for $i = 1, \ldots, n$. But then $W(u_1(\mathbf{x}_1'), \ldots, u_n(\mathbf{x}_n')) > W(u_1(\mathbf{x}_1^*), \ldots, u_n(\mathbf{x}_n^*))$. ∎

Since welfare maxima are Pareto efficient, they must satisfy the same first-order conditions as Pareto efficient allocations; furthermore, under convexity assumptions, every Pareto efficient allocation is a competitive equilibrium, so the same goes for welfare maxima: every welfare maximum is a competitive equilibrium for some distribution of endowments.

This last observation gives us one further interpretation of the competitive prices: they are also the Kuhn-Tucker multipliers for the welfare maximization problem. Applying the envelope theorem, we see that the competitive prices measure the (marginal) social value of a good: how much welfare would increase if we had a small additional amount of the good. However, this is true only for the choice of welfare function that is maximized at the allocation in question.

We have seen above that every welfare maximum is Pareto efficient, but is the converse necessarily true? We saw in the last section that every Pareto efficient allocation satisfied the same first-order conditions as the problem of maximizing a weighted sum of utilities, so it might seem plausible that under convexity and concavity assumptions things might work out nicely. Indeed they do.

Pareto efficiency and welfare maximization. *Let* $\mathbf{x}^*$ *be a Pareto efficient allocation with* $\mathbf{x}_i^* \gg \mathbf{0}$ *for* $i = 1, \ldots, n$. *Let the utility functions* u_i *be concave, continuous, and monotonic functions. Then there is some choice of weights* a_i^* *such that* $\mathbf{x}^*$ *maximizes* $\sum a_i^* u_i(\mathbf{x}_i)$ *subject to the resource constraints. Furthermore, the weights are such that* $a_i^* = 1/\lambda_i^*$ *where* λ_i^* *is the* i^{th} *agent's marginal utility of income; that is, if* m_i *is the value of agent* i's *endowment at the equilibrium prices* $\mathbf{p}^*$, *then*

$$\lambda_i^* = \frac{\partial v_i(\mathbf{p}^*, m_i)}{\partial m_i}.$$

Proof. Since $\mathbf{x}^*$ is Pareto efficient, it is a Walrasian equilibrium. There therefore exist prices $\mathbf{p}$ such that each agent is maximized on his or her budget set; this in turn implies

$$\mathbf{D}u_i(\mathbf{x}_i^*) = \lambda_i \mathbf{p}^* \quad \text{for } i = 1, \ldots, n.$$

Consider now the welfare maximization problem

$$\max \sum_{i=1}^{n} a_i u_i(\mathbf{x}_i)$$

$$\text{such that } \sum_{i=1}^{n} x_i^1 \leq \sum_{i=1}^{n} x_i^{1*}$$

$$\vdots$$

$$\sum_{i=1}^{n} x_i^k \leq \sum_{i=1}^{n} x_i^{k*}.$$

According to the sufficiency theorem for concave constrained maximization problems (Chapter 27, page 504), $\mathbf{x}^*$ solves this problem if there exist nonnegative numbers $(q_1, \ldots, q_k) = \mathbf{q}$ such that

$$a_i \mathbf{D} u_i(\mathbf{x}_i^*) = \mathbf{q}.$$

If we choose $a_i = 1/\lambda_i$, then the prices $\mathbf{p}$ serve as the appropriate nonnegative numbers and the proof is done. ∎

The interpretation of the weights as reciprocals of the marginal utilities of income makes good economic sense. If some agent has a large income at some Pareto efficient allocation, then his marginal utility of income will be small and his weight in the implicit social welfare function will be large.

The above two propositions complete the set of relationships between market equilibria, Pareto efficient allocations, and welfare maxima. To recapitulate briefly:

(1) competitive equilibria are always Pareto efficient;

(2) Pareto efficient allocations are competitive equilibria under convexity assumptions and endowment redistribution;

(3) welfare maxima are always Pareto efficient;

(4) Pareto efficient allocations are welfare maxima under concavity assumptions for some choice of welfare weights.

Inspecting the above relationships we can see the basic moral: a competitive market system will give efficient allocations but this says nothing about distribution. The choice of distribution of income is the same as the choice of a reallocation of endowments, and this in turn is equivalent to choosing a particular welfare function.

Notes

The general equilibrium model was first formulated by Walras (1954). The first proof of existence was due to Wald (1951); more general treatments of existence were provided by McKenzie (1954) and Arrow & Debreu (1954). The definitive modern treatments are Debreu (1959) and Arrow & Hahn (1971). The latter work contains numerous historical notes.

The basic welfare results have a long history. The proof of the first welfare theorem used here follows Koopmans (1957). The importance of convexity in the Second Theorem was recognized by Arrow (1951) and Debreu (1953). The differentiable treatment of efficiency was first developed rigorously by

Samuelson (1947). The relationship between welfare maxima and Pareto efficiency follows Negisihi (1960).

The revealed preference proof of the Second Welfare Theorem is due to Maskin & Roberts (1980).

Exercises

17.1. Consider the revealed preference argument for the Second Welfare Theorem. Show that if preferences are strictly convex, then $x'_i = x^*_i$ for all $i = 1, \ldots, n$.

17.2. Draw an Edgeworth box example with an infinite number of prices that are Walrasian equilibria.

17.3. Consider Figure 17.6. Here x^* is a Pareto efficient allocation, but x^* cannot be supported by competitive prices. Which assumption of the Second Welfare Theorem is violated?

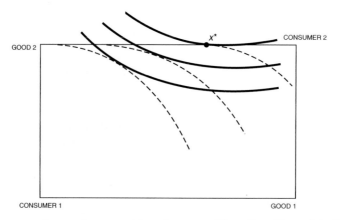

Figure 17.6   **Arrow's exceptional case.** The allocation x^* is Pareto efficient but there are no prices at which x^* is a Walrasian equilibrium.

17.4. There are two consumers A and B with the following utility functions and endowments:

$$u_A(x_A^1, x_A^2) = a \ln x_A^1 + (1 - a) \ln x_A^2 \quad \boldsymbol{\omega}_A = (0, 1)$$
$$u_B(x_B^1, x_B^2) = \min(x_B^1, x_B^2) \quad \boldsymbol{\omega}_B = (1, 0).$$

Calculate the market clearing prices and the equilibrium allocation.

17.5. We have n agents with identical strictly concave utility functions. There is some initial bundle of goods $\boldsymbol{\omega}$. Show that equal division is a Pareto efficient allocation.

17.6. We have two agents with *indirect* utility functions:

$$v_1(p_1, p_2, y) = \ln y - a \ln p_1 - (1 - a) \ln p_2$$
$$v_2(p_1, p_2, y) = \ln y - b \ln p_1 - (1 - b) \ln p_2$$

and initial endowments

$$\boldsymbol{\omega}_1 = (1, 1) \qquad \boldsymbol{\omega}_2 = (1, 1).$$

Calculate the market clearing prices.

17.7. Suppose that all consumers have quasilinear utility functions, so that $v_i(\mathbf{p}, m_i) = v_i(\mathbf{p}) + m_i$. Let $\mathbf{p}^*$ be a Walrasian equilibrium. Show that the aggregate demand curve for each good must be downward sloping at $\mathbf{p}^*$. More generally, show that the gross substitutes matrix must be negative semidefinite.

17.8. Suppose we have two consumers A and B with identical utility functions $u_A(x_1, x_2) = u_B(x_1, x_2) = \max(x_1, x_2)$. There are 1 unit of good 1 and 2 units of good 2. Draw an Edgeworth box that illustrates the strongly Pareto efficient and the (weakly) Pareto efficient sets.

17.9. Consider an economy with 15 consumers and 2 goods. Consumer 3 has a Cobb–Douglas utility function $u_3(x_3^1, x_3^2) = \ln x_3^1 + \ln x_3^2$. At a certain Pareto efficient allocation x^*, consumer 3 holds (10,5). What are the competitive prices that support the allocation $\mathbf{x}^*$?

17.10. If we allow for the possibility of satiation, the consumer's budget constraint takes the form $\mathbf{px}_i \leq \mathbf{p\omega}_i$. Walras' law then becomes $\mathbf{pz}(\mathbf{p}) \leq 0$ for all $\mathbf{p} \geq 0$. Show that the proof of existence of a Walrasian equilibrium given in the text still applies for this generalized form of Walras' law.

17.11. Person A has a utility function of $u_A(x_1, x_2) = x_1 + x_2$ and person B has a utility function $u_B(x_1, x_2) = \max(x_1, x_2)$. Agent A and agent B have identical endowments of $(1/2, 1/2)$.

(a) Illustrate this situation in an Edgeworth box diagram.

(b) What is the equilibrium relationship between p_1 and p_2?

(c) What is the equilibrium allocation?

CHAPTER 18

PRODUCTION

The previous chapter dealt only with a pure exchange economy. In this chapter we will describe how one extends such a general equilibrium model to an economy with production. First we will discuss how to model firm behavior, then how to model consumer behavior, and finally how the basic existence and efficiency theorems need to be modified.

18.1 Firm behavior

We will use the representation for technologies described in Chapter 1. If there are k goods, then a net output vector for firm j is a k-vector $\mathbf{y}_j$, and the set of feasible net output vectors—the production possibilities set—for firm j is Y_j. Recall that a net output vector has negative entries for net inputs and positive entries indicating net outputs. Examples of production possibilities sets are described in Chapter 1.

We will deal exclusively with competitive, price-taking firms in this chapter. If $\mathbf{p}$ is a vector of prices of the various goods, $\mathbf{p}\mathbf{y}_j$ is the profit associated with the production plan $\mathbf{y}_j$. Firm j is assumed to choose a production plan $\mathbf{y}_j^*$ that maximizes profits.

In Chapter 2 we dealt with the consequences of this model of behavior. There we described the idea of the net supply function $\mathbf{y}_j(\mathbf{p})$ of a competitive firm. This is simply the function that associates to each vector $\mathbf{p}$ the profit-maximizing net output vector at those prices. Under certain assumptions the net supply function of an individual firm will be well-defined and nicely behaved. If we have m firms, the **aggregate net supply function** will be $\mathbf{y}(\mathbf{p}) = \sum_{j=1}^{m} \mathbf{y}_j(\mathbf{p})$. If the individual net supply functions are well-defined and continuous functions then the aggregate net supply function is well-defined and continuous.

We can also consider the **aggregate production possibilities set**, Y. This set indicates all feasible net output vectors for the economy as a whole. This aggregate production possibilities set is the sum of the individual production possibility sets so that we can write

$$Y = \sum_{j=1}^{m} Y_j.$$

It is a good idea to remind yourself of what this notation means. A production plan $\mathbf{y}$ is in Y if and only if $\mathbf{y}$ can be written as

$$\mathbf{y} = \sum_{j=1}^{m} \mathbf{y}_j,$$

where each production plan $\mathbf{y}_j$ is in Y_j. Hence, Y represents all production plans that can be achieved by some distribution of production among the firms $j = 1, \ldots, m$.

Aggregate profit maximization. *An aggregate production plan,* $\mathbf{y}$, *maximizes aggregate profit, if and only if each firm's production plan* $\mathbf{y}_j$ *maximizes its individual profit.*

Proof. Suppose that $\mathbf{y} = \sum_{j=1}^{m} \mathbf{y}_j$ maximizes aggregate profit but some firm k could have higher profits by choosing $\mathbf{y}'_k$. Then aggregate profits could be higher by choosing the same plan $\mathbf{y}'_k$ for firm k and doing exactly what was done before for the other firms.

Conversely, let $(\mathbf{y}_j)$ for $j = 1, \ldots, m$ be a set of profit-maximizing production plans for the individual firms. Suppose that $\mathbf{y} = \sum_{j=1}^{m} \mathbf{y}_j$ is not profit-maximizing at prices $\mathbf{p}$. This means that there is some other production plan $\mathbf{y}' = \sum_{j=1}^{m} \mathbf{y}'_j$ with $\mathbf{y}'_j$ in Y_j that has higher profits:

$$\sum_{j=1}^{m} \mathbf{p}\mathbf{y}'_j = \mathbf{p}\sum_{j=1}^{m} \mathbf{y}'_j > \mathbf{p}\sum_{j=1}^{m} \mathbf{y}_j = \sum_{j=1}^{m} \mathbf{p}\mathbf{y}_j.$$

But by inspecting the sums on each side of this inequality, we see that some individual firm must have higher profits at $\mathbf{y}'_j$ than at $\mathbf{y}_j$. ∎

The proposition says that if each firm maximizes profits, then aggregate profits must be maximized, and, conversely, that if aggregate profits are maximized, then each firm's profits must be maximized. The argument follows from the assumption that aggregate production possibilities are simply the sum of the individual firms' production possibilities.

It follows from this proposition that there are two ways to construct the aggregate net supply function: either add up the individual firms' net supply functions, or add up the individual firms' production sets and then determine the net supply function that maximizes profits on this aggregate production set. Either way leads to the same function.

18.2 Difficulties

It is convenient to assume that the aggregate net supply function is well-behaved, but a more detailed analysis would derive this from underlying properties of the production sets. If production sets are strictly convex and suitably bounded, it is not hard to show that the net supply functions will be well-behaved. Conversely, if the production sets have nonconvex regions this will lead to discontinuities in the net supply "functions." The quotes are to emphasize the fact that in the presence of nonconvexities demand functions will not be well-defined; at some prices there may be several profit-maximizing bundles. If the discontinuities are "small" this may not matter much, but it is hard to make general statements.

The in-between case is the constant-returns-to-scale case. We've already seen in Chapter 2 that the net supply behavior in this case may be rather unpleasant: zero, infinity, or a whole range of outputs may be supplied, depending on the prices. Despite this apparently bad behavior, the net supply "functions" associated with constant-returns-to-scale technologies turn out to depend more-or-less continuously on prices.

The first point to make is that net supply "functions" will not be functions at all. The definition of a function requires that there be a *unique* point in the range associated with each point in the domain. If the production set exhibits constant returns to scale, then if some net output vector $\mathbf{y}$ yields maximal profits of zero, then so does $t\mathbf{y}$ for any $t \geq 0$. Hence there is an infinity of bundles that are optimal net supplies.

Mathematically, this is handled by defining a type of generalized function called a **correspondence**. A correspondence associates with each point in its domain a *set* of points in its range. If the set of points is convex, then we say that we have a **convex correspondence.** Of course a function is a special case of a convex correspondence.

It is not hard to show that if the production set is convex, then the net supply correspondence is a convex correspondence. Furthermore, it turns out that the net supply correspondence changes in an appropriately continuous way as prices change. Almost all the results for net supply functions that we use in this chapter can be extended to the case of correspondences. Interested readers may consult the references at the end of the chapter for details. However, we will limit our analysis to the case of net supply functions in order to keep the discussion as simple as possible.

18.3 Consumer behavior

Production introduces two new complications into our model of consumer behavior: labor supply and profit distribution.

Labor supply

In the pure exchange model the consumer was assumed to own some initial endowment $\boldsymbol{w}_i$ of commodities. If the consumer sells this vector of commodities, he receives an income of $\mathbf{p}\boldsymbol{w}_i$. It is immaterial whether the consumer sells his entire bundle and buys some goods back, or whether he sells only part of his bundle. The observed amount of income may differ, but the economic income is the same.

If we introduce labor into the model, we introduce a new possibility: consumers can supply different amounts of labor depending on the wage rates.

We examined a simple model of labor supply in Chapter 9, page 145. In that model the consumer has $\overline{L}$ of "time" available which he has to divide between labor, ℓ, and leisure, $L = \overline{L} - \ell$. The consumer cares about leisure, L, and a consumption good, c. The price of labor—the wage rate—is denoted by w and the price of the consumption good is denoted by p. The consumer may already own an endowment of the consumption good $\overline{c}$, which contributes to his nonlabor income.

We can write the consumer's maximization problem as

$$\max u(c, L)$$
$$\text{such that } pc = p\overline{c} + w(\overline{L} - L).$$

It is often more convenient to write the budget constraint as

$$pc + wL = p\overline{c} + w\overline{L}.$$

The second way of writing the budget constraint treats leisure as just another good: one has an endowment of it, $\overline{L}$, and one "sells" the endowment to a firm at a price w, then "buys back" some of the leisure at the same price w.

The same strategy can be used in the more complex case where the consumer has many different types of labor. For any vector of prices of goods and labor, the consumer can consider selling off his or her endowment and then buying back the desired bundle of goods and leisure. When we view the labor supply problem in this way, we see that it fits exactly into the previous model of consumer behavior. Given an endowment vector $\boldsymbol{\omega}$ and a price vector $\mathbf{p}$, the consumer solves the problem

$$\max u(\mathbf{x})$$
$$\text{such that } \mathbf{px} = \mathbf{p}\boldsymbol{\omega}.$$

The only complication is that there are now more constraints on the problem; for example, the total amount of leisure consumed has to be less than 24 hours a day. Formally, such constraints can be incorporated into the definition of the consumption set described in Chapter 7, page 94.

Distribution of profits

We now turn to the question of profit distribution. In a capitalist economy, consumers own firms and are entitled to a share of the profits. We will summarize this ownership relation by a set of numbers (T_{ij}), where T_{ij} represents consumer i's share of the profits of firm j. For any firm j we require that $\sum_{i=1}^{n} T_{ij} = 1$, so that it is completely owned by individual consumers. We will take the ownership relations as being historically given, although more complicated models can incorporate the existence of a stock market for shares.

At a price vector $\mathbf{p}$ each firm j will choose a production plan that will yield a profit of $\mathbf{py}_j(\mathbf{p})$. The total profit income received by consumer i is just the sum of the profits he receives from each of the firms: $\sum_{j=1}^{m} T_{ij}\mathbf{py}_j(\mathbf{p})$. The budget constraint of the consumer now becomes

$$\mathbf{px}_i = \mathbf{p}\boldsymbol{\omega}_i + \sum_{j=1}^{m} T_{ij}\mathbf{py}_j(\mathbf{p}).$$

We assume that the consumer will choose a utility-maximizing bundle that satisfies this budget constraint. Hence, consumer i's demand function can be written as a function of the price vector $\mathbf{p}$. Again it is necessary to make an assumption of strict convexity of preferences to ensure $\mathbf{x}_i(\mathbf{p})$ is a (single-valued) function. However, we have seen in Chapter 9 that under such an assumption $\mathbf{x}_i(\mathbf{p})$ will be continuous, at least at strictly positive prices and income.

18.4 Aggregate demand

Adding together all of the consumers' demand functions gives the aggregate consumer demand function $\mathbf{X}(\mathbf{p}) = \sum_{i=1}^{n} \mathbf{x}_i(\mathbf{p})$. The aggregate supply vector comes from adding together the aggregate supply from consumers, which we denote by $\boldsymbol{\omega} = \sum_{i=1}^{n} \boldsymbol{\omega}_i$, and the aggregate net supply of firms, $\mathbf{Y}(\mathbf{p})$. Finally, we define the aggregate excess demand function by

$$\mathbf{z}(\mathbf{p}) = \mathbf{X}(\mathbf{p}) - \mathbf{Y}(\mathbf{p}) - \boldsymbol{\omega}.$$

Notice that the sign convention for supplied commodities works out nicely: a component of $\mathbf{z}(\mathbf{p})$ is negative if the relevant commodity is in net excess supply and positive if the commodity is in net excess demand.

An important part of the existence argument in a pure exchange economy was the application of Walras' law. Here is how Walras' law works in an economy with production.

Walras' law.   *If* $\mathbf{z}(\mathbf{p})$ *is as defined above, then* $\mathbf{pz}(\mathbf{p}) = 0$ *for all* $\mathbf{p}$.

Proof. We expand $\mathbf{z}(\mathbf{p})$ according to its definition.

$$\mathbf{pz}(\mathbf{p}) = \mathbf{p}\left[\mathbf{X}(\mathbf{p}) - \mathbf{Y}(\mathbf{p}) - \boldsymbol{\omega}\right]$$

$$= \mathbf{p}\left[\sum_{i=1}^{n} \mathbf{x}_i(\mathbf{p}) - \sum_{j=1}^{m} \mathbf{y}_j(\mathbf{p}) - \sum_{i=1}^{n} \boldsymbol{\omega}_i\right]$$

$$= \sum_{i=1}^{n} \mathbf{p}\mathbf{x}_i(\mathbf{p}) - \sum_{j=1}^{m} \mathbf{p}\mathbf{y}_j(\mathbf{p}) - \sum_{i=1}^{n} \mathbf{p}\boldsymbol{\omega}_i.$$

The budget constraint of the consumer is $\mathbf{p}\mathbf{x}_i = \mathbf{p}\boldsymbol{\omega}_i + \sum_{j=1}^{m} T_{ij}\mathbf{p}\mathbf{y}_j(\mathbf{p})$. Making this replacement

$$\mathbf{pz}(\mathbf{p}) = \sum_{i=1}^{n} \mathbf{p}\boldsymbol{\omega}_i + \sum_{i=1}^{n}\sum_{j=1}^{m} T_{ij}\mathbf{p}\mathbf{y}_j(\mathbf{p}) - \sum_{j=1}^{m} \mathbf{p}\mathbf{y}_j(\mathbf{p}) - \sum_{i=1}^{n} \mathbf{p}\boldsymbol{\omega}_i$$

$$= \sum_{j=1}^{m} \mathbf{p}\mathbf{y}_j(\mathbf{p})\sum_{i=1}^{n} T_{ij} - \sum_{j=1}^{m} \mathbf{p}\mathbf{y}_j(\mathbf{p})$$

$$= \sum_{j=1}^{m} \mathbf{p}\mathbf{y}_j(\mathbf{p}) - \sum_{j=1}^{m} \mathbf{p}\mathbf{y}_j(\mathbf{p}) = 0,$$

since $\sum_{i=1}^{n} T_{ij} = 1$ for each j. ∎

Walras' law holds for the same reason that it holds in the pure exchange case: each consumer satisfies his budget constraint, so the economy as a whole has to satisfy an aggregate budget constraint.

18.5 Existence of an equilibrium

If $z(p)$ is a continuous function defined on the price simplex that satisfies Walras' law, the argument of Chapter 17 can be applied to show that there exists a p^* such that $z(p^*) \leq 0$. We have seen that continuity follows if the production possibilities set for each firm is strictly convex. It is not too hard to see that we only need to have the *aggregate* production possibilities set convex. Even if the individual firms have technologies that exhibit slight nonconvexities, such as a small region of increasing returns to scale, the induced discontinuities may be smoothed out in the aggregate.

Recall that the argument for existence we have sketched here is valid only when we are dealing with demand *functions*. The only serious restriction that this imposes is that it rules out constant-returns-to-scale technologies, which we have argued is a rather important case. Therefore, we will state an existence theorem for the general case and discuss the economic meaning of the assumptions.

Existence of an equilibrium. *An equilibrium exists for an economy if the following assumptions are satisfied:*

(1) Each consumer's consumption set is closed, convex, and bounded below;

(2) There is no satiation consumption bundle for any consumer;

(3) For each consumer $i = 1, \ldots, n$, the sets $\{x_i : x_i \succeq_i x_i'\}$ and $\{x_i : x_i' \succeq_i x_i\}$ are closed;

(4) Each consumer holds an initial endowment vector in the interior of his consumption set;

(5) For each consumer i, if x_i and x_i' are two consumption bundles, then $x_i \succ_i x_i'$ implies $tx_i + (1-t)x_i' \succ_i x_i'$ for any $0 < t < 1$;

(6) For each firm j, 0 is an element of Y_j;

(7) $Y = \sum_{j=1}^{m} Y_j$ is closed and convex;

(8) $Y \cap (-Y) \subset \{0\}$

(9) $Y \supset (-\mathbf{R}_+)$.

Proof. See Debreu (1959). ∎

Although the proof of this theorem is beyond the scope of this book, we can at least make sure we understand the purpose of each assumption. Assumptions (1) and (3) are needed to establish the existence of a utility-maximizing bundle. Assumptions (1)–(5) are needed to establish the continuity of the consumer's demand correspondence.

Assumption (6) is an assumption that a firm can always go out of business: this ensures that equilibrium profits will be nonnegative. Assumption (7) is needed to guarantee continuity of each firm's (multivalued) net supply function. Assumption (8) ensures that production is irreversible in the sense that you can't produce a net output vector **y** and then turn around and use the outputs as inputs and produce all the inputs as outputs. It is used to guarantee the feasible set of allocations will be bounded. Finally, assumption (9) says that any production plan that uses all goods as inputs is feasible; this is essentially an assumption of free disposal; it implies that the equilibrium prices will be nonnegative.

18.6 Welfare properties of equilibrium

An allocation $(\mathbf{x}, \mathbf{y})$ is feasible if *aggregate* holdings are compatible with the aggregate supply:

$$\sum_{i=1}^{n} \mathbf{x}_i - \sum_{j=1}^{m} \mathbf{y}_j - \sum_{i=1}^{n} \boldsymbol{\omega}_i = \mathbf{0}.$$

As before, a feasible allocation $(\mathbf{x}, \mathbf{y})$ is Pareto efficient if there is no other feasible allocation $(\mathbf{x}', \mathbf{y}')$ such that $\mathbf{x}'_i \succ_i \mathbf{x}_i$ for all $i = 1, \ldots, n$.

First Theorem of Welfare Economics.   *If $(\mathbf{x}, \mathbf{y}, \mathbf{p})$ is a Walrasian equilibrium, then $(\mathbf{x}, \mathbf{y})$ is Pareto efficient.*

Proof. Suppose not, and let $(\mathbf{x}', \mathbf{y}')$ be a Pareto dominating allocation. Then since consumers are maximizing utility we must have

$$\mathbf{p}\mathbf{x}'_i > \mathbf{p}\boldsymbol{\omega}_i + \sum_{j=1}^{m} T_{ij}\mathbf{p}\mathbf{y}_j \quad \text{for all } i = 1, \ldots, n.$$

Summing over the consumers $i = 1, \ldots, n$, we have

$$\mathbf{p}\sum_{i=1}^{n} \mathbf{x}'_i > \sum_{i=1}^{n} \mathbf{p}\boldsymbol{\omega}_i + \sum_{j=1}^{m} \mathbf{p}\mathbf{y}_j.$$

Here we have used the fact that $\sum_{i=1}^{n} T_{ij} = 1$. Now we use the definition of feasibility of $\mathbf{x}'$ and replace $\sum_{i=1}^{n} \mathbf{x}'_i$ by $\sum_{j=1}^{m} \mathbf{y}'_j + \sum_{i=1}^{n} \boldsymbol{\omega}_i$:

$$\mathbf{p}\left[\sum_{j=1}^{m} \mathbf{y}'_j + \sum_{i=1}^{n} \boldsymbol{\omega}_i\right] > \sum_{i=1}^{n} \mathbf{p}\boldsymbol{\omega}_i + \sum_{j=1}^{m} \mathbf{p}\mathbf{y}_j$$

$$\sum_{j=1}^{m} \mathbf{p}\mathbf{y}'_j > \sum_{j=1}^{m} \mathbf{p}\mathbf{y}_j.$$

But this says that aggregate profits for the production plans $(\mathbf{y}'_j)$ are greater than aggregate profits for the production plans $(\mathbf{y}_j)$ which contradicts profit maximization by firms. ∎

The other basic welfare theorem is just about as easy. We will content ourselves with a sketch of the proof.

Second Theorem of Welfare Economics. *Suppose* $(\mathbf{x}^*, \mathbf{y}^*)$ *is a Pareto efficient allocation in which each consumer holds strictly positive amounts of each good, and that preferences are convex, continuous, and strongly monotonic. Suppose firms' production possibility sets,* Y_j, *for* $j = 1, \ldots, m$ *are convex. Then there exists a price vector* $\mathbf{p} \geq \mathbf{0}$ *such that:*

(1) if $\mathbf{x}'_i \succ_i \mathbf{x}^*_i$, *then* $\mathbf{p}\mathbf{x}'_i > \mathbf{p}\mathbf{x}^*_i$ *for* $i = 1, \ldots, n$;

(2) if $\mathbf{y}'_j$ *is in* Y_j, *then* $\mathbf{p}\mathbf{y}^*_j \geq \mathbf{p}\mathbf{y}'_j$ *for* $j = 1, \ldots, m$.

Proof. (Sketch) As before, let P be the set of all aggregate preferred bundles. Let F be the set of all *feasible* aggregate bundles; that is,

$$F = \left\{ \boldsymbol{\omega} + \sum_{j=1}^{m} \mathbf{y}_j : \mathbf{y}_j \text{ is in } Y_j \right\}.$$

Then F and P are both convex sets, and, since $(\mathbf{x}^*, \mathbf{y}^*)$ is Pareto efficient, F and P are disjoint. We can therefore apply the separating hyperplane theorem in Chapter 26, page 483, and find a price vector $\mathbf{p}$ such that

$$\mathbf{p}\mathbf{z}' \geq \mathbf{p}\mathbf{z}'' \text{ for all } \mathbf{z}' \text{ in } P \text{ and } \mathbf{z}'' \text{ in } F.$$

Monotonicity of preferences implies that $\mathbf{p} \geq \mathbf{0}$. We can use the construction given in the pure exchange proof to show that at these prices each consumer is maximizing preferences and each firm is maximizing profits. ∎

The above proposition shows that every Pareto efficient allocation can be achieved by a suitable reallocation of "wealth." We determine the allocation $(\mathbf{x}^*, \mathbf{y}^*)$ that we want, then determine the relevant prices $\mathbf{p}$. If we give consumer i income $\mathbf{p}\mathbf{x}^*_i$, he or she will not want to change his or her consumption bundle.

We can interpret this result in several ways: first, we can think of the state as confiscating the consumers' original endowments of goods and leisure and redistributing the endowments in some way compatible with the desired income redistribution. Notice that this redistribution may involve a redistribution of goods, profit shares, and leisure.

On the other hand, we can think of consumers as keeping their original endowments but being subject to a lump sum tax. This tax is unlike usual taxes in that it is levied on "potential" income rather than "realized" income; that is, the tax is levied on endowments of labor rather than on labor sold. The consumer has to pay the tax regardless of his actions. In a pure economic sense, taxing an agent by a lump sum tax and giving the proceeds to another agent is the same as giving some of the first agent's labor to the other agent and letting him sell it at the going wage rate.

Of course, agents may differ in ability, or—equivalently—in their endowments of various kinds of potential labor. In practice it may be very difficult to observe such differences in ability so as to know how to levy the appropriate lump sum taxes. There are substantial problems involved in efficient redistribution of income when abilities vary across individuals.

A revealed preference argument

Here is a simple but somewhat indirect proof of the Second Welfare Theorem based on a revealed preference argument that generalizes the similar theorem given in Chapter 17.

Second Theorem of Welfare Economics. *Suppose that* $(\mathbf{x}^*, \mathbf{y}^*)$ *is a Pareto efficient allocation and that preferences are locally nonsatiated. Suppose further that a competitive equilibrium exists from the initial endowments* $\boldsymbol{\omega}_i = \mathbf{x}_i^*$ *with profit shares* $T_{ij} = 0$ *for all* i *and* j, *and let it be given by* $(\mathbf{p}', \mathbf{x}', \mathbf{y}')$. *Then in fact,* $(\mathbf{p}', \mathbf{x}^*, \mathbf{y}^*)$ *is a competitive equilibrium.*

Proof. Since $\mathbf{x}_i^*$ satisfies each consumer's budget constraint by construction, we must have $\mathbf{x}_i' \succeq_i \mathbf{x}_i^*$. Since $\mathbf{x}^*$ is Pareto efficient, this implies that $\mathbf{x}_i' \sim_i \mathbf{x}_i^*$. Thus, if $\mathbf{x}_i'$ provides maximum utility on the budget set, so does $\mathbf{x}_i^*$.

Due to the nonsatiation assumption, each agent will satisfy his budget constraint with equality so that

$$\mathbf{p}'\mathbf{x}_i' = \mathbf{p}'\mathbf{x}_i^* \qquad i = 1, \ldots, n.$$

Summing over the agents $i = 1, \ldots, n$ and using feasibility, we have

$$\mathbf{p}'\left(\sum_{j=1}^{m} \mathbf{y}_j' + \sum_{i=1}^{n} \boldsymbol{\omega}_i\right) = \mathbf{p}'\left(\sum_{j=1}^{m} \mathbf{y}_j^* + \sum_{i=1}^{n} \boldsymbol{\omega}_i\right),$$

or

$$\mathbf{p}'\sum_{j=1}^{m} \mathbf{y}_j' = \mathbf{p}'\sum_{j=1}^{m} \mathbf{y}_j^*.$$

Hence, if $\mathbf{y}'$ maximizes aggregate profits, then $\mathbf{y}^*$ maximizes aggregate profits. By the usual argument, each individual firm must be maximizing profits. ∎

This proposition states that if an equilibrium *exists* from the Pareto efficient allocation $(\mathbf{x}^*, \mathbf{y}^*)$, then $(\mathbf{x}^*, \mathbf{y}^*)$ is *itself* a competitive equilibrium. We may well ask what is required for an equilibrium to exist. According to the earlier discussion concerning existence, two assumptions are sufficient: (1) that all demand functions be continuous; and (2) that Walras' law be satisfied. The continuity of demand will follow from the convexity of preferences and production sets. Walras' law can be checked by the following calculation:

$$\mathbf{pz}(\mathbf{p}) = \mathbf{pX}(\mathbf{p}) - \mathbf{p}\omega - \mathbf{pY}(\mathbf{p})$$
$$= \mathbf{pX}(\mathbf{p}) - \mathbf{pX}^* - \mathbf{pY}(\mathbf{p})$$
$$= 0 - \mathbf{pY}(\mathbf{p}) \le 0.$$

We see in this model that the value of excess demand is always nonpositive. This occurs because we did not give the consumers a share of the firms' profits. Since these profits are being "thrown away," the value of excess demand may well be negative. However, an inspection of the proof of the existence of equilibrium in Chapter 17, page 321, shows that we didn't really need to use the assumption that $\mathbf{pz}(\mathbf{p}) \equiv 0$; it is enough to have $\mathbf{pz}(\mathbf{p}) \le 0$.

This result shows that the crucial conditions for the second welfare theorem are simply the conditions that a competitive equilibrium exists—i.e., the convexity conditions.

18.7 Welfare analysis in a productive economy

It should come as no surprise that the analysis of welfare maximization in a productive economy proceeds in much the same way as in the pure exchange case. The only real issue is how to describe the feasible set of allocations in the case of production.

The easiest way is to use the transformation function mentioned in Chapter 1, page 4. Recall that this is a function that picks out efficient production plans in the sense that $\mathbf{y}$ is an efficient production plan if and only if $T(\mathbf{y}) = 0$. It turns out that nearly any reasonable technology can be described by means of a transformation function.[1]

The welfare maximization problem can then be written as

$$\max W(u_1(\mathbf{x}_1), \ldots, u_n(\mathbf{x}_n))$$
$$\text{such that } T(X^1, \ldots, X^k) = 0.$$

---

[1] We can incorporate the resource endowments into the definition of the transformation function.

where $X^g = \sum_{i=1}^{n} x_i^g$ for $g = 1, \ldots, k$. The Lagrangian for this problem is

$$\mathcal{L} = W(u_1(\mathbf{x}_1), \ldots, u_n(\mathbf{x}_n)) - \lambda T(\mathbf{X}) = 0,$$

and the first-order conditions are

$$\frac{\partial W}{\partial u_i} \frac{\partial u_i(\mathbf{x}_i^*)}{\partial x_i^g} - \lambda \frac{\partial T(\mathbf{X}^*)}{\partial X^g} = 0 \qquad i = 1, \ldots, n$$

$$g = 1, \ldots, k.$$

These conditions can be rearranged to yield

$$\frac{\dfrac{\partial u_i(\mathbf{x}_i^*)}{\partial x_i^g}}{\dfrac{\partial u_i(\mathbf{x}_i^*)}{\partial x_i^h}} = \frac{\dfrac{\partial T(\mathbf{X}^*)}{\partial X^g}}{\dfrac{\partial T(\mathbf{X}^*)}{\partial X^h}} \qquad i = 1, \ldots, n$$

$$g = 1, \ldots, k$$
$$h = 1, \ldots, k.$$

The conditions characterizing welfare maximization require that the marginal rate of substitution between each pair of commodities must be equal to the marginal rate of transformation between those commodities.

18.8 Graphical treatment

There is an analog of the Edgeworth box that is very helpful in understanding production and general equilibrium. Suppose that we consider a one-consumer economy. The consumer leads a rather schizophrenic life: on the one hand he is a profit-maximizing producer who produces a consumption good from labor inputs while on the other hand he is a utility-maximizing consumer who owns the profit-maximizing firm. This is sometimes called a **Robinson Crusoe economy**.

In Figure 18.1 we have drawn the production set of the firm. Note that labor is measured as a negative number since it is an input to the production process and that the technology exhibits constant returns to scale.

There is some maximum amount of labor that can be supplied, $\overline{L}$. For simplicity, we assume that the initial endowment of the consumption good is zero. The consumer has preferences over consumption-leisure bundles which are given by the indifference curves in the diagram. What will the equilibrium wage be?

If the real wage is given by the slope of the production set, the consumer's budget set will coincide with the production set. He will demand the bundle that gives him maximal utility. The producer is willing to supply

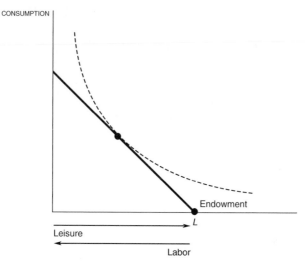

CONSUMPTION

Endowment

L

Leisure

Labor

Figure
18.1

Robinson Crusoe economy with constant returns. Labor is measured as a negative number and the technology exhibits constant returns to scale.

the bundle since he gets zero profits. Hence, both the consumption and the labor markets clear.

Notice the following interesting point: the real wage is determined entirely by the technology while the final production and consumption bundle is determined by consumer demand. This observation can be generalized to the **Nonsubstitution Theorem** which states that, if there is only one nonproduced input to production and the technology exhibits constant returns to scale, then the equilibrium prices are independent of tastes—they are determined entirely by technology. We will prove this theorem in Chapter 18, page 354.

The decreasing returns to scale case is depicted in Figure 18.2. We can find the equilibrium allocation by looking for the points where the marginal rate of substitution equals the marginal rate of transformation. The slope at this point gives us the equilibrium real wage.

Of course, at this real wage the budget line of the consumer does not pass through the endowment point $(0, \overline{L})$. The reason is that the consumer is receiving some profits from the firm. The amount of profits the firm is making, measured in units of the consumption good, is given by the vertical intercept. Since the consumer owns the firm, he receives all of these profits as "nonlabor" income. Thus, his budget set is as indicated, and both markets do indeed clear.

This brings up an interesting point about profits in a general equilibrium model. In the treatment above, we have assumed that the technology exhibits decreasing returns to labor without any particular explanation of why this might be so. A possible reason for such decreasing returns to

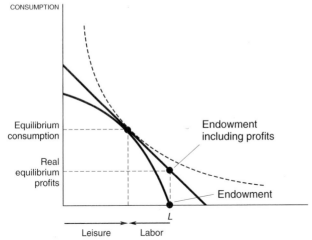

CONSUMPTION

Equilibrium consumption

Real equilibrium profits

Endowment including profits

Endowment

L

Leisure   Labor

Robinson Crusoe economy with decreasing returns. The budget line of the consumer does not pass through $(0, \bar{L})$ since he receives some of the profits from the firm.

Figure 18.2

labor might be the presence of some fixed factor—land, for example. In this interpretation Robinson's production function for consumption depends on the (fixed) land input, T, and the labor input, L. The production function may well exhibit constant returns to scale if we increase both factors of production, but, if we fix the land input and look at output as a function of labor alone, we would presumably see decreasing returns to labor. We have seen in Chapter 1, page 16, that every decreasing-returns-to-scale technology can be thought of as a constant-returns-to-scale technology by postulating a fixed factor.

From this point of view the "profits"—or nonlabor income—can be interpreted as **rent** to the fixed factor. If we do use this interpretation, then profits broadly speaking are zero—the value of the output must be equal to the value of the factors, almost by definition. Whatever is left over is automatically counted as a factor payment, or rent, to the fixed factor.

EXAMPLE: The Cobb-Douglas constant returns economy

Suppose we have one consumer with a Cobb-Douglas utility function for consumption, x, and leisure, R: $u(x, R) = a \ln x + (1 - a) \ln R$. The consumer is endowed with one unit of labor/leisure and there is one firm with a constant-returns-to-scale technology: $x = aL$.

By inspection we see that the equilibrium real wage must be the marginal product of labor; hence, $w^*/p^* = a$. The maximization problem of the consumer is

$$\max\ a \ln x + (1 - a) \ln R$$
$$\text{such that } px + wR = w.$$

In writing the budget constraint, we have used the fact that equilibrium profits are zero. Using the by now familiar result that the demand functions for a Cobb-Douglas utility function have the form $x(p) = am/p$ where m is money income, we find

$$x(p, w) = a \frac{w}{p}$$

$$R(p, w) = (1 - a) \frac{w}{w} = 1 - a.$$

Hence, equilibrium supply of labor is a, and the equilibrium output is a^2.

EXAMPLE: A decreasing-returns-to-scale economy

Suppose the consumer has a Cobb-Douglas utility function as in the last example, but the producer has a production function $x = \sqrt{L}$. We arbitrarily normalize the price of output to be 1. The profit maximization problem is

$$\max\ L^{1/2} - wL.$$

This problem has first-order condition:

$$\frac{1}{2} L^{-\frac{1}{2}} - w = 0.$$

Solving for the firm demand and supply functions,

$$L = (2w)^{-2}$$
$$x = (2w)^{-1}.$$

The profit function is found by substitution:

$$\pi(w) = (2w)^{-1} - w(2w)^{-2}$$
$$= (4w)^{-1}.$$

The income of the consumer now includes profit income so that the demand for leisure is

$$R(w) = \frac{(1 - a)}{w} \left(w + \frac{1}{4w} \right) = (1 - a) \left(1 + \frac{1}{4w^2} \right).$$

By Walras' law we only need find a real wage that clears the labor market:

$$\frac{1}{4w^2} = 1 - (1 - a) \left(1 + \frac{1}{4w^2} \right).$$

Solving this equation, we find

$$w^* = \left(\frac{2-a}{4a}\right)^{1/2}.$$

The equilibrium level of profits is therefore

$$\pi^* = \frac{1}{4}\left(\frac{2-a}{4a}\right)^{-1/2}.$$

Here is an alternative way to solve the same problem. As indicated earlier, the decreasing-returns-to-scale feature of the technology is presumably due to the presence of a fixed factor. Let us call this factor "land" and measure it in units so that the total amount of land is $\overline{T} = 1$. Let the production function be given by $L^{\frac{1}{2}}T^{\frac{1}{2}}$. Note that this function exhibits constant returns to scale and coincides with the original technology when $T = 1$. The price of land will be denoted by q.

The profit maximization problem of the firm is

$$\max L^{1/2}T^{1/2} - wL - qT,$$

which has first-order conditions

$$\frac{1}{2}L^{-1/2}T^{1/2} - w = 0$$

$$\frac{1}{2}L^{1/2}T^{-1/2} - q = 0.$$

In equilibrium the land market will clear so that $T = 1$. Inserting this into the above equations gives

$$L = (2w)^{-2}$$

$$L = (2q)^2.$$

These equations together imply $q = 1/4w$.

The consumer's income now consists of his income from his endowment of labor, $w\overline{L} = w$, plus his income from his endowment of land, $q\overline{T} = q$. His demand for leisure is therefore given by

$$R = (1-a)\frac{m}{w} = (1-a)\frac{(w+q)}{w}.$$

Setting demand for labor equal to supply of labor yields the equilibrium real wage

$$w^* = \left(\frac{2-a}{4a}\right)^{1/2}.$$

The equilibrium rent to land is

$$q^* = \frac{1}{4}\left(\frac{2-a}{4a}\right)^{-1/2}.$$

Note that this is the same as the earlier solution.

18.9 The Nonsubstitution Theorem

Here we will present an argument for the Nonsubstitution Theorem mentioned earlier. We will assume that there are n industries producing outputs y_i, $i = 1, \ldots, n$. Each industry produces only a single output; no joint production is allowed. There is only one nonproduced input to production denoted by y_0. We generally think of this nonproduced good as labor. The prices of the $n + 1$ goods will be denoted by $\mathbf{w} = (w_0, w_1, \ldots, w_n)$.

As usual, the equilibrium prices will only be determined as relative prices. We will assume that labor is a necessary input to each industry. Thus in equilibrium $w_0 > 0$, and we can choose it as numeraire; that is, we can arbitrarily set $w_0 = 1$.

We will assume that the technology exhibits constant returns to scale. We have seen in Chapter 5, page 66, that this implies that each industry's cost function can be written as $c_i(\mathbf{w}, y_i) = c_i(\mathbf{w}) y_i$ for $i = 1, \ldots, n$. The functions $c_i(\mathbf{w})$ are the **unit cost functions**—how much it costs to produce one unit of output at the prices $\mathbf{w}$, measured in terms of the numeraire price w_0.

We also assume that labor is indispensable to production so that the unit factor demand for labor is strictly positive. Using x_i^0 to denote firm i's demand for factor 0 when $y = 1$, we can use the derivative property of the cost function to write

$$x_i^0(\mathbf{w}) = \frac{\partial c_i(\mathbf{w})}{\partial w_0} > 0.$$

Note that this implies that the cost functions are *strictly* increasing in w_0. Since the cost functions strictly increase in at least one of the prices, $c_i(t\mathbf{w}) = tc_i(\mathbf{w}) > c_i(\mathbf{w})$ for $t > 1$.

Nonsubstitution Theorem. *Suppose there is only one nonproduced input to production, this input is indispensable to production, there is no joint production, and the technology exhibits constant returns to scale. Let $(\mathbf{x}, \mathbf{y}, \mathbf{w})$ be a Walrasian equilibrium with $y_i > 0$ for $i = 1, \ldots, n$. Then $\mathbf{w}$ is the unique solution to $w_i = c_i(\mathbf{w})$, $i = 1, \ldots, n$.*

Proof. If $\mathbf{w}$ is an equilibrium price vector in a constant-returns-to-scale economy, then profits must be zero in each industry; that is:

$$w_i y_i - c_i(\mathbf{w}) y_i = 0 \qquad i = 1, \ldots, n.$$

Since $y_i > 0$ for $i = 1, \ldots, n$ this condition can be written as

$$w_i - c_i(\mathbf{w}) = 0 \qquad i = 1, \ldots, n.$$

This says that any equilibrium price vector must satisfy the condition that price equals average cost. Since $w_0 > 0$ and labor is an indispensable factor of production, we must have $c_i(\mathbf{w}) > 0$. This in turn implies that $w_i > 0$ for $i = 0, \ldots, n$. In other words, all equilibrium price vectors are strictly positive.

We will show that there is only one such equilibrium price vector. For suppose $\mathbf{w}'$ and $\mathbf{w}$ were two distinct solutions to the above system of equations. Define

$$t = \frac{w'_m}{w_m} = \max_i \frac{w'_i}{w_i}.$$

Here the maximum ratio of the components of the two vectors occurs at component m at which w'_m is t times as large as w_m.

Suppose that $t > 1$. Then we have the following string of inequalities:

$$w'_m =_1 t w_m =_2 t c_m(\mathbf{w}) =_3 c_m(t\mathbf{w}) >_4 c_m(\mathbf{w}') =_5 w'_m.$$

The justifications for these equalities and inequalities are as follows:

(1) definition of t;

(2) assumption that $\mathbf{w}$ is a solution;

(3) linear homogeneity of cost function;

(4) definition of t, assumption $t > 1$, and strict monotonicity of cost function in the vector of factor prices;

(5) assumption that $\mathbf{w}'$ is a solution.

The result of assuming $t > 1$ is a contradiction, so $t \leq 1$, and thus $\mathbf{w} \geq \mathbf{w}'$. The role of $\mathbf{w}$ and $\mathbf{w}'$ is symmetric in the above argument so we also have $\mathbf{w}' \geq \mathbf{w}$. Putting these two inequalities together, we have $\mathbf{w}' = \mathbf{w}$, as required. ∎

This theorem says that, if there is an equilibrium price vector for the economy, it must be the solution to $w_i = c_i(\mathbf{w})$ for $i = 1, \ldots, n$. The surprising thing is that $\mathbf{w}$ does not depend on demand conditions at all; i.e., $\mathbf{w}$ is completely independent of preferences and endowments.

Let us use the term **technique** to refer to the factor demands necessary to produce one unit of output. Let $\mathbf{w}^*$ be the vector of prices that satisfies the zero-profit conditions. Then we can determine the equilibrium technique for firm i by differentiating the cost function with respect to each of the factor prices j:

$$x_i^j(\mathbf{w}^*) = \frac{\partial c_i(\mathbf{w}^*)}{\partial w_j}.$$

Since the equilibrium prices are independent of demand conditions, the equilibrium choice of technique will be independent of demand conditions. No matter how consumer demands change the firm will not substitute away from the equilibrium technique; this is the reason for the name *nonsubstitution* theorem.

18.10 Industry structure in general equilibrium

Recall that the number of firms is a given in the Walrasian model. In Chapter 13 we argued that the number of firms in an industry was a variable. How can we reconcile these two models?

Let us consider first the constant-returns case. Then we know that the only profit-maximizing level of profits compatible with equilibrium is that of zero profits. Furthermore, at the prices compatible with zero profits, the firms are willing to operate at any level. Hence, the industry structure of the economy is indeterminate—firms are indifferent as to what market share they hold. If the number of firms is a variable, it is also indeterminate.

Consider now the decreasing-returns case. If all technology is decreasing returns, we know that there will be some equilibrium profits. In the general equilibrium model as we have described it up until now, there is no reason to have constant profits across firms. The usual argument for constant profits is that firms will enter the industry with the highest profits; but if the number of firms is fixed this cannot occur.

What would in fact happen if the number of firms were variable? Presumably we would see entry occur. If the technology really exhibits decreasing returns to scale, the optimum size of the firm is infinitesimal, simply because it is always better to have two small firms than one large one. Hence, we would expect continual entry to occur, pushing down the profit level. In long-run equilibrium we would expect to see an infinite number of firms, each operating at an infinitesimal level.

This seems rather implausible. One way out is to return to the argument we mentioned in Chapter 13: if we can always replicate, the only sensible long-run technology is a constant-returns-to-scale technology. Hence, the decreasing-returns-to-scale technology really must be due to the presence of some fixed factor. In this interpretation the equilibrium "profits" should really be regarded as returns to the fixed factor.

Notes

See Samuelson (1951) for the nonsubstitution theorem. The treatment here follows von Weizsäcker (1971).

Exercises

18.1. Consider an economy in which there are two nonproduced factors of production, land and labor, and two produced goods, apples and bandannas. Apples and bandannas are produced with constant returns to scale. Bandannas are produced using labor only, while apples are produced using labor and land. There are N identical people, each of whom has an initial endowment of fifteen units of labor and ten units of land. They all have utility functions of the form $U(A, B) = c \ln A + (1 - c) \ln B$ where $0 < c < 1$ and where A and B are a person's consumption of apples and bandannas, respectively. Apples are produced with a fixed-coefficients technology that uses one unit of labor and one unit of land for each unit of apples produced. Bandannas are produced using labor only. One unit of labor is required for each bandanna produced. Let labor be the *numeraire* for this economy.

(a) Find competitive equilibrium prices and quantities for this economy.

(b) For what values (if any) of the parameter c is it true that small changes in the endowment of land will not change competitive equilibrium prices?

(c) For what values (if any) of the parameter c is it true that small changes in the endowment of land will not change competitive equilibrium consumptions?

18.2. Consider an economy with two firms and two consumers. Firm 1 is entirely owned by consumer 1. It produces guns from oil via the production function $g = 2x$. Firm 2 is entirely owned by consumer 2; it produces butter from oil via the production function $b = 3x$. Each consumer owns 10 units of oil. Consumer 1's utility function is $u(g, b) = g^{.4} b^{.6}$ and consumer 2's utility function is $u(g, b) = 10 + .5 \ln g + .5 \ln b$.

(a) Find the market clearing prices for guns, butter, and oil.

(b) How many guns and how much butter does each consumer consume?

(c) How much oil does each firm use?

CHAPTER **19**

TIME

In this chapter we discuss some topics having to do with the behavior of a consumer and an economy over time. As we will see, behavior over time can, in some cases, be regarded as a simple extension of the static model discussed earlier. However, time also imposes some interesting special structure on preferences and markets. Given the inherent uncertainty of the future, it is natural to examine some issues involving uncertainty as well.

19.1 Intertemporal preferences

Our standard theory of consumer choice is perfectly adequate to describe intertemporal choice. The objects of choice—the consumption bundles—will now be streams of consumption over time. We assume that the consumer has preferences over these consumption streams that satisfy the usual regularity conditions. It follows from the standard considerations that there will generally exist a utility function that will represent those preferences.

However, just as in the case of expected utility maximization, the fact that we are considering a particular kind of choice problem will imply that the preferences have a special structure that generates utility functions of a particular form. One particularly popular choice is a utility function that is additive over time, so that

$$U(c_1, \ldots, c_T) = \sum_{t=1}^{T} u_t(c_t).$$

Here $u_t(c_t)$ is the utility of consumption in period t. This function can also be further specialized to the time-stationary form

$$U(c_1, \ldots, c_T) = \sum_{t=1}^{T} \alpha^t u(c_t).$$

In this case we use the same utility function in each period; however, period t's utility is multiplied by a **discount factor** α^t.

Note the close analogy with the expected utility structure. In that model, the consumer has the same utility in each state of nature, and the utility in each state of nature was multiplied by the probability that that state would occur. Indeed, a mechanical rewording of the axioms of expected utility theory can be used to justify time-additive utility functions of this sort in terms of restrictions on the underlying preferences.

Suppose that consumption possibilities in the future are uncertain. As we've seen earlier, a natural set of axioms implies that we can choose a representation of utility that is additive across states of nature. However, it may easily be the case that one monotonic transform of utility is additive across states of nature and a *different* monotonic transform is additive across time. There is no reason that there should be one representation of preferences that is additive for both intertemporal and uncertain choices. Despite this, the most common specification is to assume that the intertemporal utility function is additive across both time and states of nature. This is not particularly realistic, but it does make for simpler calculations.

19.2 Intertemporal optimization with two periods

We have studied a simple two-period portfolio optimization model in Chapter 11, page 184. Here we investigate how to extend this model to several periods. This example serves to illustrate the method of **dynamic programming**, a technique for solving multi-period optimization problems by breaking them into two-period optimization problems.

We first review the two-period model. Denote consumption in each of the two periods by (c_1, c_2). The consumer has an initial endowment of w_1 in period 1, and can invest his wealth in two assets. One asset pays a certain return of R_0; the other asset pays a *random* return of $\tilde{R}_1$. It is convenient to think of these returns as *total* returns; that is, one plus the rate of return.

Suppose that the consumer decides to consume c_1 in the first period and to invest a fraction x of his wealth in the risky asset and a fraction $1 - x$ in the certain asset. In this portfolio the consumer has $(w_1 - c_1)x$ dollars earning a return $\tilde{R}_1$ and $(w_1 - c_1)(1 - x)$ dollars earning a return R_0. Therefore, his second-period wealth—which equals his second-period consumption—is

$$\tilde{w}_2 = \tilde{c}_2 = (w_1 - c_1)[\tilde{R}_1 x + R_0(1 - x)] = (w_1 - c_1)\tilde{R}.$$

Here $\tilde{R} = \tilde{R}_1 x + R_0(1 - x)$ is the consumer's **portfolio return**. Note that it is, in general, a random variable since $\tilde{R}_1$ is a random variable.

Since the portfolio return is uncertain, the consumer's second-period consumption is uncertain. We suppose that the consumer has a utility function of the form

$$U(c_1, \tilde{c}_2) = u(c_1) + \alpha E u(\tilde{c}_2),$$

where $\alpha < 1$ is a discount factor.

Let $V_1(w_1)$ be the maximum utility the consumer can achieve if he has wealth w_1 in period 1:

$$V_1(w_1) = \max_{c_1, x} \ u(c_1) + \alpha E u[(w_1 - c_1)\tilde{R}]. \qquad (19.1)$$

The function $V_1(w_1)$ is essentially an indirect utility: it gives maximized utility as a function of wealth.

Differentiating equation (19.1) with respect to c_1 and x, we have the first-order conditions

$$u'(c_1) = \alpha E u'(\tilde{c}_2)\tilde{R} \qquad (19.2)$$
$$E u'(\tilde{c}_2)(\tilde{R}_1 - R_0) = 0. \qquad (19.3)$$

Equation (19.2) is an intertemporal optimization condition: it says that the marginal utility of consumption in period 1 must be equal to the discounted expected marginal utility of consumption in period 2. Equation (19.3) is a portfolio optimization condition: it says that the expected marginal utility of moving a small amount of money from the safe to the risky asset should be zero. We analyzed a similar first-order condition in Chapter 11, page 184.

Given these two equations in two unknowns, x and c_1, we can, in principle, solve for the optimal consumption and portfolio choice. We give an example of this below as part of a solution to the T-period problem.

19.3 Intertemporal optimization with several periods

Suppose now that there are T periods. If $(\tilde{c}_1, \ldots, \tilde{c}_T)$ is some (possibly random) stream of consumption, we assume that the consumer evaluates it according to the utility function

$$U(\tilde{c}_1, \ldots, \tilde{c}_T) = \sum_{t=0}^{T} \alpha^t E u(\tilde{c}_t).$$

If the consumer has wealth at time t of w_t, and invests a fraction x_t in the risky asset, his wealth in period $t+1$ is given by

$$\tilde{w}_{t+1} = [w_t - c_t]\tilde{R},$$

where $\tilde{R} = x_t \tilde{R}_1 + (1 - x_t)R_0$ is the (random) portfolio return between period t and $t+1$.

In order to solve this intertemporal optimization problem, we use the method of **dynamic programming** to break it into a sequence of two-period optimization problems. Consider period $T-1$. If the consumer has wealth w_{T-1} at this point, the maximum utility he can get is

$$V_{T-1}(w_{T-1}) = \max_{c_{T-1}, x_{T-1}} u(c_{T-1}) + \alpha Eu[(w_{T-1} - c_{T-1})\tilde{R}]. \qquad (19.4)$$

This is just equation (19.1) with $T-1$ replacing 1. The first-order conditions are

$$u'(c_{T-1}) = \alpha Eu'(\tilde{c}_T)\tilde{R} \qquad (19.5)$$
$$Eu'(\tilde{c}_T)(\tilde{R}_1 - R_0) = 0. \qquad (19.6)$$

We have already seen how to solve this problem, in principle, and determine the indirect utility function $V_{T-1}(w_{T-1})$.

Now go back to period $T-2$. If the consumer chooses (c_{T-2}, x_{T-2}), then in period $T-1$ he will have (random) wealth of

$$\tilde{w}_{T-1} = [w_{T-2} - c_{T-2}]\tilde{R}.$$

From this wealth he will achieve an expected utility of $V_{T-1}(w_{T-1})$. Hence, the consumer's maximization problem at period $T-2$ can be written as

$$V_{T-2}(w_{T-2}) = \max_{c_{T-2}, x_{T-2}} u(c_{T-2}) + \alpha E V_{T-1}[(w_{T-2} - c_{T-2})\tilde{R}].$$

This is just like the problem (19.4), but "second-period" utility is given by the *indirect* utility function $V_{T-1}(w_{T-1})$ rather than the direct utility function.

The first-order conditions for period $T - 2$ are

$$u'(c_{T-2}) - \alpha EV'(\tilde{w}_{T-1})\tilde{R} = 0 \tag{19.7}$$

$$EV'(\tilde{w}_{T-1})(\tilde{R}_1 - R_0) = 0. \tag{19.8}$$

Again (19.7) is an intertemporal optimization condition: the marginal utility of current consumption has to equal the discounted *indirect* marginal utility of future wealth, and (19.8) is a portfolio optimization condition.

We can use these conditions to solve for $V_{T-2}(w_{T-2})$ and so on. Given the indirect utility function $V_t(w_t)$ the T-period intertemporal optimization problem is just a sequence of two-period problems.

EXAMPLE: Logarithmic utility

Suppose that $u(c) = \log c$. Then the first-order conditions (19.5) and (19.6) become

$$\frac{1}{c_{T-1}} = \alpha E \frac{\tilde{R}}{[w_{T-1} - c_{T-1}]\tilde{R}} = \frac{\alpha}{[w_{T-1} - c_{T-1}]} \tag{19.9}$$

$$0 = E\left[\frac{\tilde{R}_1 - R_0}{[w_{T-1} - c_{T-1}]\tilde{R}}\right]. \tag{19.10}$$

Note that the portfolio return cancels out of equation (19.9), a very convenient property of logarithmic utility.

Solving equation (19.9) for c_{T-1}, we have

$$c_{T-1} = \frac{w_{T-1}}{1 + \alpha}.$$

We substitute this into the objective function to determine the indirect utility function:

$$V_{T-1}(w_{T-1}) = \ln\frac{w_{T-1}}{1 + \alpha} + \alpha E \ln\frac{\alpha w_{T-1}\tilde{R}}{1 + \alpha}.$$

Using the properties of the logarithm,

$$V_{T-1}(w_{T-1}) = (1 + \alpha)\ln w_{T-1} + \alpha E \ln \tilde{R} + \alpha \ln \alpha - (1 + \alpha)\ln(1 + \alpha).$$

Note the important feature that the indirect utility function V_{T-1} is logarithmic in wealth. The random return affects V_{T-1} additively; it doesn't influence the *marginal* utility of wealth, and therefore doesn't enter into the appropriate first-order conditions.

It follows that the first-order conditions for period $T - 2$ will have the form

$$\frac{1}{c_{T-2}} = \frac{\alpha(1 + \alpha)}{[w_{T-2} - c_{T-2}]} \tag{19.11}$$

$$0 = E\left[\frac{\tilde{R}_1 - R_0}{[w_{T-2} - c_{T-2}]\tilde{R}}\right]. \tag{19.12}$$

These are very similar to the conditions for period $T-1$; equation (19.11) has an extra factor of $1 + \alpha$ on the right-hand side, and equation (19.12) is exactly the same. It follows from this observation that each period the consumer chooses the same portfolio he would choose if he were solving a two-period problem and that the consumption choice in period $T - 1$ is always proportional to wealth in that period.

19.4 General equilibrium over time

As mentioned earlier, the concept of a good in the Arrow-Debreu general equilibrium model is very general. Goods can be distinguished by any characteristic that agents care about. If agents care about when a good is available, then goods that are available at different times should be re-garded as different goods. If agents care about the circumstances under which goods are available, then goods can be distinguished by the state of nature in which they will be provided.

When we distinguish goods in these ways, we can understand the role of equilibrium prices in new and deeper ways. For example, let us con-sider a simple general equilibrium model with one good, consumption, that is available at different times $t = 1, \ldots, T$. In light of the preceeding re-marks, we view this good as being T different goods, and let c_t indicate consumption available at time t.

In a pure exchange model, agent i would be endowed with some con-sumption at time t, $\bar{c}_{it}$. In a production model, there would be a technol-ogy available to transform consumption at time t into consumption at other times in the future. By sacrificing consumption at one time, the consumer can enjoy consumption at some future time.

Agents have preferences over consumption streams, and there are mar-kets available for trading consumption at different points of time. One way that such markets might be organized is through the use of **Arrow-Debreu securities**. These are securities of a special form: security t pays off \$1 when date t arrives and zero at every other date. Securities of this sort exist in the real world; they are known as **pure discount bonds**. A pure discount bond pays off a certain amount of money (e.g., \$10,000) at a particular date.

This model has all the pieces of the standard Arrow-Debreu model: preferences, endowments, and markets. We can apply the standard existence results to show that there must exist equilibrium prices (p_t) for the Arrow-Debreu securities that clear all markets. Note that p_t is the price paid at time zero for the delivery of the consumption good at time t. In this model all the financial transaction take place at the beginning and consumption is carried out over time.

In real-life intertemporal markets we often use a different way to measure future prices, namely **interest rates**. Imagine that there is a bank that offers the following arrangement: for each dollar it receives at time 0 it will pay $1 + r_t$ dollars at time t. We say that the bank is offering an interest rate of r_t. What is the relationship between the interest rate r_t and the Arrow-Debreu price p_t?

Suppose that some agent holds one dollar at time 0. He may invest it in the bank, in which case he gets $1 + r_t$ dollars at time t. Alternatively, he may invest the dollar in Arrow-Debreu security t. If the price of Arrow-Debreu security t is p_t, then he can buy $1/p_t$ units of it. Since each unit of this security will be worth $1 at time t, it follows that he will have $1/p_t$ dollars at time t. Clearly, the amount of money that the agent will have at time t must be the same regardless of which investment plan he follows; hence,

$$1 + r_t = \frac{1}{p_t}.$$

This means that interest rates are just the reciprocals of the Arrow-Debreu prices, minus 1.

We can use Arrow-Debreu prices to value consumption streams in the usual way. For example, the budget constraint of a consumer takes the form

$$\sum_{t=1}^{T} p_t c_t = \sum_{t=1}^{T} p_t \bar{c}_t.$$

Using the relationship between prices and interest rates, we can also write this as

$$\sum_{t=1}^{T} \frac{c_t}{1 + r_t} = \sum_{t=1}^{T} \frac{\bar{c}_t}{1 + r_t}.$$

Hence, the budget constraint takes the form that the **discounted present value** of consumption must equal the discounted present value of the endowment.

Given that the setup is exactly the same as the standard Arrow-Debreu model described earlier, the same theorems hold: under various convexity assumptions equilibrium will exist and be Pareto efficient.

Infinity

In many applications it does not seem appropriate to use a finite time horizon, since agents might reasonably expect an economy to continue "indefinitely." However, if an infinite time period is used, certain difficulties arise with the existence and welfare theorems.

The first set of problems are technical ones: what is the appropriate definition of a continuous function with an infinite number of arguments? What is an appropriate fixed point theorem or separating hyperplane theorem? These questions can be addressed using various mathematical tools; most of the issues that arise are purely technical in nature.

However, there are also some fundamental peculiarities of models with an infinite number of time periods. Perhaps the most famous example comes in the **overlapping generations model**, which is also known as the **pure consumption-loan model**. Consider an economy with the following structure. Each period, n agents are born, each of whom lives for two time periods. Hence, at any time after the first period $2n$ agents are alive: n young agents and n old agents. Each agent has an endowment of 2 units of consumption when he is born, and is indifferent between consumption when he is young and when he is old.

In this simple case there is no problem with existence of equilibrium. Clearly one equilibrium is for each agent to consume his endowment. This equilibrium is supported by prices $p_t = 1$ for all t. However, it turns out that this equilibrium is not Pareto efficient!

To see this, suppose that each member of generation $t + 1$ transfers one unit of its endowment to generation t. Now generation 1 is better off since it receives 3 units of consumption in its lifetime. None of the other generations are worse off since they are compensated when they are old for the transfers they made when they were young. This means that we have found a Pareto improvement on the original equilibrium!

It is worthwhile thinking about what goes wrong with the argument for the First Welfare Theorem in the model. The problem is that there are an infinite number of goods; if the equilibrium prices are all 1, then the value of both the aggregate consumption stream and the aggregate endowment is infinite. The contradiction in the last step of the proof of the First Welfare Theorem no longer holds, and the proof fails.

This example is very simple, but the phenomenon is quite robust. One should be very careful in extrapolating results of models with finite horizons to models with infinite horizons.

19.5 General equilibrium over states of nature

We have remarked earlier that agents may care about the circumstances, or **state of nature** under which goods become available. After all, an umbrella when it is raining is a very different good than when it is not raining!

Let us suppose that markets are open at time 0, but there is some uncertainty about what will happen at time 1, when the trades are actually supposed to be carried out. To be specific, suppose that there are two possible states of nature at time 1, either it rains or it shines.

Suppose that agents issue **contingent contracts** of the form: "Agent i will deliver one unit of good j to the holder of this contract if and only if it rains." The trade at time 0 is trade in *contracts*, that is, promises to provide some good or service in the future, if some state of nature prevails.

We can imagine that there is a market in these contracts and that at any price vector for the contracts, agents can consult their preferences and their technologies and determine how much they wish to demand and supply of the various contracts. Note that contracts are traded and paid for at time 0 but will only be exercised at time 1 if the appropriate state of the world occurs. As usual an equilibrium price vector is one where there is no excess demand for any contract. From the viewpoint of the abstract theory the contracts are just goods like any other goods. The standard existence and efficiency results apply.

It is important to understand the efficiency result correctly. Preferences are defined over the space of lotteries. If the von Neumann-Morgenstern axioms are met, the preferences over random events can be summarized by an expected utility function. To say that there is no other feasible allocation that makes all consumers better off is to say that there is no pattern of contingent contracts that increases each agent's *expected utility*.

There are real-life analogs of contingent contracts. Perhaps the most common is insurance contracts. Insurance contracts offer to deliver a certain amount of money if and only if some event occurs. However, it must be admitted that contingent contracts are rather rare in practice.

Notes

See Ingersoll (1987) for several worked-out examples of dynamic portfolio optimization models. Geanakoplos (1987) has a nice survey of the overlapping generations model.

Exercises

19.1. Consider the logarithmic utility example in Chapter 19, page 362. Show that consumption in an arbitrary period t is given by

$$c_t = w_t/[1 + \alpha + \alpha^2 \ldots \alpha^{T-t}] = \frac{1 - \alpha}{1 - \alpha^{T-t+1}} w_t.$$

19.2. Consider the following scheme for "rent stabilization." Each year landlords are allowed to increase their rents by 3/4 of the rate of inflation. Owners of newly constructed apartments can set their initial rent at any price they please. Advocates of this plan claim that since the initial price of new apartments can be set at any level, the supply of new housing will not be discouraged. Let us analyze this claim in a simple model.

Suppose that apartments last for 2 periods. Let r be the nominal rate of interest and π be the rate of inflation. Assume that in the absence of rent stabilization the rent in period 1 will be p and the rent in period 2 will be $(1 + \pi)p$. Let c be the constant marginal cost of constructing new apartments and let the demand function for apartments in each period be given by $D(p)$. Finally, let K be the supply of rent controlled apartments.

(a) In the absence of rent stabilization, what must be the equilibrium relationship between the period 1 rental price p and the marginal cost of constructing a new apartment?

(b) If the rent stabilization plan is adopted, what will this relationship have to be?

(c) Draw a simple supply-demand diagram and illustrate the number of new apartments without rent stabilization.

(d) Will the rent stabilization plan result in more or fewer new apartments being built?

(e) Will the equilibrium price of new apartments be higher or lower under this rent stabilization plan?

CHAPTER **20**

ASSET
MARKETS

The study of asset markets demands a general equilibrium approach. As we will see below, the equilibrium price of a given asset depends critically on how its value correlates with the values of other assets. Hence, the study of multi-asset pricing inherently involves general equilibrium considerations.

20.1 Equilibrium with certainty

In the study of asset markets the focus is on what determines the differences in prices of assets. In a world of certainty, the analysis of asset markets is very simple: the price of an asset is simply the present discounted value of its stream of returns. If this were not so, there would be a possibility for riskless **arbitrage**.

Consider, for example, a two-period model. We suppose that there is some asset that earns a sure **total return** of R_0. That is, one dollar invested in asset 0 today will pay R_0 dollars next period for certain. If R_0 is the total return on asset 0, $r_0 = R_0 - 1$ is the **rate of return**.

There is another asset a that will have a value V_a next period. What will be the equilibrium price of asset a today?

In a world of certainty, the answer to this question is easy: the price of asset a today must be given by its present value,

$$p_a = \frac{V_a}{R_0} = \frac{V_a}{r_0 + 1}. \qquad (20.1)$$

If this were not so, then someone would have a sure way to make money. If $p_a > V_a/R_0$, then anyone who owned asset a could sell one unit and invest the proceeds in the riskless asset. Next period he would have $p_a R_0 > V_a$. Since at least one person would want to sell asset a, it follows that p_a is not an equilibrium price.

Another way to write the equilibrium condition (20.1) is in terms of the return on asset a. The return on asset a is defined by $R_a = V_a/p_a$. If we divide both sides of (20.1) by p_a, and rearrange the resulting expression, we have

$$R_a = \frac{V_a}{p_a} = R_0. \qquad (20.2)$$

This equation simply says that in equilibrium, all assets with a certain return must have the *same* return—since no one would hold an asset that was expected to have a smaller return than another.

20.2 Equilibrium with uncertainty

In a world where asset returns are not certain, the expected returns to assets will differ depending on the riskiness of the asset. Normally, we would think that the riskier the asset, the less one would pay for it, other things being equal. Put another way, this means that the riskier the asset, the higher the expected return has to be in order to induce people to hold that asset.

By analogy to equation (20.2), we can write

$$\overline{R}_a = R_0 + \text{risk premium for asset } a.$$

The left-hand side of this expression is the **expected return** on asset a. The right-hand side is the risk-free return plus the risk premium for asset a. We also can express this condition as

$$\overline{R}_a - R_0 = \text{risk premium for asset } a.$$

The left-hand side of this equation is called the **excess return** on asset a, and the equation asserts that in equilibrium the excess return on each asset is equal to its risk premium.

These equations are, of course, simply definitions. Economic theories of asset markets attempt to derive explicit expressions for the risk premium terms in terms of "fundamentals" such as consumer preferences and the pattern of asset returns.

This analysis involves considerations of general equilibrium since the value of a risky asset inherently depends on the presence or absence of other risky assets which serve as complements or substitutes with the asset in question. Therefore, in most models of asset pricing, the value of an asset ends up depending on how it **covaries** with other assets.

What is surprising is how generally this insight emerges in models that are seemingly very different. In this chapter we will derive and compare several models of asset pricing.

20.3 Notation

We collect here the notation we will use in this chapter. This will make it easy to look back and remind yourself of the definitions of various symbols as needed. Some of the terms will be defined in more detail in the appropriate section.

We will generally consider a two-period model, with the present being period 0. The values of the various assets in period 1 are uncertain. We model this uncertainty using the notion of **states of nature**. That is, we suppose that there are various possible outcomes indexed by $s = 1, \ldots, S$, and the value of each of the assets next period depends on which outcome actually occurs.

i individual investor, $i = 1, \ldots, I$

W_i wealth of investor i in period 0

c_i consumption in period 0

$W_i - c_i$ amount invested in period 0 by investor i

s states of nature $s = 1, \ldots, S$ in the second period

π_s the probability of occurrence of state s. We assume that all consumers have the same probability beliefs; this is the case of **homogeneous expectations**.

C_{is} consumption by individual i in state s in the second period

$\tilde{C}_i$ consumption by individual i in the second period regarded as a random variable

Note that we can view consumption in two different ways: either as the list of possible consumptions in each state of nature, (C_{is}), or as the random variable $\tilde{C}_i$, which takes on the value (C_{is}) with probabilities π_s.

$u_i(c_i) + \delta E u_i(\tilde{C}_i)$ von Neumann-Morgenstern utility function for investor i. Note that we assume that this function is additively separable over time with discount factor δ.

p_a price of asset a for $a = 0, \ldots, A$

X_{ia} amount purchased of asset a by investor i

x_{ia} fraction of investor i's investment wealth that is held in asset a. If W_i is the total amount invested in all assets, $x_{ia} = p_a X_{ia}/W_i$, and therefore $\sum_{a=0}^{A} x_{ia} = 1$.

$(x_{i0}, \ldots, x_{iA})$ portfolio of assets held by investor i. Note that a portfolio is denoted by the fraction of wealth invested in each of the given assets.

V_{as} value of asset a in state of nature s in the second period

$\tilde{V}_a$ value of asset a in the second period regarded as a random variable

R_{as} the (total) return on asset a in state s. By definition, $R_{as} = V_{as}/p_a$.

$\tilde{R}_a$ the total return on asset a regarded as a random variable. The random variable $\tilde{R}_a$ takes on the value R_{as} with probability π_s.

$\overline{R}_a = \sum_{s=1}^{S} \pi_s R_{as} = E\tilde{R}_a$ the expected return on asset a

R_0 the total return on a risk-free asset

$\sigma_{ab} = \text{cov}(\tilde{R}_a, \tilde{R}_b)$ the covariance between the returns on assets a and b

20.4 The Capital Asset Pricing Model

We will analyze the various models of asset markets in roughly historical order, so we start with the grandfather of them all, the celebrated **Capital Asset Pricing Model**, or **CAPM**. The CAPM starts with a particular specification of utility, namely that utility of a random distribution of wealth depends only on the first two moments of the probability distribution, the mean and the variance.

This is compatible with the expected utility model only in certain circumstances; for example, when all assets are Normally distributed, or when the expected utility function is quadratic. However, the mean-variance may serve as a rough approximation to a general utility function in a broader variety of cases. In this context "risk aversion" means that an increase in expected consumption is a good and an increase in the variance of consumption is a bad.

We first derive the budget constraint. A similar budget constraint will be used in several of the models we examine. Omitting the investor subscript

i for notational convenience, second-period consumption is given by

$$\tilde{C} = (W - c) \sum_{a=0}^{A} x_a \tilde{R}_a = (W - c) \left[x_0 R_0 + \sum_{a=1}^{A} x_a \tilde{R}_a \right].$$

Since the portfolio weights must sum to one, so that $x_0 = 1 - \sum_{a=1}^{A} x_a$, we can also write the budget constraint as

$$\tilde{C} = (W - c) \left[R_0 + \sum_{a=1}^{A} x_a (\tilde{R}_a - R_0) \right]. \tag{20.3}$$

The expression in square brackets is the **portfolio return**. Given our assumptions about the mean-variance utility function, whatever the level of investment, the investor would like to have the least possible variance of the portfolio return for a given expected value. That is, the investor would like to purchase a portfolio that is **mean-variance efficient**. *Which* portfolio is actually chosen will depend on the investor's utility function; but whatever it is, it must minimize variance for a given level of expected return.

Before proceeding further, let us examine the first-order conditions for this minimization problem. We want to minimize the variance of the portfolio return subject to the constraints that we achieve a specified expected return, $\overline{R}$, and that we satisfy the budget constraint $\sum_{a=0}^{A} x_a = 1$.

$$\min_{x_0, \ldots, x_A} \sum_{a=0}^{A} \sum_{b=0}^{A} x_a x_b \sigma_{ab}$$

$$\text{such that } \sum_{a=0}^{A} x_a \overline{R}_a = \overline{R}$$

$$\sum_{a=0}^{A} x_a = 1.$$

In this problem we allow x_a to be positive or negative. This means that the consumer can hold a long or a short position in any asset, including the riskless asset.

Letting λ be the Lagrange multiplier for the first constraint and μ the Lagrange multiplier for the second constraint, the first-order conditions take the form

$$2 \sum_{b=0}^{A} x_b \sigma_{ab} - \lambda \overline{R}_a - \mu = 0 \quad \text{for } a = 0, \ldots, A. \tag{20.4}$$

Since the objective function is convex and the constraints are linear, the second-order conditions are automatically satisfied.

These first-order conditions can be used to derive a nice equation describing the pattern of expected returns. The derivation that we use is elegant, but somewhat roundabout. Let $(x_1^e, \ldots, x_A^e)$ be some portfolio consisting entirely of *risky* assets that is known to be mean-variance efficient. Suppose that one of the risky assets available to the investors—say asset e—is a "mutual fund" that holds this efficient portfolio (x_a^e). Then the portfolio that invests 0 in every asset except for asset e and 1 in asset e is mean-variance efficient. This means that such a portfolio must satisfy the conditions given in equation (20.4) for each asset $a = 0, \ldots, A$.

Noting that for this portfolio $x_b = 0$ for $b \neq e$, we see that the ath first-order condition becomes

$$2\sigma_{ae} - \lambda \overline{R}_a - \mu = 0. \tag{20.5}$$

Two special cases occur when $a = 0$ and when $a = e$:

$$-\lambda R_0 - \mu = 0$$
$$2\sigma_{ee} - \lambda \overline{R}_e - \mu = 0.$$

When $a = 0$, σ_{ae} is zero since asset 0 is not risky. When $a = e$, $\sigma_{ae} = \sigma_{ee}$ since the covariance of a variable with itself is simply the variance of the random variable.

Solving these two equations for λ and μ yields

$$\lambda = \frac{2\sigma_{ee}}{\overline{R}_e - R_0}$$
$$\mu = -\lambda R_0 = -\frac{2\sigma_{ee} R_0}{\overline{R}_e - R_0}.$$

Substituting these values back into (20.5) and rearranging yields

$$\overline{R}_a = R_0 + \frac{\sigma_{ae}}{\sigma_{ee}}(\overline{R}_e - R_0). \tag{20.6}$$

This equation says that the expected return on any asset is equal to the risk-free rate plus a "risk premium" that depends on the covariance of the asset's return with some efficient portfolio of risky assets. This equation must hold for *any* efficient portfolio of risky assets.

In order to give this equation empirical content, we need to be able to identify some particular efficient portfolio. In order to do this we examine the structure of the efficient portfolios graphically. In Figure 20.1 we have plotted the expected returns and the **standard deviations** that can be generated by some particular set of risky assets.[1] The set of mean-standard

---

[1] The standard deviation of a random variable is just the square root of its variance.

deviation efficient portfolios that consist entirely of risky assets can be shown to have the hyperbolic shape depicted in Figure 20.1, but the fact that it has this particular shape isn't necessary for the following argument.

We want to construct the set of efficient portfolios that use both the risky assets and the risk-free asset. To do this draw the line that passes through the risk-free rate R_0 and just touches the hyperbola in Figure 20.1. Call the point where it touches this set $(\overline{R}_m, \sigma_m)$. This point is the expected return and standard deviation of some portfolio we shall call portfolio m. I claim that every combination of expected return and standard deviation on this straight line can be achieved by taking convex combinations of two portfolios: the risk-free portfolio and portfolio m.

For example, to construct a portfolio that has an expected return of $\frac{1}{2}(\overline{R}_m - R_0)$ and a standard deviation of $\frac{1}{2}\sigma_m$, we simply put half of our wealth in portfolio m and half in the riskless asset. This shows how to achieve any mean-standard deviation combination to the left of $(\overline{R}_m, \sigma_m)$. To generate return combinations to the right of the point $(\overline{R}_m, \sigma_m)$, we have to *borrow* money at the rate R_0 and invest it in portfolio m.

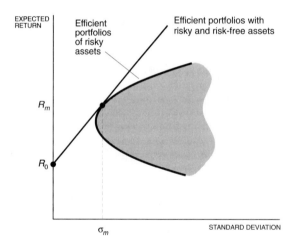

Figure 20.1   **Set of risky returns and standard deviations.** All mean-variance efficient portfolios can be constructed by combining the portfolios whose returns are R_0 and $\overline{R}_m$.

This geometric argument shows that the structure of the set of efficient portfolios is very simple indeed: it can be constructed entirely of two portfolios, one being the portfolio consisting of the riskless asset and one being portfolio m. The only remaining issue is to give empirical content to this particular portfolio of risky assets.

Let the fraction of wealth invested in asset a in portfolio m be denoted by x_a^m. Of course, we must have $\sum_{a=1}^{A} x_a^m = 1$. Let W_i denote the amount of wealth that individual i invests in the risky portfolio. Let X_{ia} be the number of shares that individual i invests in risky asset a, and let p_a denote the price of asset a. Since each investor holds the *same* portfolio of risky assets, we must have

$$x_a^m = \frac{p_a X_{ia}}{W_i} \quad \text{for } i = 1, \ldots, I.$$

Multiply each side of this equation by W_i and sum over i to find

$$x_a^m = \frac{p_a \sum_{i=1}^{I} X_{ia}}{\sum_{i=1}^{I} W_i}.$$

The numerator of this expression is the total market value of asset a. The denominator is the total value of all risky assets. Hence, x_a^m is just the fraction of wealth invested in risky assets that is invested in asset a. This portfolio is known as the **market portfolio of risky assets**. This is a potentially observable portfolio—as long as we can measure the aggregate holdings of risky assets.

Since the market portfolio of risky assets is one particular mean-standard deviation efficient portfolio, we can rewrite equation (20.6) as

$$\overline{R}_a = R_0 + \frac{\sigma_{am}}{\sigma_{mm}} (\overline{R}_m - R_0).$$

This is the fundamental result of the CAPM. It gives empirical content to the risk premium: the risk premium is the covariance of asset a with the market portfolio divided by the variance of the market portfolio times the excess return on the market portfolio.

The term σ_{am}/σ_{mm} can be recognized as the theoretical regression coefficient resulting from a regression of $\tilde{R}_a$ on $\tilde{R}_m$. For this reason, this term is typically written as β_a. Making this substitution gives us the final form of the CAPM:

$$\overline{R}_a = R_0 + \beta_a (\overline{R}_m - R_0). \tag{20.7}$$

The CAPM says that to determine the expected return on any asset, we simply need to know that asset's "beta"—its covariance with the market portfolio. Note that the variance of the asset return is irrelevant; it is not the "own risk" of an asset that matters, but how this return on an asset contributes to the overall portfolio risk of the agents. Since everybody holds the *same* portfolio of risky assets in the CAPM model, the risk that matters is how an asset influences the riskiness of the market portfolio.

The appealing feature of the CAPM is that it involves things that appear to be empirically observable: the expected return on the market portfolio of risky assets, and the regression coefficient of a regression relating the return on a specific asset and the return on the market portfolio. However, it must be remembered that the relevant theoretical construction is the portfolio of *all* risky assets; this may not be so easy to observe.

20.5 The Arbitrage Pricing Theory

The CAPM starts with a specification of consumer tastes; the Arbitrage Pricing Theory (APT) starts with a specification of the process generating asset returns. In this sense the CAPM is a demand-side model, while the APT is a supply-side model.

It is commonly observed that most asset prices move together; that is, there is a high degree of covariance among asset prices. It is natural to think of writing the returns on assets as a function of a few common factors and some asset-specific risks. If there are only two factors, for example, we could write

$$\tilde{R}_a = b_{0a} + b_{1a}\tilde{f}_1 + b_{2a}\tilde{f}_2 + \tilde{\epsilon}_a. \quad \text{for } a = 1, \dots, A.$$

Here we think of $(\tilde{f}_1, \tilde{f}_2)$ as being "macroeconomic," economy-wide factors that influence all asset returns. Each asset a has a particular "sensitivity" b_{ia} to factor i. The asset-specific risk, $\tilde{\epsilon}_a$, is, by definition, independent of the economy wide factors $\tilde{f}_1$ and $\tilde{f}_2$.

Because of the presence of the "constant term" b_{0a}, the factors $\tilde{f}_i$, $i = 1, 2$ and the asset-specific risks, $\tilde{\epsilon}_a$ for $a = 1, \dots, A$, can always be assumed to have a zero expectation. (If the expectations aren't zero, just incorporate them into b_{0a}.) We also suppose that the $E\tilde{f}_1\tilde{f}_2 = 0$, that is that the factors are truly *independent* factors.

Let us first examine some special cases of the APT in which there is no asset-specific risk. We start with the case in which there is only one risk factor, so that

$$\tilde{R}_a = b_{0a} + b_{1a}\tilde{f}_1 \text{ for } a = 0, \dots, A.$$

As usual, we seek to explain the expected returns on the assets in terms of a risk premium. By construction, we have $\overline{R}_a = b_{0a}$, so this reduces to examining the behavior of b_{0a} for $a = 1, \dots, A$.

Suppose that we construct a portfolio of two assets a and b where we hold x in asset a and $1 - x$ in asset b. The return on this portfolio will be

$$x\tilde{R}_a + (1 - x)\tilde{R}_b = [xb_{0a} + (1 - x)b_{0b}] + [xb_{1a} + (1 - x)b_{1b}]\tilde{f}_1.$$

Let us choose x^* so that the second term in brackets is zero. This implies

$$x^* = \frac{b_{1b}}{b_{1b} - b_{1a}}. \tag{20.8}$$

Note that to do this we must assume $b_{1b} \neq b_{1a}$, which means that assets a and b do not have the same sensitivity.

The resulting portfolio is by construction a riskless portfolio. Hence, its return must be equal to the risk-free rate, which implies that

$$x^*b_{0a} + (1 - x^*)b_{0b} = R_0,$$

or

$$x^*(b_{0a} - b_{0b}) = R_0 - b_{0b}.$$

Substituting from equation (20.8) and rearranging, we have

$$\frac{b_{0b} - R_0}{b_{1b}} = \frac{b_{0b} - b_{0a}}{b_{1b} - b_{1a}}. \qquad (20.9)$$

Interchanging the role of a and b in this argument gives us

$$\frac{b_{0a} - R_0}{b_{1a}} = \frac{b_{0a} - b_{0b}}{b_{1a} - b_{1b}}. \qquad (20.10)$$

Observe that the right-hand sides of equations (20.9) and (20.10) are the same. Since this is true for all assets a and b, it follows that

$$\frac{b_{0a} - R_0}{b_{1a}} = \lambda_1$$

for some constant λ_1 for all assets a. Using the fact that $\overline{R}_a = b_{0a}$ and rearranging gives us the final form of the one-factor APT:

$$\overline{R}_a = R_0 + b_{1a}\lambda_1. \qquad (20.11)$$

Equation (20.11) says that the expected return on any asset a is the risk-free rate plus a risk premium which is given by the sensitivity of asset a to the common risk factor times a constant. The constant can be interpreted as the risk premium paid on a portfolio that has sensitivity 1 to the kind of risk represented by factor 1.

Two factors

Suppose now that we consider a two-factor model:

$$\tilde{R}_a = b_{0a} + b_{1a}\tilde{f}_1 + b_{2a}\tilde{f}_2.$$

Now we construct a portfolio (x_a, x_b, x_c) with three assets a, b, and c which satisfies three equations:

$$x_a b_{1a} + x_b b_{1b} + x_c b_{1c} = 0$$
$$x_a b_{2a} + x_b b_{2b} + x_c b_{2c} = 0$$
$$x_a + x_b + x_c = 1.$$

The first equation says that the portfolio eliminates the risk from factor 1, the second equation says that the portfolio eliminates the risk from factor 2, and the third equation says that the sum of the asset shares is 1—that we do indeed have a portfolio.

It follows that this portfolio has zero risk. Therefore it must earn the riskless return, so $x_a b_{0a} + x_b b_{0b} + x_c b_{0c} = R_0$. Writing these conditions in matrix form gives us

$$
\begin{pmatrix}
b_{0a} - R_0 & b_{0b} - R_0 & b_{0c} - R_0 \\
b_{1a} & b_{1b} & b_{1c} \\
b_{2a} & b_{2b} & b_{2c}
\end{pmatrix}
\begin{pmatrix}
x_a \\
x_b \\
x_c
\end{pmatrix}
=
\begin{pmatrix}
0 \\
0 \\
0
\end{pmatrix}.
$$

The vector (x_a, x_b, x_c) does not consist of all zeroes since it sums to 1. It follows that the matrix on the left must be singular. If the last two rows are not collinear (which we will assume), it must be that the first row is a linear combination of the last two rows. That is, each entry on the top row is a linear combination of the corresponding entries in the next two rows. This implies that

$$
\overline{R}_a - R_0 = b_{1a}\lambda_1 + b_{2a}\lambda_2 \quad \text{for all } a = 1, \ldots, A. \tag{20.12}
$$

The λ's have the same interpretation as before: they are the excess returns on portfolios that have sensitivity 1 to the particular type of risk indicated by the appropriate factor. This is the natural generalization of the 1-factor case: the excess return on asset a depends on its sensitivity to the two risky factors.

Asset-specific risk

We have seen that if the number of factors is small relative to the number of assets, and there are no asset-specific risks, then it is possible to construct riskless portfolios. These riskless portfolios must earn the riskless return, which puts certain restrictions on the set of expected returns.

But the constructions of these riskless portfolios of risky assets can only be accomplished if *all* risk is due to the macroeconomic factors. What happens if there is asset-specific risk in addition to economy-wide risk?

By definition asset-specific risks are independent of the economy-wide risk factors, and are independent of each other. The Law of Large Numbers then implies that the risk of a highly diversified portfolio of firms must involve very little asset-specific risk. This argument suggests that we can ignore the asset-specific risks, and that the linear relationship of expected returns to factors can still be expected to hold, at least as a good approximation. The interested reader can consult the references given at the end of the chapter for the details of this argument.

20.6 Expected utility

Let us now consider a model of asset pricing based on intertemporal expected utility maximization. Consider the following two-period problem:

$$\max_{c, x_1, \ldots, x_A} \ u(c) + \alpha E \left[u \left((W - c) \left(R_0 + \sum_{a=1}^{A} x_a (\tilde{R}_a - R_0) \right) \right) \right].$$

Again, we have dropped the subscript for investor i for notational convenience.

This problem asks us to determine first-period savings, $W - c$, and the portfolio investment pattern, $(x_1, \ldots, x_A)$, so as to maximize discounted expected utility.

Letting $\tilde{R} = (R_0 + \sum_{a=1}^{A} x_a (\tilde{R}_a - R_0))$ be the portfolio return, and $\tilde{C} = (W - c)\tilde{R}$, we can write the first-order condition for this problem as

$$u'(\dot{c}) = \alpha E u'(\tilde{C})\tilde{R}$$
$$0 = E u'(\tilde{C})(\tilde{R}_a - R_0) \qquad \text{for } a = 1, \ldots, A.$$

The first condition says that the marginal utility of consumption in the first period should equal the discounted expected marginal utility of consumption in the second period. The second set of conditions say that the expected marginal utility from shifting the portfolio away from the safe asset into asset a must be zero for all assets $a = 1, \ldots, A$.

Let us focus on the second set of conditions and see what their implications are for asset pricing. Using the covariance identity, from Chapter 26, page 486, we can write these conditions as

$$E u'(\tilde{C})(\tilde{R}_a - R_0) = \text{cov}(u'(\tilde{C}), \tilde{R}_a) + E u'(\tilde{C})(\overline{R}_a - R_0) = 0 \text{ for } a = 1, \ldots, A.$$

Rearranging, we have

$$\overline{R}_a = R_0 - \frac{1}{E u'(\tilde{C})} \text{cov}(\tilde{R}_a, u'(\tilde{C})). \tag{20.13}$$

This equation is reminiscent of the pricing equation from the CAPM, equation (20.7), but with a few differences. Now the risk premium depends on the covariance with marginal utility, rather than with the market portfolio of risky assets.

If an asset is positively correlated with consumption, then it will be negatively correlated with the marginal utility of consumption, since $u'' < 0$. This means that it will have a positive risk premium—it must command a higher expected return in order to be held. Just the reverse holds for assets that are negatively correlated with consumption.

As it stands, this equation holds only for an individual investor i. However, under certain conditions, the condition can be aggregated. For example, suppose that all assets are Normally distributed. Then consumption will also be Normally distributed, and we can apply a theorem due to Rubinstein (1976) which says

$$\text{cov}(u'(\tilde{C}), \tilde{R}_a) = Eu''(\tilde{C})\text{cov}(\tilde{C}, \tilde{R}_a).$$

Applying this to equation (20.13), and adding the subscript i to distinguish the individual investors, we have

$$\overline{R}_a = R_0 + \left(-\frac{Eu_i''(\tilde{C}_i)}{Eu_i'(\tilde{C}_i)} \right) \text{cov}(\tilde{C}_i, \tilde{R}_a). \tag{20.14}$$

The term multiplying the covariance is sometimes known as the **global risk aversion** of agent i. Exploiting this analogy, we will denote it by r_i. Cross-multiplying equation (20.14), we have

$$\frac{1}{r_i}(\overline{R}_a - R_0) = \text{cov}(\tilde{C}_i, \tilde{R}_a).$$

Summing over all investors $i = 1, \ldots, I$, and using $\tilde{C} = \sum_{i=1}^{I} \tilde{C}_i$ to denote aggregate consumption gives us

$$(\overline{R}_a - R_0) \sum_{i=1}^{I} \frac{1}{r_i} = \text{cov}(\tilde{C}, \tilde{R}_a).$$

This can also be written as

$$\overline{R}_a = R_0 + \left[\sum_{i=1}^{I} \frac{1}{r_i} \right]^{-1} \text{cov}(\tilde{C}, \tilde{R}_a). \tag{20.15}$$

Now the risk premium is proportional to the covariance of *aggregate* consumption and the asset return. The proportionality factor is a measure of average risk aversion.

We can also express this proportionality factor as the excess return on a particular asset. Suppose that there is an asset c that is perfectly correlated with aggregate consumption. (This asset may itself be a portfolio of other assets.) Then the return on this asset c, R_c, must satisfy equation (20.15):

$$\overline{R}_c = R_0 + \left[\sum_{i=1}^{I} \frac{1}{r_i} \right]^{-1} \text{cov}(\tilde{C}, \tilde{R}_c) = R_0 + \left[\sum_{i=1}^{I} \frac{1}{r_i} \right]^{-1} \text{var}(\tilde{C}).$$

Solving this equation for the average risk aversion, we have

$$\left[\sum_{i=1}^{I}\frac{1}{r_i}\right]^{-1}=\frac{\overline{R}_c-R_0}{\sigma_{cc}}.$$

This allows us to rewrite the asset pricing equation (20.15) as

$$\overline{R}_a=R_0+\frac{\sigma_{ca}}{\sigma_{cc}}(\overline{R}_c-R_0).\qquad(20.16)$$

The ratio of covariances in this expression is sometimes known as the **consumption beta** of an asset. It is the theoretical regression coefficient between the return on asset a and the return on an asset that is perfectly correlated with aggregate consumption. It has the same interpretation as the "market beta" in our study of the CAPM. In fact, the resemblance between (20.16) and (20.7) is so striking that one wonders whether there is really any difference between them.

In a two-period model there isn't. If there are only two periods, then aggregate wealth (that is, the market portfolio) in the second period is equal to aggregate consumption. However, in a multiperiod model, wealth and consumption may differ.

Although we derived our equation in a two-period model, it is actually valid in a multiperiod model. To see this, consider the following experiment. In period t move a dollar from the safe asset into asset a. In period $t+1$ change your consumption by an amount equal to $x_a(\tilde{R}_a-R_0)$. If you have an optimal consumption plan, the expected utility from this action must be zero. But this condition and Normality of the return distribution were the only conditions we used to derive (20.16)!

EXAMPLE: Expected utility and the APT

Since the APT places restrictions on the characteristics of the returns, and the expected utility model only places restrictions on the preferences, we can combine the results of the two models to provide an interpretation of the factor-specific risks.

The expected utility model in (20.13) says

$$\overline{R}_a=R_0-\frac{1}{Eu'(\tilde{C})}\mathrm{cov}(\tilde{R}_a,u'(\tilde{C})),\qquad(20.17)$$

and the APT postulates

$$\tilde{R}_a=b_{0a}+b_{1a}\tilde{f}_1+b_{2a}\tilde{f}_2.$$

Substituting this equation into equation (20.13) gives us

$$\overline{R}_a=R_0-\frac{1}{Eu'(\tilde{c})}\left[b_{1a}\mathrm{cov}(u'(\tilde{C}),\tilde{f}_1)+b_{2a}\mathrm{cov}(u'(\tilde{C}),\tilde{f}_2)\right].$$

Comparing this to equation (20.12), we see that λ_1 and λ_2 are proportional to the covariance between marginal utility of consumption and the appropriate factor risk.

20.7 Complete markets

We consider now a different model of asset valuation. Suppose that there are S different states of nature and for each state of nature s there is an asset that pays off $1 if state s occurs and zero otherwise. An asset of this form is known as an **Arrow-Debreu security**. Let p_s be the equilibrium price of Arrow-Debreu security s.

Now consider an arbitrary asset a with value V_{as} in state s. How much is this asset worth in period 0? Consider the following argument: construct a portfolio holding V_{as} units of Arrow-Debreu security s. Since Arrow-Debreu security s is worth $1 in state s, this portfolio will be worth V_{as} in state s. Hence, this portfolio has exactly the same pattern of payoffs as asset a. It follows from arbitrage considerations that the value of asset a must be the same as the value of this portfolio. Hence,

$$p_a = \sum_{s=1}^{S} p_s V_{as}.$$

This argument shows that the value of any asset can be determined from the values of the Arrow-Debreu assets.

Letting π_s be the probability of state s, we can write

$$p_a = \sum_{s=1}^{S} \frac{p_s}{\pi_s} V_{as} \pi_s = E \frac{\tilde{p}}{\tilde{\pi}} \tilde{V}_a,$$

where E is the expectation operator. This formula says that the value of asset a is the expectation of the product of the value of asset a and the random variable (p/π). Using the covariance identity, from Chapter 26, page 486, we can rewrite this expression as

$$p_a = \mathrm{cov}\left(\frac{\tilde{p}}{\tilde{\pi}}, \tilde{V}_a\right) + E\frac{\tilde{p}}{\tilde{\pi}} E\tilde{V}_a. \tag{20.18}$$

By definition

$$E\frac{\tilde{p}}{\tilde{\pi}} = \sum_{s=1}^{S} \frac{p_s}{\pi_s} \pi_s = \sum_{s=1}^{S} p_s.$$

Hence, $E(\tilde{p}/\tilde{\pi})$ is the value of a portfolio that pays off $1 for certain next period. Letting R_0 be the risk-free return on such a portfolio, we have

$$E\frac{\tilde{p}}{\tilde{\pi}} = \frac{1}{R_0}.$$

Substituting this into equation (20.18) and rearranging slightly, we have

$$p_a = \frac{\overline{V}_a}{R_0} + \mathrm{cov}(\tilde{p}/\tilde{\pi}, \tilde{V}_a). \tag{20.19}$$

Hence the value of asset a must be its discounted expected value plus a risk premium.

All of this is simply manipulating definitions; now we add a behavioral assumption. If agent i purchases c_{is} units of Arrow-Debreu security s, he must satisfy the first-order condition

$$\pi_s u_i'(c_{is}) = \lambda p_s,$$

or

$$\frac{u_i'(c_{is})}{\lambda_i} = \frac{p_s}{\pi_s}.$$

It follows that p_s/π_s must be proportional to the marginal utility of consumption of investor i. The left-hand side of this expression is a strictly decreasing function of consumption, due to risk aversion. Let f_i be the inverse of u_i'/λ_i; this is also a decreasing function. We can then write

$$c_{is} = f_i(p_s/\pi_s).$$

Summing over i, and using C_s to denote aggregate consumption in state s we have

$$C_s = \sum_{i=1}^{I} f_i(p_s/\pi_s).$$

Since each f_i is a decreasing function, the right-hand side of this expression is a decreasing function. Hence, it has an inverse F, so we can write

$$\frac{p_s}{\pi_s} = F(C_s),$$

where $F(C_s)$ is a decreasing function of aggregate consumption.

Substituting this into (20.19) we have

$$p_a = \frac{\overline{V}_a}{R_0} + \operatorname{cov}(F(\tilde{C}), \tilde{V}_a). \tag{20.20}$$

Hence, the value of asset a is the discounted expected value adjusted by a risk premium that depends on the covariance of the value of the asset with a decreasing function of aggregate consumption. Assets that are positively correlated with aggregate consumption will have a negative adjustment; assets that are negatively correlated will have a positive adjustment, just as in the other models.

20.8 Pure arbitrage

Finally, we consider an asset-pricing model with the absolute minimum of assumptions: we only require that there be no opportunities for pure arbitrage.

Arrange the set of assets as an $A \times S$ matrix where the entry V_{sa} measures the value of asset a in state of nature s. Call this matrix $\mathbf{V}$. Let $\mathbf{X} = (X_1, \ldots X_A)$ be a pattern of holdings of the A assets. Then the value of this pattern of investment second period will be an S-vector given by the matrix product $\mathbf{VX}$.

Suppose that $\mathbf{X}$ results in a nonnegative payoff in every state of nature: $\mathbf{VX} \geq \mathbf{0}$. Then it seems reasonable to suppose that the value of this investment pattern should be nonnegative: that is, that $\mathbf{pX} \geq 0$. Otherwise, there would be an obvious arbitrage opportunity. We state this condition as

No arbitrage principle. If $\mathbf{VX} \geq \mathbf{0}$, then $\mathbf{pX} \geq 0$.

This is essentially a requirement that there be "no free lunches." It turns out that one can show that the no arbitrage principle implies that there exists a set of "state price" $\rho_s \geq 0$, for $s = 1, \ldots, S$, such that the value of any asset a is given by

$$p_a = \sum_{s=1}^{S} \rho_s V_{as}. \tag{20.21}$$

Since the proof is not directly of interest to us, we give it in an appendix. Here we explore the implications of this condition for asset pricing.

Recalling that π_s measures the probability that state s occurs, we can write equation (20.21) as

$$p_a = \sum_{s=1}^{S} \frac{\rho_s}{\pi_s} V_{as} \pi_s.$$

The right-hand side of this equation is just the expectation of the product of two random variables. Let $\tilde{Z}$ be the random variable that takes on the values ρ_s/π_s, and let $\tilde{V}_a$ be the random variable that takes on the values V_{as}.

Then, applying the covariance identity, we have

$$p_a = E\tilde{Z}\tilde{V}_a = \mathrm{cov}(\tilde{Z}, \tilde{V}_a) + \overline{Z}\,\overline{V}_a.$$

By definition

$$\overline{Z} = \sum_{s=1}^{S} \frac{\rho_s}{\pi_s} \pi_s = \sum_{s=1}^{S} \rho_s.$$

The right-hand side of this expression is the value of a security that pays 1 in each state of nature—that is, it is the value of a riskless bond. By definition, this value is $1/R_0$.

Making this substitution and rearranging, we have

$$\overline{V}_a = p_a R_0 - R_0 \mathrm{cov}(\tilde{Z}, \tilde{V}_a).$$

Dividing through by p_a to convert this to an expression involving asset returns yields

$$\overline{R}_a = R_0 - R_0 \mathrm{cov}(\tilde{Z}, \tilde{R}_a).$$

From this equation, we see that under very general conditions the risk premium for each asset depends on the covariance of asset return with a single random variable—the same one for all assets.

In the different models we have investigated we have found different expressions for $\tilde{Z}$. In the case of the CAPM, $\tilde{Z}$ was the return on the market portfolio of risky assets. In the case of the consumption-beta model, $\tilde{Z}$ was the marginal utility of consumption. In the Arrow-Debreu model, $\tilde{Z}$ is a particular function of aggregate consumption.

APPENDIX

We want to show that the No Arbitrage Principle given in the text implies the existence of the nonnegative state prices $(\rho_1, \ldots, \rho_S)$. In order to attack this question, let us consider the following linear programming problem:

$$\min \quad \mathbf{pX}$$
$$\text{such that} \quad \mathbf{VX} \geq \mathbf{0}.$$

This linear program problem asks us to find the cheapest portfolio that gives a vector of all nonnegative returns. Certainly $\mathbf{X} = \mathbf{0}$ is a feasible choice for this problem, and the No Arbitrage Principle implies that it indeed minimizes the objective function. Thus the linear programming problem has a finite solution.

The dual of this linear program is

$$\max \quad \mathbf{0}\boldsymbol{\rho}$$
$$\text{such that} \quad \boldsymbol{\rho}\mathbf{V} = \mathbf{p},$$

where $\boldsymbol{\rho}$ is the S-dimensional nonnegative vector of dual variables. Since the primal has a finite feasible solution, so does the dual. Thus we have found that a necessary implication of the No Arbitrage Condition is that there must exist a nonnegative S-dimensional vector $\boldsymbol{\rho}$ such that

$$\mathbf{p} = \boldsymbol{\rho}\mathbf{V}.$$

Notes

Our treatment of the CAPM follows Ross (1977). The APT model is due to Ross (1976); the treatment here follows Ingersoll (1987). The asset pricing formula for the Arrow-Debreu model follows Rubinstein (1976). The pure arbitrage analysis follows Ross (1978), but we use the proof from Ingersoll (1987).

Exercises

20.1. The first-order condition for portfolio choice in the expected utility model was $Eu'(\tilde{C})(\tilde{R}_a - R_0) = 0$ for all assets a. Show that this could also be written as $Eu'(\tilde{C})(\tilde{R}_a - \tilde{R}_b) = 0$ for any assets a and b.

20.2. Write equation (20.20) in terms of the rate of return on asset a.

CHAPTER 21

EQUILIBRIUM ANALYSIS

In this chapter we discuss some topics in general equilibrium analysis that don't conveniently fit in the other chapters. Our first topic concerns the core, a generalization of the Pareto set, and its relationship to Walrasian equilibrium. We follow this by a brief discussion of the relationship between convexity and size. Following this we discuss conditions under which there will be only one Walrasian equilibrium. Finally, the chapter ends with a discussion of the stability of general equilibrium.

21.1 The core of an exchange economy

We have seen that Walrasian equilibria will generally exist and that they will generally be Pareto efficient. But the use of a competitive market mechanism system is only one way to allocate resources. What if we used some other social institution to facilitate trade? Would we still end up with an allocation that was "close to" a Walrasian equilibrium?

In order to examine this question we consider a "market game" where each agent i comes to the market with an initial endowment of ω_i. Instead of using a price mechanism, the agents simply wander around and make tentative arrangements to trade with each other. When all agents have made the best arrangement possible for themselves, the trades are carried out.

As described so far the game has very little structure. Instead of specifying the game in sufficient detail to calculate an equilibrium we ask a more general question. What might be a "reasonable" set of outcomes for this game? Here is a set of definitions that may be useful in thinking about this question.

Improve upon an allocation. *A group of agents S is said to* **improve upon** *a given allocation* **x** *if there is some allocation* **x'** *such that*

$$\sum_{i \in S} \mathbf{x}'_i = \sum_{i \in S} \boldsymbol{\omega}_i,$$

and

$$\mathbf{x}'_i \succ_i \mathbf{x}_i \quad \text{for all } i \in S.$$

If an allocation **x** can be improved upon, then there is some group of agents that can do better by not engaging in the market at all; they would do better by only trading among themselves. An example of this might be a group of consumers who organize a cooperative store to counteract high prices at the grocery store. It seems that any allocation that can be improved upon does not seem like a reasonable equilibrium—some group would always have an incentive to split off from the rest of the economy.

Core of an economy. *A feasible allocation* **x** *is in the* **core** *of the economy if it cannot be improved upon by any coalition.*

Notice that, if **x** is in the core, **x** must be Pareto efficient. For if **x** were not Pareto efficient, then the coalition consisting of the entire set of agents could improve upon **x**. In this sense the core is a generalization of the idea of the Pareto set. If an allocation is in the core, every group of agents gets some part of the gains from trade—no group has an incentive to defect.

One problem with the concept of the core is that it places great informational requirements on the agents—the people in the dissatisfied coalition have to be able to find each other. Furthermore, it is assumed that there are no costs to forming coalitions so that, even if only very small gains can be made by forming coalitions, they will nevertheless be formed.

A geometrical picture of the core can be obtained from the standard Edgeworth box diagram for the two-person, two-good case. See Figure 21.1. In this case the core will be the subset of the Pareto set at which each agent does better than by refusing to trade.

Will the core of an economy generally be nonempty? If we continue to make the assumptions that ensure the existence of a market equilibrium, it will, since the market equilibrium is always contained in the core.

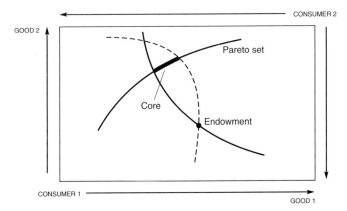

Core in an Edgeworth box. In the Edgeworth box diagram, the core is simply that segment of the Pareto set that lies between the indifference curves that pass through the initial endowment.

Figure 21.1

Walrasian equilibrium is in core. *If* $(\mathbf{x}^*, \mathbf{p})$ *is a Walrasian equilibrium with initial endowments* $\boldsymbol{\omega}_i$*, then* $\mathbf{x}^*$ *is in the core.*

Proof. Assume not; then there is some coalition S and some feasible allocation $\mathbf{x}'$ such that all agents i in S strictly prefer $\mathbf{x}'_i$ to $\mathbf{x}^*_i$ and furthermore

$$\sum_{i \in S} \mathbf{x}'_i = \sum_{i \in S} \boldsymbol{\omega}_i.$$

But the definition of the Walrasian equilibrium implies

$$\mathbf{px}'_i > \mathbf{p}\boldsymbol{\omega}_i \quad \text{for all } i \text{ in } S$$

so

$$\mathbf{p}\sum_{i \in S} \mathbf{x}'_i > \mathbf{p}\sum_{i \in S} \boldsymbol{\omega_i}$$

which contradicts the first equality. ∎

We can see from the Edgeworth box diagram that generally there will be other points in the core than just the market equilibrium. However, if we allow our 2-person economy to grow we will have more possible coalitions and hence more opportunities to improve upon any given allocation. Therefore, one might suspect that the core might shrink as the economy grows. One problem with formalizing this idea is that the core is a subset of the allocation space and thus as the economy grows the core keeps changing dimension. Thus we want to limit ourselves to a particularly simple type of growth.

We will say two agents are of the same **type** if both their preferences and their initial endowments are the same. We will say that one economy is a **replica** of another if there are r times as many agents of each type in one economy as in the other. This means that if a large economy replicates a smaller one, it is just a "scaled up" version of the small one. For simplicity we will limit ourselves to only two types of agents, type A and type B. Consider a fixed 2-person economy; by the r-core of this economy, we mean the core of the rth replication of the original economy.

It turns out that all agents of the same type must receive the same bundle at any core allocation. This result makes for a much simpler analysis.

Equal treatment in the core. *Suppose agents' preferences are strictly convex, strongly monotonic, and continuous. Then if* x *is an allocation in the r-core of a given economy, then any two agents of the same type must receive the same bundle.*

Proof. Let x be an allocation in the core and index the $2r$ agents using subscripts $A1, \ldots, Ar$ and $B1, \ldots, Br$. If all agents of the same type do not get the same allocation, there will be one agent of each type who is most poorly treated. We will call these two agents the "type-A underdog" and the "type-B underdog." If there are ties, select any of the tied agents.

Let $\overline{x}_A = \frac{1}{r}\sum_{j=1}^{r} x_{A_j}$ and $\overline{x}_B = \frac{1}{r}\sum_{j=1}^{r} x_{B_j}$ be the average bundle of the type-A and type-B agents. Since the allocation x is feasible, we have

$$\frac{1}{r}\sum_{j=1}^{r} x_{A_j} + \frac{1}{r}\sum_{j=1}^{r} x_{B_j} = \frac{1}{r}\sum_{j=1}^{r} \omega_{A_j} + \frac{1}{r}\sum_{j=1}^{r} \omega_{B_j}$$

$$= \frac{1}{r} r\omega_A + \frac{1}{r} r\omega_B.$$

It follows that

$$\overline{x}_A + \overline{x}_B = \omega_A + \omega_B,$$

so that $(\overline{x}_A, \overline{x}_B)$ is feasible for the coalition consisting of the two underdogs. We are assuming that at least for one type, say type A, two of the type-A agents receive different bundles. Hence, the A underdog will strictly prefer $\overline{x}_A$ to his present allocation by strict convexity of preferences (since it is a weighted average of bundles that are at least as good as x_A), and the B underdog will think $\overline{x}_B$ is at least as good as his present bundle. Strong monotonicity and continuity allows A to remove a little from $\overline{x}_A$, and bribe the type-B underdog, thus forming a coalition that can improve upon the allocation. ∎

Since any allocation in the core must award agents of the same type with the same bundle, we can examine the cores of replicated two-agent economies by use of the Edgeworth box diagram. Instead of a point x in the core representing how much A gets and how much B gets, we think of $\mathbf{x}$ as telling us how much *each* agent of type A gets and how much *each* agent of type B gets. The above lemma tells us that all points in the r-core can be represented in this manner.

The following proposition shows that any allocation that is not a market equilibrium allocation must eventually not be in the r-core of the economy. This means that core allocations in large economies look just like Walrasian equilibria.

Shrinking core. *Assume that preferences are strictly convex and strongly monotonic, and that there is a unique market equilibrium* $\mathbf{x}^*$ *from initial endowment* $\boldsymbol{\omega}$. *Then if* $\mathbf{y}$ *is not the market equilibrium, there is some replication* r *such that* $\mathbf{y}$ *is not in the* r-core.

Proof. Refer to the Edgeworth box in Figure 21.2. We want to show that a point like $\mathbf{y}$ can eventually be improved upon. Since $\mathbf{y}$ is not a Walrasian equilibrium, the line segment through $\mathbf{y}$ and $\boldsymbol{\omega}$ must cut at least one agent's indifference curve through $\mathbf{y}$. Thus it is possible to choose a point such as $\mathbf{g}$ which, for example, agent A prefers to $\mathbf{y}$. There are several cases to treat, depending on the location of $\mathbf{g}$; however, the arguments are essentially the same, so we treat only the case depicted.

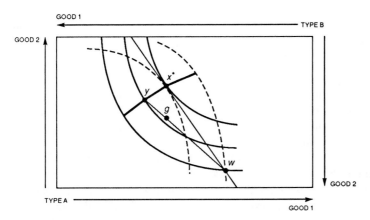

The shrinking core. As the economy replicates, a point like y will eventually not be in the core.

Figure 21.2

Since $\mathbf{g}$ is on the line segment connecting $\mathbf{y}$ and $\boldsymbol{\omega}$, we can write

$$\mathbf{g} = \theta\boldsymbol{\omega}_A + (1 - \theta)\mathbf{y}_A$$

for some $\theta > 0$. By continuity of preference, we can also suppose that $\theta = T/V$ for some integers T and V. Hence,

$$\mathbf{g}_A = \frac{T}{V}\boldsymbol{\omega}_A + \left(1 - \frac{T}{V}\right)\mathbf{y}_A.$$

Suppose the economy has replicated V times. Then form a coalition consisting of V consumers of type A and $V - T$ consumers of type B, and consider the allocation $\mathbf{z}$ where agents of type A in the coalition receive $\mathbf{g}_A$ and agents of type B receive $\mathbf{y}_B$. This allocation is preferred to $\mathbf{y}$ by all members of the coalition (we can remove a little from the A agents and give it to the B agents to get strict preference). We will show that it is feasible for the members of the coalition. This follows from the following calculation:

$$
\begin{aligned}
V\mathbf{g}_A &+ (V - T)\mathbf{y}_B \\
&= V\left[\frac{T}{V}\boldsymbol{\omega}_A + \left(1 - \frac{T}{V}\right)\mathbf{y}_A\right] + (V - T)\mathbf{y}_B \\
&= T\boldsymbol{\omega}_A + (V - T)\mathbf{y}_A + (V - T)\mathbf{y}_B \\
&= T\boldsymbol{\omega}_A + (V - T)[\mathbf{y}_A + \mathbf{y}_B] \\
&= T\boldsymbol{\omega}_A + (V - T)[\boldsymbol{\omega}_A + \boldsymbol{\omega}_B] \\
&= T\boldsymbol{\omega}_A + V\boldsymbol{\omega}_A - T\boldsymbol{\omega}_A + (V - T)\boldsymbol{\omega}_B \\
&= V\boldsymbol{\omega}_A + (V - T)\boldsymbol{\omega}_B.
\end{aligned}
$$

This is exactly the endowment of our coalition since it has V agents of type A and $(V - T)$ agents of type B. Thus, this coalition can improve upon $\mathbf{y}$, proving the proposition. ∎

Many of the restrictive assumptions in this proposition can be relaxed. In particular we can easily get rid of the assumptions of strong monotonicity and uniqueness of the market equilibrium. Convexity appears to be crucial to the proposition, but, as in the existence theorem, that assumption is unnecessary for large economies. Of course, we can also allow for there to be more than only two types of agents.

In the study of Walrasian equilibrium we found that the price mechanism leads to a well-defined equilibrium. In the study of Pareto efficient allocations we found that nearly all Pareto efficient allocations can be obtained through a suitable reallocation of endowments and a price mechanism. And here, in the study of a general pure exchange economy, prices appear in a third and different light: the only allocations that are in the core of a large economy are market equilibrium allocations. The shrinking core theorem shows that Walrasian equilibria are robust: even very weak equilibrium concepts, like that of the core, tend to yield allocations that are close to Walrasian equilibria for large economies.

21.2 Convexity and size

Convexity of preference has come up in several general equilibrium models. Usually, the assumption of strict convexity has been used to assure that the demand function is well-defined—that there is only a single bundle demanded at each price—and that the demand function be continuous—that small changes in prices give rise to small changes in demand. The convexity assumption appears to be necessary for the existence of an equilibrium allocation since it is easy to construct examples where nonconvexities cause discontinuities of demand and thus nonexistence of equilibrium prices.

Consider, for example, the Edgeworth box diagram in Figure 21.3. Here agent A has nonconvex preferences while agent B has convex preferences. At the price p^*, there are two points that maximize utility; but supply is not equal to demand at either point.

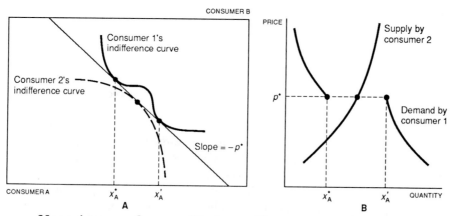

Nonexistence of an equilibrium with nonconvex prefer-   **Figure**
ences. Panel A depicts an Edgeworth box example in which   **21.3**
one agent has nonconvex preferences. Panel B shows the associated aggregate demand curve, which will be discontinuous.

However, perhaps equilibrium is not so difficult to achieve as this example suggests. Let us consider a specific example. Suppose that the total supply of the good is just halfway between the two demands at p^* as in Figure 21.3B. Now think what would happen if the economy would replicate once so that there were two agents of type A and two agents of type B. Then at the price p^*, one type-A agent could demand x_A^* and the other type-A agent could demand x_A'. In that case, the total demand by the agents would in fact be equal to the total amount of the good supplied. A Walrasian equilibrium exists for the replicated economy.

It is not hard to see that a similar construction will work no matter where the supply curve lies: if it were two-thirds of the way between x_A^* and x_A', we would just replicate three times, and so on. We can get aggregate demand arbitrarily close to aggregate supply just by replicating the economy a sufficient number of times.

This argument suggests that in a large economy in which the scale of nonconvexities is small relative to the size of the market, there will generally be a price vector that results in demand being close to supply. For a large enough economy small nonconvexities do not cause serious difficulties.

This observation is closely related to the replication argument described in our discussion of competitive firms behavior. Consider a classic model of firms with fixed costs and U-shaped average cost functions. The supply functions of individual firms will typically be discontinuous, but these discontinuities will be irrelevant if the scale of the market is sufficiently large.

21.3 Uniqueness of equilibrium

We know from the section on existence of general equilibrium that under appropriate conditions a price vector will exist that clears all markets; i.e., there exists a $\mathbf{p}^*$ such that $\mathbf{z}(\mathbf{p}^*) \leq \mathbf{0}$. The question we ask in this section is that of uniqueness: when is there only one price vector that clears all markets?

The free goods case is not of great interest here, so we will rule it out by means of the desirability assumption: we will assume that the excess demand for each good is strictly positive when its relative price is zero. Economically this means that, when the price of a good goes to zero, everyone demands a lot of it, which seems reasonable enough. This has the obvious consequence that at all equilibrium price vectors the price of each good must be strictly positive.

As before, we will want to assume $\mathbf{z}$ is continuous, but now we need even more than that—we want to assume continuous differentiability. The reasons for this are fairly clear; if indifference curves have kinks in them, we can find whole ranges of prices that are market equilibria. Not only are the equilibria not unique, they aren't even *locally* unique.

Given these assumptions, we have a purely mathematical problem: given a smooth mapping $\mathbf{z}$ from the price simplex to R^k, when is there a unique point that maps into zero? It is too much to hope that this will occur in general, since one can construct easy counterexamples, even in the two-dimensional case. Hence, we are interested in finding restrictions on the excess demand functions that ensure uniqueness. We will then be interested in whether these restrictions are strong or weak, what their economic meaning is, and so on.

We will here consider two restrictions on $\mathbf{z}$ that ensure uniqueness. The first case, that of **gross substitutes**, is interesting because it has clear economic meaning and allows a simple, direct proof of uniqueness. The second case, that of **index analysis**, is interesting because it is very general. In fact it contains almost all other uniqueness results as special cases. Unfortunately, the proof utilizes a rather advanced theorem from differential topology.

Gross substitutes

Roughly speaking, two goods are gross substitutes if an increase in the price of one of the goods causes an increase in the demand for the other good. In elementary courses, this is usually the definition of substitutes. In more advanced courses, it is necessary to distinguish between the idea of **net substitutes**—when the price of one good increases, the Hicksian demand for the other good increases—and **gross substitutes**—which replaces "Hicksian" with "Marshallian" in this definition.

Gross substitutes.   *Two goods, i and j, are gross substitutes at a price vector* $\mathbf{p}$ *if* $\dfrac{\partial z_j(\mathbf{p})}{\partial p_i} > 0$ *for* $i \neq j$.

This definition says that two goods are gross substitutes if an increase in price i brings about an increase in the excess demand for good j. If all goods are gross substitutes, the Jacobian matrix of $\mathbf{z}$, $\mathbf{Dz}(\mathbf{p})$, will have all positive off-diagonal terms.

Gross substitutes implies unique equilibrium.   *If all goods are gross substitutes at all prices, then if* $\mathbf{p}^*$ *is an equilibrium price vector, it is the unique equilibrium price vector.*

Proof. Suppose $\mathbf{p}'$ is some other equilibrium price vector. Since $\mathbf{p}^* \gg 0$ we can define $m = \max\ p_i'/p_i^* \neq 0$. By homogeneity and the fact that $\mathbf{p}^*$ is an equilibrium, we know that $\mathbf{z}(\mathbf{p}^*) = \mathbf{z}(m\mathbf{p}^*) = \mathbf{0}$. We know that for some price, p_k, we have $mp_k^* = p_k'$ by the definition of m. We now lower each price mp_i^* other than p_k successively to p_i'. Since the price of each good other than k goes down in the movement from $m\mathbf{p}^*$ to $\mathbf{p}'$, we must have the demand for good k going down. Thus $z_k(\mathbf{p}') < 0$ which implies $\mathbf{p}'$ cannot be an equilibrium. ∎

Index analysis

Consider an economy with only two goods. Choose the price of good 2 as the numeraire, and draw the excess demand curve for the good 1 as a function of its own price. Walras' law implies that, when the excess demand for good 1 is zero, we have an equilibrium. The desirability assumption we have made implies that, when the relative price of good 1 is large, the excess demand for good 1 is negative; and when the relative price of good 1 is small, the excess demand for good 1 is positive.

Refer to Figure 21.4, where we have drawn some examples of what can happen. Note that (1) the equilibria are usually isolated; (2) and (3) the cases where they are not isolated are not "stable" with respect to minor perturbations; (4) there is usually an odd number of equilibria; (5) if the excess demand curve is downward sloping at all equilibria, there can be only one equilibrium, and if there is only one equilibrium, the excess demand curve must be downward sloping at the equilibrium.

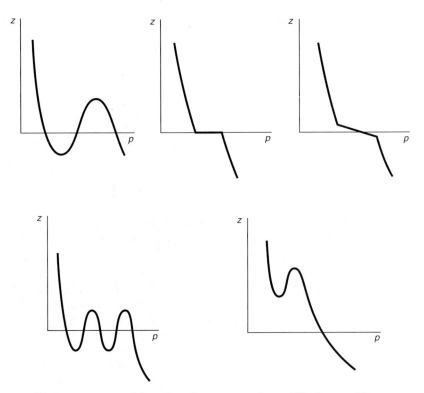

Figure 21.4   **Uniqueness and local uniqueness of equilibrium.** These panels depict some examples used in the discussion of uniqueness of equilibrium.

In the above one-dimensional case note that if $dz(p)/dp < 0$ at all equilibria, then there can be only one equilibrium. Index analysis is a way of generalizing this result to k dimensions so as to give us a simple necessary and sufficient condition for uniqueness.

Given an equilibrium $\mathbf{p}^*$, define the **index** of $\mathbf{p}^*$ in the following way: write down the negative of the Jacobian matrix of the excess supply function $-\mathbf{Dz}(\mathbf{p}^*)$, drop the last row and column, and take the determinant of the resulting matrix. Assign the point $\mathbf{p}^*$ an index $+1$, if the determinant is positive, and assign $\mathbf{p}^*$ an index -1 if the determinant is negative. (Removing the last row and column is equivalent to choosing the last good to be numeraire just as in our simple one-dimensional example.)

We also need a boundary condition; there are several general possibilities, but the simplest is to assume $z_i(\mathbf{p}) > 0$ when $p_i = 0$. In this case, a fundamental theorem of differential topology states that, if all equilibria have positive index, there can be only one of them. This immediately gives us a uniqueness theorem.

Uniqueness of equilibrium.   *Suppose* $\mathbf{z}$ *is a continuously differentiable aggregate excess demand function on the price simplex with* $z_i(\mathbf{p}) > 0$ *when* p_i *equals zero. If the* $(k-1)$ *by* $(k-1)$ *matrix* $(-\mathbf{Dz}(\mathbf{p}^*))$ *has positive determinant at all equilibria, then there is only one equilibrium.*

This uniqueness theorem is a purely mathematical result. It has the advantage that the theorem can be applied to a number of different equilibrium problems. If an equilibrium existence theorem can be formulated as a fixed point problem, then we can generally use an index theorem to find conditions under which that equilibrium is unique. However, the theorem has the disadvantage that it is hard to interpret what it means in economic terms.

In the case we are examining here, we are interested in the determinant of the aggregate excess supply function. We can use Slutsky's equation to write the derivative of the aggregate excess supply function as

$$-\mathbf{Dz}(\mathbf{p}) = -\sum_{i=1}^{n} \mathbf{D_p h}_i(\mathbf{p}, u_i) - \sum_{i=1}^{n} \mathbf{D_m x}_i(\mathbf{p}, \mathbf{p}\omega_i)[\omega_i - \mathbf{x}_i].$$

When will the matrix on the left-hand side have a positive determinant? Let's look at the right-hand side of the expression. The first term on the right-hand side works out nicely; the substitution matrix is a negative semidefinite matrix, so the (negative) of the $(k-1) \times (k-1)$ principal minor of that matrix will typically be a positive definite matrix. The sum of positive definite matrices is positive definite, and will therefore have a positive determinant.

The second term is more problematic. This term is essentially the covariance of the excess supplies of the goods with the marginal propensity to consume the goods. There is no reason to think that it would have any particular structure in general. All we can say is that if these income effects are small relative to the substitution effects, so that the first term dominates, it is reasonable to expect that equilibrium will be unique.

21.4 General equilibrium dynamics

We have shown that under plausible assumptions on the behavior of economic agents there will always exist a price vector that equates demand and supply. But we have given no guarantee that the economy will actually operate at this "equilibrium" point. What forces exist that might tend to move prices to a market-clearing price vector? In this section we will examine some of the problems encountered in trying to model the price adjustment mechanism in a competitive economy.

The biggest problem is one that is the most fundamental, namely the paradoxical relationship between the idea of competition and price adjustment: if all economic agents take market prices as given and outside their control, how can prices move? Who is left to adjust prices?

This puzzle has led to the erection of an elaborate mythology which postulates the existence of a "Walrasian auctioneer" whose sole function is to search for the market clearing prices. According to this construction, a competitive market functions as follows:

> At time zero the Walrasian auctioneer calls out some vector of prices. All agents determine their demands and supplies of current and futures goods at those prices. The auctioneer examines the vector of aggregate excess demands and adjusts prices according to some rule, presumably raising the price of goods for which there is excess demand and lowering the price of goods for which there is excess supply. The process continues until an equilibrium price vector is found. At this point, all trades are made including the exchanges of contracts for future trades. The economy then proceeds through time, each agent carrying out the agreed upon contracts.

This is, of course, a very unrealistic model. However, the basic idea that prices move in the direction of excess demand seems plausible. Under what conditions will this sort of adjustment process lead one to an equilibrium?

21.5 Tatonnement processes

Let's consider an economy that takes place over time. Each day the market opens and people present their demands and supplies to the market. At an arbitrary price vector $\mathbf{p}$, there will in general be excess demands and supplies in some markets. We will assume that prices adjust according to the following rule, the so-called law of supply and demand.

Price adjustment rule. $\dot{p}_i = G_i(z_i(\mathbf{p}))$ *for* $i = 1, \ldots, k$ *where* G_i *is some smooth sign-preserving function of excess demand.*

It is convenient to make some sort of desirability assumption to rule out the possibility of equilibria at a zero price, so we will generally assume that $z_i(\mathbf{p}) > 0$ when $p_i = 0$.

It is useful to draw some pictures of the dynamical system defined by this price adjustment rule. Let's consider a special case where $G_i(z_i)$ equals the identity function for each $i = 1, \ldots, k$. Then, along with the boundary assumption, we have a system in R^k defined by:

$$\dot{\mathbf{p}} = \mathbf{z}(\mathbf{p})$$

From the usual considerations we know that this system obeys Walras' law, $\mathbf{pz}(\mathbf{p}) \equiv 0$. Geometrically, this means that $\mathbf{z}(\mathbf{p})$ will be orthogonal to the price vector $\mathbf{p}$.

Walras' law implies a very convenient property. Let's look at how the the Euclidean norm of the price vector changes over time:

$$\frac{d}{dt}\left(\sum_{i=1}^{k} p_i^2(t) \right) = \sum_{i=1}^{k} 2p_i(t)\dot{p}_i(t) = 2\sum_{i=1}^{k} p_i(t)z_i(\mathbf{p}(t)) = 0$$

by Walras' law. Hence, Walras' law requires that the sum-of-squares of the prices remains constant as the prices adjust. This means that the paths of prices are restricted on the surface of a k-dimensional sphere. Furthermore, since $z_i(\mathbf{p}) > 0$ where $p_i = 0$, we know that the paths of price movements always point inwards near the points where $p_i = 0$. In Figure 21.5 we have some pictures for $k = 2$ and $k = 3$.

The third picture is especially unpleasant. It depicts a situation where we have a unique equilibrium, but it is completely unstable. The adjustment process we have described will almost never converge to an equilibrium. This seems like a perverse case, but it can easily happen.

Debreu (1974) has shown essentially that *any* continuous function that satisfies Walras' law is an excess demand function for some economy; thus the utility maximization hypothesis places no restrictions on *aggregate* demand behavior, and any dynamical system on the price sphere can arise from our model of economic behavior. Clearly, to get global stability results one has to assume special conditions on demand functions. The value of the results will then depend on the economic naturalness of the conditions assumed.

We will sketch an argument of global stability for one such special assumption under a special adjustment process, namely the assumption that aggregate demand behavior satisfies the Weak Axiom of Revealed Preference described in Chapter 8, page 133. This says that if $\mathbf{px}(\mathbf{p}) \geq \mathbf{px}(\mathbf{p}^*)$ we must have $\mathbf{p}^*\mathbf{x}(\mathbf{p}) > \mathbf{p}^*\mathbf{x}(\mathbf{p}^*)$ for all $\mathbf{p}$ and $\mathbf{p}^*$. Since this condition holds for all $\mathbf{p}$ and $\mathbf{p}^*$, it certainly must hold for equilibrium values of $\mathbf{p}^*$. Let us derive the implications of this condition for the *excess* demand function.

Subtracting $\mathbf{p}\omega$ and $\mathbf{p}^*\omega$ from each of these inequalities yields the following implication:

$$\mathbf{px}(\mathbf{p}) - \mathbf{p}\omega \geq \mathbf{px}(\mathbf{p}^*) - \mathbf{p}\omega \text{ implies } \mathbf{p}^*\mathbf{x}(\mathbf{p}) - \mathbf{p}^*\omega > \mathbf{p}^*\mathbf{x}(\mathbf{p}^*) - \mathbf{p}^*\omega.$$

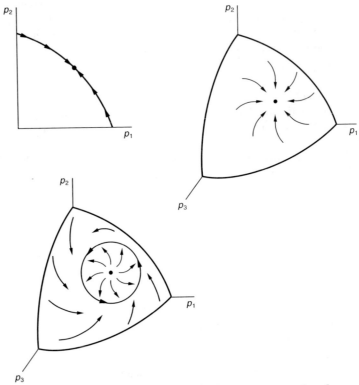

**Figure
21.5**

Examples of price dynamics. The first two examples show
a stable equilibrium; the third example has a unique unstable
equilibrium.

Using the definition of excess demand, we can write this expression as

$$\mathbf{pz}(\mathbf{p}) \geq \mathbf{pz}(\mathbf{p}^*) \text{ implies } \mathbf{p}^*\mathbf{z}(\mathbf{p}) > \mathbf{p}^*\mathbf{z}(\mathbf{p}^*). \qquad (21.1)$$

Now observe that the condition on the left side of (21.1) must be satisfied by any *equilibrium* price vector $\mathbf{p}^*$. To see this simply observe that
Walras' law implies that $\mathbf{pz}(\mathbf{p}) \equiv 0$, and the definition of equilibrium implies $\mathbf{pz}(\mathbf{p}^*) = 0$. It follows that the right-hand side must hold for any
equilibrium $\mathbf{p}^*$. Hence, we must have $\mathbf{p}^*\mathbf{z}(\mathbf{p}) > 0$ for all $\mathbf{p} \neq \mathbf{p}^*$.

WARP implies stability. *Suppose the adjustment rule is given by*
$\dot{p}_i = z_i(\mathbf{p})$ *for* $i = 1, \ldots, k$ *and the excess demand function obeys the Weak
Axiom of Revealed Preference; i.e., if* $\mathbf{p}^*$ *is an equilibrium of the economy,
then* $\mathbf{p}^*\mathbf{z}(\mathbf{p}) > 0$ *for all* $\mathbf{p} \neq \mathbf{p}^*$. *Then all paths of prices following the
above rule converge to* $\mathbf{p}^*$.

Proof. (Sketch) We will construct a Liaponov function for the economy. (See Chapter 26, page 485.) Let $V(\mathbf{p}) = \sum_{i=1}^{k}[(p_i - p_i^*)^2]$. Then

$$\frac{dV(\mathbf{p})}{dt} = \sum_{i=1}^{k} 2(p_i - p_i^*)\dot{p}_i(t) = 2\sum_{i=1}^{k}(p_i - p_i^*)z_i(\mathbf{p})$$

$$= 2\sum_{i=1}^{k}[p_i z_i(\mathbf{p}) - p_i^* z_i(\mathbf{p})] = 0 - 2\mathbf{p}^*\mathbf{z}(\mathbf{p}) < 0.$$

This implies that $V(\mathbf{p})$ is monotonically declining along solution paths for $\mathbf{p} \neq \mathbf{p}^*$. According to Liaponov's theorem we need only to show boundedness of $\mathbf{p}$ to conclude that $V(\mathbf{p})$ is a Liaponov function and that the economy is globally stable. We omit this part of the proof. ∎

21.6 Nontatonnement processes

The tatonnement story makes sense in two sorts of situations: either no trade occurs until equilibrium is reached, or no goods are storable so that each period the consumers have the same endowments. If goods can be accumulated, the endowments of consumers will change over time and this in turn will affect demand behavior. Models that take account of this change in endowments are known as **nontatonnement models**.

In such models, we must characterize the state of the economy at time t by the current vector of prices $\mathbf{p}(t)$ and the current endowments $(\boldsymbol{\omega}_i(t))$. We normally assume that the prices adjust according to the sign of excess demand, as before. But how should the endowments evolve?

We consider two specifications. The first specification, the **Edgeworth process**, says that the technology for trading among agents has the property that the utility of each agent must continually increase. This is based on the view that agents will not voluntarily trade unless they are made better off by doing so. This specification has the convenient property that it quickly leads to a stability theorem; we simply define the Liaponov function to be $\sum_{i=1}^{n} u_i(\boldsymbol{\omega}_i(t))$. By assumption, the sum of the utilities must increase over time, so a simple boundedness argument will give us a convergence proof.

The second specification is known as the **Hahn process**. For this process we assume that the trading rule has the property that there is no good in excess demand by some agent that is in excess supply by some other agent. That is, at any point in time, if a good is in excess demand by a particular agent, it is also in *aggregate* excess demand.

This assumption has an important implication. We have assumed that when a good is in excess demand its price will increase. This will make the *indirect* utility of agents who demand that good lower. Agents who have already committed themselves to supply the good at current prices are not affected by this price change. Hence, aggregate *indirect* utility should decline over time.

To make this argument rigorous, we need to make one further assumption about the change in endowments. The value of consumer i's endowment at time t is $m_i(t) = \sum_{j=1}^{k} p_j(t) w_i^j(t)$. Differentiating this with respect to t gives

$$\frac{dm_i(t)}{dt} = \sum_{j=1}^{k} p_j(t) \frac{dw_i^j(t)}{dt} + \sum_{j=1}^{k} \frac{dp_j(t)}{dt} w_i^j(t).$$

It is reasonable to suppose that the first term in this expression is zero. This means that the change in the endowment at any instant, valued at current prices, is zero. This is just saying that each agent will trade a dollar's worth of goods for a dollar's worth of goods. The value of the endowment will change over time due to changes in price, but not because agents managed to make profitable trades at constant prices.

Given this observation, it is easy to show that the sum of indirect utilities decreases with time. The derivative of agent i's indirect utility function is

$$\frac{dv_i(\mathbf{p}(t), \mathbf{p}(t)\boldsymbol{\omega}_i(t))}{dt} = \sum_{j=1}^{k} \frac{\partial v_i}{\partial p_j} \frac{dp_j}{dt} + \frac{\partial v_i}{\partial m_i} \left[\sum_{j=1}^{k} p_j \frac{dw_i^j}{dt} + \frac{dp_j}{dt} w_i^j \right].$$

Using Roy's law and the fact that the value of the change in the endowment at current prices must be zero, we have

$$\frac{dv_i(\mathbf{p}(t), \mathbf{p}(t)\boldsymbol{\omega}_i(t))}{dt} = -\frac{\partial v_i}{\partial m_i} \sum_{j=1}^{k} \left[x_i^j(\mathbf{p}, \mathbf{p}\boldsymbol{\omega}_i) - w_i^j \right] \frac{dp_j(t)}{dt}.$$

By assumption if good j is in excess demand by agent i, $dp_j/dt > 0$ and vice versa. Since the marginal utility of income is positive, the sign of the whole expression will be negative as long as aggregate demand is not equal to aggregate supply. Hence the indirect utility of each agent i must decrease when the the economy is not in equilibrium.

Notes

See Arrow & Hahn (1971) for a more elaborate discussion of these topics. The importance of the topological index to uniqueness was first recognized by Dierker (1972). The core convergence result was rigorously established by Debreu & Scarf (1963).

Exercises

21.1. There are two agents with identical, strictly convex preferences and equal endowments. Describe the core of this economy and illustrate it in an Edgeworth box.

21.2. Consider a pure exchange economy in which all consumers have differentiable quasilinear utility functions of the form $u(x_1, \ldots, x_n) + x_0$. Assume that $u(x_1, \ldots, x_n)$ is strictly concave. Show that equilibrium must be unique.

21.3. Suppose that the Walrasian auctioneer follows the price adjustment rule $\dot{p} = [\mathbf{Dz(p)}]^{-1}\mathbf{z(p)}$. Show that $V(\mathbf{p}) = -\mathbf{z(p)z(p)}$ is a Liaponov function for the dynamical system.

CHAPTER **22**

WELFARE

In this chapter we examine a few concepts from welfare economics that don't fit well in other parts of the book. The first concept is that of the compensation criterion which is a criterion often used in benefit-cost analysis. We then discuss a common trick used when computing welfare effects of some change in output or price. Finally, we examine the problem of optimal commodity taxation.

22.1 The compensation criterion

It is often desirable to know when a government project will improve social welfare. For example, constructing a dam may have economic benefits such as decreasing the price of electric power and water. However, against these benefits we must weigh the costs of possible environmental damage and the cost of constructing the dam. In general, the benefits and cost of a project will affect different people in different ways—the increased water supply from the dam may lower water fees in some areas and raise water fees in other areas. How should these differential benefits and costs be compared?

Previously we analyzed the problem of measuring the benefits or costs accruing to one individual due to a change in the price or quantity consumed of some good. In this section we try to extend that sort of analysis to a community of individuals, using the concepts of the **Pareto criterion** and the **compensation criterion**.

Consider two allocations, $\mathbf{x}$ and $\mathbf{x'}$. The allocation $\mathbf{x'}$ is said to **Pareto dominate** $\mathbf{x}$ if everyone prefers $\mathbf{x'}$ to $\mathbf{x}$.[1] If each individual prefers $\mathbf{x'}$ to $\mathbf{x}$, it seems noncontroversial to assert that $\mathbf{x'}$ is "better" than $\mathbf{x}$ and any projects that move us from $\mathbf{x}$ to $\mathbf{x'}$ should be undertaken. This is the **Pareto criterion**. However, projects that are unanimously preferred are rare. In the typical case, some people prefer $\mathbf{x'}$ to $\mathbf{x}$ and some people may prefer $\mathbf{x}$ to $\mathbf{x'}$. What should the decision be then?

The **compensation criterion** suggests the following test: $\mathbf{x'}$ is **potentially Pareto preferred** to $\mathbf{x}$ if there is some way to reallocate $\mathbf{x'}$ so that everyone prefers the reallocation to the original allocation $\mathbf{x}$. Let us state this definition a bit more formally: $\mathbf{x'}$ is potentially Pareto preferred to $\mathbf{x}$ if there is some allocation $\mathbf{x''}$ with $\sum_{i=1}^{n} \mathbf{x}_i'' = \sum_{i=1}^{n} \mathbf{x}_i'$ (i.e., $\mathbf{x''}$ is a reallocation of $\mathbf{x'}$) such that $\mathbf{x}_i'' \succ_i \mathbf{x}_i'$ for all agents i.

Thus, the compensation criterion only requires that $\mathbf{x'}$ be a *potential* Pareto improvement on $\mathbf{x}$. Call a person a "winner" if he prefers $\mathbf{x'}$ to $\mathbf{x}$, and call him a "loser" if he prefers $\mathbf{x}$ to $\mathbf{x'}$. Then $\mathbf{x'}$ is better than $\mathbf{x}$ in the sense of the compensation test if the winners can compensate the losers—that is, the winners can give away enough of their gains so as to ensure that everyone is made better off.

Now it seems reasonable that if the winners do *in fact* compensate the losers, the proposed change will be acceptable to everyone. But it is not clear why one should think $\mathbf{x'}$ is better than $\mathbf{x}$ merely because it is *possible* for the winners to compensate the losers.

The usual argument in defense of the compensation criterion is that the question of whether the compensation is carried out is really a question about income distribution, and the basic welfare theorems show that the question of income distribution can be separated from the question of allocative efficiency. The compensation criterion is concerned solely with allocative efficiency, and the question of proper income distribution can best be handled by alternative means such as redistributive taxation. We explore this point further in Chapter 22, page 410.

Let us restate this discussion in graphical terms. Suppose that there are only two individuals, and they are considering two allocations $\mathbf{x}$ and $\mathbf{x'}$. We associate with each allocation its utility possibility set

$$U = \{u_1(\mathbf{y}_1), u_2(\mathbf{y}_2) : \mathbf{y}_1 + \mathbf{y}_2 = \mathbf{x}_1 + \mathbf{x}_2\}$$
$$U' = \{u_1(\mathbf{y}_1), u_2(\mathbf{y}_2) : \mathbf{y}_1 + \mathbf{y}_2 = \mathbf{x}_1' + \mathbf{x}_2'\}.$$

---

[1] We use strict preference here for convenience; the ideas can easily be extended to weak preference.

The upper right-hand boundaries of these sets are called the **utility possibility frontiers**. The utility possibility frontier gives the utility distributions associated with all of the Pareto efficient reallocations of x and x'. Some examples of utility possibilities sets are depicted in Figure 22.1.

In Figure 22.1A, the allocation x' is Pareto preferred to x since $u_1(x_1') > u_1(x_1)$ and $u_2(x_2') > u_2(x_2)$. In Figure 22.1B, x' is potentially Pareto preferred to x: there is some reallocation of x' that is Pareto preferred to x, even though x' itself is not Pareto preferred. Thus, x' satisfies the compensation criterion in the sense that the winners could compensate the losers in the move from x to x'. In Figure 22.1C, x' and x are not comparable—neither the compensation test nor the Pareto test says anything about their relative desirability. In Figure 22.1D, we have the most paradoxical situation: here x' is potentially Pareto preferred to x, since x'' is Pareto preferable to x; but then x is also potentially Pareto preferred to x' since x''' is Pareto preferred to x'!

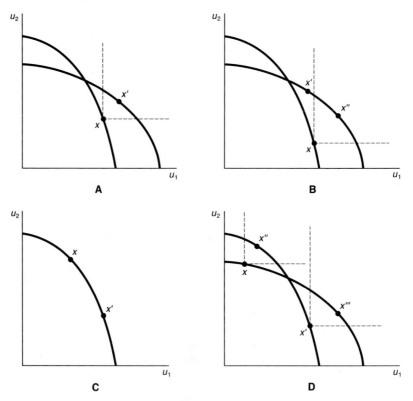

Figure 22.1   **Compensation test.** In panel A, x' is Pareto preferred to x. In panel B, x' is preferred to x in the sense of the compensation test. In panel C, x and x' are not comparable. In panel D, x is preferred to x' *and* x' is preferred to x.

Cases C and D illustrate the main defects of the compensation criterion: it gives no guidance in making comparisons between Pareto efficient allocations, and it can result in inconsistent comparisons. Nevertheless, the compensation test is commonly used in applied welfare economics.

The compensation test, as we have described it, requires that we consider the utility impact of the project on all affected consumers. On the face of it, this seems to require a detailed survey of the population. However, we show below that this may not be necessary for certain cases.

If the projects under consideration are public goods, there is not much hope to avoid explicit questioning of the community in order to make social decisions. We examine the problems with this type of questioning in chapter 23. If the projects concern private goods, we have a much nicer situation since the current prices of the private goods reflect, in some sense, their marginal value to the individual agents.

Suppose we are currently at a market equilibrium $(\mathbf{x}, \mathbf{p})$ and we are contemplating moving to an allocation $\mathbf{x}'$. Then

National income test.   *If $\mathbf{x}'$ is potentially Pareto preferred to $\mathbf{x}$, we must have*

$$\sum_{i=1}^{n} \mathbf{p}\mathbf{x}_i' > \sum_{i=1}^{n} \mathbf{p}\mathbf{x}_i.$$

That is, national income measured in current prices is larger at $\mathbf{x}'$ than at $\mathbf{x}$.

Proof. If $\mathbf{x}'$ is preferred to $\mathbf{x}$ in the sense of the compensation criterion, then there is some allocation $\mathbf{x}''$ such that $\sum_{i=1}^{n} \mathbf{x}_i'' = \sum_{i=1}^{n} \mathbf{x}_i'$ and $\mathbf{x}_i'' \succ_i \mathbf{x}_i$ for all i. Since $\mathbf{x}$ is a market equilibrium, this means that $\mathbf{p}\mathbf{x}_i'' > \mathbf{p}\mathbf{x}_i$ for all i. Summing, we have $\sum_{i=1}^{n} \mathbf{p}\mathbf{x}_i'' > \sum_{i=1}^{n} \mathbf{p}\mathbf{x}_i$. But

$$\sum_{i=1}^{n} \mathbf{p}\mathbf{x}_i'' = \mathbf{p}\sum_{i=1}^{n} \mathbf{x}_i'' = \mathbf{p}\sum_{i=1}^{n} \mathbf{x}_i'.$$

and this establishes the result. ∎

This result is useful since it gives us a one-way test of proposed projects: if national income measured at current prices declines, then the project cannot possibly be potentially Pareto preferred to the current allocation.

Figure 22.2 makes the proposition geometrically clear. The axes of the graph measure the aggregate amount of the two goods available. The current allocation is represented by some aggregate bundle $X = (X^1, X^2)$ where $X^1 = \sum_{i=1}^{n} x_i^1$ and X^2 is defined similarly. (Remember consumers are represented by subscripts and goods by superscripts.)

Let us say that an aggregate *bundle* $\mathbf{X}'$ is potentially Pareto preferred to an *allocation* $\mathbf{x}$ if $\mathbf{X}'$ can be distributed among the agents to construct

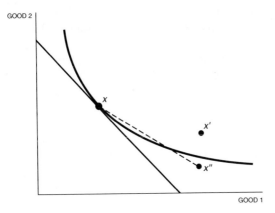

GOOD 2

GOOD 1

**Figure
22.2**

National income test. If national income decreases, the
change cannot be potentially Pareto preferred. If national income increases, the change may or may not be potentially Pareto
preferred. However, if a *small* change increases national income
then it is likely potentially Pareto preferred.

an allocation $\mathbf{x}'$ that is Pareto preferred to $\mathbf{x}$. In other words, the set of
potentially Pareto preferred aggregate bundles is given by

$$P = \left\{ \sum_{i=1}^{n} \mathbf{x}'_i : \mathbf{x}'_i \succ_i \mathbf{x}_i \text{ for all } i \right\}.$$

Figure 22.2 illustrates a typical case. The set P is nice and convex
and the aggregate bundle $\mathbf{X}$ is on its boundary. The competitive prices
separate $\mathbf{X}$ from P. From this picture it is easy to see the content of
the proposition given above: if $\mathbf{x}'$ is preferred to $\mathbf{x}$ in the sense of the
compensation criterion, then $\mathbf{X}'$ must be in P and therefore $\mathbf{pX}' > \mathbf{pX}$.

We can also see that the converse is not true. The bundle $\mathbf{X}''$ has $\mathbf{pX}'' >$
$\mathbf{pX}$, but it is not potentially Pareto preferrable to $\mathbf{x}$. However, the diagram
does present an interesting conjecture: if $\mathbf{pX}'' > \mathbf{pX}$ *and* $\mathbf{X}''$ is close
enough to $\mathbf{X}$, then $\mathbf{X}''$ must be potentially Pareto preferable to $\mathbf{x}$. More
precisely, look at the dotted line connecting $\mathbf{X}''$ and $\mathbf{X}$. All points on this
line have higher value than $\mathbf{X}$, but not all points on this line are above the
indifference curve through $\mathbf{X}$. However, points on this line that *are close
enough* to $\mathbf{X}$ are above the indifference curve. Let's try to formulate this
idea algebraically.

The argument rests on the fact that to the first order, changes in utility
for an individual are proportional to changes in income. This follows from
a simple Taylor series expansion:

$$u_i(\mathbf{x}'_i) - u_i(\mathbf{x}_i) \approx \mathbf{D}u_i(\mathbf{x}_i)[\mathbf{x}'_i - \mathbf{x}_i] = \lambda_i \mathbf{p}[\mathbf{x}'_i - \mathbf{x}_i].$$

According to this expression, small changes in the bundle $\mathbf{x}_i$ are preferred or not preferred as the change in the value of the bundle is positive or negative.

We use this idea to show that if $\mathbf{p}\sum_i \mathbf{x}'_i > \mathbf{p}\sum_i \mathbf{x}_i$ and $\mathbf{x}'_i$ is close to $\mathbf{x}_i$, then it is possible to find a redistribution of $\mathbf{x}'$—call it $\mathbf{x}''$—such that everyone prefers $\mathbf{x}''$ to $\mathbf{x}$. To show this, simply let $\mathbf{X} = \sum_i \mathbf{x}_i$ and $\mathbf{X}' = \sum_i \mathbf{x}'_i$, and define $\mathbf{x}''$ by

$$\mathbf{x}''_i = \mathbf{x}_i + \frac{\mathbf{X}' - \mathbf{X}}{n}.$$

Here each agent i is getting $1/n^{th}$ of the aggregate gain in the movement from $\mathbf{x}$ to $\mathbf{x}'$. According to the above Taylor series expansion,

$$u_i(\mathbf{x}'') - u_i(\mathbf{x}) \approx \lambda_i \mathbf{p} \left[\mathbf{x}_i + \frac{\mathbf{X}' - \mathbf{X}}{n} - \mathbf{x}_i \right]$$

$$\approx \lambda_i \mathbf{p} \left[\frac{\mathbf{X}' - \mathbf{X}}{n} \right].$$

Thus, if the right-hand side is positive—national income at the original prices increases—then it must be possible to increase every agent's utility. Of course, this only holds if the change is small enough for the Taylor approximation to be valid. The national income test is commonly used to value the impact of marginal policy changes on consumer welfare.

22.2 Welfare functions

As we mentioned earlier in this chapter, the compensation methodology suffers from the defect that it ignores distributional considerations. An allocation that is potentially Pareto preferred to the current allocation has *potentially* higher welfare. But one might well argue that *actual* welfare is what is relevant.

If one is willing to postulate some welfare function, one can incorporate distributional considerations into a cost-benefit analysis. Let us suppose that we have a linear-in-utility welfare function

$$W(u_1, \ldots, u_n) = \sum_{i=1}^{n} a_i u_i.$$

As we saw in Chapter 17, page 331, the parameters (a_i) are related to the "welfare weights" of individual economic agents. These weights can be thought of as the value judgments of the "social planner." Let us suppose we are at a market equilibrium $(\mathbf{x}, \mathbf{p})$ and are considering moving to an allocation x'. Will this movement increase welfare? If x' is close to x, we can apply a Taylor series expansion to get

$$W(u_1(x_1'), \ldots, u_n(x_n')) - W(u_1(x_1), \ldots, u_n(x_n)) \approx \sum_{i=1}^{n} a_i D u_i(x_i)(x_i' - x_i).$$

Since (x, p) is a market equilibrium, we can rewrite this as

$$W(u_1(x_1'), \ldots, u_n(x_n')) - W(u_1(x_1), \ldots, u_n(x_n)) \approx \sum_{i=1}^{n} a_i \lambda_i p(x_i' - x_i).$$

We see that the welfare test reduces to examining a weighted change of expenditures. The weights are related to the value judgments which were originally incorporated into the welfare function.

As a special case, suppose that the original allocation x is a welfare optimum. Then the results of Chapter 17, page 331, tell us that $\lambda_i = 1/a_i$. In this case we find

$$W(u_1(x_1'), \ldots, u_n(x_n')) - W(u_1(x_1), \ldots, u_n(x_n)) \approx \sum_{i=1}^{n} p(x_i' - x_i).$$

The distribution terms drop out—since distribution is already optimal—and we are left with a simple criterion: a small project increases welfare if national income (at the original prices) increases. This is exactly the criterion relevant to the compensation test.

This means that if the social planner consistently follows a policy of maximizing welfare both with respect to lump sum income distribution and with respect to other policy choices that affect allocations, then the policy choices that affect the allocations can be valued independently of the effect on the income distribution.

22.3 Optimal taxation

We saw in Chapter 8, page 118, that a lump-sum income tax is always preferable to an excise tax. However, in many cases lump-sum taxes are not feasible. What do optimal taxes look like if we are unable to use lump sum taxes?

We examine this question in a one-consumer economy. Let $u(x)$ be the consumer's direct utility function and $v(p, m)$ be his indirect utility function. We interpret p as the producer prices. If t is the vector of taxes, then the price vector faced by the consumer is $p + t$. This yields the consumer a utility of $v(p + t, m)$ and yields the government a revenue of $R(t) = \sum_{i=1}^{k} t_i x_i(p + t, m)$.

The optimal taxation problem is to maximize the consumer's utility with respect to the tax rates, subject to the constraint that the tax system raises some given amount of revenue, R:

$$\max_{t_1,\ldots,t_k} v(\mathbf{p}+\mathbf{t},m)$$

$$\text{such that } \sum_{i=1}^{k} t_i x_i(\mathbf{p}+\mathbf{t},m) = R.$$

The Lagrangian for this problem is

$$\mathcal{L} = v(\mathbf{p}+\mathbf{t},m) - \mu \left[\sum_{i=1}^{k} t_i x_i(\mathbf{p}+\mathbf{t},m) - R \right].$$

Differentiating with respect to t_i, we have

$$\frac{\partial v(\mathbf{p}+\mathbf{t},m)}{\partial p_i} - \mu \left[x_i + \sum_{j=1}^{k} t_j \frac{\partial x_j(\mathbf{p}+\mathbf{t},m)}{\partial p_i} \right] = 0 \quad \text{for } i = 1,\ldots,k.$$

Applying Roy's law, we can write

$$-\lambda x_i - \mu \left[x_i + \sum_{j=1}^{k} t_j \frac{\partial x_j(\mathbf{p}+\mathbf{t},m)}{\partial p_i} \right] = 0 \quad \text{for } i = 1,\ldots,k.$$

Solving for x_i we have

$$x_i = -\frac{\mu}{\mu+\lambda} \sum_{j=1}^{k} t_j \frac{\partial x_j(\mathbf{p}+\mathbf{t},m)}{\partial p_i}.$$

Now use the Slutsky equation on the right-hand side of this equation to get

$$x_i = -\frac{\mu}{\mu+\lambda} \sum_{j=1}^{k} t_j \left[\frac{\partial h_j}{\partial p_i} - \frac{\partial x_j}{\partial m} x_i \right].$$

After some manipulation, this expression can be written as

$$\theta x_i = \sum_{j=1}^{k} t_j \frac{\partial h_j}{\partial p_i},$$

where θ is a function of μ, λ, and $\sum_j t_j \partial x_j / \partial m$.

Applying the symmetry of the Slutsky matrix, we can write

$$\theta x_i = \sum_{j=1}^{k} t_j \frac{\partial h_i}{\partial p_j}. \tag{22.1}$$

Putting this expression into elasticity form yields

$$\theta = \sum_{j=1}^{k} \frac{\partial h_i}{\partial p_j} \frac{p_j}{x_i} \frac{t_j}{p_j} = \sum_{j=1}^{k} \epsilon_{ij} \frac{t_j}{p_j}.$$

This equation says that the taxes must be chosen so that the weighted sum of the Hicksian cross-price elasticities is the same for all goods.

In the extreme case, where $\epsilon_{ij} = 0$ for $i \neq j$, this condition becomes

$$\frac{t_i}{p_i} = \frac{\theta}{\epsilon_{ii}}. \tag{22.2}$$

so that the tax/price ratio for good i is proportional to the inverse of the elasticity of demand. This is known as the **inverse elasticity rule.** It makes good sense: you should tax goods heavily that are relatively inelastically demanded, and tax goods lightly that are relatively elastically demanded. Doing this distorts the consumer's decisions the least.

Another simplification arises when the tax rates t_i are small. In this case

$$dh_i \approx \sum_{j=1}^{k} t_j \frac{\partial h_i}{\partial p_j}.$$

Inserting this into equation (22.1) gives us

$$\frac{dh_i}{h_i} \approx \theta.$$

This equation says that the optimal set of small taxes reduces all compensated demands by the same proportion.

Notes

The material in this chapter is pretty standard; consult any text on benefit-cost analysis for elaboration. For a survey of optimal taxation theory see Mirrlees (1982) or Atkinson & Stiglitz (1980).

Exercises

22.1. In the formula for the optimal tax derived in the text, equation (22.1), show that θ is nonnegative if the required amount of revenue is positive.

22.2. A public utility produces outputs $x_1, \ldots, x_k$. These goods are consumed by a representative consumer with utility function $u_1(x_1) + \cdots + u_k(x_k) + y$, where y is a numeraire good. The utility produces good i at marginal cost c_i but has fixed costs F. Derive a formula for the optimal pricing rule that relates $(p_i - c_i)$ to the elasticity of demand for good i.

CHAPTER **23**

PUBLIC GOODS

Up until now our discussion of resource allocation has been concerned solely with **private goods**, that is, goods whose consumption only affects a single economic agent. Consider, for example, bread. You and I can consume different amounts of bread, and, if I consume a particular loaf of bread, you are excluded from consuming the same loaf of bread.

We say that a good is **excludable** if people can be excluded from consuming it. We say that a good is **nonrival** if one person's consumption does not reduce the amount available to other consumers. Rival goods are goods where one person's consumption does reduce the amount available to others. Rival goods are sometimes called **diminishable**. Ordinary private goods are both excludable and rival.

Certain goods do not have these properties. A nice example is street lights. The amount of street lights in a given area is fixed—you and I both have the same potential consumption, and the amount that I "consume" doesn't affect the amount available for you to consume. Hence, streetlights are nonrival. Furthermore, my consumption of street lights does not exclude your consumption. Goods that are not excludable and are nonrival are called **public goods**; other examples are police and fire protection, highways, national defense, lighthouses, television and radio broadcasts, clean air, and so on.

There are also many in-between cases. Consider for example, the case of a coded TV broadcast. This is nonrival—since one person's consumption doesn't reduce another person's—but it is excludable, since only people who have access to a decoder can watch the broadcast. Goods of this sort are sometimes called **club goods**.

Another class of examples are goods that are not excludable, but are rival. A crowded street is a good example: anyone can use the street, but one person's use reduces the amount of space available to someone else.

Finally, we have certain goods that are inherently private goods, but are treated as though they are public goods. Education, for example, is essentially a private good—it is excludable, and, to some extent, diminishable. However, most countries have made a political decision to provide education publicly. Often there has been a political decision to provide the same level of educational expenditure to all citizens. This constraint requires us to treat education as if it were a public good.

Resource allocation problems involving public goods turn out to be quite different from resource allocation problems involving private goods. We've seen earlier that competitive markets are an effective social institution for allocating private goods in an efficient manner. However, it turns out that private markets are often not a very good mechanism for allocating public goods. Generally, other social institutions, such as voting, must be used.

23.1 Efficient provision of a discrete public good

We begin by studying a simple example with two agents and two goods. One good, x_i, is a private good and can be thought of as money to be spent on private consumption. The other good, G, is a public good, which can be money to spend on some public good such as streetlights. The agents initially have some endowment of the private good, w_i, and determine how much to contribute to the public good. If individual i decides to contribute g_i, he will have $x_i = w_i - g_i$ of private consumption. We assume that utility is strictly increasing in consumption of both the public and the private good and write $u_i(G, x_i)$ for agent i's utility function.

Initially, we consider the case where the public good is only available in a discrete amount; either it is provided in that amount or it is not provided at all. Assume that it costs c to provide one unit of the public good so that the technology is given by

$$G = \begin{cases} 1 & \text{if } g_1 + g_2 \geq c \\ 0 & \text{if } g_1 + g_2 < c. \end{cases}$$

Later on we consider more general technologies.

We first ask when it is Pareto efficient to provide the public good. Providing the public good will Pareto dominate not providing it if there is some pattern of contributions (g_1, g_2) such that $g_1 + g_2 \geq c$ and

$$u_1(1, w_1 - g_1) > u_1(0, w_1)$$
$$u_2(1, w_2 - g_2) > u_2(0, w_2). \tag{23.1}$$

Let r_i be the maximum amount of the private good that agent i would be willing to give up to get one unit of the public good. We call this the maximum willingness-to-pay, or the **reservation price** of consumer i. (See Chapter 9, page 153.)

By definition r_i must satisfy the equation

$$u_i(1, w_i - r_i) = u_i(0, w_i). \tag{23.2}$$

Applying this definition to equation (23.1), we have

$$u_i(1, w_i - g_i) > u_i(0, w_i) = u_i(1, w_i - r_i),$$

for $i = 1, 2$. Since utility is strictly increasing in private consumption,

$$w_i - g_i > w_i - r_i$$

for $i = 1, 2$. Adding these inequalities, we see that

$$r_1 + r_2 > g_1 + g_2 \geq c.$$

Hence, if it is Pareto improving to provide the public good, we must have $r_1 + r_2 > c$. That is, the sum of the willingnesses-to-pay for the public good must exceed the cost of providing it. Note the difference from the efficiency conditions for providing a private good. In the case of a private good, if individual i is willing to pay the cost of producing a private good, it is efficient to provide it. Here we only need the weaker condition that *sum* of the willingnesses-to-pay exceeds the cost of provision.

It is not difficult to show the converse proposition. Suppose that we have $r_1 + r_2 > c$. Then choose g_i slightly less than r_i, so that the inequalities $g_1 + g_2 \geq c$ and

$$u_i(1, w_i - g_i) > u_i(0, w_i)$$

are satisfied for $i = 1, 2$. This shows when $r_1 + r_2 > c$ it is both feasible and Pareto improving to provide the public good. We summarize the discussion in the following statement: it is a Pareto improvement to provide a discrete public good if and only if the sum of the willingnesses-to-pay exceeds the cost of provision.

Private provision of a discrete public good.

Table
23.1

		Consumer 2	
		Buy	Don't buy
Consumer 1	Buy	-50,-50	-50,100
	Don't buy	100,-50	0,0

23.2 Private provision of a discrete public good

How effective is a private market at providing public goods? Suppose that $r_i = 100$ for $i = 1, 2$ and $c = 150$ so that the sum of the willingnesses-to-pay exceed the cost of provision. Each agent decides independently whether or not to buy the public good. However, since the public good is a *public* good, neither agent can exclude the other from consuming it.

We can represent the strategies and payoffs in a simple game matrix, depicted in Table 23.2.

If consumer 1 buys the good, he gets $100 worth of benefits, but has to pay $150 for these benefits. If consumer 1 buys, but consumer 2 refrains from buying, consumer 2 gets $100 worth of benefits for free. In this case we say that consumer 2 is **free riding** on consumer 1.

Note that this game has a structure similar to the **Prisoner's Dilemma** described in Chapter 15, page 261. The dominant strategy equilibrium in this game is (don't buy, don't buy). Neither consumer wants to buy the good because each prefers to free-ride on the other consumer. But the net result is that the good isn't provided at all, even though it would be efficient to do so.

This shows that we cannot expect that purely independent decisions will necessarily result in an efficient amount of the public good being provided. In general it will be necessary to use more complicated mechanisms.

23.3 Voting for a discrete public good

The amount of a public good is often determined by voting. Will this generally result in an efficient provision? Suppose that we have three consumers who decide to vote on whether or not to provide a public good which costs $99 to provide. If a majority votes in favor of provision, they will split the cost equally and each pay $33. The reservation prices of the three consumers are $r_1 = 90$, $r_2 = 30$, and $r_3 = 30$.

Clearly, the sum of the reservation prices exceeds the cost of provision. However, in this case only consumer 1 will vote in favor of providing the public good, since only consumer 1 receives a positive net benefit if the good is provided. The problem with majority voting is that it only measures the ordinal preferences for the public good, whereas the efficiency condition requires a comparison of willingness-to-pay. Consumer 1 would be willing to compensate the other consumers to vote in favor of the public good, but this possibility may not be available.

Another sort of voting involves individuals stating their willingness-to-pay for the public good, with the rule that the public good will be provided if the sum of the stated willingnesses-to-pay exceeds the cost of the public good. If the cost shares are fixed, then there is typically no equilibrium to this game. Consider the example of the three voters given above. In this case, voter 1 is made better off if the good is provided, so he may as well announce an arbitrarily large positive number. Similarly agents 2 and 3 may as well announce arbitrarily large negative numbers.

Another sort of voting for a good involves each person announcing how much they are willing to pay for the public good. If the sum of the stated prices is at least as large as the cost of the public good, the good will be provided and each person must pay the amount he announced. In this case if provision of the public good is Pareto efficient, then this is an equilibrium of the game. Any set of announcements such that each agent's announcement is no larger than his reservation price and that sum up to the cost of the public good is an equilibrium. However, there are many other *inefficient* equilibria of the game as well. For example, all agents announcing zero willingness-to-pay for the public good will typically be an equilibrium.

23.4 Efficient provision of a continuous public good

Let us now suppose that the public good can be provided in any continuous amount; we continue to consider only 2 agents for simplicity. If $g_1 + g_2$ is contributed to the public good, then the amount of the public good is given by $G = f(g_1 + g_2)$, and the utility of agent i is given by $U_i(f(g_1 + g_2), w_i - g_i)$. We may as well incorporate the production function into the utility function and just write $u_i(g_1 + g_2, w_i - g_i)$, where $u_i(G, x_i)$ is defined to be $U_i(f(G), x_i)$. Incorporating the technology into the utility function doesn't result in loss of generality since ultimately utility depends on the total contributions to the public good.

We know that the first-order conditions for efficiency can be found by maximizing a weighted sum of utilities:

$$\max_{g_1, g_2} a_1 u_1(g_1 + g_2, w_1 - g_1) + a_2 u_2(g_1 + g_2, w_2 - g_2).$$

The first-order conditions for g_1 and g_2 can be written as

$$a_1 \frac{\partial u_1(G, x_1)}{\partial G} + a_2 \frac{\partial u_2(G, x_2)}{\partial G} = a_1 \frac{\partial u_1(G, x_1)}{\partial x_1}$$
$$a_1 \frac{\partial u_1(G, x_1)}{\partial G} + a_2 \frac{\partial u_2(G, x_2)}{\partial G} = a_2 \frac{\partial u_2(G, x_2)}{\partial x_2}. \tag{23.3}$$

It follows that $a_1 \partial u_1 / \partial x_1 = a_2 \partial u_2 / \partial x_2$. Dividing the left-hand sides of (23.3) by the right-hand sides, and using this equality, we have

$$\frac{\frac{\partial u_1(G, x_1)}{\partial G}}{\frac{\partial u_1(G, x_1)}{\partial x_1}} + \frac{\frac{\partial u_2(G, x_2)}{\partial G}}{\frac{\partial u_2(G, x_2)}{\partial x_2}} = 1, \tag{23.4}$$

or,

$$MRS_1 + MRS_2 = 1.$$

The condition for efficiency in the case of continuous provision of the public good is that the sum of the *marginal* willingnesses-to-pay equals the *marginal* cost of provision. In this case the marginal cost is 1 since the public good is simply the sum of the contributions.

As usual, there will typically be a whole range of allocations (G, x_1, x_2) where this efficiency condition is satisfied. Since in general the marginal willingness-to-pay for a public good depends on the amount of private consumption, the efficient level of G will typically depend on x_1 and x_2.

However, under one special case, the case of quasilinear utility, the efficient amount of the public good will be *independent* of the level of private consumption. To see this, suppose that the utility functions have the form $u_i(G) + x_i$. Then the efficiency condition (23.4) can be written as $u_1'(G) + u_2'(G) = 1$, which will normally determine a unique level of the public good.[1]

EXAMPLE: Solving for the efficient provision of a public good

Suppose that the utility functions have the Cobb-Douglas form $u_i(G, x_i) = a_i \ln G + \ln x_i$. In this case the MRS functions are given by $a_i x_i / G$, so the efficiency condition is

$$\frac{a_1 x_1}{G} + \frac{a_2 x_2}{G} = 1,$$

or

$$G = a_1 x_1 + a_2 x_2. \tag{23.5}$$

---

[1] This argument assumes that it is efficient to supply a positive amount of the public good. If income is very low, this may not be the case.

If the total amount of the private good available initially is w, then we also have the condition

$$x_1 + x_2 + G = w. \tag{23.6}$$

Equations (23.5) and (23.6) describe the set of Pareto efficient allocations.

Now consider quasilinear utility functions where $u_i(G, x_i) = b_i \ln G + x_i$. The first-order efficiency condition is

$$\frac{b_1}{G} + \frac{b_2}{G} = 1,$$

or

$$G = b_1 + b_2. \tag{23.7}$$

Again the allocation must be feasible so the set of Pareto efficient allocations is described by (23.6) and (23.7). Note that in the case of quasilinear utility there is a unique efficient amount of the public good, whereas in the general case there are many different efficient levels.

23.5 Private provision of a continuous public good

Suppose that each agent independently decides how much he wants to contribute to the public good. If agent 1 thinks that agent 2 will contribute g_2, say, then agent 1's utility maximization problem is

$$\max_{g_1} u_1(g_1 + g_2, w_1 - g_1)$$

such that $g_1 \geq 0$.

The constraint that $g_1 \geq 0$ is a natural restriction in this case; it says that agent 1 can voluntarily increase the amount of the public good, but he cannot unilaterally decrease it. As we will see below, this inequality constraint turns out to be important.

The Kuhn-Tucker first-order condition for this problem is

$$\frac{\partial u_1(g_1 + g_2, x_1)}{\partial G} - \frac{\partial u_1(g_1 + g_2, x_1)}{\partial x_1} \leq 0, \tag{23.8}$$

where equality holds if $g_1 > 0$. We can also write this condition as

$$\frac{\dfrac{\partial u_1(g_1 + g_2, x_1)}{\partial G}}{\dfrac{\partial u_1(g_1 + g_2, x_1)}{\partial x_1}} \leq 1.$$

If agent i contributes a positive amount, his marginal rate of substitution between the public and private good must equal his marginal cost, 1. If his marginal rate of substitution is less than his cost, then he will not want to contribute.

This condition is illustrated in Figure 23.1. Here the "endowment" of agent 1 is the point (w_1, g_2), since the amount of private consumption he receives if he contributes nothing is w_1 and the amount of the public consumption he receives is g_2. The "budget" line is the line with slope of -1 that passes through this point. The feasible points on the budget line are those where $g_1 = w_1 - x_1 \geq 0$. We have depicted two cases: in one case, agent 1 wants to contribute a positive amount, and in the other case, agent 1 wants to free ride.

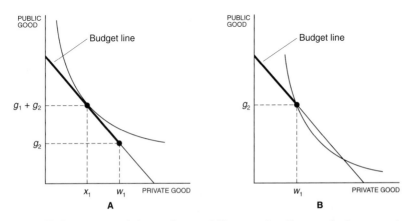

Private provision of a public good. In panel A, agent 1 is contributing a positive amount. In panel B, agent 1 finds it optimal to free ride on agent 2's contribution.

Figure 23.1

A **Nash equilibrium** to this game is a set of contributions (g_1^*, g_2^*) such that each agent is contributing an optimal amount, given the contribution of the other agent. Hence equation (23.8) must be satisfied simultaneously for both agents. We can write the conditions characterizing a Nash equilibrium as

$$\frac{\frac{\partial u_1(G^*, x_1^*)}{\partial G^*}}{\frac{\partial u_1(G^*, x_1^*)}{\partial x_1}} \leq 1$$

$$\frac{\frac{\partial u_2(G^*, x_2^*)}{\partial G^*}}{\frac{\partial u_2(G^*, x_2^*)}{\partial x_2}} \leq 1.$$

(23.9)

If a positive amount of G is provided, then at least one of these inequalities must be an equality. We could continue the analysis and attempt to find conditions under which only one of the agents contributes, when both contribute, etc.

However, there is another somewhat more useful way to describe Nash equilibrium in this case. To do this, we need to solve for the **reaction function** of agent i. This gives the amount that agent i wants to contribute as a function of the other agent's contribution.

We can write agent 1's maximization problem as

$$\max_{g_1, x_1} u_1(g_1 + g_2, x_1)$$
$$\text{such that } g_1 + x_1 = w_1 \tag{23.10}$$
$$g_1 \geq 0.$$

Using the fact that $G = g_1 + g_2$, we can rewrite this problem as

$$\max_{G, x_1} u_1(G, x_1)$$
$$\text{such that } G + x_1 = w_1 + g_2 \tag{23.11}$$
$$G \geq g_2.$$

Look carefully at the second formulation. It says that agent 1 is effectively choosing the *total* amount of the public good subject to his budget constraint, and the constraint that the amount he chooses must be at least as large as the amount provided by the other person. The budget constraint says that the total value of his consumption must equal the value of his "endowment," $w_1 + g_2$.

Problem (23.11) is just like an ordinary consumer maximization problem except for the inequality constraint. Let $f_1(w)$ be agent 1's demand for the public good as a function of his wealth, ignoring the inequality constraint. Then the amount of the public good that solves (23.10) is given by

$$G = \max\{f_1(w_1 + g_2), g_2\}.$$

Subtracting g_2 from both sides of this equation, we have

$$g_1 = \max\{f_1(w_1 + g_2) - g_2, 0\}.$$

This is the reaction function for agent 1; it gives his optimal contribution as a function of the other agent's contribution. A Nash equilibrium is a set of contributions (g_1^*, g_2^*), such that

$$g_1^* = \max\{f_1(w_1 + g_2^*) - g_2^*, 0\}$$
$$g_2^* = \max\{f_2(w_2 + g_1^*) - g_1^*, 0\}. \tag{23.12}$$

This formulation is often more useful than the formulation in (23.9) since we have a better idea of what the demand functions f_1 and f_2 might look like. We pursue this point in an example below.

It is useful to examine the form the equilibrium conditions take when utility is quasilinear. In this case we can write (23.9) as

$$u_1'(g_1^* + g_2^*) \leq 1$$
$$u_2'(g_1^* + g_2^*) \leq 1.$$

Note that in general only one of these two constraints can be binding. Suppose that agent 1 places a higher marginal value on the public good than agent 2 so that $u_1'(G) > u_2'(G)$ for all G, then only agent 1 will ever contribute—agent 2 will always free ride. Both agents will contribute only when they have the same tastes (at the margin) for the public good.

Alternatively, we note that when utility is quasilinear the demand for the public good will be independent of income, so that $f_i(w) \equiv \bar{g}_i$. Then (23.12) takes the form

$$g_1^* = \max\{\bar{g}_1 - g_2^*, 0\}$$
$$g_2^* = \max\{\bar{g}_2 - g_1^*, 0\}.$$

It follows from these equations that if $\bar{g}_1 > \bar{g}_2$, then $g_1^* = \bar{g}_1$ and $g_2^* = 0$.

EXAMPLE: Solving for Nash equilibrium provision

Consider our previous example with Cobb-Douglas utility functions. Applying the standard formula for Cobb-Douglas demand functions, we have

$$f_i(w) = \frac{a_i}{1 + a_i} w.$$

It follows that a solution to (23.12) must satisfy

$$g_1 = \max \left\{ \frac{a_1}{1 + a_1}(w_1 + g_2) - g_2, 0 \right\}$$
$$g_2 = \max \left\{ \frac{a_2}{1 + a_2}(w_2 + g_1) - g_1, 0 \right\}. \tag{23.13}$$

For the quasilinear example, we have the first-order conditions

$$\frac{b_1}{G} \leq 1$$
$$\frac{b_2}{G} \leq 1.$$

Hence, $G^* = \max\{b_1, b_2\}$. If $b_1 > b_2$, agent 1 does all the contributing and agent 2 free rides.

23.6 Voting

Suppose that a group of agents is considering voting on the amount of a public good. If the current level of the public good is G, then they take a vote to decide whether to increase or decrease the amount of the public good. If a majority votes in favor of increasing or decreasing the amount of the good, this is done. A **voting equilibrium** is an amount such that there is no majority that prefers either more or less of the public good.

Without further restrictions, it is possible that no equilibrium exists in this model. For example, suppose that there are three agents, A, B, and C and three levels of provision of the public good, 1, 2, or 3 units. A prefers 1 to 2 and 2 to 3; B prefers 2 to 3 and 3 to 1; C prefers 3 to 1 and 1 to 2. In this case there is a majority that prefers 1 to 2, a majority that prefers 2 to 3, and a majority that prefers 3 to 1. Hence, no matter what amount of the public good is provided there is a majority that wants to change it. This is an example of the well-known **paradox of voting**.

However, if we are willing to add a little more structure we can eliminate the paradox. Suppose that the agents all agree that if a majority votes in favor of an increase in the public good, agent i will pay a fraction s_i of the additional cost, and assume that all agents have quasilinear utility functions. If G units of the public good are provided, agent i receives utility $u_i(G) - s_i G$. Hence, he will vote in favor of increasing the amount of the public good if $u_i'(G) > s_i$.

We say that agent i has **single-peaked preferences** if $u_i(G) - s_i G$ has a unique maximum. Assuming this condition is satisfied, let G_i be the point where agent i's utility is maximized. Then I claim that the unique voting equilibrium is given by the **median** value of the G_i's. For simplicity, suppose that each agent has a different value of G_i and that there are an odd number of voters. If there are $n+1$ voters, then the **median voter** is that one such that $n/2$ prefer more of the public good and $n/2$ prefer less. If agent m is the median voter, the voting equilibrium level of the public good, G_v, is given by

$$u_m'(G_v) = s_m.$$

Such an equilibrium is called a **Bowen equilibrium**. It is clear that this is an equilibrium since there is no majority that wants to decrease or increase the amount of the public good. It is also not hard to show that it is unique.

One question of interest is how it compares to the efficient level of the public good. Recall that this is the level of the public good that satisfies

$$\sum_{i=1}^{n} u_i'(G_e) = 1.$$

We can also write this as

$$\frac{1}{n}\sum_{i=1}^{n} u_i'(G_e) = \frac{1}{n}.$$

The left-hand side of this equation is the derivative of the "average" utility function. The right-hand side is the average cost share. Hence, the efficient level of the public good is determined by the condition that the *average* willingness-to-pay must equal the average cost. This should be compared to the voting equilibrium condition in which the *median* willingness-to-pay is what determines the equilibrium amount of the public good. If the median consumer wants the same amount of the public good as the average consumer, the amount of the public good provided by voting will be efficient. However, in general, either too much or too little of the public good could be provided by voting depending on whether the median voter wants more or less of the public good than the average voter.

EXAMPLE: Quasilinear utility and voting

Suppose that utility takes the form $b_i \ln G + x_i$ and each person is obligated to pay an equal share $1/n$ of the public good. The efficient amount of the public good is given by $G_e = \sum_i b_i$. The voting equilibrium amount is the amount that is optimal for the median voter. Letting b_m be the taste parameter for this voter, we have

$$\frac{b_m}{G_v} = \frac{1}{n},$$

or $G_v = nb_m$. Hence

$$G_e > G_v \quad \text{if and only if} \quad \frac{1}{n}\sum_i b_i > b_m.$$

That is, the efficient amount of the public good exceeds the amount provided by majority voting if the average consumer values the public good more highly than the median consumer.

23.7 Lindahl allocations

Suppose that we try to support an efficient allocation of the public good by using a price system. We offer each consumer i the right to "buy" as much as he wants of the public good at a price p_i. Consumer i thus solves the maximization problem

$$\max_{x_i,G} u_i(G, x_i)$$

$$\text{such that } x_i + p_i G = w_i.$$

The first-order condition for this problem is

$$\frac{\frac{\partial u_i}{\partial G}}{\frac{\partial u_i}{\partial x_i}} = p_i.$$

The optimal amount of G as a function of p_i and w_i is the consumer's demand function for the public good, which we write as $G_i(p_i, w_i)$.

Is there a set of prices such that consumers will naturally choose an efficient amount of the public good? Under the standard convexity conditions, the answer is "yes." We know from our analysis of efficiency that an efficient amount of the public good must satisfy

$$\frac{\frac{\partial u_1(G^*, x_1^*)}{\partial G}}{\frac{\partial u_1(G^*, x_1^*)}{\partial x_1}} + \frac{\frac{\partial u_2(G^*, x_2^*)}{\partial G}}{\frac{\partial u_2(G^*, x_2^*)}{\partial x_2}} = 1.$$

Hence choosing

$$p_i^* = \frac{\frac{\partial u_i(G^*, x_i^*)}{\partial G}}{\frac{\partial u_i(G^*, x_i^*)}{\partial x_i}}$$

should do the trick. These prices—the prices that support an efficient allocation of the public good—are known as **Lindahl prices**.

We can also interpret these prices as tax rates. If G units of the public good are provided, then agent i must pay a tax of $p_i G$. For this reason, one sometimes sees the Lindahl prices referred to as **Lindahl taxes**.

23.8 Demand revealing mechanisms

We have seen earlier in this chapter public goods may present problems for a decentralized resource allocation mechanism. Private provision of public goods generally results in less than an efficient amount of the public good. Voting may result in too much or too little of the public good. Are there any mechanisms that result in the "right" amount of the public good being supplied?

In order to examine this question, let us return to the model of the discrete public good. Suppose that G is either 0 or 1. Let r_i be agent i's reservation price and s_i be agent i's cost share of the public good. Since the public good costs c to provide, $s_i c$ is the total amount of money that agent i must pay if the good is provided. Let $v_i = r_i - s_i c$ be agent i's **net value** for the public good. According to our previous discussion, it is efficient to provide the public good if $\sum_i v_i = \sum_i (r_i - s_i c) > 0$.

One mechanism that we might use is simply to ask each agent to report his or her net value and provide the public good if the sum of these reported values is nonnegative. The trouble with such a scheme is that it does not provide good incentives for the individual agents to reveal their true willingness to pay. For example, if agent 1's net value exceeds zero by any amount, he might as well report an arbitrarily large amount. Since his report doesn't affect how much he has to pay, but it does affect whether or not the public good is provided, he may as well report as large a value as possible.

How can we induce each agent to *truthfully* reveal his true value of the public good? Here is a scheme that works:

The Groves-Clarke mechanism

(1) Each agent reports a "bid" for the public good, b_i. This may or may not be his true value.

(2) The public good is provided if $\sum_i b_i \geq 0$, and it is not provided if $\sum_i b_i < 0$.

(3) Each agent i receives a sidepayment equal to the sum of the other bids, $\sum_{j \neq i} b_j$, if the public good is provided. (If this sum is positive, agent i receives it; if it is negative, agent i must pay this amount.)

Let us show that it is optimal for each agent to report his true value. There are n agents, each with a true value of v_i and a bid value of b_i. We want to show that it is optimal for each agent to report $b_i = v_i$ regardless of what the other agents report. That is, we want to show that truthtelling is a **dominant strategy**.

Agent i's payoff takes the form

$$\text{payoff to } i = \begin{cases} v_i + \sum_{j \neq i} b_j & \text{if } b_i + \sum_{j \neq i} b_j \geq 0 \\ 0 & \text{if } b_i + \sum_{j \neq i} b_j < 0. \end{cases}$$

Suppose that $v_i + \sum_{j \neq i} b_j > 0$. Then agent i can ensure that the public good is provided by reporting $b_i = v_i$. Suppose, on the other hand, that $v_i + \sum_{j \neq i} b_j < 0$. Then agent i can ensure that the public good is not provided by reporting $b_i = v_i$. Either way, it is optimal for agent i to tell the truth. There is never an incentive to misrepresent preferences, regardless of what the other agents do. In effect, the information-gathering mechanism has been modified so that each agent faces the social decision problem rather than the individual decision problem, and thus each agent has an incentive to reveal his own preferences correctly.

Unfortunately, the preference revelation scheme just described has a major fault. The total sidepayments may potentially be very large: they are equal to the amount that *everyone* else bids. It may be very costly to induce the agents to tell the truth!

Ideally, we would like to have a mechanism where the sidepayments sum up to zero. However, it turns out that this is not possible in general. However, it is possible to design a mechanism where the sidepayments are always nonpositive. Thus the agents may be required to pay a "tax," but they will never receive payments. Because of these "wasted" tax payments, the allocation of public and private goods will not be Pareto efficient. However, the public good will be provided if and only if it is efficient to do so.

Let us describe how this can be accomplished. The basic insight is the following: we can require each agent i to make an additional payment that depends only on what the other agents do without affecting any of i's incentives.

Let $\mathbf{b}_{-i}$ be the vector of bids, omitting the bid of agent i, and let $h_i(\mathbf{b}_{-i})$ be the extra payment made by agent i. The payoff to agent i now takes the form

$$\text{payoff to } i = \begin{cases} v_i + \sum_{j \neq i} b_j - h_i(\mathbf{b}_{-i}) & \text{if } b_i + \sum_{j \neq i} b_j \geq 0 \\ -h_i(\mathbf{b}_{-i}) & \text{if } b_i + \sum_{j \neq i} b_j < 0. \end{cases}$$

It is clear that such mechanisms give truthful revelation for exactly the reasons mentioned above. If the h_i functions are cleverly chosen, the size of the sidepayments can be significantly reduced. One nice choice for the h_i function is as follows:

$$h_i(\mathbf{b}_{-i}) = \begin{cases} \sum_{j \neq i} b_j & \text{if } \sum_{j \neq i} b_j \geq 0 \\ 0 & \text{if } \sum_{j \neq i} b_j < 0. \end{cases}$$

Such a choice gives rise to the **pivotal mechanism**, also known as the **Clarke tax**. The payoff to agent i is of the form:

$$\text{payoff to } i = \begin{cases} v_i & \text{if } \sum_i b_i \geq 0 \text{ and } \sum_{j \neq i} b_j \geq 0 \\ v_i + \sum_{j \neq i} b_j & \text{if } \sum_i b_i \geq 0 \text{ and } \sum_{j \neq i} b_j < 0 \\ -\sum_{j \neq i} b_j & \text{if } \sum_i b_i < 0 \text{ and } \sum_{j \neq i} b_j \geq 0 \\ 0 & \text{if } \sum_i b_i < 0 \text{ and } \sum_{j \neq i} b_j < 0. \end{cases} \qquad (23.14)$$

Note that agent i never receives a positive sidepayment; he may be taxed, but he is never subsidized. Adding in the sidepayment has the effect of taxing agent i only if he *changes* the social decision. Look, for example, at rows two and three of expression (23.14). Agent i has to pay a tax only when he changes the sum of the bids from positive to negative, or vice versa. The amount of the tax that i must pay is the amount by which agent i's bid damages the other agents (according to their stated bids). The price that agent i must pay to change the amount of the public good is equal to the harm that he imposes on the other agents. Note that every agent finds it advantageous to use this decision process since he is never taxed by more than the decision is worth to him.

23.9 Demand revealing mechanisms with a continuous good

Suppose now that we are concerned with the provision of a continuous public good. If G units of the public good are provided, then consumer i will have utility

$$v_i(G) = u_i(G) - s_i G,$$

where $u_i(G)$ is his (quasilinear) utility for the public good and s_i is his cost share. Suppose that agent i is asked to report the function $v_i(G)$.

Denote his reported function by $b_i(G)$. The government announces that it will provide a level of the public good, G^*, that maximizes the sum of the reported functions. Each agent i will receive a sidepayment equal to $\sum_{j \neq i} b_j(G^*)$.

In this mechanism, it is always in the interest of each agent i to truthfully report his true utility function. To see this, simply note that individual i wants to maximize

$$v_i(G) + \sum_{j \neq i} b_j(G),$$

while the government will maximize

$$b_i(G) + \sum_{j \neq i} b_j(G).$$

By reporting $b_i(G) = v_i(G)$, agent i ensures that the government will choose a G^* that maximizes his utility.

As in the discrete case, the total sidepayments can be very large. However, just as before they can be reduced by an appropriate sidepayment. The best choice in this case is the sidepayment $-\max_G \sum_{j \neq i} b_j(G)$. This leaves agent i with a net utility of

$$v_i(G) + \sum_{j \neq i} b_j(G) - \max_G \sum_{j \neq i} b_j(G).$$

Note that the sum of the last two terms must be negative. As before, agent i is taxed by the amount that he changes social welfare.

Notes

Efficiency conditions for public goods were first formulated by Samuelson (1954). The private provision of public goods has been extensively studied by Bergstrom, Blume & Varian (1986). Lindahl (1919) introduced the concept of Lindahl prices. The demand revealing mechanism was introduced by Clarke (1971) and Groves (1973).

Exercises

23.1. Consider the following game as a solution to the public goods problem in the case of a discrete public good with two agents. Each agent i states a "bid", b_i. If $b_1 + b_2 \geq c$, the good is provided and each agent pays their bid amount; otherwise, the good is not provided and neither agent pays anything. Is the efficient outcome an equilibrium to this game? Is anything else an equilibrium?

23.2. Suppose that u_1 and u_2 are both homothetic in (x_i, G). Derive the conditions for the Nash equilibrium levels of contributions.

23.3. Suppose now that the two agents have different wealths, but identical Cobb-Douglas utility functions, $u_i(G, x_i) = G^\alpha x_i^{1-\alpha}$. How big does the wealth difference between agent 1 and 2 have to be for agent 2 to contribute zero in equilibrium?

23.4. Suppose that there are n agents with identical Cobb-Douglas utility functions, $u_i(G, x_i) = G^\alpha x_i^{1-\alpha}$. There is a total amount of wealth w, which is divided among $k \leq n$ of the agents. How much of the public good is provided? How does the amount of the public good change as k increases?

23.5. Does the Clarke tax result in a Pareto efficient allocation? Does the Clarke tax result in a Pareto efficient amount of the public good?

23.6. A peculiar tribe of natives in the South Seas called the Grads consume only coconuts. They use the coconuts for two purposes: either they consume them for food, or they burn them in a public religious sacrifice. (The Grads believe that this sacrifice will help their prelim performance.)

Suppose that each Grad i has an initial endowment of coconuts of $w_i > 0$. Let $x_i \geq 0$ be the amount of coconuts that he consumes, and let $g_i \geq 0$ be the amount of coconuts that he gives to the public offering. The total number of coconuts contributed to the offering is $G = \sum_{i=1}^{n} g_i$. Grad i's utility function is given by

$$u_i(x_i, G) = x_i + a_i \ln G,$$

where $a_i > 1$.

(a) In determining his gift, each Grad i assumes that the gifts of the other Grads will remain constant and determines how much he will give on this basis. Let

$$G_{-i} = \sum_{j \neq i} g_j$$

denote the gifts other than Grad i. Write down a utility maximization problem that determines Grad i's gift.

(b) Recalling that $G = g_i + G_{-i}$ for all agents i, what will be the equilibrium amount of the public good. (Hint: not every agent will contribute a positive amount to the public good.)

(c) Who will free-ride in this problem?

(d) What is the Pareto efficient amount of the public good to provide in this economy?

CHAPTER **24**

EXTERNALITIES

When the actions of one agent directly affect the environment of another agent, we will say that there is an **externality**. In a **consumption externality** the utility of one consumer is directly affected by the actions of another consumer. For example, some consumers may be affected by other agents' consumption of tobacco, alcohol, loud music, and so on. Consumers might also be adversely affected by firms who produce pollution or noise.

In **production externality** the production set of one firm is directly affected by the actions of another agent. For example, the production of smoke by a steel mill may directly affect the production of clean clothes by a laundry, or the production of honey by a beekeeper might directly affect the level of output of an apple orchard next door.

In this chapter we explore the economics of externalities. We find that in general market equilibria will be inefficient in the presence of externalities. This naturally leads to an examination of various suggestions for alternative ways to allocate resources that lead to efficient outcomes.

The First Theorem of Welfare Economics does not hold in the presence of externalities. The reason is that there are things that people care about that are not priced. Achieving an efficient allocation in the presense of externalities essentially involves making sure that agents face the correct prices for their actions.

24.1 An example of a production externality

Suppose that we have two firms. Firm 1 produces an output x which it sells in a competitive market. However, the production of x imposes a cost $e(x)$ on firm 2. For example, suppose the technology is such that x units of output can only be produced by generating x units of pollution, and this pollution harms firm 2.

Letting p be the price of output, the profits of the two firms are given by

$$\pi_1 = \max_x \; px - c(x)$$

$$\pi_2 = -e(x).$$

We assume that both cost functions are increasing and convex as usual. (It may be that firm 2 receives profits from some production activity, but we ignore this for simplicity.)

The equilibrium amount of output, x_q, is given by $p = c'(x_q)$. However, this output is too large from a social point of view. The first firm takes account of the **private costs**—the costs that it imposes on itself—but it ignores the **social costs**—the private cost plus cost that it imposes on the other firm.

In order to determine the efficient amount of output, we ask what would happen if the two firms merged so as to **internalize** the externality. In this case the merged firm would maximize total profits

$$\pi = \max_x \; px - c(x) - e(x),$$

and this problem has first-order condition

$$p = c'(x_e) + e'(x_e). \tag{24.1}$$

The output x_e is an efficient amount of output; it is characterized by price being equal to marginal *social* cost.

24.2 Solutions to the externalities problem

There have been several solutions proposed to solve the inefficiency of externalities.

Pigovian taxes

According to this view, firm 1 simply faces the wrong price for its action, and a corrective tax can be imposed that will lead to efficient resource allocation. Corrective taxes of this sort are known as **Pigovian taxes**.

Suppose, for example, that the firm faced a tax on its output in amount t. Then the first-order condition for profit maximization becomes

$$p = c'(x) + t.$$

Under our assumption of a convex cost function we can set $t = e'(x_e)$, which leads the firm to choose $x = x_e$, as determined in equation (24.1). Even if the cost function were not convex, we could simply impose a nonlinear tax of $e(x)$ on firm 1, thus leading it to internalize the cost of the externality.

The problem with this solution is that it requires that the taxing authority know the externality cost function $e(x)$. But if the taxing authority knows this cost function, it might as well just tell the firm how much to produce in the first place.

Missing markets

According to this view, the problem is that firm 2 cares about the pollution generated by firm 1 but has no way to influence it. Adding a market for firm 2 to express its demand for pollution—or for a reduction of pollution—will provide a mechanism for efficient allocation.

In our model when x units of output are produced, x units of pollution are unavoidably produced. If the market price of pollution is r, then firm 1 can decide how much pollution it wants to sell, x_1, and firm 2 can decide how much it wants to buy, x_2. The profit maximization problems become

$$\pi_1 = \max_{x_1} \; px_1 + rx_1 - c(x_1)$$
$$\pi_2 = \max_{x_2} \; -rx_2 - e(x_2).$$

The first-order conditions are

$$p + r = c'(x_1)$$
$$-r = e'(x_2).$$

When demand for pollution equals the supply of pollution, we have $x_1 = x_2$, and these first-order conditions become equivalent to those given in (24.1). Note that the equilibrium price of pollution, r, will be a negative number. This is natural, since pollution is a "bad" not a good.

More generally, suppose that pollution and output are not necessarily produced in a one-to-one ratio. If firm 1 produces x units of output and y units of pollution, then it pays a cost of $c(x, y)$. Presumably increasing y from zero lowers the cost of production of x; otherwise, there wouldn't be any problem.

In the absence of any mechanism to control pollution, the profit maximization problem of firm 1 is

$$\max_{x,y} \; px - c(x,y),$$

which has first-order conditions

$$p = \frac{\partial c(x,y)}{\partial x}$$

$$0 = \frac{\partial c(x,y)}{\partial y}.$$

Firm 1 will equate the price of pollution to its marginal cost. In this case the price of pollution is zero, so firm 1 will pollute up to the point where the costs of production are minimized.

Now we add a market for pollution. Again, let r be the cost per unit of pollution and y_1 and y_2 the supply and demand by firms 1 and 2. The maximization problems are

$$\pi_1 = \max_{x,y_1} \; px + ry_1 - c(x,y_1)$$

$$\pi_2 = \max_{y_2} \; -ry_2 - e(y_2).$$

The first-order conditions are

$$p = \frac{\partial c(x,y_1)}{\partial x}$$

$$r = \frac{\partial c(x,y_1)}{\partial y_1}$$

$$-r = \frac{\partial e(y_2)}{\partial y_2}.$$

Equating supply and demand, so $y_1 = y_2$, we have the first-order conditions for an efficient level of x and y.

The problem with this solution is that the markets for pollution may be very thin. In the case depicted there are only two firms. There is no particular reason to think that such a market will behave competitively.

Property rights

According to this view, the basic problem is that property rights are not conducive to full efficiency. If both technologies are operated by one firm, we have seen that there is no problem. However, we will see that there is a market signal that will encourage the agents to determine an efficient pattern of property rights.

If the externality of one firm adversely affects the operation of another, it always will pay one firm to buy out the other. It is clear that by coordinating the actions of both firms one can always produce more profits than by acting separately. Therefore, one firm could afford to pay the other firm its market value (in the presence of the externality) since its value when the externality is optimally adjusted would exceed this current market value. This argument shows the market mechanism itself provides signals to adjust property rights to internalize externalities.

We have already established this claim in some generality in the proof of the First Welfare Theorem in Chapter 18, page 345. The argument there shows that if an allocation is not Pareto efficient, then there is some way that aggregate profits can be increased. A careful examination of the proof of the theorem shows that all that is necessary is that all goods that *consumers* care about are priced, or, equivalently, that consumers' preferences depend only on their own consumption bundles. There can be arbitrary sorts of production externalities and the proof still goes through up to the last line, where we show that aggregate profits at the Pareto dominating allocation exceed aggregate profits at the original allocation. If there are no production externalities, this is a contradiction. If production externalities are present, then this argument shows that there is some alternative production plan that increases aggregate profits—hence there is a market incentive for one firm to buy out the others, coordinate their production plans, and internalize the externality.

Essentially, the firm grows until it internalizes all relevant production externalities. This works well for some sorts of externalities, but not for all. For example, it doesn't deal very well with the case of consumption externalities, or the case of externalities that are public goods.

24.3 The compensation mechanism

We argued above that Pigovian taxes were not adequate in general to solve externalities due to the information problem: the taxing authority in general can't be expected to know the costs imposed by the externalities. However, it may be that the agents who generate the externalities have a reasonably good idea of the costs they impose. If so, there is a relatively simple scheme to internalize the externalities.

The scheme involves setting up a market for the externality, but it does so in a way that encourages the firms to correctly reveal the costs they impose on the other. Here is how the method works.

Announcement stage. Firm $i = 1, 2$ names a Pigovian tax t_i which may or may not be the efficient level of such a tax.

Choice stage. If firm 1 produces x units of output, then it has to pay a tax $t_2 x$, and firm 2 receives compensation in the amount of $t_1 x$. In addition, each firm pays penalty depending on the *difference* between their two announced tax rates.

The exact form of the penalty is irrelevant for our purposes; all that matters is that it is zero when $t_1 = t_2$ and positive otherwise. For purposes of exposition, we choose a quadratic penalty. In this case, the final payoffs to firm 1 and firm 2 are given by

$$\pi_1 = \max_x \; px - c(x) - t_2 x - (t_1 - t_2)^2$$
$$\pi_2 = t_1 x - e(x) - (t_2 - t_1)^2.$$

We want to show that the equilibrium outcome to this game involves an efficient level of production of the externality. In order to do this, we have to think a bit about what constitutes a reasonable equilibrium notion for this game. Since the game has two stages, it is reasonable to demand a **subgame perfect** equilibrium—that is, an equilibrium in which each firm takes into account the repercussions of its first-stage choices on the outcomes in the second stage. See Chapter 15, page 275.

As usual, we solve this game by looking at the second stage first. Consider the output choice in the second stage. Firm 1 will choose x to satisfy the condition

$$p = c'(x) + t_2 \qquad\qquad (24.2).$$

For each choice of t_2, there will be some optimal choice of $x(t_2)$. If $c''(x) > 0$, then it is straightforward to show that $x'(t_2) < 0$.

In the first stage, each firm will choose tax rates so as to maximize their profits. For firm 1, the choice is simple: if firm 2 chooses t_2, then firm 1 also wants to choose

$$t_1 = t_2. \qquad\qquad (24.3)$$

To check this, just differentiate firm 1's profit function with respect to t_1.

Things are a little trickier for firm 2, since it has to recognize that its choice of t_2 affects firm 1's output through the function $x(t_2)$. Differentiating firm 2's profit function, taking account of this influence, we have

$$\pi'_2(t_2) = (t_1 - e'(x))x'(t_2) - 2(t_2 - t_1) = 0. \qquad\qquad (24.4)$$

Putting (24.2), (24.3), and (24.4) together, we find

$$p = c'(x) + e'(x),$$

which is the condition for efficiency.

This method works by setting opposing incentives for the two agents. It is clear from (24.3) that agent 1 always has an incentive to match the announcement of agent 2. But consider agent 2's incentive. If agent 2 thinks that agent 1 will propose a large compensation rate t_1 for him, then he wants agent 1 to be taxed as little as possible—so that agent 1 will produce as much as possible. On the other hand, if agent 2 thinks that 1 will propose a small compensation rate for him, then agent 2 wants agent 1 to be taxed as much as possible. The only point where agent 2 is indifferent about the production level of agent 1 is where agent 2 is exactly compensated, on the margin, for the costs of the externality.

24.4 Efficiency conditions in the presence of externalities

Here we derive general efficiency conditions in the presence of externalities. Suppose that there are two goods, an x-good and a y-good, and two agents. Each agent cares about the other agent's consumption of the x-good, but neither agent cares about the other agent's consumption of the y-good. Initially, there are $\overline{x}$ units of the x-good available and $\overline{y}$ units of the y-good.

According to Chapter 17, page 332, a Pareto efficient allocation maximizes the sum of the utilities subject to the resource constraint

$$\max_{x_i, y_i} a_1 u_1(x_1, x_2, y_1) + a_2 u_2(x_1, x_2, y_2)$$

such that $x_1 + x_2 = \overline{x}$

$$y_1 + y_2 = \overline{y}.$$

The first-order conditions are

$$a_1 \frac{\partial u_1}{\partial x_1} + a_2 \frac{\partial u_2}{\partial x_1} = \lambda$$

$$a_1 \frac{\partial u_1}{\partial x_2} + a_2 \frac{\partial u_2}{\partial x_2} = \lambda$$

$$a_1 \frac{\partial u_1}{\partial y_1} = \mu$$

$$a_2 \frac{\partial u_2}{\partial y_2} = \mu.$$

After some manipulation, these conditions can be written as

$$\frac{\frac{\partial u_1}{\partial x_1}}{\frac{\partial u_1}{\partial y_1}} + \frac{\frac{\partial u_2}{\partial x_1}}{\frac{\partial u_2}{\partial y_2}} = \frac{\lambda}{\mu}$$

$$\frac{\frac{\partial u_1}{\partial x_2}}{\frac{\partial u_1}{\partial y_1}} + \frac{\frac{\partial u_2}{\partial x_2}}{\frac{\partial u_2}{\partial y_2}} = \frac{\lambda}{\mu}.$$

The efficiency condition is that the *sum* of the marginal rates of substitution equals a constant. When determining whether or not it is a good idea whether agent 1 should increase his consumption of good 1, we have to take into account not how much he is willing to pay for this additional consumption, but how much agent 2 is willing to pay. These are essentially the same conditions as the efficiency conditions for a public good.

It is clear from these conditions how to internalize the externality. We simply regard x_1 and x_2 as different goods. The price of x_1 is $p_1 = \partial u_2/\partial x_1$, and the price of x_2 is $p_2 = \partial u_1/\partial x_2$. If each agent faces the appropriate price for his actions, the market equilibrium will lead to an efficient outcome.

Notes

Pigou (1920) and Coase (1960) are classic works on externalities. The compensation mechanism is examined further in Varian (1989b).

Exercises

24.1. Suppose that two agents are deciding how fast to drive their cars. Agent i chooses speed x_i and gets utility $u_i(x_i)$ from this choice; we assume that $u_i'(x_i) > 0$. However, the faster the agents drive, the more likely it is that they are involved in a mutual accident. Let $p(x_1, x_2)$ be the probability of an accident, assumed to be increasing in each argument, and let $c_i > 0$ be the cost that the accident imposes on agent i. Assume that each agent's utility is linear in money.

(a) Show that each agent has an incentive to drive too fast from the social point of view.

(b) If agent i is fined an amount t_i in the case of an accident, how large should t_i be to internalize the externality?

(c) If the optimal fines are being used, what are the total costs, including fines, paid by the agents? How does this compare to the total cost of the accident?

(d) Suppose now that agent i gets utility $u_i(x)$ only if there is no accident. What is the appropriate fine in this case?

CHAPTER **25**

INFORMATION

The most rapidly growing area in economic theory in the last decade has been the area of information economics. In this chapter we will describe some of the basic themes of this subject.

Most of what we will study involves situations of **asymmetric information**, that is, situations where one economic agent knows something that another economic agent doesn't. For example, a worker might have a better idea of how much he could produce than his employer does, or a producer might have a better idea of the quality of a good he produces than a potential consumer has.

However, by carefully observing the worker's behavior, the employer might be able to infer something about his productivity. Similarly, a consumer might be able to infer something about the quality of a firm's product based on how it is sold. Good workers might want to be known as good workers, or they might not, depending on how they are paid. Producers of high-quality products would generally like to be known as such, but producers of low-quality products would also like to acquire a reputation for high-quality. Hence, studies of behavior under asymmetric information necessarily involve strategic interaction of agents.

25.1 The principal-agent problem

Many kinds of incentive problems can be modeled using the following frame-work. One person, the **principal**, wants to induce another person, the **agent**, to take some action which is costly to the agent. The principal may be unable to directly observe the action of the agent, but instead observes some output, x, that is determined, at least in part, by the actions of the agent. The principal's problem is to design an **incentive payment** from the principal to the agent, $s(x)$, that induces the agent to take the best action from the viewpoint of the principal.

The simplest example of a principal-agent problem is that of a manager and a worker. The manager wants the worker to exert as much effort as possible, in order to produce as much output as possible, while the worker rationally wants to make a choice that maximizes his own utility given the effort and incentive payment scheme.

A slightly less obvious example is that of a retail firm and a customer. The firm wants the customer to buy its product—a costly activity for the buyer. The firm would like to charge each customer his reservation price—the maximum he would be willing to pay. The firm can't observe this reservation price directly, but it can observe the amount that consumers with different tastes would purchase at different prices. The problem of the firm is then to design a pricing schedule that maximizes its profits. This is the problem a monopolist faces when it price discriminates; see Chapter 14, page 244.

We refer to this kind of problem as a **principal-agent** problem. In the following sections we will examine the manager-worker problem, but it is not hard to generalize to other contexts such as nonlinear pricing.

Let x be the output received by the principal and let a and b be possible actions that can be chosen by the agent out of some set of feasible actions, A. In some of what follows it will be convenient to suppose that there are only two feasible actions, but we do not impose that restriction at this point. Initially, we suppose that there is no uncertainty so that the outcome is completely determined by the actions of the agent, and we write this relationship as $x = x(a)$. Let $c(a)$ be the cost of action a and $s(x)$ the incentive payment from the principal to the agent.

The utility function of the principal is $x - s(x)$, the output minus the incentive payment, and the utility function of the agent is $s(x) - c(a)$, the incentive payment minus the cost of the action. The principal wants to choose a *function*, $s(\cdot)$, that maximizes his utility subject to the constraints imposed by the agent's optimizing behavior.

There are typically two sorts of constraints involving the agent. The first is that the agent may have another opportunity available to him that gives him some reservation level of utility, and that the principal must ensure that the agent gets at least this reservation level in order to be willing to participate. We call this the **participation constraint**. (This is sometimes called the **individual rationality** constraint.)

The second constraint on the problem is that of **incentive compatibility**: given the incentive schedule the principal chooses, the agent will pick the best action for himself. The principal is not able to choose the agent's action directly: he can only influence the action by his choice of the incentive payment.

We will be concerned with two sorts of principal-agent environments. The first is where there is one principal who acts as a monopolist: he sets a payment schedule which the agent will accept as long as it is expected to yield more than the agent's reservation level of utility. Here we want to determine the properties of the incentive scheme that is *optimal* from the viewpoint of the principal. The second is where there are many competing principals, who each set incentive schemes, and we wish to determine the properties of the *equilibrium* incentive payment systems.

In the monopoly problem, the reservation level of utility to the agent is exogenous: it will typically be the utility associated with some unrelated activity. In the competitive problem, the reservation level of utility is endogenous: it is the utility associated with the contracts offered by the other principals. Similarly, in the monopoly problem, the maximum achievable profits are the objective function of the problem. But in the competitive problem, we normally assume that the profits have been competed away in equilibrium. Hence a zero-profit condition becomes an important equilibrium condition.

25.2 Full information: monopoly solution

We start with the simplest example in which the principal has full information about the agent's costs and actions. In this case, the principal's goal is simply to determine what action he wants the agent to choose, and to design an incentive payment to induce the agent to choose that action. Since there is only one principal, we refer to this as the monopoly case.[1]

Let a denote various actions that the agent can take and let output be some known function of the action, $x(a)$. Let b be the action the principal wants to induce. (Think of b as being the "best" action for the principal and a the "alternative" actions.)

The problem of designing the optimal incentive scheme $s(\cdot)$ can be written as

$$\max_{b,s(\cdot)} x(b) - s(x(b))$$

---

[1] We could call this a monopsony case, since we are dealing with a single buyer rather than a single seller, but I use the term monopoly in a general sense to include the cases of both a single buyer and/or a single seller.

$$\text{such that } s(x(b)) - c(b) \geq \bar{u} \tag{25.1}$$
$$s(x(b)) - c(b) \geq s(x(a)) - c(a) \text{ for all } a \text{ in } A. \tag{25.2}$$

Condition (25.1) imposes the constraint that the agent must receive at least his reservation level of utility since one possible "action" is not to participate; this is the participation constraint. Condition (25.2) imposes the constraint that the agent will find it optimal to choose b; this is the incentive compatibility constraint. Note that the principal actually chooses the agent's action b, albeit indirectly, in his design of the incentive payment function. The constraint the principal faces is to make sure that the action that the agent wants to take is in fact the action that the principal wants him to take.

Although this maximization problem looks peculiar at first glance, it turns out to have a trivial solution. Let us ignore the incentive compatibility constraint for a moment. Focusing on the objective function and the participation constraint, we observe that for any x the principal wants $s(x)$ to be as small as possible. According to the the the participation constraint, (25.1), this means that $s(x(b))$ should be set equal to $\bar{u} + c(b)$; i.e., the payment to the agent covers the cost of the action and leaves him with his reservation utility.

Hence the optimal action, from the viewpoint of the principal, is the one that maximizes $x(b) - \bar{u} - c(b)$. Call this action b^*, and the associated output level $x^* = x(b^*)$. The question is: can we set up an incentive schedule, $s(x)$, that makes b^* the optimal choice for the agent? But this is easy: just choose any function $s(x)$ such that $s(x^*) - c(b^*) \geq s(x(a)) - c(a)$ for all a in A. For example, let

$$s(x^*) = \begin{cases} \bar{u} + c(b^*) & \text{if } x = x(b^*) \\ -\infty & \text{otherwise.} \end{cases}$$

This incentive scheme is a **target output scheme**: a target output of x^* is set and the agent is paid his reservation price if he reaches the target and otherwise receives an arbitrarily large punishment. (Actually, any payment less than the payment if the agent reaches the target would work.)

This is only one of many possible incentive schemes that solves the incentive problem. Another choice would be to choose a **linear incentive payment** and set $s(x(a)) = x(a) - F$. In this case the agent must pay a lump-sum fee F to the principal and then receives the entire output produced. This scheme works because the agent has the incentive to choose the action that maximizes $x(a) - c(a)$. The payment F is chosen so the agent just satisfies the participation constraint; i.e, $F = x(b^*) - c(b^*) - \bar{u}$. In this case the agent is the **residual claimant** to the output produced. Once the agent pays the principal the amount F, the agent gets all remaining profits.

There are a couple of things to observe about these solutions to the full-information principal-agent problem. First, the incentive compatibility constraint really isn't "binding." Once the optimal level of output is chosen, it is always possible to choose an incentive scheme that will support that as an optimizing choice by the agent. Second, since the incentive compatibility constraint is never binding, the Pareto efficient amount of output will always be produced. That is, there is no way to produce another output level that both the principal and the agent prefer. This follows from observing that the maximization problem without the incentive constraint is the standard form for Pareto optimization: maximize one agent's utility holding the other agent's utility constant.

The difficulty with these incentive schemes is that they are very sensitive to slight imperfections in information. Suppose, for example, that the relationship between input and output is not perfectly determinate. Perhaps there is some "noise" in the system, so that low output may be due to bad luck, rather than lack of effort. In this case an incentive scheme of the sort described above may not be appropriate. If the agent only gets paid when he achieves the target level of output, then his *expected* utility—averaged over the randomized outputs—may be less than his reservation level of utility. Hence he would refuse to participate.

In order to satisfy the participation constraint, the principal must offer the agent a payment scheme that yields the agent his reservation level of utility. Typically, such a scheme will involve positive payments at a number of output levels, since a number of different outputs may be consistent with the targeted level of effort. This type of problem is known as a **hidden action** incentive problem, since the action of the agent is not perfectly observable by the principal.

The second sort of imperfect information of interest is where the principal cannot perfectly observe the objective function of the agent. There may be many different types of agents with different utility functions or cost functions. The principal must design an incentive scheme that does well, on the average, whatever type of agent is involved. This type of incentive problem is known as the **hidden information** problem, since the difficulty is that the information about the type of agent is hidden to the principal. We will analyze these two sorts of incentive problems below.

25.3 Full information: competitive solution

Before turning to that discussion, it is of interest to examine the full information principal-agent problem in a competitive environment. As indicated above, one way to close the model is to add the condition that competition forces profits to zero.

To fix ideas, suppose that there is a group of producers and a group of identical workers. Each producer sets an incentive system in an attempt to attract workers to his factory. The producers must compete against one another to attract workers, and the workers must compete against each other to get jobs.

The optimization problem facing a given producer is just the same as in the monopoly case: he sees how much it will cost to induce various levels of effort, and how much it costs to attract workers to his factory, and chooses the combination that maximizes revenue minus cost.

We have seen that in this case an optimal incentive scheme may be chosen to have payment as a linear function of output, so $s(x) = x - F$. In the monopoly model, F was determined from the participation constraint

$$x(b^*) - F - c(b^*) = \bar{u},$$

where $\bar{u}$ is the level of utility available in some other activity exogenous to the model.

In a competitive model this is generally not appropriate. In this framework the way to determine F is to suppose that the participation constraint is not binding, but that competition in the industry pushes profits to zero. In this case F is determined by the condition that

$$x - (x - F) = 0,$$

which implies $F = 0$. The workers capture their entire marginal product and "monopoly rents" are driven to zero.

The fact that equilibrium rents are zero is an artifact of the constant-returns-to-scale technology. If the producers have some fixed costs K, then the equilibrium condition would require that $F = K$.

From a formal point of view, the main difference between the monopolistic and the competitive solution is how the rent F is determined. In the monopoly model it is that amount that makes the worker indifferent between working for the principal and engaging in some other activity. In the competitive model, the rent is determined by the zero-profit condition.

25.4 Hidden action: monopoly solution

In this section we will examine a simple model of a principal-agent relationship in which the actions are not directly observable. We will make a number of assumptions to make the analysis easy. In particular we will assume that there are only a finite number of possible output levels $(x_1, \ldots, x_n)$. The agent can take one of two actions, a or b, which influence the probability of occurrence of the various outputs. Thus we let π_{ia} be the probability that output level x_i is observed if the agent chooses action a and π_{ib} is the probability that x_i is observed if the agent chooses action b. Let $s_i = s(x_i)$ be the payment from the principal to the agent if x_i is observed. Then the expected profit of the principal if the agent chooses action b, say, is

$$\sum_{i=1}^{n} (x_i - s_i)\pi_{ib}. \tag{25.3}$$

As for the agent, let us suppose that he is risk averse and seeks to maximize some von Neumann-Morgenstern utility function of the payment, $u(s_i)$, and that the cost of his action, c_a, enters linearly into his utility function. Hence the agent will choose the action b if

$$\sum_{i=1}^{n} u(s_i)\pi_{ib} - c_b \geq \sum_{i=1}^{n} u(s_i)\pi_{ia} - c_a \qquad (25.4)$$

and will choose the action a otherwise. This is the incentive compatibility constraint.

We also suppose that one of the actions available to the agent is not to participate. Suppose that if the agent doesn't participate, he gets utility $\bar{u}$. Hence, the expected utility from participation must be at least $\bar{u}$:

$$\sum_{i=1}^{n} u(s_i)\pi_{ib} - c_b \geq \bar{u}. \qquad (25.5)$$

This is the participation constraint.

The principal wants to maximize (25.3) subject to the constraints (25.4) and (25.5). The maximization takes place over the action b and the payments (s_i). Note that both individuals are making optimizing choices in this problem. The agent is going to choose an action b that is best for the agent given the incentive system (s_i) set up by the principal. Understanding this, the principal wants to offer the pattern of incentive payments that is best for the principal. Thus the principal must take the subsequent actions of the agent as a constraint in the design of the incentive payments. Effectively, the principal is choosing the action for the agent that he desires, taking into account the cost of doing so—namely, that he must structure the incentive payment so that the principal's desired action is also the agent's desired action.

Agent's action can be observed

In the full information problem discussed in the last section, it was irrelevant whether the payment scheme was based on the action or the output. That was because there was a one-to-one relationship between actions and output. In this problem the distinction is crucial. If the payment can be based on the action, it is possible to implement a first-best incentive scheme, even if the output is random. All that the principal has to do is to determine the (expected) profit from inducing each possible action by the agent, and then induce the action that maximizes the principal's expected profit.

To see this mathematically, suppose that the principal can pay the agent as a function of the action the agent takes, rather than the output. Then the agent will get some payment $s(b)$. Note that this payment is certain, so that the agent's utility is $\sum_{i=1}^{n} \pi_{ib} u(s(b)) - c_b = u(s(b)) - c_b$. The incentive problem described above reduces to

$$\max_{s(b),b} \sum_{i=1}^{n} x_i \pi_{ib} - s(b)$$

such that $u(s(b)) - c_b \geq \bar{u}$
$$u(s(b)) - c_b \geq u(s(a)) - c_a.$$

This is just like the full-information problem examined earlier: the incentive compatibility constraint is inessential.

The interesting case of the principal-agent problem arises only when the actions are *hidden* so that the incentive payment can only be based on output. In this case the payments to the agent are necessarily random and the optimal incentive scheme will involve some degree of risk-sharing between the principal and the agent. The principal would like to pay the agent less when less output is produced, but the principal can't tell whether the small output is due to inadequate effort by the agent or simply to bad luck. If the principal punishes low output too much, he will impose too much risk on the agent, and will have to raise the average level of payoff to compensate for this. This is the tradeoff facing the principal in designing an optimal incentive mechanism.

Suppose that there was no incentive problem, and that the only issue is risk sharing. In this case, the principal's maximization problem is

$$\max_{(s_i)} \sum_{i=1}^{n} (x_i - s_i) \pi_{ib}$$

such that $\sum_{i=1}^{n} u(s_i) \pi_{ib} - c_b \geq \bar{u}.$

Letting λ be the Lagrange multiplier on the constraint, the first-order condition is
$$-\pi_{ib} - \lambda u'(s_i) \pi_{ib} = 0,$$

which implies $u'(s_i) = $ a constant, which means that $s_i = $ constant. Essentially, the principal fully insures the agent against all risk. This is natural since the principal is risk neutral and the agent is risk averse.

This solution will generally not be appropriate when there is some incentive constraint. If the principal provides full insurance, the agent doesn't care what outcome occurs, so there is no incentive for him to choose the action desired by the principal: if the agent receives a certain payment, regardless of his effort, why should he work hard? The determination of the optimal incentive contract involves trading off the benefits from the principal insuring the agent with the incentive costs that such insurance creates.

Analysis of the optimal incentive scheme

We will investigate the design of the optimal incentive scheme using the following strategy. First we will determine the optimal incentive scheme necessary to induce each possible action. Then we will compare the utility of these schemes to the principal to see which is the least costly scheme from his point of view. For simplicity, we suppose that only two actions are possible, a, and b, and ask how we can design a scheme to induce action b, say. Let $V(b)$ be the largest possible utility that the principal receives if he designs a scheme that induces the agent to choose action b. The maximization problem facing the principal is

$$V(b) = \max_{(s_i)} \sum_{i=1}^{n} (x_i - s_i)\pi_{ib}$$

$$\text{such that } \sum_{i=1}^{n} u(s_i)\pi_{ib} - c_b \geq \overline{u} \tag{25.6}$$

$$\sum_{i=1}^{n} u(s_i)\pi_{ib} - c_b \geq \sum_{i=1}^{n} u(s_i)\pi_{ia} - c_a. \tag{25.7}$$

Here condition (25.6) is the participation constraint and condition (25.7) is the incentive compatibility constraint.

This is a problem with a linear objective function and nonlinear constraints. Although it can be analyzed directly, it is convenient for graphical treatment to reformulate the problem as one with linear constraints and nonlinear objective. Let u_i be the utility achieved in outcome i, so that $u(s_i) = u_i$. Let f be the inverse of the utility function, and write $s_i = f(u_i)$. The function f simply indicates how much it costs the principal to provide utility u_i to the agent. It is straightforward to show that f is an increasing, convex function. Rewriting (25.6) and (25.7) using this notation, we have

$$V(b) = \max_{(u_i)} \sum_{i=1}^{n} (x_i - f(u_i))\pi_{ib}$$

$$\sum_{i=1}^{n} u_i \pi_{ib} - c_b \geq \overline{u} \tag{25.8}$$

$$\sum_{i=1}^{n} u_i \pi_{ib} - c_b \geq \sum_{i=1}^{n} u_i \pi_{ia} - c_a. \tag{25.9}$$

Here we view the problem as choosing a distribution of utility for the agent, where the cost to the principal of providing u_i is $s_i = f(u_i)$.

   This problem can be analyzed graphically when $n = 2$. In this case there are only two output levels, x_1 and x_2, and the principal only needs to set two utility levels, u_1, the utility received by the agent when the output level is x_1, and u_2, the utility received when the output level is x_2.

   The constraint set determined by (25.8)-(25.9) is shown in Figure 25.1. The agent's indifference curves if he chooses actions a or b will just be straight lines of the form

$$\pi_{1b} u_1 + \pi_{2b} u_2 - c_b = \text{constant}$$

$$\pi_{1a} u_1 + \pi_{2a} u_2 - c_a = \text{constant}.$$

Look at the incentive compatibility constraint (25.9), and consider the utility pairs (u_1, u_2) where the agent is just indifferent between action b and action a. These are points where an indifference curve for action a intersects the indifference curve for action b associated with the same level of utility. The locus of all such pairs (u_1, u_2) satisfies the equation

$$\pi_{1b} u_1 + \pi_{2b} u_2 - c_b = \pi_{1a} u_1 + \pi_{2a} u_2 - c_a.$$

Solving for u_2 as a function of u_1, we have

$$u_2 = \frac{\pi_{1a} - \pi_{1b}}{\pi_{2b} - \pi_{2a}} u_1 + \frac{c_b - c_a}{\pi_{2b} - \pi_{2a}} = u_1 + \frac{c_b - c_a}{\pi_{2b} - \pi_{2a}}. \tag{25.10}$$

The coefficient of u_1 is 1 since

$$\pi_{1a} + \pi_{2a} = \pi_{1b} + \pi_{2b} = 1.$$

It follows that the incentive compatibilty line determined in equation (25.10) has a slope of $+1$. The region where action b is preferred by the agent is the region above this line.

   The participation constraint requires that

$$\pi_{1b} u_1 + \pi_{2b} u_2 - c_b \geq \bar{u}.$$

The set of (u_1, u_2) where this condition is satisfied as an equality is simply one of the b-indifference curves for the agent. The intersection of the region satisfying incentive compatibility and the region satisfying the participation constraint is depicted in Figure 25.1.

   This figure also depicts the forty-five degree line. This line is important because it depicts those combinations of u_1 and u_2 where $u_1 = u_2$. We have seen that if there were no incentive compatibility constraint, the principal would simply insure the agent and the optimal solution satisfies the condition that $u_1 = u_2 = \bar{u}$.

   Due to the incentive compatibility constraint, the full-insurance point may not be feasible. The nature of the solution to the principal-agent

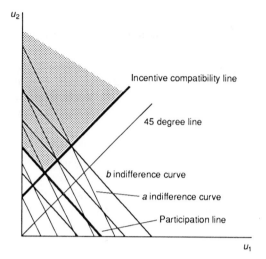

**Figure
25.1**

The feasible set for principal-agent problem with hidden action. The region to the northeast of the participation line satisfies the participation constraint. The region to the north-west of the incentive compatibility line satisfies the incentive compatibility constraint. The intersection of these two regions is the shaded area.

problem depends on whether the incentive compatibility line intercepts the vertical or the horizontal axis. We have illustrated these cases in Figure 25.2. To find the optimal solution, we simply plot the indifference curves of the principal. These will be lines of the form

$$\pi_{1b}(x_1 - f(u_1)) + \pi_{2b}(x_2 - f(u_2)) = \text{constant}.$$

The utility of the principal increases as s_1 and s_2 decrease. What do we know about the slope? The slope of the principal's indifference curves is given by

$$MRS = -\frac{\pi_{1b}f'(u_1)}{\pi_{2b}f'(u_2)}.$$

When $u_1 = u_2$, we must have $MRS = -\pi_{1b}/\pi_{2b}$. Since the agent's indifference curves are determined by the condition $\pi_{1b}u_1 + \pi_{2b}u_2 = \text{constant}$, the slope of his indifference curves when $u_1 = u_2$ is also given by $-\pi_{1b}/\pi_{2b}$. Hence the principal's indifference curve must be tangent to the agent's indifference curve along the 45-degree line. This is simply the geometric consequence of the fact that the principal will fully insure the agent if there is no incentive problem.

Hence, if the full-insurance solution is feasible, as depicted in Figure 25.2B, that will be the optimal solution. If the full-insurance solution is

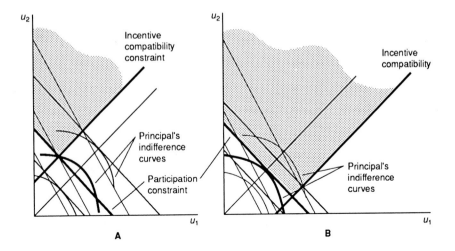

u_2

Incentive
compatibility
constraint

Principal's
indifference
curves

Participation
constraint

u_1

A

u_2

Incentive
compatibility

Principal's
indifference
curves

u_1

B

Two solutions to the principal-agent problem. In panel
A we have depicted the case where the optimal solution involves
the agent bearing some risk; panel B depicts the case where full
insurance is optimal.

**Figure
25.2**

not feasible, we find that the optimal solution will involve the agent bearing
some risk.

In order to investigate the nature of the optimal incentive scheme algebraically, we return to the n-outcome case, and set up the Lagrangian for
the maximization problem described in (25.6–25.7).

$$\mathcal{L} = \sum_{i=1}^{n} (x_i - s_i)\pi_{ib} - \lambda \left[c_b + \bar{u} - \sum_{i=1}^{n} u(s_i)\pi_{ib} \right]$$
$$- \mu \left[c_b - c_a - \sum_{i=1}^{n} u(s_i)(\pi_{ib} - \pi_{ia}) \right].$$

The Kuhn-Tucker first-order conditions can be found by differentiating this
expression with respect to s_i. This gives us

$$-\pi_{ib} + \lambda u'(s_i)\pi_{ib} + \mu u'(s_i)[\pi_{ib} - \pi_{ia}] = 0.$$

Dividing through by $\pi_{ib}u'(s_i)$ and rearranging, we have the fundamental
equation determining the shape of the incentive scheme:

$$\frac{1}{u'(s_i)} = \lambda + \mu \left[1 - \frac{\pi_{ia}}{\pi_{ib}} \right]. \tag{25.11}$$

We can generally expect that the constraint on reservation utility will be
binding so that $\lambda > 0$.

The second constraint is more problematic; as we've seen from our graphical analysis it may or may not be binding. Suppose that $\mu = 0$. Then equation (25.11) implies that $u'(s_i)$ is equal to some constant $1/\lambda$; i.e., that the payment to the agent is independent of the outcome. It follows that s_i is equal to some constant $\bar{s}$. Substituting into the incentive compatibility constraint, we find that

$$u(\bar{s}) \sum_{i=1}^{n} \pi_{ib} - c_b > u(\bar{s}) \sum_{i=1}^{n} \pi_{ia} - c_a.$$

Since each probability distribution sums to 1, this implies that

$$c_a > c_b.$$

Hence this case can only arise when the action that is preferred by the principal is also the low-cost action for the agent. This is the case depicted in Figure 25.2B in which there is no conflict of interest between the principal and the agent, and the principal simply provides insurance for the agent.

Turning to the case where the constraint is binding and consequently $\mu > 0$, we see that in general the payment to the agent, s_i, will vary with the outcome x_i. This is the case where the principal desires the action which imposes high costs on the agent, so the payment to the agent will depend on the behavior of the fraction π_{ia}/π_{ib}.

In the statistics literature, an expression of the form π_{ia}/π_{ib} is known as a **likelihood ratio**. It measures the ratio of the likelihood of observing x_i given that the agent chose a to the likelihood of observing x_i given that the agent chose b. A high value of the likelihood ratio is evidence in favor of the view that the agent chose a, while a low value of the likelihood ratio suggests that the agent chose b.

The appearance of the likelihood ratio in the formula strongly suggests that the construction of the optimal incentive scheme is closely related to statistical problems of inference. This suggests that we can bring regularity conditions from the statistics literature to bear on the problem of analyzing the behavior of optimal schemes. For example, one commonly used condition, the **Monotone Likelihood Ratio Property**, requires that the ratio π_{ia}/π_{ib} be monotone decreasing in x_i. If this condition is satisfied, then it follows that $s(x_i)$ will be a monotone increasing function of x_i. See Milgrom (1981) for details. The remarkable feature of equation (25.11) is how simple the optimal incentive scheme is: it is essentially a linear function of the likelihood ratio.

EXAMPLE: Comparative statics

As usual, we can learn some things about the optimal incentive scheme by examining the Lagrangian for this problem. The envelope theorem tells us that the the derivative of the principal's optimized value function with respect to a parameter of the problem is just equal to the derivative of the Lagrangian with respect to the same parameter.

For example, the derivatives of the Lagrangian with respect to c_a and c_b are

$$\frac{\partial \mathcal{L}}{\partial c_a} = \mu$$

$$\frac{\partial \mathcal{L}}{\partial c_b} = -(\lambda + \mu). \tag{25.12}$$

These derivatives can be used to answer the age-old question: which is better, the carrot or the stick? Think of the carrot as decreasing the cost of the chosen action b and the stick as increasing the cost of the alternative action a by the same magnitude. According to equations (25.12), a small decrease in the cost of the chosen action always increases the principal's utility by a larger amount than an increase of the same magnitude in cost of the alternative action. Effectively, the carrot relaxes two constraints, while the stick relaxes only one.

Next consider a change in the probability distribution $(d\pi_{ia})$. The effect on the principal's utility of such a change is given by

$$d\mathcal{L} = -\mu \sum_{i=1}^{n} u(s_i) d\pi_{ia}.$$

This shows that when the incentive compatibility constraint is binding so that $\mu > 0$, the interests of the principal and the agent are diametrically opposed with respect to changes in the probability distribution of the alternative action: any change that makes the agent better off must unambiguously make the principal worse off.

EXAMPLE: Principal-agent model with mean-variance utility

Here is a simple example of an incentive scheme based on Holmström & Milgrom (1987). Let the action a represent the effort of the agent and let $\tilde{x} = a + \tilde{\epsilon}$ be the output observed by the principal. The random variable $\tilde{\epsilon}$ has a Normal distribution with mean zero and variance σ^2.

Suppose that the incentive scheme chosen by the principal is linear, so that $s(\tilde{x}) = \delta + \gamma \tilde{x} = \delta + \gamma a + \gamma \tilde{\epsilon}$. Here δ and γ are the parameters to be determined. Since the principal is risk neutral, his utility is

$$E[\tilde{x} - s(\tilde{x})] = E[a + \tilde{\epsilon} - \delta - \gamma a - \gamma \tilde{\epsilon}] = (1 - \gamma)a - \delta.$$

Suppose that the agent has a constant absolute risk averse utility function, $u(w) = -e^{-rw}$, where r is absolute risk aversion and w is wealth.

The agent's wealth is simply $s(\tilde{x}) = \delta + \gamma\tilde{x}$. Since $\tilde{x}$ is Normally distributed, wealth will be Normally distributed. We have seen in Chapter 11, page 189, that in this case the agent's utility depends linearly on the mean and variance of wealth. It follows that the agent's utility associated with the incentive payment $s(\tilde{x}) = \delta + \gamma\tilde{x}$ will be given by

$$\delta + \gamma a - \frac{\gamma^2 r}{2}\sigma^2.$$

The agent wants to maximize this utility minus the cost of effort, $c(a)$:

$$\max_a \ \delta + \gamma a - \frac{\gamma^2 r}{2}\sigma^2 - c(a).$$

This gives us the first-order condition

$$\gamma = c'(a). \tag{25.13}$$

The principal's maximization problem is to determine the optimal δ and γ, subject to the constraint that the agent receive some level of reservation utility $\bar{u}$ and to the incentive constraint (25.13). This problem can be written as

$$\max_{\delta,\gamma,a} (1 - \gamma)a - \delta$$

$$\text{such that } \delta + \gamma a - \frac{\gamma^2 r}{2}\sigma^2 - c(a) \geq \bar{u}$$

$$c'(a) = \gamma.$$

Solve the first constraint for δ and the second constraint for γ and substitute into the objective function. After some simplification, this gives us

$$\max_a \ a - \frac{c'(a)^2 r}{2}\sigma^2 - c(a).$$

Differentiating, we have the first-order condition

$$1 - rc'(a)c''(a)\sigma^2 - c'(a) = 0.$$

Solving for $c'(a) = \gamma$, we find

$$\gamma = \frac{1}{1 + rc''(a)\sigma^2}.$$

This equation displays the essential features of the solution. If $\sigma^2 = 0$, so that there is no risk, we have $\gamma = 1$: the optimal incentive scheme is of the form $s = \delta + \tilde{x}$. If $\sigma^2 > 0$, we will have $\gamma < 1$ so that each agent shares some of the risk. The greater the uncertainty, or the more risk averse the agent, the smaller γ will be.

25.5 Hidden action: competitive market

What happens if there are many principals competing in the structure of their incentive contracts? In this case we may want to assume that competition will push the profits of the principals to zero, and equilibrium contracts must just break even. In this case, Figure 25.2 still applies, but we simply reinterpret the levels of the isoprofit lines and the indifference curves.

Under competition the participation constraint is not binding, and the zero-profit condition determines a particular isoprofit line for the principal. As in the monopoly case, there are two possible equilibrium configurations: full insurance or partial insurance.

In a full-insurance contract all workers are getting paid a fixed amount regardless of the output produced. They respond by putting in a minimal level of effort. In a partial-insurance equilibrium the workers get a wage that depends on output. Because the workers bear more risk, they put in a larger amount of effort, in order to increase the probability that the larger amount of output is produced.

Consider the partial-insurance case depicted in Figure 25.3. In order for this to be an equilibrium, there can be no other contract that yields higher utility to the agent and higher profits to a firm. By construction, there is no contract that induces action b with these properties; however, there may be a contract that induces action a that will be Pareto preferred—i.e., a contract that will make positive profits and be preferred by the agents.

In order to see whether such a contract exists, we draw the action a-indifference curve passing through the partial-insurance contract and the action a zero-profit line. If the zero-profit line doesn't intersect the region preferred by the worker, as in Figure 25.3a, the partial-insurance contract is an equilibrium. If the zero-profit line *does* intersect the workers' preferred region, as in Figure 25.3B, then this cannot be an equilibrium since some firm could offer a full-insurance contract that would yield positive profits and still appeal to the workers holding the partial-insurance contract. In this case no equilibrium may exist.

EXAMPLE: Moral hazard in insurance markets

In the context of an insurance market, the principal-agent problem with hidden action is known as the **moral hazard problem**. The "moral hazard" is that the purchasers of insurance policies will not take an appropriate level of care. Let us examine this problem in the context of our earlier analysis of insurance in Chapter 11, page 180.

Suppose there are many identical consumers who are contemplating buying insurance against auto theft. If a consumer's auto is stolen, he bears

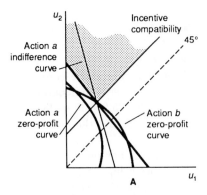

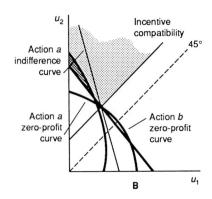

Figure 25.3

Equilibrium contracts. In panel A the partial-insurance contract is an equilibrium. In panel B it is not, since the zero-profit line under action a intersects the preferred sets for the agent.

a cost L. Let state 1 be the state of nature where the consumer's auto is stolen, and state 2 be the state where it is not. The probability that a consumer's auto is stolen depends on his actions—say whether he locks the car. Let π_{1b} be the probability of theft if the consumer remembers to lock his car, and π_{1a} be the probability of theft if the consumer forgets to lock his car. Let c be the cost of remembering to lock the car, and let s_i be the net insurance payment from the consumer to the firm in state i. Finally, let w be the wealth of the consumer.

Assuming that the insurance company wants the consumer to lock his car, the incentive problem is

$$\max_{s_1, s_2} \pi_{1b}s_1 + \pi_{2b}s_2$$

such that $\pi_{1b}u(w - s_1 - L) + \pi_{2b}u(w - s_2) - c \geq \bar{u}$
$$\pi_{1b}u(w - s_1 - L) + \pi_{2b}u(w - s_2) - c$$
$$\geq \pi_{1a}u(w - s_1 - L) + \pi_{2a}u(w - s_2).$$

If there is no incentive problem, so that the probability of the theft occurring is independent of the actions of the agent, and if competition in the insurance industry forces expected profits to zero, we have seen in Chapter 11, page 180, that the optimal solution will involve $s_2 = s_1 + L$. That is, the insurance company will fully insure the consumer, so that he has the same wealth whether or not the theft occurs.

When the probability of the loss depends on the actions of the agent, full insurance will no longer be optimal. In general, the principal wants to make the agent's consumption depend on his choices so as to leave him the incentive to take proper care. In this case the consumer's demand for insurance will be rationed. The consumer would like to buy more insurance at actuarily fair rates, but the industry will not offer such contracts since that would induce the consumer to take an inadequate level of care.

In the competitive case, the participation constraint is not binding, and the equilibrium is determined by the zero-profit condition and the incentive compatibility constraint:

$$\pi_{1b}s_1^* + \pi_{2b}s_2^* = 0$$

$$\pi_{1b}u(w - s_1^* - L) + \pi_{2b}u(w - s_2^*) - c =$$

$$\pi_{1a}u(w - s_1^* - L) + \pi_{2a}u(w - s_2^*). \tag{25.14}$$

These two equations determine the equilibrium (s_1^*, s_2^*). As usual, we have to check to make sure that there are no full-insurance contracts that can break this equilibrium. Without additional assumptions there may well be such contracts, so that no equilibrium may exist in this model.

25.6 Hidden information: monopoly

We now consider the other type of principal-agent problem, where the information about the utility or cost function of the agent is not observable. For simplicity, we suppose that there are only two types of agents who are distinguished by their cost functions and let the action of an agent be the amount of output he produces. In the context of the worker-employer model discussed previously, we now assume that output is observed perfectly by the firm, but some workers find it more costly to produce than others. The firm can perfectly observe the actions of a worker, but it can't tell how costly those actions are to the worker.

Let x_t and $c_t(x)$ be the output and cost function of an agent of type t. For definiteness, let agent 2 be the high-cost agent, so that $c_2(x) > c_1(x)$ for all x. Let $s(x)$ be the payment as a function of output and suppose that agent t's utility function is of the form $s(x) - c_t(x)$. The principal is unsure of the type of agent he faces, but he attaches a probability of π_t that it is type t. As usual, we require that each agent receive at least his reservation level of utility which we take for simplicity to be zero.

It will be convenient to make one further assumption about the cost functions, namely that the agent with higher total costs also has higher *marginal costs*; i.e., that $c_2'(x) > c_1'(x)$ for all x. This is sometimes called the **single-crossing property**, since it implies that any given indifference curve for a type 1 agent crosses any given indifference curve of a type 2 agent at most once. We observe the following simple fact, which you are asked to prove in an exercise:

Single-crossing property. Assume that $c_2'(x) > c_1'(x)$ for all x. It follows that for any two distinct levels of output x_1 and x_2, with $x_2 > x_1$, we must have $c_2(x_2) - c_2(x_1) > c_1(x_2) - c_1(x_1)$.

It is instructive to consider what the optimal incentive scheme would be if the principal could observe the cost functions. In this case the principal has full information so the solution would be essentially the target-output case examined earlier. The principal would simply maximize total output minus total cost $x_1 + x_2 - c_1(x_1) - c_2(x_2)$. The solution requires $c'_t(x^*_t) = 1$ for $t = 1, 2$. The principal would then make a payment to each agent that just satisfied that agent's reservation utility, so that $s_t - c_t(x^*_t) = 0$.

This is depicted in Figure 25.4. Here we have plotted marginal cost on the vertical axis and output on the horizontal axis. Agent t produces x^*_t, where $c'_t(x^*_t) = 1$. A principal who was able to perfectly discriminate between the two agents would simply require agent t to produce output x^*_t by presenting him with a target output scheme like that outlined earlier; i.e., agent t would get a payment such that $s_t(x^*) = c_t(x^*_t)$ and $s_t(x) < c_t(x)$ for all other values of x.

This would mean that each agent would have their total surplus extracted. In terms of the diagram, agent 1 would receive a payment of $A + B$ which is just equal to his total cost of production; similarly, agent 2 would receive $A + D$ which is equal to his total cost.

The problem with this scheme is that it doesn't satisfy incentive compatibility. If the high-cost agent just satisfies his participation constraint, the low-cost agent would necessarily prefer (s_2, x^*_2) to (s_1, x^*_1). In symbols,

$$s_2 - c_1(x^*_2) > s_2 - c_2(x^*_2) = 0 = s_1 - c_1(x^*_1)$$

since $c_1(x) < c_2(x)$ for any x. In terms of the diagram, the low-cost agent could pretend to be the high-cost agent and produce only x^*_2. This would leave him with a surplus of D.

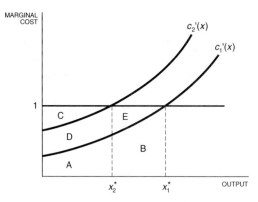

Figure 25.4 **Principal-agent problem with hidden information.** In the first-best scheme, agent 1 produces x^*_1 and agent 2 produces x^*_2.

One solution to this problem is simply to change the payments. Suppose that we pay A if the output is x_2^*, but pay $A + D$ if the output is x_1^*. This leaves the low-cost agent with a net surplus of D, which makes him indifferent between producing x_1^* and x_2^*.

This is certainly a feasible plan, but is it optimal from the viewpoint of the principal? The answer is no, and there is an interesting reason why. Suppose that we reduce the high-cost agent's target output slightly. Since he is operating where price equals marginal cost, there is only a first-order reduction in profits: the reduction in output produced is just balanced by the reduction in the amount that we have to pay agent 2.

But since x_2 and the area D are both smaller, the surplus that the low-cost agent would receive from producing at x_2 is now less. By making the high-cost agent produce less, and paying him less, we make his target output less attractive to the low-cost agent. This is *more* than a first-order effect, since the low-cost agent is operating at a point where his marginal cost is less than 1.

This is illustrated in Figure 25.5. A reduction in the target output for the high-cost agent reduces profits received from the high-cost agent by the area ΔC, but increases profits from the low-cost agent by the area ΔD. Hence the principal will find it profitable to reduce the target output for the high-cost agent to some amount *below* the efficient level. By paying the high-cost agent less, the principal reduces the amount that he has to pay the low-cost agent.

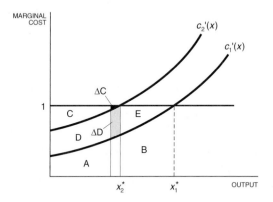

Increasing profits. By cutting the target output for the high-cost agent by a small amount, the principal can increase his profits.

Figure 25.5

In order to say more about the structure of the incentive scheme, it is convenient to formulate the problem algebraically.

As the geometric analysis indicates, the basic incentive problem is that the low-cost agent may try to "pretend" that he is a high-cost agent. If x_1 is the output that agent 1 is supposed to choose, then the principal must structure the payment plan so that agent 1's utility from choosing x_1 is higher than his utility from choosing x_2, and similarly for agent 2. These are simply a particular form of the incentive compatibility conditions which are called **self-selection constraints** in this context.

Given these observations we can write down the principal's optimization problem:

$$\max_{x_1,x_2,s_1,s_2} \pi_1(x_1 - s_1) + \pi_2(x_2 - s_2)$$

$$\text{such that } s_1 - c_1(x_1) \geq 0 \tag{25.15}$$

$$s_2 - c_2(x_2) \geq 0 \tag{25.16}$$

$$s_1 - c_1(x_1) \geq s_2 - c_1(x_2) \tag{25.17}$$

$$s_2 - c_2(x_2) \geq s_1 - c_2(x_1). \tag{25.18}$$

The first two constraints are the participation constraints. The second two constraints are the incentive compatibility or self-selection constraints. The optimal incentive plan $(x_1^*, s_1^*, x_2^*, s_2^*)$ is the solution to this maximization problem.

The first observation about this problem comes from rearranging the self-selection constraints:

$$s_2 \leq s_1 + c_1(x_2) - c_1(x_1) \tag{25.19}$$

$$s_2 \geq s_1 + c_2(x_2) - c_2(x_1). \tag{25.20}$$

These inequalities indicate that if the self-selection constraints are satisfied,

$$c_1(x_2) - c_1(x_1) \geq c_2(x_2) - c_2(x_1). \tag{25.21}$$

The single-crossing condition implies that agent 2 has a uniformly higher marginal cost than agent 1. If $x_2 > x_1$, this would contradict (25.21). Hence it must be that in the optimal solution $x_2 \leq x_1$, which means that the low-cost agent produces at least as much as the high-cost agent.

Now look at constraints (25.15) and (25.17). These can be rewritten as

$$s_1 \geq c_1(x_1) \tag{25.15'}$$

$$s_1 \geq c_1(x_1) + [s_2 - c_1(x_2)]. \tag{25.17'}$$

Since the principal wants s_1 to be as small as possible, at most one of these two constraints will be binding. From constraint (25.16) and the properties of the cost function, we see that

$$s_2 - c_1(x_2) > s_2 - c_2(x_2) = 0.$$

Hence the bracketed expression in equation (25.17′) is positive and (25.15′) cannot be binding. It follows that

$$s_1 = c_1(x_1) + [s_2 - c_1(x_2)]. \tag{25.22}$$

In the same manner, exactly one of constraints (25.16) and (25.18) will be binding. Can it be that (25.18) will be satisfied as an equality? In this case we can substitute equation (25.22) into (25.18) to find

$$s_2 = s_1 + c_2(x_2) - c_2(x_1) = s_2 + c_1(x_1) - c_1(x_2) + c_2(x_2) - c_2(x_1).$$

Rearranging, we have

$$c_1(x_2) - c_1(x_1) = c_2(x_2) - c_2(x_1),$$

which violates the single-crossing condition. It follows that the optimal policy must involve

$$s_2 = c_2(x_2). \tag{25.23}$$

Without even examining the actual optimization problem, we see that the nature of the constraints and the objective function themselves establish two important properties: the high-cost agent receives a payment that just makes him indifferent to participating, and the low-cost agent receives a surplus. The low-cost agent's surplus is just the amount necessary to discourage him from pretending to be a high-cost agent.

In order to determine the optimal actions, we substitute for s_1 and s_2 from (25.22)–(25.23) and write the principal's maximization problem as

$$\max_{x_1,x_2} \pi_1[x_1 - c_1(x_1) - c_2(x_2) + c_1(x_2)] + \pi_2[x_2 - c_2(x_2)].$$

The first-order conditions for this problem are

$$\pi_1[1 - c_1'(x_1)] = 0$$
$$\pi_1[c_1'(x_2) - c_2'(x_2)] + \pi_2[1 - c_2'(x_2)] = 0.$$

We can rewrite these conditions as

$$c_1'(x_1^*) = 1$$
$$c_2'(x_2^*) = 1 + \frac{\pi_1}{\pi_2}[c_1'(x_2^*) - c_2'(x_2^*)]. \tag{25.24}$$

The first equation implies that the low-cost agent produces the same level of output that he would if he were the only type present; i.e., the Pareto efficient level of output. Given the single-crossing property, the high-cost agent produces *less* output than he would if he were the only agent, since $c_2'(x_2^*) - c_1'(x_2^*) > 0$.

In order to depict these conditions graphically, suppose for simplicity that $\pi_1 = \pi_2 = \frac{1}{2}$. Then the second equation in (25.24) implies $2c'_2(x^*_2) = 1 + c'_1(x^*_2)$. At this point the marginal benefits from reducing x_2 a little bit just equals the marginal costs. The optimal solution is depicted in Figure 25.6. The low-cost agent produces where its marginal benefit equals marginal cost; the high-cost agent produces at a point where its marginal benefit exceed its marginal cost. The high-cost agent receives a payment of $A + D$ which extracts all of its surplus; the low-cost agent receives a payment of $A + B + D$ which makes him just indifferent to pretending to be the high-cost agent.

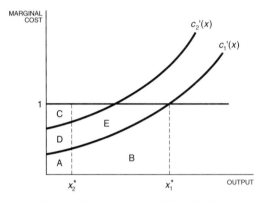

Figure 25.6

Optimal contracts. The high-cost agent produces at x^*_2 and the low-cost agent at x^*_1. The high-cost agent receives payment $A + D$, and the low-cost agent receives payment $A + B + D$.

Figure 25.7 provides another picture of the optimal incentive contract. In this diagram we depict the contracts in (s, x) space. A worker of type t has a utility function of the form $u_t = s_t - c_t(x_t)$. Hence, his indifference curves are of the form $s_t = u_t + c_t(x_t)$. By the single-crossing property the high-cost agent's indifference curves are always steeper than the low-cost agent's.

We know that the high-cost worker receives his reservation level of zero utility in equilibrium. This fixes the indifference curve and all incentive contracts (s_2, x_2) for the high-cost worker must lie on the zero utility indifference curve. The firm makes a profit on a worker of type t of $P_t = x_t - s_t$. Hence the isoprofit lines have the form $s_t = x_t - P_t$. These are parallel straight lines with slope of $+1$ and vertical intercept of $-P_t$. The total profits of the firm are $\pi_1 P_1 + \pi_2 P_2$. Note that profits increase as the profit line moves *down* to the southeast and the agent's utility increases as the indifference curves move up towards the northwest.

We know from conditions (25.24) that the low-cost worker must satisfy the condition that $c_1'(x_1^*) = 1$. This means that the isoprofit function must be tangent to the low-cost agent's indifference curve. We also know that $c_2'(x_2^*) < 1$, so the isoprofit line cuts the high-cost worker's indifference curve.

If the low-cost worker were not present, the principal would want the high-cost worker to work more, and the high-cost worker would want to do so. The shaded area in Figure 25.7 depicts the region in which both the high-cost worker and the principal could be made better off. But since the low-cost worker is present, increasing the output of the high-cost worker increases the amount that the firm has to pay the low-cost worker. In equilibrium the gains from making P_2 larger by increasing x_2 and s_2 are just counterbalanced by the decrease in P_1.

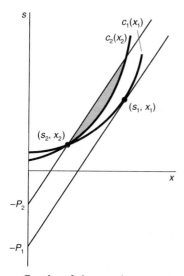

Optimal incentive contracts.   The profits of the firm are $\pi_1 P_1 + \pi_2 P_2$. The shaded area represents the inefficient use of the high-cost worker induced by the self-selection constraints.

Figure 25.7

It is this negative externality between the high-cost and the low-cost worker that leads to an inefficient equilibrium. If the monopolist were able to discriminate and offer each type of worker a distinct wage, the outcome would be fully efficient. This is analogous to the case of second degree price discrimination discussed in Chapter 14, page 244. In that model if there is only one type of consumer, the monopolist will perfectly price discriminate and make only one take-it-or-leave it offer. But if there are several types of consumers, the attempt to price discriminate will generally lead to inefficient outcomes.

25.7 Market equilibrium: hidden information

As usual, we can analyze the competitive equilibrium by adding a zero-profit condition to the model and reinterpreting the reservation utilities. As more firms enter the market, they bid up the wages of the workers and reduce the profits of the representative firm. In the monopoly problem the reservation prices determine the level of profit; in the competitive equilibrium the zero-profit condition determines the workers' utilities.

This can be seen from examining Figure 25.7. Under monopoly, the indifference curve for the high-cost agent determines the profits of the firm, $\pi_1 P_1 + \pi_2 P_2$. Under competition, the profits of the firm are forced to zero, and the agents move to higher indifference curves.

We will only examine symmetric equilibria, in which all firms offer the same set of contracts. There appear to be several possibilities for equilibrium.

(a) The representative firm offers a single contract that attracts both types of workers.

(b) The representative firm offers a single contract that attracts only one type of worker.

(c) The representative firm offers two contracts, one for each type of worker.

The case where both types of workers accept a single contract is known as a **pooling equilibrium**. The other case, where workers of different types accept different contracts is called a **separating equilibrium**.

We depict some possible equilibrium configurations in Figure 25.8. It is not hard to see it cannot be an equilibrium to offer only one type of contract, which rules out the pooling equilibrium of type (a) or the separating equilibrium of (b). If the representative firm is making zero profits, it must operate on the forty-five degree line in Figure 25.8A. If it offers only one contract, such as (s^*, x^*), this must be optimal for one of the two types; suppose that it is optimal for the low-cost type. But then a deviant firm could offer a contract in the shaded area which is preferred by the high-cost type and makes positive profits. The argument is similar if the contract is optimal for the high-cost type.

It follows that as long as both agents receive at least their reservation level of utility, the only possible equilibrium in this model is the separating equilibrium depicted in Figure 25.8B. The firm pays each worker the full value of his output and earns zero profits.

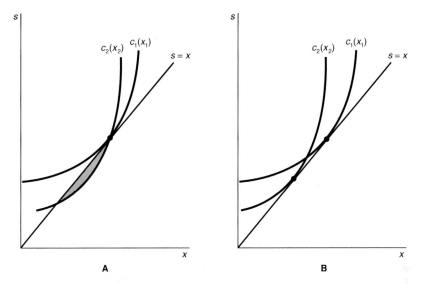

Possible equilibrium configurations. Panel A cannot be
an equilibrium by the arguments given in the text. The only
possibility is case B, where each worker receives his marginal
product.

**Figure
25.8**

EXAMPLE: An algebraic example

It is helpful to spell out the differences between the monopoly and the
competitive hidden-information model algebraically. Suppose that $c_t(x_t) = tx_t^2/2$ and $\pi_1 = \pi_2 = \frac{1}{2}$. Then the optimal solution for the monopolist is
determined by equations (25.22), (25.23), and (25.24). You should verify
that these equations have the solution

$$x_1^* = 1$$
$$x_2^* = 1/3$$
$$s_1^* = 5/9$$
$$s_2^* = 1/9.$$

The profits of the monopolist are

$$\frac{1}{2}[x_1^* - s_1^*] + \frac{1}{2}[x_2^* - s_2^*] = \frac{1}{2}[4/9] + \frac{1}{2}[2/9] = 1/3.$$

In the monopoly model the high-cost worker just receives his reservation
level of utility, which is zero. In the competitive model, the utility received
by the agents increases as firms bid up the wages.

We've seen that the competitive equilibrium involves a linear wage, so that a worker of type t wants to maximize $x_t - c_t(x_t)$. This gives us $x_1 = 1$ and $x_2 = 1/2$. The firm earns zero profits, so we must have $s_1 = x_1 = 1$ and $s_2 = x_2 = 1/2$ as well. The low-cost agent has a surplus of $1/2$, and the high-cost agent has a surplus of $1/4$.

25.8 Adverse selection

Consider a variant on the model described in the last section. Assume that the workers have different productivities in addition to having different cost functions. High-cost workers produce $v_2 x_2$ units of output, while low-cost workers produce $v_1 x_1$. We assume that $v_1 > v_2$, so that the low-cost workers are attractive for two reasons: they are more productive and they have lower cost.

What do equilibrium wage contracts look like now? As in the last section there are two logical possibilities for a symmetric equilibrium. Either the firms offer a *single* contract (s^*, x^*) to all workers or they offer two contracts $(s_1^*, x_1^*), (s_2^*, x_2^*)$. If only a single contract is offered, we call this a pooling equilibrium, and if two types are offered we call this a separating equilibrium.

Consider first the pooling equilibrium. Here all workers are getting the same compensation even though some are more productive than others. Since profits overall are zero, the firm must be making positive profits on the low-cost workers and negative profits on the high-cost workers. The total value of output produced, $(\pi_1 v_1 + \pi_2 v_2)x^*$, equals the total cost, $\pi_1 s^* + \pi_2 s^* = s^*$. Hence (s^*, x^*) must lie on the straight line $s = (\pi_1 v_1 + \pi_2 v_2)x$, whose slope is the weighted average of the productivities of the two types of agents, as illustrated in Figure 25.9.

The proposed pooling equilibrium is some point on this line. At any such point, draw the indifference curves for the two types of agents through this point. By assumption the indifference curve for the more-productive agent is flatter than the indifference curve for the less-productive agent. This means that there is some contract in the shaded area that is better for the high-productivity agents and worse for the low-productivity agents. A deviant firm could offer such a contract, and attract only high-productivity agents, thereby making a positive profit. Since this construction can be carried out at any point on the zero-profit line, no pooling equilibrium exists.

The remaining possibility is a separating equilibrium. Figure 25.10 depicts an example of both efficient and equilibrium contracts. The contracts (s_1^*, x_1^*) and (s_2^*, x_2^*) are the (full-information) efficient contracts, but they don't satisfy the self-selection constraints: the low-productivity agent prefers the contract targeted for the high-productivity agent. A firm might offer (s_2^*, x_2^*) hoping to attract only the low-cost, high-productivity workers. But this firm would experience **adverse selection**—both types of workers would find this contract attractive.

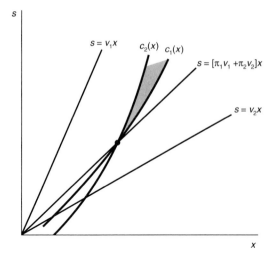

Pooling cannot be an equilibrium. If only a single contract is offered, it must be along the zero-profit line. Draw the indifference curves through such a contract and note that since the less-productive workers have steeper indifference curves, it is always possible to find a contract in the shaded area that attracts only high-productivity workers, and therefore makes a positive profit.

Figure 25.10

The solution to this adverse selection problem is to move up the zero-profit line for high-productivity workers to a point like (s'_1, x'_1). Now (s'_1, x'_1) and (s^*_2, x^*_2) is an equilibrium configuration of contracts: the low-productivity agent is just indifferent between his contract and that of the high-productivity agent. Anything above either agent's indifference curve isn't profitable for the firms, and we have an equilibrium.

However, it can also happen that no equilibrium exists. Note that the indifference curve through (s'_1, x'_1) must by construction cut the zero profit line. It follows that there will be some region like the shaded region in Figure 25.10 that is preferred by both the firm and the high-productivity workers. No contracts are offered in this area because they would attract low-productivity workers as well and therefore be unprofitable—we know such contracts are unprofitable since the zero-profit line in Figure 25.10 for the pooled workers lies below the shaded region.

But suppose that there are a lot of high-productivity workers so that the line $s = \pi_1 v_1 + \pi_2 v_2$ intersected the shaded region. In this case, offering a pooled contract in this region *would* be profitable. Hence the proposed separating equilibrium could be broken, and no pure-strategy equilibrium exists.

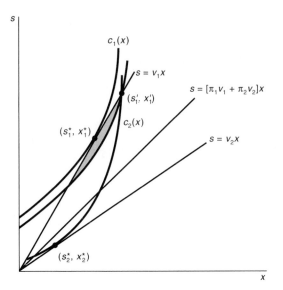

Separating equilibrium. The contracts (s_1^*, x_1^*) and (s_2^*, x_2^*) are efficient, but they don't satisfy the self-selection constraints. The contracts (s_2^*, x_2^*) and (s_1', x_1') do satisfy self-selection.

Figure 25.10

25.9 The lemons market and adverse selection

Here is another model that illustrates the possibility of nonexistence of equilibrium due to adverse selection. Consider the market for used cars. The current owner of a car presumably has better information about its quality than does a potential buyer. To the extent that buyers realize this, they may be reluctant to purchase a product that is offered for sale, because they (correctly) fear getting stuck with a lemon. If this car is so good, why is it being sold, the buyers may ask? The used-car market cars may be thin despite the presence of many potential buyers and sellers.

This simple intuition was formalized in a striking way by Akerlof (1970) in his **lemons market**. Suppose that we can index the quality of a used car by some number q, which is distributed uniformly over the interval $[0, 1]$. For later use, we will note that if q is uniformly distributed over the interval $[0, b]$, the average value of q will be $b/2$. Hence the average quality available in the market is $1/2$.

There is a large number of demanders for used cars who are willing to pay $\frac{3}{2}q$ for a car of quality q, and there are a large number of sellers who are each willing to sell a car of quality q for a price of q. Hence, if quality were observable, each used car of quality q would be sold at some price between $\frac{3}{2}q$ and q.

However, suppose that quality is not observable. Then it is sensible for the buyers of used cars to attempt to estimate the quality of a car offered to them by considering the *average* quality of the cars offered in the market. We assume that the average quality can be observed, although the quality of any given car cannot be observed. Thus the willingness to pay for a used car will be $\frac{3}{2}\bar{q}$.

What will be the equilibrium price in this market? Assume that the equilibrium price is some number $p > 0$. Then all owners of cars with quality less than p will want to offer their cars for sale, since for those owners, p is greater than their reservation price. Since quality is uniformly distributed over the interval $[0, p]$, the average quality of a car offered for sale will be $\bar{q} = p/2$. Substituting this into the formula for the reservation price of a buyer, we see that a buyer would be willing to pay $\frac{3}{2}\bar{q} = \frac{3}{2}\frac{p}{2} = \frac{3}{4}p$. This is less than p, the price at which we assumed a used car would be sold. Hence, no cars will be sold at the price p. Since the price p was arbitrary, we have shown that no used cars will be sold at any positive price. The only equilibrium price in this market is $p = 0$. At this price demand is zero and supply is zero: the asymmetric information between buyers and sellers has destroyed the market for used cars!

Any price that is attractive to the owners of good cars is even more attractive to owners of lemons. The selection of cars offered to the market is not a representative selection, but is biased towards the lemons. This is another example of adverse selection.

25.10 Signaling

In the last section we indicated how problems with hidden information could result in equilibria with adverse selection. In the lemons market too little trade takes place because the high-quality goods cannot be easily distinguished from the low-quality goods. In the labor market, the efficient set of contracts is not viable because the low-productivity workers would want to choose the contract appropriate for the high-productivity workers.

In the lemons market the sellers of good cars would like to **signal** that they are offering a good car rather than a lemon. One possibility would be to offer a warrantee—the owners of good cars would certify that they would cover the costs of any breakdowns for some time period. In effect, the sellers of the good cars would offer to insure the buyers of their cars.

In order to be consistent with equilibrium, the signal must be such that the owners of good cars could afford to offer it and the owners of lemons could not. Such a signal will allow the owners of good cars to "prove" to the potential buyers that they really have a good car. Offering the warrantee is a costly activity for the sellers of lemons, but not very costly for the sellers of good cars. Hence, this signal allows the buyers to discriminate between the two types of cars. In this case, the presence of a signal allows the market to function more effectively than it would otherwise. This need not always be the case, as we will see below.

25.11 Educational signaling

Let us return to the labor market example, with two types of workers who have productivity v_2 and v_1. Suppose that the hours worked by each type are fixed. If there are no ways to discriminate between the more-productive and less-productive workers, the workers will simply receive the average of their productivities in competitive equilibrium. This gives them a wage of

$$\bar{s} = \pi_1 v_1 + \pi_2 v_2.$$

The more-productive workers are getting paid less than their marginal product; the less-productive workers are getting paid more than their marginal product. The more-productive workers would like a way to signal that they are more productive than the others.

Suppose that there is some signal that is easier to acquire by the more-productive workers than the less-productive workers. One nice example is education—it is plausible that it is cheaper for the more-productive workers to acquire education than the less-productive workers. To be explicit, let us suppose that the cost to acquiring e years of education is $c_2 e$ for the more productive workers and $c_1 e$ for the less productive workers, and that $c_1 > c_2$.

Let us suppose that education has no effect on productivity. However, firms may still find it profitable to base wages on education since they may attract a higher-quality work force. Suppose that workers believe that firms will pay a wage $s(e)$ where s is some increasing function of e. A signaling equilibrium will be a conjectured wage profile by the workers that is actually confirmed by the firms' behavior.

Let e_1 and e_2 be the education levels actually chosen by the workers. Then a separating signaling equilibrium has to satisfy the zero-profit conditions

$$s(e_1) = v_1$$
$$s(e_2) = v_2,$$

and the self-selection conditions

$$s(e_1) - c_1 e_1 \geq s(e_2) - c_1 e_2$$
$$s(e_2) - c_2 e_2 \geq s(e_1) - c_2 e_1.$$

In general there may be many functions $s(e)$ that satisfy these conditions. We will content ourselves with exhibiting one such function.

Let e^* be some number such that

$$\frac{v_2 - v_1}{c_2} > e^* > \frac{v_2 - v_1}{c_1}.$$

Suppose that the wage function conjectured by the workers is

$$s(e) = \begin{cases} v_2 & \text{for } e > e^* \\ v_1 & \text{for } e \le e^*. \end{cases}$$

It is trivial to show that this satisfies the self-selection constraints, and hence is a wage profile consistent with equilibrium.

Note that this signaling equilibrium is wasteful in a social sense. There is no social gain to education since it doesn't change productivity. Its only role is to distinguish more-productive from less-productive workers.

Notes

The two-action case discussed above is simple, but it contains much of the insight present in the case involving many actions. For a general survey of this and other issues in the principal-agent literature see Hart & Holmström (1987). Signaling was first introduced in economics by Spence (1974). Akerlof (1970) first examined the lemons market. See Rothschild & Stiglitz (1976) for a model of market equilibrium with adverse selection. See Kreps (1990) for a more detailed discussion of equilibrium in models involving asymmetric information.

Exercises

25.1. Consider the hidden action principal-agent problem described in the text and let $f = u^{-1}$. Assume that $u(s)$ is increasing and concave, show that f is an increasing, convex function.

25.2. Let $V(c_a, c_b)$ be the utility received by the principal using the optimal incentive scheme when the costs of actions a and b are c_a and c_b, respectively. Derive an expression for $\partial V/\partial c_a$ and $\partial V/\partial c_b$ in terms of the parameters appearing in the fundamental condition, and use these expressions to interpret those parameters.

25.3. Suppose that $c_a = c_b$. What form would the optimal incentive scheme take?

25.4. Suppose in the principal-agent problem that c_b decreases while all other parameters remain constant. Show that the agent must be at least as well off.

25.5. Suppose that in the hidden action principal-agent problem the agent is risk neutral. Show that the first-best outcome can be achieved.

25.6. Consider the monopoly version of the hidden information problem. Suppose that both agents have the same cost function but different reservation levels of utility. How does the analysis change?

25.7. Prove the following implication of the single-crossing property: If $c_2'(x) > c_1'(x)$ for all x, then for any two distinct levels of output x_1 and x_2, for which $x_2 > x_1$, we must have $c_2(x_2) - c_2(x_1) > c_1(x_2) - c_1(x_1)$.

25.8. In the text it was claimed that if $c_2(x) > c_1(x)$ and $c_2'(x) > c_1'(x)$ then any two indifference curves from a type 1 and a type 2 agent intersected at most once. Prove this.

25.9. Consider the competitive equilibrium in the hidden information model described in the text. If the reservation utility of the high-cost agents is high enough, equilibrium may exist in which only the low-cost agents are employed. For what values of $\bar{u}_2$ will this occur?

25.10. Professor P has hired a teaching assistant, Mr A. Professor P cares about how many hours that Mr. A teaches and about how much she has to pay him. Professor P wants to maximize her payoff function, $x - s$, where x is the number of hours taught by Mr. A and s is the total wages she pays him. If Mr. A teaches for x hours and is paid s, his utility is $s - c(x)$ where $c(x) = x^2/2$. Mr. A's reservation utility is zero.

(a) If Professor P chooses x and s to maximize her utility subject to the constraint that Mr. A is willing to work for her, how much teaching will Mr. A be doing?

(b) How much will Professor P have to pay Mr. A to get him to do this amount of teaching?

(c) Suppose that Professor P uses a scheme of the following kind to get Mr. A to work for her. Professor P sets a wage schedule of the form $s(x) = ax + b$ and lets Mr. A choose the number of hours that he wants to work. What values of a and b should Professor P choose so as to maximize her payoff function? Could Professor P achieve a higher payoff if she were able to use a wage schedule of more general functional form?

MATHEMATICS

This chapter provides concise descriptions of most of the mathematical tools used in the text. If you forget the definition of some term, or some important property, you can look here. It is *not* appropriate for learning the concepts initially. For recommended texts for learning, consult the notes at the end of the chapter.

26.1 Linear algebra

We denote the set of all n-tuples of real numbers by R^n. The set of n-tuples of nonnegative real numbers is denoted by R^n_+. The elements of these sets will be referred to as **points** or **vectors**. Vectors will be indicated by boldface type. If $\mathbf{x} = (x_1, \ldots, x_n)$ is a vector, we denote then its ith component is x_i.

We can add two vectors by adding their components: $\mathbf{x} + \mathbf{y} = (x_1 + y_1, \ldots, x_n + y_n)$. We can perform **scalar multiplication** on a vector by multiplying every component by a fixed real number t: $t\mathbf{x} = (tx_1, \ldots, tx_n)$. Geometrically, vector addition is done by drawing $\mathbf{x}$ and translating $\mathbf{y}$ to the tail of $\mathbf{x}$; scalar multiplication is done by drawing a vector t times as long as the original.

A vector $\mathbf{x}$ is a **linear combination** of a set of n vectors A if $\mathbf{x} = \sum_{i=1}^{n} t_i \mathbf{y}_i$, where $\mathbf{y}_i \in A$ and the t_i's are scalars. A set A of n vectors is **linearly independent** if there is no set $(t_i, \mathbf{x}_i)$, with some $t_i \neq 0$ and $x_i \in A$, such that $\sum_{i=1}^{n} t_i \mathbf{x}_i = 0$. An equivalent definition is that no vector in A can be represented as a linear combination of vectors in A.

Given two vectors their **inner product** is given by $\mathbf{xy} = \sum_i x_i y_i$. The **norm** of a vector $\mathbf{x}$ is denoted by $|\mathbf{x}|$ and defined by $|\mathbf{x}| = \sqrt{\mathbf{xx}}$. Note that by the Pythagorean theorem, the norm of $\mathbf{x}$ is the distance of the point $\mathbf{x}$ from the origin; that is, it is the length of the vector $\mathbf{x}$.

There is a very important geometric interpretation of the inner product, illustrated in Figure 26.1. We have two vectors $\mathbf{x}$ and $\mathbf{y}$; the dotted line is dropped from the head of $\mathbf{y}$ to $\mathbf{x}$ and is perpendicular to $\mathbf{x}$. The vector which extends from the origin to the point where the dotted line intersects $\mathbf{x}$ is called the **projection** of $\mathbf{y}$ on $\mathbf{x}$. Certainly the projection of $\mathbf{y}$ on $\mathbf{x}$ is a vector of form $t\mathbf{x}$. Let us use the Pythagorean formula to calculate t:

$$|t\mathbf{x}|^2 + |\mathbf{y} - t\mathbf{x}|^2 = |\mathbf{y}|^2$$
$$t^2\mathbf{xx} + (\mathbf{y} - t\mathbf{x})(\mathbf{y} - t\mathbf{x}) = \mathbf{yy}$$
$$t^2\mathbf{xx} + \mathbf{yy} - 2t\mathbf{xy} + t^2\mathbf{xx} = \mathbf{yy}$$
$$t\mathbf{xx} = \mathbf{xy}$$
$$t = \frac{\mathbf{xy}}{\mathbf{xx}}.$$

Hence, if we project $\mathbf{y}$ on $\mathbf{x}$ we get a vector that points in the same direction as $\mathbf{x}$ but is only $\mathbf{xy}/\mathbf{xx}$ as long as $\mathbf{x}$. If $\mathbf{xy} = 0$, then $\mathbf{x}$ and $\mathbf{y}$ are said to be **orthogonal**.

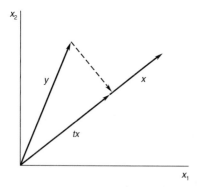

Figure 26.1 **The projection of y on x.** This illustrates the geometric interpretation the projection operation.

Let θ be the angle between $\mathbf{x}$ and $\mathbf{y}$. It is clear from elementary trigonometry that $t|\mathbf{x}| = |\mathbf{y}| \cos \theta$. If we combine this with our other formula for t, we see that $\mathbf{xy} = |\mathbf{x}||\mathbf{y}| \cos \theta$. Hence if $\theta = 90°$, $\mathbf{xy} = 0$; if $\theta > 90°$, then $\mathbf{xy} < 0$ and if $\theta < 90°$, then $\mathbf{xy} > 0$.

We can consider maps from R^n to R^m that send vectors into vectors. We denote such maps by $\mathbf{f}: R^n \to R^m$. A map is a **linear function** if $\mathbf{f}(t\mathbf{x} + s\mathbf{y}) = t\mathbf{f}(\mathbf{x}) + s\mathbf{f}(\mathbf{y})$ for all scalars s and t and vectors $\mathbf{x}$ and $\mathbf{y}$. If $\mathbf{f}$ is a linear function to R^1, we call it a **linear functional**. If $\mathbf{p}$ is a linear functional we can represent it by a vector $\mathbf{p} = (p_1, \ldots, p_n)$, and write $\mathbf{p}(\mathbf{x}) = \mathbf{px}$. A set of points of form $H(\mathbf{p}, a) = \{\mathbf{x} : \mathbf{px} = a\}$ is called a **hyperplane**.

The hyperplane $H(\mathbf{p}, 0)$ consists of all vectors $\mathbf{x}$ that are orthogonal to the vector $\mathbf{p}$. It is not hard to see that this is an $n-1$ dimensional set. The hyperplanes of the form $H(\mathbf{p}, a)$ are translations of this basic hyperplane. Hyperplanes are important in economics since $H(\mathbf{p}, a)$ consists of all vectors $\mathbf{x}$ that have value a at prices $\mathbf{p}$.

If A is a linear function $A: R^n \to R^m$, we can represent A by an m-by-n matrix $\mathbf{A} = (a_{ij})$. Then $A(\mathbf{x}) = \mathbf{Ax}$; i.e., to find the image of $\mathbf{x}$ under the map A we just apply ordinary matrix multiplication. A **symmetric** matrix has $a_{ij} = a_{ji}$ for all i and j.

We follow the following convention for inequality comparisons of vectors: $\mathbf{x} \geq \mathbf{y}$ means $x_i \geq y_i$ for all i, $\mathbf{x} \gg \mathbf{y}$ means $x_i > y_i$ for all i.

26.2 Definite and semidefinite matrices

Let $\mathbf{A}$ be a symmetric square matrix. Then if we postmultiply $\mathbf{A}$ by some vector $\mathbf{x}$ and premultiply it by the (transpose of the) same vector $\mathbf{x}$, we have a **quadratic form**. For example,

$$(x_1 \quad x_2) \begin{pmatrix} a_{11} & a_{12} \\ a_{21} & a_{22} \end{pmatrix} \begin{pmatrix} x_1 \\ x_2 \end{pmatrix} = a_{11}x_1^2 + (a_{21} + a_{12})x_1x_2 + a_{22}x_2^2.$$

Suppose that $\mathbf{A}$ is the identity matrix. In this case it is not hard to see that whatever the values of x_1 and x_2, the quadratic form must be nonnegative. In fact, if x_1 and x_2 are not both zero, $\mathbf{xAx}$ will be strictly positive. The identity matrix is an example of a **positive definite matrix**.

Definite matrices. *A square matrix $\mathbf{A}$ is:*

 (a) **positive definite** *if* $\mathbf{x}^t \mathbf{Ax} > 0$ *for all* $\mathbf{x} \neq \mathbf{0}$;
 (b) **negative definite** *if* $\mathbf{x}^t \mathbf{Ax} < 0$ *for all* $\mathbf{x} \neq \mathbf{0}$;
 (c) **positive semidefinite** *if* $\mathbf{x}^t \mathbf{Ax} \geq 0$ *for all* $\mathbf{x}$;
 (d) **negative semidefinite** *if* $\mathbf{x}^t \mathbf{Ax} \leq 0$ *for all* $\mathbf{x}$.

In some cases we do not want to require that $\mathbf{x}^t \mathbf{Ax}$ has a definite sign for *all* values of $\mathbf{x}$, but only for some restricted set of values. We say $\mathbf{A}$

is **positive definite subject to constraint bx** $= 0$ if $\mathbf{x}^t \mathbf{A} \mathbf{x} > 0$ for all $\mathbf{x} \neq 0$ such that $\mathbf{bx} = 0$. The other definitions extend to the constrained case in a natural manner.

Tests for definite matrices

It is often convenient to be able to recognize when a matrix is negative or positive semidefinite. One useful necessary condition is as follows: if a matrix is positive semidefinite, then it must have nonnegative diagonal terms. The proof is simply to note that if $\mathbf{x} = (1, 0, \ldots, 0)$, for example, then $\mathbf{x}^t \mathbf{A} \mathbf{x} = a_{11}$.

Conditions that are necessary and sufficient take a more complicated form. The **minor matrices** of a matrix A are the matrices formed by eliminating k columns and the same numbered k rows. The **naturally ordered** or **nested principal minor matrices** of A are the minor matrices given by

$$
a_{11} \qquad \begin{pmatrix} a_{11} & a_{12} \\ a_{21} & a_{22} \end{pmatrix} \qquad \begin{pmatrix} a_{11} & a_{12} & a_{13} \\ a_{21} & a_{22} & a_{23} \\ a_{31} & a_{32} & a_{33} \end{pmatrix}
$$

and so on. The **minor determinants** or **minors** of a matrix are the determinants of the minors. We denote the determinant of a matrix $\mathbf{A}$ by $\det \mathbf{A}$ or $|\mathbf{A}|$.

Suppose that we are given a square matrix $\mathbf{A}$ and a vector $\mathbf{b}$. We can **border $\mathbf{A}$ by $\mathbf{b}$** in the following way:

$$
\begin{pmatrix} 0 & b_1 & \ldots & b_n \\ b_1 & a_{11} & \ldots & a_{1n} \\ \vdots & & & \vdots \\ b_n & a_{n1} & \ldots & a_{nn} \end{pmatrix}
$$

This matrix is called the **bordered matrix**. The useful generalization of this to the minor matrices is called the **border-preserving principal minor matrices**. These are just the submatrices of this matrix, starting in the upper left-hand corner *including* the border elements. It turns out that the determinants of these submatrices give a convenient test for whether the matrix is positive or negative definite.

Tests for definite matrices. *A square matrix $\mathbf{A}$ is:*

(a) **positive definite** *if and only if the principal minor determinants are all positive;*

(b) **negative definite** *if and only if the principal minor determinants of order k have sign $(-1)^k$ for $k = 1, \ldots, n$.*

(c) **positive definite subject to** *the constraint* $\mathbf{bx} = 0$ *if and only if the border-preserving principal minors are all negative;*

(d) **negative definite subject to** *the constraint* $\mathbf{bx} = 0$ *if and only if the border-preserving principal minors have sign* $(-1)^k$ *for* $k = 2, \ldots, n$.

Note well the peculiar fact that a positive definite matrix has all positive principal minors, while a matrix that is positive definite subject to constraint has all border-preserving principal minors negative. See Chapter 27, page 500, for some examples.

Corollary.   *In the cases described above, if the naturally ordered principal minors satisfy one of the conditions (a)–(d), then all of the principal minors satisfy the appropriate condition.   Hence checking the naturally ordered principal minors is sufficient for the tests.*

26.3 Cramer's rule

Here is a convenient rule for solving linear systems of equations of the form

$$\begin{pmatrix} a_{11} & \cdots & a_{1n} \\ \vdots & & \vdots \\ a_{n1} & \cdots & a_{nn} \end{pmatrix} \begin{pmatrix} x_1 \\ \vdots \\ x_n \end{pmatrix} = \begin{pmatrix} b_1 \\ \vdots \\ b_n \end{pmatrix}.$$

We can write his system more conveniently as $\mathbf{Ax} = \mathbf{b}$.

Cramer's rule.   *To find the component x_i of the solution vector to this system of linear equations, replace the ith column of the matrix A with the column vector $\mathbf{b}$ to form a matrix $\mathbf{A}_i$. Then x_i is the determinant of $\mathbf{A}_i$ divided by the determinant of $\mathbf{A}$:*

$$x_i = \frac{|\mathbf{A}_i|}{|\mathbf{A}|}.$$

26.4 Analysis

Given a vector $\mathbf{x}$ in R^n and a positive real number e, we define an **open ball** of radius e at $\mathbf{x}$ as $B_e(\mathbf{x}) = \{\mathbf{y} \in R^n : |\mathbf{y} - \mathbf{x}| < e\}$. A set of points A is a **open set** if for every $\mathbf{x}$ in A there is some $B_e(\mathbf{x})$ which is contained in A. If $\mathbf{x}$ is in an arbitrary set and there exists an $e > 0$ such that $B_e(\mathbf{x})$ is in A, then $\mathbf{x}$ is said to be in the **interior** of A.

The **complement** of a set A in R^n consists of all the points in R^n that are not in A; it is denoted by $R^n \backslash A$.

A set is a **closed set** if $R^n \backslash A$ is an open set. A set A is bounded if there is some $\mathbf{x}$ in A and some $e > 0$ such that A is contained in $B_e(\mathbf{x})$. If a nonempty set in R^n is both closed and bounded, it is called **compact**.

A infinite **sequence** in R^n, $(\mathbf{x}^i) = (\mathbf{x}^1, \mathbf{x}^2, \ldots)$ is just an infinite set of points, one point for each positive integer. A sequence $(\mathbf{x}^i)$ is said to **converge** to a point $\mathbf{x}^*$ if for every $e > 0$, there is an integer m such that, for all $i > m$, $\mathbf{x}^i$ is in $B_e(\mathbf{x}^*)$. We sometimes say that $\mathbf{x}^i$ gets arbitrarily close to $\mathbf{x}^*$. We also say that $\mathbf{x}^*$ is the **limit** of the sequence $(\mathbf{x}^i)$ and write $\lim_{i \to \infty} \mathbf{x}^i = \mathbf{x}^*$. If a sequence converges to a point, we call it a **convergent sequence**.

Closed set. *A is a closed set if every convergent sequence in A converges to a point in A.*

Compact set. *If A is a compact set, then every sequence in A has a convergent subsequence.*

A function $\mathbf{f}(\mathbf{x})$ is **continuous** at $\mathbf{x}^*$ if for every sequence $(\mathbf{x}^i)$ that converges to $\mathbf{x}^*$, we have the sequence $(\mathbf{f}(\mathbf{x}^i))$ converging to $\mathbf{f}(\mathbf{x}^*)$. A function that is continuous at every point in its domain is called a **continuous function**.

26.5 Calculus

Calculus is a way of tying linear algebra and analysis together by approximating certain functions by linear functions. Given a function $f : R \to R$, we define its derivative at a point x^* by

$$\frac{df(x^*)}{dx} = \lim_{t \to 0} \frac{f(x^* + t) - f(x^*)}{t}$$

if that limit exists. The derivative $df(x^*)/dx$ is also denoted by $f'(x^*)$. If the derivative of f exists at x^*, we say that f is **differentiable** at x^*.

Consider the *linear* function $F(t)$ defined by

$$F(t) = f(x^*) + f'(x^*)t.$$

This is a good approximation to f near x^* since

$$\lim_{t \to 0} \frac{f(x^* + t) - F(t)}{t} = \lim_{t \to 0} \frac{f(x^* + t) - f(x^*) - f'(x^*)t}{t} = 0.$$

In the same way, given an arbitrary function $\mathbf{f}: R^n \to R^m$, we can define its derivative at $\mathbf{x}^*$, $\mathbf{Df}(\mathbf{x}^*)$, as being that linear map from R^n to R^m that approximates $\mathbf{f}$ close to $\mathbf{x}^*$ in the sense that

$$\lim_{|\mathbf{t}| \to 0} \frac{|\mathbf{f}(\mathbf{x}^* + \mathbf{t}) - \mathbf{f}(\mathbf{x}^*) - \mathbf{Df}(\mathbf{x}^*)\mathbf{t}|}{|\mathbf{t}|} = 0,$$

assuming, of course, that such a map exists. We use norm signs since both the numerator and denominator are vectors. The map $\mathbf{f}(\mathbf{x}^*) + \mathbf{Df}(\mathbf{x}^*)$ is a good approximation to $\mathbf{f}$ at $\mathbf{x}^*$ in the sense that for small vectors $\mathbf{t}$,

$$\mathbf{f}(\mathbf{x}^* + \mathbf{t}) \approx \mathbf{f}(\mathbf{x}^*) + \mathbf{Df}(\mathbf{x}^*)\mathbf{t}.$$

Given a function $f : R^n \to R$, we can also define the **partial derivatives** of f with respect to x_i evaluated at $\mathbf{x}^*$. To do this, we hold all components fixed except for the ith component, so that f is only a function of x_i, and calculate the ordinary one-dimensional derivative. We denote the partial derivative of f with respect to x_i evaluated at $\mathbf{x}^*$ by $\partial f(\mathbf{x}^*)/\partial x_i$.

Since $\mathbf{Df}(\mathbf{x}^*)$ is a linear transformation, we can represent it by a matrix, which turns out to be

$$\mathbf{Df}(\mathbf{x}^*) = \begin{pmatrix} \dfrac{\partial f_1(\mathbf{x}^*)}{\partial x_1} & \cdots & \dfrac{\partial f_1(\mathbf{x}^*)}{\partial x_n} \\ \vdots & & \vdots \\ \dfrac{\partial f_m(\mathbf{x}^*)}{\partial x_1} & \cdots & \dfrac{\partial f_m(\mathbf{x}^*)}{\partial x_n} \end{pmatrix}.$$

The matrix representing $\mathbf{Df}(\mathbf{x})$ is called the **Jacobian matrix** of $\mathbf{f}$ at $\mathbf{x}^*$. We will often work with functions from R^n to R in which case $\mathbf{Df}(\mathbf{x}^*)$ will be an n-by-1 matrix, which is simply a vector.

Higher-order derivatives

If we have a function $f: R^n \to R$, the **Hessian matrix** of that function is the matrix of mixed partial derivatives

$$\mathbf{D}^2 f(\mathbf{x}) = \left(\frac{\partial^2 f(\mathbf{x})}{\partial x_i \partial x_j} \right).$$

Note that $\mathbf{D}^2 f(\mathbf{x})$ is a symmetric matrix.

Let $f: R^n \to R$ be a differentiable function and let $\mathbf{x}$ and $\mathbf{y}$ be two vectors in R^n. Then it can be shown that

$$f(\mathbf{y}) = f(\mathbf{x}) + \mathbf{D}f(\mathbf{z})(\mathbf{y} - \mathbf{x})$$

$$f(\mathbf{y}) = f(\mathbf{x}) + \mathbf{D}f(\mathbf{x})(\mathbf{y} - \mathbf{x}) + \frac{1}{2}(\mathbf{y} - \mathbf{x})^t \mathbf{D}^2 f(\mathbf{w})(\mathbf{y} - \mathbf{x})$$

where $\mathbf{z}$ and $\mathbf{w}$ are points on the line segment between $\mathbf{x}$ and $\mathbf{y}$. These expressions are called **Taylor series** expansions of f at $\mathbf{x}$.

If $\mathbf{x}$ and $\mathbf{y}$ are close together and the derivative functions are continuous, then $\mathbf{D}f(\mathbf{z})$ and $\mathbf{D}^2 f(\mathbf{w})$ are approximately equal to $\mathbf{D}f(\mathbf{x})$ and $\mathbf{D}^2 f(\mathbf{x})$, respectively. We therefore often write the Taylor series expansions as

$$f(\mathbf{y}) \approx f(\mathbf{x}) + \mathbf{D}f(\mathbf{x})(\mathbf{y} - \mathbf{x})$$

$$f(\mathbf{y}) \approx f(\mathbf{x}) + \mathbf{D}f(\mathbf{x})(\mathbf{y} - \mathbf{x}) + \frac{1}{2}(\mathbf{y} - \mathbf{x})^t \mathbf{D}^2 f(\mathbf{x})(\mathbf{y} - \mathbf{x}).$$

26.6 Gradients and tangent planes

Consider a function $f \colon R^n \to R$. The **gradient** of f at $\mathbf{x}^*$ is a vector whose coordinates are the partial derivatives of f at $\mathbf{x}^*$:

$$\mathbf{D}f(\mathbf{x}^*) = \left(\frac{\partial f(\mathbf{x}^*)}{\partial x_1}, \ldots, \frac{\partial f(\mathbf{x}^*)}{\partial x_n} \right).$$

The gradient of f at $\mathbf{x}^*$ has the same representation as the derivative of f at $\mathbf{x}^*$ but they are conceptually somewhat different. The derivative is a linear functional on R^n; the gradient is a vector in R^n. As it happens, linear functionals can be represented by vectors so they "look" the same, even though they are really different objects. However, we will exploit appearances and use the same notation for each.

There is an important geometric interpretation of the gradient: it points in the direction that the function f increases most rapidly. To see this, let $\mathbf{h}$ be a vector of norm 1. The derivative of f in the direction $\mathbf{h}$ at $\mathbf{x}^*$ is simply $\mathbf{D}f(\mathbf{x}^*)\mathbf{h}$. Using the formula for the inner product,

$$\mathbf{D}f(\mathbf{x}^*)\mathbf{h} = |\mathbf{D}f(\mathbf{x}^*)| \cos \theta,$$

and this is clearly maximized when $\theta = 0$, i.e., when the vectors $\mathbf{D}f(\mathbf{x}^*)$ and $\mathbf{h}$ are collinear.

The **level set** of a function is the set of all $\mathbf{x}$ such that the function is constant: $Q(a) = \{\mathbf{x} : f(\mathbf{x}) = a\}$. The level set of a differentiable function $f : R^n \to R$ will generally be an $n - 1$ dimensional surface.

The **upper contour set** of a function $f : R^n \to R$ is the set of all $\mathbf{x}$ such that $f(\mathbf{x})$ is at least as large as some number: $U(a) = \{\mathbf{x} \in R^n : f(\mathbf{x}) \geq a\}$.

It is often convenient to find a formula for the **tangent hyperplane** to the level set at some point $\mathbf{x}^*$. We know that the linear map $f(\mathbf{x}^*) + \mathbf{D}f(\mathbf{x}^*)(\mathbf{x} - \mathbf{x}^*)$ closely approximates the map f near $\mathbf{x}^*$. Hence, the best linear approximation to $\{\mathbf{x} : f(\mathbf{x}) = a\}$ should be $H(a) = \{\mathbf{x} : f(\mathbf{x}^*) +$

$\mathbf{D}f(\mathbf{x}^*)(\mathbf{x} - \mathbf{x}^*) = a\}$. Since $f(\mathbf{x}^*) = a$, we have the following formula for the tangent hyperplane:

$$H(a) = \{\mathbf{x} : \mathbf{D}f(\mathbf{x}^*)(\mathbf{x} - \mathbf{x}^*) = 0\}. \tag{26.1}$$

Hyperplane.   *If* $\mathbf{x}$ *is a vector in the tangent hyperplane, then* $\mathbf{x} - \mathbf{x}^*$ *is orthogonal to the gradient of* f *at* $\mathbf{x}^*$.

This follows directly from equation 26.1 but is also quite intuitive. Along the surface $Q(a)$ the value of the function f is constant. Therefore the derivative of $f(\mathbf{x})$ in those directions should be zero.

26.7 Limits

At a couple of points in the text we use **L'Hôpital's rule** for computing limits. Suppose that we are trying to compute the limit of a fraction $f(x)/g(x)$ as $x \to 0$, but $f(0) = g(0) = 0$, so the value of the fraction at $x = 0$ is undefined. However, if f and g are differentiable, and if $g'(0) \neq 0$, L'Hôpital's rule says that

$$\lim_{x \to 0} \frac{f(x)}{g(x)} = \frac{f'(0)}{g'(0)}.$$

Hence, the limit of the ratio is the ratio of the derivatives.

26.8 Homogeneous functions

A function $f : R_+^n \to R$ is **homogeneous of degree** k if $f(t\mathbf{x}) = t^k f(\mathbf{x})$ for all $t > 0$. The two most important cases are where $k = 0$ and $k = 1$. If we double all the arguments of a function that is homogeneous of degree zero, the value of the function doesn't change. If the function is homogeneous of degree 1, the value of the function doubles.

Euler's law.   *If* f *is a differentiable function that is homogeneous of degree 1, then*

$$f(\mathbf{x}) = \sum_{i=1}^{n} \frac{\partial f(\mathbf{x})}{\partial x_i} x_i.$$

By way of proof, we note that by definition, $f(t\mathbf{x}) \equiv tf(\mathbf{x})$. Differentiating this identity with respect to t, we have

$$\sum_i \frac{\partial f(t\mathbf{x})}{\partial (tx_i)} x_i = f(\mathbf{x}).$$

Setting $t = 1$ gives us the result.

Homogeneity. *If $f(\mathbf{x})$ is homogeneous of degree $k \geq 1$, then $\partial f(\mathbf{x})/\partial x_i$ is homogeneous of degree $k - 1$.*

To see this, differentiate the identity $f(t\mathbf{x}) = t^k f(\mathbf{x})$ with respect to x_i:

$$\frac{\partial f(t\mathbf{x})}{\partial (tx_i)} t = t^k \frac{\partial f(\mathbf{x})}{\partial x_i}.$$

Dividing both sides by t yields the desired result.

An important implication of this fact is that the slopes of the level surfaces of a homogeneous function are constant along rays through the origin:

$$\frac{\dfrac{\partial f(t\mathbf{x})}{\partial x_i}}{\dfrac{\partial f(t\mathbf{x})}{\partial x_j}} = \frac{\dfrac{\partial f(\mathbf{x})}{\partial x_i}}{\dfrac{\partial f(\mathbf{x})}{\partial x_j}}, \tag{26.2}$$

for all $t > 0$.

However, there are nonhomogeneous functions that have this same property. A function is called **homothetic** if it is a positive monotonic transformation of a function that is homogeneous of degree 1. That is, a homothetic function can be written as $f(\mathbf{x}) = g(h(\mathbf{x}))$ where $h(\mathbf{x})$ is homogeneous of degree 1. It is not hard to show that homothetic functions satisfy condition (26.2).

26.9 Affine functions

A function is an **affine function** if it can be expressed in the form $f(x) = a + bx$. Affine functions are sometimes called linear functions, but, strictly speaking, this is only correct when $a = 0$.

Clearly, a differentiable function is an affine function if and only if $f''(x) \equiv 0$. Here is a useful implication of this fact: a function satisfies the condition $f(pu + (1-p)v) \equiv pf(u) + (1-p)f(v)$ for all $0 \leq p \leq 1$ if and only if $f(u)$ is affine. The proof is simply to differentiate the condition with respect to p to find $f'(pu + (1-p)v)(u-v) \equiv f(u) - f(v)$. Differentiating once more gives us $f''(pu + (1-p)v) \equiv 0$.

26.10 Convex sets

A set of points A in R^n is **convex** if $\mathbf{x}$ in A and $\mathbf{y}$ in A implies $t\mathbf{x} + (1-t)\mathbf{y}$ is in A for all t such that $0 \leq t \leq 1$. A set of points in A is **strictly convex** if $t\mathbf{x} + (1-t)\mathbf{y}$ is in the interior of A for all t such that $0 < t < 1$.

We frequently use the fact that the sum of convex sets is convex, so we prove that here. Let A_1 and A_2 be two convex sets, and let $A = A_1 + A_2$.

Let $\mathbf{x}$ and $\mathbf{y}$ be two points in A. By definition $\mathbf{x} = \mathbf{x}_1 + \mathbf{x}_2$, where $\mathbf{x}_1$ is in A_1 and $\mathbf{x}_2$ is in A_2, and similarly for $\mathbf{y}$. It follows that $t\mathbf{x} + (1-t)\mathbf{y} = t(\mathbf{x}_1 + \mathbf{x}_2) + (1-t)(\mathbf{y}_1 + \mathbf{y}_2) = [t\mathbf{x}_1 + (1-t)\mathbf{y}_1] + [t\mathbf{x}_2 + (1-t)\mathbf{y}_2]$. The bracketed expressions are in A_1 and A_2 respectively since each of these is a convex set. Hence $t\mathbf{x} + (1-t)\mathbf{y}$ is in A, which establishes that A is a convex set.

26.11 Separating hyperplanes

Let A and B be two convex sets in R^n that are disjoint; i.e., that have an empty intersection. Then it is reasonably intuitive that one can find a hyperplane that "separates" the two sets. That is, A lies on one side of the hyperplane and B lies on the other side. This is the content of the following theorem.

Separating hyperplane theorem.   *If A and B are two nonempty, disjoint, convex sets in R^n, then there exists a linear functional $\mathbf{p}$ such that $\mathbf{px} \geq \mathbf{py}$ for all $\mathbf{x}$ in A and $\mathbf{y}$ in B.*

26.12 Partial differential equations

A **system of partial differential equations** is a system of equations of the form

$$\frac{\partial f(\mathbf{p})}{\partial p_i} = g_i(f(\mathbf{p}), \mathbf{p}) \qquad i = 1, \ldots n$$

$$f(\mathbf{q}) = 0.$$

The last equation is called the **boundary condition**. General systems of PDEs can be more complicated than this, but this form is sufficient for our purposes.

A **solution** to a system of PDEs is a function $f(\mathbf{p})$ that satisfies the equations identically in $\mathbf{p}$. A necessary condition for there to exist a solution to a set of PDEs comes from the symmetry of cross-partial derivatives:

$$\frac{\partial g_i}{\partial f}\frac{\partial f}{\partial p_j} + \frac{\partial g_i}{\partial p_j} = \frac{\partial^2 f(\mathbf{p})}{\partial p_i \partial p_j} = \frac{\partial^2 f(\mathbf{p})}{\partial p_j \partial p_i} = \frac{\partial g_j}{\partial f}\frac{\partial f}{\partial p_i} + \frac{\partial g_j}{\partial p_i}.$$

It follows that

$$\frac{\partial g_i}{\partial f}\frac{\partial f}{\partial p_j} + \frac{\partial g_i}{\partial p_j} = \frac{\partial g_j}{\partial f}\frac{\partial f}{\partial p_i} + \frac{\partial g_j}{\partial p_i}$$

is a necessary condition for a *local* solution to this set of PDEs to exist. This condition is known as an **integrability condition**. (The conditions for a solution to exist globally are somewhat more complicated and depend on the topological properties of the domain.)

Solving for an explicit solution to a system of PDEs may be quite difficult, but there is one special case that is easy to handle. This is the case where $f(\mathbf{p})$ does not appear explicitly on the right-hand side of the equations. This sort of system can be solved by simple integration.

Consider, for example, what happens when there are two equations:

$$\frac{\partial f(p_1, p_2)}{\partial p_1} = g_1(p_1, p_2)$$

$$\frac{\partial f(p_1, p_2)}{\partial p_2} = g_2(p_1, p_2)$$

$$f(q_1, q_2) = 0.$$

If the integrability condition

$$\frac{\partial g_1(p_1, p_2)}{\partial p_2} = \frac{\partial g_2(p_1, p_2)}{\partial p_1}$$

is satisfied, it can be shown that the solution to this system is given by

$$f(p_1, p_2) = \int_{q_1}^{p_1} g_1(t, q_2)\, dt + \int_{q_2}^{p_2} g_2(p_1, t)\, dt.$$

It is clear that this function satisfies the boundary condition, and simple differentiation shows that $\partial f / \partial p_2 = g_2(p_1, p_2)$. We only need establish that $\partial f / \partial p_1 = g_1(p_1, p_2)$.

Taking the derivative, we find

$$\frac{\partial f(p_1, p_2)}{\partial p_1} = g_1(p_1, q_2) + \int_{q_2}^{p_2} \frac{\partial g_2(p_1, t)}{\partial p_1}\, dt.$$

Using the integrability condition

$$\frac{\partial f(p_1, p_2)}{\partial p_1} = g_1(p_1, q_2) + \int_{q_2}^{p_2} \frac{\partial g_1(p_1, t)}{\partial p_2}\, dt$$

$$= g_1(p_1, q_2) + g_1(p_1, p_2) - g_1(p_1, q_2)$$

$$= g_1(p_1, p_2).$$

26.13 Dynamical systems

The **state** of a system consists of a description of all of the variables that affect the behavior of the system. The **state space** of a system consists of all feasible states. For example, the state space of a particular economic system may consist of all possible price configurations, or all possible configurations of prices and consumption bundles.

If we denote the state space by S, we can describe a **dynamical system** by a function $\mathbf{F} : S \times R \to S$. The real line, R, is interpreted as time and $\mathbf{F}(\mathbf{x}, t)$ is the state of the system at time t if it was in state $\mathbf{x}$ at time 0.

Usually the state function $\mathbf{F}$ is not given explicitly but is given implicitly by a **system of differential equations**. For example, $\dot{\mathbf{x}} = \mathbf{f}(\mathbf{x}(t))$ is a differential equation that tells us the rate of change of $\mathbf{x}$ when the system is in state $\mathbf{x}(t)$. If $\mathbf{f}(\mathbf{x})$ satisfies certain regularity conditions, it can be shown that there is a unique dynamical system defined by $\mathbf{f}$.

A **solution** to a system of differential equations $\dot{\mathbf{x}} = \mathbf{f}(\mathbf{x})$ is a function $\mathbf{x} : R \to R^n$ such that $\dot{\mathbf{x}}(t) = \mathbf{f}(\mathbf{x}(t))$ for all t. A solution is also called a **solution curve, trajectory, orbit**, etc.

An **equilibrium** of a dynamical system is a state $\mathbf{x}^*$ such that $\mathbf{f}(\mathbf{x}^*) = \mathbf{0}$. Roughly speaking, if a dynamical system ever gets in an equilibrium state, it stays there forever.

Suppose that we are given some dynamical system $\dot{\mathbf{x}} = \mathbf{f}(\mathbf{x})$ and we start at time 0 in some arbitrary state $\mathbf{x}_0$. It is often of interest to know when the state of the system will move to some equilibrium $\mathbf{x}^*$. We say that a system is **globally stable** if $\lim_{t \to \infty} \mathbf{x}(t) = \mathbf{x}^*$ for all initial values $\mathbf{x}_0$. We note that a globally stable equilibrium must be unique.

There is a very convenient criterion for determining when a dynamical system is globally stable. We will restrict ourselves to the case where the state space S is compact, so that we know that the system will always stay in a bounded region. Suppose that we can find a differentiable function $V : S \to R$ that has the following two properties:

(1) V reaches a minimum at $\mathbf{x}^*$;

(2) $\dot{V}(\mathbf{x}(t)) < 0$ for all $\mathbf{x}(t) \neq \mathbf{x}^*$. That is, $\mathbf{D}V(\mathbf{x})\mathbf{f}(\mathbf{x}(t)) < 0$ for $\mathbf{x}(t) \neq \mathbf{x}^*$.

Such a function is called a **Liaponov function**.

Liaponov's theorem. *If we can find a Liaponov function for a dynamical system, then the unique equilibrium $\mathbf{x}^*$ is globally stable.*

26.14 Random variables

Given a random variable $\tilde{R}_a$ that takes on the value R_{as} with probability π_s, for $s = 1, \ldots, S$, we define the **expectation** of that random variable to be

$$E\tilde{R}_a = \overline{R}_a = \sum_{s=1}^{S} R_{as} \pi_s.$$

We define the **covariance** of two random variables $\tilde{R}_a$ and $\tilde{R}_b$ by

$$\text{cov}(\tilde{R}_a, \tilde{R}_b) = \sigma_{ab} = E(R_a - \overline{R}_a)(R_b - \overline{R}_b).$$

The **variance** of a random variable $\tilde{R}_a$ is given by

$$\sigma_a^2 = \sigma_{aa} = \text{cov}(\tilde{R}_a, \tilde{R}_a).$$

Let x_a, x_b, and c be nonstochastic. Then, given the definitions, the following facts follow by direct computation:

Expectation of a sum. $E(x_a \tilde{R}_a + x_b \tilde{R}_b) = x_a E\tilde{R}_a + x_b E\tilde{R}_b = x_a \overline{R}_a + x_b \overline{R}_b$. More generally,

$$E \sum_{a=1}^{A} x_a \tilde{R}_a = \sum_{a=1}^{A} x_a \overline{R}_a.$$

Covariance identity. $\text{cov}(\tilde{R}_a, \tilde{R}_b) = E\tilde{R}_a \tilde{R}_b - \overline{R}_a \overline{R}_b$.

Covariance of a sum. $\text{cov}(x_a \tilde{R}_a + c, \tilde{R}_b) = x_a \text{cov}(\tilde{R}_a, \tilde{R}_b)$.

Variance of a sum. $\text{var}(x_a \tilde{R}_a + x_b \tilde{R}_b + c) = x_a^2 \text{var}(\tilde{R}_a) + 2x_a x_b \text{cov}(\tilde{R}_a, \tilde{R}_b) + x_b^2 \text{var}(\tilde{R}_b) = x_a^2 \sigma_{aa} + 2x_a x_b \sigma_{ab} + x_b^2 \sigma_{bb}$. More generally,

$$\text{var}\left(\sum_{a=1}^{A} x_a \tilde{R}_a\right) = \sum_{a=1}^{A} \sum_{b=1}^{A} x_a x_b \sigma_{ab}.$$

Notes

There are many books on mathematics for economics that cover this material in detail. See, for example, Binmore (1982), Binmore (1983), and Blume & Simon (1991).

CHAPTER 27

OPTIMIZATION

This chapter is meant to serve as a *review* of various facts about optimization. Typically students will have spent several weeks studying these methods in a mathematics course prior to studying this text.

27.1 Single variable optimization

Let $f : R \rightarrow R$ be a function. We say that this function achieves a **maximum** at x^* if $f(x^*) \geq f(x)$ for all x. If $f(x^*) > f(x)$ for all $x \neq x^*$, then we say that x^* is a **strict maximum**. Similarly, if $f(x^*) \leq f(x)$ for all x, we say that the function achieves a **minimum**, and if $f(x^*) < f(x)$ for all $x \neq x^*$, we have a **strict minimum**.

Note that the problem of maximizing $f(x)$ with respect to x is the same as the problem of minimizing $-f(x)$.

First-order and second-order conditions

Suppose that a differentiable[1] function f achieves a maximum at x^*. Then

---

[1] In this text we will often adopt "Solow's convention:" every function is assumed to be differentiable one more time than we need it to be.

we know from elementary calculus that the first derivative of f must be equal to zero at x^* and that the second derivative of f must be less than or equal to zero at x^*. These conditions are known as the **first-order condition** and the **second-order condition**, respectively, and they can be expressed mathematically by:

$$f'(x^*) = 0$$
$$f''(x^*) \leq 0.$$

Note that these are *necessary* not sufficient conditions; a point in R that solves the maximization problem must satisfy the conditions, but there may be points that satisfy the conditions that do not solve the maximization problem.

For a minimization problem the first-order condition is the same, but the second-order condition becomes $f''(x^*) \geq 0$.

EXAMPLE: First- and second-order conditions.

Consider the function $f(x, a) = \ln x - ax$. The first-order condition for a maximum with respect to x is that $1/x - a = 0$, and the second-order condition is that $-1/x^2 \leq 0$. We see that the second-order condition is automatically satisfied, so it follows that the optimal value of x is $x^* = 1/a$.

Now let $g(x, b) = u(x) - bx$. In this case we cannot solve explicitly for the x^* that maximizes this expression, but we know that it must satisfy the two conditions $u'(x^*) = b$ and $u''(x^*) \leq 0$.

Concavity

A function of one variable is **concave** if

$$f(tx + (1 - t)y) \geq tf(x) + (1 - t)f(y)$$

for all x and y and all t such that $0 \leq t \leq 1$. See Figure 27.1 for a picture. A concave function has the property that f evaluated at a weighted average of x and y is greater than or equal to the same weighted average of $f(x)$ and $f(y)$.

If f is differentiable, then f is concave if and only if $f''(x) \leq 0$ for all x. For example, $\ln x$ is a concave function since its second derivative is always less than or equal to zero.

A function is **strictly concave** if

$$f(tx + (1 - t)y) > tf(x) + (1 - t)f(y)$$

for all x and y and all t such that $0 < t < 1$. If $f''(x) < 0$ for all x, then f is strictly concave, but the converse is not true. For example, $f(x) = -x^4$ is strictly concave, but $f''(0) = 0$.

Another property of a concave function is that

$$f(x) \le f(y) + f'(y)[x - y] \tag{27.1}$$

for all x and y. A linear function grows at a constant rate. Roughly speaking, a concave function is one that grows less rapidly at each point than the linear function that is tangent to it at that point.

If f is concave, then its second derivative is less than or equal to zero at every point. If follows that if $f'(x^*) = 0$, then x^* is a maximum of the function. The easiest proof of this is just to substitute $y = x^*$ and $f'(x^*) = 0$ in equation (27.1) to find

$$f(x) \le f(x^*) + f'(x^*)[x - x^*] = f(x^*)$$

for all x. But this inequality shows that x^* is a maximum value of f. Hence for concave functions the first-order condition is both necessary and sufficient.

A **convex** function satisfies the property that

$$f(tx + (1 - t)y) \le tf(x) + (1 - t)f(y).$$

Note that if $f(x)$ is convex, then $-f(x)$ is concave. Given this observation it is easy to establish the following facts.

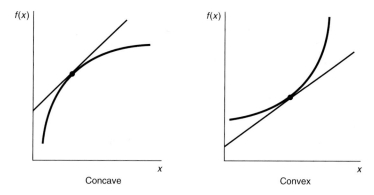

Concave and convex functions. A concave function grows less rapidly than a linear function which is tangent to it at some point; a convex function grows more rapidly than a linear function.

Figure 27.1

1) If f is a convex function, then $f''(x) \geq 0$ for all x.

2) If f is a convex function, then

$$f(x) \geq f(y) + f'(y)[x - y].$$

3) If f is a convex function and $f'(x^*) = 0$, then x^* minimizes the function f.

The envelope theorem

Suppose that $f(x, a)$ is a function of both x and a. We generally interpret a as being a parameter determined outside the problem being studied and x as the variable we wish to study. Suppose that x is chosen to maximize the function. For each different value of a there will typically be a different optimal choice of x. In sufficiently regular cases, we will be able to write the function $x(a)$ that gives us the optimal choice of x for each different value of a. For example, in some economic problem the choice variable might be the amount consumed or produced of some good while the parameter a will be a price.

We can also define the (optimal) **value function**, $M(a) = f(x(a), a)$. This tells us what the optimized value of f is for different choices of a.

EXAMPLE: The value function

We have seen above that for $f(x, a) = \ln x - ax$, the optimal value of x is $x(a) = 1/a$. Hence the value function for this problem is given by $M(a) = \ln(1/a) - a/a = -\ln a - 1$.

For the example $g(x, b) = u(x) - bx$, we have $M(b) = u(x(b)) - bx(b)$.

In economics we are often interested in how the optimized value changes as the parameter a changes. It turns out that there is a simple way to calculate this change. By definition we have

$$M(a) \equiv f(x(a), a).$$

Differentiating both sides of this identity, we have

$$\frac{dM(a)}{da} = \frac{\partial f(x(a), a)}{\partial x}\frac{\partial x(a)}{\partial a} + \frac{\partial f(x(a), a)}{\partial a}.$$

Since $x(a)$ is the choice of x that maximizes f, we know that

$$\frac{\partial f(x(a), a)}{\partial x} = 0.$$

Substituting this into the above expression, we have

$$\frac{dM(a)}{da} = \frac{\partial f(x(a), a)}{\partial a}. \qquad (27.2)$$

A better way to write this is

$$\frac{dM(a)}{da} = \frac{\partial f(x, a)}{\partial a}\bigg|_{x=x(a)}.$$

In this notation it is clear that the derivative is taken holding x fixed at the optimal value $x(a)$.

In other words: the total derivative of the value function with respect to the parameter is equal to the partial derivative *when the derivative is evaluated at the optimal choice*. This statement is the simplest form of the **envelope theorem**. It is worthwhile thinking about why this happens. When a changes there are two effects: the change in a directly affects f and the change in a affects x which in turn affects f. But if x is chosen optimally, a small change in x has a zero effect on f, so the indirect effect drops out and only the direct effect is left.

EXAMPLE: The envelope theorem

Continuing with the $f(x, a) = \ln x - ax$ example, we recall that $M(a) = -\ln a - 1$. Hence $M'(a) = -1/a$. We can also see this using the envelope theorem; by direct calculation we see that $\partial f(x, a)/\partial a = -x$. Setting x equal to its *optimal* value, we have $\partial f(x, a)/\partial a = -1/a = M'(a)$.

For the case where $M(b) = g(x(b), b) = u(x(b)) - bx(b)$, we have $M'(b) = -x(b)$.

Comparative statics

Another question of interest in economics is how the optimal choice changes as a parameter changes. Analysis of this sort is known as **comparative statics** analysis or **sensitivity analysis**. The basic calculation goes as follows. We know that the optimal choice function $x(a)$ must satisfy the condition

$$\frac{\partial f(x(a), a)}{\partial x} \equiv 0.$$

Differentiating both sides of this identity,

$$\frac{\partial^2 f(x(a), a)}{\partial x^2} \frac{dx(a)}{da} + \frac{\partial^2 f(x(a), a)}{\partial x \partial a} \equiv 0.$$

Solving for $dx(a)/da$, we have

$$\frac{dx(a)}{da} = -\frac{\partial^2 f(x(a), a)/\partial x \partial a}{\partial^2 f(x(a), a)/\partial x^2}.$$

We know that the denominator of this expression is negative due to the second-order conditions for maximization. Noting the minus sign preceding the fraction, we can conclude that

$$\text{sign } \frac{dx(a)}{da} = \text{sign } \frac{\partial^2 f(x(a), a)}{\partial x \partial a}.$$

Hence, the sign of the derivative of the optimal choice with respect to the parameter depends only on the second cross-partial of the objective function with respect to x and a.

The nice feature of this is that we don't actually have to repeat this calculation every time; we can simply use the information about the cross-partial.

EXAMPLE: Comparative statics for a particular problem

If $f(x, a) = \ln x - ax$, we saw above that $x(a) = 1/a$. By direct calculation $x'(a) < 0$. But we could have seen this without solving the maximization problem simply by observing that

$$\frac{\partial^2 f(x, a)}{\partial x \partial a} = -1 < 0.$$

In the optimization problem with the objective function $g(x, b) = u(x) - bx$, we can immediately see that

$$\text{sign } x'(b) = \text{sign } (-1) < 0.$$

This is a remarkable example: we know almost nothing about the shape of the function $u(x)$, and yet we are able to determine how the optimal choice must change as the parameter changes simply by using the properties of the *form* of the objective function. We will examine many examples of this sort in our study of microeconomics.

For minimization problems, all that changes is the sign of the denominator. Since the second-order condition for minimization implies that the second derivative with respect to the choice variable is positive, we see that the sign of the derivative of the choice variable with respect to the parameter is the *opposite* of the sign of the cross-partial derivative.

27.2 Multivariate maximization

Let us now consider the next level of complexity of maximization problems. Now we have two choice variables, x_1 and x_2. It will often be convenient to write these two variables as a vector $\mathbf{x} = (x_1, x_2)$.

In this case we write the maximization problem using the notation

$$\max_{x_1, x_2} f(x_1, x_2),$$

or, more generally, as

$$\max_{\mathbf{x}} f(\mathbf{x}).$$

First- and second-order conditions

Here the first-order conditions take the form that the partial derivative of the objective function with respect to each choice variable must vanish. If there are only two choice variables, this gives us the two necessary conditions

$$\frac{\partial f(x_1, x_2)}{\partial x_1} = 0$$

$$\frac{\partial f(x_1, x_2)}{\partial x_2} = 0.$$

If there are n choice variables, it is convenient to define the **gradient vector**, $\mathbf{D}f(\mathbf{x})$ by

$$\mathbf{D}f(\mathbf{x}) = \left(\frac{\partial f}{\partial x_1}, \ldots, \frac{\partial f}{\partial x_n} \right).$$

Using this notation we can write the n first-order conditions as

$$\mathbf{D}f(\mathbf{x}^*) = \mathbf{0}.$$

This equation simply says that at the optimal choice $\mathbf{x}^*$ the vector of partial derivatives must equal the zero vector.

The second-order conditions for the two-choice variable problem are most easily expressed in terms of the matrix of second derivatives of the objective function. This matrix, known as the **Hessian matrix**, takes the form

$$H = \begin{pmatrix} f_{11} & f_{12} \\ f_{21} & f_{22} \end{pmatrix}.$$

where f_{ij} stands for $\partial^2 f / \partial x_i \partial x_j$.

Calculus tells us that at the optimal choice $\mathbf{x}^*$, the Hessian matrix must be **negative semidefinite**. This means that for any vector (h_1, h_2), we must satisfy

$$(h_1, h_2) \begin{pmatrix} f_{11} & f_{12} \\ f_{21} & f_{22} \end{pmatrix} \begin{pmatrix} h_1 \\ h_2 \end{pmatrix} \leq 0.$$

More generally, let us think of $\mathbf{h}$ as a column vector and let $\mathbf{h}^t$ be the transpose of $\mathbf{h}$. Then we can write the condition characterizing a negative semidefinite matrix as

$$\mathbf{h}^t H \mathbf{h} \leq 0.$$

If we are examining a minimization problem rather than a maximization problem, then the first-order condition is the same, but the second-order condition becomes the requirement that the Hessian matrix be **positive semidefinite**.

Comparative statics

Suppose we want to determine how the optimal choice functions respond to changes in a parameter a. We know that the optimal choices have to satisfy the first-order conditions

$$\frac{\partial f(x_1(a), x_2(a), a)}{\partial x_1} = 0$$

$$\frac{\partial f(x_1(a), x_2(a), a)}{\partial x_2} = 0.$$

Differentiating these two expressions with respect to a, we have

$$f_{11} \frac{\partial x_1}{\partial a} + f_{12} \frac{\partial x_2}{\partial a} + f_{13} = 0$$

$$f_{21} \frac{\partial x_1}{\partial a} + f_{22} \frac{\partial x_2}{\partial a} + f_{23} = 0.$$

This is more conveniently written in matrix form as

$$\begin{pmatrix} f_{11} & f_{12} \\ f_{21} & f_{22} \end{pmatrix} \begin{pmatrix} x_1'(a) \\ x_2'(a) \end{pmatrix} = \begin{pmatrix} -f_{13} \\ -f_{23} \end{pmatrix}.$$

If the matrix on the left-hand side of this expression is invertible, we can solve this system of equations to get

$$\begin{pmatrix} x_1'(a) \\ x_2'(a) \end{pmatrix} = \begin{pmatrix} f_{11} & f_{12} \\ f_{21} & f_{22} \end{pmatrix}^{-1} \begin{pmatrix} -f_{13} \\ -f_{23} \end{pmatrix}.$$

Rather than invert the matrix, it is often easier to use **Cramer's rule**, described in Chapter 26, page 477, to solve the system of equations for $\partial x_1 / \partial a$, etc.

For example, if we want to solve for $\partial x_1/\partial a$, we can apply Cramer's rule to express this derivative as the ratio of two determinants:

$$\frac{\partial x_1}{\partial a} = \frac{\begin{vmatrix} -f_{13} & f_{12} \\ -f_{23} & f_{22} \end{vmatrix}}{\begin{vmatrix} f_{11} & f_{12} \\ f_{21} & f_{22} \end{vmatrix}}.$$

By the second-order condition for maximization, the matrix in the denominator of this expression is a negative semidefinite matrix. Elementary linear algebra tells us that this matrix must have a positive determinant. Hence the sign of $\partial x_1/\partial a$ is simply the sign of the determinant in the numerator.

EXAMPLE: Comparative statics

Let $f(x_1, x_2, a_1, a_2) = u_1(x_1) + u_2(x_2) - a_1 x_1 - a_2 x_2$. The first-order conditions for maximizing f are

$$u_1'(x_1^*) - a_1 = 0$$
$$u_2'(x_2^*) - a_2 = 0.$$

The second-order condition is that the matrix

$$H = \begin{pmatrix} u_1''(x_1^*) & 0 \\ 0 & u_2''(x_2^*) \end{pmatrix}$$

is negative semidefinite. Since a negative semidefinite matrix must have diagonal terms that are less than or equal to zero, it follows that $u_1''(x_1^*) \leq 0$ and $u_2''(x_2^*) \leq 0$.

The maximized value function is given by

$$M(a_1, a_2) \equiv \max_{x_1, x_2} u_1(x_1) + u_2(x_2) - a_1 x_1 - a_2 x_2,$$

and a simple calculation using the envelope theorem shows that

$$\frac{\partial M}{\partial a_1} = -x_1^*$$
$$\frac{\partial M}{\partial a_2} = -x_2^*.$$

The comparative statics calculation immediately above shows that

$$\text{sign } \frac{\partial x_1}{\partial a_1} = \text{sign } \begin{vmatrix} 1 & 0 \\ 0 & u_2''(x_2^*) \end{vmatrix}.$$

Carrying out the calculation of the determinant,

$$\text{sign } \frac{\partial x_1}{\partial a_1} \leq 0.$$

Note that we can determine how the choice variable responds to changes in the parameter without knowing anything about the explicit functional form of u_1 or u_2; we only have to know the *structure* of the objective function—in this case, that it is **additively separable**.

Convexity and concavity

A function $f : R^n \to R$ is **concave** if

$$f(t\mathbf{x} + (1-t)\mathbf{y}) \geq tf(\mathbf{x}) + (1-t)f(\mathbf{y})$$

for all $\mathbf{x}$ and $\mathbf{y}$ and all $0 \leq t \leq 1$. This has the same interpretation as in the univariate case; namely, that f evaluated at a weighted average of $\mathbf{x}$ and $\mathbf{y}$ is at least as large as the weighted average of $f(\mathbf{x})$ and $f(\mathbf{y})$.

It turns out that a concave function must satisfy the inequality

$$f(\mathbf{x}) \leq f(\mathbf{y}) + \mathbf{D}f(\mathbf{y})[\mathbf{x} - \mathbf{y}].$$

In the two-dimensional case, we can write this as

$$f(x_1, x_2) \leq f(y_1, y_2) + \left(\frac{\partial f(y_1, y_2)}{\partial x_1} \quad \frac{\partial f(y_1, y_2)}{\partial x_2} \right) \left(\begin{matrix} x_1 - y_1 \\ x_2 - y_2 \end{matrix} \right),$$

or, carrying out the multiplication,

$$f(x_1, x_2) \leq f(y_1, y_2) + \frac{\partial f(y_1, y_2)}{\partial x_1}[x_1 - y_1] + \frac{\partial f(y_1, y_2)}{\partial x_2}[x_2 - y_2].$$

This is a natural generalization of the one-dimensional condition.

There is also a nice generalization of the second-derivative condition for concavity. Recall that in the one-dimensional case, the second derivative of a concave function must be less than or equal to zero. In the multidimensional case, the condition for concavity is that the *matrix* of second derivatives is negative semidefinite at every point. Geometrically, this means that the graph of a concave function must "curve away" from its tangent plane in every direction. This means that the second-order conditions for maximization are automatically satisfied for concave functions. Similarly, the Hessian matrix for a convex function must be positive semidefinite.

If the Hessian matrix of a function is negative definite at every point, then the function must be strictly concave. However the converse is not true: the Hessian of a strictly concave function may be singular at some points. This is true even in one dimension; consider the function $-x^4$ at $x = 0$.

Quasiconcave and quasiconvex functions

A function $f : R^n \to R$ is **quasiconcave** if the upper contour sets of the function are convex sets. In other words, sets of the form $\{\mathbf{x} \in R^n : f(\mathbf{x}) \geq a\}$ are convex for all values of a. A function $f(\mathbf{x})$ is **quasiconvex** if $-f(\mathbf{x})$ is quasiconcave.

27.3 Constrained maximization

Consider a constrained maximization problem of the form

$$\max_{x_1, x_2} f(x_1, x_2)$$

such that $g(x_1, x_2) = 0$.

In order to state the first- and second-order conditions for this problem, it is convenient to make use of the **Lagrangian**:

$$\mathcal{L}(\lambda, x_1, x_2) = f(x_1, x_2) - \lambda g(x_1, x_2).$$

The variable λ is known as a **Lagrange multiplier**. As we shall see, it turns out to have a useful economic interpretation.

The first-order conditions require that the derivatives of the Lagrangian with respect to each of its arguments are zero.

$$\frac{\partial \mathcal{L}}{\partial x_1} = \frac{\partial f}{\partial x_1} - \lambda \frac{\partial g}{\partial x_1} = 0$$

$$\frac{\partial \mathcal{L}}{\partial x_2} = \frac{\partial f}{\partial x_2} - \lambda \frac{\partial g}{\partial x_2} = 0$$

$$\frac{\partial \mathcal{L}}{\partial \lambda} = -g(x_1, x_2) = 0.$$

There are 3 unknowns—x_1, x_2, and λ—and three equations; often one will be able to solve this system of equations for the optimizing choices.

The n-dimensional optimization problem has the same general structure. The problem is

$$\max_{\mathbf{x}} f(\mathbf{x})$$

such that $g(\mathbf{x}) = 0$,

so that the Lagrangian becomes

$$\mathcal{L} = f(\mathbf{x}) - \lambda g(\mathbf{x}),$$

and the $n + 1$ first-order conditions have the form

$$\frac{\partial \mathcal{L}}{\partial x_i} = \frac{\partial f(\mathbf{x})}{\partial x_i} - \lambda \frac{\partial g(\mathbf{x})}{\partial x_i} = 0 \quad \text{for } i = 1, \ldots, n$$

$$\frac{\partial \mathcal{L}}{\partial \lambda} = -g(\mathbf{x}) = 0.$$

The second-order conditions make use of the Hessian matrix of the Lagrangian. In the two-dimensional problem, this is

$$\mathbf{D}^2\mathcal{L}(x_1, x_2) = \begin{pmatrix} \frac{\partial^2 \mathcal{L}}{\partial x_1^2} & \frac{\partial^2 \mathcal{L}}{\partial x_1 \partial x_2} \\ \frac{\partial^2 \mathcal{L}}{\partial x_2 \partial x_1} & \frac{\partial^2 \mathcal{L}}{\partial x_2^2} \end{pmatrix}$$

$$= \begin{pmatrix} \frac{\partial^2 f}{\partial x_1^2} - \lambda \frac{\partial^2 g}{\partial x_1^2} & \frac{\partial^2 f}{\partial x_1 \partial x_2} - \lambda \frac{\partial^2 g}{\partial x_1 \partial x_2} \\ \frac{\partial^2 f}{\partial x_2 \partial x_1} - \lambda \frac{\partial^2 g}{\partial x_2 \partial x_1} & \frac{\partial^2 f}{\partial x_2^2} - \lambda \frac{\partial^2 g}{\partial x_2^2} \end{pmatrix}.$$

The second-order condition requires that this matrix must be negative semidefinite subject to a linear constraint

$$\mathbf{h}^t \mathbf{D}^2 \mathcal{L}(\mathbf{x}) \mathbf{h} \le 0 \text{ for all } \mathbf{h} \text{ satisfying } \mathbf{D}g(\mathbf{x})\mathbf{h} = 0.$$

Intuitively, this condition requires that the Hessian matrix be negative semidefinite for any change in a direction tangent to the constraint surface.

If the Hessian matrix is negative *definite* subject to the constraint, then we say that we have a **regular maximum**. A regular maximum must be a strict local maximum, but the reverse is not necessarily true.

27.4 An alternative second-order condition

There is an alternative way to state the second-order condition in the case of a *regular* local maximum. In this case seeing whether a particular matrix is negative definite subject to a linear constraint can be reduced to checking the signs of various determinants of a certain matrix.

Consider the matrix of second derivatives of the Lagrangian, *including* the various derivatives with respect to the Lagrange multiplier, λ. If there are two choice variables and one constraint, this matrix will look like this:

$$\mathbf{D}^2\mathcal{L}(\lambda, x_1, x_2) = \begin{pmatrix} \frac{\partial^2 \mathcal{L}}{\partial \lambda^2} & \frac{\partial^2 \mathcal{L}}{\partial \lambda \partial x_1} & \frac{\partial^2 \mathcal{L}}{\partial \lambda \partial x_2} \\ \frac{\partial^2 \mathcal{L}}{\partial x_1 \partial \lambda} & \frac{\partial^2 \mathcal{L}}{\partial x_1^2} & \frac{\partial^2 \mathcal{L}}{\partial x_1 \partial x_2} \\ \frac{\partial^2 \mathcal{L}}{\partial x_2 \partial \lambda} & \frac{\partial^2 \mathcal{L}}{\partial x_2 \partial x_1} & \frac{\partial^2 \mathcal{L}}{\partial x_2^2} \end{pmatrix}. \qquad (27.3)$$

It is straightforward to calculate the following derivatives using the definition of the Lagrangian and the first-order conditions:

$$\frac{\partial^2 \mathcal{L}}{\partial \lambda^2} = 0$$

$$\frac{\partial^2 \mathcal{L}}{\partial \lambda \partial x_1} = \frac{\partial^2 \mathcal{L}}{\partial x_1 \partial \lambda} = -\frac{\partial g(\mathbf{x})}{\partial x_1}$$

$$\frac{\partial^2 \mathcal{L}}{\partial \lambda \partial x_2} = \frac{\partial^2 \mathcal{L}}{\partial x_2 \partial \lambda} = -\frac{\partial g(\mathbf{x})}{\partial x_2}.$$

Inserting these expressions into (27.3) gives us the **bordered Hessian** matrix:

$$\begin{pmatrix} 0 & -\dfrac{\partial g}{\partial x_1} & -\dfrac{\partial g}{\partial x_2} \\ -\dfrac{\partial g}{\partial x_1} & \dfrac{\partial^2 \mathcal{L}}{\partial x_1^2} & \dfrac{\partial^2 \mathcal{L}}{\partial x_1 \partial x_2} \\ -\dfrac{\partial g}{\partial x_2} & \dfrac{\partial^2 \mathcal{L}}{\partial x_2 \partial x_1} & \dfrac{\partial^2 \mathcal{L}}{\partial x_2^2} \end{pmatrix}.$$

Note that this matrix has the form

$$\begin{pmatrix} 0 & b_1 & b_2 \\ b_1 & h_{11} & h_{12} \\ b_2 & h_{21} & h_{22} \end{pmatrix},$$

where the "border terms" are the negative of the first derivatives of the constraint, and the h_{ij} terms are the second derivatives of the Lagrangian with respect to the choice variables. If there are n choice variables and 1 constraint, the bordered Hessian will be an $n + 1$ dimensional square matrix. We give an example with four choice variables below.

It turns out that in the case of a regular maximum with $b_1 \neq 0$, the second-order conditions given above imply that the bordered Hessian has a positive determinant. The proof of this fact is not difficult, but is rather tedious, and is omitted.

It is worth observing that the sign of the determinant of the bordered Hessian will not change if we multiply the first row and column by -1. This operation will eliminate the minus signs on the border and make for a somewhat neater looking expression. Some authors write the bordered Hessian this way to start with. However, if you do that it is not so obvious that the bordered Hessian is just the Hessian matrix of the Lagrangian, including the derivatives with respect to λ.

If there are n choice variables, and one constraint, the bordered Hessian will be a $n + 1$ by $n + 1$ matrix. In this case, we have to look at the determinants of various submatrices of the bordered Hessian. We illustrate this calculation in the case of a 4 by 4 bordered Hessian. Denote the border terms by b_i and the Hessian terms by h_{ij}, as above, so that the bordered Hessian is

$$\begin{pmatrix} 0 & b_1 & b_2 & b_3 & b_4 \\ b_1 & h_{11} & h_{12} & h_{13} & h_{14} \\ b_2 & h_{21} & h_{22} & h_{23} & h_{24} \\ b_3 & h_{31} & h_{32} & h_{33} & h_{34} \\ b_4 & h_{41} & h_{42} & h_{43} & h_{44} \end{pmatrix}.$$

Consider the case of a regular maximum, where the Hessian is negative definite subject to constraint, and assume $b_1 \neq 0$. Then an equivalent set of second-order conditions is that the following determinant conditions must hold:

$$\det \begin{pmatrix} 0 & b_1 & b_2 \\ b_1 & h_{11} & h_{12} \\ b_2 & h_{21} & h_{22} \end{pmatrix} > 0$$

$$\det \begin{pmatrix} 0 & b_1 & b_2 & b_3 \\ b_1 & h_{11} & h_{12} & h_{13} \\ b_2 & h_{21} & h_{22} & h_{23} \\ b_3 & h_{31} & h_{32} & h_{33} \end{pmatrix} < 0$$

$$\det \begin{pmatrix} 0 & b_1 & b_2 & b_3 & b_4 \\ b_1 & h_{11} & h_{12} & h_{13} & h_{14} \\ b_2 & h_{21} & h_{22} & h_{23} & h_{24} \\ b_3 & h_{31} & h_{32} & h_{33} & h_{34} \\ b_4 & h_{41} & h_{42} & h_{43} & h_{44} \end{pmatrix} > 0.$$

The same pattern holds for an arbitrary number of factors. We express this condition by saying that *naturally ordered principal minors of the bordered Hessian must alternate in sign.*

The analogous second-order condition for a regular local minimum is that the same set of determinants must all be *negative*.

How to remember the second-order conditions

You may have trouble remembering all the determinant conditions involving second-order conditions—at least, I do. So here is a simple way to think about the conditions.

The simplest example of a positive definite matrix is the identity matrix. Calculating the determinants, it is easy to see that the principal minors of the identity matrix are all positive.

The simplest example of a negative definite matrix is the *negative* of the identity matrix. It is not hard to see that the principal minors of this matrix must alternate in sign:

$$\begin{vmatrix} -1 & 0 \\ 0 & -1 \end{vmatrix} > 0$$

$$\begin{vmatrix} -1 & 0 & 0 \\ 0 & -1 & 0 \\ 0 & 0 & -1 \end{vmatrix} = -1 \begin{vmatrix} -1 & 0 \\ 0 & -1 \end{vmatrix} < 0.$$

Suppose that we have a matrix that is positive definite subject to linear constraint. The easiest case of this is an identity matrix subject to the constraint $(h_1, h_2)(1, 1) = 0$. This gives us the bordered Hessian

$$\begin{pmatrix} 0 & 1 & 1 \\ 1 & 1 & 0 \\ 1 & 0 & 1 \end{pmatrix}.$$

The upper-left minor is

$$\begin{vmatrix} 0 & 1 \\ 1 & 1 \end{vmatrix} = -1 < 0.$$

The determinant of the whole matrix is found by expanding along the first column:

$$-1\begin{vmatrix} 1 & 1 \\ 0 & 1 \end{vmatrix} + 1\begin{vmatrix} 1 & 1 \\ 1 & 0 \end{vmatrix} = -2.$$

Hence, the condition for a matrix to be positive definite subject to constraint is that all principal minors of the bordered Hessian are negative.

We next examine a matrix that is negative semidefinite subject to constraint. Again, take the simplest example: the negative of the identity matrix and the constraint $(h_1, h_2)(1, 1) = 0$. This gives us the bordered Hessian

$$\begin{pmatrix} 0 & 1 & 1 \\ 1 & -1 & 0 \\ 1 & 0 & -1 \end{pmatrix}.$$

The two principal minors are

$$\begin{vmatrix} 0 & 1 \\ 1 & -1 \end{vmatrix} = -1 < 0,$$

and

$$\begin{vmatrix} 0 & 1 & 1 \\ 1 & -1 & 0 \\ 1 & 0 & -1 \end{vmatrix} = -\begin{vmatrix} 1 & 1 \\ 0 & -1 \end{vmatrix} + \begin{vmatrix} 1 & 1 \\ -1 & 0 \end{vmatrix} = 2 > 0.$$

Hence we want the principal minors to alternate in sign.

The envelope theorem

Consider a parameterized maximization problem of the form

$$M(a) = \max_{x_1, x_2} g(x_1, x_2, a)$$

$$\text{such that } h(x_1, x_2, a) = 0.$$

The Lagrangian for this problem is

$$\mathcal{L} = g(x_1, x_2, a) - \lambda h(x_1, x_2, a),$$

and the first-order conditions are

$$\frac{\partial g}{\partial x_1} - \lambda \frac{\partial h}{\partial x_1} = 0$$

$$\frac{\partial g}{\partial x_2} - \lambda \frac{\partial h}{\partial x_2} = 0 \tag{27.4}$$

$$h(x_1, x_2, a) = 0.$$

These conditions determine the optimal choice functions $(x_1(a), x_2(a))$, which in turn determine the maximum value function

$$M(a) \equiv g(x_1(a), x_2(a), a). \qquad (27.5)$$

The **envelope theorem** gives us a formula for the derivative of the value function with respect to a parameter in the maximization problem. Specifically, the formula is

$$\frac{dM(a)}{da} = \frac{\partial \mathcal{L}(\mathbf{x}, a)}{\partial a}\Big|_{\mathbf{x}=\mathbf{x}(a)}$$
$$= \frac{\partial g(x_1, x_2, a)}{\partial a}\Big|_{\mathbf{x}=\mathbf{x}(a)} - \lambda \frac{\partial h(x_1, x_2, a)}{\partial a}\Big|_{\mathbf{x}=\mathbf{x}(a)}.$$

As before, the interpretation of the partial derivatives needs special care: they are the derivatives of g and h with respect to a *holding x_1 and x_2 fixed at their optimal values.*

The proof of the envelope theorem is a straightforward calculation. Differentiate the identity (27.5) to get

$$\frac{dM}{da} = \frac{\partial g}{\partial x_1}\frac{dx_1}{da} + \frac{\partial g}{\partial x_2}\frac{dx_2}{da} + \frac{\partial g}{\partial a},$$

and substitute from the first-order conditions (27.4) to find

$$\frac{dM}{da} = \lambda \left[\frac{\partial h}{\partial x_1}\frac{dx_1}{da} + \frac{\partial h}{\partial x_2}\frac{dx_2}{da} \right] + \frac{\partial g}{\partial a}. \qquad (27.6)$$

Now observe that the optimal choice functions must identically satisfy the constraint $h(x_1(a), x_2(a), a) \equiv 0$. Differentiating this identity with respect to a, we have

$$\frac{\partial h}{\partial x_1}\frac{dx_1}{da} + \frac{\partial h}{\partial x_2}\frac{dx_2}{da} + \frac{\partial h}{\partial a} \equiv 0. \qquad (27.7)$$

Substitute (27.7) into (27.6) to find

$$\frac{dM}{da} = -\lambda \frac{\partial h}{\partial a} + \frac{\partial g}{\partial a},$$

which is the required result.

27.5 Constrained maximization with inequality constraints

In many problems in economics it is natural to use inequality constraints. Here we examine the appropriate form of the first-order conditions for such problems.

Let $f: R^n \to R$ and $g_i: R^n \to R$ for $i = 1, \ldots, k$, and consider the optimization problem

$$\max f(\mathbf{x})$$
$$\text{such that } g_i(\mathbf{x}) \leq 0. \qquad i = 1, \ldots, k \qquad (27.8)$$

The set of points $\{\mathbf{x} : g_i(\mathbf{x}^*) \leq 0 \quad i = 1, \ldots, k\}$ is called the **feasible set**. If at a particular $\mathbf{x}^*$ we have $g_i(\mathbf{x}^*) = 0$, we say that the ith constraint is a **binding constraint**; otherwise, we say that the ith constraint is not binding, or is a **slack constraint**.

Let $G(\mathbf{x}^*)$ be the set of gradients of the binding constraints at $\mathbf{x}^*$:

$$G(\mathbf{x}^*) = \{\mathbf{D}g_i(\mathbf{x}^*) : \text{ for all } i \text{ such that } g_i(\mathbf{x}^*) = 0.\}.$$

Then we say that the **constraint qualification** holds if the set of vectors $G(\mathbf{x}^*)$ is linearly independent.

Kuhn-Tucker Theorem.   *If $\mathbf{x}^*$ solves (27.8) and the constraint qualification holds at $\mathbf{x}^*$, then there exists a set of **Kuhn-Tucker multipliers** $\lambda_i \geq 0$, for $i = 1, \ldots, k$ such that*

$$\mathbf{D}f(\mathbf{x}^*) = \sum_{i=1}^{k} \lambda_i \mathbf{D}g_i(\mathbf{x}^*).$$

*Furthermore, we have the **complementary slackness** conditions:*

$$\lambda_i \geq 0 \quad \text{for all } i,$$
$$\lambda_i = 0 \quad \text{if } g_i(\mathbf{x}^*) < 0.$$

Comparing the Kuhn-Tucker theorem to the Lagrange multiplier theorem, we see that the major difference is that the signs of the Kuhn-Tucker multipliers are nonnegative while the signs of the Lagrange multipliers can be anything. This additional information can occasionally be very useful.

The Kuhn-Tucker theorem is, of course, only a necessary condition for a maximum. However, in one important case it is necessary and sufficient.

Kuhn-Tucker sufficiency.   *Suppose that f is a concave function and g_i is a convex function for $i = 1, \ldots, k$. Let $\mathbf{x}^*$ be a feasible point and suppose that we can find nonnegative numbers λ_i consistent with complementary slackness such that $\mathbf{D}f(\mathbf{x}^*) = \sum_{i=1}^{k} \lambda_i \mathbf{D}g(\mathbf{x}^*)$. Then $\mathbf{x}^*$ solves the maximization problem stated in (27.8).*

Proof. Let $\mathbf{x}$ be a feasible point. Since f is concave we can write

$$f(\mathbf{x}) \leq f(\mathbf{x}^*) + \mathbf{D}f(\mathbf{x}^*)(\mathbf{x} - \mathbf{x}^*).$$

Using the hypothesis of the theorem, we can write this as

$$f(\mathbf{x}) \leq f(\mathbf{x}^*) + \sum_{i=1}^{k} \lambda_i \mathbf{D} g_i(\mathbf{x}^*)(\mathbf{x} - \mathbf{x}^*). \tag{27.9}$$

Since $g_i(\mathbf{x})$ is convex, we have

$$g_i(\mathbf{x}) \geq g_i(\mathbf{x}^*) + \mathbf{D} g_i(\mathbf{x}^*)(\mathbf{x} - \mathbf{x}^*). \tag{27.10}$$

If constraint i is binding, $g_i(\mathbf{x}) \leq g_i(\mathbf{x}^*) = 0$; since $\lambda_i \geq 0$ $\lambda_i \mathbf{D} g_i(\mathbf{x}^*)(\mathbf{x} - \mathbf{x}^*) \leq 0$ for all binding constraints. If constraint i is slack, $\lambda_i = 0$. Applying these observations to inequality (27.9), we see that each term in the sum is less than or equal to zero so $f(\mathbf{x}) \leq f(\mathbf{x}^*)$, as required.

27.6 Setting up Kuhn-Tucker problems

The Lagrange conditions for a constrained maximum and a constrained minimum problem are the same, since they deal only with first-order conditions. The Kuhn-Tucker conditions are also the same, *if the problem is set up in the correct way.* In general, this may require some manipulation before applying the theorem.

Recall that we stated the Kuhn-Tucker conditions for a maximization problem of the form

$$\max_{\mathbf{x}} f(\mathbf{x})$$

$$\text{such that } g_i(\mathbf{x}) \leq 0 \quad \text{for } i = 1, \ldots, k.$$

The Lagrangian for this problem is

$$\mathcal{L} = f(\mathbf{x}) - \sum_{i=1}^{k} \lambda_i g_i(\mathbf{x}).$$

When the problem is set up in this way, the Kuhn-Tucker multipliers are guaranteed to be nonnegative.

In some problems the constraints require that some function be *greater than* or equal to zero. In this case we must multiply the constraint through by -1 to put it in the proper form to apply the Kuhn-Tucker conditions. For example, suppose that we had the problem

$$\max_{\mathbf{x}} f(\mathbf{x})$$

$$\text{such that } h_i(\mathbf{x}) \geq 0 \quad \text{for } i = 1, \ldots, k.$$

This is equivalent to the problem

$$\max_{\mathbf{x}} f(\mathbf{x})$$

$$\text{such that } -h_i(\mathbf{x}) \leq 0 \quad \text{for } i = 1, \ldots, k,$$

which is of the required form.

For this problem the Lagrangian becomes

$$\mathcal{L} = f(\mathbf{x}) - \sum_{i=1}^{k} \lambda_i(-h_i(\mathbf{x})) = f(\mathbf{x}) + \sum_{i=1}^{k} \lambda_i(h_i(\mathbf{x})).$$

Since the transformed problem has the proper form, the multipliers (λ_i) are guaranteed to be nonnegative.

Suppose that we are studying a *minimization* problem. Then to get the Kuhn-Tucker multipliers to have the right (nonnegative) signs, we have to set the problem up to have the form

$$\min_{\mathbf{x}} f(\mathbf{x})$$

$$\text{such that } g_i(\mathbf{x}) \geq 0 \quad \text{for } i = 1, \ldots, k.$$

Note that a minimization problem requires greater-than inequalities, while a maximization problem requires less-than inequalities.

27.7 Existence and continuity of a maximum

Consider a parameterized maximization problem of the form

$$M(a) = \max f(\mathbf{x}, a)$$
$$\text{such that } \mathbf{x} \text{ is in } G(a) \tag{27.11}$$

Existence of an optimum.   *If the constraint set $G(a)$ is nonempty and compact, and the function f is continuous, then there exists a solution $\mathbf{x}^*$ to this maximization problem.*

Uniqueness of optimum.   *If the function f is strictly concave and the constraint set is convex, then a solution, should it exist, is unique.*

Let $\mathbf{x}(a)$ be a solution to problem (27.11). It is often of interest to know when $\mathbf{x}(a)$ is well-behaved. The first problem we must face is that $\mathbf{x}(a)$ may not in general be a function: there may, in general, be several points that solve the optimization problem. That is, for each a, $\mathbf{x}(a)$ will be a *set* of points. A **correspondence** is a rule that associates to each a a set of $\mathbf{x}$'s. We want to examine how a set of points $\mathbf{x}(a)$ changes as a changes; in particular we want to know when $\mathbf{x}(a)$ changes "continuously" as a changes.

It turns out that there are two definitions of continuity that are appropriate for correspondences. If the set $\mathbf{x}(a)$ does not "explode" when a changes slightly then we say the correspondence is **upper-semicontinuous**. If the set $\mathbf{x}(a)$ does not "implode" when a changes slightly, then we say the correspondence is **lower-semicontinuous**. If a correspondence is both upper- and lower-semicontinuous, then it is said to be **continuous**.

Theorem of the maximum. *Let $f(\mathbf{x}, a)$ be a continuous function with a compact range and suppose that the constraint set $G(a)$ is a nonempty, compact-valued, continuous correspondence of a. Then (1) $M(a)$ is a continuous function and (2) $\mathbf{x}(a)$ is an upper-semicontinuous correspondence.*

If the correspondence $\mathbf{x}(a)$ happens to be single-valued, so that $\mathbf{x}(a)$ is a *function*, then it will be a continuous function.

Notes

See Dixit (1990) for an intuitive discussion and examples of optimization in economics. See Blume & Simon (1991) for a more in-depth treatment. See Berge (1963) and Hildenbrand & Kirman (1988) for more on topological properties of correspondences.

REFERENCES

Abreu, D. (1986). Extremal equilibria of oligopolistic supergames. *Journal of Economic Theory*, *39*, 191–225.

Afriat, S. (1967). The construction of a utility function from expenditure data. *International Economic Review*, *8*, 67–77.

Akerlof, G. (1970). The market for lemons: Quality uncertainty and the market mechanism. *Quarterly Journal of Economics*, *89*, 488–500.

Anscombe, F. & Aumann, R. (1963). A definition of subjective probability. *Annals of Mathematical Statistics*, *34*, 199–205.

Arrow, K. (1951). An extension of the basic theorems of classical welfare economics. In P. Newman (Ed.), *Readings in Mathematical Economics*. Baltimore: Johns Hopkins Press.

Arrow, K. (1970). *Essays in the Theory of Risk Bearing*. Chicago: Markham.

Arrow, K. & Debreu, G. (1954). Existence of equilibrium for a competitive economy. *Econometrica*, *22*, 265–290.

Arrow, K. & Hahn, F. (1971). *General Competitive Analysis*. San Francisco: Holden-Day.

Atkinson, T. & Stiglitz, J. (1980). *Lectures on Public Economics*. New York: McGraw-Hill.

Aumann, R. (1987). Game theory. In J. Eatwell, M. Milgate, & P. Newman (Eds.), *The New Palgrave*. London: MacMillan Press.

Berge, C. (1963). *Topological Spaces*. New York: Macmillan.

Bergstrom, T., Blume, L., & Varian, H. (1986). On the private provision of public goods. *Journal of Public Economics*, *29*(1), 25–49.

Binmore, K. (1982). *Mathematical Analysis* (2 ed.). Cambridge: Cambridge University Press.

Binmore, K. (1983). *Calculus*. Cambridge: Cambridge University Press.

Binmore, K. (1991). *Fun and Games*. San Francisco: Heath.

Binmore, K. & Dasgupta, P. (1987). *The Economics of Bargaining.* Oxford: Basil Blackwell.

Blackorby, C., Primont, D., & Russell, R. (1979). *Duality, Separability and Functional Structure: Theory and Economic Applications.* Amsterdam: North-Holland.

Blackorby, C. & Russell, R. R. (1989). Will the real elasticity of substitution please stand up. *American Economic Review, 79*(4), 882–888.

Blume, L. & Simon, C. (1991). *Mathematics for Economists.* New York: W. W. Norton & Co.

Clarke, E. (1971). Multipart pricing of public goods. *Public Choice, 11,* 17–33.

Coase, R. (1960). The problem of social cost. *Journal of Law and Economics, 3,* 1–44.

Cook, P. (1972). A one-line proof of the Slutsky equation. *American Economic Review, 42,* 139.

Davidson, C. & Deneckere, R. (1986). Long-run competition in capacity, short-run competition in price, and the Cournot model. *RAND Journal of Economics, 17,* 404–415.

Deaton, A. & Muellbauer, J. (1980). *Economics and Consumer Behavior.* Cambridge: Cambridge University Press.

Debreu, G. (1953). Valuation equilibrium and Pareto optimum. In K. Arrow & T. Scitovsky (Eds.), *Readings in Welfare Economics.* Homewood, Ill.: Irwin.

Debreu, G. (1959). *Theory of Value.* New York: Wiley.

Debreu, G. (1964). Continuity properties of Paretian utility. *International Economic Review, 5,* 285–293.

Debreu, G. (1974). Excess demand functions. *Journal of Mathematical Economics, 1,* 15–22.

Debreu, G. & Scarf, H. (1963). A limit theorem on the core of an economy. *International Economic Review, 4,* 235–246.

Dierker, E. (1972). Two remarks on the number of equilibria of an economy. *Econometrica, 40,* 951–953.

Diewert, E. (1974). Applications of duality theory. In M. Intriligator & D. Kendrick (Eds.), *Frontiers of Quantitative Economics.* Amsterdam: North-Holland.

Dixit, A. (1986). Comparative statics for oligopoly. *International Economic Review, 27,* 107–122.

Dixit, A. (1990). *Optimization in Economic Theory* (2 ed.). Oxford: Oxford University Press.

Dowrick, S. (1986). von Stackelberg and Cournot duopoly: Choosing roles. *Rand Journal of Economics, 17*(1), 251–260.

Friedman, J. (1971). A noncooperative equilibrium for supergames. *Review of Economic Studies, 38*, 1–12.

Frisch, R. (1965). *Theory of Production*. Chicago: Rand McNally.

Fudenberg, D. & Tirole, J. (1991). *Game Theory*. Cambridge: MIT Press.

Geanakoplos, J. (1987). Overlapping generations model of general equilibrium. In J. Eatwell, M. Milgate, & P. Newman (Eds.), *The New Palgrave*. London: MacMillan Press.

Gorman, T. (1953). Community preference fields. *Econometrica, 21*, 63–80.

Groves, T. (1973). Incentives in teams. *Econometrica, 41*, 617–631.

Harsanyi, J. (1967). Games of incomplete information played by Bayesian players. *Management Science, 14*, 159–182, 320–334, 486–502.

Hart, O. & Holmström, B. (1987). The theory of contracts. In T. Bewley (Ed.), *Advances in Economic Theory*. Cambridge: Cambridge University Press.

Herstein, I. & Milnor, J. (1953). An axiomatic approach to measurable utility. *Econometrica, 21*, 291–297.

Hicks, J. (1932). *Theory of Wages*. London: Macmillan.

Hicks, J. (1946). *Value and Capital*. Oxford, England: Clarendon Press.

Hicks, J. (1956). *A Revision of Demand Theory*. London: Oxford University Press.

Hildenbrand, W. & Kirman, A. (1988). *Equilibrium Analysis*. Amsterdam: North-Holland.

Holmström, B. & Milgrom, P. (1987). Aggregation and linearity in the provision of intertemporal incentives. *Econometrica, 55*, 303–328.

Hotelling, H. (1932). Edgeworth's taxation paradox and the nature of demand and supply function. *Political Economy, 40*, 577–616.

Hurwicz, L. & Uzawa, H. (1971). On the integrability of demand functions. In J. Chipman, L. Hurwicz, M. Richter, & H. Sonnenschein (Eds.), *Preferences, Utility, and Demand*. New York: Harcourt, Brace, Jovanovich.

Ingersoll, J. (1987). *Theory of Financial Decision Making*. Totowa, New Jersey: Rowman & Littlefield.

Kierkegaard, S. (1938). *The Journals of Soren Kierkegaard*. Oxford: Oxford University Press.

Koopmans, T. (1957). *Three Essays on the State of Economic Science*. New Haven: Yale University Press.

Kreps, D. (1990). *A Course in Microeconomic Theory*. Princeton University Press.

Kreps, D. & Scheinkman, J. (1983). Quantity pre-commitment and Bertrand competition yield Cournot outcomes. *Bell Journal of Economics, 14*, 326–337.

Ledyard, J. (1986). The scope of the hypothesis of Bayesian equilibrium. *Journal of Economic Theory, 39*, 59–82.

Lindahl, E. (1919). Just taxation—a positive solution. In R. Musgrave & A. Peacock (Eds.), *Classics in the Theory of Public Finance*. London: Macmillan.

Machina, M. (1982). 'Expected utility' analysis without the independence axiom. *Econometrica, 50*, 277–323.

Marshall, A. (1920). *Principles of Economics*. London: Macmillan.

Maskin, E. & Roberts, K. (1980). On the fundamental theorems of general equilibrium. Technical Report 43, Cambridge University, Cambridge, England.

McFadden, D. (1978). Cost, revenue, and profit functions. In M. Fuss & D. McFadden (Eds.), *Production Economics: A Dual Approach to Theory and Applications*. Amsterdam: North-Holland.

McFadden, D. & Winter, S. (1968). *Lecture Notes on Consumer Theory*. University of California at Berkeley: Unpublished.

McKenzie, L. (1954). On equilibrium in Graham's model of world trade and other competitive systems. *Econometrica, 22*, 147–161.

McKenzie, L. (1957). Demand theory without a utility index. *Review of Economic Studies, 24*, 183–189.

Milgrom, P. (1981). Good news and bad news: Representation theorems and applications. *Bell Journal of Economics, 13*, 380–391.

Milgrom, P. & Roberts, J. (1982). Limit pricing and entry under incomplete information: An equilibrium analysis. *Econometrica, 50*, 443–459.

Mirrlees, J. (1982). The theory of optimal taxation. In K. Arrow & M. Intriligator (Eds.), *Handbook of Mathematical Economics*, volume II. Amsterdam: North-Holland.

Myerson, R. (1986). An introduction to game theory. In S. Reiter (Ed.), *Studies in Mathematical Economics*. Mathematical Association of America.

Myerson, R. (1991). *Game Theory*. Cambridge: Harvard University Press.

Nash, J. (1950). Equilibrium points in n-person games. *Proceedings of the National Academy of Sciences, 36*, 48–49.

Nash, J. (1951). Non-cooperative games. *Annals of Mathematics, 54*, 286–295.

Negisihi, T. (1960). Welfare economics and the existence of an equilibrium for a competitive economy. *Metroeconomica, 12*, 92–97.

Neumann, J. & Morgenstern, O. (1944). *Theory of Games and Economic Behavior*. Princeton, NJ: Princeton University Press.

Novshek, W. (1980). Cournot equilibrium with free entry. *Review of Economic Studies, 47*, 473–486.

Pigou, A. (1920). *The Economics of Welfare*. London: Macmillan.

Pollak, R. (1969). Conditional demand functions and consumption theory. *Quarterly Journal of Economics, 83*, 60–78.

Pratt, J. (1964). Risk aversion in the small and in the large. *Econometrica, 32*, 122–136.

Rasmusen, E. (1989). *Games and Information*. Oxford: Basil Blackwell.

Ross, S. (1976). The arbitrage theory of capital asset pricing. *Journal of Economic Theory, 13*, 341–360.

Ross, S. (1977). The capital asset pricing model (CAPM), short sales restrictions and related issues. *Journal of Finance, 32*, 177–183.

Ross, S. (1978). A simple approach to the valuation of risky streams. *Journal of Business, 51*, 453–475.

Rothschild, M. & Stiglitz, J. (1976). Equilibrium in competitive insurance markets: An essay on the economics of imperfect information. *Quarterly Journal of Economics, 80*, 629–649.

Roy, R. (1942). *De l'utilité*. Paris: Hermann.

Roy, R. (1947). La distribution de revenu entre les divers biens. *Econometrica, 15*, 205–225.

Rubinstein, M. (1976). The valuation of uncertain income streams and the pricing of options. *Bell Journal of Economics, 7*, 407–25.

Samuelson, P. (1947). *Foundations of Economic Analysis*. Cambridge, Mass.: Harvard University Press.

Samuelson, P. (1948). Consumption theory in terms of revealed preference. *Econometrica*, *15*, 243–253.

Samuelson, P. (1951). Abstract of a theorem concerning substitutability in an open Leontief model. In T. Koopmans (Ed.), *Activity Analysis of Production and Consumption*. New York: Wiley.

Samuelson, P. (1954). The pure theory of public expenditure. *The Review of Economics and Statistics*, *64*, 387–389.

Samuelson, P. (1974). Complementarity: An essay on the 40th anniversary of the Hicks-Allen revolution in demand theory. *Journal of Economic Literature*, *64*(4), 1255–1289.

Scarf, H. (1973). *The Computation of Economic Equilibrium*. New Haven: Yale University Press.

Shafer, W. & Sonnenschein, H. (1982). Market demand and excess demand functions. In K. Arrow & M. Intriligator (Eds.), *Handbook of Mathematical Economics*. Amsterdam: North-Holland.

Shapiro, C. (1989). Theories of oligopoly behavior. In R. Schmalensee & R. Willig (Eds.), *Handbook of Industrial Organization*, volume 1. Amsterdam: North-Holland.

Shephard, R. (1953). *Cost and Production Functions*. Princeton, NJ: Princeton University Press.

Shephard, R. (1970). *Cost and Production Functions*. Princeton, NJ: Princeton University Press.

Silberberg, E. (1974). A revision of comparative statics methodology in economics. *Journal of Economic Theory*, *7*, 159–172.

Silberberg, E. (1990). *The Structure of Economics*. New York: McGraw–Hill.

Singh, N. & Vives, X. (1984). Price and quantity competition in a differentiated duopoly. *Rand Journal of Economics*, *15*, 546–554.

Sonnenschein, H. (1968). The dual of duopoly is complementary monopoly: or, two of Cournot's theories are one. *Journal of Political Economy*, *36*, 316–318.

Spence, M. (1974). *Market Signaling*. Cambridge, Mass.: Harvard University Press.

Spence, M. (1975). Monopoly, quality and regulation. *Bell Journal of Economics*, *6*(2), 417–429.

Tirole, J. (1988). *The Theory of Industrial Organization*. Cambridge: MIT Press.

Varian, H. (1980). A model of sales. *American Economic Review, 70*, 651–659.

Varian, H. (1982). The nonparametric approach to demand analysis. *Econometrica, 50*, 945–973.

Varian, H. (1984). The nonparametric approach to production analysis. *Econometrica, 52*, 579–597.

Varian, H. (1985). Price discrimination and social welfare. *American Economic Review, 75*(4), 870–875.

Varian, H. (1989a). Price discrimination. In *Handbook of Industrial Organization*. Amsterdam: North-Holland.

Varian, H. (1989b). A solution to the problem of externalities when agents are well-informed. Technical report, University of Michigan, Ann Arbor.

Varian, H. (1990). Goodness-of-fit in optimizing models. *Journal of Econometrics, 46*, 125–140.

von Weizsacker, C. (1971). *Steady State Capital Theory*. New York: Springer-Verlag.

Wald, A. (1951). On some systems of equations in mathematical economics. *Econometrica, 19*, 368–403.

Walras, L. (1954). *Elements of Pure Economics*. London: Allen and Unwin.

Willig, R. (1976). Consumer's surplus without apology. *American Economic Review, 66*, 589–597.

Wold, H. (1943). A synthesis of pure demand analysis, I-III. *Skandinavisk Aktuarietidskrift, 26*, 27.

Yaari, M. (1969). Some remarks on measures of risk aversion and their uses. *Journal of Economic Theory, 1*, 315–329.

Yokoyama, T. (1968). A logical foundation of the theory of consumer's demand. In P. Newman (Ed.), *Readings in Mathematical Economics*. Baltimore: Johns Hopkins Press.

A8 REFERENCES

ANSWERS

1 Technology

1.1 False. There are many counterexamples. Consider the technology generated by a production function $f(x) = x^2$. The production set is $Y = \{(y, -x) : y \leq x^2\}$ which is certainly not convex, but the input requirement set is $V(y) = \{x : x \geq \sqrt{y}\}$ which is a convex set.

1.3 $\epsilon_1 = a$ and $\epsilon_2 = b$.

1.5 Substitute tx_i for $i = 1, 2$ to get

$$f(tx_1, tx_2) = [(tx_1)^\rho + (tx_2)^\rho]^{\frac{1}{\rho}} = t[x_1^\rho + x_2^\rho]^{\frac{1}{\rho}} = tf(x_1, x_2).$$

This implies that the CES function exhibits constant returns to scale and hence has an elasticity of scale of 1.

1.7 Let $f(\mathbf{x}) = g(h(\mathbf{x}))$ and suppose that $g(h(\mathbf{x})) = g(h(\mathbf{x}'))$. Since g is monotonic, it follows that $h(\mathbf{x}) = h(\mathbf{x}')$. Now $g(h(t\mathbf{x})) = g(th(\mathbf{x}))$ and $g(h(t\mathbf{x}')) = g(th(\mathbf{x}'))$ which gives us the required result.

1.9 Note that we can write

$$(a_1 + a_2)^{\frac{1}{\rho}} \left[\frac{a_1}{a_1 + a_2} x_1^\rho + \frac{a_2}{a_1 + a_2} x_2^\rho \right]^{\frac{1}{\rho}}.$$

Now simply define $b = a_1/(a_1 + a_2)$ and $A = (a_1 + a_2)^{\frac{1}{\rho}}$.

1.11.a This is closed and nonempty for all $y > 0$ (if we allow inputs to be negative). The isoquants look just like the Leontief technology except we are measuring output in units of $\log y$ rather than y. Hence, the shape of the isoquants will be the same. It follows that the technology is monotonic and convex.

1.11.b This is nonempty but not closed. It is monotonic and convex.

1.11.c This is regular. The derivatives of $f(x_1, x_2)$ are both positive so the technology is monotonic. For the isoquant to be convex to the origin, it is sufficient (but not necessary) that the production function is concave. To check this, form a matrix using the second derivatives of the production function, and see if it is negative semidefinite. The first principal minor of the Hessian must have a negative determinant, and the second principal minor must have a nonnegative determinant.

$$\frac{\partial^2 f(x)}{\partial x_1^2} = -\frac{1}{4} x_1^{-\frac{3}{2}} x_2^{\frac{1}{2}} \qquad \frac{\partial^2 f(x)}{\partial x_1 \partial x_2} = \frac{1}{4} x_1^{\frac{-1}{2}} x_2^{-\frac{1}{2}}$$

$$\frac{\partial^2 f(x)}{\partial x_2^2} = -\frac{1}{4} x_1^{\frac{1}{2}} x_2^{\frac{-3}{2}}$$

$$\text{Hessian} = \begin{bmatrix} -\frac{1}{4} x_1^{-3/2} x_2^{1/2} & \frac{1}{4} x_1^{-1/2} x_2^{-1/2} \\ \frac{1}{4} x_1^{-1/2} x_2^{-1/2} & -\frac{1}{4} x_1^{1/2} x_2^{-3/2} \end{bmatrix}$$

$$D_1 = -\frac{1}{4} x_1^{-3/2} x_2^{1/2} < 0$$

$$D_2 = \frac{1}{16} x_1^{-1} x_2^{-1} - \frac{1}{16} x_1^{-1} x_2^{-1} = 0.$$

So the input requirement set is convex.

1.11.d This is regular, monotonic, and convex.

1.11.e This is nonempty, but there is no way to produce any $y > 1$. It is monotonic and weakly convex.

1.11.f This is regular. To check monotonicity, write down the production function $f(x) = ax_1 - \sqrt{x_1 x_2} + bx_2$ and compute

$$\frac{\partial f(x)}{\partial x_1} = a - \frac{1}{2} x_1^{-1/2} x_2^{1/2}.$$

This is positive only if $a > \frac{1}{2}\sqrt{\frac{x_2}{x_1}}$, thus the input requirement set is not always monotonic.

Looking at the Hessian of f, its determinant is zero, and the determinant of the first principal minor is positive. Therefore f is not concave. This alone is not sufficient to show that the input requirement sets are not convex. But we can say even more: f is *convex*; therefore, all sets of the form

$$\{x_1, x_2 : ax_1 - \sqrt{x_1 x_2} + bx_2 \le y\} \quad \text{for all choices of } y$$

are convex. Except for the border points this is just the complement of the input requirement sets we are interested in (the inequality sign goes in the wrong direction). As complements of convex sets (such that the border line is not a straight line) our input requirement sets can therefore not be themselves convex.

1.11.g This function is the successive application of a linear and a Leontief function, so it has all of the properties possessed by these two types of functions, including being regular, monotonic, and convex.

2 Profit Maximization

2.1 For profit maximization, the Kuhn-Tucker theorem requires the following three inequalities to hold

$$\left(p \frac{\partial f(\mathbf{x}^*)}{\partial x_j} - \mathbf{w}_j \right) x_j^* = 0,$$

$$p \frac{\partial f(\mathbf{x}^*)}{\partial x_j} - \mathbf{w}_j \leq 0,$$

$$x_j^* \geq 0.$$

Note that if $x_j^* > 0$, then we must have $w_j/p = \partial f(\mathbf{x}^*)/\partial x_j$.

2.3 In the text the supply function and the factor demands were computed for this technology. Using those results, the profit function is given by

$$\pi(p, w) = p \left(\frac{w}{ap} \right)^{\frac{a}{a-1}} - w \left(\frac{w}{ap} \right)^{\frac{1}{a-1}}.$$

To prove homogeneity, note that

$$\pi(tp, tw) = tp \left(\frac{w}{ap} \right)^{\frac{a}{a-1}} - tw \left(\frac{w}{ap} \right)^{\frac{1}{a-1}} = t\pi(p, w),$$

which implies that $\pi(p, w)$ is a homogeneous function of degree 1.

Before computing the Hessian matrix, factor the profit function in the following way:

$$\pi(p, w) = p^{\frac{1}{1-a}} w^{\frac{a}{a-1}} \left(a^{\frac{a}{1-a}} - a^{\frac{1}{1-a}} \right) = p^{\frac{1}{1-a}} w^{\frac{a}{a-1}} \phi(a),$$

where $\phi(a)$ is strictly positive for $0 < a < 1$.

The Hessian matrix can now be written as

$$D^2\pi(p, \omega) = \begin{pmatrix} \frac{\partial^2 \pi(p,w)}{\partial p^2} & \frac{\partial^2 \pi(p,w)}{\partial p \partial w} \\ \frac{\partial^2 \pi(p,w)}{\partial w \partial p} & \frac{\partial^2 \pi(p,w)}{\partial w^2} \end{pmatrix}$$

$$= \begin{pmatrix} \frac{a}{(1-a)^2} p^{\frac{2a-1}{1-a}} w^{\frac{a}{a-1}} & -\frac{a}{(1-a)^2} p^{\frac{a}{1-a}} w^{\frac{1}{a-1}} \\ & \\ -\frac{a}{(1-a)^2} p^{\frac{a}{1-a}} w^{\frac{1}{a-1}} & \frac{a}{(1-a)^2} p^{\frac{1}{1-a}} w^{\frac{2-a}{a-1}} \end{pmatrix} \phi(a).$$

The principal minors of this matrix are

$$\frac{a}{(1-a)^2} p^{\frac{2a-1}{1-a}} w^{\frac{a}{a-1}} \phi(a) > 0$$

and 0. Therefore, the Hessian is a positive semidefinite matrix, which implies that $\pi(p, w)$ is convex in (p, w).

2.5 From the previous exercise, we know that

$$\ln(w_2 x_2 / w_1 x_1) = \ln(w_2 / w_1) + \ln(x_2 / x_1),$$

Differentiating, we get

$$\frac{d \ln(w_2 x_2 / w_1 x_1)}{d \ln(w_2 / w_1)} = 1 - \frac{d \ln(x_2 / x_1)}{d \ln |TRS|} = 1 - \sigma.$$

2.7.a We want to maximize $20x - x^2 - wx$. The first-order condition is $20 - 2x - w = 0$.

2.7.b For the optimal x to be zero, the derivative of profit with respect to x must be nonpositive at $x = 0$: $20 - 2x - w < 0$ when $x = 0$, or $w \geq 20$.

2.7.c The optimal x will be 10 when $w = 0$.

2.7.d The factor demand function is $x = 10 - w/2$, or, to be more precise, $x = \max\{10 - w/2, 0\}$.

2.7.e Profits as a function of output are

$$20x - x^2 - wx = [20 - w - x]x.$$

Substitute $x = 10 - w/2$ to find

$$\pi(w) = \left[10 - \frac{w}{2}\right]^2.$$

2.7.f The derivative of profit with respect to w is $-(10 - w/2)$, which is, of course, the negative of the factor demand.

3 Profit Function

3.1.a Since the profit function is convex and a decreasing function of the factor prices, we know that $\phi_i'(w_i) \leq 0$ and $\phi_i''(w_i) \geq 0$.

3.1.b It is zero.

3.1.c The demand for factor i is only a function of the ith price. Therefore the marginal product of factor i can only depend on the amount of factor i. It follows that $f(x_1, x_2) = g_1(x_1) + g_2(x_2)$.

3.3 The first-order conditions are

$$a_1 \frac{p}{x_1} - w_1 = 0$$

$$a_2 \frac{p}{x_2} - w_2 = 0,$$

which can easily be solved for the factor demand functions. Substituting into the objective function gives us the profit function.

3.5 If w_i is strictly positive, the firm will never use more of factor i than it needs to, which implies $x_1 = x_2$. Hence the profit maximization problem can be written as

$$\max \; px_1^a - w_1 x_1 - w_2 x_2.$$

The first-order condition is

$$pax_1^{a-1} - (w_1 + w_2) = 0.$$

The factor demand function and the profit function are the same as if the production function were $f(x) = x^a$, but the factor price is $w_1 + w_2$ rather than w. In order for a maximum to exist, $a < 1$.

4 Cost Minimization

4.1 Let $\mathbf{x}^*$ be a profit-maximizing input vector for prices $(p, \mathbf{w})$. This means that $\mathbf{x}^*$ must satisfy $pf(\mathbf{x}^*) - \mathbf{w}\mathbf{x}^* \geq pf(\mathbf{x}) - \mathbf{w}\mathbf{x}$ for all permissible $\mathbf{x}$. Assume that $\mathbf{x}^*$ does not minimize cost for the output $f(\mathbf{x}^*)$; i.e., there exists a vector $\mathbf{x}^{**}$ such that $f(\mathbf{x}^{**}) \geq f(\mathbf{x}^*)$ and $\mathbf{w}(\mathbf{x}^{**} - \mathbf{x}^*) < 0$. But then the profits achieved with $\mathbf{x}^{**}$ must be greater than those achieved with $\mathbf{x}^*$:

$$pf(\mathbf{x}^{**}) - \mathbf{w}\mathbf{x}^{**} \geq pf(\mathbf{x}^*) - \mathbf{w}\mathbf{x}^{**}$$
$$> pf(\mathbf{x}^*) - \mathbf{w}\mathbf{x}^*,$$

which contradicts the assumption that $\mathbf{x}^*$ was profit-maximizing.

4.3 Following the logic of the previous exercise, we equate marginal costs to find

$$y_1 = 1.$$

We also know $y_1 + y_2 = y$, so we can combine these two equations to get $y_2 = y - 1$. It appears that the cost function is $c(y) = 1/2 + y - 1 = y - 1/2$. However, on reflection this can't be right: it is obviously better to produce everything in plant 1 if $y_1 < 1$. As it happens, we have ignored the implicit constraint that $y_2 \geq 0$. The actual cost function is

$$c(y) = \begin{cases} y^2/2 & \text{if } y < 1 \\ y - 1/2 & \text{if } y > 1. \end{cases}$$

4.5 The cost of using activity a is $a_1w_1 + a_2w_2$, and the cost of using activity b is $b_1w_1 + b_2w_2$. The firm will use whichever is cheaper, so

$$c(w_1, w_2, y) = y \min\{a_1w_1 + a_2w_2, b_1w_1 + b_2w_2\}.$$

The demand function for factor 1, for example, is given by

$$x_1 = \begin{cases} a_1y & \text{if } a_1w_2 + a_2w_2 < b_1w_1 + b_2w_2 \\ b_1y & \text{if } a_1w_2 + a_2w_2 > b_1w_1 + b_2w_2 \\ \text{any amount between} & \\ \quad a_1y \text{ and } b_1y & \text{otherwise.} \end{cases}$$

The cost function will not be differentiable when

$$a_1w_2 + a_2w_2 = b_1w_1 + b_2w_2.$$

4.7 No, the data violate WACM. It costs 40 to produce 100 units of output, but at the same prices it would only cost 38 to produce 110 units of output.

5 Cost Function

5.1 The firm wants to minimize the cost of producing a given level of output:

$$c(y) = \min_{y_1, y_2} y_1^2 + y_2^2$$

$$\text{such that } y_1 + y_2 = y.$$

The solution has $y_1 = y_2 = y/2$. Substituting into the objective function yields
$$c(y) = (y/2)^2 + (y/2)^2 = y^2/2.$$

5.3 Consider the first technique. If this is used, then we need to have $2x_1 + x_2 = y$. Since this is linear, the firm will typically specialize and set $x_2 = y$ or $x_1 = y/2$ depending on which is cheaper. Hence the cost function for this technique is $y \min\{w_1/2, w_2\}$. Similarly, the cost function for the other technique is $y \min\{w_3, w_4/2\}$. Since both techniques must be used to produce y units of output,

$$c(w_1, w_2, y) = y \left[\min\{w_1/2, w_2\} + \min\{w_3, w_4/2\}\right].$$

5.5 The input requirement set is not convex. Since $y = \max\{x_1, x_2\}$, the firm will use whichever factor is cheaper; hence the cost function is

$c(w_1, w_2, y) = \min\{w_1, w_2\}y$. The factor demand function for factor 1 has the form

$$x_1 = \begin{cases} y & \text{if } w_1 < w_2 \\ \text{either } 0 \text{ or } y & \text{if } w_1 = w_2 \\ 0 & \text{if } w_1 > w_2 \end{cases}.$$

5.7 Set up the minimization problem

$$\min x_1 + x_2$$
$$x_1 x_2 = y.$$

Substitute to get the unconstrained minimization problem

$$\min x_1 + y/x_1.$$

The first-order condition is

$$1 - y/x_1^2,$$

which implies $x_1 = \sqrt{y}$. By symmetry, $x_2 = \sqrt{y}$. We are given that $2\sqrt{y} = 4$, so $\sqrt{y} = 2$, from which it follows that $y = 4$.

5.9.a $d\pi/d\alpha = py > 0$.

5.9.b $dy/d\alpha = p/c''(y) > 0$.

5.9.c $p'(\alpha) = n[y + \alpha p/c'']/[D'(p) - n\alpha/c''] < 0$.

5.11.a $\mathbf{x} = (1, 1, 0, 0)$.

5.11.b $\min\{w_1 + w_2, w_3 + w_4\}y$.

5.11.c Constant returns to scale.

5.11.d $\mathbf{x} = (1, 0, 1, 0)$.

5.11.e $c(w, y) = [\min\{w_1, w_2\} + \min\{w_3, w_4\}]y$.

5.11.f Constant.

5.13.a Factor demand curves slope downward, so the demand for unskilled workers must decrease when their wage increases.

5.13.b We are given that $\partial l/\partial p < 0$. But by duality, $\partial l/\partial p = -\partial^2\pi/\partial p\partial w = -\partial^2\pi/\partial w\partial p = -\partial y/\partial w$. It follows that $\partial y/\partial w > 0$.

5.15 By the linearity of the function, we know we will use either x_1, or a combination of x_2 and x_3 to produce y. By the properties of the Leontief function, we know that if we use x_2 and x_3 to produce y, we must use 3 units of both x_2 and x_3 to produce one unit of y. Thus, if the cost of using one unit of x_1 is less than the cost of using one unit of both x_2 and x_3, then we will use only x_1, and conversely. The conditional factor demands can be written as:

$$x_1 = \begin{cases} 3y & \text{if } w_1 < w_2 + w_3 \\ 0 & \text{if } w_1 > w_2 + w_3 \end{cases}$$

$$x_2 = \begin{cases} 0 & \text{if } w_1 < w_2 + w_3 \\ 3y & \text{if } w_1 > w_2 + w_3 \end{cases}$$

$$x_3 = \begin{cases} 0 & \text{if } w_1 < w_2 + w_3 \\ 3y & \text{if } w_1 > w_2 + w_3 \end{cases}$$

if $w_1 = w_2 + w_3$, then any bundle (x_1, x_2, x_3) with $x_2 = x_3$ and $x_1 + x_2 = 3y$ (or $x_1 + x_3 = 3y$) minimizes cost.

The cost function is

$$c(w, y) = 3y \min(w_1, w_2 + w_3).$$

5.17.a $y = \sqrt{ax_1 + bx_2}$

5.17.b Note that this function is exactly like a linear function, except that the linear combination of x_1 and x_2 will produce y^2, rather than just y. So, we know that if x_1 is relatively cheaper, we will use all x_1 and no x_2, and conversely.

5.17.c The cost function is $c(w, y) = y^2 \min(\frac{w_1}{a}, \frac{w_2}{b})$.

6 Duality

6.1 The production function is $f(x_1, x_2) = x_1 + x_2$. The conditional factor demands have the form

$$x_i = \begin{cases} y & \text{if } w_i < w_j \\ 0 & \text{if } w_i > w_j \\ \text{any amount between 0 and } y & \text{if } w_i = w_j. \end{cases}$$

6.3 The cost function must be increasing in both prices, so a and b are both nonnegative. The cost function must be concave in both prices, so a and b are both less than 1. Finally, the cost function must be homogeneous of degree 1, so $a = 1 - b$.

7 Utility Maximization

7.1 The preferences exhibit local nonsatiation, *except* at $(0,0)$. The consumer will choose this consumption point when faced with positive prices.

7.3 The expenditure function is $e(p_1, p_2, u) = u \min\{p_1, p_2\}$. The utility function is $u(x_1, x_2) = x_1 + x_2$ (or any monotonic transformation), and the demand function is

$$
x_1 = \begin{cases}
m/p_1 & \text{if } p_1 < p_2 \\
\text{any } x_1 \text{ and } x_2 \text{ such that } p_1 x_1 + p_2 x_2 = m & \text{if } p_1 = p_2 \\
0 & \text{if } p_1 > p_2
\end{cases}
$$

7.5.a Quasilinear preferences.

7.5.b Less than $u(1)$.

7.5.c $v(p_1, p_2, m) = \max\{u(1) - p_1 + m, m\}$

8 Choice

8.1 We know that

$$
x_j(\mathbf{p}, m) \equiv h_j(\mathbf{p}, v(\mathbf{p}, m)) \equiv \partial e(\mathbf{p}, v(\mathbf{p}, m))/\partial p_j. \tag{27.12}
$$

(Note that the partial derivative is taken with respect to the *first* occurrence of p_j.) Differentiating equation (27.12) with respect to m gives us

$$
\frac{\partial x_j}{\partial m} = \frac{\partial^2 e(\mathbf{p}, v(\mathbf{p}, m))}{\partial p_j \partial u} \frac{\partial v(p, m)}{\partial m}.
$$

Since the marginal utility of income, $\partial v/\partial m$, must be positive, the result follows.

8.3 The equation is $d\mu/dt = at + b\mu + c$. The indirect money metric utility function is

$$
\mu(q, p, m) = e^{b(q-p)} \left[m + \frac{c}{b} + \frac{a}{b^2} + \frac{c}{b} p \right] - \frac{c}{b} - \frac{a}{b^2} - \frac{aq}{b}.
$$

8.5 Write the Lagrangian

$$
\mathcal{L}(\mathbf{x}, \lambda) = \frac{3}{2} \ln x_1 + \ln x_2 - \lambda(3x_1 + 4x_2 - 100).
$$

(Be sure you understand why we can transform u this way.) Now, equating the derivatives with respect to x_1, x_2, and λ to zero, we get three equations in three unknowns

$$\frac{3}{2x_1} = 3\lambda,$$

$$\frac{1}{x_2} = 4\lambda,$$

$$3x_1 + 4x_2 = 100.$$

Solving, we get

$$x_1(3, 4, 100) = 20, \text{ and } x_2(3, 4, 100) = 10.$$

Note that if you are going to interpret the Lagrange multiplier as the marginal utility of income, you must be explicit as to which utility function you are referring to. Thus, the marginal utility of income can be measured in original '*utils*' or in 'ln *utils*'. Let $u^* = \ln u$ and, correspondingly, $v^* = \ln v$; then

$$\lambda = \frac{\partial v^*(\mathbf{p}, m)}{\partial m} = \frac{\frac{\partial v(\mathbf{p}, m)}{\partial m}}{v(\mathbf{p}, m)} = \frac{\mu}{v(\mathbf{p}, m)},$$

where μ denotes the Lagrange multiplier in the Lagrangian

$$L(\mathbf{x}, \mu) = x_1^{\frac{3}{2}} x_2 - \mu(3x_1 + 4x_2 - 100).$$

Check that in this problem we'd get $\mu = \frac{20^{\frac{3}{2}}}{4}$, $\lambda = \frac{1}{40}$, and $v(3, 4, 100) = 20^{\frac{3}{2}} 10$.

8.7 Instead of starting from the utility maximization problem, let's now start from the expenditure minimization problem. The Lagrangian is

$$\mathcal{L}(\mathbf{x}, \mu) = p_1 x_1 + p_2 x_2 - \mu((x_1 - \alpha_1)^{\beta_1}(x_2 - \alpha_2)^{\beta_2} - u);$$

the first-order conditions are

$$p_1 = \mu\beta_1(x_1 - \alpha_1)^{\beta_1 - 1}(x_2 - \alpha_2)^{\beta_2},$$

$$p_2 = \mu\beta_2(x_1 - \alpha_1)^{\beta_1}(x_2 - \alpha_2)^{\beta_2 - 1},$$

$$(x_1 - \alpha_1)^{\beta_1}(x_2 - \alpha_2)^{\beta_2} = u.$$

Divide the first equation by the second

$$\frac{p_1 \beta_2}{p_2 \beta_1} = \frac{x_2 - \alpha_2}{x_1 - \alpha_1},$$

using the last equation

$$x_2 - \alpha_2 = \left((x_1 - \alpha_1)^{-\beta_1} u\right)^{\frac{1}{\beta_2}};$$

substituting and solving,

$$h_1(\mathbf{p}, u) = \alpha_1 + \left(\frac{p_2\beta_1}{p_1\beta_2} u^{\frac{1}{\beta_2}}\right)^{\frac{\beta_2}{\beta_1+\beta_2}},$$

and

$$h_2(\mathbf{p}, u) = \alpha_2 + \left(\frac{p_1\beta_2}{p_2\beta_1} u^{\frac{1}{\beta_1}}\right)^{\frac{\beta_1}{\beta_1+\beta_2}}.$$

Verify that

$$\frac{\partial h_1(\mathbf{p}, m)}{\partial p_2} = \left(\frac{u}{\beta_1 + \beta_2} \left(\frac{\beta_1}{p_1}\right)^{\beta_2} \left(\frac{\beta_2}{p_2}\right)^{\beta_1}\right)^{\frac{1}{\beta_1+\beta_2}} = \frac{\partial h_2(\mathbf{p}, m)}{\partial p_1}.$$

The expenditure function is

$$e(\mathbf{p}, u) = p_1 \left(\alpha_1 + \left(\frac{p_2\beta_1}{p_1\beta_2} u^{\frac{1}{\beta_2}}\right)^{\frac{\beta_2}{\beta_1+\beta_2}}\right) + p_2 \left(\alpha_2 + \left(\frac{p_1\beta_2}{p_2\beta_1} u^{\frac{1}{\beta_1}}\right)^{\frac{\beta_1}{\beta_1+\beta_2}}\right).$$

Solving for u, we get the indirect utility function

$$v(\mathbf{p}, m) =$$
$$\left(\frac{\beta_1}{\beta_1 + \beta_2} \left(\frac{m - \alpha_2 p_2}{p_1} - \alpha_1\right)\right)^{\beta_1} \left(\frac{\beta_2}{\beta_1 + \beta_2} \left(\frac{m - \alpha_1 p_1}{p_2} - \alpha_2\right)\right)^{\beta_2}.$$

By Roy's law we get the Marshallian demands

$$x_1(\mathbf{p}, m) = \frac{1}{\beta_1 + \beta_2} \left(\beta_1\alpha_2 + \beta_2\frac{m - \alpha_1 p_1}{p_2}\right),$$

and

$$x_2(\mathbf{p}, m) = \frac{1}{\beta_1 + \beta_2} \left(\beta_2\alpha_1 + \beta_1\frac{m - \alpha_2 p_2}{p_1}\right).$$

8.9 By definition, the Marshallian demands $\mathbf{x}(\mathbf{p}, m)$ maximize $\phi(\mathbf{x})$ subject to $\mathbf{px} = m$. We claim that they also maximize $\psi(\phi(\mathbf{x}))$ subject to the same budget constraint. Suppose not. Then, there would exist some other choice $\mathbf{x}'$ such that $\psi(\phi(\mathbf{x}')) > \psi(\phi(\mathbf{x}(\mathbf{p}, m)))$ and $\mathbf{px}' = m$. But since applying the transformation $\psi^{-1}(\cdot)$ to both sides of the inequality will preserve it, we would have $\phi(\mathbf{x}') > \phi(\mathbf{x}(\mathbf{p}, m))$ and $\mathbf{px}' = m$, which contradicts our initial assumption that $\mathbf{x}(\mathbf{p}, m)$ maximized $\phi(\mathbf{x})$ subject to $\mathbf{px} = m$. Therefore $\mathbf{x}(\mathbf{p}, m) = \mathbf{x}^*(\mathbf{p}, m)$. (Check that the reverse proposition also holds—i.e., the choice that maximizes u^* also maximizes u when the the same budget constraint has to be verified in both cases.)

$$v^*(\mathbf{p}, m) = \psi(\phi(\mathbf{x}^*(\mathbf{p}, m))) = \psi(\phi(\mathbf{x}(\mathbf{p}, m)) = \psi(v(\mathbf{p}, m)),$$

the first and last equalities hold by definition and the middle one by our previous result; now

$$\begin{aligned}
e^*(\mathbf{p}, u^*) &= \min\{\mathbf{px} : \psi(\phi(\mathbf{x})) = u^*\} \\
&= \min\{\mathbf{px} : \phi(\mathbf{x}) = \psi^{-1}(u^*)\} \\
&= e(\mathbf{p}, \psi^{-1}(u^*));
\end{aligned}$$

again, we're using definitions at both ends and the properties of $\psi(\cdot)$ — namely that the inverse is well defined since $\psi(\cdot)$ is monotonic— to get the middle equality; finally using definitions and substitutions as often as needed we get

$$\begin{aligned}
\mathbf{h}^*(\mathbf{p}, u^*) &= \mathbf{x}^*(\mathbf{p}, e^*(\mathbf{p}, u^*)) = \mathbf{x}(\mathbf{p}, e^*(\mathbf{p}, u^*)) \\
&= \mathbf{x}(\mathbf{p}, e(\mathbf{p}, \psi^{-1}(u^*))) = \mathbf{h}(\mathbf{p}, \psi^{-1}(u^*)).
\end{aligned}$$

8.11 No, because his demand behavior violates GARP. When prices are $(2, 4)$ he spends 10. At these prices he could afford the bundle $(2, 1)$, but rejects it; therefore, $(1, 2) \succ (2, 1)$. When prices are $(6, 3)$ he spends 15. At these prices he could afford the bundle $(1, 2)$ but rejects it; therefore, $(2, 1) \succ (1, 2)$.

8.13.a Draw the lines $x_2 + 2x_1 = 20$ and $x_1 + 2x_2 = 20$. The indifference curve is the northeast boundary of this X.

8.13.b The slope of a budget line is $-p_1/p_2$. If the budget line is steeper than 2, $x_1 = 0$. Hence the condition is $p_1/p_2 > 2$.

8.13.c Similarly, if the budget line is flatter than $1/2$, x_2 will equal 0, so the condition is $p_1/p_2 < 1/2$.

8.13.d If the optimum is unique, it must occur where $x_2 - 2x_1 = x_1 - 2x_2$. This implies that $x_1 = x_2$, so that $x_1/x_2 = 1$.

8.15 Use Slutsky's equation to write: $\frac{\partial L}{\partial w} = \frac{\partial L^s}{\partial w} + (\overline{L} - L)\frac{\partial L}{\partial m}$. Note that the substitution effect is always negative, $(\overline{L} - L)$ is always positive, and hence if leisure is inferior, $\frac{\partial L}{\partial w}$ is necessarily negative. Thus the slope of the labor supply curve is positive.

9 Demand

9.1 If preferences are homothetic, demand functions are linear in income, so we can write $x_i(\mathbf{p})m$ and $x_j(\mathbf{p})m$. Applying Slutsky symmetry, we have

$$\frac{\partial x_i(\mathbf{p})}{\partial p_j} + x_i(\mathbf{p})x_j(\mathbf{p})m = \frac{\partial x_j}{\partial p_i} + x_j(\mathbf{p})x_i(\mathbf{p})m.$$

Subtracting $x_i(\mathbf{p})x_j(\mathbf{p})m$ from each side of the equation establishes the result.

9.3 We have to solve

$$\frac{d\mu(p; q, m)}{dp} = a + bp + c\mu(p; q, m).$$

The homogeneous part has a solution of the form Ae^{cp}. A particular solution to the nonhomogeneous equation is given by

$$\bar{\mu} = -\frac{(a + bp)c + b}{c^2}.$$

Therefore the general solution to the differential equation is given by

$$\mu(p; q, m) = Ae^{cp} - \frac{(a + bp)c + b}{c^2}.$$

Since $\mu(q; q, m) = m$ we get

$$\mu(p; q, m) = \left(m + \frac{(a + bq)c + b}{c^2}\right)e^{c(p-q)} - \frac{(a + bp)c + b}{c^2}.$$

Hence, the indirect utility function is

$$v(q, m) = \left(m + \frac{(a + bq)c + b}{c^2}\right)e^{-cq}.$$

(Verify that using Roy's identity we get the original demand function.)
    To get the direct utility function, we must solve

$$\min_q \left(m + \frac{(a + bq)c + b}{c^2}\right)e^{-cq}$$

such that $qx + z = m$.

The optimal value is given by

$$q^* = \frac{x - cz - a}{b + cx},$$

which implies that

$$u(x, z) = \frac{b + cx}{c^2} \exp\left\{ \frac{ac - cx + c^2 z}{b + cx} \right\}.$$

(Again, substitute z by $m - px$ above, equate the derivative of the resulting expression with respect to x to zero, solve for x and recover the original demand function.)

9.5 To get the direct utility function we must solve

$$u(\mathbf{x}, z) = \min_{\mathbf{q}}\{v(\mathbf{q}, m) : z + q_1 x_1 + q_2 x_2 = m\}.$$

After a few minutes of algebraic fun, we get

$$q_1^* = \frac{b_2(x_1 - a_1) - b(x_2 - a_2)}{b_1 b_2 - b^2},$$

and

$$q_2^* = \frac{b_1(x_2 - a_2) - b(x_1 - a_1)}{b_1 b_2 - b^2}.$$

Substituting these values back into $v(\cdot)$, we get

$$u(\mathbf{x}, z)$$
$$= z + \frac{b_2(x_1 - a_1)^2 + b_1(x_2 - a_2)^2}{2(b_1 b_2 - b^2)} + \frac{b(a_1 x_2 + a_2 x_1 - x_1 x_2 - a_1 a_2)}{b_1 b_2 - b^2}$$
$$= z + \frac{1}{2(b_1 b_2 - b^2)} [x_1 - a_1, x_2 - a_2] \begin{bmatrix} b_2 & -b \\ -b & b_1 \end{bmatrix} \begin{bmatrix} x_1 - a_1 \\ x_2 - a_2 \end{bmatrix}.$$

9.7 The function is weakly separable, and the subutility for the z-good consumption is $z_2^b z_3^c$. The conditional demands for the z-goods are Cobb-Douglas demands:

$$z_1 = \frac{b}{b + c} \frac{m_z}{p_2}$$

$$z_2 = \frac{c}{b + c} \frac{m_z}{p_3}.$$

9.9.a The function $V(x, y) = \min\{x, y\}$, and $U(V, z) = V + z$.

9.9.b The demand function for the z-good is $z = m/p_z$ if $p_z < p_x + p_y$. If $p_z > p_x + p_y$, then the demand for the x-good and the y-good is given by $x = y = m/(p_x + p_y)$. If $p_z = p_x + p_y$, then take any convex combination of these demands.

9.9.c The indirect utility function is

$$v(p_x, p_y, p_z, m) = \max \left\{ \frac{m}{p_x + p_y}, \frac{m}{p_z} \right\}.$$

9.11.a There are a variety of ways to solve this problem. The easiest is to solve for the indirect utility function to get $v_1(p_1, p_2, m_1) = m_1(p_1 p_2)^{-1/2}$. Now use Roy's identity to calculate:

$$x_1 = \frac{1}{2} \frac{m_1}{p_1}$$

$$x_2 = \frac{1}{2} \frac{m_1}{p_2}.$$

Note that these are Cobb-Douglas demands.

Recognizing that person 2 has Cobb-Douglas utility, we can write down the demands immediately:

$$x_1 = \frac{3}{3 + a} \frac{m_2}{p_1}$$

$$x_2 = \frac{a}{3 + a} \frac{m_2}{p_2}.$$

9.11.b We must have the marginal propensity to consume each good the same for each consumer. This means that

$$\frac{1}{2} = \frac{3}{3 + a},$$

which implies that $a = 3$.

10 Consumers' Surplus

10.1 We saw that in this case the indirect utility function takes the form $v(\mathbf{p}) + m$. Hence the expenditure function takes the form $e(\mathbf{p}, u) = u - v(\mathbf{p})$. The expenditure function is necessarily a concave function of prices, which implies that $v(\mathbf{p})$ is a convex function.

11 Uncertainty

11.1 The proof of Pratt's theorem established that

$$\pi(t) \approx \frac{1}{2} r(w) \sigma^2 t^2.$$

But the $\sigma^2 t^2$ is simply the variance of the gamble $t\tilde{\epsilon}$.

11.3 We have seen that investment in a risky asset will be independent of wealth if risk aversion is constant. In an earlier problem, we've seen that constant absolute risk aversion implies that the utility function takes the form $u(w) = -e^{-rw}$.

11.5.a The probability of heads occurring for the first time on the jth toss is $(1-p)^{j-1}p$. Hence the expected value of the bet is $\sum_{j=1}^{\infty}(1-p)^{j-1}p2^j = \sum_{j=1}^{\infty}2^{-j}2^j = \sum_{j=1}^{\infty}1 = \infty$.

11.5.b The expected utility is

$$\sum_{j=1}^{\infty}(1-p)^{j-1}p\ln(2^j) = p\ln(2)\sum_{j=1}^{\infty}j(1-p)^{j-1}.$$

11.5.c By standard summation formulas:

$$\sum_{j=0}^{\infty}(1-p)^j = \frac{1}{p}.$$

Differentiate both sides of this expression with respect to p to obtain

$$\sum_{j=1}^{\infty}j(1-p)^{j-1} = \frac{1}{p^2}.$$

Therefore,

$$p\ln(2)\sum_{j=1}^{\infty}j(1-p)^{j-1} = \frac{\ln(2)}{p}.$$

11.5.d In order to solve for the amount of money required, we equate the utility of participating in the gamble with the utility of not participating. This gives us:

$$\ln(w_0) = \frac{\ln(2)}{p},$$

Now simply solve this equation for w_0 to find

$$w_0 = e^{\ln(2)/p}.$$

11.7 Risk aversion implies a concave utility function. Denote by $\alpha \in [0,1]$ the proportion of the initial wealth invested in asset 1. We have

$$E[u(\alpha w_0(1+R_1)+(1-\alpha)w_0(1+R_2))]$$

$$= \int\int u(\alpha w_0(1+r_1)+(1-\alpha)w_0(1+r_2))f(r_1)f(r_2)dr_1dr_2$$

$$> \int\int [\alpha u(w_0(1+r_1))+(1-\alpha)u(w_0(1+r_2))]f(r_1)f(r_2)dr_1dr_2$$

$$= \int u(w_0(1+r_1))f(r_1)dr_1 = \int u(w_0(1+r_2))f(r_2)dr_2 =$$

$$= E[u(w_0(1+R_1))] = E[u(w_0(1+R_2))].$$

The inequality follows from the concavity of $u(\cdot)$.

For part b, proceed as before reversing the inequality since now $u(\cdot)$ is convex.

11.9 Initially the person has expected utility of

$$\frac{1}{2}\sqrt{4+12}+\frac{1}{2}\sqrt{4+0}=3.$$

If he sells his ticket for price p, he needs to get at least this utility. To find the breakeven price we write the equation

$$\sqrt{4+p}=3.$$

Solving, we have $p=5$.

11.11 We want to solve the equation

$$\frac{p}{w_1}+\frac{1-p}{w_2}=\frac{1}{w}.$$

After some manipulation we have

$$w=\frac{w_1 w_2}{pw_2+(1-p)w_1}.$$

13 Competitive Markets

13.1 The first derivative of welfare is $v'(p)+\pi'(p)=0$. Applying Roy's law and Hotelling's lemma, we have $-x(p)+y(p)=0$, which is simply the condition that demand equals supply. The second derivative of this welfare measure is $-x'(p)+y'(p)$ which is clearly positive; hence, we have a welfare minimum rather than a welfare maximum.

The intuition behind this is that at any price other than the equilibrium price, the firm wants to supply a different amount than the consumer wants to demand; hence, the "welfare" associated with all prices other than the equilibrium price is not attainable.

13.3.a The average cost curve is just

$$\frac{c(\mathbf{w}, y)}{y} = \frac{y^2 + 1}{y} w_1 + \frac{y^2 + 2}{y} w_2.$$

You should verify that it is a convex function that has a unique minimum at

$$y_m = \sqrt{\frac{w_1/w_2 + 2}{w_1/w_2 + 1}}.$$

The derivative of y_m with respect to w_1/w_2 is negative, so the minimum of the average cost shifts to the left (right) as w_1/w_2 increases (decreases). In fact it converges to 1 as the ratio approaches ∞ and to $\sqrt{2}$ as it goes down to 0.

13.3.b The marginal cost is

$$\frac{\partial c(\mathbf{w}, y)}{\partial y} = 2y(w_1 + w_2),$$

so short-run supply schedule is given by

$$y(p) = \frac{p}{2(w_1 + w_2)}.$$

13.3.c The long-run supply curve is

$$Y(p) = \begin{cases} \text{arbitrarily large amount} & \text{if } p > 2y_m(w_1 + w_2) \\ 0 & \text{otherwise.} \end{cases}$$

13.3.d From the cost function we have that $x_1 = y^2 + 1$ and $x_2 = y^2 + 2$. Also, we see that x_1 and x_2 are not substitutes at any degree. Therefore, the input requirement set for an individual firm is

$$V(y) = \left\{ (x_1, x_2) \in [1, \infty) \times [2, \infty) : y \le \min \left\{ \sqrt{x_1 - 1}, \sqrt{x_2 - 2} \right\} \right\}.$$

13.5.a In order to offset the output subsidy, the U.S. should choose a tax of the same size as the subsidy; that is, choose $t(s) = s$.

13.5.b In the case of the capital subsidy, the producers receive $p - t(s)$. If y^* is to remain optimal, we must have $p - t(s) = \partial c(w, r - s, y^*)/\partial y$.

13.5.c Differentiate the above expression to get

$$t'(s) = \frac{\partial^2 c(w, r - s, y^*)}{\partial y \partial r} = \frac{\partial K(w, r - s, y^*)}{\partial y}.$$

13.5.d Since $K(w, r - s, y) = K(w, r - s, 1)y$, the formula reduces to $t'(s) = K(w, r - s, 1)$.

13.5.e In this case $\partial K/\partial y < 0$ so that an increase in the subsidy rate implies a decrease in the tariff.

13.7.a $y_m = 500$

13.7.b $p = 5$

13.7.c $y_c = 50 \times 5 = 250$

14 Monopoly

14.1 The profit-maximizing level of output is 5 units. If the monopolist only has 4 to sell, then it would find it most profitable to charge a price of 6. This is the same as the competitive solution. If, however, the monopolist had 6 units to sell, it would be most profitable to dispose of one unit and only sell 5 units at a price of 5.

14.3 For this constant elasticity demand function revenue is constant at 10, regardless of the level of output. Hence output should be as small as possible—that is, a profit-maximizing level of output doesn't exist.

14.5 The monopolist's profit maximization problem is

$$\max_y \; p(y, t)y - cy.$$

The first-order condition for this problem is

$$p(y, t) + \frac{\partial p(y, t)}{\partial y} y - c = 0.$$

According to the standard comparative statics calculations, the sign of dy/dt is the same as the sign of the derivative of the first-order expression with respect to t. That is,

$$\text{sign} \; \frac{dy}{dt} = \text{sign} \; \frac{\partial p}{\partial t} + \frac{\partial p^2}{\partial y \partial t} y.$$

For the special case $p(y,t) = a(p) + b(t)$, the second term on the right-hand side is zero.

14.7 Since the elasticity of demand is -1, revenues are constant at any price less than or equal to 20. Marginal costs are constant at c so the monopolist will want to produce the smallest possible output. This will happen when $p = 20$, which implies $y = 1/2$.

14.9 The integral to evaluate is

$$\int_0^x \frac{\partial^2 u(z,q)}{\partial z \partial q}\, dz < \int_0^x \frac{\partial p(x,q)}{\partial q}\, dz.$$

Carrying out the integration gives

$$\frac{\partial u(x,q)}{\partial q} < \frac{\partial p(x,q)}{\partial q} x,$$

which is what is required.

14.11 The figure depicts the situation where the monopolist has reduced the price to the point where the marginal benefit from further reductions just balance the marginal cost. This is the point where $p_2 = 2p_1$. If the high-demand consumer's inverse demand curve is *always* greater than twice the low-demand consumer's inverse demand curve, this condition cannot be satisfied and the low-demand consumer will be pushed to a zero level of consumption.

14.13 This is equivalent to the price discrimination problem with $x = q$ and $w_t = r_t$. All of the results derived there translate on a one-to-one basis; e.g., the consumer who values quality the more highly ends up consuming the socially optimal amount, etc.

14.15 Under the *ad valorem* tax we have

$$(1 - \tau)P_D = \left(1 + \frac{1}{\epsilon}\right) c.$$

Under the output tax we have

$$P_D - t = \left(1 + \frac{1}{\epsilon}\right).$$

Solve each equation for P_D, set the results equal to each other, and solve for t to find

$$t = \frac{\tau k c}{1 - \tau} \qquad k = \frac{1}{1 + \frac{1}{\epsilon}}$$

14.17.a Differentiating the first-order conditions in the usual way gives

$$\frac{\partial x_1}{\partial t_1} = \frac{1}{p_1' - c_1''} < 0$$

$$\frac{\partial x_2}{\partial t_2} = \frac{1}{2p_2' + p_2'' x_2 - c_2''} < 0.$$

14.17.b The appropriate welfare function is $W = u_1(x_1) + u_2(x_2) - c_1(x_1) - c_2(x_2)$. The total differential is

$$dW = (u_1' - c_1')dx_1 + (u_2' - c_2')dx_2.$$

14.17.c Somewhat surprisingly, we should tax the competitive industry and subsidize the monopoly! To see this, combine the answers to the first two questions to get the change in welfare from a tax policy (t_1, t_2).

$$dW = (p_1 - c_1')\frac{dx_1}{dt_1}dt_1 + (p_2 - c_2')\frac{dx_2}{dt_2}dt_2.$$

The change in welfare from a small tax or subsidy on the competitive industry is zero, since price equals marginal cost. But for the monopolized industry, price exceeds marginal cost, so we want the last term to be positive. But this can only happen if dt_2 is negative—i.e., we subsidize industry 2.

14.19.a The profit-maximizing choices of p_1 and p_2 are

$$p_1 = a_1/2b_1$$
$$p_2 = a_2/2b_2.$$

These will be equal when $a_1/b_1 = a_2/b_2$.

14.19.b We must have $p_1(1 - 1/b_1) = c = p_2(1 - 1/b_2)$. Hence $p_1 = p_2$ if and only if $b_1 = b_2$.

14.21 Under the *ad valorem* tax we have

$$(1 - \tau)P_D = \left(1 + \frac{1}{\epsilon}\right)c.$$

Under the output tax we have

$$P_D - t = \left(1 + \frac{1}{\epsilon}\right).$$

Solve each equation for P_D, set the results equal to each other, and solve for t to find

$$t = \frac{\tau k c}{1 - \tau} \qquad k = \frac{1}{1 + \frac{1}{\epsilon}}$$

14.23.a If $c < 1$, then profits are maximized at $p = 3/2 + c/2$ and the monopolist sells to both types of consumers. The best he can do if he sells only to Type A consumers is to sell at a price of $2 + c/2$. He will do this if $c \geq 1$.

14.23.b If a consumer has utility $ax_1 - x_1^2/2 + x_2$, then she will choose to pay k if $(a - p)^2/2 > k$. If she buys, she will buy $a - p$ units. So if $k < (2 - p)^2/2$, then demand is $N(4 - p) + N(2 - p)$. If $(2 - p)^2 < k < (4 - p)^2/2$, then demand is $N(4 - p)$. If $k > (4 - p)^2/2$, then demand is zero.

14.23.c Set $p = c$ and $k = (4 - c)^2/2$. The profit will be $N(4 - c)^2/2$.

14.23.d In this case, if both types of consumers buy the good, then the profit-maximizing prices will have the Type B consumers just indifferent between buying and not buying. Therefore $k = (2 - p)^2/2$. Total profits will then be $N((6 - 2p)(p - c) + (2 - p)^2/2)$. This is maximized when $p = 2(c + 2)/3$.

15 Game Theory

15.1 There are no pure strategy equilibria and the unique mixed strategy equilibrium is for each player to choose Head or Tails with probability $1/2$.

15.3 The unique equilibrium that remains after eliminating weakly dominant strategies is (Bottom, Right).

15.5.a $a \geq e$, $c \geq g$, $b \geq d$, $f \geq h$

15.5.b Only $a \geq e$, $b \geq d$.

15.5.c Yes.

15.7 If one player defects, he receives a payoff of π_d this period and π_c forever after. In order for the punishment strategy to be an equilibrium the payoffs must satisfy

$$\pi_d + \frac{\pi_c}{r} \leq \pi_j + \frac{\pi_j}{r}.$$

Rearranging, we find

$$r \leq \frac{\pi_j - \pi_c}{\pi_d - \pi_j}.$$

15.9.a (Top, Left) and (Bottom, Right) are both equilibria.

15.9.b Yes. (Top, Left) dominates (Bottom, Right).

15.9.c Yes.

15.9.d (Top, Left).

16 Oligopoly

16.1 The Bertrand equilibrium has price equal to the *lowest* marginal cost, c_1, as does the competitive equilibrium.

16.3 Let $\delta = \beta_1\beta_2 - \gamma^2$. Then by direct calculation: $a_i = (\alpha_i\beta_j - \alpha_j\gamma)/\delta$, $b_i = \beta_j/\delta$, and $c = \gamma/\delta$.

16.5 The argument is analogous to the argument given on page 297.

16.7 In a cartel the firms must equate the marginal costs. Due to the assumption about marginal costs, such an equality can only be established when $y_1 > y_2$.

16.9 In the Prisoner's Dilemma, (Defect, Defect) is a dominant strategy equilibrium. In the Cournot game, the Cournot equilibrium is only a Nash equilibrium.

16.11.a $P(Y) + P'(Y)y_i = c + t_i$

16.11.b Sum the first order conditions to get $nP(Y) + P'(Y)Y = nc + \sum_{i=1}^{n} t_i$, and note that industry output Y can only depend on the sum of the taxes.

16.11.c Since total output doesn't change, Δy_i must satisfy

$$P(Y) + P'(Y)[y_i + \Delta y_i] = c + t_i + \Delta t_i.$$

Using the original first order condition, this becomes $P'(Y)\Delta y_i = \Delta t_i$, or $\Delta y_i = \Delta t_i/P'(Y)$.

17 Exchange

17.1 In the proof of the theorem, we established that $\mathbf{x}_i^* \sim_i \mathbf{x}_i'$. If $\mathbf{x}_i^*$ and $\mathbf{x}_i'$ were distinct, a convex combination of the two bundles would be feasible and strictly preferred by every agent. This contradicts the assumption that $\mathbf{x}^*$ is Pareto efficient.

17.3 Agent 2 holds zero of good 2.

17.5 There is no way to make one person better off without hurting someone else.

17.7 The Slutsky equation for consumer i is

$$\frac{\partial x_i}{\partial p_j} = \frac{\partial h_i}{\partial p_j}.$$

17.9 In equilibrium we must have $p_2/p_1 = x_3^2/x_3^1 = 5/10 = 1/2$.

17.11.a The diagram is omitted.

17.11.b We must have $p_1 = p_2$.

17.11.c The equilibrium allocation must give one agent all of one good and the other agent all of the other good.

18 Production

18.1.a Consider the following two possibilities. (i) Land is in excess supply. (ii) All land is used. If land is in excess supply, then the price of land is zero. Constant returns requires zero profits in both the apple and the bandanna industry. This means that $p_A = p_B = 1$ in equilibrium. Every consumer will have income of 15. Each will choose to consume $15c$ units of apples and $15(1-c)$ units of bandannas. Total demand for land will be $15cN$. Total demand for labor will be $15N$. There will be excess supply of land if $c < 2/3$. So if $c < 2/3$, this is a competitive equilibrium.

If all land is used, then the total outputs must be 10 units of apples and 5 units of bandannas. The price of bandannas must equal the wage which is 1. The price of apples will be $1 + r$ where r is the price of land. Since preferences are homothetic and identical, it will have to be that each person consumes twice as many apples as bandannas. People will want to consume twice as much apples as bandannas if $p_A/p_B = \frac{c}{(1-c)}(1/2)$. Then it also must be that in equilibrium, $r = (p_A/p_B) - 1 \geq 0$. This last inequality will hold if and only if $c \geq 2/3$. This characterizes equilibrium for $c \geq 2/3$.

18.1.b For $c < 2/3$.

18.1.c For $c < 2/3$.

19 Time

19.1 See Ingersoll (1987), page 238.

20 Asset Markets

20.1 The easiest way to show this is to write the first-order conditions as

$$Eu'(\tilde{C})\tilde{R}_a = Eu'(\tilde{C})R_0$$
$$Eu'(\tilde{C})\tilde{R}_b = Eu'(\tilde{C})R_0$$

and subtract.

21 Equilibrium Analysis

21.1 The core is simply the initial endowment.

21.3 Differentiating $V(p)$, we have

$$\frac{dV(p)}{dt} = -2\mathbf{z}(\mathbf{p})\mathbf{Dz}(\mathbf{p})\dot{\mathbf{p}}$$
$$= -2\mathbf{z}(\mathbf{p})\mathbf{Dz}(\mathbf{p})\mathbf{Dz}(\mathbf{p})^{-1}\mathbf{z}(\mathbf{p})$$
$$= -2\mathbf{z}(\mathbf{p})\mathbf{z}(\mathbf{p}) < 0.$$

22 Welfare

22.1 We have the equation

$$\theta x_i = \sum_{j=1}^{k} t_j \frac{\partial h_j}{\partial p_i}.$$

Multiply both sides of this equation by t_i and sum to get

$$\theta R = \theta \sum_i t_i x_i = \sum_{j=1}^{k} \sum_{i=1}^{k} t_i t_j \frac{\partial h_j}{\partial p_i}.$$

The right-hand side of expression is nonpositive (and typically negative) since the Slutsky matrix is negative semidefinite. Hence θ has the same sign as R.

23 Public goods

23.1 Suppose that it is efficient to provide the public good together, but neither agent wants to provide it alone. Then any set of bids such that $b_1 + b_2 = c$ and $b_i \leq r_i$ is an equilibrium to the game. However, there are also many *inefficient* equilibria, such as $b_1 = b_2 = 0$.

23.3 Agent 1 will contribute $g_1 = \alpha w_1$. Agent 2's reaction function is $f_2(w_2 + g_1) = \max\{\alpha(w_2 + g_1) - g_1, 0\}$. Solving $f_2(w_2 + \alpha w_1) = 0$ yields $w_2 = (1 - \alpha)w_1$.

23.5 The allocation is not in general Pareto efficient, since for some patterns of preferences some of the private good must be thrown away. However, the amount of the public good provided will be the Pareto efficient amount: 1 unit if $\sum_i r_i > c$, and 0 units otherwise.

24 Externalities

24.1.a Agent 1's utility maximization problem is

$$\max_{x_1} \; u_1(x_1) - p(x_1, x_2)c_1,$$

while the social problem is

$$\max_{x_1, x_2} \; u_1(x_1) + u_2(x_2) - p(x_1, x_2)[c_1 + c_2].$$

Since agent 1 ignores the cost he imposes on agent 2, he will generally choose too large a value of x_1.

24.1.b By inspection of the social problem and the private problem, agent 1 should be charged a fine $t_1 = c_2$.

24.1.c If the optimal fines are being used, then the total costs born by the agents in the case of an accident are $2[c_1 + c_2]$, which is simply twice the total cost of the accident.

24.1.d Agent 1's objective function is

$$(1 - p(x_1, x_2))u_1(x_1) - p(x_1, x_2)c_1.$$

This can also be written as

$$u_1(x_1) - p(x_1, x_2)[u_1(x_1) + c_1].$$

This is just the form of the previous objective function with $u_1(x_1) + c_1$ replacing c_1. Hence the optimal fine for agent 1 is $t_1 = u_2(x_2) + c_2$.

25 Information

25.1 By construction we know that $f(u(s)) \equiv s$. Differentiating one time shows that $f'(u)u'(s) = 1$. Since $u'(s) > 0$, we must have $f'(u) > 0$. Differentiating again, we have

$$f'(u)u''(s) + f''(u)u'(s)^2 = 0.$$

Using the sign assumptions on $u'(s)$, we see that $f''(u) > 0$.

25.3 In this case it is just as costly to undertake the action preferred by the principal as to undertake the alternative action. Hence, the incentive constraint will not be binding, which implies $\mu = 0$. It follows that $s(x_i)$ is constant.

25.5 In this case the maximization problem takes the form

$$\max \sum_{i=1}^{n} (x_i - s_i)\pi_{ib}$$

$$\text{such that } \sum_{i=1}^{n} s_i \pi_{ib} - c_b \geq \bar{u}$$

$$\sum_{i=1}^{n} s_i \pi_{ib} - c_b \geq \sum_{i=1}^{n} s_i \pi_{ia} - c_a.$$

Assuming that the participation constraint is binding, and ignoring the incentive-compatibility constraint for a moment, we can substitute into the objective function to write

$$\max \sum_{i=1}^{m} s_i \pi_{ib} - c_b - \bar{u}.$$

Hence, the principal will choose the action that maximizes expected output minus (the agent's) costs, which is the first-best outcome. We can satisfy the incentive-compatibility constraint by choosing $s_i = x_i + F$, and choose F so that the participation constraint is satisfied.

25.7 Since $c_2'(x) > c_1'(x)$, we must have

$$\int_{x_1}^{x_2} c_2'(x)\,dx > \int_{x_1}^{x_2} c_1'(x)\,dx.$$

The result now follows from the Fundamental Theorem of Calculus.

25.9 For only low-cost workers to be employed, there must be no profitable contract that appeals to the high-cost workers. The most profitable contract to a high-cost worker maximizes $x_2 - x_2^2$, which implies $x_2^* = 1/2$. The cost of this to the worker is $(1/2)^2 = 1/4$. For the worker to find this acceptable, $s_2 - 1/4 \geq \bar{u}_2$, or $s_2 = \bar{u}_2 + 1/4$. For the firm to make a profit, $x_2^* \geq s_2$. Hence we have $1/2 \geq \bar{u}_2 + 1/4$, or $\bar{u}_2 \leq 1/4$.

INDEX